THE MANAGED
Health Care Handbook

Second Edition

Peter R. Kongstvedt, MD, FACP
Partner
Ernst & Young
Washington, DC

AN ASPEN PUBLICATION®
Aspen Publishers, Inc.
Gaithersburg, Maryland
1993

Library of Congress Cataloging-in-Publication Data

The managed health care handbook / edited by Peter R. Kongstvedt.—
2nd ed.
p.   cm.
Includes bibliographical references and index.
ISBN: 0-8342-0355-3
1. Managed care plans (Medical care)—Management. I. Kongstvedt,
Peter R. (Peter Reid)
[DNLM: 1. Delivery of Health Care—economics—United States.
2. Managed Care Programs. W 84 AA1 M26]
RA413.M28 1993
368.3'82'0068—dc20
DNLM/DLC
for Library of Congress
92-49421
CIP

Editorial Resources: Ruth Bloom

Library of Congress Catalog Card Number: 92-49421
ISBN: 0-8342-0355-3

Printed in the United States of America

4   5

To My Father,

Gerald Nicholas Kongstvedt

Table of Contents

Contributors

Allison A. Alkire, MBA, MPS
Senior Research Specialist
Towers Perrin
Valhalla, New York

Donald F. Anderson, PhD
Principal
William M. Mercer, Inc.
San Francisco, California

John P. Anton
Vice President, National Marketing
CIGNA Employee Benefits Companies
Atlanta, Georgia

Jeffrey L. Berlant, MD, PhD
Medical Director, Psychiatric Services
St. Alphonsus Regional Medical Center
Boise, Idaho

Henry F. Blissenbach, PharmD
President
Diversified Pharmaceutical Services
Minneapolis, Minnesota

John F. Boyer, PhD
Director, Coordinated Care Policy
Health Services Financing
Office of the Assistant Secretary of Defense (Health
  Affairs)
The Pentagon
Washington, DC

Garry Carneal, Esq.
Associate General Counsel
Group Health Association of America, Inc.
Washington, DC

Elisabeth A. Handley, MA
Deputy Director
Office of Prepaid Health Care Operations and
  Oversight
Washington, DC

Erling Hansen, Esq.
General Counsel
Group Health Association of America, Inc.
Washington, DC

R. Robert Herrick, MS
President
Robert Herrick Associates, Inc.
Nashville, Tennessee

Gregory N. Herrle, FSA
Principal and Consulting Actuary
Milliman & Robertson, Inc.
Brookfield, Wisconsin

David S. Iskowe, CPA
President and Chief Operating Officer
Focus Healthcare Management
Brentwood, Tennessee

Mark S. Joffe, Esq.
Law Offices of Mark S. Joffe
Washington, DC

William G. Kopit, Esq.
Epstein Becker and Green
Washington, DC

Jean D. LeMasurier
Director, Division of Policy and Evaluation
Office of Coordinated Care Policy and Planning
Health Care Financing Administration
Washington, DC

Mark E. Lutes, Esq.
Epstein Becker and Green
Washington, DC

Gordon K. MacLeod, MD, FACP
Professor of Health Services Administration and
   Clinical Professor of Medicine
University of Pittsburgh
Pittsburgh, Pennsylvania

Jan Malcolm
Vice President, Public Policy and Programs
Group Health, Inc.
Minneapolis, Minnesota

Joel L. Michaels, Esq.
Michaels and Wishner, PC
Washington, DC

Margaret E. O'Kane, MHS
President
National Committee for Quality Assurance
Washington, DC

Elizabeth Brennfleck Pascuzzi
Principal
Pascuzzi & Associates
Pittsburgh, Pennsylvania

Michael Pine, MD, MBA
Michael Pine and Associates
Chicago, Illinois

Christine C. Rinn, Esq.
Michaels and Wishner, PC
Washington, DC

Larry Sobel, Esq.
Deputy Director, Coordinated Care Operations
Health Services Financing
Office of the Assistant Secretary of Defense (Health
   Affairs)
The Pentagon
Washington, DC

Sidney W. Stolz, MBA
Principal
Towers Perrin
Rosslyn, Virginia

Roger S. Taylor, MD, MPH
National Leader, Health Care
The Wyatt Company
Washington, DC

James L. Touse, Esq.
AEtna Life Insurance Company
Walnut Creek, California

Eric R. Wagner, MBA
Senior Manager
Ernst & Young
Washington, DC

David L. Ward, CPA
President and Chief Executive Officer
CapitalCare, Inc.
Vienna, Virginia

Carlos Zarabozo
Director, Operational Analysis Staff
Office of Prepaid Health Care Operations and
   Oversight
Health Care Financing Administration
Washington, DC

Preface

The American health care system is in a state of flux unlike ever before. Some have used the phrase *permanent white water* to describe the conditions under which health care systems must now be managed. The rate of change is nearly exponential, or at least it feels that way to those of us in operations. The reasons for this condition are neither simple nor few.

Health care costs are escalating at an alarming rate as a result of a multiplicity of causes, including:

- rapidly developing (and usually expensive) technology
- cost shifting by providers to pay for care rendered to patients who either cannot pay or are covered by systems that do not pay the full cost of care
- shifting demographics as our population ages
- high (and not unreasonable) expectations for a long and healthy life
- the current legal environment, which has led to defensive medicine
- administrative costs related to the care that is delivered
- wide variations in efficiencies and quality of care that is rendered by all types of providers (professional and institutional)
- serious inequities and variations in incomes among all types of providers (regardless of efficiency or quality)
- a myriad other reasons

Clearly, there are no simple answers to the issues that face us in health care today. The prospect of national health reform, which is being debated as this book is written, will likely complicate matters even further. Under all scenarios, managing the triad of access to care, cost of care, and quality of care remains the challenge that we must face.

An analogy from the world of physics used in the first edition of this book remains valid. The laws of physics prevail in management as much as in the physical world, and there is a managerial corollary to the second law of thermodynamics. Paraphrased, the second law of thermodynamics states that order will proceed toward chaos unless energy is pumped into a system (ie, entropy); the same holds for health care delivery. In health care, much of the energy has traditionally been in the form of money. Now that the nation's monetary resources are bumping up against their limits, the energy that must be pumped into the health care system is in the form of management. To that end, this book has been written.

In the 4-year interval between the publication of the first edition of this book and this edition, there have been enough changes in the health care system to warrant a considerable revision and expansion of this reference text. Many chapters have been entirely rewritten, and some have been modified and added to; other topics are addressed for the first time.

The primary mission of this book remains unchanged: to provide an operational resource for managers in the field. It is based on actual operations of managed care plans rather than on purely theoretical models. In a field this complex many topics may be discussed, but not always to the degree one would like or with the emphasis that all would find appropriate. Information in this book is not intended to be the total, final, or best answer to any issue in managed health care. Rather, what is presented are possible solutions and multiple approaches to problems as well as information of which managers should be aware when running managed care operations.

Beyond its primary mission, this book is intended to be a useful resource to managers who are considering entering the field, to middle managers in the field who are trying to advance their careers, to senior executives in the industry with a little less experience than they would like, to medical directors new to managed care, to physicians in group practice who are charged with managing their peers and colleagues in a risk-based arrangement with a managed care plan, to hospital administrators trying to cope with the plethora of health care plans banging on their doors, to corporate benefits managers charged with controlling health care costs for employees, to academicians or students working to gain an understanding of how these things work, and to regulators who must administer the rules of play.

The chapters do not really need to be read in order, although they are presented in a logical order. Neither do all chapters need to be read to gain understanding. Chapters cross-reference each other when necessary. There is a glossary in the back of the book; in addition to that, there are two terms with specific meanings attached to them that are necessary to know to understand the text:

1. *Member*—This term is used synonymously with the terms *patient* and *covered insured*. A member is any individual or dependent who is enrolled in and covered by a managed health care plan.

2. *Plan*—This means a managed health care plan. This term is used to refer to any type of managed care plan (health maintenance organization, preferred provider organization, point-of-service, and so forth).

The book is intended to provide practical advice that is based on the experiences, both first-hand and observed, of managers in the industry as it exists today. The book is also highly biased: my biases as well as those of the contributing authors. There is no shortage of impassioned opinions in this industry, and many of those opinions are held with nearly-religious zeal. That means that there will be those who disagree with what they read here, and some of what will be presented in the following pages will become outdated, perhaps even as the book is published. Still, the information in this book has been forged and tempered in the crucible of one of the most revolutionary, volatile, and highly charged fields of endeavor in the country: managed health care.

Peter Reid Kongstvedt
McLean, Virginia

Acknowledgments

I wish to express my gratitude to the following individuals. First and most important, thanks to my wife, Sheryl Kongstvedt, for being there at the right times. I also wish to thank the following persons for affording me guidance along the way and the opportunity to grow: Dick Easley, Richard Cooper, John Austin, Frank McGrath, Sim Pace, and Ben Giuliani. A very special thanks to Nina Lane and Erin Carlson of the Group Health Association of America (GHAA) library for their help with reference sourcing; the GHAA library is the most comprehensive resource available for information about managed health care. Thanks to Ron Klar for intellectually stimulating discussions about the use of data. I would also like to thank Jack Bruggeman and Ruth Bloom at Aspen Publishers, Inc. Finally, thanks to the many excellent people in the managed care industry with whom I have had the privilege and good fortune to work over the years.

Part I

Introduction to Managed Care

You know more than you think you do.

Benjamin Spock, MD
Baby and Child Care (1945)

Chapter 1

An Overview of Managed Health Care

Gordon K. MacLeod

ROOTS OF MANAGED CARE

The number of managed health care enrollees has increased dramatically over the past 20 years, in sharp contrast to a much slower evolution during the preceding 40 years. By 1992, more than 1 million Americans had been enrolled in managed care plans; total enrollment in health maintenance organizations (HMOs) reached 36,482,090 by July 1991.[1] In addition, the number of employees covered by preferred provider organizations (PPOs) grew from zero in the late 1970s to an estimated 37,117,051, not including an equal number of dependents, by December 1991.[2] To explain the phenomenal growth of managed health care in the last two decades, it is necessary to explore the progression of corporate practice in American institutions.

The 20th century in the United States witnessed the transformation of society from rural to urban, from an individual orientation to insti-tutional domination, from an agricultural to a manufacturing economy, and from self-employment to employee status in increasingly larger corporations. During the same time period, medical practice made the transition from generalist to specialist, from solo to group practice, from direct payment for health care to group insurance, and from a predominantly cottage industry to increasing emphasis on the corporate management of medical care. Although these forces affecting medical practice are well documented, they reflect only some of the ongoing changes in organizing and financing health and medical care in recent years.

In commenting on the development of corporate management, Peter Drucker begins the first paragraph in the first chapter of his management text with the following statement:[3(p3)]

> During the last fifty years, society in every developed country has become a society of institutions. Every major social task, whether economic performance *or health care* [italics added], education or the protection of the environment, the pursuit of new knowledge or defense, is today being entrusted to big organizations, designed for perpetuity and managed by their own managements.

Gordon K. MacLeod, MD, FACP, is Professor of Health Services Administration and Clinical Professor of Medicine at the University of Pittsburgh, Pittsburgh, Pennsylvania. He is the founding director of the Health Maintenance Organization Service, US Department of Health, Education, and Welfare (1971–1973).

He goes on to warn that "on the performance of these institutions, the performance of modern society—if not the survival of each individual—increasingly depends."[3(p3)] His comments are particularly relevant to managed health care plans as we approach the beginning of the 21st century.

The transition from general practitioner to medical specialist was made with relative ease. It was signaled by the formation of specialty societies. The first one was formed by ophthalmologists in 1864. Five additional specialty societies were founded by 1888.[4] By 1940, 25% of all physicians called themselves specialists.

In 1932, in remarkable concordance with future developments, the Committee on the Costs of Medical Care recommended the linkage of group practice to prepayment for health services but opposed compulsory health insurance. The committee was chaired by Ray Lyman Wilbur, MD, a past president of the American Medical Association (AMA). The majority of the committee members believed that a compulsory national health insurance program would furnish a medical service limited in scope and deficient in quality; furthermore, it was held that any such plan would block normal developments in medical care delivery.

World War II served to catalyze the training of specialists, with the result that enormous demands were made on medical training facilities after the war ended. Nearly two thirds of the physicians leaving the armed forces after World War II planned to take residency training in one specialty or another by using their entitlement from veterans' educational benefits. By 1966, some 70% of physicians called themselves specialists.[5]

After World War II, there began a significant shift from solo to group practice that has continued to reshape medical practice until the present day. Organized medicine's opposition to group practice, however, did not deter its advocates from responding to the scientific, technological, professional, political, and economic forces that were about to transform medical care delivery.[6]

The 2.6% of physicians engaged in group practice in 1946 increased exponentially over the next four decades, so that today approxi-mately one third of all physicians are practicing in some 16,000 groups, with more than 60% of them in multispecialty settings. The AMA defines group practice as "three or more physicians who deliver patient care, make joint use of equipment and personnel, and divide income by a prearranged formula."[4(p503)]

Until early in the 20th century, physicians in the private practice of medicine almost universally billed the patient directly on a fee-for-service basis. Physicians introduced prepaid group practice into the American medical care system during the second quarter of the 20th century, which then offered them a choice between two systems of patient care, but the early growth of managed medical care delivery was relatively slow.

The corporate practice of medicine in the traditional health care system, whether investor owned or not for profit, was advanced by action of the federal government through enactment of the Medicare and Medicaid laws in 1965. Medicare and Medicaid legislation prompted the development of investor-owned hospital chains and stimulated the growth of university medical centers, both of which furthered the corporate practice of medicine by increasing the number of management personnel and physicians employed by hospitals and medical schools.

Indeed, these new health care financing laws for the elderly and the poor laid the groundwork for increased corporate control of medical care delivery by third-party payers through government mandated regulation of fee-for-service and indemnity payments for health care services. After years of unchecked health care inflation, third-party payers were authorized by the government, thus imposing additional corporate cost controls on hospitals, physicians, and patients, such as diagnosis-related groups, prospective pricing, and a resource-based relative value scale.

Further federal support for the corporate practice of medicine resulted from passage of the HMO Act in 1973 with its ensuing amendments that enabled managed medical care plans to increase in numbers and expand enrollments through health care programs financed by grants, contracts, and loans.

After passage of the HMO Act, strong support for the health maintenance organization (HMO) concept came from business; the executive, legislative, and judicial branches of government; and several states where managed care proliferated, such as California, and some northeast states, and particularly Minneapolis-St. Paul, Minnesota.[7] Bipartisan support for managed care was based on the concept that HMOs can decrease costs and encourage free-market competition in the medical care arena with only limited government intervention. Perhaps one measure of the success of this policy can be found in the virtual disappearance of some 17 national health insurance bills introduced into Congress in the early 1970s.

GROWTH AND DEVELOPMENT OF MANAGED CARE

Managed medical care is strictly an outgrowth of the private sector, dating back some 60 years. In the 1970s, so-called prepaid group and solo practice plans were recast into a popular marketable entity called an HMO, with development of PPOs later in the same decade. Some say PPOs are HMOs in transition. The history of these types of plans predates the 1970s, however.

The year 1929 had been a signal year for medical care organization in the United States when it witnessed the establishment of a rural farmers' cooperative health plan by Michael Shadid, MD, in Elk City, Oklahoma, a community of some 6,000 persons without any medical specialists. Shadid formed a lay organization composed of leading farmers, sold shares at $50.00 each to raise money for a new hospital, and then provided each shareholder with medical care at a discount rate. Despite opposition from the county medical society, an annual dues schedule was devised that covered the cost of medical care, surgery, and house calls for $1.00 plus $0.10/ mile each way if one lived out in the country. Dental services were made available, with fillings costing $1.00, crowns $7.00, and full dentures $25.00 to $35.00 depending on style. By 1934, 600 family memberships assisted in supporting a medical staff consisting of Dr. Shadid plus four new specialists and a dentist. That same year, two California physicians in Los Angeles, Donald Ross, MD and H. Clifford Loos, MD, entered into a prepaid contract to provide comprehensive health services to about 2,000 water company employees.[8] These two plans were harbingers of managed care eventually serving about 40% of the American public in the early 1990s.[1,2]

Several other prepaid group practice plans started up between 1930 and 1960; they enjoyed many years of successful growth although again not without strong opposition from organized medicine. Prominent among these plans founded in the next several decades were the Group Health Association in Washington, DC in 1937, the Kaiser-Permanente Medical Care Program in 1942 (by far the largest, most widely distributed nationally, and best known HMO prototype), the Group Health Cooperative of Puget Sound in Seattle in 1947, the Health Insurance Plan of Greater New York in 1947, and the Group Health Plan of Minneapolis in 1957.[9]

A variant of the prepaid group practice plan appeared in 1954, when a prototype IPA (individual practice association) was established by the San Joaquin County Foundation for Medical Care in Stockton, California. Fearing competition from Kaiser-Permanente, the San Joaquin County Medical Society set up a prepaid foundation for medical care (later to be called an IPA) in the same community. A relative value fee schedule for guaranteeing payment was adopted, all grievances were heard by a voluntary board of physicians, and a sincere attempt was made to monitor the quality of care.[8] Over the past 10 to 15 years the IPA/HMO has grown much more rapidly than either group practice or staff model HMOs.

Both prepaid group and individual practice associations were the opening wedge for a new kind of health care delivery in the United States, whereby physicians shared the risk of financing health care for an enrolled population and in which physicians were offered a choice between billing and collecting a fee-for-service from the patient or having the HMO pay the physician directly out of a prepaid per capita payment (capitation) for health care services. These models led to widespread dissemination of managed care plans. HMOs assumed responsibility for providing a comprehensive range of health services to voluntarily enrolled populations at a fixed annual premium.

A major factor in the overall success of HMOs was the willingness of physicians to accept financial risk in providing health and medical care services to groups of subscribers. If HMO physicians incurred expenses exceeding budgeted costs, then part or all of the shortfall would have to be absorbed by the physicians. On the other hand, any excess in revenues over expenditures could be shared by physicians. In addition, enrollees achieved considerable savings in health insurance premiums mainly by reduction in the number of unnecessary hospital admissions and length of hospital stays.

By combining coverage for outpatient and inpatient care in a single premium, HMOs were also able to reduce hospitalization utilization simply by shifting some services appropriately to a less expensive ambulatory setting. By contrast, traditional fee-for-service physicians had little or no economic incentive to reduce access to hospitalization. Indeed, many hospital administrators were economically motivated to encourage fee-for-service physicians to keep beds fully occupied by patients who otherwise might be treated on an outpatient basis. The increase in indemnity coverage likewise increased both volume and profits for health insurance companies. It is important to note that many physicians preferred to retain the concept of fee-for-service payments for patient care and resisted sharing in the financial risk of the HMO group practice or staff models; physicians more willingly accepted the fee-for-service IPA model, however.

HMO physicians share the risk for overutilization of medical care whether they work on a contract basis (group model), on salary (staff model), on capitation (some IPAs, networks, and direct contract capitated models), or on fee-for-service (some IPAs and direct contract fee-for-service models). They are also subject to other corporate influences, such as those arising from mergers, buyouts, diversification, as well as to having their services marketed to the public. In actuality, managed health care is consigned to institutional sponsorship.

During the developmental years of managed care plans, most hospital administrators viewed HMOs as a threat because they believed that managed care could drastically reduce the number of admissions compared to the effect of other kinds of health insurance. By 1973, only some 5,000,000 people had been enrolled in prepaid group practice plans.[9] Including dependents of employees signed up in PPOs, it is estimated that about 100,000,000 people are now enrolled in managed care plans.[1,2] Under managed care, many thousands of physicians have switched to the corporate practice of medicine, although some have done so reluctantly.

The evolution of these pioneer prepaid group and individual practice plans in the private sector was one of the most extraordinary developments in the history of medical care organization in the world. Prepaid plans went on to serve as a template for financing and organizing health care services for the American people; at the very least they ushered in a new era of corporate influence into the practice of medicine. Physicians are now given career choices between the Scylla of fee-for-service practice in what some call a cottage industry and the Charybdis of payment under corporate control. So began the race for freestanding managed care corporations to sell physician, hospital and other health care services to corporate benefit managers.

Managed health care was not the only contributor to the trend toward the corporate practice of medicine in the United States. At about the same time that managed medical care first appeared, Duke University Medical School was organizing its Private Diagnostic Clinic (PDC). In 1931, the PDC was established and served as a harbinger of faculty practice plans (FPPs). After a period of relatively slow growth, revenues from Medicare payments spurred dramatic growth in FPPs. After passage of the Medicare Act, FPPs grew from 6 in 1965 to 118 in 1980 in the 127 US medical schools, almost all of which now participate in managed care systems or have organized their own.[10] Some 60,000 physicians are now employed in FPPs in academic health centers.[11] In fact, FPPs form the largest block of full-time physicians directly employed by corporations. FPPs may well have spurred the growth of managed care by providing medical students and residents with role models of physicians pursuing seemingly satisfying and successful careers in a corporate mode.

Variations in corporate practice can also be found in trade union clinics, diagnostic centers, university health services, and employee medical service plans.

Indirect incursion into fee-for-service practice came from health insurance companies such as Blue Cross, Blue Shield, and commercial carriers. In 1929, the same year that HMOs first appeared, a group of teachers sponsored the first Blue Cross plan in Dallas, Texas, to cover hospital costs. Blue Shield's forerunners for the reimbursement of physicians' costs were medical bureaus set up by state medical societies, the first of which was established in 1933 in Washington State.

In addition, many federal and state hospital systems such as Veterans Administration hospitals and state mental hospitals are essentially corporate models with management decisions made centrally. Some 20,000 physicians are employed by the federal government.[12]

In addition to physicians participating in corporately sponsored managed care plans and FPPs, other hospital-based physicians outside academic health centers today account for a considerable amount of patient care, especially in connection with teaching programs based in the community hospitals. These physicians are increasingly subject to corporate influences because many of them are directly employed either part or full time by the hospital and are frequently involved in operating or participating in their own managed care systems. The corporate practice of medicine has had a further impact upon hospital-based physicians and other health care professionals with the advent of vertically integrated, multi-institutional health care systems.

In the private sector, moreover, there has been a dramatic increase in both horizontal and vertical integration of hospital systems. Some 40% of the nation's community hospitals are operated as multi-hospital systems.[13] In addition, both not-for-profit and investor-owned companies are now involved in a wide variety of health care markets, including long-term care, wellness programs, HMOs, and PPOs.

PPOs, as a recent development in managed care, are often considered to be evolving HMOs. Although many variations exist, the PPO in its simplest form is a contractual arrangement between professional and/or institutional health care providers and employers, insurance carriers, or third-party administrators to provide health care services, often at discounted rates. Although the physician is not usually at risk in the PPO, some mixed forms have incorporated elements of the IPA model, such as physician capitation, into the contractual arrangement.

The PPO first appeared in the medical marketplace in the late 1970s. This corporate model offers a discount, usually about 15% to 20% less than what competitors charge, to enrollees who agree to use the services of selected sets of physicians and hospitals.[14] Unlike the HMO, however, the PPO reimburses the patient for covered services obtained from any provider at the discounted rate set for preferred providers; the patient then has to pay out of pocket the balance between the scheduled fee and the billed amount.

Although HMOs have organizational mechanisms to assume corporate responsibility for cost containment and quality assessment, PPOs do not include such intrinsic controls. Many PPOs have unbundled HMO utilization controls, however, such as prior approval screens, preadmission certification, second surgical opinions, retrospective review, and concurrent length of stay review, and adapted them to fee-for-service payments. Moreover, PPOs have used other HMO administrative maneuvers for controlling costs, such as negotiated provider discounts, selective contracting, utilization management, and even fixed per capita pricing in some PPOs.

Presently, managed health care plans are giving more attention to price and patient satisfaction. Some managed health care plans now permit payment to nonparticipating physicians at the point of service. Under this arrangement, the patient is responsible (a) in an IPA or PPO for charges by nonparticipating physicians beyond that allowed by a fee schedule or (b) in a group or staff model HMO for direct payment to non-participants until a substantial deductible is met.

In contrast to the United States, several European national health insurance plans had been around for several decades before 1929. Since then, these European governmental programs have done little to stimulate innovation in health care delivery although they have addressed problems with cost and access to health care fairly effectively. In fact, many governments in countries across the northern tier of Europe eventually socialized medical care delivery and created national health services that actually thwarted any further change in organizing medical care by the private sector, whereas here in the United States, medical care organization continues to evolve without direct government control. The current international trend toward privatization of national health programs has prompted many governments to examine the US experience with managed care.

MANAGEMENT FUNCTIONS IN MANAGED CARE

Managed health care elements found in HMOs, PPOs, and indemnity arrangements that have unbundled corporate responsibilities for quality assessment and cost containment are intended to control the inappropriate use of health care services. Further development of managed health care will remain a prime objective of those advocates of a pluralistic health care system who favor the concept of corporate medical care. It is readily acknowledged that competition for market share now exists between noncontractual fee-for-service/direct service payment programs and any system that uses the managed care label. It is generally accepted that the mission of managed health care is to deliver high-quality health and medical care services at a competitive price. The management functions of planning, organizing, directing, controlling, and coordinating lend themselves to carrying out the stated mission in alternative provider systems such as HMOs and PPOs.[15]

The planning functions in HMOs and PPOs as alternative provider systems lend themselves to strategic planning, resource planning, facility planning, and financial planning. Unlike those who use widely decentralized fee-for-service direct or indemnity payment systems, the managed health care manager is uniquely positioned to design a set of objectives for the organization. The process calls for continuous input from physicians, hospitals, and consumers in response to changes in the internal and external environment of the plan.

Strategic planning is the process of setting long-term objectives for the future. Accurate long-range forecasting for the future of alternative provider systems has propagated some extraordinarily successful outcomes. Strategic planning, when carried out effectively, necessarily influences the future professional and business prospects of a managed medical care plan. Risks are involved in strategic planning, but even greater risk results from not planning strategically.

With the degree of institutionalization of medical care delivery that we see today in managed medical care plans and the rapid growth in popularity of HMOs as an alternative provider system, the prediction made by the federal government's HMO program in the 1970s of making HMOs available to 90% of the population does not seem so far-fetched.

Resource planning involves the acquisition and allocation of fixed capital, equipment capital, human capital, and operating capital in the health care arena in which the managed care process must function. In these alternative provider systems, managers must give physician recruitment and retention a very high priority.

Facility planning in most managed health care plans necessarily shifts attention from hospital to ambulatory care. At present, such care is not encumbered by the high degree of regulation we find in the hospital setting. Accordingly, managed medical care plans are able to optimize the use of outpatient services at a lower cost than inpatient care. In addition, these plans can consider various settings for care other than the hospital, such as skilled nursing facilities, personal care homes, home, or the physician's office. In the case of IPAs and PPOs, facility planning is usually limited to administrative activity. In every instance, however, consideration of time and travel needs for staff and subscribers as well as overhead costs for facilities is essential for a successful outcome in the planning process.

Financial planning in managed health care has many facets but has to focus on the budget as its main planning tool. The opportunity for innovation in management-oriented cost accounting is not impeded by the traditional encumbrances of hospital accounting. This planning function in managed health care plans, although risky, is often untapped. Investment in innovation may provide exceptionally good opportunities to enhance the performance of managed health care in general and to improve the quality of medical care in particular. The ability to communicate the importance of financial planning to the physician staff may tax even the most creative and energetic manager, but making low-cost and high-quality health care accessible to patients must remain the paramount goal for managed medical care plans.

Shifting the responsibility for medical care delivery from each individual practitioner to corporate control raises issues of an ethical nature in many physicians' minds. There is an inherent conflict between prepayment and underutilization just as there is between fee-for-service and overutilization of patient care. Both of these conflicts are mitigated by the high degree of professionalism characteristic of physicians. These conflicts can challenge the leadership and organizational skills of managers, however, and can result in problems affecting cost, quality of care, and professional performance. Perhaps the best way to measure quality of care is by evaluating health and medical care outcomes when a defined population is served, which is uniquely possible in HMOs. Professional performance in all settings is somewhat more difficult to assess than outcome measurements, and is discussed in Chapters 16 and 18.

Organizational skills are essential for the successful operation of any medical practice and are especially important in managed health care plans. Increasingly, physicians with organizational skills are being recruited to assume responsibility for top level managerial positions, for motivating others, for assessing performance, and for developing good working relationships with other health professionals, nonprofessional employees, and subscribers and patients alike. Physicians are uniquely prepared to manage specific problems arising from clinical practice, diagnostic procedures, and therapeutic interventions. The role of the physician manager has been variously appreciated in managed health care plans, however, and will remain a challenge until enough physicians are recruited or trained to function as managers as well as clinicians. Obviously, peer review and outcome performance assessment require physician participation and management.

The directing function in managed health care plans requires skill in delegating authority appropriately while continuing to assume responsibility for both operating activities and clinical care. The problem of distinguishing authority from responsibility can be resolved by observing that one can delegate the authority to perform tasks but one cannot be relieved of the responsibility for them. Some say it is a truism that the manager must always retain responsibility for any task assigned to a subordinate. Although the nonphysician manager can delegate the authority for delivering patient care services to a physician, only a licensed physician can provide such care; thus the conundrum. The nonphysician manager must relinquish some degree of responsibility for the clinical aspects of patient care. Perhaps it is more important to understand different styles of management than it is to ponder the authority/responsibility conundrum. A direct management style makes clear the rewards and punishments affecting the quality of performance. A middle approach offers subordinates the manager's friendship, concern, and approachability; this can be very effective when a physician or other health care worker is assigned a difficult task. A variant of this approach finds the manager consulting with the employee about how to carry out a specific task. At the other end of the spectrum, a positive management style assumes that an employee has the capability to perform a task and will accept responsibility for carrying it out, thus creating a sense of confidence in the employee. Many health professionals, especially physicians, are trained to perform with a minimum of supervision and a high degree of autonomy when undertaking clinical tasks. Under these circumstances, a highly directive management style is not always very effective.

Management's responsibility for the recruitment and further training of professional health workers should take into account the candidate's credentials and the kind of leadership necessary to manage other health professionals. Because physicians, nurses, and some other health care workers must be licensed to practice their profession, this clearly limits recruitment opportunities to those qualified by virtue of their training and credentialing.

Various control formulations exist. A fair and competitive income comparable to that of others in the organization and the community usually tops the list of controls. Feedback on performance is a prerequisite for improving productivity and quality. Employee benefits and amenities, where applicable, are other controls that should help maintain satisfactory performance. Management training along with participation in management decisions has been shown to be effective in intentionally involving employees in controlling the operation of the organization.

Even though it must be recognized that many physicians do not wish to work as managers, appropriately trained or experienced physicians can avoid or resolve many of the operational problems that occur in managed care systems. Most, if not all, of the challenges and opportunities faced by managed health care plans can be addressed effectively by competent physician managers with appropriate administrative direction or support. In staff model HMOs where the medical director is an employee, however, it is essential that a nonphysician chief executive officer delegate full clinical authority to that person. It should be pointed out that the nonphysician manager may be held legally liable for contracting for physician services or for defects in the design or implementation of cost containment mechanisms.

The importance of the coordinating ability of the manager cannot be overemphasized. Ambiguity and conflict constitute core characteristics of complex organizations such as managed care plans. This is particularly true for the multi-setting, multiprofessional, and multifunctional managed medical care plan. Competition for time, patients, position, personnel, programs, space, and money generates differences that need to be reconciled continuously. Great skill is often required in minimizing internal organizational conflicts. In addition, coordinating functions are essential for opening and maintaining vertical and horizontal lines of communication.

CONCLUSION

The following chapters describe how to grapple with managed medical care plans as they develop further in this era of specialization, institutionalization, and corporate practice. Federal and state regulation of managed care plans has become increasingly perplexing. The recent growth and development of managed medical care involving ambulatory medical care, hospitalization, and health insurance has created a variety of complex organizations requiring the finest management skills available. The available pool of existing and future management personnel will find much of value in this book to use in furthering the goals of cost containment, accessibility, high-quality comprehensive health care, subscriber satisfaction, and career opportunities in managed medical care.

REFERENCES

1. Parker MJ, Ball PA, Kraus N. *InterStudy Competitive Edge*. 1992;1:10.
2. *Directory of Operational PPOs*. Chicago: SMG Marketing Groups; 1992.
3. Drucker PF. *Management Tasks, Responsibilities, Practices*. New York: Harper & Row; 1974.
4. Campion FD. *The AMA and US Health Policy*. Chicago: Chicago Review Press; 1984:435, 503.
5. Rothstein WG. *American Medical Schools*. New York: Oxford University Press; 1978:187–188.
6. Committee on the Costs of Medical Care. *Medical Care for the American People*. Chicago: University of Chicago Press; 1932:128.
7. Starr P. *The Social Transformation of American Medicine*. New York: Basic Books; 1982.
8. MacColl WA. *Group Practice and Prepayment of Medi-*

cal Care. Washington, DC: Public Affairs Press; 1966:20–24.

9. MacLeod GK, Prussin JA. The continuing evolution of health maintenance organizations. *N Engl J Med.* 1973;288:439–443.

10. MacLeod GK, Schwarz MR. Faculty practice plans: Profile and critique. *JAMA.* 1986;256:58–62.

11. Jonas HS, Etzel SI, Barzansky B. Educational programs in US medical schools. *JAMA.* 1991; 266:914.

12. Roback G, Randolph L, Seidman B. *Physician Charac-*

teristics and Distribution in the U.S. Chicago: American Medical Association; 1990:8.

13. Griffith JR. *The Well-Managed Community Hospital.* Ann Arbor, MI: Health Administration Press; 1987:134.

14. Barger SB, Hillman DG, Garland HR. *The PPO Handbook.* Gaithersburg, MD: Aspen Publishers; 1985:25–26.

15. Gabel J, Jacich C, Williams K, et al. The commercial health insurance industry in transition. *Health Affairs.* 1987;6:47–48.

Chapter 2

Types of Managed Care Organizations

Eric R. Wagner

The various types of managed health care organizations were reasonably distinct when the first edition of this book was conceived. Those distinctions had blurred considerably by the time the first edition was published. Since then the differences between traditional forms of health insurance and managed care organizations have narrowed further.

Originally, health maintenance organizations (HMOs), preferred provider organizations (PPOs), and traditional forms of indemnity health insurance were distinct, mutually exclusive products and mechanisms for providing health care coverage. Today, an observer may be hard pressed to uncover the differences between products that bill themselves as HMOs, PPOs, or managed care overlays to health insurance. For example, many HMOs, which traditionally limited their members to a designated set of participating providers, now allow their members to

Eric R. Wagner is a Senior Manager in the Washington, DC, office of Price Waterhouse, an international accounting and professional services firm. He has worked with clients on all phases of managed health care evaluation, development, management, and acquisition and has authored several publications related to the managed care field.

use nonparticipating providers at a reduced coverage level. Such point-of-service (POS) plans combine both HMO-like systems with indemnity systems, allowing individual members to choose which system they wish to access at the point where they need the medical service. Similarly, some PPOs, which historically provided unrestricted access to physicians and other health care providers, have implemented primary care case management or gatekeeper systems and have added elements of financial risk to their reimbursement systems. Finally, many indemnity insurance (or self-insurance) plans have included utilization management features in their plans that were once found only in HMOs or PPOs.

As a result of these recent changes, the descriptions of the different types of managed care systems that follow provide only a guideline for determining the form of managed care organization that is observed. In many cases, the managed health care organization will be a hybrid of several specific types.

Some controversy exists about whether the term *managed care* accurately describes the new generation of health care delivery and financing mechanisms. Those commentators who object to the term raise questions about what it is that is managed by a managed care organization. These commentators ask: Is the individual patient's medical care being managed or is the organization simply managing the composition and reimbursement of the provider delivery system?

Observers who favor the term *managed care* hold that managing the provider delivery system can be equivalent in its outcomes to managing the medical care delivered to the patient. In contrast to historical methods of financing health care delivery in the United States, the current generation of financing mechanisms includes far more active management of both the delivery system through which care is provided and the medical care that is actually delivered to individual patients. Although the term *managed care* may not perfectly describe this current generation of financing vehicles, it provides a convenient shorthand description for the range of alternatives to traditional indemnity health insurance.

A simplistic but useful concept regarding managed care is the continuum. On one end of the continuum is managed indemnity with simple precertification of elective admissions and large case management of catastrophic cases, superimposed on a traditional indemnity insurance plan. Similar to indemnity is the service plan, which has contractual relationships with providers addressing maximum fee allowances, prohibiting balance billing, and using the same utilization management techniques as managed indemnity (the nearly universal examples of service plans are Blue Cross and Blue Shield plans). Further along the continuum are PPOs, POS, open panel [individual practice association (IPA) type] HMOs, and finally closed panel (group and staff model) HMOs. As you progress from one end of the continuum to the other, you add new and greater elements of control and accountability, you tend to increase both the complexity and the overhead required to operate the plan, and you achieve greater potential control of cost and quality.

This chapter provides a description of the different types of managed health care organizations and the common acronyms used to represent them. A brief explanation is provided for each type of organization. In addition, this chapter includes descriptions of the five most common forms of HMOs—the original managed care organizations—and their relationships with physicians.

TYPES OF MANAGED CARE ORGANIZATIONS AND COMMON ACRONYMS

The managed care industry has spawned a large number of acronyms to describe its distinctive organizations; many people have described these acronyms as a confusing alphabet soup of initials. Nevertheless, knowledge of a few key acronyms makes an understanding of the managed care environment easier.

Health Maintenance Organization

HMOs are organized health care systems that are responsible for both the financing and the delivery of a broad range of comprehensive health services to an enrolled population. The original definition of an HMO also included the aspect of financing health care for a prepaid fixed fee, but that portion of the definition is no longer absolute, although it is still common.

In many ways, an HMO can be viewed as a combination of a health insurer and a health care delivery system. Whereas traditional health care insurance companies are responsible for reimbursing covered individuals for the cost of their health care, HMOs are responsible for providing health care services to their covered members through affiliated providers who are reimbursed under various methods (see Chapters 4, 6, 7, and 8).

As a result of their responsibility for providing covered health services to their members, HMOs must ensure that their members have access to covered health care services. In addition, HMOs generally are responsible for assuring the quality and appropriateness of the health services they provide to their members.

The five common models of HMOs are staff, group practice, network, IPA, and direct contract. The primary differences among these models are based on how the HMO relates to its participating physicians. These relationships are described in more detail in a subsequent section of this chapter.

Preferred Provider Organization

PPOs are entities through which employer health benefit plans and health insurance carriers contract to purchase health care services for covered beneficiaries from a selected group of participating providers. Typically, participating providers in PPOs agree to abide by utilization management and other procedures implemented by the PPO and agree to accept the PPO's reimbursement structure and payment levels. In return, PPOs often limit the size of their participating provider panels and provide incentives for their covered individuals to use participating providers instead of other providers. In contrast to traditional HMO coverage, individuals with PPO coverage are permitted to use non-PPO providers, although higher levels of coinsurance or deductibles routinely apply to services provided by these nonparticipating providers.

PPOs sometimes are described as preferred provider arrangements (PPAs). The definition of a PPA is usually the same as the definition of a PPO. Some observers, however, use the term *PPA* to describe a less formal relationship than would be described by a PPO. The term *PPO* implies that an organization exists, whereas a PPA may achieve the same goals as a PPO through an informal arrangement among providers and payers.

The key common characteristics of PPOs include the following:

- *Select provider panel.* PPOs typically contract with selected providers in a community to provide health services for covered individuals. Most PPOs contract directly with hospitals, physicians, and other diagnostic facilities. Providers are selected to participate on the basis of their cost efficiency, community reputation, and scope of services. Some PPOs assemble massive databases of information about potential providers, including costs by diagnostic

category, before they make their contracting decisions.
- *Negotiated payment rates.* Most PPO participation agreements require participating providers to accept the PPO's payments as payment in full for covered services (except for applicable coinsurance or deductibles). PPOs attempt to negotiate payment rates that provide them with a competitive cost advantage relative to charge-based payment systems. These negotiated payment rates usually take the form of discounts from charges, all-inclusive per diem rates, or payments based on diagnosis-related groups.
- *Rapid payment terms.* Some PPOs are willing to include prompt payment features in their contracts with participating providers in return for favorable payment rates. For example, a PPO may commit to pay all clean claims submitted by its providers within 15 days of submittal in return for a 5% discount from charges.
- *Utilization management.* Many PPOs implement utilization management programs to control the utilization and cost of health services provided to their covered beneficiaries. In the more sophisticated PPOs, these utilization management programs resemble the programs operated by HMOs.
- *Consumer choice.* Unlike traditional HMOs, PPOs generally allow covered beneficiaries to use non-PPO providers instead of PPO providers when they need health services. Higher levels of beneficiary cost sharing, often in the form of higher copayments, typically are imposed when PPO beneficiaries use non-PPO providers.

Exclusive Provider Organization

Exclusive provider organizations (EPOs) are similar to PPOs in their organization and purpose. Unlike PPOs, however, EPOs limit their beneficiaries to participating providers for any health care services. In other words, beneficiaries covered by an EPO are required to receive all their covered health care services from providers that participate with the EPO. The EPO does not cover services received from other providers.

Some EPOs parallel HMOs in that they not only require exclusive use of the EPO provider network but also use a gatekeeper approach to authorizing nonprimary care services. In these cases, the primary difference between an HMO and an EPO is that the former is regulated under HMO laws and regulations, whereas the latter is regulated under insurance laws and regulations.

EPOs usually are implemented by employers whose primary motivation is cost saving. These employers are less concerned about the reaction of their employees to severe restrictions on the choice of health care provider and offer the EPO as a replacement for traditional indemnity health insurance coverage. Because of the severe restrictions on provider choice, only a few large employers have been willing to convert their entire health benefits programs to an EPO format.

Point-of-Service Plan

Capitated and Primary Care Preferred Provider Organizations

These are hybrids of more traditional HMO and PPO models. The following are characteristics of these types of plans:

- Primary care physicians are reimbursed through capitation payments (ie, a fixed payment per member per month) or other performance-based reimbursement methods (see Chapter 6).
- There is often an amount withheld from physician compensation that is paid contingent upon achievement of utilization or cost targets.
- The primary care physician acts as a gatekeeper for referral and institutional medical services.
- The member retains some coverage for services rendered that either are not authorized by the primary care physician or are delivered by nonparticipating providers. Such coverage is typically significantly lower than coverage for authorized services de-

livered by participating providers (eg, 100% compared to 60%).

Traditional HMOs may offer similar benefit options through an out-of-plan benefits rider or POS option.

Open-Access or Point-of-Service Health Maintenance Organizations

Many HMOs have recognized that the major impediment to enrolling additional members and expanding market share has been the reluctance of individuals to forfeit completely their ability to receive reimbursement for using nonparticipating providers. These individuals consider the possibility that they would need the services of a renowned specialist for a rare (and expensive to treat) disorder and believe that the HMO would not refer them for care or reimburse their expenses. This possibility, no matter how unlikely, overshadows all the other benefits of HMO coverage in the minds of many individuals.

An expanding number of HMOs (and insurance carriers with both HMOs and indemnity operations) have adopted a solution to this problem: They provide some level of indemnity-type coverage for their members. HMO members covered under these types of benefit plans may decide whether to use HMO benefits or indemnity-style benefits for each instance of care. In other words, the member is allowed to make a coverage choice at the point of service.

The indemnity coverage available under POS options from HMOs typically incorporates high deductibles and coinsurance to encourage members to use HMO services instead of out-of-plan services. Members who use the non-HMO benefit portion of the benefit plan may also be subject to utilization review (eg, preadmission certification and continued stay review). Despite the availability of out-of-network benefits, most POS plans experience between 65% and 85% in-network usage, thus retaining considerable cost control.

As discussed in Chapter 23, this hybrid form of health benefit coverage represents an attractive managed care option for many employers and their covered employees, particularly when the employer is looking toward POS as a consolidation of existing indemnity coverage and multiple HMOs in the group (ie, total replacement coverage).

Self-Insured and Experience-Rated Health Maintenance Organizations

Historically, HMOs offered community-rated premiums to all employers and individuals who enrolled for HMO coverage. The federal HMO Act originally mandated community rating for all HMOs that decided to pursue federal qualification. Community rating was eventually expanded to include rating by class, where premium rates for an individual employer group could be adjusted prospectively on the basis of demographic characteristics that were associated with utilization differences. Such characteristics often included the age and sex distributions of the employer's work force and the standard industrial classification of the employer.

Although community rating by class provided HMOs with some flexibility to offer more attractive rates to selected employer groups, many employers continued to believe that their group-specific experience would be better than the rates offered by HMOs. Some HMOs developed self-insured or experience-rated options in response to the needs expressed by these employers.

Under a typical self-insured benefit option, an HMO receives a fixed monthly payment to cover administrative services (and profit) and variable payments that are based on the actual payments made by the HMO for health services. There is usually a settlement process at the end of a specified period, during which a final payment is calculated (either to the HMO by the group or to the group by the HMO). Variations in the payment arrangement exist and are similar in structure to the different forms of self-funded insurance programs.

Under experience-rated benefit options, an HMO receives monthly premium payments much as it would under traditional premium-based plans. There typically is a settlement process where the employer is credited with some

portion (or all) of the actual utilization and cost of its group to arrive at a final premium rate. Refunds or additional payments are then calculated and made to the appropriate party.

The HMO regulations of some states and federal HMO qualification regulations preclude HMOs from offering self-insured or experience-rated benefit plans. HMOs avoid these prohibitions by incorporating related corporate entities that use the HMO's negotiated provider agreements, management systems, utilization protocols, and personnel to service the self-insured line of business.

Rating methodologies are discussed in detail in Chapter 26.

Specialty Health Maintenance Organizations

Specialty HMOs have developed in some states to provide the benefits of the HMO model to limited components of health care coverage. Dental HMOs have become more common during the last 5 years as an option to indemnity dental insurance coverage. Specialty HMOs serving other health care needs (eg, mental health) have also developed in certain states where they are permitted under the insurance or HMO laws and regulations. One challenge to the formation of such HMOs is that state laws usually define a broad range of health services that are required to be offered by licensed HMOs.

Managed Care Overlays to Indemnity Insurance

The perceived success of HMOs and other types of managed care organizations in controlling the utilization and cost of health services has prompted entrepreneurs to develop managed care overlays that can be combined with traditional indemnity insurance, service plan insurance, or self-insurance (the term *indemnity insurance* is used to refer to all three forms of coverage in this context). These managed care overlays are intended to provide cost control for insured plans while retaining the individual's freedom of choice of provider and coverage for out-of-plan services.

The following types of managed care overlays currently exist:

- *General utilization management.* These companies offer a complete menu of utilization management activities that can be selected by individual employers or insurers. Some offer or can develop panels of participating providers within individual markets and bear strong resemblances to PPOs.
- *Specialty utilization management.* Firms that focus on utilization review for specialty services have become common. Mental health and dental care are two common types of specialty utilization management overlays.
- *Catastrophic or large case management.* Some firms have developed to assist employers and insurers with managing catastrophic cases regardless of the specialty involved. This service includes screening to identify cases that will become catastrophic, negotiation of services and reimbursement with providers who can treat the patient's condition, development of a treatment protocol for the patient, and ongoing monitoring of the treatment.
- *Workers' compensation utilization management.* In response to the rapid increases in the cost of workers' compensation insurance, firms have developed managed care overlays to address what they claim are the unique needs of patients covered under workers' compensation benefits. Managed care and workers' compensation programs are discussed in detail in Chapter 33.

HEALTH MAINTENANCE ORGANIZATION MODELS

The five commonly recognized models of HMOs are staff, group, network, IPA, and direct contract. The major differences among these models pertain to the relationship between the HMO and its participating physicians. Until recently, individual HMOs usually could be neatly categorized into a single model type for descriptive purposes. Currently, many HMOs have different relationships with different groups of physicians. As a result, many HMOs cannot easily be classified as a single model type, although such plans are occasionally referred to as mixed models.

The following paragraphs provide brief descriptions of the five common HMO model types. Further discussion may be found in Chapters 4, 5, and 6.

Staff Model

In a staff model HMO, the physicians who serve the HMO's beneficiaries are employed by the HMO. These physicians typically are paid on a salary basis and may also receive bonus or incentive payments that are based on their performance and productivity. Staff model HMOs must employ physicians in all the common specialties to provide for the health care needs of their members. These HMOs may contract with selected subspecialists in the community for infrequently needed health services.

Staff model HMOs are also known as closed panel HMOs because most participating physicians are employees of the HMO and community physicians are unable to participate. Some well-known examples of staff model HMOs include Group Health Association in Washington, DC, and Group Health Cooperative of Puget Sound in Seattle, Washington.

Physicians in staff model HMOs usually practice in one or more centralized ambulatory care facilities. These facilities, which often resemble outpatient clinics, contain physician offices and ancillary support facilities (eg, laboratory and radiology) to support the health care needs of the HMO's beneficiaries. Staff model HMOs usually contract with hospitals and other inpatient facilities in the community to provide nonphysician services for their members.

Staff model HMOs can have an advantage relative to other HMO models because they have a greater degree of control over the practice patterns of their physicians. As a result, it can be easier for staff model HMOs to manage and control the utilization of health services. They also offer the convenience of one-stop shopping for their members because the HMO's facilities tend to be full service (ie, have laboratory, radiology, and other departments).

Offsetting this advantage are several disadvantages for staff model HMOs. First, staff model HMOs are usually more costly to develop and implement because of the small membership and the large fixed salary expenses the HMO must incur for staff physicians and support staff. Second, staff model HMOs provide a limited choice of participating physicians from which potential HMO members may select. Many potential members are reluctant to change from their current physician and find the idea of a clinic setting uncomfortable. Finally, it is expensive for staff model HMOs to expand their services into new areas because of the need to construct new ambulatory care facilities.

Group Model

In group model HMOs, the HMO contracts with a multispecialty physician group practice to provide all physician services to the HMO's members. The physicians in the group practice are employed by the group practice and not by the HMO. In some cases, these physicians may be allowed to see both HMO patients and other patients, although their primary function may be to treat HMO members.

Physicians in a group practice share facilities, equipment, medical records, and support staff. The group may contract with the HMO on an all-inclusive capitation basis to provide physician services to HMO members. Alternatively, the group may contract on a cost basis to provide its services.

There are two broad categories of group model HMOs as described below.

Captive Group

In the captive group model, the physician group practice exists solely to provide services to the HMO's beneficiaries. In most cases, the HMO formed the group practice to serve its members and recruited physicians and now provides administrative services to the group. The most prominent example of this type of HMO is

the Kaiser Foundation Health Plan, where the Permanente Medical Groups provide all physician services for Kaiser's members. The Kaiser Foundation Health Plan, as the licensed HMO, is responsible for marketing the benefit plans, enrolling members, collecting premium payments, and performing other HMO functions. The Permanente Medical Groups are responsible for rendering physician services to Kaiser's members under an exclusive contractual relationship with Kaiser. Kaiser is sometimes mistakenly thought to be a staff model HMO because of the close relationship between itself and the Permanente Medical Groups.

Independent Group

In the independent group model HMO, the HMO contracts with an existing, independent, multispecialty physician group to provide physician services to its members. In many cases, the independent physician group is the sponsor or owner of the HMO. An example of the independent group model HMO is Geisinger Health Plan of Danville, Pennsylvania. The Geisinger Clinic, which is a large, multispecialty physician group practice, is the independent group associated with the Geisinger Health Plan.

Typically, the physician group in an independent group model HMO continues to provide its non-HMO services while it participates in the HMO. Although the group may have an exclusive relationship with the HMO, this relationship usually does not prevent the group from engaging in non-HMO business.

Common Features of Group Models

Both types of group model HMOs are also referred to as closed panel HMOs because physicians must be members of the group practice to participate in the HMO; as a result, the HMO is considered closed to physicians who are not part of the group. Both types of group model HMOs share the advantages of staff model HMOs of making it somewhat easier to conduct utilization management because of the integration of physician practices and of providing broad services at its facilities. In addition, group practice HMOs may have lower capital needs than staff model

HMOs because the HMO does not have to support the large fixed salary costs associated with staff physicians.

Group model HMOs have several disadvantages in common with staff model HMOs. Like staff model HMOs, group model HMOs provide a limited choice of participating physicians for potential HMO members to select from. The limited physician panel can be a disadvantage in marketing the HMO. The limited number of office locations for the participating medical groups may also restrict the geographic accessibility of physicians for the HMO's members. The lack of accessibility can make it difficult for the HMO to market its coverage to a wide geographic area. Finally, group practices may be perceived by some potential HMO members as offering an undesirable clinic setting. Offsetting this disadvantage may be the perception of high quality associated with many of the physician group practices that are affiliated with HMOs.

Network Model

In network model HMOs, the HMO contracts with more than one group practice to provide physician services to the HMO's members. These group practices may be broad-based, multispecialty groups, in which case the HMO resembles the group practice model described above. An example of this type of HMO is Health Insurance Plan of Greater New York, which contracts with many multispecialty physician group practices in the New York area.

Alternatively, the HMO may contract with several small groups of primary care physicians (ie, family practice, internal medicine, pediatrics, and obstetrics/gynecology), in which case the HMO can be classified as a primary care network model. An example of this type of HMO is West Michigan HealthCare Network in Grand Rapids, Michigan.

In the primary care network model, the HMO contracts with several groups consisting of 7 to 15 primary care physicians representing the specialties of family practice and/or internal medicine, pediatrics, and obstetrics/gynecology to provide physician services to its members. Typi-

cally, the HMO compensates these groups on an all-inclusive physician capitation basis. The group is responsible for providing all physician services to the HMO's members assigned to the group and may refer to other physicians as necessary. The group is financially responsible for reimbursing other physicians for any referrals it makes. In some cases, the HMO may negotiate participation arrangements with specialist physicians to make it easier for its primary care groups to manage their referrals.

In contrast to the staff and group model HMOs described previously, network models may be either closed or open panel plans. If the network model HMO is a closed panel plan, it will only contract with a limited number of existing group practices. If it is an open panel plan, participation in the group practices will be open to any physician who meets the HMO's and group's credentials criteria. In some cases, network model HMOs will assist independent primary care physicians with the formation of primary care groups for the sole purpose of participating in the HMO's network.

Network model HMOs address many of the disadvantages associated with staff and group model HMOs. In particular, the broader physician participation that is usually identified with network model HMOs helps overcome the marketing disadvantage associated with the closed panel staff and group model plans. Nevertheless, network model HMOs usually have more limited physician participation than either IPA model or direct contract model plans.

Individual Practice Association Model

IPA model HMOs contract with an association of physicians—the IPA—to provide physician services to their members. The physicians are members of the IPA, which is a separate legal entity, but they remain individual practitioners and retain their separate offices and identities. IPA physicians continue to see their non-HMO patients and maintain their own offices, medical records, and support staff. IPA model HMOs are open panel plans because participation is open to all community physicians who meet the HMO's and IPA's selection criteria.

Generally, IPAs attempt to recruit physicians from all specialties to participate in their plans. Broad participation of physicians allows the IPA to provide all necessary physician services through participating physicians and minimizes the need for IPA physicians to refer HMO members to nonparticipating physicians to obtain services. In addition, broad physician participation can help make the IPA model HMO more attractive to potential HMO members.

IPA model HMOs usually follow one of two different methods of establishing relationships with their IPAs. In the first method, the HMO contracts with an IPA that has been independently established by community physicians. These types of IPAs often have contracts with more than one HMO on a nonexclusive basis. In the second method, the HMO works with community physicians to create an IPA and to recruit physicians to participate in it. The HMO's contract with these types of IPAs is usually on an exclusive basis because of the HMO's leading role in forming the IPA.

IPAs may be formed as large communitywide entities where physicians can participate without regard to the hospital with which they are affiliated. Alternatively, IPAs may be formed so that only physicians from one or two hospitals are eligible to participate in the IPA.

Hospital-based IPAs are sometimes preferred by HMOs over larger community-based IPAs for at least two reasons. First, hospital-based IPAs can restrict the panel of the IPA to physicians who are familiar with each other's practice patterns. This familiarity can make the utilization management process easier. Second, by using several hospital-based IPAs an HMO can limit the impact of a termination of one of its IPA agreements to a smaller group of physicians.

Most HMOs compensate their IPAs on an all-inclusive physician capitation basis to provide services to the HMO's members. The IPA then compensates its participating physicians on either a fee-for-service basis or a combination of fee-for-service and primary care capitation. In the fee-for-service variation, IPAs pay all their participating physicians on the basis of a fee schedule or a usual, customary, or reasonable (UCR) charge approach and withhold a portion of each payment for incentive and risk-sharing purposes.

Under the primary care capitation approach, IPAs pay their participating primary care physicians on a capitation basis and pay their specialist physicians on the basis of a fee schedule or UCR approach. The primary care capitation payments are based on fixed amounts per member per month and usually vary depending on the HMO member's age and sex. The IPA typically withholds a portion of both the capitation and fee-for-service payments for risk-sharing and incentive purposes. Compensation for primary care is discussed in Chapter 6.

IPA model HMOs overcome all the disadvantages associated with staff, group, and network model HMOs. They require less capital to establish and operate. In addition, they can provide a broad choice of participating physicians who practice in their private offices. As a result, IPA model HMOs offer marketing advantages in comparison to the staff and group model plans.

There are two major disadvantages of IPA model HMOs from the HMO's perspective. First, the development of an IPA creates an organized forum for physicians to negotiate as a group with the HMO. The organized forum of an IPA can help its physician members achieve some of the negotiating benefits of belonging to a group practice. Unlike the situation with a group practice, however, individual members of an IPA retain their ability to negotiate and contract directly with managed care plans. Because of their acceptance of combined risk through capitation payments, IPAs are generally immune from antitrust restrictions on group activities by physicians as long as they do not prevent or prohibit their member physicians from participating directly with an HMO.

Second, the process of utilization management is generally more difficult in an IPA model HMO than it is in staff and group model plans because physicians remain individual practitioners with little sense of being a part of the HMO. As a result, IPA model HMOs may devote more administrative resources to managing inpatient and outpatient utilization than their staff and group model counterparts.

Direct Contract Model

As the name implies, direct contract model HMOs contract directly with individual physicians to provide physician services to their members. With the exception of their direct contractual relationship with participating physicians, direct contract model HMOs are similar to IPA model plans. A well-known example of a direct contract model HMO is US Healthcare and its subsidiary HMOs.

Direct contract model HMOs attempt to recruit broad panels of community physicians to provide physician services as participating providers. These HMOs usually recruit both primary care and specialist physicians and typically use a primary care case management approach (also known as a gatekeeper system).

Like IPA model plans, direct contract model HMOs compensate their physicians on either a fee-for-service basis or a primary care capitation basis. Primary care capitation is somewhat more commonly used by direct contract model HMOs because it helps limit the financial risk assumed by the HMO. Unlike IPA model HMOs, direct contract model HMOs retain most of the financial risk for providing physician services; IPA model plans transfer this risk to their IPAs.

Direct contract model HMOs have most of the same advantages as IPA model HMOs. In addition, direct model HMOs eliminate the potential of a physician bargaining unit by contracting directly with individual physicians. This contracting model reduces the possibility of mass termination of physician participation agreements.

Direct contract model HMOs have several disadvantages. First, the HMO assumes additional financial risk for physician services relative to an IPA model HMO, as noted above. This additional risk exposure can be expensive if primary care physicians generate excessive referrals to specialist physicians.

Second, it can be more difficult and time consuming for a direct contract model HMO to recruit physicians because it lacks the physician leadership inherent in an IPA model plan. It is difficult for nonphysicians to recruit physicians, as several direct contract model HMOs have discovered in their attempts to expand into new markets.

Finally, utilization management may be more difficult in direct contract model HMOs because all contact with physicians is on an individual basis and there may be little incentive for physicians to participate in the utilization management programs.

CONCLUSION

Managed care is on a continuum, with a number of plan types offering an array of features that vary in their abilities to balance access to care, cost, quality control, benefit design, and flexibility. Managed care plans continue to evolve, with features from one type of plan appearing in others and new features continually being developed. There is no one single definition of the term *managed care*.

SUGGESTED READING

Boland P. *Making Managed Healthcare Work: A Practical Guide to Strategies and Solutions.* New York: McGraw-Hill; 1991.

Hale JA. *From HMO Movement to Managed Care Industry: The Future of HMOs in a Volatile Healthcare Market.* Minneapolis: InterStudy; 1988.

Rahn GJ. *Hospital-Sponsored Health Maintenance Organizations.* Chicago: American Hospital Publishing; 1987.

Shouldice RG. *Introduction to Managed Care.* Arlington, VA: Information Resources Press; 1991.

Wagner ER. *A Practical Guide to Evaluating Physician Capitation Payments.* Washington, DC: American Society of Internal Medicine; 1987.

Wagner ER, Hackenberg VJ. *A Practical Guide to Physician-Sponsored HMO Development.* Washington, DC: American Society of Internal Medicine; 1986.

Chapter 3

Elements of Management Control Structure

Peter R. Kongstvedt

It is not really possible to deal comprehensively with the topic of the elements of management control structure in one chapter of a book. There are myriad courses, texts, and other learning resources available to the reader that deal with the basic elements of management. For the purposes of this chapter, it is assumed that the reader has a working knowledge of business and management, so that certain fundamental aspects of management will not be discussed here (eg, how to read a balance sheet, write a job description, or construct an organizational chart). What follows in this chapter is a brief overview of certain management control elements as they pertain specifically to managed care. Detailed discussions of these activities are the topics of much of this book.

Ironically, there is no standardization of management governance or control structure in managed care; for example, the function, or even the very presence, of a board of directors will vary from plan to plan. The function of key officers or managers, as well as of committees, will likewise vary depending on the type of organization, the ownership, and the motivations and skills of the individuals involved. Because each plan will construct its own management control structure to suit its needs, only a few of the most common elements are described in this chapter.

BOARD OF DIRECTORS

Many, although not all, types of managed care plans will have a board of directors. The makeup and function of the board will be influenced by many factors (discussed below), but the board has the final responsibility for governance of the operation.

Examples of plans or managed care operations that would not necessarily have their own boards would include the following:

- preadmission certification and medical case management operations of insurance companies
- preferred provider organizations (PPOs) developed by large insurance companies
- PPOs developed for single employers by an insurance company
- employer sponsored/developed plans (PPOs, precertification operations)
- health maintenance organizations (HMOs) or exclusive provider organizations (EPOs) set up as a line of business of an insurance company

These operations or plans are subsidiaries of larger companies; those companies do have boards of directors, but their boards are involved with oversight of the entire company and not the subsidiary operation. PPOs or HMOs that are divisions of insurance companies may be required to list a board on their licensure forms, but that board may have little real operational role.

Board Make-up

All HMOs have boards, although not all those boards are particularly functional. This is especially true for HMOs that are part of large national companies. Each local HMO is incorporated and required to have a board, but it is not uncommon for the chains to use the same two corporate officers (perhaps with one local representative; see below) as the board for every HMO. Again, the board fulfills its legal function and obligation, but the actual operation of the HMO is controlled through the management structure of the company rather than through a direct relationship between the plan director and the board.

There are legal requirements for boards, particularly for HMOs. Those requirements are spelled out in each state's laws and regulations; for federally qualified HMOs, there are federal regulations as well. A common (although recently less so) requirement for HMOs is the necessity for member representation; new start-up operations may be exempt from that requirement for a period of time. Many state regulations require that at least one third of the board be members of the plan. In the case of the national HMO companies, that often translates into one individual who meets periodically with two corporate officers for brief board meetings. In the case of community-based HMOs, that may mean that multiple board seats (up to one third) are held by members.

Board make-up will also vary depending on whether the plan is for-profit, in which case the owners' or shareholders' representatives may hold the majority of seats, or not-for-profit, in which case there will probably be broader community representation.[*] The use of outside directors rather than plan officers as directors in either case will be dictated by local events and company bylaws. Provider-sponsored plans will usually have majority representation by providers and so must take special precautions to avoid

antitrust problems. The issue of antitrust is also discussed in Chapter 37.

Regardless of how the board is made up, it is important for there to be adequate director and officer liability insurance as well as insurance for errors and omissions. The need for such insurance may be attenuated by certain provisions in the company's or plan's bylaws holding the board members and officers harmless from liability. This issue requires review by legal counsel.

Function of the Board

As stated earlier, the function of the board is governance: overseeing and maintaining final responsibility for the plan. In a real sense, the buck stops with the board. Final approval authority of corporate bylaws rests with the board. It is the bylaws that govern the basic structure of power and control not only of the plan officers but of the board itself.

The fiduciary responsibility of the board in an operating plan is paramount. General oversight of the profitability or reserve status rests with the board, as does oversight and approval of significant fiscal events such as a major acquisition or a significant expenditure. In a for-profit plan, the board has fiduciary responsibility to protect the interests of the stockholders.

Legal responsibilities of the board also may include review of reports and document signing. For example, a board officer may be required to sign the quarterly financial report to the state regulatory agency, the board chairperson may be required to sign any acquisition documents, and the board is responsible for the veracity of financial statements to stockholders.

Setting and approving policy is another common function of an active board. This may be as broad as determining the overall policy of using a gatekeeper system, or it may be as detailed as approving organizational charts and reporting structures. Although most policies and procedures will be the responsibility of the plan offic-

---

[*]Some not-for-profit HMOs are actually organized as cooperatives, with the entire board being made up of members.

ers, an active board may set a policy regarding what operational policies must be brought to the board for approval or change.

In HMOs and many other types of managed care plans, the board has a special responsibility for oversight of the quality management (QM) program and for the quality of care delivered to members. Usually this responsibility is discharged through board (or board subcommittee) review of the QM documentation (including the overall QM plan and regular reports on findings and activities) and through feedback to the medical director and plan QM committee.

In freestanding plans, the board also has responsibility for hiring the chief executive officer (CEO) of the plan and for reviewing that officer's performance. The board in such plans often sets the CEO's compensation package, and the CEO reports to the board.

Active boards generally have committees to take up certain functions. Common board committees may include an executive committee (for rapid access to decision making and confidential discussions), a compensation committee (to set general compensation guidelines for the plan, set the CEO's compensation, and approve and issue stock options), a finance committee (to review financial results, approve budgets, set and approve spending authorities, review the annual audit, review and approve outside funding sources, and so forth), and a QM committee (as noted above).

KEY MANAGEMENT POSITIONS

The roles and titles of the key managers in any plan will vary depending on the type of plan, its legal organization, its line of business, its complexity, whether it is freestanding or a satellite of another operation, and the local needs and talent. There is little consistency in this area from plan to plan. How each key role is defined (or even whether it will be present at all) is strictly up to the management of each plan. What follows, then, is a general overview of certain key roles.

Executive Director/Chief Executive Officer

Most plans have at least one key manager. Whether or not that individual is called a CEO, an executive director, a general manager, or a plan manager is a function of the items mentioned earlier in this chapter (eg, scope of authority, reporting structure of the company, and the like). For purposes of discussion, this key manager will be referred to as an executive director.

The executive director is usually responsible for all the operational aspects of the plan, although that is not always the case. For example, some large companies (eg, insurance companies or national HMO chains) have marketing reporting vertically to a regional marketing director rather than through the plan manager. A few companies take that to the extreme of having each functional area reporting vertically to regional managers rather than having all operations coordinated at the local level by a single manager; thus reporting is a function of the overall environment, and there is little standardization in the industry.

In freestanding plans and traditional HMOs, the executive director is responsible for all areas. The other officers and key managers report to the executive director, who in turn reports to the board (or to a regional manager in the case of national companies). The executive director also has responsibility for general administrative operations and public affairs.

Medical Director

Almost by definition, managed care plans will have a medical director. Whether that position is a full-time manager or a community physician who comes in a few hours per week is determined by the needs of the plan. The medical director usually has responsibility for provider relations, provider recruiting, QM, utilization management, and medical policy.

Some plans (eg, simple PPOs) may only use the medical director, or a medical consultant, to review claims or perhaps to approve physician applications and to review patterns of utilization. The spectrum of medical director involvement parallels the intensity of medical management activities. Usually the medical director reports to the executive director.

As a plan grows in size, particularly if it is a complex plan such as an HMO, the need for the medical director to leverage time becomes crucial. If the medical director gets bogged down in day-to-day minutia, the ability to provide leadership in the critical areas of utilization, quality, network management, and medical policy becomes dramatically reduced.

There are two approaches commonly employed to deal with this problem. The most common is bringing in an associate medical director. An associate medical director usually starts as a part-time position, but as the plan grows in size and complexity the position may evolve into a full-time function, and in fact there may be many associate medical directors in large plans. The role of the associate medical director is often defined as a subset of the overall duties of the medical director; for example, this person may focus primarily on utilization management or QM. This concept of adding qualified staff is not different from basic management practices for any specialized activity, but health plan managers are occasionally slow to realize the value of adding physician managers when they may be quick to realize the value of adding multiple layers of management in other operational areas.

The second approach to the issue of dealing with medical management in a large plan is to decentralize certain functions. For example, in a closed panel plan (eg, a staff model HMO or a multisite group practice) it is common practice to assign management responsibilities to a physician at each geographic site. This on-site physician manager may have responsibility for utilization and staffing at the site or other duties as necessary. In an open panel setting (eg, an open panel HMO), the network may be divided up into regions, and associate medical directors may be assigned responsibilities for designated regions. In either case, management must be realistic about the time and resources required for these associate medical directors to do their jobs. The skills, motivations, and compensation for decentralized or delegated medical management must be carefully thought through, and of course the medical director retains ultimate accountability.

Finance Director

In freestanding plans or large operations, it is common to have a finance director or chief financial officer. That individual is generally responsible for oversight of all financial and accounting operations. In some plans, that may include functions such as billing, management information services (MIS), enrollment, and underwriting as well as accounting, fiscal reporting, and budget preparation. This position usually reports to the executive director, although once again some national companies use vertical reporting.

Marketing Director

This person is responsible for marketing the plan. Responsibility generally includes oversight of marketing representatives, advertising, client relations, and enrollment forecasting. A few plans have marketing generating initial premium rates, which are then sent to finance or underwriting for review, but that is uncommon. This position reports to the executive director or vertically, depending on the company.

Operations Director

In larger plans, it is not uncommon to have an operations director. This position usually oversees claims, MIS, enrollment, underwriting (unless finance is doing so), member services, office management, and any other traditional back room functions. This position usually reports to the executive director.

COMMITTEES

Again, there is little consistency from plan to plan regarding committees. Nonmedical committees may be limited to the member grievance committee (see Chapter 19). Other nonmedical committees are often ad hoc, convened to meet a specific need and then dissolved. Most plans tend to have standing committees to address management issues in defined areas, but that is idiosyncratic from plan to plan.

In the medical management area, committees serve to diffuse some elements of responsibility (which can be beneficial for medical-legal reasons) and allow important input from the field into procedure and policy or even into case-specific interpretation of existing policy. These aspects are discussed in greater detail in Chapter 38.

Some examples of common medical management committees are given below. The actual formation, role, responsibility, and activity of any committee is a local call. More information about each of these areas may be found in the pertinent chapters of this book.

Quality Management Committee

This topic is discussed in Chapters 15 and 38. This is one area where a committee is essential for oversight of the QM activity, setting of standards, review of data, feedback to providers, follow-up, and approval of sanctions. A peer review committee may be a subset of the QM committee, or it may be separate.

Credentialing Committee

This important topic is discussed in Chapters 5, 37, and 38. This committee may also be a subset of the QM committee, or it may be separate. In new plans with heavy credentialing needs, it is probably best for the committee to be separate.

Medical Advisory Committee

Many plans have a medical advisory committee whose purpose is to review general medical management issues brought to it by the medical director. Such issues may include changes in the contract with providers, compensation, changes in authorization procedures, and so on. This committee serves as a sounding board for the medical director. Occasionally it has voting authority, but that is rare because such authority is really vested with the board.

Utilization Review Committee

This committee reviews utilization issues brought to it by the medical director. Often this committee approves or reviews policy regarding coverage. This committee is also the one that reviews utilization patterns of providers and approves or reviews the sanctioning process (for utilization reasons) against providers.

Sometimes this committee gets involved in resolving disputes between the plan and a provider regarding utilization approval and may be involved in reviewing cases for medical necessity. In large plans, this function may be further subdivided into various specialty panels for review of consultant utilization. This committee may be a subset of the medical advisory committee or it may be freestanding.

Pharmacy and Therapeutics Committee

Plans with significant pharmacy benefits often have a pharmacy and therapeutics committee. Pharmacy is discussed in Chapter 14. This committee is usually charged with developing a formulary, reviewing changes to that formulary, and reviewing abnormal prescription utilization patterns by providers. This committee is usually freestanding.

MANAGEMENT CONTROL STRUCTURE

Control structure refers to issues such as reporting responsibility, spending (and other commitment) authority, hiring and firing, the conduct of performance evaluations of employees, and so forth. Each plan will set these up to fit its situation and needs. Although these issues are too diverse to be addressed in this chapter, a wealth of material on all these functions can be found in the general management literature.

One item that is of special significance is the monthly operating report (MOR). Most tightly run managed care plans develop an MOR to use as the basic management tool. The typical MOR reports the month- and year-to-date financial status of the plan. Those data are backed up with details regarding membership, premium revenue, other revenue, medical costs (usually total and broken out into categories such as hospital, primary care, referral care, ancillary services, and so forth), marketing costs, administrative costs, other expenses, taxes (if appropriate), and the bottom line. Results are generally reported in terms of whole dollars and per member per month. This issue is discussed in detail in Chapter 25.

How much detail is reported routinely or on an ad hoc basis is a local call. The point here is that managed care, especially in tightly run plans, is so dynamic that managers cannot wait for quarterly results. Managers must have current and reliable data from which to manage. Sutton's Law dictates that you must "go where the money is," and that can only be done if the MOR tells you where to look. In the case of hospital utilization, one cannot even wait for the MOR but must have daily reporting (see Chapter 16).

Various other types of reports are described throughout this book. What reports and routine reviews a manager needs to run the business is a decision each plan must make. If the plan is not producing an MOR, however, it is probably not managing optimally.

CONCLUSION

The basic functions of governance and control in HMOs are similar to those in any business, although the specifics regarding the board of directors, plan officers, and responsibilities of key managers vary tremendously from plan to plan.

SUGGESTED READING

Boland P. *Making Managed Healthcare Work: A Practical Guide to Strategies and Solutions.* New York: McGraw-Hill; 1991.

Curry W, ed. *The Physician Executive.* American College of Physician Executives; 1988.

Drucker P. *Management Tasks, Responsibilities, Practices.* New York: Harper & Row; 1974.

Rahn G, ed. *Hospital Sponsored Health Maintenance Organizations: Issues for Decision Makers.* Chicago: American Hospital Publishing; 1987.

Part II

The Health Care Delivery System

When one's all right, he's prone to spite
The doctor's peaceful mission.
But when he's sick, it's loud and quick
He bawls for a physician.

Eugene Field
(1850–1895)
Doctors, st 2, 1890

Chapter 4

Primary Care in Closed Panels

Peter R. Kongstvedt

This chapter deals with issues involving primary care physicians (PCPs) in closed panel health plans; that is, group and staff model health maintenance organizations (HMOs) or large group practices that have a high proportion of managed care in their practice. Although primary medical care can and is delivered by consultants, this chapter will restrict its scope to PCPs.

Conventional definitions of primary care encompass internal medicine, family practice, and pediatrics. Obstetrics/gynecology (Ob/Gyn) is generally considered specialty care, although it is not uncommon for HMOs to allow self-referral by members to Ob/Gyn physicians for certain services (eg, Pap smears). In that context, many of the comments regarding PCPs will hold equally well for Ob/Gyn physicians in closed panels, because issues of recruiting, compensation, and so forth will be similar.

Last, issues germane to primary care in closed panels may also hold relevance in open panels, particularly for private medical groups of 10 or more physicians that have a significant level of managed care participation.

NEEDS ASSESSMENT

To assess a closed panel's needs for PCPs you must look at realistic staffing ratios, availability, scope of practice, and acceptance.

Staffing Ratios

In closed panel HMOs, staffing ratios look at the number of PCPs to the number of members. There are significant differences in staffing ratios depending on the size of the health plan and whether there is a considerable Medicare population being served. Staffing ratios are also occasionally addressed in state regulations; for example, in Pennsylvania a staffing ratio of 1 physician per 1,600 members is required. Staffing ratios will be discussed in terms of full-time equivalents (FTEs), although most closed panel plans in fact use part-time providers on their staff. There are two common units of measurement for staffing: members per physician (eg, 1:1,300) and physicians per 1,000 members (eg, 0.8:1,000). This chapter will use the latter convention.

Large, mature closed panel plans that serve a primarily commercial population have an average PCP staffing ratio of 0.8:1,000 and an average physician staffing ratio of 1.3:1,000. Plans that are smaller may have more than twice those ratios. The ratios per 1,000 members, by specialty type, are 0.3 for full-time general/family practice, 0.3 for internal medicine, 0.2 for pediatrics, and 0.1 for Ob/Gyn.[1]

These figures may vary considerably from plan to plan. Some private, for-profit closed panel plans have used primary care staffing ratios of 0.6:1,000, and some large, well-known closed panel plans use ratios closer to 1.2:1,000.

The size of a health plan has a clear impact on staffing ratios. Economies of scale are achievable in large plans. Plans that have a large medical staff also have the ability to cover clinic sites more easily, so that there is less need for overstaffing simply to ensure the presence of a provider at a site. Smaller plans not only need to ensure site coverage (assuming that they have more than one site to cover) but must staff for growth as well.

The scope of clinical practice by the PCPs has an effect on staffing. If PCPs are performing many procedures that might otherwise go out to referral specialists, there will be a need for more generous staffing. For example, if family practitioners are performing obstetrical services, some of their time will be taken up with prenatal care and deliveries, so that greater staffing will be required to meet the primary care needs of the members.

Medicare members utilize far more services than non-Medicare commercial members. Members younger than 65 have an average of 3.6 physician encounters per year; Medicare members average 7 encounters per year.[1] This statistic refers to total physician encounters, not necessarily those for primary care only. Nevertheless, the implications for staffing are clear: Staffing needs are greatly increased when a substantial Medicare population is served.

Closed panel plans are more likely to use nonphysician providers (ie, physician assistants, nurse practitioners, or nurse-midwives) to deliver some primary medical care to their members.[2] The scope of that primary care is somewhat limited in comparison to that provided by a licensed physician but is adequate for the responsibilities with which these providers are charged. Well-qualified midlevel practitioners are generally found to be a great asset to a plan in that they are able to deliver excellent primary care, tend to spend more time with patients, and receive generally good acceptance from most members.

Fully 86% of closed panel plans reported using nonphysician providers (compared with 48% of open panel plans); 52% of plans used physician assistants, 52% of plans used nurse practitioners, and 28% of plans used nurse-mid-

wives.[1] Most plan managers use slightly different staffing ratios for nonphysician providers than for PCPs. For example, a nonphysician provider may be considered 0.8 of an FTE for PCP staffing purposes. The primary reasons for this are the tendency for nonphysician providers to spend more time with their patients (which often accounts for their popularity with their patients) and the need for the nonphysician provider to staff cases with a physician. The physician who staffs such cases may also have a slightly diminished productivity strictly from the point of view of personally seeing patients.

Staffing ratios are useful guides for management to use when addressing recruiting needs, but they are also useful when addressing issues of efficiency and productivity. Ratios that are lean may, over time, erode the level of service and cost effectiveness of a plan. For example, if you run at 0.5:1,000 or tighter for an extended period, the stress level of the PCPs will rise as they try to meet the demand for services by members. When that happens, the harried PCPs will have less time and patience for evaluating problems and will be inclined to refer the member to a consultant to deal with any but the most routine care. Furthermore, the attitude of the PCPs will degenerate and be reflected back to members during office visits.

Ratios that are significantly richer may over time become an insupportable overhead cost. If overstaffing continues for too long, productivity could take a nose dive, and efforts to improve it will be met with resistance. Once low productivity levels become institutionalized, it is often quite difficult to improve them because you are demanding more work for no increase in compensation, and the usual result is a retort, stating that plan management's demands for greater productivity will have a serious negative impact on patient care quality. A more detailed discussion of productivity is presented later in this chapter.

Availability

The availability of high-quality physicians may have an impact on staffing ratios. Although there are many things that may affect physician availability, two important elements are the cycle of physician training and the desirability of your practice situation.

Virtually all residency programs begin and end in midsummer. Usually a resident fresh out of training will want to decompress for a few weeks or more, so that physicians from training programs often are not available to start until August or September. Even for physicians a few years out of training, it is not uncommon for them to have signed 1-year contracts, so that they also may not be available until the late summer. If a physician has been out of training for a number of years and is in private practice or is coming out of the military, there is much more variability in availability.

The desirability of your practice opportunity also affects the availability of physicians. Geographic location, climate, plan size and history, reputation, and lifestyle potential will all have an impact. The presence of other well-qualified and congenial physicians on your staff will also improve your recruiting potential because a collegial atmosphere with support from fellow physicians is an important element in making your plan desirable from the PCP's standpoint.

If you are in a situation where there is sufficient variation in physician availability to make recruiting difficult, you may have to overstaff in the summer and fall to be able to serve projected increases in membership in January and February because many open enrollments occur in the fall.

Scope of Practice

The scope of clinical skills that the physicians in your group have will also affect your staffing needs. If the PCPs perform a large variety of procedures or if supervision of midlevel practitioners is required (eg, family practitioners performing routine obstetric procedures, internists performing stress tests and reading the electrocardiograms, or PCPs supervising physician's assistants), there will be an incremental decrease in the amount of time available for regular office care.

You may wish to recruit a PCP with special skills rather than recruit a consultant, and this too may have an effect on your staffing ratios. For example, your PCPs may be sending all the routine flexible proctosigmoidoscopies out to a gastroenterologist. If your plan is large enough, you may consider recruiting specifically for an internist skilled in that procedure, even though it would alter your staffing ratios slightly downward. The same argument may exist for stress testing or a number of other high-volume procedures that a well-trained PCP can perform as well as a consultant.

One concern with this idea, which applies equally to adding consultants (see Chapter 7), is that once such a resource becomes easily available utilization tends to rise. The service is often seen as free and other PCPs will tend to request it more readily. Furthermore, if a physician truly enjoys doing the procedure, he or she may tend to recommend it more often as an unconscious means of displacing other less enjoyable clinical activities (eg, routine health assessments).

Acceptance

Your needs may be affected by the acceptability of your current PCPs by your target markets, the medical community as a whole, and your membership. For example, you may require the addition of only one PCP according to the staffing ratios, but your plan is located in a community where family physicians are not generally accepted. To provide adequate coverage, you may have to consider adding an internist and a pediatrician, even though it makes your staffing ratios too high for half the year.

RECRUITING

Timing

New managers who are recruiting physicians for the first time often underestimate how long it takes to recruit well-qualified PCPs. Although physicians coming out of training programs are usually not available until middle to late summer, they frequently have decided where they are going by the preceding fall or winter. There are always exceptions, and there are certainly excellent physicians who have not decided by the time they are done with their residency programs, but that is not the norm.

Even for PCPs who have been in practice and desire to make a change, the process is a long one. Physicians, like other people, do not wish to contemplate another change, so they will take their time in choosing their next location. If they are well qualified, they can afford to be choosy and explore many opportunities.

In general, the window for recruiting is most open between November and April, although opportunities do exist all year long. As a rule of thumb, it is best to plan on beginning the recruiting process at least 5 to 9 months before new physicians are required to be on board. This gestation period may be cut short if you are lucky, in which case you may have to decide whether you are willing to add the new PCP(s) to your staff early.

Sources

Spontaneous inquiries occur randomly. If your plan is in a desirable location, you can count on frequent inquiries. If a physician is already in your community or once lived there and wishes to return, he or she may contact you directly.

Advertisements in professional journals are perhaps the most common method of making contact with PCPs interested in making a change. The lead time for getting the ad in the periodical can be quite long, so plan ahead. Some managers hold that it is enough to run the ads every other issue rather than every issue. State medical societies also have journals, which are good places to run ads, especially in your home state and the states surrounding your plan. Examples of national medical journals that routinely run advertisements include the following:

- *American Journal of Obstetrics and Gynecology*
- *Annals of Internal Medicine*
- *Journal of the American Medical Association*
- *Journal of Family Practice*
- *Pediatrics*
- *New England Journal of Medicine*

Newspaper advertisements are less useful, although some widely circulated newspapers such as the *New York Times* do run ads for physicians in their areas. Military publications such as the *Military Press* and *Stars and Stripes* may reach physicians who will be completing their service and are looking for civilian practice opportunities.

Letters to cooperative residency programs may be useful, especially if the program director is willing to post your letter on a common bulletin board where residents can see it. Recruiting physicians on site at a training program is rarely allowed, so some large plans host informal off-site gatherings for residents of area programs. If your plan participates as a training site for a residency program, you will have a reasonably good chance of recruiting some of the residents who rotated through.

Direct mail can be quite effective. Mailing labels may be obtained from a number of sources such as the American Medical Association and Business Mailers, Inc. Preparing a professional-looking brochure is important, although a well-written letter will still have an impact. Because preparing a direct mailing can be labor intensive, you may wish to contract with an outside agency to collate the material, stuff the envelopes, and so on.

Your brochure or letter should contain, at a minimum, the following elements:

- a description of the health plan in terms of its size, the number of medical facilities (or clinics, if you use that term), medical services available, current physicians on staff, and any unique points about the plan
- a description of the hospitals, their location, their size, their services, and so forth
- a description of the community and its positive points such as colleges or universities, special cultural and recreational offerings, religious and social organizations, shopping and dining, and the weather

Professional Recruiting Agencies

A carefully selected professional agency can be an invaluable resource in locating and recruiting high-quality physicians. When you do your own recruiting, you will be dismayed at the number of responses you get from poorly qualified candidates. Separating out the well-qualified candidates from the unqualified, as well as weeding out the tire kickers, can be an exhausting chore for someone not trained in it. Even worse, you may inadvertently pass over an important piece of information about a candidate, or not look for it at all, and have a disastrous outcome.

Professional recruiters will not be able to guarantee a placement, nor can they guarantee that a candidate who does get placed with you will ultimately work out. They can, however, remove a great deal of the burden from you in the recruiting process. They may also have access to candidates who are looking to change but who do not wish to contact anyone directly for fear of compromising their current position.

Such help does not come cheap, although fees for placements are quite variable. The most you might see is 30% of the physician's first-year salary, but lesser fees are more common. For example, a recruiter may charge a straight fee of $12,000 or $15,000 for a placement. Some recruiters require a retainer to be paid at the beginning, with the balance contingent on placement, whereas others work strictly on contingency. It is common for a recruiter to give you a discount for multiple placements in a year. Fees are sometimes negotiable, although if you negotiate the fee down too low the recruiter may be less motivated to help you.

In selecting a recruiting agency, be sure to check the agency's references. Try to get an idea of how many physicians it has placed, whether it has successfully placed PCPs in groups similar to your own, how long it took on average, and whether the physicians are still there. If you are unfamiliar with contracts, be sure to have the agency's contract reviewed by an attorney before signing.

Initial Selection of Candidates To Consider

After you have responses from candidates, you need to select whom you will consider asking in for an interview. Although this process

will be easier if you have been using a professional recruiter, it cannot be eliminated entirely.

The curriculum vitae is the first source of data for you to use and should describe the physicians' credentials and current situation, their training, where they went to medical school, where their postgraduate training took place, and specialty board certification or eligibility (some specialties such as Ob/Gyn require a certain amount of practice experience before certification is given).

From either the cover letter or a phone call, try to ascertain the professional goals and needs of the PCP. For example, a physician may simply be looking for someplace to park for a year while a spouse finishes training. In that case, you need to decide whether that is acceptable or not.

The process of checking the credentials of a candidate should be thorough; shortcuts must not be taken even if your group is suffering from understaffing. Failure to perform credentials checking properly not only opens the group up to a serious legal liability but may compromise care to the members, cause a serious embarrassment to the group, and result in the need to recruit again under even more stress. A more thorough discussion of physician credentials checking is found in Chapters 5 and 37; the process in closed panels should contain all the elements found in open panels plus those items discussed specifically in this chapter.

Finding out the malpractice history is an important exercise. Usually it is enough simply to ask the candidates to list any malpractice claims that were judged against them or settled with an award. It is not uncommon for a physician to have been sued or even to have settled a case to avoid costly and lengthy litigation, even though the physician may have been perfectly innocent. Do not allow the presence of a malpractice history alone to deter you from considering a candidate, but look closely at that history for evidence of a pattern or of a truly malfeasant act.

You should find out what type of malpractice insurance the potential candidate currently has. You want to know who the carrier is, whether it is on a claims made or occurrence basis, and whether the candidate has or will purchase tail coverage if necessary. In other words, if candidates have the occurrence type of malpractice insurance (which is becoming uncommon), they are covered for any claim arising against them in the future for events that occurred during the time they had the policy. If they have the claims made type of coverage (the most common type), their coverage ends as soon as the premiums stop. To continue coverage for future claims arising from events that occurred during the policy period, they must buy tail coverage. Tail coverage can be quite expensive (for example, an Ob/Gyn in practice for 10 years may have to pay well over $75,000 for tail coverage), and you need to determine whether your plan would have to provide it to attract the candidate. If you do provide it, you may want to consider a 3-year forgiveness of the cost. In other words, you will pay for the coverage, but its cost is considered a loan to the new physician. For each year the physician practices with your group, you forgive a third of the original loan. If the physician leaves before 3 years are up, he or she has to repay whatever portion of the loan remains.

Under no circumstances may you refuse to consider a candidate for reasons of age, sex, religious beliefs, race, or any other elements considered under the Equal Employment Opportunity Act.

Before inviting a physician to your plan for an interview, conduct a telephone interview first. This may reveal, for example, that the candidate has little or no communication skills, is unable to speak the same language as your members, or has unreasonable demands. This will also give you an opportunity to explore further reasons why the candidate wants to be considered for your group.

Reference checks are usually done at this point but are occasionally done after the candidate has come in for an interview. There are two types of reference checks: formal letters of reference and telephone reference checks. Ask your candidates to submit three letters of reference from physicians who have known them professionally in their current position. If that is not possible for reasons of confidentiality, reserve the right to check those references after a job offer has been made, and ask for references from the next most recent position.

It is unusual in this litigious era for reference letters to do anything except either state what percentage of the time the candidate spends walking on water or simply confirm employment, revealing no information whatsoever except that the candidate was employed.

Telephone reference checks are more useful because they are confidential and you may sometimes be able to read between the lines. The most useful telephone conversations occur between physicians. When nonphysicians question physicians about the competence of another physician, negative responses are likely to be muted. Again, it is unusual for a reference to say negative things for fear of a lawsuit, even after you have assured him or her of complete confidentiality.

You may wish to telephone references who have not been provided by the candidate (only after the candidate has given permission for you to do reference checks; it could be devastating if the current employer does not know that the candidate is looking to leave). Such references could include the president of the candidate's local medical society, the chief of staff where the candidate currently has active privileges, or, in the case of physicians just completing training, the director of the residency program.

The National Practitioner Data Bank

A special type of reference check was created by the Health Care Quality Improvement Act of 1986. In addition to providing immunity from antitrust lawsuits, the Act requires hospitals, health plans, malpractice carriers, and state licensure boards to report settled or lost malpractice suits and adverse acts, sanctions, or restrictions against the practice privileges of a physician. The reporting aspect of the Act is further discussed in Chapters 9 and 37.

The Act also states that any hospital or HMO may contact the National Practitioner Data Bank to obtain information about a physician and that, if the hospital or health plan fails to do so, it will be assumed that it did so anyway. In other words, there is a potential for liability on the part of the plan if it fails to check with the National Practitioner Data Bank and hires a physician who has a poor record as reported in the Data Bank and there is a malpractice problem later on. As this book is being written, there are relatively few cases in the Data Bank, making it rather spare as a repository of information. It is likely that over the course of time, however, the Data Bank will indeed become a useful reference check for network managers.

Information about the National Practitioner Data Bank may be obtained by writing to:

National Practitioner Data Bank
PO Box 6048
Camarillo, CA 93011-6048

Interview Process

After candidates to interview are selected, the next step is to invite them to the plan. The trip should be arranged so that as little work as possible is required of the candidates. You should prepay the airfare, arrange to have someone meet them at the airport, have the hotel arranged, and so forth. It is good form to invite spouses as well, but that may be delayed until a second interview.

The interview should be carefully scheduled. Plan for the candidate to meet with other PCPs in the plan, the chief of staff of the appropriate medical department, and other plan executives as necessary (eg, the marketing director, the nursing or operations director, the executive director, and so forth).

A visit to the main hospital that the PCP would be using is also important. Hospitals are usually quite accommodating about giving tours to prospective new physicians. If there is time, an informal tour of the community is helpful, with an emphasis on the types of neighborhoods that are available to live in. If the candidate and spouse have both come, you may wish to arrange for a real estate agent to give the spouse a tour while the candidate is interviewing.

Try not to leave large blocks of time where the candidate has nothing to do and feels adrift. The same goes for the spouse (unless the spouse wants to be left alone; inquire first). This carries over to the evening if the candidate is staying over night. A dinner invitation is appropriate, al-

though the candidate may feel too tired and may wish to decline, in which case you should graciously accept the refusal.

After the initial interview is complete, be sure to follow up promptly. If you are no longer interested, it is still good form to send a letter thanking the candidates and indicating that the final selection did not include them but that you appreciate their interest and wish them luck. If you are still interested, arrange for a second visit, this time for the candidate and spouse to see the community. Assuming that you have satisfactorily completed the reference check, you will want to make an offer of employment at that time. The candidate may wish to think it over and review the contract. If that is the case, ask for an answer within a fixed time frame, such as 3 weeks.

When offering a contract, you will wish to include a provision that if the candidate has falsified any information, or has failed to provide complete information, you have the right to terminate the contract. If you have not been able to complete the reference check because of confidentiality issues, you will wish to be able to contact references at the candidate's current location upon the candidate's acceptance of your offer, and final acceptance by you is contingent upon that last reference check.

COMPENSATION

The basic tenet of compensation for PCPs in closed panels is that they should be on approximate parity with their fee-for-service colleagues. This does not refer to gross income but includes benefits (eg, malpractice insurance, health and life insurance, retirement, and so forth), duty requirements (eg, frequency of being on call, hours worked, and so forth), bonus pay, and net take-home pay. Because physicians do not look at gross dollars alone when assessing a practice opportunity, neither should you. Further discussion about factors leading to physician retention is found later in this chapter.

Straight Salary

A straight salary is the most common payment mechanism in staff model HMOs and is often found in group models as well, where the group's salary costs are passed back directly to the plan. Some private group practice groups use straight salary, although usually as a base after which productivity, medical costs, or other modifiers are then applied. Bonus arrangements are commonly attached to salary plans as well.

Capitation

Some group model closed panel plans capitate a medical group (or groups) that make up the physician panel. In that case, the plan negotiates the overall capitation rate with the group, and the group then decides how to compensate the physicians. Again, salary with a bonus plan is the most common arrangement within the group, although some groups use fee-for-service, and a few capitate individual providers. A more thorough discussion of both capitation and fee-for-service in managed care is found in Chapter 6.

Benefits

Benefits are a vital part of the total compensation package. Whether the plan pays straight salary and provides the benefits directly to the physicians or the group is capitated and provides the benefits itself, benefits are an integral part of compensation.

Exhibit 4-1 lists benefits that are almost universally provided to physicians as part of their compensation. Exhibit 4-2 lists benefits that are quite commonly provided as well, but perhaps not in every case. Exhibit 4-3 lists some benefits that are not routinely provided but that you may wish to consider for special circumstances.

Exhibit 4-1 Routine Benefits

- Malpractice insurance
- Life insurance
- Health insurance
- Continuing medical education time and funds
- Professional licensure fees
- Vacation and sick leave

Exhibit 4-2 Common Benefits

- Dental insurance
- Disability insurance
- Auto allowance and parking fees at hospitals
- Professional society dues
- Retirement plan
  —401(k)
  —Simplified employee pension plan (SEP) IRA
  —Tax deferred annuity (TDA)

Risk and Bonus Arrangements

Bonus plans are common in closed panels, whereas risk arrangements are less so. In capitated groups, there is the inherent risk that the capitation payment represents all the money there is; in a sense that is a clear risk.

The most common mechanism to deal with risk in a closed panel is a withhold. In a withhold, part of the capitation payment (eg, 20%) or salary (eg, 10%) is withheld until the end of the year. That withhold is used to cover excess medical expenses. If there is still money in the withhold, the physicians receive it. For a more complete discussion of risk arrangements, refer to Chapter 6.

Exhibit 4-3 Uncommon Benefits

- Book and journal allowance (separate from continuing medical education (CME) funds)
- Paid time off for nonplan activities
  —Research
  —Jury duty
  —Military leave
  —Volunteer work
- Compensation time
- Extended leave without pay
- In-plan moonlighting
  —Extended hours
  —Urgent care
- Sabbatical program
- Paternity leave (maternity leave is assumed to be provided)
- Deferred compensation
- Profit sharing
- Low-interest, unsecured loans

Bonus plans are most often based either on total plan performance or on medical cost alone. When bonus is based on total plan performance, it may be affected by things outside the physician's control, such as membership growth, underwriting criteria, premium yield, and so forth. This will be perceived as unfair in the event that no bonus is paid. On the other hand, it clearly points out that everyone is in it together.

Bonus based on medical expense only is more closely related to actions under the control of the physicians. For example, if the plan outperforms budget on per member cost for medical services, 10% of the total base salary is paid as a bonus. When medical expense is measured on a per member per month or per member per year basis rather than on whole dollars, there can be no charge that the bonus is based on anything outside the physician's control.

Bonus plans may pay straight bonus to every physician, or they may be tied to performance evaluations. It is unwise to pay bonus on the basis of a few single criteria for individual PCPs because any single criterion can be manipulated to the benefit of the PCP but to the detriment of the plan. If bonus is to be paid to PCPs on a differential basis, you are better off using a broader performance evaluation system. See Chapter 18 for a complete discussion of formal performance appraisals for physicians.

The amount of bonus available may be calculated as a percentage of the total base salary paid during the year or as a percentage of savings over budget. If a percentage of savings is used, you need to determine whether there will be an upper limit on the bonus. For example, you may wish to share savings of per member per month medical expenses on a 50:50 basis with the physician group, but only to a maximum of 20% of the total base salary paid.

If you intend to pay a bonus on the basis of making the budget targets (eg, paying 10% of base salary if the per member per month medical expense targets are met), be sure to include the amount of the bonus payment in your overall accruals for physician salary and benefits. If you are going to pay on the basis of exceeding budget only, then you will not have to face an unexpected expense.

CREDENTIALING

The process of credentialing new physicians in closed panels is basically one of making sure that they have the necessary documents to allow them to practice with your group. This use of the term *credentialing* differs from its use in open panels. In the open panel setting, *credentialing* refers primarily to checking references and documentation (eg, licensure verification, malpractice insurance, and so forth). In open panels, it is the physician's responsibility to have the necessary documentation; in closed panels, it is the plan's responsibility to obtain it for the physician. Because some of the documents require a lengthy lead time, you should plan to begin as soon as the physician has signed an employment contract.

Obtaining a state license to practice medicine takes the longest amount of time. If the physician has licenses in many other states, it lengthens the process because the state must check with each other state to determine whether the PCP's license is valid.

The Drug Enforcement Agency (DEA) number allows a physician to prescribe scheduled narcotics. Although it is a federally issued permit, the number is good only for one state location. Therefore, even if the physician has a DEA number from another state, he or she must reapply for a new number. Some states also issue narcotics numbers as well.

After state licensure has been obtained, the physician must obtain malpractice insurance. If your plan has a group policy, it is a simple matter to add the newcomer. If candidates had claims made malpractice insurance, they will need a tail coverage policy to cover against suits that may haunt them from the past. Your carrier may insist on seeing evidence of such coverage before issuing a new policy, and you should as well.

Once state licensure and malpractice coverage have been obtained, the physician must apply for hospital privileges at your participating hospitals. An application for membership in the county and state medical societies may also be made at that time.

ORIENTATION

Time invested in proper orientation will be well spent. If your plan has been understaffed for some time, there will be pressure to get the new PCP seeing patients as soon as possible, or perhaps after half a day of brief overview. The new PCP will learn the ropes eventually, but if you want to foster a good attitude and help the new PCP learn his or her way around more efficiently, spend the time with a good orientation program.

Plan the orientation to expose new PCPs to all the personnel with whom they will be interacting in the future. Have those individuals review the important elements of their areas. When new PCPs understand what is expected of them and what to expect from others in the plan as well as the technical components of practicing in your group, they will be more comfortable. Consider orientation to be administrative preventive medicine. Exhibit 4-4 lists some topics that may be appropriate for an orientation program.

Although you may spend 3 or 4 days going over orientation material, there is no way a new PCP will be able to absorb all the information about your plan in that short time. Therefore, for the first few weeks it is best to schedule a reduced patient load. For example, you may want to schedule only half the normal number of appointments for the new PCP to see. It is also helpful to assign an experienced nurse to the new PCP to help explain the forms, assist in getting laboratory and radiology studies, help with preadmission requirements, and so forth. After 2 or 3 weeks, the new PCP may be assigned a permanent nurse or aide if such a change is necessary.

Many groups use a buddy system for the first few weeks as well. This means that an experienced plan physician in the same specialty as the new PCP is designated to help the new PCP acclimate to the system. This extends to the new PCP taking phone calls with the experienced PCP (the first call, actually; the new PCP takes the call and then, if more than advice is needed, the new PCP in turn calls the experienced PCP to

Exhibit 4-4 Suggested Topics for Orientation of Closed Panel Physicians

- Expectations
  —Of the plan for the physician
  —Of the physician for the plan
- Plan practice manual or principles of practice
- Appointment system, including control of the schedule
- Scheduling of procedures
- Schedule of regular hours and on-call hours
- Patient responsibilities and clinical duties
- Productivity
- Authorization policies and procedures
- Forms and paperwork
- Affiliated providers
- Consultants
- Institutions
- Ancillary services
- Nonclinical duties
- Meetings and committees
- Continuing medical education
- Quality management program and peer review
- Plan subscription agreement and plan schedule of benefits
- Plan member grievance procedures

review procedure). By designating another physician to help out the new PCP, there is less chance of the new PCP feeling reluctant to ask for help.

PRODUCTIVITY

Measuring outpatient productivity in closed panel managed care plans is far more complicated than measuring it in a standard fee-for-service setting. Because the economic incentives in fee-for-service are so straightforward, productivity is a simple product of how much a physician bills and collects. In managed care, one is trying to practice cost effectively and yet provide high-quality care. Therefore, the measures must be modified.

One common unit of measurement involves looking at the number of patient visits per unit time (eg, visits per day). Other common measures are visits per hour, per session (usually half a day, but that can be subtly altered), per week, per month, or per year. The larger the time scale, the less the influence of minor factors. For example, if you measure visits per session but fail to define a session rigidly, you will not know whether all the visits are occurring in the space of 2 hours, 3 hours, and so on. The problem with larger time scales is that they are slow to respond to changes and will be less sensitive indicators of current productivity. A reasonable combination is to look at visits per day or per week on average for a month and then have a rolling 12-month average for the year to date.

In the fee-for-service setting in 1990, the mean for outpatient productivity by PCPs was 79.7 office visits per week, with the variation by specialty going from 64.3 visits per week for internal medicine (including Medicare visits) to 105.1 visits per week for pediatrics and 112.5 visits per week for family practice.[3] Hospital rounds add to these numbers as follows: The mean number of hospital rounds per week in 1990 was 24.2, with the variation by specialty going from 36.2 rounds per week for internal medicine (including Medicare visits) to 21.7 rounds per week for pediatrics and 17.7 rounds per week for family practice.[3]

It is perfectly reasonable to expect somewhere around this level of productivity from PCPs on your staff. Using productivity as an absolute measure, however, can cause problems. Just as in an uncontrolled fee-for-service setting, if you pressure the PCPs too heavily to get productivity up, the easiest thing for them to do is start churning the patients (eg, refer sick patients out and schedule 35 blood pressure checks per day). This is obviously counterproductive in a managed health care plan.

The point is to have a reasonable expectation of PCP productivity and stick to it but not rely inappropriately on productivity in measuring how well the plan is doing. If studies of appointment availability show reasonable accessibility to care and if the medical expenses are well controlled (including salary and benefits for the medical staff), you may feel little need to apply pressure to improve productivity.

RETENTION OF QUALITY PHYSICIANS

Physician retention is a recurrent problem in some closed panel HMOs and, to a lesser extent, in private group practices. The reasons for this are unclear, although it is possible to speculate.

Issues of physician autonomy tend to rise quickly to the surface in tightly managed closed panels. Because tight medical management equates with frequent physician management, some physicians grow uncomfortable with practicing in a fishbowl environment. They would prefer a practice where there is no retrospective secondary evaluation of their decisions and where they are the unquestioned authority. Situations such as this are becoming more rare with increasing intervention by third-party payers, but the image of the autonomous, hard-working, and well-compensated physician is one that is placed in front of physicians as the ideal throughout training and beyond.

Another common problem in closed panels is that there is no real entry or exit barrier. Few closed panels require new physicians to ante up $50,000 for a partnership or place physicians in the position of trying to sell their equity stake if they leave. Because of that, group and staff model HMOs are convenient places for physicians to practice for a few years while trying to figure out what they ultimately want to do.

Although one can argue that new physicians cost less than experienced ones (thus reducing overhead), the cost to the plan of high physician turnover is large. When one factors in recruiting costs such as recruiter's fees, advertising, time spent interviewing candidates, travel costs, and so forth, the costs are considerable. New physicians also do not know the system as well, which reduces efficiency in medical management. Last, problems of member satisfaction and plan reputation are markedly exacerbated by high physician turnover.

Exhibit 4-5 represents ideas that may be incorporated in your closed panel to promote retention of high-quality physicians. One key caution is not to develop a system that entrenches a few senior physicians with all the longevity benefits and allows new physicians little hope of attaining those benefits, thereby continuing the turnover problem.

CONCLUSION

The development and maintenance of a high-quality medical staff in a closed panel health

Exhibit 4-5 Items To Consider for Physician Retention in Closed Panels

- Longevity-related benefits, within limits (must use great care so as not to make physicians with less longevity into second-class citizens, or attrition will occur from below)
  —Cafeteria style
  —Flex time of some sort
  —On-call responsibilities
   1. Amount
   2. When
  —Participation in profit sharing
  —Vesting schedule for tail malpractice insurance and relocation expenses
  —Sabbatical time
  —Tuition aid for dependents
  —Increasing vacation time
  —Stock options
  —Preferential opportunity for investment in plan
  —Personal financial counseling
  —Retirement plan with vesting schedule on plan matching contributions
- On-call responsibilities for all physicians
  —Outside back-up
  —After-hours telephone triage system
- Physician input into support staff
- Staff development for physicians beyond CME
  —Telephone skills

  —Stress management
  —Coping skills
  —Handling difficult patients
   1. Entitled demanders
   2. Other hateful patients
  —Communications skills
  —Time management skills
- Formal recognition programs
- Career path development
- Encouragement of academic affiliation
- Social events with professionals
- Utilization of group or staff physicians for larger task force objectives
- Participation in and encouragement of research
- Professional newsletter
- Development of survey instruments
  —Structured exit interviews
  —Profile of high-quality physicians likely to remain with group
- Training programs for ancillary and support staff
  —Telephone skills
  —Stress management
  —Coping skills
  —Handling difficult patients (as above)
  —Communications skills
  —Time management skills

plan takes a great deal of thoughtful attention and work, but the reward is high. Ensuring that compensation (both monetary and nonmonetary) is comparable to the community norms, properly orienting new physicians, paying considerable attention to proper incentive programs and performance requirements, and keeping in touch with the short- and long-term needs of the medical staff are necessary management tasks.

REFERENCES

1. Group Health Association of America. *HMO Industry Profile, Vol 2: Physician Staffing and Utilization Patterns.* Washington, DC: Group Health Association of America; 1991.

2. Packer-Thursman J. The role of midlevel practitioners. *HMO Mag.* March/April 1992: 28–34.

3. American Medical Association. *Socioeconomic Characteristics of Medical Practice 1990/1991.* Chicago: American Medical Association; 1991.

SUGGESTED READING

American College of Physician Executives. *Physician Managers and the Law.* Tampa, FL: American College of Physician Executives; 1987.

American Medical Association. *Socioeconomic Characteristics of Medical Practice 1990/1991.* American Medical Association, 1991.

Curry W, ed. *The Physician Executive.* Tampa, FL: American College of Physician Executives; 1988.

Shouldice RG. *Introduction to Managed Care.* Arlington, VA: Information Resources Press; 1991.

Chapter 5

Primary Care in Open Panels

Peter R. Kongstvedt

DEFINITIONS

One must begin with definitions about what will be considered primary care. In virtually all systems, care rendered by physicians in the specialties of family practice, internal medicine, and pediatrics is considered primary care.

Many obstetrics/gyneocology (Ob/Gyn) specialists feel that they too deliver primary care to their patients. They argue that they are often the only physician a young woman sees for many years. This is true in the case of generally healthy young women, but it is not always so when medical problems not involving the female reproductive tract occur. Still, a number of plans that capitate primary care (ie, use a gatekeeper system) also include Ob/Gyn as primary care and split the care (and perhaps the capitation) between the Ob/Gyn and an internist or family practitioner. Plans that use this method must define what services are to be delivered by each. For example, the Ob/Gyn may be seen without referral for Pap smears and pelvic examinations, for pregnancy, and for sterilization procedures. For any other problems, the member must see the primary care physician (PCP) for either treatment by or referral to any other specialist and perhaps even for referral back to the Ob/Gyn whom she has chosen for services be-yond those defined as being allowed under the self-referral option.

In general, it is probably easier to define Ob/Gyn as a specialty service and treat it as any other specialty. For marketing reasons as well as medical acceptability in the community, however, most plans make special arrangements for routine Pap smears and obstetric services while still requiring coordination with the PCP for all other care.

NETWORK DEVELOPMENT

Young or newly forming plans will concentrate primarily on network development. Mature plans will concentrate more on network maintenance (discussed later in this chapter), although recruiting to fill in areas with suboptimal access will always be an ongoing process, particularly during periods of high growth.

The ease of developing a network is influenced by many factors. Markets that are heavily saturated with managed care plans may have great difficulty recruiting PCPs (or consultants) if those providers see no need to sign up with yet another plan. Conversely, competition may be so fierce, or there may be so many (under-utilized) providers, that recruiting will be easier. In any event, recruiting PCPs for open panels is best done by means of an orderly approach. Without proper planning, the time line will be substantially drawn out, and the physician panel may not complement hospital choices or market needs.

Setting Priorities

If you are beginning from scratch, you are likely to start with a few easy recruits (often friends of the medical director or physicians with whom contact has already been made). That will rarely be sufficient by itself, so that there is a need to recruit systematically to achieve an acceptable panel size and configuration.

Consider geographic needs first. This generally breaks down into two main considerations: the need to target potential new members and the need to use certain hospitals (discussed in Chapter 8).

In the first case, you should already have identified your primary target markets (eg, a large and growing suburban-industrial community). In the second case, you may have selected a high-quality hospital and need to recruit physicians from that medical staff in preference to physicians who practice only at a noncontracting hospital, even if it is in the targeted area.

Priorities will also be affected by the availability, acceptability (to you, to your potential members, and to the rest of the medical panel), scope of practice, and practice capacities of physicians in target areas. If you have more than one geographic high priority for recruiting but there is a major difference in the ease with which you will be able to recruit qualified and acceptable physicians, you will want to give early attention to the area from which it will be the easiest to recruit. This is for two reasons. First, the success of your physician recruiters will be enhanced with the amount of successful experience they have, and second, there is often a chain reaction when your panel reaches critical mass. In other words, when there are enough physicians already on your panel, it becomes more acceptable or even competitively necessary for physicians to join.

Access Needs

In addition to the broad geographic needs and hospital-related needs, it is important to assess accessibility in general. There are a number of traditional ways to do this. One method is to look at the number of physicians per 1,000 members. One large survey reported the mean total physicians per 1,000 members in mature open panel plans to be 36.92, and the mean total PCPs per 1,000 members was reported as 14.43.[1] This last ratio equates to 71 members per physician, which may represent an average enrollment but does not necessarily predict capacity; it is more useful to look at the number of members whom each physician must accept (on the basis of contractual terms, see Chapter 36), such as 200 members per PCP. The ratios of physicians to members in open panels can vary tremendously depending on age of the plan, geographic access needs, maturity of the marketplace in general, number of open practices, and marketing needs.

A more useful measure is geographic accessibility. This is generally calculated through one of two methods: drive time, and number of PCPs by geographic availability. Drive time refers to how long members in the plan's service area have to drive to reach a PCP (or a PCP with an open practice; that is, one still accepting new patients). In general, drive time should be no more than 15 to 20 minutes, although 30 minutes may be appropriate for certain rural areas. A drive time of 20 minutes may be acceptable for access from a purely medical viewpoint, but it may not be as acceptable in a heavily urbanized market.

Analyzing the number of PCPs by geographic availability is also useful. Generally, you want to be able to provide at least two PCPs within 2 or 3 miles of each ZIP code from which your plan will be drawing members (the density is usually greater in urban areas and less in rural areas). Another measure of geographic availability is the radius from where the members live (eg, two PCPs within an 8-mile radius for urban areas and two PCPs within a 20-mile radius for rural areas). Again, these ratios may represent a minimum configuration and will not necessarily be acceptable in your marketplace.

Identification of Candidates

Selection of candidates to recruit is based on a number of sources. First is the personal acquaintances of the medical director. These are often the easiest physicians to recruit, but they are relatively few in number.

Second, the list of physicians with privileges at the hospitals with which you are contracting should be used. The hospital administrator will frequently be able to guide you toward those physicians you should approach early and those you should avoid. The hospital executive staff is often helpful in enhancing the environment for recruiting because in many situations the physicians will value highly the judgment of the hospital administration. An important caveat is in order here. Sometimes the reason a physician is considered desirable from the hospital's point of view is the fact that the physician admits a lot of patients, and a heavy user of hospital services is not always the most desirable from the point of view of a managed care plan. It is therefore crucial that the plan retain independent judgment about whom to recruit and why.

A third source for identification of candidates is the physician list of your competitors. In general, unless your competition has signed the physicians to an exclusive agreement, you will have an easier time signing these physicians up because they have already made the commitment to join a managed health care plan panel.

Fourth, the local county or state medical society may be a good source for obtaining mailing labels. You can rent the list for a single label run, or the society may actually provide the labels for a reasonable fee. If possible, you want this broken down by primary care and by ZIP code.

Last, if all else fails (or simply as a back-up), there are the Yellow Pages. Although the phone book provides the most complete list, it is absolutely unselective and must be used only with extreme caution.

One special method of identifying candidates is available only to large insurance carriers, and that is claims data. A large carrier may already have sufficient data on hand from indemnity business to be able to make an initial evaluation of which physicians practice cost effectively and which physicians have been pillaging the system for years. Claims data may also provide a crude method of assessing quality, for example, by identifying physicians with abnormally high rates of certain procedures (eg, hysterectomies) or those who frequently use outmoded treatments (eg, routine tonsillectomies). Although interpretation of indemnity claims history is not as easy as it first appears, clear outliers are not difficult to identify if there are sufficient data to draw statistically valid conclusions. In other words, a large database is of no value if there are insufficient transactions at the level of individual providers in an area. The subject of provider profiling is addressed in greater detail in Chapter 16.

Timing

You need to develop a realistic time frame within which to work. You also need to give the physician recruiters a reference to use in recruiting so as not to let one step of the recruiting process overshadow the others. Each aspect of physician recruiting should have set goals for both number and duration. Begin the time frame with first contact and continue through successful completion, which occurs when both the physician and your plan sign the contract. In a new start-up, you may want to begin the time frame with the start of the enterprise and include physician identification as the first step.

Each plan and community will have its own special characteristics, but in general the time between the first letter to the physician and the first telephone contact should be no more than 7 to 10 days. If it is longer than that, the physician will have forgotten you.

The time between the first telephone contact and the first visit should likewise be no more than 7 to 10 days, although a busy physician's schedule may necessitate a slightly longer lead time. Try to avoid scheduling the first visit during normal office hours, because the physician, who is under pressure to see patients, will be unable to give enough time and thought to the discussion. A lunch meeting (you bring the deli tray) or a meeting on an afternoon off or just after office hours is best. This first visit should last about 1 hour and involve explaining the concept and the contract, determining the level of interest, and obtaining initial information about the physician and the practice. This is also the time for the recruiter to obtain an initial impression of the ambiance of the physician's office for marketing purposes.

If possible, you wish to obtain closure (actually, contingent closure) on the second visit. Generally, allow 1 or 2 weeks between the first and second visits, and make the appointment for the second visit during the first one. In some cases, physicians will want to have their attorney look at the contract, and you will need to allow sufficient time for that. In any event, have a definite time for follow-up and potential closure.

In general, it is best to keep the pressure on. If you allow too much time to elapse between contacts or steps, your ease in getting a signed contract will be diminished. It is preferable to keep the entire time from first letter to signed contract or signed letter of intent to 2 months or less.

As discussed below under credentialing, the contract or letter of intent is contingent on the credentialing process. If a physician does not meet the standards of your plan, you reserve the right not to add that physician to your panel.

Role of the Recruiter

The key personnel in this process are the physician recruiters. In some plans, recruiters are drawn from the marketing department; in others, they are part of the provider relations department. The use of marketing representatives for physician recruiting may be necessary during the first few months of a new start-up plan, but the function is really best carried out by people who have more understanding and empathy with physicians and who will be responsible for maintaining the relationship after a physician has joined the panel. The recruiters are supervised by a director or manager of provider relations.

The recruiters make the telephone calls and do the leg work. They must be able to explain to the physician and the physician's support staff any necessary details to facilitate an informed decision. This includes all the aspects of physician compensation, best and worst case scenarios, the scope of covered services, covered benefits to members, benefits to the physician for joining, operational policies such as authorization systems and preadmission requirements, and any other pertinent information. A detailed understanding of the reimbursement system is, of course, critical (compensation models are discussed in Chapter 6).

The number of recruiters will depend on the number of physicians you hope to add to the panel and the geographic area you want to cover. In the early phases of a start-up, when there is an intense need for physician recruiting, you may need three to five individuals. Later, during a controlled growth phase, recruiting is handled by the regular provider relations staff.

Role of the Medical Director

In addition to making the personal contacts in the recruiting process, the medical director has at least two other primary responsibilities in recruiting (as opposed to credentialing, as discussed below).

First, the medical director adds prestige and legitimacy to the endeavor. The medical director endorses the plan, both explicitly and implicitly, by being medical director. If the medical director has been in the area for some time, this local endorsement may be the deciding factor in new plans looking to recruit physicians.

It is important for the medical director to understand the plan and its policies. This seems obvious, but there have been cases where medical directors have been recruited solely to add prestige and were unaware of how the plan actually operated. This poses two serious problems. The medical director may promise things that are not possible, and the medical director may quit in an embarrassing huff after finding out how things really work. Fortunately, over the past few years, the level of management expertise found in medical directors of open panels has increased significantly, and the medical director is much more likely to be able to manage the process than have to be managed.

The second primary recruiting responsibility is closing certain difficult cases. There will be times when the physician recruiter has done all the preparatory work but a sought-after physician will be hesitant about signing. In these cases, the medical director's personal contact may be the deciding factor.

TYPES OF CONTRACTING SITUATIONS

There are a number of possible types of contracting situations with which an open panel may have to deal in developing a network. The subject of the contract itself is addressed in Chapter 36, and reimbursement is discussed in Chapter 6. This discussion focuses on the types of situations that may present themselves, regardless of specific contracting and reimbursement issues.

Individual Physicians

This is the most common category of contracting in open panels, which is not surprising given the large number of solo practitioners in many parts of the country. In this model, the physician contracts directly with the health plan and not through any third party or intermediary. The advantage to the plan is that there is a direct relationship with the physician, which makes it cleaner and simpler to interact. The disadvantage is that it is only one physician, and therefore the effort to obtain and maintain that relationship is disproportionately great.

Small Groups

Not substantially different from individual physicians, small groups usually operate relatively cohesively. The advantage to the plan is that the same amount of effort to obtain and maintain a small group yields a higher number of physicians. Plans generally prefer to contract with small groups for that reason. The disadvantage is that, if the relationship with the group needs to be terminated (for whatever reason, theirs or yours), there is greater disruption in patient care.

Multispecialty Groups

Multispecialty groups represent a special category. Relatively uncommon in certain parts of the country, they are occasionally the dominant practices in certain areas. The advantage of contracting with multispecialty groups is that you obtain not only PCPs but specialty consultants as well. This provides for broader access (including specialists to whom other PCPs may refer) and allows for existing referral patterns to continue.

One disadvantage is that multispecialty groups sometimes are dominated by the specialty or referral physicians in the group, which may lead to inappropriate overutilization of referral services. Another potential disadvantage is the case where, by accepting the group, you are forced to accept a specialist whose cost or quality is not what you desire (although not so bad as to prevent contracting with the group). Again, as a general rule, if relations with large groups founder, there is a greater likelihood that there will be disruptions in patient care.

Independent Practice Associations

The independent practice association (IPA) is the original form of open panel plan. In the early 1970s, it was envisioned that open panel plans would all be IPA model plans. In this situation, there is actually a legal entity of an IPA, which contracts with physicians, and the IPA in turn contracts with the health plan. The advantage to the plan is that a large number of providers come along with the contract. Furthermore, if relations between the IPA and the health plan are close, there may be a confluence of goals, which benefits all parties.

There are two primary disadvantages to contracting with IPAs. The first is that an IPA can function somewhat as a union. If relations between the IPA and the health plan are arm's length or problematic, the IPA can hold a considerable portion (or perhaps all) of the delivery system hostage to negotiations. This fact has not been lost on the Justice Department of the federal government. IPAs that function as anticompetitive forces may encounter difficulties with the law. Antitrust issues are discussed in Chapter 37.

The second disadvantage is that the plan's ability to select and deselect individual physicians is much more limited when contracting through an IPA than when contracting directly with the providers. If the IPA is at risk for medical expenses, there may be a confluence of objectives between the plan and the IPA to bring in cost-effective and high-quality providers and to remove those providers whose cost or quality is not acceptable. Unfortunately, the IPA has its own internal political structure, so that defining who is cost effective or high quality, as well as dealing with outliers, may not match exactly between the plan and the IPA. If the plan has the contractual right to refuse to accept or to departicipate individual providers in the IPA, that obstacle may be avoided, although the purely political obstacles remain.

Hospital-Centered Organizations

Many hospitals have been exploring methods of developing organizations that will legally and structurally bond the physicians to the hospital. Sometimes these are referred to as medical staff hospital organizations or physician-hospital organizations (PHOs). The positive and negative ramifications that apply to IPAs are identical to those for hospital-based organizations (including their antitrust risk) and have been discussed above. In addition to those issues, there are two other broad issues that relate specifically to the hospital-based nature of the organization.

First is the link between a hospital's own willingness to do business with a plan and the plan's willingness to do business with the PHO. In other words, the hospital may refuse to contract with the plan or may not provide favorable terms unless the plan brings in the PHO, perhaps even on an exclusive basis. That obviously removes control of that entire portion of the delivery system (physicians and hospital), leaving the plan at the mercy (or abilities) of the PHO to achieve the goals of the plan. If the PHO is at significant risk for medical expenses, there may be confluence of goals, but it is unusual for there to be such risk.

The second issue relates to the reasons that the PHO formed in the first place. If the hospital has the goals of keeping beds filled and keeping the medical staff happy (and busy), the selection process for choosing which providers are in the PHO may be weighted toward those physicians who admit a lot of patients to the hospital, a criterion that may not be ideal from the plan's perspective. Another reason that the PHO may have formed was to circle the wagons, that is, to resist aggressive managed care. In that event, there may be a real mismatch between how the plan wants to perform medical management and how the PHO will allow it to occur. Issues of control of utilization management, quality management, and provider selection become difficult to resolve.

Nonetheless, hospital-centered organizations can function effectively. If the organization is formed with a genuine understanding of the goals of managed care, a genuine willingness to deal with difficult issues of utilization, quality, and provider selection, and a willingness to share control with the health plan, it is possible to work together.

Faculty Practice Plans

Faculty practice plans (FPPs) are medical groups that are organized around teaching programs, primarily at university hospitals. An FPP may be a single entity or may encompass multiple entities defined along specialty lines (eg, cardiology or anesthesiology). Plans generally contract with the legal group representing the FPP rather than with individual physicians within the FPP, although that varies from plan to plan.

FPPs represent special challenges for various reasons. First, many teaching institutions and FPPs tend to be less cost effective in their practice styles than private physicians. This probably relates to the primary missions of the teaching program: to teach and to perform research. Cost effectiveness is a secondary goal only (if a goal at all).

A second challenge is that an FPP, like a medical group, comes all together or not at all. This again means that the plan has little ability to select or deselect the individual physicians within the FPP. Related to that is the lack of detail regarding claims and encounter data. Many FPPs simply bill the plan, accept capitation, or collect encounter data in the name of the FPP rather than in the name of the individual provider who performed the service. This means that the plan has little ability to analyze data to the same level of detail that is afforded in the rest of the network.

A third major challenge is the use of house officers (interns and residents in training) and medical students to deliver care. In teaching hospitals, the day-to-day care is actually delivered by house officers rather than by the attending faculty physician, who functions as a teacher and supervisor. House officers and medical students, because they are learning how to practice medicine, tend to be profligate in their use of medical resources; they are there to learn medicine, not simply to perform direct service to patients. Furthermore, experience does allow physicians to learn what is cost effective, and house officers and medical students have yet to gain such experience. Nevertheless, there is some evidence that intensive attention to utilization management by faculty can have a highly beneficial effect on house staff.[2]

The last major issue with teaching programs and FPPs is the nature of how they deliver services. Most teaching programs are not really set up for case management. It is far more common to have multiple specialty clinics (eg, pulmonary, cardiology, or vascular surgery) to which patients are referred for each specific problem. Such a system takes on characteristics of a medical pinball machine, where the members ricochet from clinic to clinic, having each organ system attended to with little regard for the totality of care. This leads to enormous run-ups in cost as well as continuity problems and a clear lack of control or accountability.

Despite these difficulties, there are good reasons for health plans to contract with teaching programs and FPPs other than the societal good derived from the training of medical practitioners. Teaching programs and FPPs provide not only routine care but tertiary and highly specialized care as well, care that the plan will have to find means to provide in any event. Teaching programs also add prestige to the plan by virtue of their reputation for providing high-quality care, although that can be a two-edged sword in that the participation of a teaching program may draw adverse selection in membership.*

Most teaching programs and FPPs recognize the problems cited above and are willing to work with plans to ameliorate them. For example, they may be willing to extend a deep discount to a managed care plan in the recognition that the plan's ability to control utilization is limited and therefore must be made up on price. Teaching programs may occasionally be willing to accept a high level of risk for medical expenses, but that can be a problem for them because of the risk of adverse selection mentioned above. Risk for defined services (eg, laboratory or radiology) may be more acceptable.

CREDENTIALING

It is not enough to get physicians to sign contracts. Without performing proper credentialing, you will have no knowledge of the quality or acceptability of physicians, nor will you have any idea whether they will actually be an asset to your plan. Furthermore, in the event of a legal action against a physician, the plan may expose itself to some liability by having failed to carry out proper credentialing. The credentialing process is a critical one, and should be carried out during the recruiting process and, if necessary, after the contract or letter of intent is signed. Periodic recredentialing (eg, every 2 years) should also take place, although recredentialing will generally be less extensive than primary credentialing. In most plans, the medical director bears ultimate responsibility for credentialing.

If the credentialing process is incomplete at the time the physician is ready to sign, then a provision must be included in the signed docu-

---

*In other words, if there is more than one health plan competing in a single group account (ie, an employer group) for membership, members with serious illnesses may choose the health plan affiliated with a teaching program to ensure access to high-quality tertiary care. That means that sicker members join that health plan and less sick members join the health plan that does not have such an affiliation. This issue does not come up if the plan is the sole carrier in an account or if all the competing plans use the teaching program, but it is a clear problem if there are multiple plans competing freely for members in a single account.

ment (either the contract or the letter of intent) indicating that the final contract is contingent upon the plan's completing the credentialing process. If the predetermined standards are not met, then you will be unable to accept that physician in your panel. A word of warning: It is more difficult than one might imagine to tell physicians that the plan is not going to accept them after they have signed a contract.

The elements illustrated in Exhibits 5-1 and 5-2 are some examples of data that should be captured in the credentialing process. Primary verification of the elements in Exhibit 5-1 should also be performed as appropriate.

National Practitioner Data Bank

A special type of credentialing requirement and reference check was created by the Health Care Quality Improvement Act of 1986. This act, an important law for managed care plans, is discussed in Chapters 4 and 37. The reader is urged to refer to those chapters and to become familiar with the credentialing aspects of this Act.

Exhibit 5-1 Basic Elements of Credentialing

- Training (copy of certificates)
  - —Location of training
  - —Type of training
- Specialty board eligibility or certification (copy of certificate)
- Current state medical license (copy of certificate)
  - —Restrictions
  - —History of loss of license in any state
- Drug Enforcement Agency (DEA) number (copy of certificate)
- Hospital privileges
  - —Name of hospitals
  - —Scope of practice privileges
- Malpractice insurance
  - —Carrier name
  - —Currency of coverage (copy of face sheet)
  - —Scope of coverage (financial limits and procedures covered)
- Malpractice history
  - —Pending claims
  - —Successful claims against the physician, either judged or settled
- National Practitioner Data Bank status

Exhibit 5-2 Additional Elements of Credentialing

- Medicare, Medicaid, and federal tax identification numbers
- Social Security number
- Location and telephone numbers of all offices
- Hours of operation
- Yes/no questions regarding:
  - —Limitations or suspensions of privileges
  - —Suspension from government programs
  - —Suspension or restriction of DEA license
  - —Malpractice cancellation
  - —Felony conviction
  - —Drug or alcohol abuse
  - —Chronic or debilitating illnesses
- Provisions for emergency care and back-up
- Use of nonphysician (ie, midlevel) practitioners
- In-office surgery capabilities
- In-office testing capabilities
- Areas of special medical interest
- Record of continuing medical education

Office Evaluation

There are two main items to evaluate in a physician's office: capacity to accept new members and office ambiance. This evaluation is best accomplished by having the recruiter visit the office and may be performed in one fairly short visit.

In addition to asking physicians directly how many new members they will accept (and usually including that in the contract), the recruiter should ask to examine the appointment book. In this way, the recruiter can get a reasonably good idea of how much appointment availability the physician has. For example, if there are no available appointment slots for a physical examination for 6 weeks or more, the physician may be overestimating his or her ability to accept more work.

The recruiter can also get an idea of how easy it is for a patient with an acute problem to be put on the schedule. This may be examined by looking at the number of acute slots left open each day and by looking at the number of double-booked appointments that were put in at the end of each day.

In addition, the recruiter can assess less tangible items such as cleanliness of the office, friendliness of the staff toward patients, and general atmosphere. Hours of operation can be verified, as can provisions for emergency care and in-office equipment capabilities.

MEDICAL RECORD REVIEW

Many plans insist on a review of sample medical records by the medical director. The purpose of this is to assure the medical director that physicians do indeed practice high-quality medicine and that their practice is already cost effective. Some physicians object to submitting to this review, but if it is required for participation, and if the physician is assured that it is strictly confidential and not a witch hunt, there should be fewer problems.

If the plan already has a quality assurance program that involves chart review, a physician should agree to the initial review as a matter of course. Sometimes it is not objections by the physicians that form the impediment to this review but rather the embarrassment of the medical director in having to perform it.

COMPENSATION

Compensation of PCPs in open panels is discussed in detail in Chapter 6.

ORIENTATION

In all enterprises, time invested in the beginning to ensure real understanding is time well spent. Therefore, a planned approach to orientation of a newly added PCP will pay off in improved compliance with your plan's procedures and policies, in increased professional satisfaction on the part of the PCP, and in increased member satisfaction. Orientation is aimed at two audiences: the PCP and the PCP's office staff. Exhibit 5-3 lists some topics to consider in orienting physicians, and Exhibit 5-4 lists some topics for orienting their office staff.

NETWORK MAINTENANCE

Maintenance of the professional relationship with physicians in the network recently has assumed a far greater role in managed care than at

Exhibit 5-3 Suggested Topics for Orientation of Open Panel Physicians

- Plan subscription agreement and schedule of benefits
- Authorization policies and procedures
- Forms and paperwork
- Utilization and financial data supplied by plan
- Committees and meetings
- Quality management program and peer review
- Recredentialing requirements
- Member transfer in or out of practice
  —Member initiated
  —Physician initiated
- Plan member grievance procedure
- Schedule of compensation from plan
- Contact persons in plan
- Affiliated providers
  —Primary care
  —Consultants
  —Institutions
  —Ancillary services

any previous time in the industry's history. The saturation of managed care plans in some communities, coupled with increasing interventions by third-party payers (commercial, Medicare, and Medicaid) limiting providers' ability to cost

Exhibit 5-4 Suggested Topics for Orientation of Office Staff

- Plan subscription agreement and schedule of benefits
- Authorization policies and procedures
- Forms and paperwork
- Member transfer in or out of practice
  —Member initiated
  —Physician initiated
- Plan member grievance procedure
- Member eligibility verification
- Member identification card
- Current member list and eligibility verification
- Affiliated providers
  —Primary care
  —Consultants
  —Institutions
  —Ancillary services
- Contact persons in plan
  —Names
  —Telephone numbers
- Hours of operation

shift to other fee-for-service payers, has placed increasing strain on physicians and has clearly colored how they view participation with managed care plans. Failure to service the network properly can lead to defections or closure of practices to your plan, difficulty with new recruiting, and a slow downward spiral. Even for those plans that have not properly maintained their networks, however, it is never too late to put in the effort because it is certainly possible to recover from a poor history.

The Physician's View of Managed Care

To maintain the network, it is first important to understand how physicians view managed care. These issues are discussed at length in Chapter 9 but are mentioned briefly here. An understanding of these elements allows provider relations staff to key in on those items that are important to physicians.

In general, physicians see managed care as a general threat and pain in the neck. The issue of loss of or impingement on autonomy is perhaps the most emotionally charged issue there is. There are organizational demands on physicians as well: compliance with a restricted referral and hospital panel, increased bureaucratic overhead, multiple plans that use different forms and procedures, and an inability to rid themselves easily of difficult patients (so-called entitled demanders[3,4]).

Managed care often places the physician in an adversarial relationship with a patient (actually less often than one would think, but it only takes a few). This is uncomfortable because physicians are not trained for it.[5] This most often comes up in the guise of clearly unnecessary or medically marginal care that is demanded by the patient, but it may also occur when something is medically necessary but not a covered benefit; this issue most often appears under the term *patient advocacy.*

Some physicians have a real fear that managed care can lead to decreased quality of care. This has never really been proven, and there are now some data specific to open panel plans that show good quality of care along with lower utilization.[6–9] Nevertheless the fear remains, and coupled with this is a fear of increased malpractice liability. The Wickline case (discussed in Chapter 38), combined with threats of legal action by members demanding certain services, has increased the anxiety level of practicing physicians.

Managed care often results in a demand to discount fees or, more important, restricts the ability of a physician to cost shift into the plan as other payers (especially government programs) squeeze down. In plans with capitation or withhold mechanisms some income is placed at risk, a situation generally not greeted with enthusiasm.

Last, most managed care plans are quite poor at providing appropriate feedback to physicians. Feedback is often sporadic, usually coinciding with annual payouts (or lack thereof) of risk pools. Routine useful information such as the status of risk pools and utilization data is often inadequate. In fact, in some plans the physicians hear from the plan only when there is a problem, such as overutilization, and never at all when performance is good.

In the face of all these issues, many physicians in fact are quite satisfied with their participation in managed care. Their incomes are maintained or enhanced,[10] their patients are able to receive medical care without economic barriers to access, and they enjoy participating in a more structured delivery system that has the ability to deal with issues of cost and quality. In general, physicians who are satisfied with their participation have been able to make an attitudinal adjustment more successfully than their colleagues who are not satisfied.[11]

Maintaining the Network

This topic is so important that most of the key elements are discussed in a separate chapter. The reader is referred to Chapter 9 on changing provider behavior because changing behavior involves many issues important to network maintenance. The issues of data and feedback, the use of positive feedback, translation of goals and objectives, autonomy needs, quality of care, role conflict, understanding the insurance functions of the plan, plan differentiation in the marketplace, and discipline and sanctioning will not be repeated here.

In most plans, there are individuals who are solely responsible for maintaining communications with the physician panel, both PCPs and consultants, and both the physicians and their office staff. The roles of these provider relations representatives are to elicit feedback from the physicians and office staff, to update them on changes, to troubleshoot, and generally to keep things running smoothly.

The importance of this function cannot be overstated. Some care must be taken in selecting the individuals who will fill this role. Unless provider relations staff are mature and experienced, they may fall into the trap of forgetting for whom they are actually working. It is appropriate and necessary for them to represent the PCPs' point of view to plan management, but it is inappropriate if they find themselves siding against the health plan in the event of a dispute. The provider relations staff must seek to prevent rifts, not to foster them.

Provider relations is similar to customer relations; but an even better metaphor is that of business partner. In a customer relation, the customer is always right; in a health plan, neither the plan nor the physician is always right. It is perhaps more useful to strive to be seen as a reliable and desirable business partner to the providers with whom you do business under contracts and agreements. Provider relations must therefore be proactive rather than simply reactive.

In addition to the items discussed in Chapter 9, the plan should have a well-developed early warning system for troubleshooting. Such a system could include regular on-site visits by provider relations staff (and occasionally by the medical director) and regular two-way communications vehicles. Changes in patterns, particularly patterns in utilization and compliance with plan policy and procedure, will often be a sign that the relationship is going awry. Last, close monitoring of the member services complaints report can yield crucial information; physicians will often tell their patients what they think and

what they intend to do long before they tell the plan.

Culling the Network

Beyond the elements referred to above, another function of network maintenance is the determination of who not to keep in the plan. In any managed care plan, there will be physicians who simply cannot or will not work within the system and whose practice style is clearly cost ineffective or of poor quality. Quality is discussed in Chapter 15, and sanctions for reasons of poor quality are discussed in Chapters 9 and 37; quality-related actions will not be repeated here. The point of this section is not whether those physicians practice poor medicine (that judgment need not be made) but whether their practice style is one that the plan can afford.

Regarding the issue of unacceptably costly practice style, the plan must develop a mechanism for identification of such practitioners that uses a combination of claims and utilization data (see Chapter 16) and some type of formal performance evaluation system (see Chapter 18). If identified providers are reluctant to change, even after the medical director has worked closely with them, then serious consideration should be given to terminating them from the panel. In fact, if a plan is in serious financial difficulties stemming from the behavior of the network providers, management may decide to act unilaterally (assuming that the contract between the plan and the providers allows either party to terminate without cause upon adequate notice) and to departicipate those (presumably few) providers whose practice behavior is so far out of line that there will be an immediate positive impact on plan performance.

There are any number of objections to removing a physician from the panel. Asking the members to change physicians is not easy or pleasant, benefits managers get upset, and invariably the physician in question is in a strategic location. The decision often comes down to whether you want to continue to subsidize that physician's poor practice behavior from the earnings of the other physicians (in capitated or risk/bonus types of reimbursement systems) and from the plan's earnings or drive the rates up to uncompetitive levels. If those are unacceptable alternatives, then the separation must occur.

Once the decision has been made to departicipate a provider from the network, it is best to act promptly. Some health maintenance organizations, however, contractually require a physician to participate until the entire membership has had a chance to change plans (which may take a year unless the physician's member panel is small), but that option can be quite costly because the physician will have no incentive to control cost once he or she has been notified of termination. In those cases, the contract usually also allows the plan to increase the amount of withhold (eg, from 20% up to 50%) to cover excess costs. In preferred provider organizations there is usually no need for such arrangements because the member may still see that physician, albeit at a higher level of coinsurance.

CONCLUSION

Network development requires an orderly project management approach. It is equally important to invest in proper orientation of new physicians and their office staff. Maintenance of the relationship between the physicians and the plan is a key element of success that is gaining increasing importance as plans become ever more competitive in the marketplace. The plan must be willing to departicipate a provider in certain circumstances to deliver the proper combination of quality and cost effectiveness that is a requirement of managed care.

REFERENCES

1. Group Health Association of America. *HMO Industry Profile, Vol 2: Physician Staffing and Utilization Patterns.* Washington, DC: Group Health Association of America; 1991.

2. Woodside JR, Bodne R, et al. Intensive, focused utilization management in a teaching hospital: an exploratory study. *Qual Assur Util Rev.* 1991;6:47–50.

3. Friedson E. Prepaid group practice and the new "demanding patient." *Milbank Mem Fund Q.* 1973;51.

4. Groves JE. Taking care of the hateful patient. *N Engl J Med.* 1978;298:883–887.

5. Daniels N. Why saying no to patients in the United States is so hard. *N Engl J Med.* 1986;314:1380–1383.

6. Ware JE, Brook RH, et al. Comparison of health outcomes at a health maintenance organization with those of fee-for-service care. *Lancet.* 1986;1017–1022.

7. Udvarhelyi IS, Jennison K, et al. Comparison of the quality of ambulatory care for fee-for-service and prepaid patients. *Ann Intern Med.* 1991;115:394–400.

8. Sloss EM, Keller EB, et al. Effect of a health maintenance organization on physiologic health. *Ann Intern Med.* 1987;106:130–138.

9. Clancy CM, Hillner BE. Physicians as gatekeepers—the impact of financial incentives. *Arch Intern Med.* 1989;149:917–920.

10. Schulz R, Scheckler WE, et al. Physician adaptation to health maintenance organizations and implications for management. *Health Serv Res.* 1990;25:43–64.

11. Reames HR, Dunstone DC. Professional satisfaction of physicians. *Arch Intern Med.* 1989;149:1951–1956.

Chapter 6

Compensation of Primary Care Physicians in Open Panels

Peter R. Kongstvedt

There are two basic ways to compensate primary care physicians (PCPs) in open panels for services: capitation and fee-for-service. One recent large survey reported that 60% of open panel plans use capitation and that the remainder use fee-for-service (with a rare and puzzling 1% exception for salary).[1] With the rapid rise in popularity of point-of-service (POS) plans, the relative ratio of capitation to fee-for-service could change over time (this issue is discussed later in this chapter). Capitation and fee-for-service each have variations and permutations that are discussed in this chapter. There are any number of sources of information about each, so only an overview is given here.

CAPITATION

Capitation is prepayment for services on a per member per month (PMPM) basis. In other words, a PCP is paid the same amount of money every month for a member regardless of whether that member receives services or not and regardless of how expensive those services are.

Scope of Covered Services

To determine an appropriate capitation, you must first define what will be covered in the scope of primary care services. Include all services that the PCP will be expected to deliver, including preventive services, outpatient care, and hospital visits. Certain areas are difficult to define, for example, diagnostic testing, prescriptions, surgical procedures (what if the same procedure is performed by the PCP and by a referral physician?), and so forth. Other services such as immunizations, office care, and so forth are easier to define. If a plan is unable to define primary care services easily, an excellent reference is published by Milliman and Robertson, a national actuarial firm.[2] Defining the scope of covered services forms the basis for estimating the total costs of primary care.

Most performance-based compensation systems also hold the PCP accountable for nonprimary care services, either through risk programs or through positive incentive programs, both of which are discussed later in this chapter. For such programs, the same exercise of categorizing what and how services are defined should be carried out for specialty or referral services, institutional care, and ancillary services. Essentially, you need to be able to estimate costs for each of the categories you will capitate or track for capitated or at-risk PCPs.

Calculation of Capitation Payments

The issue of expected costs in defined categories is discussed in greater detail in Chapter 26. If you have been in operation for some time and have a data system capable of tracking the detail, estimating costs in categories is simply a matter of collating the existing data. If you do not have that experience or cannot draw upon it, you will have a more difficult time. In those cases, it is frequently necessary to have an actuary develop the data on the basis of your geographic area, the benefits you will offer, and the controls you will put in place. In fact, it may be best to consult an actuary in any case, even though it is not inexpensive.

A plan wishing to convert from a fee-for-service system to capitation will have to calculate the capitation equivalent of average fee-for-service revenues for the physicians. In other words, calculate what physicians would receive from fee-for-service for that membership base, assuming appropriate utilization.* This figure may then be discounted or not, depending on your situation. In plans where you fully expect the PCPs to receive a substantial bonus from control of utilization, a discount may be appropriate. In most cases, however, you will not wish to discount PCP services heavily.

As a rough example, if a physician receives approximately $45.00 per visit (collected, not just billed) and you can reasonably estimate a visitation rate of three primary care visits per member per year (PMPY), then multiplying $3 \times$ 45.00 and dividing the result by 12 (to get the revenue per month) yields $11.25 PMPM. That could approximate the capitation rate. This example is crude and does not take into account any particular definition of scope of covered services, actual visitation rates for an area, visit rate differences by age and sex, average collections by a physician, effect of copays, or differences in mean fees among different specialties, so it should not be used in capitating primary care services.

If your plan uses a risk/bonus arrangement, it is useful to be able to demonstrate to physicians that if utilization is controlled they will receive

more than they would have under fee-for-service. For example, if your plan uses a blended capitation rate of $11.25 PMPM and there are in fact three visits PMPY, and if good utilization control yields a bonus of $2.25 PMPM from the risk pools, then the physician receives a year-end reconciliation that blends out to $13.50 PMPM, or $54.00 per visit.

Variations by Age and Gender

Most capitation systems vary payments by the age and gender of the enrolled member to take into account the differences in average utilization of medical services in those categories. For example, the capitation rate for a member younger than 18 months of age might be $34.00 PMPM to reflect the high utilization of services by newborns.* The capitation rate may then fall to $8.00 PMPM for members 1 to 2 years of age, $6.00 PMPM for members 2 to 18 years of age, $10.00 PMPM for male members 18 to 45 years of age and $14.00 PMPM for female members 18 to 45 years of age (reflecting the higher costs for women in their childbearing years), and so forth. Examples of age- and sex-based utilization rates may be found in Chapter 26.

Those plans without the capability of capitating by age and gender must take special care in developing capitation rates. This is a particular problem when one is recruiting pediatricians because utilization of services by members in the first 18 months of life is quite high. In plans that capitate an independent practice association (IPA) with a single payment, the issue will remain. Unless the IPA has worked out an equitable method of distributing funds, the plan may need to provide support in this area.

Variations by Other Factors

It is possible, although not common, to vary capitation by factors other than age and sex. One example would be to vary capitation on the basis of experience, either expected or real. In this case, the capitation calculations would need to

---

*In other words, if high utilization is one of the primary reasons to convert from fee-for-service, it would not be appropriate simply to memorialize the high utilization rates when calculating a capitation equivalent; it is more appropriate to calculate the capitation on the basis of what utilization *should* be.

---

*This includes immunizations unless the plan carves immunization costs out of the capitation rate; this is discussed later in the chapter.

factor in the experience of each account group. In other words, if an account had an unusually healthy population of enrollees (eg, all healthy, young nonsmokers who use seat belts and advocate nonviolence), the capitation would be factored downward; the reverse would be true for a group with high expected utilization (eg, all hypertensive, overweight asbestos workers who smoke and drink heavily before racing their motorcycles, sans helmets, to buy illegal drugs). On a prospective basis, this could be done with standard industry codes in a manner similar to that used in developing premium rates under some forms of community rating. In the case of actual experience, a commercial account's retrospective experience could be used to adjust capitation payments up or down on a prospective basis. In all cases, the calculation of capitation would be highly complex compared to simple age and sex adjustments.

Another more easily analyzed factor is geography. Even in the same statistical metropolitan area, there may be considerable differences in utilization. For example, in the Washington, DC, metropolitan area there are highly significant differences in utilization among some counties in Maryland, Northern Virginia, and the District of Columbia (Blue Cross Blue Shield of the National Capital Area, unpublished data, 1989–1992). In such situations, it may be appropriate to factor in geographic location when capitation payments are calculated.

Practice type may occasionally be a legitimate capitation factor. As an example, internists argue that the case mix they get is different from the case mix family practitioners get. This has not been borne out in any research, but there is some evidence that even in the same strata of age and sex, specialty internists (eg, cardiologists) have sicker patients than general internists[3] [it must also be pointed out that the same investigators noted that after adjustment for patient mix, there was a whopping 41% higher level of utilization in unmanaged fee-for-service systems compared to health maintenance organizations (HMOs)[4]]. The actual mix of services delivered in the office may also differ by specialty type (Blue Cross Blue Shield of the National Capital Area, unpublished data, 1989–1992). University teaching programs tend to attract adverse selection from the membership base and may have a legitimate claim in that regard.

There may be straightforward business adjustments to capitation as well. One example that occurs in certain plans is an adjustment for exclusivity. In this case, the plan pays a higher capitation rate to those providers who do not sign up with any other managed care plans (there are usually no restrictions against participating with government programs or indemnity carriers). Such arrangements may raise the potential for antitrust actions (see Chapter 37), but that is dependent on the particular situation.

In any event, if factors other than age and sex are to be used to adjust capitation, the calculations become highly complex, and communicating these factors to the participating providers becomes far more difficult. The plan must also guard against an imbalance in factors that lead to a higher than expected (or rated for) capitation payout over the entire network. In other words, most adjustments lead not only to increases in capitation but to decreases as well.

Carve-Outs

Occasionally, capitation systems allow for certain services normally considered covered to be carved out of the capitation payment. For example, immunizations may not be paid under capitation but may be reimbursed on a fee schedule. As a general rule, carve outs should only be used for those services that are not subject to discretionary utilization. In the case of immunizations, the medical guidelines for administering them are relatively clear cut but subject to change (eg, there may be an increase in the number of immunizations that are to be given in the first years of life), and there is little question about their use. That would not be the case, for example, for office-based laboratory testing. If your plan reimburses capitation for all services, but pays fees for office-based laboratory work, you may see a rise in routine testing.

Capitation Pools for Referral and Institutional Services

When capitation exists for primary care services, payment for referral services and institutional services is often made from capitation funds as well. The services themselves may be paid for under a number of mechanisms (fee-for-service, per diem, capitation, and the like), but the expense is drawn against a capitated fund or pool.

For example, the PCP receives a $11.25 PMPM blended capitation rate for primary care services (in other words, the blend of all the age and sex capitation rates for that physician's membership base comes out to $11.25 PMPM). For each member, $17.00 PMPM is added to a capitated pool for referral services, and $35.00 PMPM is added to a capitated pool for hospital or institutional inpatient and outpatient services. The PCP does not actually receive the money in those pools; the plan holds on to it. Any medical expenses incurred by members in that PCP's panel will be counted against the appropriate pool of funds. At the end of the year, a reconciliation of the various pools is made (see below).

As with primary care, the scope of covered services must first be defined. For example, will home health be covered under institutional or referral (probably institutional because it reduces institutional costs), and will hospital-based professionals (radiology, pathology, and anesthesia) be covered under institutional or referral? The same exercise is carried out with any category for which capitated funds will be accrued, for example, ancillary services such as pharmacy expenses.

Medical Expenses for Which the Primary Care Physician Is Not at Risk

Even in plans that use withholds and risk/bonus arrangements (see below), there are sometimes certain medical expenses for which PCPs will not be at risk. For example, a plan may negotiate a capitated laboratory contract; laboratory capitation is then backed out of the referral and primary care capitation amounts and accounted for separately. If the PCP orders laboratory services from another vendor, that cost is deducted from his or her referral pool; otherwise, lab cost and use has no effect on the PCP's compensation.

Other examples of such nonrisk services might include any type of rider benefit (eg, vision or dental) or services over which PCPs have little control, such as obstetrics. Another example would be defined catastrophic conditions (eg, persistent vegetative state), where the PCP is taken out of the case management function by the plan and the plan's case management system takes over the coordination of care. The danger here is that there will be pressure to include too much in this category, thereby gutting the entire concept of capitation. Once a service has been taken out of the at-risk category, it is exceedingly difficult to put it back in.

Withholds and Risk/Bonus Arrangements

It is common to develop withhold and risk/bonus arrangements around the different capitation pools. One common arrangement is the withhold. One large survey recently reported that approximately 60% of HMOs use withholds,[5] although that survey combined both closed and open panel plans. A withhold is simply a percentage, for example, 20%, of the primary care capitation that is withheld every month and used to pay for cost overruns in referral or institutional services. In the earlier example of $11.25 PMPM, a 20% withhold would be $2.25. The PCP would actually receive a check each month for the difference between the capitation rate and the withhold, in this case $9.00; the remainder, in this case $2.25, is held by the plan and used at year end (or whenever) for reconciliation of cost overruns. The amount of payment withheld varied from 5% to 20% in the survey cited, with few plans reporting routine withholds greater than 20% (in fact, concern was registered that withholds greater than 20% could have a risk of incenting inappropriate underutilization).[5]

Many plans also have a clause in their physician's contract that states that the plan may increase the amount of withhold in the event of cost excesses beyond what is already being withheld. For example, the withhold can be increased from 20% to 30% if referral costs are out of control. The general guideline is to cover the actual and accrued expenses through the capitated pools and the withhold.

Although there are a few plans that have attempted to put the entire PCP capitation payment at risk for cost overruns, this is very unwise. If a PCP's entire capitation payment is withheld, that is tantamount to indentured servitude and may lead to serious service problems. It is better to limit the maximum risk at which the primary care capitation may be placed (eg, 50%, although even that level of withhold cannot be sustained for long).

If the withhold is used to pay for excess expenses in the referral pool or institutional services pool, the natural question is whether the PCP should be responsible for expenses related to members who are part of a different physician's practice. In other words, why should a PCP have to pay for overutilization by another physician? In the survey noted earlier, 25% of plans reported using individual risk pools, 12% reported using risk pools of 2 to 50 physicians, and 63% used risk pools of more than 50 physicians.[5] In those plans that do track risk pools individually, it is more common for only one pool (usually referral), if any, to be tracked on an individual basis while the withhold, if any, and hospital pool are aggregate.

One reason that individual risk pools have fallen out of favor over the past few years is the danger that a physician will be tempted to underutilize services inappropriately because of too close attention to the risk. This is not a danger in most cases, but it only takes one or two instances to cause serious problems. If the risk is spread out, any single action has less direct impact.

Another reason is that the element of chance is always operating, especially when a capitation pool is small. If a physician has 100 members under capitation, one case of acquired immunodeficiency syndrome (AIDS) could wipe out all the pools. By spreading the risk in these pools to all physicians, or to a large enough subset (say the northeast quadrant or five large medical groups), then chance has less of an impact.

What if not all the withhold is used or there is actually a surplus in either the referral pool or the institutional services pool? First, any surplus in a pool is generally first used to pay for any excess expenses in the other pool. For example, if there is money left in the referral pool but the institutional pool has cost overruns, the extra funds in the referral pool are first applied against

the excessive expenses in the hospital pool, and vice versa.

After both funds are covered, any excess money is shared with or paid to the physicians. In general, only those physicians with positive balances in their own risk pools receive any money. For example, a PCP has referral services funds tracked for his or her own patients. If the cost of services for those members leaves a positive balance in the referral pool, and if there is money left in the institutional services pool on a planwide basis, the PCP receives a pro rata share of the money. In other words, risk is shared with all physicians in the plan, but reward may be tracked individually. In another example, some plans have decided to disburse positive balances in referral and institutional funds on the basis of both utilization and measures of quality and member satisfaction (see Chapter 18).

The degree to which an individual PCP's pools will have an impact on year-end bonus disbursements may vary. If the decision is to minimize risk to individual PCPs, then you will want to set low thresholds (see below) and minimize or even stop tracking expenses against an individual PCP's pools while those expenses are still low.

For example, if a PCP has a member with AIDS, the referral expenses will be paid either out of the planwide referral capitation pool or out of a separate stop-loss fund and will not count against the individual PCP's referral risk fund after referral expenses have reached $2,500. In this way, high-cost cases, which could wipe out an individual PCP's risk pool, will have less effect than that PCP's ability to control overall referral expenses in the rest of the member panel.

It is common, although not absolute, for a plan to pay out all extra funds in the referral pool but only half the funds in the hospital pool. In some cases, there is an upper limit on the amount of bonus a PCP can receive from the hospital pool. The justification for this is that the plan stands a considerably greater degree of risk for hospital services and therefore deserves a greater degree of reward. Furthermore, it is often a combination of utilization controls and effective negotiating that yields a positive result, and the plan does most of the negotiating.

Reinsurance and Stop-Loss or Threshold Protection

The degree of risk to which any physician is exposed needs to be defined. As mentioned earlier, it is common for a plan to stop deducting expenses against an individual PCP's pool after a certain threshold is reached for purposes of the year-end reconciliation. There are two forms of threshold protection: costs for individual members and aggregate protection.

As an example of individual case cost protection, if a PCP has a member with leukemia, after the referral expenses reach $4,000, it will no longer be counted against the PCP's referral pool, or more commonly only 20% of expenses in excess of $4,000 will be counted against the referral pool; the uncounted expenses will be paid either from an aggregate pool or from a specially allocated stop-loss fund.

It is possible to vary the amount of threshold protection by the size of a PCP's member base to reduce the element of chance. For example, if a PCP has fewer than 300 members, the threshold is $2,000; if the PCP has more than 300 members, the threshold is $4,000. It is equally common for a threshold to exist for hospital services, although the level is much higher, for example, $30,000. As alluded to earlier, the lower the threshold, the less the effect of high-cost cases on individual capitation funds and the greater the effect of overall medical management. On the other hand, if it is too low there may be a perverse incentive to run up expenses to get them past the threshold. Multitiered thresholds also create an artificial barrier to the PCPs' acceptance of new members. For example, if the threshold for 300 members or fewer is less than that for 301 members or more, PCPs may resist adding members above the 300 limit so as to protect the lower threshold level. Tiered thresholds can be time limited to prevent this problem.

Aggregate protection is not as common. As an example of aggregate protection, the plan may reduce deductions to 20% or even stop deducting referral expenses after total expenses for an individual PCP reach 150% of the capitation amount. Providing aggregate stop-loss protection on the basis of a percentage of total capita-

tion allows such protection to be tied to the membership base of the PCP. This is another way of ensuring that a PCP's capitation will not be totally at risk.

The combination of threshold protection and risk sharing across the physician panel serves to reduce any individual PCP's exposure to events outside his or her control. It is frustrating to manage properly all your cases but receive no reward because one seriously ill patient had high expenses.

In any case, providing threshold protection to an individual physician is important, and you need to remember to budget for its cost. Although such stop-loss protection can be paid from the aggregate of all the physician's referral funds, that ensures that there will be a draw on the withhold (if there is one). Because positive referral balances will be paid back to PCPs, negative balances will need to be funded through the withhold, so there can never be a full return of the withhold. Therefore, it is preferable to budget a line item for stop-loss expense and to reduce the referral allocations by that amount.

It is likewise important for there to exist a mechanism for peer review of excess expenses to determine whether they were due to bad luck or poor case management. In the latter situation, the plan must have recourse to recovering all or part (up to the contractually agreed upon maximum individual physician risk) of the excess costs from a physician who failed to provide proper case management.

Problems with Capitation Systems

The most common problem with capitation involves chance. As mentioned earlier, a significant element of chance is involved when there are too few members in an enrolled base to make up for bad luck (or good luck, but nobody ever complains about that). Physicians with fewer than 100 members may find that the dice simply roll against them, and they will have members who need bypass surgery or have cancer, AIDS, or a host of other expensive medical problems. The only way to assuage that is to spread the risk for expensive cases through common risk-sharing pools for referral and institutional expenses and to provide stop-loss or threshold protection for expensive cases.

Another frequent problem is in the perception of the physicians and their office staff. Although many practices have now acclimated to capitation, there is a feeling that capitation is really funny money. When PCPs are receiving a capitation payment of $11.25, this is sometimes unconsciously (or consciously) confused with the office charge. In their minds, it appears as though everyone is coming in for service and demanding the most expensive care possible, all for an office charge of $11.25. It is easy to forget that many of the members who have signed up with that physician are not even coming in at all. It only takes 10% of the members to come in once per month to make it seem as if there is a never-ending stream of entitled demanders in the waiting room. The best approach to this is to make sure that the plan collects data on encounters so that the actual reimbursement per visit can be calculated.

The last major perceived problem is inappropriate underutilization. An argument made against capitation in general and risk/bonus arrangements in particular is that you are paying physicians not to do something, and that is dangerous.[6-10] Although there has been one spectacular case of fraud in south Florida, where providers were placed on individual risk arrangements and serious quality problems were noted, that was a failure of management and regulation. In fact, not only is there no real evidence that capitation or risk/bonus systems have led to poor quality (a fact that the references noted earlier in this paragraph have themselves all conceded), but there is some evidence that managed care systems have provided equal or better care to members than uncontrolled fee-for-service systems.[11-14]

Under a well-crafted capitation program, you are not paying physicians to underutilize services; you are sharing the savings of cost-effective care. In an unmanaged fee-for-service system, there is a direct relationship between doing something and getting paid for it; under capitation, the reward is removed from the action. In other words, the capitation check does not change each month depending on services. Fur-

thermore, by carefully constructing a stop-loss or threshold protection program, you can attenuate the effect of high-cost cases on capitation funds. Spreading the risk over more than one physician can lower the effect of single cases on a physician's reimbursement, but at the cost of not recognizing individual performance.

In the final analysis, it is the obligation of plan management to monitor the quality of services and to ensure that there is no inappropriate underutilization of services. One can argue that in a well-managed plan identification of poor quality is easier because there is more access to data and a tighter quality assurance system, and that is exactly how the plan must approach this issue.

One last issue should be raised, although it is not a problem per se but something to be aware of. In a capitated system, savings from decreased utilization may not always result in direct savings to the plan. In other words, if primary care services undergo a reduction in utilization, the capitation payments will not go down, just as they will not go up when there is increased utilization. If a system uses capitation extensively for primary care, specialty care, and hospitalization, there may be no reduction in expenses even if controls result in a dramatic lowering of utilization rates. On the other hand, such reductions will result in less pressure to increase capitation rates the next year.

CAPITATING AN INDIVIDUAL PRACTICE ASSOCIATION

Some HMOs capitate an IPA for all professional medical services. In that case, the plan calculates what all such services will cost and capitates the IPA, but the IPA is free to reimburse the participating physicians in any way it chooses. Some IPAs use a fee-for-service arrangement (discussed later in this chapter), whereas others recapitate the individual physicians just as though the plan were capitating directly. In the latter case, the main difference is that the plan has laid off the entire risk for professional services to the IPA rather than remain at risk for any costs beyond what was budgeted into the risk pools and reinsurance.

EFFECT OF BENEFITS DESIGN ON REIMBURSEMENT

Benefits design may have a great effect on reimbursement to PCPs, primarily in capitated programs, although the effect may be felt in any reimbursement system that relies on performance. The three major categories of benefits design that have such an impact are reductions in benefits, copayment levels, and POS plans.

Benefits Reductions

Because many managed care plans have adopted greater flexibility in benefits design in response to marketplace demands, the underpinnings of actuarial assumptions that were used to build capitation rates have become less reliable. If a plan has adopted exclusions for pre-existing conditions, has imposed waiting periods, or does not offer benefits that have usually been covered, the related expenses for those conditions are no longer applicable to the reimbursement rate. In other words, the capitation rate may now be higher than actually required. The impact of benefits reductions on primary care services is usually not so great as to warrant changing previously acceptable capitation rates, but that is not an absolute.

Benefits changes have a greater impact on risk pools. For example, if mental health and chemical dependency coverage is carved out of the PCP managing system and turned over to a dedicated management function (a common occurrence in managed care; see Chapter 13), then concomitant reductions in the referral and hospital risk pools are warranted. The same is true if an account wanted to carve out pharmacy services to another vendor (eg, a national company that administers a card and mail order program; see Chapter 14).

Copayment Levels

Copayment levels can have an immediate impact on capitation rates, both for PCP capitation and for risk pool allocations. The amount of capitation due a PCP will be different with a

$3.00 copay compared to a $10.00 copay. For example, if a capitation rate was calculated to be $11.25 on the basis of three visits PMPY at $45.00 per visit, then application of a $10.00 copay would reduce the capitation amount to $8.75 ($45.00 − $10.00 = $35.00; 3 visits × $35.00 = $105.00; $105.00 ÷ 12 months = $8.75 PMPM).

The same issue applies for calculating contributions to referral risk pools and hospital risk pools. For example, if consultant care has a $10.00 copay, then estimated consultant visit costs would have to take the copay into account. The same is true for hospital care if copays of $100.00 or $200.00 are applied.

The effect of copays and cost sharing on utilization is real, although it differs with respect to the amount of out-of-pocket expense to which the member is exposed.[15–17] It should be noted, however, that cost sharing does not necessarily selectively reduce inappropriate hospitalization (in other words, although total utilization may be reduced with cost sharing, the change in utilization may not reflect a change in whether the utilization was appropriate in the first place).[18] Deciding whether to adjust capitation rates on the basis of expected utilization differences from copays is difficult. Explaining such adjustments to PCPs is no easy task either because changes in utilization are population based, and any individual member may or may not change his or her behavior.

Adjusting capitation rates for copays is not easily done if there are widespread differences in copay amounts among different accounts. For example, if 50% of the members have a $3.00 copay, 35% have a $5.00 copay, and 15% have a $10.00 copay for primary care services (not to mention different copays for referral services), calculating the appropriate capitation can be difficult. Even so, it is usually worth doing unless the variations are minor or infrequent.

Point-of-Service Plans

For the purposes of this discussion, POS plans are those that allow members to obtain a high level of benefits by using the HMO or gatekeeper system while still having insurance type benefits available if they choose to use providers without going through the managed care system. For a discussion of POS, see Chapter 2.

Because members with POS benefits are not totally locked in to the managed care plan, utilization occurs both in network and out of network. Although the plan can actuarially determine the level of in-network and out-of-network use for the entire enrolled group (see Chapter 26), that cannot be said for an individual physician's member panel. This has an obvious impact on capitation rates.

Some plans attempt to adjust capitation rates on the basis of prospective in-network utilization. That usually means a reduction in the capitation rate. Other plans attempt to make adjustments on a retrospective basis, although this is a terribly difficult exercise in provider relations. In either event, it is no easy task to explain to a PCP who feels underpaid anyway that you are going to pay even less. An alternative is not to reduce the capitation rate, but that can result in a windfall for the PCP whose POS members never come in for services (or, on a more pernicious note, for the PCP who does not provide adequate access for POS members, thereby driving them out of network for services). This has become so difficult that many plans capitate PCPs for pure HMO (ie, not POS) members and pay fee-for-service for POS members.

POS makes it difficult to measure performance of PCPs as well. For example, if performance is based only on in-network utilization, one good way to look like a stellar performer is subtly to encourage POS members to seek services out of network. If PCPs are held accountable for all services, both in network and out of network, then they may argue that it is not fair that they are held accountable for utilization that is completely out of their control. Although this issue is not easily resolved, many plans with extensive experience in POS have chosen to fold out-of-network utilization into the performance-based reimbursement system, whether capitation or fee-for-service. To attenuate the problem of lack of control by an individual PCP, the risk or reward system is spread out among groups of PCPs or the entire network, thereby maintaining actuarial integrity.

FEE-FOR-SERVICE

There are some veterans of managed health care who hold that the fee-for-service system of American medicine is the root of all the problems we face with high costs. Although that is simplistic, there is some truth to it, particularly when there are no controls in place. In a system where economic reward is predicated on how much one does, particularly if procedural services pay more than cognitive ones, it is only human nature to do more, especially when it pays more. The reward is immediate and tangible: A large bill is made out, and it usually gets paid. Doing less results in getting paid less.

On the other side of the argument, fee-for-service results in distribution of payment on the basis of expenditure of resources. In other words, a physician who is caring for sicker patients will be paid more, reflecting that physician's greater investment of time, energy, and skills.

In a managed health care plan, fee-for-service may be used to compensate physicians and may be the method of choice in certain situations. For example, in a simple preferred provider organization (PPO) fee-for-service will be virtually the only option available. There are a number of managed and successful HMOs and IPAs that use fee-for-service for primary care, but there appears to be a greater risk of failure with a fee-for-service HMO than with a capitated one. Nevertheless, with the rise in popularity of POS plans (discussed earlier), there is an increased need to use fee-for-service in managed care.

Standing Risk

In a fee-for-service plan, determining who will stand risk for services is a major issue. This may run from a situation where the plan stands virtually all the risk, such as in a simple PPO or indemnity plan, to a system where the risk is shared fully with the providers, such as in an HMO. The no balance billing clause (see Chapter 36) is highly important to a tightly managed fee-for-service plan.

This clause states that the physician will only look to the plan for payment of services and will accept payment by the plan as payment in full. In other words, if the plan has to reduce or otherwise alter the amount of payment, the physician will not look to the member for any additional fees.

Determination of Fees

Usual, Customary, or Reasonable

The most prevalent method of fee determination is the usual, customary, or reasonable (UCR) fee. In some cases, this is really a euphemism for the physician sending a bill and the plan paying it. There is little uniformity to UCR because it represents what the physician usually bills for that service, and there can be tremendous discrepancies among physician's fees for the same service. One common methodology for determining UCR is to collect data for charges by current procedural terminology (CPT) code, calculate the charge that represents the 90th percentile, and call that the UCR maximum. When a claim is submitted, it is paid in full if it is lower than the 90th percentile; if it is higher than the 90th percentile, it is paid at the UCR maximum. Some plans use different technologies to determine what is reasonable, and arrive at allowances different than the 90th percentile. Still other plans negotiate a further percentage discount of the UCR (eg, 20%) and use that to pay claims.

The advantage to using a percentage of UCR is that it is extremely easy to obtain. Most physicians will gladly accept a discount on fees if it ensures rapid and guaranteed payment. The problem is that there is nothing to prevent the physician from increasing the fees by the same percentage as the discount, although excessive fee hikes will bump into the fee maximum. Some plans require the physician to notify the plan of a fee hike, but in truth there is little that the plan can or will do if it has no real clout.

The other problem is that it has become increasingly common for standard indemnity insurance plans to require a percentage copay (usually 20%) and deductible (eg, $200.00) for services, so the cost of services in a managed care plan that has obtained a percentage discount off UCR may not be significantly less than that of an insurance plan if the managed care plan has only small office copays. There is also the problem of increased utilization when the barrier of the copayment or cost sharing has been eliminated.

Relative Value Scales

The use of a relative value scale (RVS) has gained popularity in fee-for-service plans. In this system, each procedure, as defined in CPT, has a relative value associated with it. The plan pays the physician on the basis of a monetary multiplier for the RVS value. For example, if a procedure has a value of 4 and the multiplier is $12, the payment is $48.

A classic problem in using an RVS and negotiating the value of the multiplier has been the imbalance between procedural and cognitive services. Until recently, in most available RVS systems, as in fee-for-service in general, procedures have more monetary value than cognitive services. In other words, there is less payment to a physician for performing a careful history and physical examination and thinking about the patient's problem than for doing a procedure involving needles, scalpels, or machines. This has changed with the adoption of the resource based relative value scale (RBRVS) by the Health Care Financing Administration (HCFA) for Medicare.

RBRVS has addressed to some extent the imbalance between cognitive and procedural services, lowering the value of invasive procedures (eg, cardiac surgery) and raising the value of cognitive ones (eg, office visits). HCFA has imposed this on all physicians for Medicare recipients. Some large insurers are following suit in setting their determination of reasonable fees, but they lack the statutory ability to require acceptance of that fee as payment in full unless there is a contractual agreement to do so by the provider. Without such contracts, it is likely that RBRVS will actually result in great cost shifting to the private sector by those physicians whose incomes have been affected by lowered reimbursement for Medicare patients. In a managed care plan with appropriate contracts (see Chapter 36), RBRVS represents a rational method for setting fees.

Negotiated Fee Schedule, Fee Maximum, or Fee Allowance

Fee allowance schedules are quite useful and common. In this case, the plan determines what it considers the correct fees for services, usually on the basis of CPT codes, and the physician agrees to accept those fees as payment in full. This has the advantage of allowing the plan to control determination of payment for services on a uniform basis. In essence, this is an RVS that has already been multiplied. It is common practice to pay a percentage discount off charges subject to the fee schedule maximum. As mentioned above, the use of RBRVS is becoming a common method of building the fee allowance schedule.

Of special concern in the use of a fee schedule or RVS is the possibility of an antitrust violation. This is of particular concern in physician-sponsored plans. You do not really want a group of competing physicians to get together and set fees. It is preferable to use nonphysicians or an outside agency to perform this task.

Global Fees

A variation on fee-for-service is the global fee. A global fee is a single fee that encompasses all services delivered in an episode. Common examples of global fees include obstetrics, in which a single fee is supposed to cover all prenatal visits, the delivery itself, and at least one postnatal visit, and certain surgical procedures, in which a single surgical fee pays for preoperative care, the surgery itself, and postoperative care.

Some plans are using global fees to cover primary care as well. In this case, the plan must statistically analyze what goes into primary care to calculate the global fee. That analysis must include the range of visit codes as well as all covered services that occur during primary care visits (eg, electrocardiography, simple laboratory tests, spirometry, and so forth). The analysis will vary by specialty type (ie, internal medicine, family practice, and pediatrics).

The analysis then builds by specialty a composite type of visit. The average type of visit for internal medicine, for example, may be an inter-mediate visit, and 20% of the time an electrocardiogram is performed, 30% of the time a urinalysis is performed, and so forth (these figures are fictitious and should not be used for actual fee calculations). The plan then builds up the global fee by putting together the pieces; for example, $42 for the office visit, $7.00 for the electrocardiogram ($35.00 × 0.2), and so forth.

The chief value of a global fee is that it protects against problems of unbundling and upcoding. With unbundling, the physician now bills separate charges for services once included in a single fee; for example, the office visit is $45.00, the bandage is $10.00, starch in the nurses uniform is $3.00, and so forth. Upcoding refers to billing for a procedure that yields greater revenue than that actually performed; an example is coding for an office visit that was longer than the time actually spent with the patient. Global fees offer no protection against churning, which is the practice of seeing patients more often than is medically necessary to generate more bills; in fact, global fees, if not managed correctly, may exacerbate a problem with churning.

Plans that use global fees often tie them to performance. For example, utilization targets may be set for all medical services. How a PCP or group of PCPs performs against these targets may be used to set the global fees. For example, PMPM targets are set for primary care, referral care, institutional care, and ancillary services. Performance of a group of PCPs is measured against those targets on a rolling 12-month basis, and performance against those targets is used to adjust prospectively the next quarter's global fee up or down. Targets are modified by age, sex, product type (eg, pure HMO versus POS), or any other variables that are appropriate. Targets are also modified for the effect of stop loss against catastrophic cases. In other words, measurement of performance is similar to that used in capitated systems.

A performance-based global fee system is a hybrid of capitation and fee-for-service. Unlike capitation, there are generally no payouts from capitated risk pools (eg, referral pools), so there is no dollar-for-dollar relationship between utilization and reimbursement. Like capitation,

PMPM targets in all categories of medical expense are monitored, and reimbursement is still associated with good performance; also like capitation, there is a statistical build-up to determine reimbursement. Like fee-for-service, payment is only made if services are rendered, and no payments are made if there are no services.

This last feature makes such systems attractive to employer groups that have much lower than normal utilization (ie, those that have healthy employees and dependents who require fewer services than a typical capitation calculation assumes) and to POS plans where the plan desires to reward performance but needs to address both in-network and out-of-network utilization. As discussed earlier, under capitation you run the risk of paying twice for services under POS, once through capitation and again through out-of-network claims.

One central issue facing plan management in applying performance-based fee-for-service under POS is determining whether to include out-of-network costs in the performance evaluation of PCPs. At first blush, it does not seem fair to do so because such expenses are not under the control of the PCP. The best way to make one's performance profile look good, however, is to force members to seek care out of network (through poor service), thereby subverting the ultimate goal of cost control. Therefore, most plans are now including out-of-network expenses into performance evaluations and are working with PCPs to encourage in-network use by members. Related to that, it is important for plans to set performance parameters accurately that vary by product type; in other words, if you expect 30% out-of-network use by members under POS, that assumption must find its way into the PMPM standards against which you measure a PCP's performance.

Withholds

As with capitation, many plans that use fee-for-service withhold a certain percentage of the fee to cover medical cost overruns. For example, the plan may be using a negotiated fee schedule that amounts to a 20% discount for most physician fees. The plan then withholds an additional

20% in a risk pool until the end of the year. In effect, physicians receive what amounts to 60% of their usual fee but may receive an additional 20% at the end of the year if there were no excess medical costs.

It is possible to try to create profiles of physicians' utilization patterns to distribute more equitably the withhold funds in the event that some, but not all, of the withhold is used to cover extra medical costs. Unfortunately, this is difficult in a fee-for-service system if there is no gatekeeper model in place. Most plans simply return remaining withhold funds on a straight pro rata basis, although some plans return withhold on a preferential basis to PCPs as opposed to consultants.

Mandatory Reductions in All Fees

In a plan where risk for medical cost is shared with all the physicians and where straight CPT codes are used to reimburse on a fee-for-service basis, there must exist a mechanism whereby fees may be reduced unilaterally by the plan in the event of cost overruns. This is the usual method in an HMO and may be employed in a strongly controlled preferred provider organization as well.

For example, the plan may be using a fee schedule that is equivalent to a 20% discount on the most common fees in the area. In the event that medical expenses are over budget and there is not enough money in the risk withhold fund to cover them, all physician's fees are reduced by a further percentage, say an additional 10%, to cover the expenses. At this point, the effective discount is 30%, although this would really be 50% in the event that a withhold system was in place, all of the withhold funds had been used, and there were still excess medical liabilities.

Budgeted Fee-for-Service

Related to mandatory fee reductions, budgeted fee-for-service is used in a few plans. In this variation, the plan budgets a maximum amount of money that may be spent in each specialty category. This maximum may be expressed either as a PMPM amount or as a percentage of revenue (eg, 5.6% of premium revenue). As costs in that specialty category approach or exceed the budgeted amount, the withhold in that specialty, not across all specialties, is increased.

This approach has the advantage of focusing the reimbursement changes on those specialties in which excess costs occur rather than on all specialties in the network. The disadvantage is that this may not be provider specific; in other words, all specialists are treated the same, and there is no specific focus on individual outliers. Plans that do not use gatekeepers to managed care may find this type of approach useful. This type of system may also be amenable to formal performance evaluations (see Chapter 18).

Sliding Scale Individual Fee Allowances

Related to budgeted fee-for-service is the sliding scale individual fee allowance. In this model, PCP performance is again measured against benchmark targets in all categories of medical expense, with appropriate protection for expensive outlier cases. On the basis of performance, the PCP's reimbursement may vary from 70% of allowable charges up to 110% if performance exceeds targets.[19] Although this system still allows for upcoding and unbundling, it does vary by individual on the basis of performance and could be applied to groups of physicians as well as to individuals.

Problems with Fee-for-Service in Managed Health Care Plans

There are two significant problems with using fee-for-service in managed health care plans. These problems can become markedly exacerbated if the plan starts to get into financial trouble.

The first problem is churning. This simply means that physicians perform more procedures than are really necessary and schedule patient revisits at frequent intervals. Because most patients depend on the physician to recommend when they should come back and what tests should be done, it is easy to have a patient come back for a blood pressure check in 2 weeks instead of a month and to have serum electrolytes measured (unless laboratory services are capitated) in the physician's office at the same time. Few patients will argue, and the physician collects for the work.

Few physicians consciously churn, but it does happen, even if unconsciously. The serious problem comes when the plan reduces the fees because of medical expense overruns. When this happens, a feeding frenzy can occur. In effect, physicians start to feel that they have to get theirs first. If the fees are lowered 10% this month, what might happen next month? Better to get in as many visits as possible this month because next month may bring a 20% fee reduction. This creates a self-fulfilling prophecy, and the inevitable downward spiral begins.

The only effective approach to churning is tight management (or switching to capitation). Some plans develop physician peer review committees to review utilization. These committees have the authority to sanction physicians who abuse the system. This has some slowing effect if there are enough reviewers and not too many physicians to review. The actions of such committees should follow a process that includes warnings and a probationary period in which expectations for improvement are clearly outlined. Other plans apply differential withholds selectively on those providers whose utilization is clearly out of line, although defining that takes some care.

Better still, manage the plan such that few sanctions are necessary. This means controlling referrals, controlling hospital and institutional utilization, and negotiating effective discounts with providers and hospitals. It also means closely monitoring utilization and billing patterns by PCPs and acting when necessary. Performance-based programs such as those described earlier can also be applied to lessen the impact of churning, but this problem still remains in any fee-for-service plan.

On the other hand, if cost overruns bring fees down to grossly unacceptable low levels, utilization may decrease simply because the plan does not pay enough to get providers to do the work. That is a potentially problematic situation that can lead to inappropriate underutilization.

The second major problem is upcoding (sometimes referred to as CPT creep) and unbundling. As mentioned earlier, *upcoding* refers to a slow creeping upward of CPT codes that pay more; for example, a routine office visit becomes an extended one, a Pap smear and pelvic examination become a full physical examination, or a cholecystectomy becomes a laparotomy. *Unbundling* refers to charging for services that were previously included in a single fee without lowering (or lowering sufficiently) the original fee.

These problems are best monitored by the claims department in coordination with whichever department is responsible for data analysis. There are two useful approaches. The first is to look for trends by providers. Individuals who are trying to game the system will usually stand out. If there is one physician who has 40% extended visits compared to 20% for all the other physicians in the panel, it may be worth further review (this topic is addressed in Chapter 16). The second approach is to automate the claims system to rebundle unbundled claims and to separate for review any claims that appear to have a gross mismatch between services rendered and the clinical reason for the visit (this topic is ad-dressed in Chapter 20). The problems of upcoding and unbundling are also addressed through the use of global fees, as discussed earlier in this chapter.

CONCLUSION

In a tightly managed plan, such as an HMO, capitation will be more consistent with the overall goal of controlling costs. Although capitation is initially harder to calculate, and although it is harder to gain acceptance for it from physicians, this system has less likelihood of leading to overutilization than fee-for-service. Problems of inappropriate underutilization must be guarded against with effective monitoring and an effective quality assurance system.

Fee-for-service can be used as well but requires a different set of management skills. It is easier to install and is more acceptable to physicians but can quickly get out of control unless it is watched carefully. New products such as POS require new approaches to reimbursement because classic approaches are not ideally suited. As managed care evolves (or as federal legislation occurs), reimbursement may be expected to evolve further.

REFERENCES

1. Group Health Association of America. *HMO Industry Profile, Vol 2: Physician Staffing and Utilization Patterns.* Washington, DC: Group Health Association of America; 1991.

2. Doyle RL, Feren AP. *Healthcare Management Guidelines, Vol 3: Ambulatory Care Guidelines.* Milliman & Robertson; 1991.

3. Kravitz RL, Greenfield S, Rogers W, et al. Differences in the mix of patients among medical specialties and systems of care: results from the medical outcomes study. *JAMA.* 1992;267:1617–1623.

4. Greenfield S, Nelson EC, Zubkoff M, et al. Variations in resource utilization among medical specialties and systems of care: results from the medical outcomes study. *JAMA.* 1992;267:1624–1630.

5. Hillman AL, Pauly MV, Kerman K, Martinek CR. HMO manager's views on financial incentives and quality. *Health Affairs.* Winter 1991:207–219.

6. Hillman AL. Health maintenance organizations, finan-cial incentives, and physician's judgments. *Ann Intern Med.* 1990;112:891–893.

7. Hillman AL. Financial incentives for physicians in HMOs—is there a conflict of interest? *New Engl J Med.* 1987;317:1743–1748.

8. Hillman AL, Pauly MV, Kerstein JJ. How do financial incentives affect physicians' clinical decisions and the financial performance of health maintenance organizations? *N Engl J Med.* 1989;321:86–92.

9. Reagan MD. Toward full disclosure of referral restrictions and financial incentives by prepaid health plans. *N Engl J Med.* 1987;317:1729–1734.

10. *Medicare: Physician Incentive Payments by Prepaid Health Plans Could Lower Quality of Care.* Washington, DC: General Accounting Office; 1988. General Accounting Office publication GAO/HRD-89-29.

11. Ware JE, Brook RH, et al. Comparison of health outcomes at a health maintenance organization with those of fee-for-service care. *Lancet.* 1986;1017–1022.

12. Udvarhelyi IS, Jennison K, et al. Comparison of the quality of ambulatory care for fee-for-service and prepaid patients. *Ann Intern Med.* 1991;115:394–400.

13. Sloss EM, Keeler EB, et al. Effect of a health maintenance organization on physiologic health. *Ann Intern Med.* 1987;106:130–138.

14. Clancy CM, Hillner BE. Physicians as gatekeepers—the impact of financial incentives. *Arch Intern Med.* 1989;149:917–920.

15. Shapiro MF, Hayward RA, Freeman HE, Sudman S, Corey CR. Out-of-pocket payments and use of care for serious and minor symptoms. *Arch Intern Med.* 1989;149:1645–1648.

16. Newhouse JP, Manning WG, Morris CN, et al. Some interim results from a controlled trial of cost sharing in health insurance. *N Engl J Med.* 1981;305:1501–1507.

17. O'Grady KF, Manning WG, Newhouse JP, Brook RH. The impact of cost sharing on emergency department use. *N Engl J Med.* 1985;313:484–490.

18. Siu AL, Sonnenberg FA, et al. Inappropriate use of hospitals in a randomized trial of health insurance plans. *N Engl J Med.* 1986;315:1259–1266.

19. Church DE, Bokor A, McCain DD. An alternative to primary care capitation in an IPA-model HMO. *Med Interface.* November 1989: 37–42.

Chapter 7

Negotiating and Contracting with Consultants

Peter R. Kongstvedt

There are many reasons why a managed health care plan will need to negotiate and contract with consultants (this term refers not only to physician consultants but to nonphysicians as well, such as psychologists, physical therapists, and the like). Contract-based networks are a hallmark of managed care, and the provision of health care services from providers who are not under contract can be a real barrier to effective medical management if the volume of such services is high.

REASONS TO CONTRACT

Perhaps the most obvious reason for your plan to contract is to save money by having an advantageous agreement such as a discount. There are other reasons in addition to obtaining discounts. For a health maintenance organization (HMO), the issue of subordinated funds for uncovered liabilities is very real. Regulatory reserve requirements include calculations that are based on the number of real or expected visits to outside providers who have not signed a contract containing the National Association of Insurance Commissioners (NAIC) no balance billing clause (see Chapter 36 for a discussion of this issue).

Just as important, contractual arrangements will aid in getting and holding a consultant's attention, will help in the administration of an authorization system, will allow you to forecast and budget medical expenses more accurately, and will help ensure access to care for the members of the health plan.

Why would a consultant want to contract with a plan? At first blush it would appear that consultants would prefer simply to charge their fees and not bother signing a contract. That may be so in some cases, but there are some powerful reasons for them to contract.

A consultant will be acutely interested in the total volume of referrals. If you intend to or already significantly restrict the size of your referral panel, and if you have a reasonable membership base, you can easily calculate the expected number of referrals. Translating this into whole dollars could put you into a relatively strong position.

Time really is money. Most consultants will value your plan's ability to turn around a claim quickly. If consultants do not understand the value of rapid claim turnaround, their office manager will. Of course, if you cannot turn the claim around in a reasonable amount of time (eg,

30 days or sooner), you will have considerable difficulty in negotiating and maintaining contracts.

In tightly managed plans with well-functioning prospective authorization systems, being able to guarantee payment for authorized services for covered benefits is valuable. Elimination of uncertainty will be worth a measure of peace of mind to most consultants. If your plan depends heavily on retrospective review and claims adjudication, however, you may not be able to guarantee payment.

Some contracts will provide a regular revenue stream for the consultant. This is most valuable in capitated arrangements but holds for other arrangements as well. Depending on the payment mechanism you agree on and the volume of work that the consultant will do for you, this can be a powerful incentive, especially in an overcrowded medical market or to a consultant just getting started.

A consultant may also hope to see an increase in fee-for-service referrals. This is important only in open panel arrangements or in those closed panels that do a significant amount of fee-for-service work. Because most physicians prefer to work with those consultants whom they know and trust, a contractual arrangement that leads to that type of relationship will be valuable. The reverse is also true: A consultant may contract with your plan to prevent the disruption of fee-for-service referrals or as a favor to a valued primary care physician (PCP) who has been a good source of referrals.

Last, a consultant may contract simply to prevent a competitor from getting there first. There is often fierce competition among consultants, although most physicians are reluctant to admit it. This point must be discussed delicately if at all because many professionals may find the notion offensive, even if it is prevalent.

How many consultants of each type are necessary to contract with is not an easy question to answer. Many plans have between two and three times as many consultants as PCPs, but that number tells nothing about distribution by specialty or geographic area. Certain specialties such as general surgery, orthopedics, and obstetrics and gynecology and some of the medical

subspecialties (eg, cardiology and gastroenterology) need to be adequately represented at each major hospital with which you contract. Other specialties such as neurosurgery or cardiothoracic surgery need only be represented at those hospitals to which the plan refers members for appropriate treatment.

CLOSED PANELS: IN-HOUSE AND OUTSIDE CONTRACTS

Closed panel plans such as staff or group model HMOs (or large group practices with a significant managed care practice) must carefully weigh the advantages and disadvantages of bringing a consultant in house to join the medical staff rather than contracting out for services. The need to bring a consultant in house may arise if the volume of referrals is high, if the plan is unable to obtain satisfactory contracts outside, if there are questions about the quality of care being delivered by outside consultants and there are no good alternatives, if there is patient dissatisfaction, or if there are problems with proper utilization control.

Balanced against this are issues that may militate against the decision to bring a consultant in house. Providing adequate on-call coverage could be a problem. If there is only one of that type of consultant and cross-coverage with another in-house consultant is not possible, the consultant could burn out; if coverage previously had been provided by outside consultants who now no longer receive referrals, they may be less than cooperative about sharing calls.

Another potential problem can arise if there is a large geographic area to cover. If the plan uses multiple hospitals covering a wide territory, or if there are multiple medical centers, the consultant may not be able to provide sufficient coverage and the volume of referrals coming back inside may decrease. Even if referrals can be tightened up on an outpatient basis, attention must be paid to emergency care, especially for surgery, obstetrics, orthopedics, and cardiology.

Depending on your plan's current situation, it may also be more politic to use prominent outside consultants. Sometimes the same operational results can be achieved by asking a consultant to come to your facility on a regular basis.

TYPES OF REIMBURSEMENT ARRANGEMENTS

There are a number of mechanisms to reimburse consultants for services. Exhibit 7-1 lists some of the common (and less common) methods. The most appropriate method for use in any given situation will be predicated on the goals of the plan, the consultant, and each party's ability to actually manage within the terms of the agreement.

Charges and Discounts

The easiest arrangement to understand is straight fee-for-service. The consultant sends a claim and you pay it. Then why bother to contract at all? The answer is to get the consultant to agree to the NAIC sole source of payment clause (see Chapter 36). This is certainly not a preferred arrangement, but sometimes it is all you can get, particularly in high-cost specialties such as neurosurgery or in small start-up plans without a significant enrollment. Paying straight charges is obviously a fallback position.

A common arrangement is discounted fee-for-service. There are two variations here: first, a straight discount on charges, such as 20%; and

---

Exhibit 7-1 Models for Reimbursing Consultants

- Charges
- Discounts
- Fee allowances
- Capitation (with and without carve-outs)
- Retainer
- Hourly and salary
- Global fees
- Bundled case rates
- Outpatient and professional diagnostic-related groups or ambulatory patient groups
- Periodic interim payments or cash advances
- Withholds
- Penalties
- Changing schedules on the basis of performance

---

second, a discount based on volume or a sliding scale. In this latter type, the degree of discount is based on an agreed upon set of figures. For example, for an obstetrician who performs 0 to 5 deliveries per month there is a 10% discount, for 6 to 10 per month there is a 15% discount, and so forth. The sliding scale is used much less with consultants than with hospitals because the straight discount is easier for everyone to understand, agree to, and administer. Many plans combine a discount arrangement with a fee maximum. The fee maximum is a fee allowance schedule (see below); the plan pays the lesser of the consultant's discounted charges or the maximum allowance.

Relative Value Scale or Fee Allowance Schedule

If you have the systems capability to support it, using a relative value scale (RVS) such as the resource based relative value scale (RBRVS) or a fee allowance schedule can be useful, especially in an open panel. The RBRVS is discussed in Chapter 6. The difference between the two is that in an RVS each procedure is assigned a relative value, usually on the basis of Current Procedural Terminology—Revision 4 (CPT-4). That value is then multiplied by another figure (the multiplier) to arrive at a payment. Rather than negotiate separate fees, one negotiates the multiplier. In a fee allowance schedule, the fees for procedures (again, usually on the basis of CPT-4) are explicitly laid out, and the consultant agrees to accept those fees as full payment unless the discounted charges are less than the fee schedule, in which case the plan pays the lesser of the two.

The real utility with these is the avoidance of unanticipated fee hikes. If you have simply negotiated a discount on charges, the discount can easily be made up by raising fees. This may be partially offset by contractually requiring notice for any fee increases, assuming that you can and will actually spot the stray fee hike, but that still leaves you with the problem of administering a jumble of different agreements. It is far preferable to have one uniform method of handling claims.

The other advantage of a fee allowance schedule or RVS is in negotiations. Presenting a document with a list of printed fees has the power of legitimacy. Because you are not haggling fees, and it is right there on paper, it is more likely to be seen as acceptable.

A variation on fee-for-service is the global fee, flat rate, or case rate. These are discussed later in this chapter.

Capitation

Capitation is a popular and powerful method of reimbursing consultants. There are dangers involved, and you must carefully evaluate your current situation before capitating, particularly if you have a lot of point-of-service (POS) benefits in your plan (see Chapter 2 for a discussion of POS). If done properly, capitation can be valuable both to the consultant and to your plan, a genuine win-win situation. If done poorly, it can be a chronic headache.

Capitation is simply paying a provider a set amount of money per member per month (PMPM). You first must calculate the expected volume of referrals, the average cost, your ability to control utilization, and your relative negotiating strength. Your plan may have past data to guide you, or you may need to depend on an actuary or your best assumptions to derive the correct capitation amount. Please refer to Chapters 6 and 26 for more discussion on capitation and utilization rates.

Capitation has the advantages of allowing you to budget for expected medical costs and to place a degree of risk and reward on the consultant, and the financial incentives encourage the consultant to be a more active participant in controlling utilization.

In open panels it is possible, although not common, to allow for voluntary participation with capitation of consultant services. Once you have determined the correct capitation amount, you may negotiate an arrangement whereby the consultant agrees to capitation but understands that each capitated PCP is free to participate or not in the arrangement on a year-to-year basis. If the PCP does not agree to the capitated arrangement, the consultant does not receive capitation payments for that PCP's members, and referrals are paid on a fee-for-service basis. This approach works well when PCPs are at individual or small group risk for their referral funds, but it becomes meaningless if referral risk is aggregated across the entire network.

In fee-for-service plans, it is probably not a good idea to capitate consultants before capitating PCPs. If you do so to any great degree, you may find that you have obligated more money than you intended to consultant capitations, to the detriment of primary care and hospital funds. There may be exceptions to this, such as physical therapy or mental health and chemical dependency, but those are infrequent.

There are some common problems that need to be addressed before you capitate consultants. If you fail to explore these issues, you may find yourself in the position of having to live with a year-long arrangement that is to your disadvantage.

The pressure to capitate frequently comes as a result of uncontrolled utilization. Referrals are high, expenses are out of control, and there is high negative variance to budget. The pressure to capitate is to prevent costs from going even higher and to bring some predictability to medical expenses. This is usually the wrong time to capitate. Be assured that the consultant knows exactly how much you have been paying and will not eagerly agree to a capitation rate that amounts to a substantial discount, unless the plan (and the PCPs) are willing to change consultants. It is far preferable to control utilization before negotiating a capitation rate. If you do not, you will be locked in to the higher rate for at least a year. Of course, if the consultant, not the PCP, is the cause of inappropriately high utilization, then you really should look for a new consultant.

Another common problem is being able to control the flow of referrals. It is easy to assume that, once you cut a deal with a consultant, all you need to do is notify the PCPs and/or members and your problems are solved. This is not so. Disrupting old referral patterns is tough, and you may find that you do not have the system capabilities to respond proactively to referrals outside the capitated system. Furthermore, your capitated consultant may not be able to provide adequate geographic or emergency coverage. When referrals go outside your capitated system, you are essentially paying for them twice. This problem virtually defines a POS plan, which is why capitating consultants in a POS plan is problematic.

One possible approach to the geographic coverage problem is to capitate only for an appropriate geographic primary care base. This balkanization of the specialty base frequently is more acceptable, unless the capitating specialty group has wide coverage.

Capitation may actually serve to increase utilization. If the PCPs who are controlling the referrals, and perhaps even the medical director of the plan, see capitation as putting a lid on expenses, there is far less pressure to control utilization because it appears that the service costs the same regardless of use; you could almost say that it is free!

If you fail to control utilization of capitated services as though they were fee-for-service, you will have a most unpleasant surprise when the contract comes up for renegotiation. Most consultants will keep careful track of what they would have made in fee-for-service equivalents. If you have failed to control utilization, the capitation rate may be equivalent to an unacceptable discount on charges. You will either have to give in, find a new consultant, or hang tough. In each of those cases, someone loses.

The last major problem encountered in capitation is the issue of carve-outs. A carve-out is a particular service that the consultant does not include in the capitation rate. For example, ophthalmologists may capitate for all services except cataract extractions, for which they will give you a 25% discount on charges. The problem here is that you may find yourself with an unexplainably high rate of cataract extractions. If the service is one that only the consultant can reasonably judge the need for, and that service is a carve-out, you have a potential problem. In all fairness, it is unlikely that you will be the victim of outright fraud, but it still makes for some uneasiness.

A variation of the carve-out problem arises when the consultant cannot or will not handle all the services. If you capitate for all services, but

the consultant refers out for the delivery of some of those services you may wish to consider deducting those costs from the capitation payment. There are no consistent guidelines here. If the service is one that the consultant truly cannot perform (eg, an ophthalmologist who does not do retinal surgery), then you can probably budget properly and not roll that expense into the capitation rate, thereby avoiding having to adjust the rate frequently and pressuring the consultant (perhaps inappropriately) not to refer cases. On the other hand, if the consultant can perform the service but simply does not (eg, an ophthalmologist who is never available on Wednesday afternoons), then it is appropriate to deduct those expenses from the capitation payment. If you intend to do so, you must be clear about your intentions from the start and place appropriate language in the contract.

Retainer

A retainer is identical to what is commonly used with law firms. You simply pay a set amount to a consultant every month and reconcile at periodic intervals on the basis of actual utilization, either as a prenegotiated discount on charges or on some other objective measure. This ensures availability of the consultant to members and provides for the steady income desired by the consultant while still allowing payment on the basis of actual utilization. One issue to address early is whether the reconciliation goes both ways or whether it only goes up. That issue surfaces more often than one would expect.

Hourly and Salary

Just as it sounds, with hourly and salary arrangements the plan pays a consultant an hourly rate or salary for performing services. In essence, you are buying block time. This works to your advantage if you contract with an already busy consultant because there will be little incentive for him or her to stretch out sessions. This type of arrangement is common in emergency departments or other settings when a physician needs to be available for a defined time period. This also works if you need to buy on-call coverage to back up an in-house consultant. Hourly and salary arrangements lend themselves more to closed panel than open panel plans.

Flat Rate, Case Rate, or Global Fee for Procedures

If you are not using a fee schedule, you may want to negotiate a flat rate for a well-defined set of procedures. This is usually done as part of a negotiation for a discount on charges. For example, you may negotiate a 20% discount on charges with an obstetrician but a flat rate for normal vaginal deliveries or cesarean sections. The charge for those procedures will be the same regardless of how much or how little time and effort are spent. In this example, many plans use the same flat rate for either a vaginal delivery or a cesarean section, thereby eliminating any financial incentive to perform one or the other.

Related to the flat rate is the global fee. A global fee is a flat rate that encompasses more than a single type of service. For example, a global fee for surgery may include all preoperative and postoperative care as well as one or two follow-up office visits. A global fee for obstetrics may include all prenatal and postnatal care.

Global fees must be carefully defined as to what they include and what may be billed outside them. For example, if ultrasound is billed outside the global fee for a delivery, you will need to monitor its use to determine whether any providers are using (and billing for) an abnormally high number of ultrasounds per case.

Bundled Case Rates

Bundled case rates refer to a reimbursement that combines both the institutional and the professional charges into a single payment. For example, a plan may negotiate a bundled case rate of $20,000 for cardiac bypass surgery. That fee covers the charges from the hospital, the surgeon, the pump technician, and the anesthesiologist as well as all preoperative and postoperative care. Bundled case rates sometimes have outlier provisions for cases that become catastrophic and grossly exceed expected utilization.

Diagnosis-Related Groups and Ambulatory Patient Groups

These are important topics for hospital reimbursement but currently have limited utility in consultant reimbursement other than through bundled case rates, as discussed above. Further discussion on these two methods is found in Chapter 8.

Periodic Interim Payments and Cash Advances

Occasionally a plan may use periodic interim payments (PIPs) or cash advances with consultants. In the case of PIPs, the plan advances the provider a set amount of cash equivalent to a defined time period's expected reimbursable charges. As claims come in from that consultant, the claims are taken against the PIP, but the PIP is routinely replenished. In this way, the consultant gets a positive cash flow as well as the use of the plan's money interest free. Cash advances are simply that: The plan advances the provider a set amount of cash and then carries it as a receivable on the books. In the event that the relationship between the consultant and the plan terminates, the final claims are taken against the cash advance.

Neither of these techniques can be recommended for routine use. In either case, the advanced cash may not be treated as a liability by the consultant but rather simply as a payment, which makes it difficult to recover the funds. Furthermore, a special deal with a few providers has the potential of making relations with the rest of the network rather testy.

RISK/BONUS ARRANGEMENTS

In addition to whatever reimbursement arrangement you make with a consultant, there are times when it is mutually advantageous to add an element of risk and reward. This is almost always done in the context of utilization but could conceivably be tied to other objectives as well. These types of arrangements are best suited to those specialties in which the consultants themselves control a major aspect of utilization and in which there is a sufficient volume of referrals to rule out random chance playing too large a role in the results. Risk and reward arrangements are far easier to do in a pure HMO environment than in a preferred provider organization or a POS plan.

In setting risk and reward levels, keep in mind that you do not want to make the risk or reward so great that it has the potential of having a serious negative impact on clinical decision making. It is better policy to devise a reimbursement mechanism that fairly compensates a consultant up front for appropriate and judicious use of clinical resources and then sets a risk or bonus level that, while still being attention getting, is not potentially seriously injurious to the fiscal health of the consultant. You do not want to put the consultant, the plan member, or yourself in the position of having economics override proper medical care. What you do want is a risk or bonus arrangement that will help focus the attention of the consultant on controlling unnecessary utilization.

Set Targets

There are a number of objective criteria that one can use in setting targets for risk and bonus arrangements. A frequent one is average length of stay (eg, setting a target of 1 or 2 days average length of stay for normal vaginal deliveries). A variation would be total bed days per 1,000 members (eg, all surgical bed days per 1,000 members for the total plan membership, or whatever geographic base you choose).

Another possibility is PMPM cost. You need to define carefully the cost area, such as professional, hospital, all inclusive, and so on. If you have the systems capabilities to track accurately, this method has the advantage of being more directly tied to the bottom line of your plan.

Another method is to look at a particular medical expense as a percentage of premium revenue. This is less useful because, although it ties directly to your plan's margin, it can lead to disputes that are based on your premium rates and yield. Theoretically you could claim that everyone is in the enterprise together, but in actual practice it appears as though you are trying to buy market share and take it out on the backs of the providers.

Avoid setting targets for productivity. If you set a risk or bonus on the basis of seeing a certain number of patients per hour or any of the other usual fee-for-service incentives, you could have the problem of churning.

Define the Risk or Bonus

You must define the amount of payment that will be at risk or the amount that will potentially be available for bonus. For example, in a capitation situation it may be 10% or 20% of the total capitation payments for the year (in whole dollars). Next you must choose between a straight bonus arrangement for exceeding goals or a risk/bonus band in which the consultant is at risk for failing to meet goals and may achieve a bonus for exceeding them (in other words, a withhold on payment, possibly combined with a bonus plan).

After you have set the goals and amount of risk and reward, determine the spread of bonus payments. For example, achieving a 2% reduction in length of stay yields a 1% bonus up to a maximum of 10% of the total payments for the year. Be as specific as possible to avoid disputes later, and be absolutely sure that you can accurately track whatever objectives you set.

A simple warning here: Be sure that you have done a financial model of the possible outcomes of a bonus arrangement. You do not want to set up an arrangement where the bonus negates any savings achieved from meeting the goals. If the bonus will be paid simply for meeting goals and you have included those goals in your budget, be sure to include the bonus in your budget and reported medical benefit expenses as well. This should be obvious, but it occasionally is overlooked.

A frequently encountered criticism of bonus arrangements is that you are paying a provider to deliver reduced (ie, inferior) care. This should simply not be the case. You are sharing the savings that high-quality, cost-effective medical care produces; furthermore, any providers caught trying to line their pockets by delivering inferior care will be terminated from participation in your plan. It is the consultant's responsibility to provide high quality care. It is your responsibility to make sure that the consultant is properly reimbursed and to monitor the quality of care delivered.

PROHIBITION OF SUBAUTHORIZATIONS

In a tightly controlled managed care plan with a primary care authorization system, you will want a clear understanding (including contract language) that the consultant is not allowed to authorize services for a member but must obtain authorization from the PCP or the health plan. This includes hospitalizations, ancillary testing, and referrals to other consultants.

There are some common occurrences of this problem. One example is the consultant who owns an expensive piece of diagnostic equipment; although there is usually no genuine plan to do unnecessary testing, there is still a subtle pressure to use the machine and generate some revenue from it. If such self-authorizations are prohibited contractually, the consultant will either be forced to contact the PCP and discuss the need for the test, or the consultant will not be allowed to bill for the test (remember the sole source of payment clause).

Another common occurrence is the consultant choosing to hospitalize the member. Although hospitalization may be appropriate, your ability to manage the case is severely hampered if you do not know about it until it is all over. In most managed health care plans, hospitalization requires either preadmission review by the plan's utilization management department or authorization from the PCP and health plan. It is crucial to ensure that you will be able to manage hospital cases concurrently, and that means preadmission notification and authorization. See Chapter 10 for further discussion about utilization management.

The last common occurrence is the problem of referrals to other consultants. If you allow a consultant to refer to another consultant without obtaining authorization, the member can start getting shunted from one consultant to another. Not only is that an inefficient and expensive way to deliver medical care, but the lack of continuity has implications for the quality of care as well.

How tightly you enforce this will vary in certain circumstances. For example, an obstetrician may only need to notify the plan when a member is admitted for a delivery and may not require PCP preauthorization at all. If a consultant is capitated for all office services, that capitation may include office procedures and tests as well (eg, office radiology for an orthopedist). Even without capitation, you may decide to allow selected consultants to perform certain studies because it is simply necessary for the delivery of care (eg, allowing neurologists to order magnetic resonance imaging). These exceptions must be carefully thought through, and reimbursement for them should not encourage overutilization.

The point of this is not to make a system so rigid that it becomes impossible to deliver proper care but to have a system that allows you to manage the health care that is delivered by timely intervention when it is appropriate and to direct the care in the most cost-effective way possible. It is certainly possible that a tightly run plan could allow consultants to function as managing physicians in certain circumstances (eg, for active acquired immunodeficiency syndrome cases), but that is an analysis that each plan must make for itself.

CONCLUSION

Medical care delivered by consultants is a crucial element in the cost and quality of health care. Reimbursement arrangements and contracts are tools that codify and clarify the responsibilities of each party to the other. They will not solve your problems and will not take the place of good management. Remember: A 20% discount will not make up for poor utilization control, and nothing will make up for poor quality of care.

Chapter 8

Negotiating and Contracting with Hospitals and Institutions

Peter R. Kongstvedt

Although there are a few states (eg, Maryland and New Jersey) that are so heavily regulated that there is little or no latitude allowed in reimbursing hospitals, in general this represents an area of tremendous potential for creativity. Hospital contracting is one of the most important tasks that an executive director and other appropriate plan managers face.

REASONS TO CONTRACT

The reasons for a plan to contract with hospitals are much the same as those for contracting with consultants; this is discussed in Chapter 7 and will not be repeated here. It should be noted that because of the amount of money involved with hospital care the issues take on greater importance. This is particularly true for both required reserves for uncovered liabilities and discounts. In some cases, failure to have adequate contracts with hospitals will lead to a rejection of state licensure or federal qualification (for health maintenance organizations).

The reasons for a hospital to agree to a contractual arrangement are likewise similar to those of a consultant. The hospital will be acutely interested in improving, or in some cases holding on to, a volume of inpatient days and outpatient procedures. This becomes crucial if the hospital is suffering from a low occupancy rate. A hospital will also be interested in a plan's ability to turn around a claim; the time value of money is even more important to a hospital than to a consultant because the amount of money is so much greater and because the public sector (ie, Medicare and Medicaid) are notoriously slow payers.

Guaranteed payments for authorized services for covered benefits will also be valuable, especially if the hospital has been absorbing losses as a result of denial of payments from a retrospective review process. As with consultants in an open panel, a hospital may hope to see an increase in regular fee-for-service patients; because physicians prefer not to perform rounds in multiple hospitals, this is a genuine possibility.

Last, a hospital will contract to shut out a competitor. Competition among hospitals is usually much more open than competition among physicians and is usually a regional issue; a hospital will have a reasonably defined service area from which most of its admissions come. If you are planning (or willing) to limit the number of participating hospitals in each service area, this becomes a strong negotiating point.

SELECTING HOSPITALS

Selecting which hospitals to approach is done by balancing a number of variables. In a small market there may be a limited choice. In most cases, though, there will be some latitude. Before you begin the selection process, you must first decide how much you are willing to limit the choices in your plan.

Generally, the more you are willing to limit the number of participating hospitals, the greater your leverage in negotiating. Limiting the number has serious disadvantages as well. If you strictly limit yourself to just a few hospitals, you may have a competitive disadvantage in the marketplace because prospective members and accounts often use hospitals as a means of judging whether to join a managed care health plan. If you fail to include a sufficient selection of hospitals, you may see disappointing marketing results. On the other hand, if you refuse to limit the number of hospitals, you may have considerable difficulty in extracting favorable agreements.

A certain number of hospitals will be required to cover your service area effectively. In some small communities, a single hospital may be able to serve the entire population, but that is rare. It is important to map out the hospital locations relative to your defined service area and to look for overlap among competing hospitals.

Selecting which hospitals to approach first in a service area is a combination of hard data—such as occupancy, cost, and services offered—with your judgment about the hospital's willingness to negotiate and the perception of the public and physician community about the hospital's quality. It does little good to make an agreement with a hospital that is perceived as inferior. Likewise, it is less than optimal to contract with a hospital that does not do high-volume obstetrics if there is a regional competitor that does because your plan will be less attractive to young families.

If the hospital is a sponsor or joint venture partner in your plan, the choice factors become rather clear. If a hospital is an enthusiastic supporter, or if there is a long history of a good working relationship, that should also be taken into consideration.

NEGOTIATING STRATEGY

General Strategy

Your ability to negotiate successfully with the hospitals in your area will depend on a number of things. Chief among them are the personal abilities of the negotiator, the size of your plan, your ability actually to shift patient care, and your past track record in being able to deliver what you promise. A new start-up operation has considerably less clout than an existing large plan. If the new start-up can demonstrate genuine potential for significant growth, that may help offset the weakness of having little to offer but promises.

Setting an overall strategy is important to the ultimate success of your plan. It is certainly possible to approach the project of hospital negotiations by using the managerial equivalent of Brownian motion, but your end results could be disappointing.

The strategic plan should address both regional and planwide issues. You may have one set of criteria for primary care services in a service area and a different set for tertiary services. After you have selected the hospital you wish to approach first, select the hospitals you will approach next if the initial hospital either is unwilling to come to agreement or offers too little to make the agreement worth the risk. You may find that you will want to approach some hospitals for tertiary services on a much wider regional basis than for primary care. If you do not intend significantly to restrict your hospital panel, then first select those hospitals with the most marketing value.

Data Development

After you have selected individual hospitals to approach, make a worksheet for each and one for the entire service area as well. Estimate the hospital's occupancy rate (these data may be available from your local or state health department or the American Hospital Association[1]) and operating margin (this too may be available at the health department or may be published in the hospital's annual report).

Estimate the total number of bed days you currently have in the hospital. If you are a new start-up, estimate the total number of bed days you believe you will control and over what time span (be honest here). Estimate as well the number of bed days you can realistically shift into the hospital or, if necessary, away from the hospital. This estimate will be affected by geographic accessibility and acceptability of such case shifting by members and physicians.

Last, calculate the whole dollars associated with all the above estimations or facts. You will want to know what whole dollar amount you represent to the hospital now and in the future. Calculate what happens if you shift into and out of the hospital and what percentage of the hospital's gross income you represent.

Goal Setting

It is axiomatic that medical services are bought at the margin. As with purchasing an automobile or furniture, it is unusual to pay the sticker price. This goes for primary care, consultant care, and, most important, hospital services. If a hospital ward is fully staffed but running at less than full occupancy, the marginal cost of filling another bed on that ward is minor compared to the revenue. It is unlikely that the hospital will call in extra nurses, hire extra support staff, buy new equipment, or take out more insurance to care for a 10% increase in bed days. Those costs are relatively fixed. The marginal costs (such as laundry, food, drugs and supplies, and the like) are less than the fixed overhead.

Because of this, a hospital has room to maneuver in negotiating. This does not mean that you can expect a hospital to reduce its charges by half (unless its charges are grossly inflated to begin with), but you can reasonably expect effective discounts of 20% to 30% if you are able to deliver sufficient volume. Certain for-profit hospitals are actually managed to show a profit at less than 50% occupancy. In those cases, even greater discounts may sometimes be obtained because much of the added revenue to the hospital goes right to the bottom line. Conversely, such high-margin hospitals may feel little pressure to increase their occupancy if they have a

decent market share and may be difficult to deal with because they hope to freeze you out.

After you have developed the worksheet referred to above, take your assumptions regarding how much you can shift into the hospital and apply the desired discount. If a hospital has a low occupancy rate, or if it has less than a full occupancy rate but is enjoying healthy profit margins (or reserves if it is not-for-profit), and you can deliver or remove a significant volume of patients, you may be able to achieve a good discount. If the hospital is running above 90% occupancy, your prospects of substantial savings are not as good.

Include outpatient procedures in your calculations. It is increasingly common to find that outpatient procedures are actually more expensive than identical procedures done in an inpatient setting. Hospital managers have not been idly watching utilization shift to the outpatient department; they have adjusted charges to enhance revenues.

Setting goals should be done by using the various payment mechanisms discussed in the next section. Modeling discounted charges, per diem rates, and so forth will allow you to have a working knowledge of the many opportunities you have for a mutually satisfactory agreement. Failing to look at all the alternatives may lead you to stalemate if the hospital administrator does not like the reimbursement model you are proposing, even though he or she may very well agree to a different proposal that would actually yield the same result.

Responsibilities and Timing

The project must be mapped out and managed with standard project management techniques. Considering the money involved, great attention should be paid to assigning roles and schedules in the negotiating process.

The key players in hospital negotiations are the executive director, the medical director, and the finance director. It is the responsibility of the executive director to initiate the contact, set the stage or tone, and be sure that the executive director of the hospital feels comfortable with the plan's commitment to proceed fairly, openly, and honestly. It is not always necessarily the role of the executive director actually to negotiate the details of the agreement, because it is unlikely that the executive director of the hospital will be doing so. In small plans or in early start-ups, however, or sometimes for political reasons, the executive director may end up carrying the ball all the way through.

The role of the finance director is to work closely with the plan's executive director and the hospital's finance director or controller. It is common for the actual negotiation to take place at this level. The finance director should not have the authority actually to sign off on the agreement because the controller of the hospital will surely not have this authority, and it further serves a useful purpose to be able to break the negotiations to confer with the executive director back at the plan. Because the hospital may not believe your numbers, it falls to the finance director of your plan to present those numbers in a credible and understandable way (not only the numbers now but the numbers you expect).

In addition to evaluating the quality of the institution and helping understand the political climate, the medical director needs to be able to convince the hospital administrator that the plan will genuinely shift the patient caseload as necessary. If the medical director cannot persuade the hospital that the plan is able to move patients in or out, you will have lost a key advantage in the negotiations. This need not be done in a heavy-handed way or as a naked threat. It suffices for this issue to be brought out in a businesslike and unemotional way, perhaps with assurances that it is clearly your preference to use the fine hospital with which you are negotiating.

Last, set a realistic time schedule. The degree to which you achieve success in your hospital negotiations will be reflected in the amount of effort you put into the negotiating process. It is not realistic to think that you can obtain sizeable discounts and contracts with a number of hospitals in less than 2 or 3 months (and perhaps considerably longer). It will take time for you to do your preplanning work, for the hospital to digest what you are proposing, for the hospital to make a counteroffer and for you to counter that, and so on. After that, each side's lawyers will want to review the contract language. When you have finally reached an agreement, the hospital may have to take it to its board for final approval.

Conversely, try not to let too much dust collect on the proposal before either following up or approaching another hospital as an alternative. There is no reason for the hospital to hurry the process unless it believes that to delay will mean losing the contract. If you are paying full charges or have proposed a reduction in what you are currently paying, the hospital will obviously prefer to keep collecting that revenue as long as possible unless you are promising a sizeable increase in volume that it is not now getting.

TYPES OF REIMBURSEMENT ARRANGEMENTS

There are a number of reimbursement methodologies available in contracting with hospitals, except in those states where regulations prohibit creativity. Exhibit 8-1 lists a number of methods that have been used by plans but is not exhaustive. Lack of imagination is the only real impediment to negotiating, although many plans have found that their inability to handle administratively what is otherwise a bright idea has led to problems. A brief discussion of these methodologies follows.

Exhibit 8-1 Models for Reimbursing Hospitals

- Charges
- Discounts
- Sliding scales for discounts and per diems
- Per diems
- Differential by day in hospital
- Diagnosis related groups (DRGs)
- Differential by service type
- Case rates
  —Institutional only
  —Bundled
- Bed leasing
- Capitation or percentage of revenue
- Periodic interim payments or cash advances
- Penalties and withholds
- Ambulatory patient groups (APGs) for outpatient care

Straight Charges

The easiest payment mechanism in health care is straight charges. It is also obviously the most expensive and the least desirable mechanism, after the option of no contract at all. This is a fallback position to be agreed to only in the event that you are unable to obtain any form of discount at all, but it is still desirable to have a contract with a no balance billing clause in it (see Chapter 36).

Straight Discount on Charges

As with consultants, a common arrangement with hospitals is a straight percentage discount on charges. In this case, the hospital submits its claim in full and your plan discounts it by the agreed-to percentage and then pays it. The hospital accepts this payment as payment in full. The amount of discount you can obtain will depend on the factors discussed above.

Sliding Scale Discount on Charges

It is more common to see sliding scale discounts with hospitals than with consultants. It is also more appropriate because the services delivered by the hospital are not under the hospital's direct control but rather under the control of the attending physicians. There are fewer means for the hospital to overutilize inappropriately, so it is less risky to use this technique. This method also recognizes the primary financial goals of both parties.

With a sliding scale, the percentage discount is reflective of total volume of admissions and outpatient procedures. Whether you lump the two categories together or deal with them separately is not as important as making sure that you deal with them both. With the rapidly climbing cost of outpatient charges, savings from reduction of inpatient utilization could be negated by an unanticipated overrun in outpatient charges.

An example of a sliding scale is a 10% reduction in charges for 0 to 500 total bed days per year with incremental increases in the discount up to a maximum percentage. An interim per diem charge could be negotiated as well, or your plan could simply adjust the discount as the year progresses (this is not preferred because you would lose the present value of the money).

How you track is also negotiable. You may wish to vary the discount on a month-to-month basis rather than yearly. You may wish to track total bed days, number of admissions, or whole dollars spent. Whatever you finally agree to, be sure that it is a clearly defined and measurable objective.

The last issue to look at in a sliding scale is timeliness of payment. It is likely that the hospital will demand a clause in the contract spelling out your requirement to process claims in a timely manner, usually 30 days or sooner. In some cases you may wish to negotiate a sliding scale, or a modifier to your main sliding scale, that applies a further reduction based on your plan's ability to turn a clean claim around quickly. For example, you may receive an additional 4% discount for paying a clean claim within 14 days of receipt. Conversely, the hospital may demand a penalty for clean claims that are not processed within 30 days.

Straight Per Diem Charges

Unlike straight charges, a negotiated per diem is a single charge for a day in the hospital regardless of any actual charges or costs incurred. In this very common type of arrangement, you negotiate a per diem rate with the hospital and pay that rate without adjustments. For example, your plan will pay $800 for each day regardless of the actual cost of the service.

Hospital administrators are sometimes reluctant to add days in the intensive care unit or obstetrics to the arrangement unless there is sufficient volume of regular medical-surgical cases to make the ultimate cost predictable. In a small plan, or in one that is not limiting the number of participating hospitals, the hospital administrator is concerned that the hospital will be used for expensive cases at a low per diem while competitors will be used for less costly cases. In such cases, you may choose to negotiate multiple sets of per diem charges based on service type (eg, medical-surgical, obstetrics, intensive care, neonatal intensive care, rehabilitation, and so forth) or a combination of per diem and flat case rate for obstetrics.

The key to making a negotiated per diem work is predictability. If you can accurately predict the number and mix of cases, you can accurately calculate a per diem. The per diem is simply an estimate of the charges (or costs) for an average day in that hospital minus the amount of discount you feel is appropriate.

A disadvantage of the per diem approach, however, is that the per diem must be paid even if the billed charges are less than the per diem rate. For example, if the plan has a per diem arrangement that pays $800 per day for medical admissions and the total allowable charges (billed charges less charges for noncovered items provided during the admission) for a 5-day admission are $3,300, the hospital is reimbursed $4,000 for the admission ($800 per day times 5 days). This is acceptable as long as the average per diem represents an acceptable discount.

A plan may also negotiate to reimburse the hospital for expensive surgical implants provided at the hospital's actual cost of the implant. Such reimbursement would be limited to a defined list of implants (eg, cochlear implants) where the cost to the hospital for the implant is far greater than is recoverable under the per diem or outpatient arrangement. Under this reimbursement methodology, the hospital is able to generate a reasonable profit on the facility and ancillary charges and to recover its cost of the implant.

Sliding Scale Per Diem

Like the sliding scale discount on charges discussed above, the sliding scale per diem is also based on total volume. In this case, you negotiate an interim per diem that you will agree to pay for each day in the hospital. Depending on the total number of bed days in the year, you will either pay a lump sum settlement at the end of the year or withhold an amount from your final payment for the year to adjust for an additional reduction in the per diem from an increase in total bed days.

You will probably want to make an arrangement whereby on a quarterly or semiannual basis you will adjust the interim per diem so as to reduce any disparities caused by unexpected changes in utilization patterns.

Differential by Day in Hospital

This simply refers to the fact that most hospitalizations are more expensive on the first day. For example, the first day for surgical cases includes operating suite costs, the operating surgical team costs (nurses and recovery), and so forth. This type of reimbursement method is generally combined with a per diem approach, but the first day is paid at a higher rate. For example, the first day may be $1,000 and each subsequent day is $600.

Diagnosis-Related Groups

As with Medicare, you can use diagnosis-related groups (DRGs) to pay for inpatient care. There are publications of DRG categories, criteria, outliers, and trim points (ie, the cost or length of stay that causes the DRG payment to be supplemented or supplanted by another payment mechanism) to enable you to negotiate a payment mechanism for DRGs based on Medicare rates or, in some cases, state regulated rates. First, though, you need to assess whether it will be to your benefit.

If it is your intention to reduce unnecessary utilization, there will not necessarily be concomitant savings if you use straight DRGs. If the payment is fixed on the basis of diagnosis, any reduction in days will go to the hospital and not to your plan. Furthermore, unless you are prepared to perform careful audits of the hospital's DRG coding, you may experience code creep. On the other hand, DRGs do serve to share risk with the hospital, thus making the hospital an active partner in controlling utilization and making plan expenses more manageable. DRGs are perhaps better suited to plans with loose controls than plans that tightly manage utilization.

Service-Related Case Rates

Like DRGs, service-related case rates are a cruder cut. In this reimbursement mechanism, various service types are defined (eg, medicine, surgery, intensive care, neonatal intensive care, psychiatry, obstetrics, and the like), and the hospital receives a flat per-admission reimbursement for whatever type of service the patient is admitted to (eg, all surgical admissions cost $6,100). If services are mixed, a prorated payment may be made (eg, 50% of surgical and 50% of intensive care).

Case Rates

Whatever mechanism you use for hospital reimbursement, you may still need to address certain categories of procedures and negotiate special rates. The most common of these is obstetrics. It is common to negotiate a flat rate for a normal vaginal delivery and a flat rate for a cesarean section or a blended rate for both. In the case of blended case rates, the expected reimbursement for each type of delivery is multiplied by the expected (or desired) percentage of utilization. For example, a case rate for vaginal delivery is $1,800, and for cesarean section it is $2,300. Utilization is expected to be 80% vaginal and 20% cesarean section, and therefore the case rate is $1,900 ($1,800 × 0.8 = $1,440; $2,300 × 0.2 = $460; $1,440 + $460 = $1,900).

Case rates are certainly not necessary if you can get them included into your negotiated per diem, but you will probably want to use them if you have negotiated a discount on charges. This is because the delivery suite or operating room is substantially more costly to operate than a regular hospital room. For example, you may negotiate a flat rate of $1,900 per delivery. The downside of this arrangement is that you achieve no added savings from decreased length of stay. The upside is that it makes the hospital a much more active partner in controlling utilization.

Another area for which you will want to negotiate flat rates is specialty procedures at tertiary hospitals, for example, coronary artery bypass surgery or heart transplants. These procedures, although relatively infrequent, are tremendously costly.

A broader variation is the bundled case rate. As discussed in Chapter 7, the bundled case rate refers to an all-inclusive rate paid for both insti-

tutional and professional services. The plan negotiates a flat rate for a procedure (eg, bypass surgery), and that rate is used to pay all parties who provide services connected with that procedure. Bundled case rates are not uncommon in teaching facilities where there is a faculty practice plan that works closely with the hospital.

Bed Leasing

A relatively uncommon reimbursement mechanism is bed leasing. This refers to a plan actually leasing beds from an institution, for example, paying the hospital $350 per bed for 10 beds regardless of whether those beds are used or not. This ensures revenue flow to the hospital, ensures access to beds (at least some beds) for the plan, and is budgetable. It is perhaps best used in those situations where a plan is assured of a steady number of bed days with little or no seasonality. The problem with bed leasing is that there is no real savings from reducing utilization unless contract terms allow the plan to lease back the beds to the hospital if they are not being used.

Capitation or Percentage of Revenue

Capitation refers to reimbursing the hospital on a per member per month (PMPM) basis to cover all institutional costs for a defined population of members. The payment may be varied by age and sex but does not fluctuate with premium revenue. *Percentage of revenue* refers to a fixed percentage of premium revenue (ie, a percentage of the collected premium rate) being paid to the hospital, again to cover all institutional services. The difference between percentage of revenue and capitation is that percentage of revenue may vary with the premium rate charged and the actual revenue yield. In both cases, the hospital stands the entire risk for institutional services for the defined membership base; if the hospital cannot provide the services itself, the cost for such care is deducted from the capitation payment.

For this type of arrangement to work, a hospital must know that it will serve a clearly defined segment of a plan's enrollment and that it can provide most of the necessary services to those members. In these cases, the primary care physician is clearly associated with just one hospital. Alternatively, if you are dealing with a multihospital chain with multiple facilities in your plan's service area, it may be reasonable to expect that the hospitals in the chain can care for the plan's members on an exclusive basis. Capitation may also be tied to the percentage of admissions to that hospital. For example, the capitation rate is $25 PMPM. The plan has 10,000 members, and 50% of admissions go to that hospital that month. The payment therefore is $25 × (10,000 × 0.5) = $125,000. This is quite uncommon, however.

The advantage of this type of payment mechanism is that it is not only budgetable but succeeds in laying off all or most of the risk for institutional expenses. The hospital becomes a full partner in controlling utilization, and you have less need to control. The problem is that you will see none of the savings for improved utilization control. Another problem can arise if the hospital refuses to share any of the savings (calculated as though there were a per diem or discounted charges model) with the physicians who are controlling the cases; if you pursue such an arrangement, you may want to include provisions for a bonus plan between the hospital and the physicians.

Point-of-service (POS) plans with an out-of-network benefit make capitation methods difficult to use. As discussed in Chapters 6 and 7, capitation in POS may mean having to pay twice for a service, once under capitation and again if the member seeks service outside the network. In areas where there are no real alternatives to a certain hospital (eg, a rural area or an area where a hospital enjoys a monopoly) this problem may not be material, but that is the exception. Capitation tied to the percentage of admissions to that hospital, as mentioned earlier in this chapter, may also attenuate this problem.

The other issue of which you need to be aware in this arrangement is that some state insurance departments may consider this degree of risk abatement too much. It may be reasoned that, if the health plan is not actually assuming the risk for services, then it is not really a health plan at all but only a marketing organization. In such a case, there may be a question as to who should really hold the certificate of authority or license to operate the health plan.

Periodic Interim Payments and Cash Advances

Periodic interim payments (PIPs) and cash advances are methods whereby the plan advances a hospital cash to cover expected claims. This cash advance is periodically replenished if it gets below a certain amount. Claims may be applied directly against the cash advance or may be paid outside it, in which case the cash advance serves as an advance deposit. The value of this to a hospital is obvious: positive cash flow. PIPs and cash advances are quite valuable to a hospital and will generate a discount in and of themselves.

Penalties and Withholds

As with physician services (see Chapters 6 and 7), occasionally penalties or withholds are used in hospital reimbursement methods. As an example, a plan may negotiate with a hospital to allow the hospital's own utilization management department to perform all the utilization management functions (see Chapter 10). As part of that negotiation, goals are set for average length of stay and average admission rate. Part of the payment to the hospital may be withheld, or conversely the plan may set aside a bonus pool. In any event, if the goals are met or exceeded, the hospital receives its withhold or bonus, and vice versa. One complication with this is the possibility that a hospital can make its statistics look good by simply sending patients to other hospitals; this is similar to problems encountered with physician capitation. If a service area is clearly defined, or if the hospital is capitated, then it may be easier to apply a risk or reward program.

OUTPATIENT PROCEDURES

As mentioned earlier, the shift from inpatient to outpatient care has not gone unnoticed by hospital administrators. As care has shifted, so have charges. It is not uncommon to see outpatient charges exceeding the cost of an inpatient day unless steps are taken to address that imbalance.

Discounts on Charges

Either straight discounts or sliding scale discounts may be applied to outpatient charges. Some hospitals argue that the cost to deliver highly technical outpatient procedures actually is greater than an average per diem, primarily because the per diem assumes more than a single day in the hospital, thereby spreading the costs over a greater number of reimbursable days. Some plans have responded by simply admitting patients for their outpatient surgery, paying the per diem, and sending the patient home. Many plans negotiate the cost of outpatient surgery to never exceed the cost of an inpatient day, whereas other plans concede the problem of frontloading surgical services and agree to cap outpatient charges at a fixed percentage of the per diem (eg, 125% of the average per diem).

Bundled Charges

Plans may negotiate bundled charges for outpatient procedures. In this method of reimbursement, all the various charges are bundled into one single charge, thereby reducing the problem of unbundling and exploding (ie, charging for multiple codes or brand-new codes where previously only one code was used). Plans may use their own data to develop the bundled charges, or they may use outside data (an excellent source is published by Milliman and Roberston,[2] a national actuarial firm). Bundled charges are generally tied to the principal procedure code used by the facility. Bundled charges may also be added together in the event that more than one procedure is performed, although the second procedure is discounted because the patient was already in the facility and using services.

Ambulatory Patient Groups

Ambulatory patient groups (APGs) were developed by 3M Health Systems under a contract with the Health Care Financing Administration, primarily for use with Medicare.[3] At the time this book is being written, APGs have not yet been put into use, but there is every indication that they will be.

APGs are to outpatient services what DRGs are to inpatient ones (although APGs are based on procedures rather than simply on diagnoses). As with bundled charges (discussed above), under APGs all the services associated with a given procedure or visit are bundled into the APG reimbursement. More than one APG may be billed if more than one procedure is performed, but there is significant discounting for additional APGs. Plans need to pay attention to this method of reimbursement because, like DRGs, APGs have the potential for driving cost shifting.

CONCLUSION

As with consultants, reimbursement mechanisms and contracts with hospitals are tools. The importance of these tools cannot be overestimated, and you must craft these tools with all the skills you have available. It is possible and desirable to develop win-win situations with hospitals, and that can be a pivotal issue in the ultimate success of your plan.

REFERENCES

1. American Hospital Association. *American Hospital Association Guide to the Health Care Field.* Chicago: American Hospital Association; 1992.

2. Doyle RL, Feren AP. *Healthcare Management Guidelines, Vol. 3: Ambulatory Care Guidelines.* Milliman & Robertson; 1991.

3. Averill RF, Goldfield NI, McGuire TE, et al. *Design and Evaluation of a Prospective Payment System for Ambulatory Care, Final Report.* Health Care Financing Administration Cooperative Agreement no 17-C-99369/1-02.

SUGGESTED READING

Feldman R, Kralewski J, Shapiro J, Chan HC. Contracts between hospitals and health maintenance organizations. *Health Care Manage Rev.* 1990;15:47–60.

Lewis JB. How to evaluate managed care contracts. *Healthcare Financ Manage.* 1990;44:32–42.

Melnick GA, Zwanziger J, Verity-Guerra A. The growth and effects of hospital selective contracting. *Health Care Manage Rev.* 1989;14: 57–64.

Shelton N. Competitive contingencies in selective contracting for hospital services. *Med Care Rev.* 1989;46:271–293.

Part III

Medical Management

You can't always get what you want.
But if you try sometimes
You just might find
You get what you need.

Mick Jagger (1969)

Chapter 9

Changing Provider Behavior in Managed Care Plans

Peter R. Kongstvedt

The practice behavior of physicians* in a managed health care plan is the most important element in controlling cost and quality. As has been mentioned in Chapters 4 and 5, this process begins at the front door. Selecting physicians who already practice high-quality, cost-effective medicine is the best way to achieve success, although profiling physicians, as discussed in Chapter 16, is no easy task. Even in the best of worlds, however, one cannot be assured that every physician participating in the plan will be solid gold, and realities of marketing and delivery system needs dictate that adequate geographic coverage be present, even when that means accepting some B players rather than all A players.

The best contractual arrangements in the world will be of little value if there are poor utilization patterns or a lack of cooperation with plan policies and procedures. There will be some physicians in the medical community who will not modify their practice behavior. There will also be some physicians who are frankly hostile and some who, for various reasons, you will not want participating in your plan regardless of

how friendly or cooperative they are. The majority of physicians, however, will cooperate and be valued participants.

Given these realities, the purpose of this chapter is to present some of the issues involved in modifying the practice behavior of those participating physicians who can and will work with the plan. Financial incentives are clearly a useful method of influencing behavior[1,2] and are discussed separately in Chapters 4, 6, and 7; nonfinancial approaches are the topic of this chapter. A word of caution: One cannot overtly manipulate physicians, at least not successfully for long, so a more reasoned approach is warranted.

GENERAL APPROACHES

Before looking at specific issues in changing practice behavior in physicians, a few general approaches should be kept in mind.

Role of Data

As has been mentioned in other chapters, particularly Chapter 16, data regarding utilization and cost are an integral part of a managed care plan. The value of data is not restricted to plan managers; data are equally important to indi-

---

* For convenience, the terms *physician* and *provider* are used interchangeably, in recognition of the fact that there are nonphysician providers as well.

vidual physicians. If the only data physicians get are letters at the end of the year informing them that all their withhold is used up, they can credibly argue that they have been blindsided.

Providing regular and accurate data about an individual physician's performance, from both a utilization and (for risk/bonus models) an economic standpoint, is vital to changing behavior. Most physicians will want to perform well, but they can only do so when they can judge their own performance against that of their peers or against plan norms, and feedback must be regular to sustain the changed behavior.[3–10]

Practice Guidelines

Practice guidelines refer to codified approaches to medical care. Guidelines may be for both diagnostic and therapeutic modalities, and they may be used to guide physicians in the care of patients with defined diseases or symptoms or as surveillance tools to monitor practice on a retrospective basis.

Many physicians have an initial negative reaction to practice guidelines. They feel that guidelines make for cookbook medicine and do not allow for judgment or that guidelines represent a high risk in the case of a malpractice suit (because guidelines provide a template against which all actions will be judged). Nevertheless, practice guidelines have been gaining in popularity, at least among medical managers.

Implementing practice guidelines is not always easy, particularly in an open panel setting. There is frequent lack of enthusiasm on the part of the physicians, and the plan's ability actually to monitor the guidelines is limited. Generally, the plan's quality management (QM) process is best able to monitor the use of guidelines (see Chapter 15), although there may be some ability to use the claims system to do so as well.

Attempting to put comprehensive practice guidelines into place in a managed care plan is a daunting task. In an open panel, it will be exponentially more difficult. There is some evidence that simple publication of practice guidelines alone may predispose physicians to consider changing their behavior but that such guidelines by themselves are unlikely to effect rapid change.[11] The reader is urged to explore the topic of practice guidelines in greater detail.[*]

Translating Goals and Objectives

A useful way of looking at communications between plan management and physicians is to consider the concept of translation. It is easy to overlook the fact that managers and physicians may have radically different ways of viewing matters relating to the delivery of health care services to plan members.

For example, the area of cost containment is rife with possibilities for opposing views. Physicians frequently look upon cost containment measures as unnecessary intrusions into their domain, whereas nonphysician managers view the same measures as the only way to control headstrong physicians. Translating the goal of cost containment into terms that are both understandable and acceptable to both parties will take you far toward obtaining cooperation and acceptance. To ensure that the economic resources will be available to compensate providers and to make services available at all to patients, cost containment must take place.

Rewards Are More Effective Than Sanctions

A tenet of behavior modification theory is that positive interactions or rewards are more effective at achieving long-term changes in behavior than negative interactions or sanctions. Furthermore, it is rarely good policy for managers to impose their will on others in an arbitrary manner. In some cases it is necessary, but if it is done as a matter of course cooperation will not be enthusiastic. In the worst case, it can lead to widespread dissatisfaction and defection from the plan. Even without such attrition, overt cooperation can occur, but covert sabotage undoes any progress made. This can be especially true with physicians. Unlike regular employees, physicians (even in closed panel operations) behave with a great deal of autonomy and power.

---

[*] For a reasonably concise introductory discussion of practice guidelines as they relate to health plans, see *Quality Review Bulletin, Journal of Quality Assurance,* Vol 16, Number 2, February 1990.

In the context of this discussion, rewards refer primarily to forms of positive feedback and communication about good performance. Clearly, good case management should yield economic rewards as well, but positive feedback from plan management will be a reward system all its own. Other rewards could include continuing education seminars about managed care, small gifts or acknowledgments for good work, and so forth.

Although it is unrealistic to expect that every physician will embrace every policy and procedure the plan has, the odds of cooperation will increase when the interactions between the physician and the plan are more positive than negative. This is not to be confused with capitulation on necessary policies and procedures: There were once plenty of physician-friendly health plans that are now little more than smoking rubble. Rather, this is to emphasize that too heavy a hand will eventually cause problems.

Be Involved

It is shocking how often managers of health plans fail to maintain an active involvement with the participating physicians. Frequently the only communications with the physicians are occasional newsletters or memos, claims denials, and calls from the utilization management department harassing the physicians about hospital cases. Those types of interactions will not add to the luster of plan management in the physicians' eyes.

Frequent and regular contact, either through scheduled meetings, personal visits, or telephone calls, will help create an environment for positive change. If the only time physicians hear from the plan is when there is a problem, they will try to avoid contact in the future and will tend to have decreased responsiveness to the plan's needs.

Offer advice, suggestions, and alternatives, not just demands to change something. Ask intelligent questions about the clinical issues at hand, and solicit advice about alternative ways to provide the care. Work to get to the point where physicians will be asking themselves the same questions you would ask without your having to ask them.

Involvement is a two-way proposition. It is fair and reasonable to expect the practicing physicians to participate in plan committees to help set medical policy, monitor quality, and so forth. Soliciting active participation in such functions helps promote a sense of ownership on the part of the involved physicians and will clearly give the plan some valuable input. Whether the plan compensates the physicians for the time spent on such activities is a local decision, but an honorarium is common.

Stepwise Approach to Changing Behavior Patterns

Changing provider behavior involves a stepwise approach. The first and most common step is collegial discussion. Discussing cases and utilization patterns in a nonthreatening way, colleague to colleague, is generally an effective method of bringing about change.

Far less common is positive feedback. This is an even more effective tool for change but one that most managers fail to use to any great degree. Positive feedback does not refer to mindless or misleading praise but to letting a physician know when things are done well. Most managers get so involved in firefighting that they tend to neglect sending positive messages to those providers who are managing well. In the absence of such messages, providers have to figure out for themselves what they are doing right (the plan will usually tell them what they are doing wrong), and that may not be optimal.

Persuasion is also commonly used. Somewhat stronger than collegial discussion, persuasion refers to plan managers persuading providers to act in ways that the providers may not initially choose themselves. For example, if a patient requires intravenous antibiotics for osteomyelitis but is otherwise doing well, that patient is a candidate for home intravenous therapy. Some physicians will resist discharging the patient to home therapy because it is inconvenient to follow the case; keeping the patient in the hospital is a lot easier in terms of rounding. The physician must then be persuaded to discharge the patient because of the cost effectiveness of home therapy.

Firm direction of plan policies, procedures, and requirements is the next step after persuasion. If a physician refuses to cooperate with the plan to deliver care cost effectively and discussions and persuasion have failed, a medical director may be required to give a physician firm direction, reminding him or her of the contractual agreement to cooperate with plan policies and procedures. Behind firm direction is the implied threat of refusal to pay for services or even more severe sanctions. It is clearly a display of power and should not be done with a heavy hand. When giving firm direction, it is best to not allow oneself to be drawn into long and unresolvable arguments. Presumably the discussions and even the arguments have already occurred, so it is pointless to keep rehashing them. This is sometimes called a broken record type of response because, rather than respond to old arguments, the medical director always gives the same response: firm direction.

The last steps are sanctions and termination. Sanctioning should rarely be required, and termination is so serious that these topics are discussed separately at the end of this chapter.

One last thought in this section: Avoid global responses to individual problems. When managers are uncomfortable confronting individual physicians about problems in behavior, a dysfunctional response is to make a global change in policy or procedure because of the actions of one or two physicians. That type of response frequently has the effect of alienating all the other physicians who have been cooperating while failing to change the behavior of the problem providers. If a policy change is required, make it. If the problem is really just with a few individuals, however, deal with them and do not harass the rest of the panel.

INHERENT DIFFICULTIES IN MODIFYING PHYSICIAN BEHAVIOR

Physicians are professionals with an inordinately large set of built-in biases. This is due to their training, the current environment of medical practice today, and the types of pressures now being brought to bear upon them. There is also great heterogeneity in attitudes and prior training in cost containment.[12] None of these is-

sues is unique to the medical profession, but their combination and depth make for a number of inherent difficulties in changing behavior.

What follows is a brief discussion of some of the more important issues. It is wise for managers to be sensitive to these issues, although that does not mean that they should fail to apply proper management and control techniques.

Strong Autonomy and Control Needs

There is perhaps no more emotionally charged issue than autonomy and control. Physicians are trained to function in an autonomous way, to stand up for themselves, and to be the authority. It is difficult for them to accept a role in which another entity has control over their professional activities. Physicians participating in managed care plans often feel antagonistic when they perceive that their control has been lost or lessened. By definition, managed care introduces elements of management control into the arena of health care delivery, management that clearly reduces the physician's autonomy. In one large study, physicians who entered into contracts with health maintenance organizations (HMOs) expected lower earnings, lower quality of care, and lessened autonomy; neither earnings nor quality declined, but there remained a general perception that physician autonomy did decline.[13]

There has been an increase in the amount of external control over the years. HMOs, preferred provider organizations (PPOs), indemnity plans with managed care elements (eg, preadmission authorization requirements), Medicare, and Medicaid are all programs that have been increasing their control over medical practice as health care costs have risen. The degree of control will vary considerably depending on the type of program involved, but managed health care, particularly tightly managed HMOs, currently exerts the greatest degree of external control outside medical residency training. The greater the degree of external control, the greater the danger of overt or covert resistance to achieving the goals of the plan.

All the issues discussed at the beginning of this chapter are pertinent to ameliorating some of the anxieties that arise in dealing with control issues. It is also helpful to reinforce the plan's commitment to supporting and strengthening the role of primary care. It is probably not unreasonable to point out that failure of the private sector and the physician community to control medical costs in the nation will lead to even greater interventions by nonphysicians charged with bringing medical costs under control.

Enlisting the physician's help in achieving the plan's goals is possible by empowering the physicians within the system. Suggestions for some specific approaches to the issues of control needs follow.

Control of Where Care Is Received

Virtually all managed care plans will have some controls over where members receive their care. In a simple PPO, that control will be confined to a differential in benefits that is based on whether a member uses participating hospitals and physicians. In a tightly managed HMO, the plan will allow only the use of participating providers, and even then only for certain services. For example, the HMO may have an exclusive contract for mammography; even though all the participating hospitals have the ability to perform mammography, only one provider will be allowed to do it and get paid.

If a plan intends to have a highly restricted panel of participating providers, it is sometimes helpful to elicit the opinions of those physicians already in the panel, even though the final decision will still rest with the plan. For example, if the decision has been made to use only two or three orthopedic groups to provide services, the primary care physicians could be canvassed for nominations of groups to approach. The plan should clearly state that it is not having a majority rule vote but is looking for people to approach; the final selection will be based on a combination of the plan's regular credentialing process, the group's willingness to cooperate with plan policies and procedures, and cost.

Control of Patient Care

Much more volatile than the above, control of patient care is a real hot button with most physicians. This control can range from the retrospective review of claims that is found in most plans to the mandatory preauthorization of all non-

primary care services that is found in tightly managed HMOs. The greater the degree of plan involvement in clinical decision making, the greater the chances of antagonism between physicians and plan managers, but also the greater the degree of medical cost control.

Because this management of medical services is the hallmark of managed care, it is neither possible nor desirable to eliminate it. How that control is exercised will have a great effect on its acceptance and success, however. If the plan intervenes in an arbitrary and heavy-handed manner, there will be problems. If interventions are done with some element of understanding and respect, there should be greater cooperation.

The techniques described earlier are particularly important here. Frequent and regular contact, both positive and negative, will help a great deal. Discussing cases and suggesting and soliciting alternatives for case management will yield better results than arbitrary demands for improvement.

Control of Quality

The most common objection that physicians will actually voice about managed care is that it reduces the quality of care. Regardless of whether that argument is often a smoke screen for purely economic concerns, the issue is still a valid one. Any system that requires the use of a restricted network of providers and has an authorization system has the potential of reducing the quality of care delivered. A more detailed discussion of QM programs is found in Chapter 15.

The best approach here is to place responsibility for participating with the plan's QM program squarely with the physicians themselves. It is vital to have a properly constructed QM program so that participation is meaningful. A solid QM program will allow the physicians to feel that the plan genuinely does have an interest in quality and should allow for some pride in participation.

Role Conflict

It is often stated that physicians are trained to be the patient's advocate. This is partially true, but that notion presupposes a system whereby a patient, like a plaintiff or defendant in a lawsuit, needs an advocate. In fact, physicians are trained to be the patient's caregiver, that is, the coordinator and deliverer of medical care.

The issue of advocacy arises when a physician feels that the needs of the plan and the needs of the patient are in conflict. When that happens, the physician feels genuinely torn between being the patient's advocate and the plan's advocate. This most frequently comes up when patients request or demand a service that is not really necessary or is medically marginal. Physicians feel on the spot if they must deny the service, putting themselves in a role conflict with their patients: "Just whose side are you on, anyway?" This is a difficult situation that is handled better by some physicians than others.[14]

Plan managers need to acknowledge this conflict, even though there may be less conflict in reality than in perception. Because of poor provider understanding of the insurance function (discussed below), the conflict may come up when the physician feels a service is medically necessary that in fact is not a covered benefit. In some cases, there is poor understanding of the difference between what is actually medically necessary and what is essentially a convenience. The health plan is not in the business of denying truly needed services, assuming that they are covered under the schedule of benefits; denial of such services would be ethically and financially foolish.

What the health plan is in the business of doing is cutting the fat out of the system. The physician is charged with conserving the resources, primarily economic, of the plan to ensure availability of those resources to those who truly need them. It is the physician who will best be able to determine what is really needed and what is really not, and that will help provide more appropriate allocation of those resources. The plan's utilization management efforts are (or should be) aimed at aiding the physician in carrying out that function.

Poor Understanding of the Insurance Function of the Plan

As mentioned above, some of the problems of role conflict stem from a poor understanding of the insurance aspect of the plan. HMOs in particular are marketed as offering comprehensive benefits, even though there are clearly certain exclusions and limitations, just as there are for any form of health care coverage. Physicians often do not differentiate between what is medically necessary and what is a covered benefit.

Every plan has certain exclusions and limitations of coverage. For example, a member may require 3 months of inpatient psychiatric care, but the plan only covers 30 days. Another example is an experimental transplant procedure. In each case an argument can be made that the treatment is necessary, but it is not a covered benefit under the plan's schedule of benefits.

Plan management may make exceptions to the exclusions and limitations policy, but that should only be done rarely and after much thought. In some cases it will be clearly cost effective to do so (eg, providing 30 days of home durable medical equipment to avoid a hospitalization). In other cases it will not be. If frequent exceptions are made, it can lead to an open-ended commitment to provide lifetime services, a commitment that the plan cannot afford if it is to remain in business.

Helping a physician understand the insurance nature of the plan and that there are limitations to coverage will be a wise investment on the part of the plan managers. It is often of great help for the plan to play the role of the black hat here; in other words, plan management contacts the member in such cases to reinforce that it is a contract (ie, schedule of benefits) issue and not a matter of the physician being callous and hard hearted.

Bad Habits

All of us have habits and patterns in our lives. Most physicians have habits and patterns in their practices that are not cost effective but are difficult to change. One example is the practice of not seeing patients or making rounds on Wednesdays; the physician's partner may not feel comfortable discharging a partner's patient, so the stay is lengthened by an extra day. Another example is a physician who keeps a routine, uncomplicated cholecystectomy in for 5 days, stating "That's the way I've always done it and it's worked just fine for me!"

This problem is a touchy one. It is usually poor form bluntly to accuse a physician of bad practice habits. The frontal assault is generally met with the indignant question, "Are you questioning my judgment?" You are not, of course; you are questioning a bad habit.

It is preferable to lead physicians to the appropriate conclusion themselves. If you discuss the issue objectively, present supporting information, and ask physicians to examine critically the difference in practice behavior, a number of physicians will arrive at the conclusion that their old habits must change. By allowing physicians gracefully and quietly to make the change, you run less risk of creating the need for a rigid defensive posture on their part.

In some cases, that will not work. If calm and rational discussions fail to effect a change, firmer action is needed; physicians may cooperate but may tell the patient that the health plan is making them do it. In most cases, that type of grumbling will go away after a short while. If it does not, the medical director must counsel these physicians about appropriate behavior, especially in this litigious era. If there is an adverse outcome, even though it had nothing to do with the changed practice pattern, the chances of a lawsuit are probably heightened if those types of comments have been made.

Poor Understanding of Economics

Even though physicians and their business managers are becoming more sophisticated about managed care, there is still a surprising lack of understanding of the economics, especially in capitated or other performance-based reimbursement systems. There may be little understanding of the withholds and incentive pools, or physicians may feel so distant from those pools that there is little or no effect on behavior.

It is worthwhile to have continual re-education about the economics of the plan as it relates to the physician's income. Related to this is the need for accurate and timely feedback to the physicians about their economic status on the basis of payments and utilization. Inaccurate feedback is far worse than no feedback at all.

The hoary old cliche that money talks is absolutely true. Because of that, plan management should always be aware of the whole dollars involved in compensating physicians. A small number, such as an $11.25 per member per month capitation payment, may seem like funny money to a physician, but if that $11.25 per member per month really means $40,000 per year, that has a considerable impact on the financial health of a practice. Helping physicians realize the contribution that the plan is making to their bottom line can be eye opening.

Poor Differentiation among Competing Plans

Considerable difficulty arises when there is little or no differentiation among competing plans; this is essentially a problem in open panels. In federally qualified HMOs, the benefits may be the same and the provider network may be similar or the same; the only difference is the rates (in other words, any flavor as long as it's vanilla).

This becomes a problem when each plan has different internal policies and procedures with which the physicians and their office staff must comply. If a physician is contracting with three or more plans, the frustration involved with trying to remember which one wants what can be quite high. This problem is exacerbated when the same patient changes to a different managed care plan. For example, on Friday Mr. Jones was with the ABC Health Plan, but when he came in for his return appointment on Monday he had switched to the XYZ Health Plan; the office staff did not take notice, which resulted in claims or authorization denials. This can be a real morale problem with the physician's office staff. When frustration rises, compliance falls.

This is best addressed by increased attention and service to the physicians and their office staff. Frequent and timely communications will help, and the more that is done in person the better because newsletters have a way of getting to the bottom of the parakeet cage without getting read.

In this area, nonmonetary issues can have as much impact as monetary ones. Examples include difficult-to-use forms that require a lot of unnecessary writing, frequent busy signals on service lines, and inconsistencies in responses to questions. It cannot be overstressed that prompt and courteous responsiveness to questions and concerns is required. You do not have to give the answer that you think physicians will want to hear; you do have to give an answer or response that is consistent, clear, and reasonably fair.

DISCIPLINE AND SANCTIONS

This section discusses the most serious form of behavior modification. Sanctions or threats of sanctions are only applied when the problem is so serious that action must be taken and when the provider fails to cooperate. In some cases the provider may be willing to cooperate, but the offense is so serious that sanctions must be taken anyway. An example of this is a serious problem in quality of care, such as malpractice resulting in death or serious morbidity. In any event, the sanctioning process has legal overtones that must be kept in mind. The reader is referred to Chapters 37 and 38 for additional discussion.

Plan management may initiate disciplinary actions short of a formal sanctioning process. In most cases, such discipline is helpful in creating documentation of chronic problems or failure to cooperate. Discipline may involve verbal warnings or letters; in either case, the thrust of the action is to document the offensive behavior and to describe the consequences of failure to cooperate.

One example of discipline is sometimes called ticketing. It is called that because it is similar to getting a ticket from a traffic cop. This is a verbal reprimand about a specific behavior; the behavior and corrective action are described, as are the consequences of failure to carry out the corrective action. The manager refuses to get into an argument at that time and requires the offending provider to make an appointment at a future date to discuss the issue (similar to a court date). This allows tempers to cool off a bit and ensures that the disciplinary message does not get muddied up with other issues. When a manager issues a ticket, there should be a document to file that describes what transpired.

A more formal approach is an actual disciplinary letter. Like a ticket, the letter describes the offending behavior and the required corrective action and invites the provider to make an appointment to discuss the issue. In the case of a verbal ticket or a disciplinary letter, the consequence of failure to change errant ways is initiation of the formal sanctioning process.

Formal sanctioning has potentially serious legal overtones. Due process, or a policy regarding rights and responsibilities of both parties, is a requirement for an effective sanctioning procedure, at least when one is sanctioning for reasons of quality. The Health Care Quality Improvement Act of 1986 has formalized due process in the sanctioning procedure as it relates to quality and must be adhered to in order to maintain protection from antitrust action. Although this Act was primarily aimed at hospital peer review activities, HMOs are specifically mentioned, and other forms of managed care may be implied in the future.

The Health Care Quality Improvement Act of 1986 describes the requirements of due process as follows:[15]

> (a)...a professional review action must be taken
>
> (1) in the reasonable belief that the action was in the furtherance of quality health care,
>
> (2) after a reasonable effort to obtain the facts of the matter,
>
> (3) after adequate notice and hearing procedures are afforded to the physician involved and after such other procedures as are fair to the physician under the circumstances, and
>
> (4) in the reasonable belief that the action was warranted by the facts known after such reasonable effort to obtain facts and after meeting the requirements of paragraph (3)....
>
> (b)...A health care entity is deemed to have met the adequate notice and hearing requirement of subsection (a)(3) with respect to a physician if the following conditions are met (or

are waived voluntarily by the physician):

(1) Notice of Proposed Action—The physician has been given notice stating—

(A)(i) that a professional review action has been proposed to be taken against the physician,

(ii) reasons for the proposed action,

(B)(i) that the physician has the right to request a hearing on the proposed action,

(ii) any time limit (of not less than 30 days) within which to request such a hearing, and

(C) a summary of the rights in the hearing under paragraph (3).

(2) Notice of Hearing—If a hearing is requested on a timely basis under paragraph (1)(B), the physician involved must be given notice stating—

(A) the place, time, and date of the hearing, which date shall not be less than 30 days after the date of the notice, and

(B) a list of the witnesses (if any) expected to testify at the hearing on behalf of the profession review body.

(3) Conduct of Hearing and Notice—...

(A)...the hearing shall be held (as determined by the health care entity)—

(i) before an arbitrator mutually acceptable to the physician and the health care entity,

(ii) before a hearing officer who is appointed by the entity and who is not in direct economic competition with the physician involved, or

(iii) before a panel of individuals who are appointed by the entity and are not in direct economic competition with the physician involved;

(B) the right to the hearing may be forfeited if the physician fails, without good cause, to appear;

(C) in the hearing the physician involved has the right—

(i) to representation by an attorney or other person of the physician's choice,

(ii) to have a record made of the proceedings, copies of which may be obtained by the physician upon payment of any reasonable charges associated with the preparation thereof,

(iii) to call, examine, and cross-examine witnesses,

(iv) to present evidence determined to be relevant by the hearing officer, regardless of its admissibility in a court of law, and

(v) to submit a written statement at the close of the hearing; and

(D) upon completion of the hearing, the physician has the right—

(i) to receive the written recommendation of the arbitrator, officer, or panel, including a statement of the basis for the recommendations, and

(ii) to receive a written decision of the health care entity, including a statement of the basis for the decision.

Following the requirements of the Act regarding due process is cumbersome and is obviously the final step before removing a physician from the panel for reasons of poor quality care. Because it is such a drastic step, compliance with the Act, including the reporting requirements (see Chapter 37), is the best protection the plan has against a legal action.

It should be emphasized that the Act is in regard to peer review activities resulting in actions against physicians for quality problems. If a physician fails to cooperate with contractually agreed-to plan policies and procedures, the plan may have reason to terminate the contract with the physician for cause. Even in that case, it may be wise to have a due process policy that allows for formal steps to be taken in the event that the plan contemplates termination. Presentation of facts to a medical advisory committee made up of physicians who are not in direct economic competition with the involved physician provides a back-up to plan management. Such a committee may be able to effect changes by the physician where the medical director may not. Finally, the backing of a committee underscores that severe sanctions are not arbitrary but the result of failure on the part of the physician, not plan management.

There may arise situations where a physician's utilization performance is such that there is a clear mismatch with managed care practice philosophy; in other words, the plan simply cannot afford to keep the physician in the panel. The quality of the physician's medical care may be adequate, and there may have been no gross lack of cooperation with plan policies and procedures, but the physician simply practices medicine in such a style that medical resources are heavily and inappropriately overutilized. In such cases, the medical director must assess whether the physician can change his or her behavior. Assuming that the medical director concludes that the provider in question cannot change (or change sufficiently) or has failed to change despite warnings and feedback, the plan may choose to terminate the relationship solely on the basis of contractual terms that allow either party to terminate without cause when adequate notice is given (see Chapter 36).

When the plan departicipates a physician in this way, it is often not subject to a due process type of review. The reason is that the separation is based on practice style and fit, not accusations of rule breaking or poor quality. Although this may not seem fair at first blush, in point of fact most contracts certainly allow physicians to terminate if they feel the fit is poor; plans have the same right, even if they do not exercise it frequently. Terminating physicians in this manner has the potential for creating adverse relations in the network if there is the perception that the plan is acting arbitrarily and without reason. On the other hand, assuming that the terminated physician does indeed practice profligately, the other physicians in the network are probably aware of it, so that there may not be as much shock and surprise as one might think. Even so, such steps are drastic and should not be done frequently or lightly.

CONCLUSION

Changing physician behavior is crucial to the success of any managed care plan. Physicians are unique with their strong need for autonomy and control, potential for role conflicts, uneven understanding of the economics or insurance functions of managed care, and ingrained practice habits. Plan managers can exacerbate the difficulties in changing physician behavior by failing to be responsive and consistent, failing to differentiate their plan from other plans, failing to provide positive feedback, failing to address specific problems with providers early, and failing to take a stepwise approach to managing change.

When reasonable efforts to get a physician to change are unsuccessful and the problems are serious, discipline and sanctions must be applied. Due process must be followed before termination for poor quality, and it may be useful in other settings as well. In the final analysis, it is the plan's responsibility to effect changes in provider behavior that will benefit all the parties concerned and to take action when necessary.

REFERENCES

1. Hillman AL, Pauly MV, Kerman K, Martinek CR. HMO managers' views on financial incentives and quality. *Health Affairs.* Winter 1991:207–219.

2. Hillman AL, Pauly MV, Kersten JJ. How do financial

incentives affect physicians' clinical decisions and the financial performance of health maintenance organizations? *N Engl J Med.* 1989;321:86–92.

3. Dyck FJ, Murphy FA, Murphy JK, et al. Effect of sur-

veillance on the number of hysterectomies in the province of Saskatchewan. *N Engl J Med.* 1977;296:1326–1328.

4. Myers SA, Gleicher N. A successful program to lower cesarean section rates. *N Engl J Med.* 1989;319:1511–1516.

5. Wennberg JE, Blowers L, Parker R, Gittelsohn AM. Changes in tonsillectomy rates associated with feedback and review. *Pediatrics.* 1977;59:821–826.

6. Frazier LM, Brown JT, Divine GW, et al. Academia and clinic: can physician education lower the cost of prescription drugs? A prospective, controlled trial. *Ann Intern Med.* 1991;15:116–121.

7. Soumerai SB, McLaughlin TJ, Avorn J. Improving drug prescribing in primary care: a critical analysis of the experimental literature. *Milbank Q.* 1989;67:268–317.

8 Marton KI, Tul V, Sox HC. Modifying test-ordering behavior in the outpatient medical clinic. *Arch Intern Med.* 1985;145:816–821.

9. Berwick DM, Coltin KL. Feedback reduces test use in a health maintenance organization. *JAMA.* 1986; 255: 1450–1454.

10. Martin AR, Wolf MA, Thibodeau LA, et al. A trial of two strategies to modify the test-ordering behavior of medical residents. *N Engl J Med.* 1980;303:1330–1336.

11. Lomas J, Anderson GM, Domnik-Pierre K, et al. Do practice guidelines guide practice? The effect of a consensus statement on the practice of physicians. *N Engl J Med.* 1989;321:1306–1311.

12. Greene HL, Goldberg RJ, Beattie H, et al. Physician attitudes toward cost containment: the missing piece of the puzzle. *Arch Intern Med.* 1989;149:1966–1968.

13. Schulz R, Scheckler WE, Girard C, Barker K. Physician adaptation to health maintenance organizations and implications for management. *Health Serv Res.* 1990; 25:43–64.

14. Anderson RO. How do you manage the demanding (difficult) patient? *HMO Pract.* 4:15–16.

15. *Healthcare Quality Improvement Act of 1986.* 45 US Code §11101–11152. Sec 412, Standards for Professional Review Actions.

SUGGESTED READING

Curry W, ed. *The Physician Executive.* Tampa, FL: American College of Physician Executives; 1988.

Eisenberg JM. *Doctors' Decisions and the Cost of Medical Care.* Ann Arbor, MI: Health Administration Press; 1986.

Chapter 10

Controlling Hospital Utilization

Peter R. Kongstvedt

Utilization of hospital (or more accurately institutional) services usually accounts for up to 40% or more of the total expenses in a managed health care plan. That amount can be even greater when utilization is excessive. Control of these expenses is therefore prominent among most managers' priorities.

The expense of any medical service is a product of the price of that service times the volume of services delivered. Pricing for institutional services is discussed in Chapter 8; this chapter focuses on managing the volume of institutional services. Simple reduction of bed days may be of value but can lull the inexperienced manager into a sense of complacency. Control of institutional utilization is therefore to be understood in context with control of other areas of utilization as well. This chapter will concentrate on medical/surgical care; mental health and substance abuse services are unique and are discussed separately in Chapter 13.

MEASUREMENTS

Definition of the Numbers

First you must choose exactly what you will measure and how you will define that measurement. It is common for most plans to measure

bed days per 1,000 plan members per year (a formula to calculate this is given below). Deciding what to count as a bed day is not always straightforward, however.

In some plans, outpatient surgery will be counted as a single day in the hospital. This is done on the assumption that an outpatient procedure will cost the plan nearly the same as or sometimes more than a single inpatient day. Some plans count skilled nursing home days in the total, and some add commercial, Medicare, Medicaid, and fee-for-service into the total calculation. In some plans the day of discharge is counted; in most it is not (unless it is charged for by the hospital). Whether to count nursery days in the total when the mother is still in the hospital or only if the newborn is boarding over or in intensive care also needs to be decided.

As a general rule of thumb, most plans count commercial days separately from any other days, especially Medicare days. If you have a significant Medicaid population, you may wish to track it both separately and together with commercial. Most plans do not count outpatient surgery as an inpatient day but report out that number separately; likewise, most plans report skilled nursing days separately.

How to count nursery days is a difficult decision. If you use the assumption that skilled nursing days are not counted as hospital days because the cost is so much less, the same assumption may be made for nursery days while the mother is in the hospital. In most hospitals, the nursery charges for a normal newborn are relatively low. If the newborn requires a stay beyond the mother's discharge, the charges usually are higher. If the neonate is in the intensive care unit, charges will obviously be quite high. If you have negotiated an all-inclusive per diem rate or a case rate that takes normal nursery days into account while the mother is in the hospital, you may have no need to count them separately. If you must pay a high rate for nursery, you will probably want them counted in the total.

Further discussion about utilization reports may be found in Chapter 16.

Formulas To Calculate Institutional Utilization

The standard formula to calculate bed days per 1,000 members per year is relatively straightforward. You may use it to calculate the annualized bed days per 1,000 members for any time period you choose (eg, for the day, the month to date, the year to date, and so forth).

When calculating bed days per 1,000, use the assumption of a 365-day year as opposed to a 12-month year to prevent variations that are due solely to the length of the month. The formula is as follows:

$$[A \div (B \div 365)] \div (C \div 1,000)$$

where A is gross bed days per time unit, B is days per time unit, and C is plan membership.

This may be broken into steps. Exhibit 10-1 illustrates the calculation for bed days per 1,000 on a single day; Exhibit 10-2 illustrates the calculation for bed days per 1,000 for the month to date.

Expected Variations

There are two common reasons for variations in hospital utilization rates across the country. One reason is easily understood; the other is not. Easily understood is the relationship between how tight the utilization management (UM) pro-

gram you have is and its results. The tighter you make the program, and the more actual medical management is going on, the lower your utilization numbers will be. Conversely, if you choose for various reasons not to enforce a UM program stringently (eg, you may not be marketing a tight system), you will have proportionate increases in the hospitalization rate.

Less easily understood are the profound geographic variations in inpatient utilization. Rates of utilization on the East Coast are consistently and significantly higher than those on the West Coast.[1] In fact, there are geographic variations in utilization in cities of similar size that are not ter-

Exhibit 10-1 Example of Bed Days for a Single Day

Assume: Current hospital census = 10
Plan membership = 12,000

Step 1: Gross days = $10 \div (1 \div 365)$
= $10 \div 0.00274$
= 3,649.635

Step 2: Days per 1,000 = $3,649.635 \div (12,000 \div 1,000)$
= $3,649.635 \div 12$
= 304 (rounded)

Therefore, the days per 1,000 for that single day equal 304

Exhibit 10-2 Example of Bed Days for the Month to Date (MTD)

Assume: Total gross hospital bed days in MTD = 300
Plan membership = 12,000
Days in MTD = 21

Step 1: Gross days MTD = $300 \div (21 \div 365)$
= $300 \div 0.0575$
= 5,217.4

Step 2: Days per 1,000 in MTD = $5,217.4 \div (12,000 \div 1,000)$
= $5,217.4 \div 12$
= 435

Therefore, the days per 1,000 for the MTD equal 435

ribly far apart[2-6] and even significant geographic variations in a single metropolitan service area (Blue Cross and Blue Shield of National Capital Area, unpublished data). There is no rational explanation for this from the standpoint of the patients. The answer must lie with the practice habits of physicians in different areas. At the very least, this perplexing disparity based on geography points out that significant improvement in utilization may be achieved, especially in the eastern U.S.

FINANCIAL INCENTIVES

Financial incentives are important tools for helping manage hospital utilization. This topic is addressed in Chapters 4, 6, and 8, and the reader is referred to those chapters.

COMMON METHODS FOR DECREASING UTILIZATION

Control of institutional utilization may be best presented by discussing the key categories for managing the process: prospective, concurrent, and retrospective review and large (ie, catastrophic) case management (LCM). Prospective review means review of a case *before* it even happens, concurrent review means review occurs *while* the case is active, and retrospective review occurs *after* the case is finished. Large case management refers to managing cases that are expected to result in very large costs, so as to provide coordination of care that results in both proper care and cost savings.

Prospective Review

Precertification

Precertification refers to a requirement on the part of the admitting physician (and often the hospital) to notify the plan before a member is admitted for inpatient care or an outpatient procedure. There is a widespread and rather erroneous belief that the primary role of precertification is to prevent unnecessary cases from occurring. Although that may occasionally happen (particularly in workers' compensation

cases; see Chapter 33), it is not the chief reason for precertification.

There are three primary reasons for precertification. The first is to notify the concurrent review system that a case will be occurring. In that way, the UM system will be able to prepare discharge planning (discussed below) ahead of time as well as look for the case during concurrent review rounds. In some instances, the LCM function (see below) may be notified if the admission diagnosis raises the possibility that it will be a highly expensive case (eg, a bone marrow transplant).

The second major reason for precertification is to ensure that care takes place in the most appropriate setting. Perhaps an inpatient case is diverted to the outpatient department, or a case is diverted from a nonparticipating hospital to a participating one or to a facility that has been designated as a center of excellence for a selected procedure.

The third reason is to capture data for financial accruals. Although it is unlikely that a plan can capture every case before or while it is taking place, a mature plan that is running well can capture the vast majority of cases, perhaps 90% to 95%. By knowing the number and nature of hospital cases as well as potential catastrophic cases, the plan may more accurately accrue for expenses rather than have to wait for claims to come in. This allows management to take action early and to avoid nasty financial surprises. Accrual methodology is discussed in Chapter 25.

In any case, for inpatient cases the plan usually assigns a length of stay guideline at the time the admission is certified. This topic of length of stay is discussed below. The plan may also use the precertification process to verify eligibility of coverage for the member, although most plans have a disclaimer stating that ultimate eligibility for coverage will be determined at the time the claim is processed.

In the case of an emergency or urgent admission, it is obviously not possible to obtain precertification. In that event, there is usually a contractual requirement to notify the plan by the next business day or within 24 hours if the plan has 24-hour-per-day UM staffing. Most plans have contractual language with both the physicians and the hospitals imposing financial penalties (eg, a percentage of their fee or a flat penalty) for failure to obtain certification. For plans that allow members to seek care from noncontracted providers (eg, in point-of-service plans), the responsibility to contact the plan rests with the members if they choose not to see a network physician; in such cases, most plans impose benefits penalties (eg, a higher coinsurance or a flat penalty rate) on a member who fails to obtain proper precertification.

Preadmission Testing and Same Day Surgery

One of the easiest and also the most common methods for cost control is preadmission testing and same day surgery. A member who is going to be hospitalized on an elective basis has routine preoperative tests done as an outpatient and is admitted the same day as the surgery is to be performed. Both these policies are confirmed at the time of precertification.

For example, a member has elective gallbladder surgery scheduled for 10:00 AM on Thursday. On Tuesday the member goes to the hospital for the preoperative tests. The results are made available to the admitting physician, who performs the admission history and physical as an outpatient and either delivers the results to the hospital or calls them in on an outside line to the hospital's transcription department. The member arrives at the hospital at 6:00 AM on Thursday, is admitted, and has surgery as scheduled.

In many health plans, the plan has made arrangements for laboratory work to be done with a contracted laboratory at reduced rates or will have in-house capabilities to perform the laboratory work. Occasionally, a hospital will refuse to accept the results of these laboratories. If the laboratory is accredited and licensed, the hospital has little grounds to require you to use its laboratory, electrocardiography, and radiology services for preoperative admission testing. In these cases it falls to the plan's management team to discuss this with the hospital administrator and negotiate an agreement for the hospital to accept your laboratory work or to agree to perform the work at equivalent costs to you. If they refuse to cooperate, you need to decide whether

you want to direct the elective cases to another, more cooperative hospital.

Mandatory Outpatient Surgery

It has become popular for health plans to produce mandatory outpatient surgery lists. These are essentially lists of procedures that may only be performed on an outpatient basis unless prior approval is obtained from the plan medical director. This is used by so many third party payers that you do not need to make one from scratch if you do not wish to; simply look at what other similar plans or even Medicare are using. One byproduct of this popularity is that no two lists are identical, which causes some confusion with physicians and hospitals. Although there is consensus on many common procedures (eg, a carpal tunnel release), there are always procedures that are migrating from inpatient to outpatient (eg, at the time this book was written, outpatient cardiac catheterization had only become popular in the last few years). That confusion probably tends to encourage the use of outpatient surgery when physicians are in doubt.

As mentioned earlier in this chapter and elsewhere, be sure that you will actually achieve the desired savings before instituting mandatory outpatient surgery requirements. In some cases, hospitals or freestanding outpatient surgery facilities have charges that are equal to or greater than those for an inpatient day. In other cases, the facility charge may be lower, but the unbundled charges for anesthesia, recovery, supplies, and so on can drive the cost higher than anticipated. These issues are discussed in Chapter 8.

Concurrent Review

Concurrent review means managing utilization during the course of a hospitalization (as opposed to an outpatient procedure). Common techniques for concurrent review involve assignment and tracking of length of stay, review and rounding by UM nurses, and discharge planning. The roles of the medical director, the primary care physician (PCP), and the attending or consulting physicians are discussed later in this chapter, as is the relationship between concurrent review and LCM.

Assignment of Length of Stay

A common approach to hospital utilization control is the assignment of a maximum allowable length of stay (MaxLOS), which sometimes appears in the guise of an estimated length of stay, but with teeth. With the MaxLOS, the plan assigns a length of stay on the basis of the admission diagnosis, and that is all the plan will authorize for payment. For example, an admission for gallbladder surgery may be assigned 3 days. It is assumed that the patient will be admitted on the day of surgery and go home 3 days later. Any stay beyond that day is not covered. In those plans that cannot or will not restrict payment, the MaxLOS is used only to trigger greater involvement by the medical director.

The MaxLOS is determined by International Classification of Diseases, Ninth Revision, Clinical Modification (ICD-9-CM) code, or diagnostic code, although diagnosis-related groups (DRGs) are similar in concept. Selecting a norm for the MaxLOS is not always easy given the regional variations. Looking at the local fee-for-service experience may or may not be helpful, depending on your area's history in achieving good control of utilization. Looking at the experience of other local managed health care plans is useful. Although competitors frequently object to allowing rival health plans to review their data, many states require plans to report key data such as utilization and financial performance on a quarterly basis to the state insurance department.

If you have no other source, use the length of stay data[1] for the western United States and take the lengths of stay at the 50th percentile or below. Somewhat more aggressive length of stay guidelines are available through Milliman and Robertson, a national actuarial firm.[7] Either of these will at least put you into an acceptable range until you can develop your own data or get access to better data than you have now.

The advantage of using MaxLOS designations is threefold. First, it allows you to cover a relatively large geographic area with few personnel, which may be necessary in a new start-up open panel plan. Second, such a list has the power of legitimacy and does not require that you negotiate every time. Third, it is relatively

mechanical and requires less training of plan personnel. This last may be true for the person issuing the MaxLOS designation, but it is still important to verify, usually through the UM nurse, that the diagnosis is accurate.

The problem with using MaxLOS designations is also threefold. First, it is easy to get complacent. If you choose certain values for MaxLOS designations, you may fail to evaluate continually if those are in fact the correct values. Second, designated time becomes free time. In other words, there is less incentive to evaluate critically every day in the hospital for appropriateness and alternatives if plan personnel and the physician feel that there is still time on the meter. Third, using such a mechanical system often achieves less than optimal results. Intensive medical management by qualified personnel should produce better control of utilization, but such personnel are not always available. The topic of concurrent review against criteria is discussed below.

You must also know what the consequences of exceeding the MaxLOS will be. In many plans, exceeding the MaxLOS results in either a denial of payment for services rendered after the MaxLOS has been reached or a reduction in payment, usually by a percentage amount. If you have failed to inform your membership of a MaxLOS program and you do not have sole source of payment clauses with your providers and hospitals (see Chapter 36), you may not be able to enforce a MaxLOS designation easily.

Role of the Utilization Management Nurse

The one individual who is crucial to the success of a managed care program is the UM nurse. It is the UM nurse who will be the eyes and ears of the medical management department, who will generally coordinate the discharge planning, and who will facilitate all the activities of utilization control.

Staffing levels for UM nurses will vary depending on the size of the geographic area, the number of hospitals, the size of the plan, and the intensity with which UM will be performed (eg, by on-site hospital rounding). It is common for plans to staff one UM nurse for every 8,500 to 12,000 members, assuming that the UM nurses will be making rounds on all hospitalized patients and that utilization is reasonably tightly controlled, but not on a 24-hour-per-day basis. Plans that perform telephone review only may staff at ratios that are twice that. It is also necessary to provide clerical support to do intake, to follow up on discharge planning needs, to take care of filing, and so forth.

The scope of responsibilities of the UM nurse will vary depending on the plan and the personalities and skills of the other members of the medical management team. In some plans, the role simply involves telephone information gathering. In other plans, there will be a more proactive role, including frequent communication with attending physicians, the medical director, the hospitals, and the hospitalized members and their families; discharge planning and facilitation; and a host of other activities, including active hospital rounding.

Information gathering. The one fundamental function of the UM nurse is information gathering. Information about hospital cases must be obtained in an accurate and timely fashion. It falls to the UM nurse to be the focal point of this information and to ensure that it is obtained and communicated to the necessary individuals in medical management and the claims department.

Necessary information includes admission date and diagnosis, the type of hospital service to which the patient was admitted (eg, medical, surgical, maternity, and so forth), the admitting physician, consultants, planned procedures (type and timing), expected discharge date, needed discharge planning, and any other pertinent information the plan managers may need.

Telephone rounding. In some plans, information gathering is done strictly by telephone; in other plans, hospital rounding is done in person by the UM nurse. When the telephone is used, it is used first to check with the admitting office to determine whether any plan members were admitted and then to check with the hospital's own UM department to obtain any further information.

Telephone rounding is usually done in cases where there is too much geographic area to cover and the plan cannot yet justify adding more UM nurses [eg, in a start-up individual provider association or preferred provider organization (PPO) covering five counties]. It may also be done in those instances where a hospital refuses to give the UM nurse rounding privileges on hospitalized plan members. There are certain instances where a plan may in fact delegate rounding and review to the hospital's UM department, but those are rare; examples include arrangements where the hospital is at significant financial risk (eg, through capitation or DRGs). The other time telephone rounding is used is when there are not tight controls on utilization, and the function is one of looking for clear outliers rather than trying to achieve optimal utilization control.

Hospital rounding. Rounding in person is far superior to telephone rounding. When rounds are conducted daily by a UM nurse on every hospitalized member, you will obtain the most accurate and timely information, and you will obtain information that you might not get otherwise.

For example, in a good quality management program (see Chapter 15) the rounding UM nurse will be able to watch for quality problems or significant events that would trigger a quality assurance audit. A rounding nurse will also be able to pick up information about a patient's condition that may affect discharge planning, information that the attending physician may have failed to communicate (eg, the need for home durable equipment that must be ordered).

The UM nurse may also be able to detect practice behavior that increases utilization simply for the convenience of the physician or hospital. For example, a patient may be ready for discharge but the physician missed making rounds that morning and will not be back until the next day, or the hospital rescheduled surgery for its own reasons and the patient will have to spend an extra and unnecessary day. In situations such as these, the UM nurse must not be put into an adversarial position but should refer such cases to the medical director.

Personal rounding by your plan's UM nurse has the added advantage of increasing member satisfaction. Many people feel uncomfortable talking to physicians and welcome the chance to express their fears or feelings to the UM nurse.

In other cases, inquiring about how members are feeling can let them know that you care about them as people and that you are not simply trying to get them out as fast as you can.

In the situation where a hospital refuses to grant rounding privileges to the UM nurse, a frequent excuse is that there is already a UM department in the hospital. That is usually not adequate for your needs and does not address the specific member satisfaction and quality assurance needs of your plan. Another frequent excuse is protecting the confidentiality of the patients. That does not hold if the plan's UM nurse is only rounding on plan members (who have agreed in their application to allow access to records). If a hospital refuses to cooperate with you on allowing the plan's UM nurse to round, you must seriously question your willingness to do business with that hospital. In most cases, a hospital will cooperate fully and willingly.

Review against criteria. The heart of concurrent review is the evaluation of each hospital case against established criteria. Many plans, especially open panel plans and PPOs, use published or commercially available criteria for such reviews[7–10] to facilitate evaluation by the UM nurses. Experienced nurses use such criteria as an aid in managing utilization, but they do not blindly depend on it. It is possible to keep a patient in the hospital for less than adequate reasons but still meet criteria; the seasoned UM nurse is able to evaluate each case on its merits.

Most plans have now automated this function to improve the efficiency of the UM nurses. Software allows the MaxLOS to be generated automatically from the admission diagnosis or procedure. Member and benefit eligibility is checked, diagnostic and procedure codes are generated from entered text, review criteria are automatically displayed for both admission and concurrent review, unlimited text may be entered to allow tracking, census reports are produced, statistics are generated, and so forth. UM software also links to the claims system so that claims are properly processed, including special instructions from the nurses.

Discharge planning and follow-up. Good discharge planning starts as soon as a patient is admitted into the hospital, or even before. The physician and the UM nurse should be considering discharge planning as part of the overall treatment plan from the outset. This planning includes an estimate of how long the patient will be in the hospital, what the expected outcome will be, whether there will be any special requirements on discharge, and what needs to be facilitated early on.

For example, if a patient is admitted with a fractured hip and it is known from the outset that many weeks of rehabilitation will be necessary, it is helpful to contact the facility where the rehabilitation will take place to ensure that a bed will be available at the time of transfer. If it is known that a patient will need durable medical equipment, the equipment should be ordered early so that the patient does not spend extra days in the hospital waiting for it to arrive.

An often overlooked aspect of discharge planning is informing the patient and family. If the patient and family do not know what to expect, they may be surprised when the physician tells them that the patient is being discharged. This is especially true if the patient has received hospital care in the past and has certain expectations. Informing the patient and family from the start about when they can expect discharge, how the patient will be feeling, what they might need to prepare for at home, and how follow-up will occur will all help smooth things considerably.

In the case of short stay obstetrics, if the patient and family are not prepared for the homecoming, there may be tremendous pressure on the physician to keep the mother and child in the hospital so that everyone can get a little more rest. Unfortunately, the hospital is far too expensive for that. Active discharge planning for short stay obstetrics is crucial. If your plan offers a home health visit to mothers who have had a short stay delivery, that should be confirmed on admission.

Discharge planning is an ongoing effort beginning with admission or preadmission screening. The UM nurse is in the ideal position to coordinate discharge planning. In addition to making sure that all goes smoothly to effect a smooth and proper discharge from the hospital, the UM nurse can follow up with the member by telephone after discharge to ensure that all is well.

Primary Care Physician's Responsibilities

There are two basic models for managing hospital cases: the PCP model and the attending physician model. In the PCP model, the PCPs are expected to manage the care of their patients in the hospital even when patients are hospitalized for care delivered primarily by consultants or specialists; most commonly this occurs when either the patient is hospitalized for surgery or when the patient has a drawn out course of treatment (eg, recovery from a stroke). In the PCP model, the most important functions of the member's PCP are also the most obvious: to make rounds every day and to coordinate the patient's care.

In the first cited instance, care from a consultant, it is all the more important for the PCP to round daily. This serves a number of purposes. First, it helps ensure continuity of care while the patient is in the hospital (eg, the PCP may be able to add pertinent clinical information as needed). Second, it provides a comforting presence for the patient, a presence that results not only in better bonding between physician and patient but in providing emotional support. Third, it allows for continuity after discharge because the PCP is aware of the clinical course and discharge planning. Fourth, it helps control unnecessary utilization.

Utilization control by the PCP is highly effective in the setting of a member receiving hospital care from a consultant. The PCP is able to discuss the case with the consultant and suggest ways to decrease the length of stay (eg, home nursing care) that the consultant is not used to considering. The PCP will presumably know the patient well enough to determine the patient's ability to do well in alternative situations.

The PCP will also be able to communicate effectively with a consultant in the event that the consultant failed to see the patient on rounds. For example, if a busy surgeon misses a patient on rounds because the patient was in the bathroom, the surgeon, because of a heavy operating room schedule, may not make it back to see that patient until late at night. If the patient is actually ready for discharge, the PCP can communicate with the surgeon that morning and arrange for discharge.

There will be situations where the PCP is unable to make rounds in person. This happens most frequently when a member is admitted to a tertiary hospital where the PCP does not have privileges. For example, cardiac bypass surgery may be done at a teaching hospital with a closed medical staff. In these situations, it is important for the PCP to be in frequent telephone contact with the attending physician on the case to keep up with developments and to aid in the discharge planning process. For example, the PCP may be comfortable in accepting the patient back in transfer during the recovery period or may be able to suggest home nursing care. In addition to controlling utilization, this helps ensure continuity of care, and the attending physician will almost always remark to the patient about how attentive the PCP has been about the case.

Equally important to good medical management is for the PCP to avoid the trap of "That's the way it's always been done and it's good enough for me!" The PCP has responsibility not only over the physical health of the member but over the financial health of the plan as well. The PCP must be open to evaluating new methods of treatment and considering high-quality but cost-effective ways of caring for people.

As a corollary, PCPs must be confident and assertive about their own abilities. It is an unfortunate byproduct of the highly specialized nature of medicine that there are times when a PCP is looked down upon by a consultant. Certainly a consultant who depends on the PCP for referrals will not knowingly exhibit behavior that the PCP will find offensive, but there often remains an unspoken agreement that the consultant will call the shots once the patient is admitted.

There are a number of objections that a PCP may raise concerning getting involved with patients admitted to a consultant's service. First, the PCP may feel intimidated by the consultant's knowledge about the medical problem. When this happens, there is no reason why the PCP cannot read up on the subject, at least in a major medical text, and ask questions. Also, it is the

PCP's patient, and the consultant is a consultant. It is the role and responsibility of the PCP to follow the care of the patient and to be aware of the medical issues involved. The simple act of asking the consultant questions about that care is appropriate and necessary and will frequently result in improved understanding by all parties as well as improved utilization control.

There is the possibility that the PCP will view such questioning as confrontational and will be unwilling to question the competence of the consultant. It is important to point out that the PCP is not questioning the consultant's competence (assuming that the consultant is indeed competent) but rather is discussing the case and asking the consultant his or her opinion about alternatives. The fear of such confrontations is far greater than the reality. The PCP has nothing to be shy about; PCPs are trained physicians specializing in primary care, and the consultant is helping care for the PCP's patient, not vice versa.

Consultant's Responsibilities

Primary care physician model. Even in a PCP model as discussed above, the consultant has responsibilities as well as the PCP. The interaction between consultant and PCP is highly important to good medical management and utilization control. Beyond that, it is reasonable for the plan, through the medical director, to communicate certain expectations of all consultants.

First, you expect all consultants to be aware of and to cooperate with your plan's policy on testing, procedures, and primary care case management. Second, plans that use PCPs as gatekeepers or managing physicians should expect consultants to be in communication with PCPs about their patients and to provide written reports on consultations (some plans go as far as to refuse payment to a consultant until the PCP receives a written report). Third, care should be directed back to the PCP as soon as it is possible to do so, and the consultant will reinforce the plan's philosophy of primary care. Last, the consultant will not subauthorize further care for the member without first discussing the case with the PCP involved. The PCP may already have worked up a problem that the consultant is seeing for the first time, or the PCP may be able to

perform the medical duties that the consultant is requesting; for example, a surgeon may call a cardiologist to evaluate chest pain even though the PCP is an internist who is aware of the patient's condition.

Attending physician model. Some plans use an attending physician model of hospital management. In these plans, it is not practical for the PCP to follow all cases in the hospital. Reasons may include high use of teaching hospitals with closed medical staffs, communities where PCPs simply do not hospitalize cases (which can occur in both urban and rural areas), or plans that do not use a PCP gatekeeper system. In any case, the attending physician is usually a specialist or consultant and has responsibility to manage the case and to interact with the plan.

The responsibilities of the attending physician in this model are little different from those of the PCP. Interaction with the plan is necessary, and the consultant needs to cooperate with plan policies and procedures. The main difference in this model is the person with whom the UM nurse and medical director interact.

In a loosely controlled plan there will be fewer expectations of the consultant than in a tightly controlled plan. As has been mentioned numerous times, the better the control of utilization you hope to achieve, the more you have to deal with practice patterns and physician behavior. Consultants are able to add significantly to the cost of care not only from their own fees but through additional fees generated by extra days in the hospital and through testing, procedures, and secondary referrals to other consultants.

Medical Director's Responsibilities

In addition to monitoring all the elements discussed in this chapter, there are a few specific functions that the medical director should be performing.

Communications

The medical director will have to become involved in the most difficult cases from a management standpoint. This does not necessarily refer to those cases where the difficulty is medical but rather to those cases where there is difficulty with the PCP, a consultant, a hospital, or the member or member's family. There are times when the medical director must deal with uncooperative individuals, and this is certainly a difficult responsibility. The medical director must take a compassionate, caring, but firm stance when dealing with difficult people. It is often easiest simply to give in, but that can only be done so many times before it becomes a habit that damages the plan's effectiveness. The ability to empathize and sympathize with someone's point of view and to recognize what the real issues are in a dispute is not the same as acquiescing. Although there are indeed times when the medical director will want to loosen the reins, it is important for the medical director to remain firm when the situation is clear and to back up his or her subordinates and the PCPs when they are right.

If the medical director is only heard from when there is a problem, his or her effectiveness will be diminished. It is important for there to be reasonably frequent contact with PCPs and important consultants even when all is well. This can be especially useful when discussing cases. If the medical director discusses cases, suggesting alternatives if appropriate even when there is no pressing need to make a change, the participating plan physicians will be much more accepting of the medical director's opinions when change is needed (assuming that the medical director has useful opinions in the first place, of course).

The usefulness of frequent contact cannot be underestimated. By asking thoughtful questions in a nonthreatening manner, and by constantly stimulating thought regarding cost-effective clinical management, the medical director may slowly reinforce appropriate patterns of care. The most successful outcome of such contacts occurs when physicians begin asking themselves the questions the medical director would ask and begin improving their practice patterns on that basis.

Daily Review of Utilization

A task that the medical director should perform for optimal utilization control is reviewing the hospital log daily. This may seem an onerous task, and it can be, but it is the only way the medical director will consistently spot problems in time to do something about them. For example, finding that surgery was not done on the same day as admission may prompt a call to the PCP or surgeon to prevent that same thing happening again. If possible, it is even better for the medical director to review the hospital log with the UM nurse early enough in the day for meaningful action to be taken, which is usually before noon, when many hospitals automatically charge for another day. Large plans with highly competent UM nurses and UM departments may get to a point where the medical director need not review every case every day but simply will review any problem cases or outliers. Even in these situations, the medical director should periodically review every case to be certain that the UM department is performing as well as expected.

Retrospective Review

Retrospective review occurs after the case is finished and the patient is discharged. Retrospective review takes on two primary forms: claims review and pattern review.

Claims Review

Claims review refers to examining claims for improprieties or mistakes. For example, it is common for plans to review large claims to verify whether services were actually delivered or whether mistakes were made in collating the claims data. In such large cases, the plan may actually send a representative on site to the hospital to review the medical record against the claims record. The topic of claims review is also discussed in Chapter 20.

Pattern Review

This refers to examining patterns of utilization to determine where action must be taken. For example, if three hospitals in the area perform coronary artery bypass surgery, the plan may look to see which one has the best clinical outcomes, the shortest length of stay, and the lowest charges. The plan may then preferentially send all such cases to that hospital. Pattern review also allows the plan to focus UM efforts primarily on those areas needing greater attention (ie, Sutton's Law: Go where the money is!).

One other use of pattern review is to provide feedback to providers. Although not as powerful as active UM by the plan's own department, feedback can have an effect in and of itself.[11] When combined with other management functions and financial incentives, feedback can be a useful management tool.

Alternatives to Acute Care Hospitalization

There are many instances where patients are ill or disabled but not to the extent that they need to be in an acute care hospital. Despite that, that is where they often stay. The reasons for this are many.

In some cases, the patient started out needing the services of an acute care hospital (eg, a patient had surgery but the recovery phase requires far fewer resources than are available in the hospital). In other cases, there is simply no place for the patient to go (eg, a patient is recovering from a broken femur but lives alone). In a few cases, a patient is kept in the hospital for the convenience of a physician who does not want to make house calls or rounds at another institution. Last, there are times when a patient is kept in the hospital simply because "That's the way it's always been done!"

Skilled or Intermediate Nursing Facilities

A useful alternative to consider is the skilled or intermediate nursing facility. This is most suited for prolonged convalescence or recovery cases. For example, if a patient with a broken femur requires more traction than can be provided safely at home and requires many months to recover, the cost for a bed day in a nursing facility will be greatly reduced compared to the acute care hospital. The same goes for rehabilitation cases such as stroke or trauma to the brain when the damage is too extensive for the patient to go home immediately. Although there are few (if any) reasons anymore to admit someone for uncomplicated back pain, if one of your physicians does so a nursing facility is the most appropriate place for the bed rest to take place.

The main problem with this alternative is objections from the patient or the family, particularly in the case of young patients. There is a stigma attached to nursing homes that makes some people associate them with warehouses for the elderly. To overcome this, you need to take a proactive approach.

First, contract only with those nursing facilities that meet your (and implicitly your members') demands for pleasant surroundings. You may find a better price elsewhere, but try to imagine yourself or your loved ones staying at the facility for a month and see if it would be acceptable. A good nursing facility will be interested in working with you on making the option acceptable by ensuring that your patients will be given a private room (a private room in a nursing facility is still less costly than a semiprivate bed in an acute care hospital) or at least will be placed in a room with another patient with a similar functional status.

Second, discuss the alternative with the patient and the family well in advance of the actual move. Nothing is as distressing as suddenly finding out that you will be shipped out in the morning to a nursing home. If possible, have the family visit the nursing facility to meet the staff and see the environment before the patient is transferred.

Last, do not abandon the patient. In other words, have someone, preferably the physician and the UM nurse, visit the patient on a regular basis. It is easy to rationalize that, because the patient is in the nursing facility for long-term care, you do not need to visit often; after all, the nurse would call if there was a problem. That may be true from a medical standpoint, but it is not true from a human relations standpoint.

How you handle using a nursing facility will have an impact on your marketing. If you coldly shunt people into a nursing facility simply to save money, you will rapidly get a reputation for placing your needs over those of your members. Members will complain to their benefits managers or to other potential members, and you will develop problems in enrollment. If, however, you handle the option with caring and compassion, taking the time to alleviate the emotional distress that may be caused, you will find that most people are quite understanding and accepting of this alternative.

The other issue to consider in the use of nursing facilities is monitoring the case in regard to your benefit structure. It is easy for a case to go from prolonged recovery to permanent placement or custodial care. It can be emotionally wrenching both for the member's family and for you to face up to the end of benefits. The problem of who will pay for long-term custodial care is a national dilemma, and it becomes personal when a family is faced with high costs because the benefits your plan offers do not continue indefinitely.

If it is possible or likely that benefits will end, it is wise early on to make the benefits structure clear to the family. This does not have to be done in a cold and calculating manner but rather by laying out all the possibilities so that the family may begin early planning themselves.

Step-Down Units

As an alternative to freestanding nursing facilities, many hospitals with excess capacity have developed step-down units. Even if they have not, many hospital administrators are willing to consider it in your negotiations.

In essence, a step-down unit is a ward or section of a ward that is used in much the same way as a skilled nursing facility. A patient who requires less care and monitoring, such as someone recovering from a hip replacement (after all the drains have been removed), may need only bed rest, traction, and minimal nursing care. In recognition of the lesser resource needs, the charge per day is less.

The step-down unit has the advantage of being convenient for the physician and UM nurse and is more acceptable to the patient and family. It also does not require transfer outside the facility. Although the cost per day is sometimes slightly higher than that of a nursing facility, the difference may be worth it in terms of member acceptability.

Outpatient Procedure Units

In many instances, performing a procedure in an outpatient unit is less expensive than admitting a patient for a 1-day stay. This is not always true because, with the increased popularity of outpatient surgery, some hospitals have raised their outpatient unit charges to make up the lost revenue. As discussed in Chapter 8, you must pay attention to outpatient charges when negotiating with hospitals.

Free-standing outpatient facilities are also an alternative. These may be affiliated with a hospital or may be independent. As with hospitals, you can and should negotiate the charge structure so that you indeed save the costs that outpatient surgery should allow.

Hospice Care

Hospice care is that care given to terminally ill patients. It tends to be supportive care and is used most often when such care cannot be given in the home. It is not always covered by health plans, but it does sometimes take the place of acute care hospitalization and should be considered when appropriate.

Home Health Care

Home health agencies are proliferating and home care is becoming increasingly accepted. Services that are particularly amenable to home health care include nursing care for routine reasons (eg, checking weights, changing dressings, and the like), home intravenous treatment (eg, for osteomyelitis, certain forms of chemotherapy, or home intravenous nutrition), home physical therapy, respiratory therapy, and rehabilitation care.

You should have little trouble negotiating and contracting with home health agencies for services. It is becoming popular for hospitals to have home health care services to aid with caring for patients discharged from their facility, and you may be able to negotiate those services with your overall contract. Furthermore, as Medicare continues to tighten down payments for home care, many agencies are looking for alternative sources of revenue. As with hospitals or any other providers of care, home health and high-technology home care agencies need to be evaluated in terms beyond simple pricing breaks. An active quality management program, the presence of a medical director, and evidence of attention to the changes that are constantly occurring in the field are all requisites for contracting.

A warning about home health services is in order. Because the physician and UM nurse seldom visit the patient receiving home health care, it often defaults to the home health nurse to determine how often and how long the patient should receive services, and this can lead to some surprising bills. It is highly advisable to have a firm policy regarding how many home health visits may be covered under a single authorization and that continued authorization requires physician review.

Large Case Management

LCM, also referred to as catastrophic case management, refers to specialized techniques for identifying and managing cases that are disproportionately high in cost. For example, active acquired immunodeficiency syndrome can be an expensive disease process, as can a high cervical spinal cord injury, a bone marrow transplant, and many other events.

Identification of cases may be straightforward because the patients are in the hospital the first time you identify them. This is the case for trauma. Other cases may be identified before they are ever hospitalized. For example, examining the claims system for use of dialysis services may identify an end-stage renal disease patient. Proactively contacting patients with potentially catastrophic illnesses not only can save the plan considerable expense by managing the care cost effectively but can also result in better medical care because the services are coordinated.

Prenatal care is a specialized form of LCM because active coordination occurs before the newborn is delivered. Prenatal LCM involves identification of high-risk pregnancies early enough to intervene to improve the chances of a good outcome. With the staggering costs of neonatal intensive care, it only takes a few improved outcomes to yield dramatic savings. Methods for identifying cases include sending out information about pregnancy to all members, reviewing the claims system for pregnancy-related claims, asking (or requiring) the PCPs and obstetricians to notify the plan when a delivery is expected, and so forth. After the UM department is in-

formed of the case, the member may be proactively contacted, and a questionnaire may be given to assess for risk factors (eg, very young maternal age, diabetes, medical problems, and so forth). If risk factors are noted, then the plan coordinates prenatal care in a very proactive manner. Although it is impossible to force a member to seek care and to follow up problems, it is possible to increase the amount and quality of prenatal care that is delivered. A special problem exists when the pregnant patient is also abusing drugs; close coordination with the substance abuse program must then occur.

The degree to which the plan can become involved in LCM is in part a function of the benefits structure. In a tightly run managed health care plan, it is common for the UM department to be proactive in LCM; in simple PPOs, LCM is often voluntary on the part of the member (in other words, if the member chooses not to cooperate, there is little impact on benefits). Even in situations requiring strictly voluntary cooperation by the members and physicians, it is surprising how often LCM can be highly effective.

In addition to the standard methods of managing utilization, LCM often involves two other techniques. First is the use of community resources. Some catastrophic cases require support structures to help the member function or even return home. Examples of such support include family members, social service agencies, churches, special foundations, and so forth. One way to find out about such resources is to consult the *Case Management Resource Guide,*[12] and more definitive guides should be developed for each geographic area as appropriate.

The other common technique is to go beyond the contractual benefits to manage the case. For example, if the benefits structure of the group has only limited coverage for durable medical equipment, it may still be in the plan's interest to cover such expenses to get the patient home and out of the hospital. In self-funded groups, the group administrator may actually be willing to fund extracontractual benefits simply as a benefit for an employee or dependent who is experiencing a terrible medical problem.

In all events, the hallmark of LCM is longitudinal management of the case by a single UM nurse or department. Management spans hospital care, rehabilitation, outpatient care, professional services, home care, ancillary services, and so forth. It is in the active coordination of care that both quality and cost effectiveness are maintained.

CONCLUSION

The control of hospital or institutional utilization is one of the most important aspects of controlling overall health care costs. The methods used to control hospital utilization vary from relatively weak and mechanical to tightly controlled, longitudinally integrated, and highly labor intensive. The control of hospital utilization is a function that must be attended to every day to achieve optimal results, and special attention must be paid to LCM to produce the greatest savings.

REFERENCES

1. *Length of Stay by Diagnosis and Operation*. Ann Arbor, MI: Health Care Knowledge Resources; 1991.
2. Chassin MR, Brook RH, Park RE, et al. Variations in the use of medical and surgical services by the Medicare population. *N Engl J Med.* 1986;314:285–290.
3. Smits HL. Medical practice variations revisited. *Health Affairs.* Fall 1986:91–96.
4. Wennberg J, Gittelsohn A. Variations in medical care among small areas. *Sci Am.* April 1982:120–135.
5. Wennberg JE, Freeman JL, Culp WJ. Are hospital services rationed in New Haven or over-utilized in Boston? *Lancet.* 1987;1:1185–1189.
6. Chassin MR, Kosecoff J, Park RE, et al. Does inappropriate use explain geographic variations in the use of health care services? A study of three procedures. *JAMA.* 1987;258:2533–2537.
7. Doyle RL. *Healthcare Management Guidelines, Vol. 1: Inpatient and Surgical Care.* Milliman & Robertson; 1990.
8. *The ISD-A Review System with Adult Criteria.* Chicago: InterQual; 1991.
9. *Surgical Indications Monitoring SIM III.* Chicago: InterQual; 1991.
10. *Managed Care Appropriateness Protocol (MCAP).* Wellesley, MA: Utilization Management Associates; 1991.
11. Billi JE, Hejna GF, Wolf FM, et al. The effects of a cost-education program on hospital charges. *J Gen Intern Med.* 1987;2:306–311.
12. *Case Management Resource Guide.* Irvine, CA: Center for Consumer Healthcare Information; 1992.

Chapter 11

Controlling Referral/Consultant Utilization

Peter R. Kongstvedt

The control of utilization of referral physicians and consultants (both physicians and nonphysicians) is an area of great importance. In most managed health care plans, the costs associated with nonprimary care professional services will be substantially greater than the cost of primary care services; often between 1.5 and 2.0 times as high. This is due to the increased fees associated with consultant services and to the hospital-intensive nature of those services; in other words, more than half the costs of consultant services may be associated with hospital cases.

Often overlooked are the associated utilization costs generated by consultants. It is not only the fees of the consultants themselves that add to the cost of care but also the cost of services ordered by consultants, such as diagnostic studies, facility charges for procedures, and so forth. One 1987 study in a nonmanaged care environment found that each referral from a primary care physician (PCP) generated nearly $3,000 in combined hospital charges and professional fees within a 6-month period after the referral.[1] It may be safely assumed that the value of a referral has increased considerably since 1987. These costs are not routinely added to the cost of consultant services when data are compiled, but control of consultant services will often lead to control of these outside services as well.

DEFINITIONS

The definition of referral or consultant services includes physician's fees that are not considered primary care, in other words all physician's fees that are not from general internists, family physicians, and general pediatricians. If you have chosen to include obstetrics and gynecology (Ob/Gyn) as primary care, then you will need to decide which of the services provided by Ob/Gyn (eg, surgery, routine Pap smears and pelvic examinations, colposcopy, and so forth) are included as primary care and which are consultant care.

In general, most managed care plans count consultant physicians and nonphysician professionals (eg, psychologists) in the consultant cost category, and ancillary services (eg, laboratory, radiology, pharmacy, and the like) are dealt with separately. In keeping with that, control of ancillary services utilization is addressed separately in Chapter 12.

DATA

To manage consultant services, you must first be able to capture utilization and cost data and to capture them in an accurate and timely manner. If you do not have that ability, your efforts to control utilization in this category will be severely hampered. The issue of data capture and reporting is discussed further in Chapter 16.

There is no set standard for reporting data on referral utilization as there is for hospital utilization. Nevertheless, certain measures are used frequently and found useful by managers.

In health maintenance organizations (HMOs) that do not have any benefits for services provided without an authorization from a PCP, a useful measure is referrals per 100 encounters per PCP. In this measure, one counts the total number of referrals made by a PCP for every 100 primary care encounters. This correlates to a referral percentage. For example, 11 referrals per 100 encounters per PCP equals a referral rate of 11%.

More commonly used is the referral rate per 1,000 members per year. Like the measurement of hospitalization rate, this looks at an annualized referral rate for every 1,000 members. Although this is less directly related to a PCP encounter than referrals per 100 primary care encounters, the nomenclature is standard across many types of plans.

It is important to know whether you are counting initial referrals or total visits to a referral consultant. In other words, if you are only counting the initial referral or authorization, you may be missing a large portion of the actual utilization. It is not uncommon, especially in loosely controlled systems, for a single referral to generate multiple visits to a consultant. For example, if a PCP refers a member with the request to evaluate and treat, this is carte blanche for the consultant to take over the care of the patient, and succeeding visits will be to the consultant and not to the PCP.

It is therefore far more useful to track actual visits. Better yet is to track both initial referrals and actual visits because that will give you a clearer idea of how the consultants are really handling the cases. In a tightly controlled system, such as an HMO with a strict policy granting authorization for one visit only for any referral, the numbers may be close to being the same. In a system with loose controls, the number of actual visits may exceed the initial referral rate by two to three times.

SELECTION OF REFERRAL AND CONSULTING PROVIDERS

As mentioned in Chapter 7 and discussed in Chapter 16, the ability to select providers on the basis of a demonstrated pattern of practice can have a considerable impact on referral expenses. There are large differences in the efficiency of practice between providers within each specialty, and if patients are preferentially sent to those consultants and referral specialists who demonstrate cost-effective practice, the plan can achieve considerable savings.

This is especially important in plans that allow self-referral to consultants by members, such as preferred provider organizations or point-of-service (POS) plans; see Chapter 2 for a description of these types of plans. If you have a loose system that allows open access to any consultant at any time other than through selection of providers, you can exert little control except perhaps by making fee adjustments after enough documentation of overutilization. The problem with using fee adjustments to control utilization (ie, adjusting a consultant's, or the entire provider panel's, fees downward as utilization goes up) is that it can lead to an "I'd better get mine first" mentality. In that situation, providers may begin churning visits and increasing utilization to increase revenues, worried that next month the fees may be adjusted even lower. This issue is discussed in Chapter 6.

The ability to evaluate referral practice behavior is no easy task and must be done over a long period of time on a significant number of events. Please see Chapter 16 for further discussion on this topic.

AUTHORIZATION SYSTEM

Authorization systems are discussed in detail in Chapter 17. The utility of an authorization system is mentioned here because without one you have a markedly diminished chance of effectively controlling referral utilization. Through educative techniques, you may be able to decrease consultant utilization somewhat, but unless there is a primary care gatekeeper or case manager system in place it is not likely that you will achieve optimal results. If you have been able carefully to select consultants through practice pattern analysis, you may get improvement in referral expenses, but not to the same degree that a PCP authorization system will allow.

The corollary to this is the possibility that a PCP can deliver many of the same services as a consultant, but at considerable savings and in a more appropriate setting. Even in nonmanaged care systems, PCPs manage a substantial proportion of their patients' care.[2] Therefore, the reason for a PCP authorization system to manage consultant costs is twofold: to reduce consultant utilization through services delivered by the PCP and to manage those referrals that are made.

The remainder of this chapter will assume that there is some type of authorization system in place. That system can be rigid or loose.

METHODS TO ACHIEVE TIGHT CONTROL

Single Visit Authorizations Only

As discussed in Chapter 17, a system that allows only one visit per authorization is necessary for optimal control. There are common exceptions to that, which are listed below. In essence, every time a member is referred to a consultant, the PCP gatekeepers (or care coordinators, or whatever you choose to call them) must issue a unique authorization. That authorization is good for one visit and will only be used to pay one claim. Claims submitted by the consultant with multiple charges will be compared to what was authorized, and only the authorized services will be reimbursed.

This sounds strong in theory, and it is strong. Unfortunately, it is sometimes difficult to enforce. A mechanism for review of claims that do not exactly match the authorization must be put in place so that you do not penalize members and consultants if the PCP fails to document the authorization correctly. It is also sometimes difficult in practice to pull out overcharges or addons to a claim, particularly when the claims adjudicators get overworked. Nonetheless, this system is both workable and necessary for optimal control.

It is vital to inform members through full and fair disclosure of such a system before their enrolling in your plan. The usual methods of informing members include enrollment literature, new member kits, the identification card issued by your plan, the evidence of coverage certificate that you issue to a member, the referral form itself, the plan newsletter, and even signs in your consultants' offices. Consultants will usually agree to allow signs in their offices when they understand that improving compliance with authorization procedures will enhance their revenue both by speeding up claims processing and by a decreased bad debt load.

After you have informed members, you must periodically reinform them. Most people will not remember everything they hear, even after hearing it multiple times. There will always be some who deny ever knowing about the need for authorization, but you can only do the best you can.

As noted above, there are common exceptions to the rule of one authorization one visit. These include chemotherapy and radiation therapy for cancer, obstetrics, mental health and chemical dependency therapy, physical therapy, and rehabilitation therapy. You may choose other exceptions in your plan. For example, you may automatically allow one or two home health visits after short stay obstetrics.

Even for these exceptions, however, you should not have open-ended authorizations. There should be an absolute limit on the number of visits that can be authorized at once. For example, you may wish to limit initial mental health referrals to two or three visits and then require the therapist to discuss the case with the PCP or mental health case manager before any further authorizations are allowed (see Chapter 13). Physical therapy should likewise be limited to an initial number of visits, and then the therapist must discuss the case with the physician before any further authorizations are issued. For chemotherapy cases, the oncologist should discuss the case with the PCP and outline the exact course of treatment, which could then be authorized all at once. The overriding principle is that open-ended authorizations are simply blank checks. If you allow them, you will pay the price.

Prohibition of Secondary Referrals and Authorizations

Another facet of controlling referral utilization is the prohibition of secondary referrals by consultants. This means that a consultant cannot authorize anything for a member. In other words, if a consultant feels that a patient needs to see another consultant, that must be communicated back to the PCP, who is the only one able to issue an authorization for services.

This extends to revisits back to the consultant and to testing and procedures as well. For example, if a consultant has an expensive piece of diagnostic equipment in the office, there may be a subtle pressure to use it to make it pay for itself. One widely noted study looking at physician ownership of radiology equipment documented a fourfold increase in imaging examinations as well as significant increases in charges among physicians who used their own equipment compared to physicians who referred such studies to radiologists.[3] Similar results have been reported for laboratory services[4] and a wide variety of ancillary services.[5]

The issue of physician-owned diagnostic and therapeutic equipment or services is a difficult one to address and one that is coming under increasing pressure from government regulation, at least for Medicare.[6] Perhaps the best method for dealing with this issue is simply to prohibit or markedly restrict the use of such services. Most managed care plans contract with a limited number of vendors for such ancillary services and may limit referral to only those vendors. The topic of ancillary services is discussed in Chapter 12.

Even in the absence of those types of pressures, secondary referrals may simply be unnecessary. For example, an endocrinologist may be concerned about a referred patient's chest pain and may refer the patient to a cardiologist when in fact the patient's PCP had worked up the problem and was tracking it carefully. This hap-

pens more often than one might think because a patient may not always communicate or even understand what previous care they have received, and the PCP may not have considered it necessary to put that information into the referral letter or form.

Last, the prohibition on secondary authorizations extends to procedures, including hospitalizations. A consultant must obtain the authorization from the PCP or the plan (depending on the plan's policy about precertification) before any procedures (eg, colonoscopy) or admission to the hospital. This is not to be punitive but to ensure that such things are done in the most cost-effective manner possible. For example, a referral surgeon may not be aware of the preadmission testing program, may use a noncontracting hospital, or may be used to admitting the patient the day before surgery simply as a convenience. By requiring authorization, such problems can be detected and dealt with easily.

Review of Reasons for Referral

It is the responsibility of the medical director to review the reasons for referral by the PCPs. In the tightest of all systems, this review takes place before the actual referral is made. In other words, the medical director or associate medical director must approve any authorization prospectively. This system is obviously cumbersome and may be seen as demeaning to the PCPs, but it is definitely tight, even if prohibitively expensive. It is perhaps most suitable for a tightly controlled closed panel or a training program where interns and residents are involved.

More acceptable is retrospective review of referrals. In this case, the medical director or associate medical director reviews referral forms after the fact, although preferably not long after. Reviews may be of all referrals, which potentially achieves tight control but is unrealistic, or of randomly selected referrals, which will be less tight but still quite useful. More useful is to evaluate PCP referral rates and patterns as well as utilization patterns of referral physicians to determine where retrospective review will have the greatest potential.

The preferred vehicle for review is the referral form (or authorization form), which contains the reasons for referral. If the referral form does not contain clinical information, or if referral authorizations are captured electronically, then periodic chart review, similar to a quality assurance audit, needs to be used.

In this review, the medical director is looking at reasons for referral that are inappropriate or poorly thought out. It is surprising how often one encounters reasons for referral such as "Please evaluate and treat." This is a blank check. Another commonly encountered referral is one in which the patient's complaints are simply echoed (eg, "Patient complains of pain in foot"). In these cases, one is not sure what the referring physician even bothered to do.

A referral should be made after adequate thought and course of action have been taken. The referring PCP should indicate why the patient is being referred, what the PCP thinks the diagnosis is or what he or she is concerned about, what has already been done, and what exactly the PCP wants the consultant to do. By failing to indicate the results of their own work-up or significant findings on the patient's history and physical examination, PCPs make themselves look lazy and make the job of the consultant that much more inefficient.

When the medical director encounters sloppy reasons for referral, it is not necessary to reprimand or embarrass the PCP. It is more appropriate to discuss the case clinically, suggesting options that the PCP may have tried before referring or ways in which the referral could have been more effective. The ultimate goal of these discussions is to foster that type of internal questioning behavior in the PCP so that the medical director will not have to do it. You want each PCP to consider all the options before making a referral and to make referrals count. This often means breaking old habits, but then that is what medical management is about.

Self-Referrals by Members

It is a chronic problem in managed care plans with authorization systems to have members referring themselves to consultants for care. In

POS plans that have benefits for self-referral, plan design allows this. In either an HMO or a POS plan, new members who are not used to the system and signed up because of the benefits offered may not recall or note the requirements for authorization and are more apt to self-refer and later be surprised that there is reduced or no coverage for the service.

In these situations, you need to consider your policy on first offenders. Many HMOs will pay for the first self-referral if it is a new member, if the plan recently changed to an authorization system, or if plan managers want to be nice. In such cases the plan documents a warning so that benefits for self-referral may be denied on subsequent occurrences. Most POS plans do not cover any self-referrals at the higher level of benefits, but some will remind the member via their explanation of benefits statement that the benefits would have been higher if the member had obtained authorization.

Large Case Management

Even in HMO or POS plans, there may be times when the plan may wish to have a referral specialist function as a PCP. This would occur when a member has a chronic and high-cost problem that is clearly outside the scope of a PCP's training and practice. In those events, the plan's large case management (LCM) function becomes proactive in managing the case (see Chapter 10). As part of the case management the patient may no longer be the responsibility of a PCP, but care may be coordinated with a specialist who functions as the PCP for that case only. For example, a member with active and aggressive acquired immunodeficiency syndrome may be better cared for by an infectious disease specialist rather than a PCP, although that assumption may not hold in every case. The point is that the plan's LCM function may choose this route on occasion rather than force the PCP to manage catastrophic cases.

Financial Arrangements

Financial arrangements are discussed in detail in Chapter 7, so only two pertinent issues are reiterated.

Capitation is a powerful and effective tool for controlling consultant utilization but can be a trap if not used wisely. You are urged to review the section on capitation in Chapter 7 before using it. Simple capitation arrangements alone without proper controls on utilization, such as an authorization system and review of reasons for referral, can lead to serious overutilization unless the referral physician is able to exert strong controls on utilization without managerial controls.

Financial incentives or risk/bonus arrangements for PCPs and contracting consultants can be quite useful, especially incentives for PCPs. As discussed elsewhere, this is not an attempt to bribe a physician but to share the savings of cost-effective practice. Incentives should not be so great as to raise the danger of inappropriate underutilization but should be enough to have a genuine effect.

CONCLUSION

The control of referral and consultant services affects not only professional expenses but costs associated with testing and procedures, including hospitalization, that may be generated by the consultant. The ability to select only those consultants and referral specialists who practice cost effectively can yield cost savings, but optimal control depends on an authorization system, and lack of such a system will hamper your abilities meaningfully to decrease consultant utilization over the long term.

REFERENCES

1. Glenn JK, Lawler FH, Hoerl MS. Physician referrals in a competitive environment: an estimate of the economic impact of a referral. *JAMA.* 1987;258:1920–1923.

2. Dietrich AJ, Nelson EC, Kirk JW, et al. Do primary physicians actually manage their patients' fee-for-service care? *JAMA.* 1988;259:3145–3149.

3. Hillman BJ, Joseph CA, Mabry MR, et al. Frequency and costs of diagnostic imaging in office practice—a comparison of self-referring and radiologist-referring physicians. *N Engl J Med.* 1990;323:1604–1608.

4. Office of the Inspecter General. *Financial Arrangements between Physicians and Health Care Businesses: Report to Congress.* Washington, DC: Dept. of Health and Human Services; 1989. Dept. of Health and Human Services Publication no. OAI-12-88-01410.

5. State of Florida Health Care Cost Containment Board. *Joint Ventures among Health Care Providers in Florida.* Tallahassee, FL: State of Florida;1991;2.

6. *The Ethics in Patient Referrals Act—Omnibus Budget Reconciliation Act of 1989.*

Chapter 12

Controlling Utilization of Ancillary and Emergency Services

Peter R. Kongstvedt

Ancillary services are divided into diagnostic and therapeutic services. Examples of ancillary diagnostic services include laboratory, radiology, nuclear testing, computed tomography (CT), magnetic resonance imaging (MRI), electroencephalography (EEG), electrocardiography, cardiac testing (including plain and nuclear stress testing, other cardiac nuclear imaging, invasive imaging, echocardiography, and Holter monitoring), and so forth. Examples of ancillary therapeutic services include cardiac rehabilitation, noncardiac rehabilitation, physical therapy (PT), occupational therapy, speech therapy, and so forth.

Pharmacy services are a special form of ancillary services that account for a significant measure of cost and have been subject to tremendous inflation. This important topic is discussed separately in Chapter 14.

Ancillary services are unique in that they are rarely sought out by the patient without a referral by a physician. For example, it is certainly possible that an individual could self-refer to a rehabilitation center, but it is likely that the center would require a referral from a physician before accepting the individual into the program. Diagnostic studies almost universally require physician referral. One exception is the free-standing diagnostic center that has medical staff whose sole purpose is to guide a patient through the diagnostic work-up that the patient seeks (eg, a freestanding cardiac testing center whose advertisements appeal to people who want those tests done). Because those types of centers are out of your control, as are freestanding urgent/convenience care centers, your only real way to control them is economic. If those centers do not have a contract with your plan, or if you require authorization from a contracted physician to pay in full, you do not have to pay such freestanding centers. In the case of a health maintenance organization (HMO), you do not have to pay at all. For a preferred provider organization (PPO), a point-of-service (POS) plan, or a managed indemnity plan, you may or may not have a partial payment liability, depending on your service agreement and schedule of benefits.

Because most ancillary services require an order from a physician, it is logical that control of such services is dependent on changing the utilization patterns of physicians. As discussed below, the other primary method of controlling costs of ancillary services is to contract for such services in such a way as to make costs predictable. Even with favorable contracts, controlling utilization of ancillary services by physicians remains an essential ingredient to long-term cost control.

PHYSICIAN-OWNED ANCILLARY SERVICES

There is compelling evidence that physician ownership of diagnostic or therapeutic equipment or services, whether owned individually or through joint ventures or partnerships, can lead to significant increases in utilization of those services. As mentioned in Chapter 11, there are three recent studies that documented this phenomenon in diagnostic imaging,[1] laboratory,[2] and a remarkably wide range of other services.[3] Physician self-referral is now severely restricted by the Health Care Financing Administration for Medicare services,[4] and many private plans have followed suit.

Actually tracing ownership or fiduciary relationships is not always easy to do. The ancillary services may have a completely separate provider name and tax identification number, may have a separate billing address (perhaps not even in the same geographic area), and may otherwise appear to be an independent vendor. Tracking unusually high rates of referral to a given provider of ancillary services (see Chapter 16) may be the only clue to such potential utilization abuse. Many plans are also clearly prohibiting physician self-referral in their provider contracts (unless expressly allowed by the plan) and are requiring the physicians to disclose any fiduciary relationship with such providers.

It is neither practical nor desirable to place too heavy a restriction on physicians' ability to use services or equipment that they own. For example, orthopedists cannot properly care for their patients if they cannot obtain radiographs. In some cases, a physician may be the only available provider of a given service (eg, in a rural area). In other cases, it may actually be more cost effective to allow physicians to use their own facility. The point here is that physician-owned services must not be allowed to become a lucrative profit center, one that is subject to abuse.

Managed care plans deal with this issue in a number of ways. One method is to have an outright ban on self-referral other than for carefully designated services. For example, a cardiologist may be allowed to perform in-office exercise tolerance testing but be prohibited from referring to a freestanding cardiac diagnostic center in which he or she has a fiduciary relationship. Another method is to reimburse for such physician self-referred services at a low margin (not so low as to cause the physician to lose money but low enough to prevent any profit). The last common method is to contract for all ancillary services through a very limited network of providers; this is discussed later in this chapter.

DATA CAPTURE

The ability to control utilization of ancillary services will be directly related to your ability to capture accurate and timely data (see Chapters 16 and 25). If you have a tight authorization system (see Chapter 17), you may get prospective data. If your claims management system is capable, you should be able to get retrospective data. If you have no way to capture data regarding ancillary services, you will have great difficulty controlling utilization. Lack of data will also make contracting problematic because no vendor will be willing to contract aggressively without having some idea of projected utilization.

Data elements that you need to capture include who ordered the service [this is sometimes different than the physician of record; for example, a member may have signed up with a primary care physician (PCP), but the referral physician ordered the tests], what was ordered, what is being paid for (in other words, are you paying for more than was ordered?), and how much it is costing.

The ability to look at patterns of usage in ancillary services is quite valuable. For example, it would be useful to know that of 10 family practitioners there is 1 who routinely orders double the number of radiographs compared to the other 9. There may be a perfectly good reason for this, but you will never know unless you can identify that pattern and look for the reasons.

FINANCIAL INCENTIVES

Ancillary services utilization is commonly incorporated into primary care reimbursement systems that are performance based (eg, capitation or performance-based fee-for-service). This topic is discussed in Chapters 4 and 6.

FEEDBACK

The issue of monetary gain leading to excessive use of ancillary services has been discussed earlier in this chapter, but there are a number of nonmonetary causes of excessive testing; such causes include the quest for diagnostic certainty, peer pressure, convenience, patient demands, and fear of malpractice claims.[5]

There is evidence that physicians will modify their use of ancillary services when given feedback on their performance. Simple feedback regarding test ordering behavior has led to modest reductions in use.[6] This response has been confirmed for simple feedback, and somewhat greater decreases have been seen when feedback was combined with other written guidelines or peer review.[7,8]

Feedback to physicians regarding their use of ancillary services is therefore a worthwhile endeavor. Feedback should include comparisons to their peers and should be properly adjusted for factors that affect utilization (eg, age and sex of patients, specialty type, and the like). Feedback should also contain adequate data to allow a physician to know where performance may be improved. See Chapter 16 for further discussion about reports.

CONTROL POINTS

Irrespective of physician self-regulation of the use of ancillary services, many plans apply additional controls over ancillary utilization.

Indications for Use

The first control point to discuss is indications for use of services. This is not an easy means of controlling ancillary services, but it has the potential of producing the best control and fostering high quality. In essence, this means using standards of care. Like protocols, standards of care outline the events and thought processes that should occur before physicians refer for ancillary or consultant services.

Standards of care are especially useful in certain types of services. Theoretically, one could develop standards of care for virtually any service, but because review of such standards is time consuming it is not worth it in all cases. For example, unless your plan is experiencing a tremendous cost overrun connected with urinalyses, there will be marginal benefits to developing a protocol for when a urinalysis is required and when a urine dip test will do.

Cardiac testing is another matter. Cardiac testing, particularly stress testing and imaging, is quite expensive and increasingly common. Indications for cardiac testing have been published in medical journals, and texts and algorithms are available, but the ordering of cardiac testing sometimes defies rationality. As mentioned earlier in this chapter, a scattershot approach may be used by some physicians that results in test ordering simply as an effort to turn something up. Concentration on this service via chart reviews for appropriateness may yield interesting results and give you direction in developing standards for ordering.

In this example, it is best to approach one or more highly respected cardiologists to develop the algorithm, protocol, or standards rather than impose them from without. A well-reasoned, referenced, and well-presented approach to cardiac disease will benefit the patient and result in lower costs.

The problem with using standards of care is that it exposes you to charges of practicing cookbook medicine. If you are simply imposing arbitrary requirements on physicians, that charge has the ring of truth. If, however, you are using the best and latest in medical intelligence as well as respected journals and experts to develop the standards, then you are simply expecting high-quality medical practice and thoughtful care of the patient.

Test of Reasonableness

If you do not have standards developed, or if you choose not to do so, there are still other approaches. The first is a continual test of reasonableness: Will the test or therapy help? In other words, will the test provide a piece of information that will have an effect on the care of the patient, or at least on the diagnosis or prognosis? In too many cases, tests are ordered only because they have always been ordered. A good example of that is the routine admission chest radiograph. Despite multiple articles in the medical literature,[9-11] admission chest radiographs get ordered for many people who do not need them. The same issue may apply to many other routine studies (eg, preoperative electrocardiograms[12] or laboratory screening[13] for otherwise healthy patients).

Another example is long-term PT for patients who no longer show improvement but who continually complain to their physician. For example, a patient may complain of lower back pain, and a diagnostic work-up has yielded a negative result. The patient may not be losing weight or exercising as instructed but is still demanding that something be done. The physician orders PT because it is easy to do and because the patient likes the attention. This is clearly not cost effective, but it happens.

Limits on Authority To Authorize

Limiting the authority to authorize ancillary services will also help control their use. If your plan is an HMO, you can limit the authority to authorize services to the PCP only. In that case, a consultant must discuss the case with the PCP, and the PCP must actually order the test or therapy. This is not always practical, and there are legitimate reasons in some plans to allow certain consultants to order ancillary services; for example, orthopedists need to be able to order x-rays.

On the other hand, as discussed earlier in this chapter, you need to watch out for the physician who has purchased an expensive piece of equipment and is hoping to increase revenue from its use. In those cases, allowing the physician to bill the plan for tests or procedures done with that equipment may cause problems. Again, one must be reasonable in this. Certain specialists use certain pieces of equipment routinely (eg, gastroenterologists use colonoscopes), and you

may not want to hamper that unduly. What you do want to avoid is paying for someone else's amortization needs.

Limits on Services Authorized

Another standard feature of managed care is limiting the number of visits for therapy without prior approval. This refers not only to having a limited number of visits that are covered in your schedule of benefits but to having a limitation on the number of visits that a member may receive without reauthorization.

For example, you may allow up to three or four visits to PT, but for any more the PCP must receive a case report or the therapist must discuss the case with the physician or the plan's case manager. At that point a treatment plan is developed and the correct number of visits is authorized.

There will be exceptions to this last technique. In cases where the absolute treatment need is known, proper authorizations for the entire course of treatment may be made. An example is radiation therapy or home intravenous treatments. In such cases, the treatment plan is worked out in detail before therapy is initiated. The number of treatments required and their duration is known and may be authorized at the beginning.

Failure to control prospectively the use of ancillary therapy may result in the number of treatments or visits required in a particular type of therapy exactly equaling the level of benefits your plan offers. Much preferred is a rational approach to treatment with review of the case by the member's physician or the plan's case management function (as appropriate) and a definite treatment plan with periodic reassessments required.

CONTRACTING

Closed panels have the option of bringing certain ancillary services in house. It is up to management to do the cost-benefit analysis to determine whether that is the best course of action. One thing to keep in mind, though, is that controlling utilization is no less difficult when the service is in house because referral for that service is often seen as free and certainly as convenient.

For open panel plans or closed panels that do not have the services in house, the services must be contracted for. A plan usually has its choice of hospital-based (sometimes that is the only choice), freestanding or independent, or office-based service. The choice will be made on the basis of a combination of quality, cost, access, service (eg, turnaround time for testing), and convenience for members. Unlike physician services, ancillary services usually may be limited to a small subset of providers. This allows for greater leverage in negotiating as well as greater control of quality and service.

In HMOs or plans that have absolute limitations on benefits for ancillary services, ancillary services often lend themselves to capitation. When capitating for ancillary services, you need to calculate the expected frequency of need for the service and the expected or desired cost and then spread this over the membership base on a monthly basis. Plans that allow significant benefits for out-of-network use (eg, a POS plan) may still capitate, but only for the in-network portion; out-of-network costs will have to be paid through the regular fee allowances. Simple PPOs generally are unable to capitate and must therefore depend on fee allowances.

Capitating for ancillary services clearly makes the provider of the service a partner in controlling costs and helps you budget and forecast more accurately. The benefit to the provider of the service is a guaranteed source of referrals and a steady income. In diagnostic services, great economies of scale will often be present. In those services where the provider delivering the service may be determining the need for continued services (eg, PT), capitation will remove the fee-for-service incentives that may lead to inappropriately increased utilization. As with all capitation contracts, you must take care that the service is not seen by the providers as free, which may lead to uncontrolled utilization. Again, as with all capitation arrangements, be sure that you can direct all (or at least a defined portion) of the care to the capitated provider and do not allow referrals to noncontracted providers.

Plans that do not have the option of capitating may still achieve considerable savings from discounts. Because ancillary services are often high-margin businesses, it is usually not difficult to obtain reasonable discounts or to have a negotiated fee schedule accepted for ancillary services. The exception is when there are a limited number of providers offering the service. Outside of exotic testing and therapy, this is usually not the case unless the plan is located in a rural area.

EMERGENCY DEPARTMENT

Exactly opposite the situation with ancillary services, use of the emergency department (ED) is usually at the discretion of the members themselves rather than due to referral from a physician. Physicians do refer patients to the ED, but that is only a source of inappropriate expense if the physician is using the ED as a way of avoiding seeing the patient. For the most part, when a patient is sent to the ED by a physician, it is because there is a legitimate concern that there may be a significant medical problem. There are, however, concerns about cost effective use of the ED even in that circumstance, and these are discussed later in this chapter. In those plans where the physicians are at risk for medical services, the cost of ED care must be built into that risk arrangement.

Prior Approval

Managed care plans that use PCPs to coordinate care have the opportunity to bring some measure of control to ED use. There have been some studies documenting decreased usage of ED services in PCP case manager plans,[14,15] but these studies have been most positive when looking at Medicaid populations. There is evidence that good access to primary care in and of itself lowers use of ED services,[16] so the positive effect in the Medicaid population may be more related to accessibility to care in a population with chronic access problems than to a structural method to lower utilization. In fact, there is one study involving children that was able to document only a modest reduction in ED use despite the presence of a gatekeeper system.[17] Requiring members to seek authorization from PCPs (in an

HMO or POS system) may thus yield some savings in utilization, but results may not be what you would hope to see.

Some plans ask members to call a central advice line before seeking care. This is occasionally referred to as triage, a term first used in the military to sort out which patients need immediate care and which can wait (and, in the case of war, which are going to die regardless). This function may offer advice to the member that results in avoidance of an ED visit, or it may authorize ED services but then follow up with the ED to determine the member's disposition. This latter feature has the added value to the plan of tracking possible admissions in order to notify the utilization review system.

Alternatives to the Emergency Department

There are alternatives to ED care that you may wish to explore. Late office hours will provide a lot of the care that members go to EDs to receive. If not all physicians or offices offer evening and weekend hours, those that do may wish to cover for those that do not (with appropriate compensation, of course). Freestanding urgent care centers are found in most communities. These are sometimes less expensive than EDs, but not always. Ancillary services or professional fees can erode any savings from the room charge, and again you have no control of the case. Nonetheless, you may consider contracting with an urgent care center if you can negotiate a good fee structure or a flat fee and ensure that the service will not be abused. Urgent care facilities or late office hours have a way of becoming predominantly for convenience care, and that can be expensive.

Contracting

Many plans contract for special rates with both freestanding urgent care centers and EDs of hospitals. A plan may negotiate a flat rate for all cases to remove the incentive to unbundle and upcode charges. That rate may be deeply discounted if the plan agrees preferentially to send urgent care visits to that facility through the plan's after-hours advice line, through the PCPs, or through the provider directory sent to each

member. This has the added value of service to the members because, if the discount is deep enough, the plan may be more willing to allow urgent care visits than if it is paying full charges at an ED.

Self-Referral

Except for serious or life-threatening conditions, when a person goes to an ED without seeking advice from the physician first, the cost can be quite high for a problem that did not need to be cared for in that setting, unless the plan has negotiated a deeply discounted flat rate, as discussed above.

One effective approach to the problem of members inappropriately self-referring themselves to the ED is a limitation on coverage. It has been shown that adding a deductible or copay for ED visits can reduce ED utilization without having an adverse effect on health.[18] Some plans have a higher copayment or coinsurance for ED visits than for visits to contracting urgent care centers (some of which may actually be hospital EDs) to direct where members seek care. Most plans waive the ED copay if admission is required.

Most plans also review ED claims that come in cold (ie, there is no prior authorization). If the ED visit is not found to be medically necessary, then coverage is denied. Some plans may elect to pay the claim for the first offense, especially for a new member of the plan. If that happens, the member should always get a letter explaining that payment was made but that he or she will have to get authorization first (unless it is a life-threatening condition) or future claims will be denied.

Education may have some effect on members' use of ED services. Educating members is done through the usual means of newsletters, pamphlets, the member identification card, and so forth. Some plans also promote self-help through education, self-help medical reference manuals, and the like.

Hidden Costs

There are hidden costs associated with ED visits. The ED charges themselves are made up of the room charge, testing, therapy, a professional component, and take-home items or medication. That in itself routinely runs several hundred dollars. The hidden expenses come from losing control of the patient's care.

When a member is seen in the ED, the care is often rendered by the ED medical staff. If the member needs admission, he or she may be admitted to a physician who is not participating in your plan. When that happens, you have lost control of the care of the patient and will have less impact on future events.

In those cases, you may have the option of refusing to pay the charges or paying only part of them. That will help achieve some savings, but at the cost of goodwill from the member, and you have still not controlled the actual use of services. It is far better to work hard to develop and maintain a notification system that functions reliably.

The goal of a notification system is to educate both the plan members and the staff of the local EDs that a plan physician must be notified for all cases involving plan members. When hospital administrators know that the level of reimbursement (or even reimbursement at all) will be dependent on plan notification, that will provide a strong incentive for the staff of the ED to work with you. Notification will allow participating plan physicians to gain immediate control of the case and to direct care in the most appropriate fashion.

You must take care not to make the system so difficult that proper medical care is hampered. The ED staff must understand that in serious cases, or when there is sufficient concern, they must take action as necessary. In those cases, the patient should be evaluated and treatment initiated if necessary, but the plan physician or the plan's utilization management department should be notified as soon as possible without jeopardizing the care of the patient. Certainly the ED receptionist can notify the plan physician in those cases where the ED physician is unable to leave the patient's side.

In cases where the physician has referred the member to the ED, you still want to have a system where the physician is kept aware of the course of events. At an absolute minimum, the plan physician should be required to handle an admission from the ED to avoid losing control of the care of the patient. That requirement also allows for continuity of care, and patients have a positive reaction when their own physician handles the case. Latitude must be given for the realities of covering on call. It will not always be possible for any single physician to handle all admissions, but that physician should have a coverage mechanism worked out that provides for this.

Out of Area Emergencies

Out of area emergency services are necessary to cover and present special difficulties. Fortunately, the amount of out of area expense is usually quite low in most plans, but the problem can become acute when someone is hospitalized out of area. When that happens and there is little hope that the patient will be discharged quickly, you need to make arrangements to transfer the patient to one of your participating hospitals and physicians as soon as medically feasible.

If the admission is only for a few days, or if the patient is too ill to be transferred, you will not be able to transfer the patient. If you can, however, transferring the patient back to your plan will allow you to control the case, and that can mean cutting the cost of care in half, even when the transportation is taken into account. Many plans, primarily HMOs, have specific language regarding out of area coverage that requires the member to cooperate in such transfers to maintain financial coverage.

CONCLUSION

Control of ancillary services requires controlling physicians' practice behavior. Authorization systems, standards of care, capitation arrangements, limitations of coverage, and risk/bonus arrangements are all useful. Control of the use of emergency services requires controlling member behavior. Copays, limitations on coverage, member education, and alternative settings for urgent care are all potentially useful.

REFERENCES

1. Hillman BJ, Joseph CA, et al. Frequency and costs of diagnostic imaging in office practice—a comparison of self-referring and radiologist-referring physicians. *N Engl J Med.* 1990;323:1604–1608.

2. Office of the Inspector General. *Financial Arrangements between Physicians and Health Care Businesses: Report to Congress.* Washington, DC: Dept. of Health and Human Services; 1989. Dept. of Health and Human Services Publication no. OAI-12-88-01410.

3. State of Florida Health Care Cost Containment Board. *Joint Ventures among Health Care Providers in Florida.* Tallahassee, FL: State of Florida; 1991:2.

4. *The Ethics in Patient Referrals Act—Omnibus Budget Reconciliation Act of 1989.*

5. Kassirer JP. Our stubborn quest for diagnostic certainty: a cause of excessive testing. *N Engl J Med.* 1989; 320:1489-1491.

6. Berwick DM, Coltin KL. Feedback reduces test use in a health maintenance organization. *JAMA.* 1986;255: 1450-1454.

7. Marton KI, Tul V, Sox HC. Modifying test-ordering behavior in the outpatient medical clinic. *Arch Intern Med.* 1985;145:816-821.

8. Martin AR, Wolf MA, Thibodeau LA, et al. A trial of two strategies to modify the test-ordering behavior of medical residents. *N Engl J Med.* 1980;303:1330-1336.

9. Tape TG, Mushlin AI. The utility of routine chest radiographs. *Ann Intern Med.* 1986;104:663-670.

10. Hubble FA, Greenfield S, Tyler JL, et al. The impact of routine admission chest x-ray films on patient care. *N Engl J Med.* 1985;312:209.

11. Food and Drug Administration. *The Selection of Patients for X-Ray Examinations: Chest X-Ray Screening Examinations.* Rockville, MD: National Center for Devices and Radiological Health; 1983. Dept of Health and Human Services Publication no. 83-8204.

12. Gold BS, Young ML, Kinman JL, et al. The utility of preoperative electrocardiograms in the ambulatory surgical patient. *Arch Intern Med.* 1992;152:301–305.

13. Narr BJ, Hansen TR, Warner MA. Preoperative laboratory screening in healthy Mayo patients: cost-effective elimination of tests and unchanged outcomes. *Mayo Clin Proc.* 1991;66:155–159.

14. Hurley R, Freund D, Taylor D. Emergency room use and primary care case management: evidence from four Medicaid demonstration programs. *Am J Public Health.* 1989;79:843–846.

15. Long S, Settle R. An evaluation of Utah's primary care case management program for Medicaid recipients. *Med Care.* 1988;26:1021–1032.

16. Kelman HR, Lane DS. Use of hospital emergency room in relation to use of private physicians. *Am J Public Health.* 1976;66:1189–1191.

17. Glotzer D, Sager A, Socolar D, Weitzman M. Prior approval in the emergency room. *Pediatrics.* 1991; 88:674–680.

18. O'Grady KF, Manning WG, Newhouse JP, Brook RH. The impact of cost sharing on emergency department use. *N Engl J Med.* 1985;313:484–490.

Chapter 13

Managed Mental Health and Substance Abuse Services

Donald F. Anderson and Jeffrey L. Berlant

Management of mental health and substance abuse (MH/SA) treatment and costs presents special challenges. Unique factors contributing to the challenges include the following:

- destigmatization of mental illness and chemical dependency, leading to a greater willingness on the part of the general public to seek help for these problems

- erosion of social support systems, including fragmentation of traditional extended and nuclear family structures

- increased complexity and stress in society, leading to increased incidence and expression of MH/SA symptoms

- advances in medication and psychological therapeutic techniques, resulting in ability to treat more disorders effectively

Donald F. Anderson is national practice leader for mental health benefits at William M. Mercer, Inc, a human resources consulting organization. He has extensive experience in the evaluation of managed mental health and substance abuse programs.

Jeffrey L. Berlant is medical director of psychiatric services at St Alphonsus Regional Medical Center in Boise, Idaho. He has broad experience in evaluation of both public and private sector managed mental health and substance abuse programs.

- proliferation of private hospitals as a result of high profit margins, cheap capital investment, lifting of certificate of need laws in several large states, and exemption from diagnosis-related groups

- aggressive advertising campaigns paid for by private hospital chains, often masquerading as public service announcements

Added to these pressures is the fact that many MH/SA problems tend to be chronic and recurrent, requiring periodic treatment, sometimes intensive in nature, throughout the lifetime of the affected individual. Finally, MH/SA diagnostic categories do not lend themselves to by-the-book utilization management with standardized length of stay and treatment protocols for specified diagnoses. The range of accepted treatment approaches for a given MH/SA diagnosis can be large, and severity of illness and service requirements cannot be inferred without detailed information about social context and specific symptoms.

Substantial efforts at managing MH/SA treatment and costs first emanated from health maintenance organizations (HMOs). Early HMOs for the most part were wary of MH/SA coverage. Some plans offered only diagnosis and consultation; others arranged for discounted fee-for-service care for members. The HMO Act of 1973 required only minimal MH/SA benefits, including crisis intervention and outpatient services up to 20 visits. No inpatient care, no benefits for chronic or recurrent conditions, and no benefits for chemical dependency were required. During the 1970s and 1980s, increasing numbers of HMOs expanded MH/SA benefits as a result of consumer demand and legislation enacted in a number of states requiring richer benefits.[1]

During the late 1970s and 1980s, when insurers and self-insured employers began instituting general utilization management techniques to help control their indemnity plan health benefit costs, it became clear that these approaches were far less effective in controlling MH/SA costs than other medical benefit costs. Thus the scene was set for development of a niche industry of specialized managed MH/SA organizations to contract directly with HMOs, indemnity insurers, and self-insured employers and to apply specialized techniques in managing these costs. Because employers are the ultimate payers for most MH/SA treatment managed by specialty MH/SA entities (whether in-house HMO, insurance carrier based, or freestanding), the following pages describe managed MH/SA care as it is articulated in the employer-driven market.

KEY TREATMENT PRINCIPLES

Specialized managed MH/SA care is rooted in four key principles of clinical treatment: alternatives to psychiatric hospitalization, alternatives to restrictive treatment for substance abuse, goal-directed psychotherapy, and crisis intervention.

Alternatives to Psychiatric Hospitalization

Partial hospitalization (day, evening, and/or weekend nonresidential) programs have proved to be an effective alternative to hospital inpatient treatment in many outcome studies.[2–4] In a plan with adequate coverage of treatment alternatives to inpatient services, and with informed decision making as to who can benefit from these alternatives, economical and effective treatment can be provided to acutely ill patients in a partial hospital setting.

Alternatives to Restrictive Treatment for Substance Abuse

The weight of research evidence does not support the general superiority of inpatient or residential substance abuse treatment compared to outpatient or partial hospitalization approaches.[5,6] The central question of which patients truly need inpatient treatment and which can benefit equally well from outpatient or partial hospitalization has yet to be answered definitively. In absence of support for the superiority of inpatient programs for the general treatment population, specialized managed MH/SA systems tend to emphasize the more economical alternatives.

Goal-Directed Psychotherapy

The research literature supports the effectiveness of brief, goal-directed psychotherapeutic approaches for a number of problems.[7,8] Specialized managed MH/SA care systems generally emphasize an interpersonal rather than an intrapsychic focus of therapy and place emphasis on therapy that is designed to be brief and time limited (rather than just a truncated version of long-term therapy).

Crisis Intervention

Successful managed MH/SA systems are designed to make use of crisis intervention as a key service in the overall constellation of services. Research has demonstrated that short-term, intensive support of individuals during life crises or periodic acute episodes of psychiatric illness is an effective way to diminish the incidence of future crises and can substantially reduce the inappropriate use of psychiatric care.[9]

BENEFIT PLAN DESIGN

The starting point for any managed MH/SA program is the underlying benefit plan. MH/SA benefit design, like all health benefit design, needs to address two key issues: coverage limits and incentives.

Coverage Limits

Coverage limits are essentially a fail-safe to limit benefit cost at levels beyond which the plan will not pay, even for medically necessary cost-effective treatment. Coverage limits can include maximum days, visits, or dollar amounts and can be based on levels of care (eg, inpatient, partial hospitalization, structured outpatient), types of disorder (eg, acute psychiatric, chronic, custodial, specific diagnoses), types of treatment (eg, psychosurgery, psychoanalysis, nutritionally based therapies), and/or types of providers [eg, physician; psychologist; social worker; marriage, family, and child counselor (MFCC)]. The optimal benefit design for a managed MH/SA program will provide adequate coverage for inpatient treatment and its alternatives as well as cover treatment providers from various professional disciplines.

Levels of Care

Traditional indemnity plans and many HMO plans limit coverage to inpatient hospital care and minimal outpatient care for mental health problems and inpatient detoxification and perhaps inpatient rehabilitation for substance abuse. To support a comprehensive managed MH/SA program, the benefit should cover a number of levels of care (Table 13-1).

Day/Dollar Limits

A recent survey of specialized managed MH/SA organizations (D. Anderson and K. Anderson, unpublished data, 1991) revealed current practice regarding coverage limits in plans where some degree of specialized MH/SA management is in effect (Exhibit 13-1). When asked to characterize optimal coverage limits, respondents advocated raising deductibles (to $500 individual/$1,200 family), raising mental health outpatient annual dollar limits (to $6,000 to $8,000), raising substance abuse structured outpatient annual dollar limits (to $6,000 to $12,000), and raising the lifetime MH/SA combined maximum (to $125,000 to $130,000).

Types of Disorders

Another way that some managed MH/SA plans limit plan liability is through limiting covered disorders. Survey respondents indicated considerable variation in the types of disorders covered by plans featuring MH/SA management (Table 13-2).

Some plans also exclude from coverage specific DSM III-R diagnostic categories such as learning disorders and autism as well as medical diagnoses with potential psychiatric treatment regimens such as obesity.

Types of Treatment

Many plans built around specialized MH/SA management limit specific treatments covered. Table 13-3 indicates variation among respondents as to coverage of selected types of treatment. Many plans also exclude from coverage such treatments as biofeedback and electroconvulsive therapy.

Types of Providers

Many traditional indemnity plans have covered only the services of MDs and PhDs for outpatient MH/SA psychotherapy. HMOs and man-

---

Table 13–1 Managed Mental Health Benefits: Covered Levels of Care

Mental Health	Substance Abuse
• Hospital inpatient services	• Detoxification (inpatient, noninpatient residential, and outpatient)
• Nonhospital residential treatment	• Hospital rehabilitation
• Partial hospital/day treatment	• Nonhospital residential rehabilitation
• Individual/group outpatient treatment	• Structured outpatient rehabilitation
• Crisis intervention	• Individual/group outpatient rehabilitation
• Outreach services	

Exhibit 13-1 Typical Day/Dollar Limits in Plans with Specialized MH/SA Management

Annual deductibles	$250 individual/$750 family
Annual dollar maximum	
Mental health	
Inpatient	
Residential	$25,000–$30,000
Partial hospital	
Individual/group	
outpatient	$1,200–$3,500
Substance abuse	
Inpatient	
Residential	$15,000–$20,000
Structured outpatient	$4,000–$9,000
Individual/group	
outpatient	$1,300–$1,500
Annual day/session maximum	
Mental health	
Inpatient	35–40
Residential	45–60
Partial hospital	40–45
Individual/group	
outpatient	35–40
Substance abuse	
Inpatient	30–40
Residential	35–40
Individual/group	
outpatient	35–40

Annual family out-of-pocket limit (stop loss): $4,000
Lifetime course of treatment limit (substance abuse): 2
Lifetime maximum (MH/SA combined): $45,000–$50,000

Courtesy of William M. Mercer, Inc, San Francisco, California.

Table 13-2 Typical Coverage of Disorders in Plans with Specialized MH/SA Management

Category of Disorder	Percentage of Plans Offering Coverage
DSM III-R diagnoses	100
Chronic mental disorders	71
Sexual addiction	21
DSM III-R V codes	7
Codependency	7
Nicotine addiction	7
Custodial care	0

Courtesy of William M. Mercer, Inc, San Francisco, California.

with a plan that offers no MH/SA coverage outside the managed system. For this reason, most managed MH/SA plans tend to offer point-of-service choice with differential coverage. The typical managed indemnity plan offers a zero deductible in-network benefit with a coinsurance of 20%. Out-of-network coverage typically will feature a deductible of $250 with 50% coinsurance.

Survey respondents indicated that an optimal coinsurance differential would be 40% (eg, 10% in network and 50% out of network). Managed MH/SA plans typically do not publish a preferred provider list. For practical purposes, then, coverage differentials actually apply to the plan member accessing a gatekeeper and accepting channeling to a network provider rather than accessing a provider directly without going through the gatekeeper.

UTILIZATION MANAGEMENT

Utilization management in specialized MH/SA programs falls into two general categories:

Table 13-3 Typical Coverage of Treatment Types in Plans with Specialized MH/SA Management

Category of Treatment	Percentage of Plans Offering Coverage
Brief problem-focused therapy	93
Long-term psychodynamically oriented therapy	64
Psychosurgery	15
Nutritionally based therapies	7

aged indemnity MH/SA plans have expanded coverage to a broader range of mental health professionals. Table 13-4 indicates patterns of provider coverage for plans with specialized MH/SA management. Some plans also cover pastoral counselors and family practitioners for MH/SA services.

Incentives

The greater the incentives to access and comply with the managed MH/SA system, the greater the impact. Exclusive of HMO MH/SA coverage, most employers are not comfortable

Table 13-4 Typical Coverage of Provider Types in Plans with Specialized MH/SA Management

Category of Provider	Percentage of Plans Offering Coverage
MD	100
PhD psychologist	93
MA social worker	87
MA psychiatric nurse	87
MFCC	83
MA psychologist	73
Certified alcoholism counselor	57

Courtesy of William M. Mercer, Inc, San Francisco, California.

utilization review (UR) and case management. In practice, distinctions between the two disciplines often become blurred, but it will be instructive to discuss them separately.

Utilization Review

In the mid-1980s, when an increasing number of employers had installed UR systems to help contain costs of indemnity plans, it became clear that UR conducted by nonspecialized staff with general medical background was ineffective when applied to MH/SA cases. As a response, specialized MH/SA UR developed that employed specialized staff applying MH/SA-specific utilization criteria. Specialized UR typically includes preadmission certification of inpatient MH/SA cases and concurrent review of inpatient and residential cases, and sometimes of outpatient cases, to determine the presence or absence of medical necessity of treatment. Operational characteristics of effective specialized UR programs are as follows:

- Telephone-based treatment review is conducted by credentialed MH/SA professional reviewers, usually MA-level psychiatric nurses, MA-level social workers, and PhD- or MA-level psychologists.
- Reviewers as a group are experienced in inpatient and outpatient treatment and have experience and training spanning MH/SA adults, adolescents, and children.

- Initial and concurrent review episodes involve direct contact with the primary clinician instead of, or in addition to, the facility UR nurse.
- There is readily available high-level back-up clinical supervisory staff for front-line reviewers. Such back-up staff includes, at a minimum, board-certified adult and child/adolescent psychiatrists and a certified addictionologist.
- Medical necessity/level of care criteria employed by reviewers are age and diagnosis specific and behaviorally descriptive and encompass all levels of care, including, for example, nonhospital residential programs and partial hospitalization. Criteria are tested and retested continually and modified as needed on an ongoing basis.

UR construed narrowly as determination of medical necessity is typically installed as a means of protecting against abuses in a traditional fee-for-service plan. Although specialized MH/SA UR has proved to be somewhat more effective in containing costs than nonspecialized UR, far more effective has been utilization management in conjunction with a specialized MH/SA network with point-of-service choice.[10] This comprehensive approach to managing MH/SA care generally invokes case management as the utilization management tool of choice.

Case Management

As comprehensive managed MH/SA programs have evolved during the late 1980s and early 1990s, the case management function has crystallized as a focal point for promoting cost-effective, quality MH/SA care. MH/SA case management encompasses traditional UR but extends beyond into a broader form of patient advocacy, addressing the longitudinal course of care as well as discrete episodes of intensive treatment. Comprehensive case management includes four overlapping components:

1. *promoting correct diagnosis and effective treatment*—assisting plan members to ac-

cess the best level, type, and mix of treatment; keeping alert to opportunities for enhancing the quality and efficacy of care; acting to make provider and patient aware of these opportunities (UR strives to exclude payment for unnecessarily intensive treatment, whereas case management strives to direct patients into effective forms of treatment at appropriate levels of intensity)

2. *promoting efficient use of resources*—helping the patient/family access the most effective resources with the minimum depletion of family finances and finite available insurance dollars (directing patients into effective care may be the most potent cost-saving method of all)

3. *preventing recidivism*—monitoring progress subsequent to intensive treatment episodes; encouraging and, if necessary, helping arrange for interepisode care to prevent recidivism

4. *monitoring for and containing substandard care*—identifying potential quality of care defects during treatment; investigating and, when needed, intervening to ensure remediation.

Comprehensive case management goes beyond determination of medical necessity and seeks to promote enhancement of the quality, efficacy, and continuity of care. As such, it is a more demanding discipline than simple UR. It is practiced optimally by qualified front-line case management staff with a minimum of 5 to 10 years of relevant clinical experience who are thoroughly trained in case management techniques, backed up by readily available doctoral-level advisors with relevant clinical experience (including managed care experience), and supported by well-articulated systems to assist with the case management task. Examples of such systems include the following:

• *triage systems*—every managed MH/SA system must devise a mechanism for directing cases to the proper case manager. This includes, for example, ensuring that cases with medical issues are directed to a psy-

chiatric nurse rather than to a social worker and that substance abuse cases are directed to case managers specifically qualified and experienced in this area.

• *quality screens*—diagnosis-based criteria for the use of case managers, delineating typical best practice patterns of high-quality care for specific problems as well as screens for common quality of care defects, should be employed routinely as cases are reviewed. Such screens assist in early identification of treatment plan–diagnosis mismatch as well as pinpoint more subtle opportunities to enhance quality and efficacy of care (eg, when providers may be unaware of or unwilling to use superior treatment methods).

CHANNELING MECHANISMS

A key aspect of any managed MH/SA system is a channeling mechanism to assess initially and direct an individual to the appropriate type and intensity of treatment. This gatekeeper function is crucial to the effectiveness of the managed MH/SA program and is fraught with potential implementation problems. Who should conduct the initial assessment to determine whether there is an MH/SA problem for which an evaluation and treatment plan are in order? Who should conduct a thorough clinical evaluation and formulate a treatment plan? Who should carry out the treatment plan? The candidates for some role in the gatekeeper function may include an employee assistance program (EAP), a primary care physician (PCP) in a general managed medical system, and/or a specialized MH/SA case manager and designated assessor clinician belonging to a contracted MH/SA provider network.

In practice, the gatekeeper role in a managed MH/SA system is often divided among a number of system participants. EAP counselors may be credentialed to make direct treatment referrals for certain types of cases but be required to review decisions with a case manager before making other types of referrals. PCPs may have full authority to treat mental health problems, may have authority to refer cases directly for MH/SA treatment with notification to the MH/SA managed care system, or may yield all authority over MH/SA treatment to the MH/SA manager. It is of the utmost importance that protocols detailing roles and responsibilities of all concerned are carefully worked out, understood, and agreed to.

The Employee Assistance Program As Gatekeeper

EAPs play a unique role in corporate America, serving as a wide open point of access for employees and dependents with various problems and concerns. Before the advent of specialized MH/SA systems, EAPs were often the only reliable source of information and guidance for individuals needing MH/SA services. In this role, it has long been one of the functions of the EAP to assess an individual's MH/SA status and if necessary to make a referral for treatment.

The positive aspect of involving EAP counselors as gatekeepers for the managed MH/SA benefit is that they are numerous, generally knowledgeable, and cast a wide net; they are likely to come in contact with people early, when problems of living have not necessarily grown to become major MH/SA problems. Drawbacks of assigning gatekeeper responsibilities to EAP counselors include the fact that not all are clinically credentialed and qualified, virtually none has the medical background to enable identification of medical and medication problems that may mimic or underlie MH/SA problems, and some may not be philosophically in tune with the goals of the managed MH/SA program.

The Primary Care Physician As Gatekeeper

Many managed medical care programs (including many HMOs) restrict direct access to mental health practitioners and require the approval of the PCP before mental health specialists may be consulted. In some managed care programs, the PCP is expected to diagnose and treat common, uncomplicated mental disorders.

The advantage of investing gatekeeping responsibility with the PCP is that it encourages continuity of care and concentrates authority over preventing unnecessary use of all specialty services in the hands of one person. A major disadvantage of using PCPs as gatekeepers for MH/SA services is that medical clinicians have been shown to be dramatically less likely to detect or treat mental disorders than mental health specialists.[11] Historically, HMOs have gradually acknowledged the value of allowing direct access to mental health services. A recent longitudinal study of a large number of HMOs demonstrated that only 22% of HMOs allowed self-referral for mental health services in their first 2 years of existence, 51% allowed self-referral after 2 to 5 years, and 80% allowed self-referral after 16 years.[12]

The Mental Health/Substance Abuse Case Manager and Assessor As Gatekeepers

Most specialized managed MH/SA systems are organized to utilize some combination of case managers and designated assessor-clinicians within the contracted provider network as gatekeepers/channelers to appropriate treatment. Some systems rely on case managers to conduct a fairly detailed initial assessment over the telephone and to make referrals for treatment on that basis for all but the most complex cases, which are referred to a field clinician for further evaluation. Other systems routinely channel virtually every case to one of a group of specially designated assessors for detailed face-to-face evaluation and treatment planning.

In either instance, important triaging occurs at the outset. Many systems are able to case match referrals to assessors or treatment clinicians on the basis of the therapist's specialty interests, gender of the therapist, language and ethnicity requirements, and so forth. Among systems that encompass a broad spectrum of mental health providers (eg, MD, PhD, MSW, RN), few have developed a practical theory or usable criteria for matching cases to specific provider disciplines.

PROVIDER NETWORKS

Assembling and administering a specialized MH/SA provider network involves a more labor-intensive selection and monitoring process than is usually required for a general medical provider network. Some of the criteria could apply to any network; examples are geographic accessibility, inclusion of full continuum of care, willingness to negotiate favorable rates in exchange for channeling of patients, willingness to cooperate with utilization management procedures and standards, and structural evidence of quality such as appropriate credentials, current licensure, certification, and the like. Some other issues related to continuum of services, practice patterns, and practice philosophy are uniquely relevant to specialized MH/SA networks.

Network Development Staff

All managed MH/SA organizations offering a specialized network-based product employ network development staff dedicated to assembling and administering networks of contracted MH/SA providers. These staff may be located at a central administrative location or at several local offices throughout the region or country, but typically they reside in the local area of a network during its start-up phase. Network development staff typically includes experienced MH/SA clinicians, who are responsible for evaluating clinical skills of prospective network members, and individuals experienced in managed care administration and provider contracting, who are responsible for negotiating contract terms and administering the network after it is established.

Network Development Process

Generally, managed MH/SA organizations adhere to a network development process that includes the following steps.

Establish the Size and Scope of the Network

To pinpoint the size and scope of the network, the organization must take into account the benefit design to be administered (ie, the range of provider types covered), the demographic characteristics of the population to be served, area geographic characteristics (eg, physical or psychologic barriers to provider access), and any specific payer requirements related to the size and composition of the network.

The above factors influence the characteristics of a network in any particular area, but certain general rules of thumb apply across most specialized MH/SA networks:

1. No plan member has driving time of more than:
   - 1 hour to a full-service hospital
   - 30 minutes to an emergency room
   - 30 minutes to an outpatient SA program
   - 30 minutes to an individual provider
   - 30 minutes to an assessor
2. Network coverage ratios should be at least
   - 1 individual provider per 1,000 covered members
   - 1 assessor per 3,000 covered members
3. The distribution of network providers by discipline generally falls within these ranges: psychiatrists, 20% to 30%; PhD psychologists, 20% to 30%; MA-level providers (psychologists, social workers, nurses, MFCCs), 40% to 60%.

Assess and Determine Fees/Rates

Providers in the area to be developed are surveyed to determine current prevalent fees by discipline and sometimes by procedure within discipline. From analysis of these data, maximum fees are usually fixed at a standard by discipline across the entire network in the given geographic area. Individual provider fees are usually pegged at a level reflecting approximately a 10% discount from the median. Some organizations actually establish the maximum fee at the 75th or 80th percentile, arguing that it is more cost effective to pay close to top dollar to attract the best practitioners but to be vigilant when it comes to evaluating practice philosophy and practice patterns. Hospital and substance abuse treatment program rates typically are not fixed but are negotiated on a program-by-program basis. Typical discounts for these programs are in the range of 25% to 40% of regular charges and are usually contracted on an all-inclusive per diem basis.

Identify Targeted Providers

Once the size of the network and fees are established, the task is to identify providers who will actually be enrolled in the network. Important factors in identifying the targeted group include minimizing disruption of ongoing therapeutic relationships for the plan population to be served, identifying providers who have a good reputation in the community for quality and competence, and identifying providers who are likely to work compatibly in a managed care environment.

Good sources of information about providers include payer (employer or insurer) staff, who can identify providers historically utilized by plan members and who probably have some knowledge of specific MH/SA providers; EAP counselors, who have ongoing relationships with MH/SA providers to whom they have referred patients; and community providers with whom the MH/SA organization itself has had favorable past experience. If these sources are not available or are not sufficient to identify a large enough target group, less selective sources such as professional association listings, state licensing registers, or the phone book are used.

Contact Providers

Once a targeted group of providers is identified, contact is made by mail or telephone. Information about network requirements and potential channeling of patients is provided, and providers are invited to indicate interest. Depending on how much advance work has been done to identify likely candidates, response rates range from 10% to 50%.

*Obtain In-Depth Information via
    Application*

Providers expressing interest in network membership are asked to complete a detailed application. Although the content and length of application forms vary, forms generally cover such areas as credentials, certification, licensure, spe-

cialization/specialized training, years of experience, treatment philosophy, hours available, percentage of practice available to network subscribers, fees, and so forth.

Conduct a Site Visit/Interview

Anywhere from 10% to 30% of providers completing the application typically are eliminated as a result of failure to pass the screening process (most MH/SA organizations have a formalized set of screens that are applied to applications to narrow the field of eligible network participants). Virtually all organizations conduct an in-person site visit to facility-based programs before approving them for network membership. With individual providers, there is considerably more variation. Many organizations rely completely on written applications, some include a telephone interview, some conduct face-to-face site visits/interviews for selected providers, and a few require site visits/interviews for any individual provider admitted to the network. Some common selection criteria are listed in Exhibit 13-2.

Select Providers for Network

Results of analysis of applications, interviews, and site visits typically are reviewed formally by a credentialing committee that includes top-level clinical and administrative staff. Approved providers receive a contract, the final terms of which are negotiated by network development staff with oversight from top-level operations and legal staff. Managed MH/SA contracting issues do not differ significantly from those involved in general managed care contracting, which are dealt with in Chapters 5 and 36.

QUALITY ASSURANCE

Quality assurance (QA) refers to activities designed to prevent and/or correct quality problems. In managed MH/SA systems, core QA activities are focused on the qualifications and behavior of case managers and providers and (to some extent) on the treatment results achieved by providers. The following is a delineation of common elements of internal QA programs for

Exhibit 13-2 Common Selection Criteria for Providers

Facilities
- must provide a continuum of levels of care (not only acute inpatient)
- average length of stay for acute inpatient cases < 10 days

Psychiatrists
- accustomed to filling medication management role in conjunction with other therapists handling individual therapy
- usual practice pattern involves referring patients to psychologists and social workers for individual therapy
- work primarily with serious, complicated conditions

Psychologists
- usual practice pattern involves referring to physician for medication evaluation when appropriate
- do not routinely test all patients unless specifically indicated

Social Workers
- demonstrated experience in treating socio-familial issues
- experienced with assessment, especially in community mental health center settings

Nurses
- some general medical nursing experience
- demonstrated current knowledge of psychopharmacology

All practitioners
- knowledge, experience, and training in goal-focused, brief therapy techniques
- experienced in multidisciplinary treatment approaches
- routinely use peer support system to discuss difficult cases
- demonstrated familiarity with community resources

Courtesy of William M. Mercer, Inc, San Francisco, California.

---

managed MH/SA organizations. Medical/surgical quality assurance activities are discussed in Chapter 15.

Utilization Review/Case Management

Internal QA programs should include the following elements designed to ensure quality in the UR/case management process:

- *credentialing/recredentialing*—typical requirements are that case managers have at least MA-level MH/SA clinical credentials, have a minimum of 3 to 5 years of clinical experience, and maintain current licensure and certification to practice. Many organizations consistently exceed these standards in practice; for example, it is not uncommon for incumbent case managers in a given setting to average 10 to 15 years of clinical experience at various levels of care.

- *clinical rounds*—staff must participate in educationally oriented interdisciplinary conferences that include senior clinical staff.

- *formal supervision*—provision must be made for regular direct supervision and coaching of case managers by clinically qualified supervisors.

- *clinical audits*—routine internal audits of case management notes must be performed with attention to administrative and clinical performance, routine feedback to case managers, and individualized remedial activities when standards are not met.

- *data tracking*—staff-specific, diagnosis-specific outcome data must be tracked (eg, average length of stay) with comparison to norms, analysis of implications for case management technique, and feedback to case managers.

- *inservice training*—inservice training programs for case managers must be shaped and driven by the findings of the internal QA monitoring system.

Network Providers

Internal QA systems in MH/SA programs should include the following elements to ensure quality in the provider network:

- *credentialing/recredentialing*—minimum requirements usually include academic credentialing, licensure, certification, confirmation of criterion-level malpractice insurance, and clearing of malpractice history. Some organizations independently check licensure directly with state licensing boards and perform direct checks on legal actions concerning malpractice. Re-credentialing should be done on a continual basis (eg, every 2 years), including systematic reminders to providers when current licensure or insurance is about to expire.

- *case manager ratings*—routine global ratings of providers by case managers per contact episode must be based on cost effectiveness, quality of care, and cooperativeness with the managed care system.

- *provider profiling*—diagnosis-based provider profiling must be based on measures of cost and utilization with feedback to providers on network norms. This topic is also addressed in Chapter 16.

- *treatment chart audits*—there must be routine audits of provider treatment charts, often focused on profile outliers, with feedback to providers.

- *provider communications*—these include bulletins, newsletters, memoranda, and so forth to network providers addressing administrative and clinical issues; these are driven by findings of the internal QA system.

- *provider education*—provision must be made for formal education programs for providers driven by findings of the internal QA system.

- *provider satisfaction surveys*—the plan must conduct routine monitoring of network provider satisfaction with clinical and administrative requirements of the managed care system and provide the opportunity for constructive suggestions for system changes.

- *outcome monitoring*—there must be diagnosis-specific, provider-specific tracking of outcome measures including patient satisfaction, recidivism/relapse, mental and/or physical health status change, mental and/or physical claims costs, and functional change (through employer-based data such as absenteeism rates and productivity measures).

External Quality Assurance Monitoring

It has been suggested that the incentives and conflicts of interest inherent in a managed MH/SA program are too great to be overcome entirely by internal self-regulation. In recognition of this problem, some state and federal regulatory agencies and employer/payers have instituted routine external quality monitoring of managed MH/SA systems. This issue is also discussed in Chapters 15 and 21.

The results of such external auditing activity reveal considerable variation in performance among managed MH/SA organizations and within organizations over time and at different service delivery locations. Some examples of variation and common weaknesses in systems are as follows.

Utilization Criteria

Most organizations have criteria that specify clear behavioral criteria for various levels of care. Some organizations, however, have adopted criteria that do not provide clear guidance to the case manager. In these cases, general, nonbehavioral (sometimes tautologic) criteria are difficult to apply with any precision. In some other instances, criteria are clear but inefficient. For example, some organizations use published 50th percentile norms to assign initial lengths of stay, thus missing the opportunity to influence cases for which earlier discharge would be achievable.

Staff Qualifications

Some organizations lack case managers or even supervisory personnel with relevant MH/SA background and experience. Some lack doctoral-level advisors who can engage in matched peer review with doctoral-level treaters. Some programs have MDs without psychiatric or substance abuse background functioning as psychiatric medical directors.

Inservice Training

Some organizations select inservice training programs on the basis of apparently random or arbitrary topic selection rather than needs identified through an internal QA system. Many have no inservice training, orientation, or QA oversight applied to doctoral-level advisors. Some have no discernible inservice training program at all.

Quality of Care Problem Identification

Analysis of random samples of case management notes in more than 40 audits of managed MH/SA systems has consistently confirmed clinically significant identifiable quality of care problems in 25% to 50% of cases.[13] Problems range from misdiagnosis, to subtherapeutic or toxic medication dosages, to unexplored medical complications, to mismatch of diagnosis and treatment plan. In some programs, detection of and action on these problems occur in a small minority of cases. Action by doctoral-level advisors on problems that are identified by case managers in these programs can also be a too rare occurrence.

Provider Credentialing

In the most minimal level of QA for a provider network, the MH/SA system warrants to payers and direct consumers that all network providers meet certain baseline credentialing standards. Some programs fail thoroughly to document and independently to confirm credentialing when providers are admitted to the network, and many programs fail consistently to recredential on a continuing basis to ensure that network members continue to meet basic requirements.

Outcomes Tracking

The ultimate gateway to true continuous quality improvement in managed MH/SA programs is keyed to the reliable measurement of treatment outcomes and analysis of the relationship among treatment outcome, treatment approach, provider type, and case management technique. Many MH/SA programs have recently begun to track treatment outcomes in a number of ways. There is, however, great variation among programs in the degree of conceptual development of these approaches and in the sophistication of information systems available to put data to use in an effective QA system.

CONCLUSION

This chapter outlines some of the key aspects, issues, and recent developments in specialized managed care programs addressing MH/SA treatment. In overview, MH/SA presents unique management problems that are increasingly being addressed through specialized managed care systems with specific and separate operational guidelines, managed care personnel, provider networks, and QA approaches.

REFERENCES

1. Bennett MJ. The greening of the HMO: implications for prepaid psychiatry. *Am J Psychiatr.* 1988;145:1544–1549.

2. Schene AH, Gersons VP. Effectiveness and application of partial hospitalization. *Acta Psychiatr Scand.* 1986;74:335–340.

3. Rosie JS. Partial hospitalization: a review of recent literature. *Hosp Community Psychiatr.* 1987;38:1291–1299.

4. Mosher LR. Alternatives to psychiatric hospitalization. *N Engl J Med.* 1983;309:1579–1580.

5. Annis HM. Is inpatient rehabilitation of the alcoholic cost effective? A composition. *Adv Alcohol Subst Abuse.* 1986;5:175–190.

6. Saxe L, Goodman L. *The Effectiveness of Outpatient vs Inpatient Treatment: Updating the OTA Report.* Hartford, CT: Prudential Insurance Company; 1988.

7. Husby R, Dahl AA, Dahl CI, Heiberg AN, Olafsen OM, Weisaeth L. Short-term dynamic psychotherapy: prognostic value of characteristics of patients studies by a two-year follow-up of 39 neurotic patients. *Psychother Psychosom.* 1985;43:8–16.

8. Horowitz MJ, et al. Comprehensive analysis of change after brief dynamic psychotherapy. *Am J Psychiatr.* 1986;143:582–589.

9. Whittington HG. Managed mental health: clinical myths and imperatives. In: Feldman S, ed. *Managed Mental Health Services.* Springfield, IL: Thomas; 1992:223–243.

10. Anderson D. How effective is managed mental health care? *Bus Health.* November 1989:34–35.

11. Wells KB, et al. Detection of depressive disorder for patients receiving prepaid or fee-for-service care. *JAMA.* 1989;262:3298–3302.

12. Shadle M, Christianson JB. The organization of mental health care delivery in HMOs. *Admin Mental Health.* 1988;15:201–225.

13. National Medical Audit, proprietary managed MH/SA system audit database.

Chapter 14

Pharmaceutical Services in Managed Care

Henry F. Blissenbach

Before 1973, pharmacy, as a covered benefit, was not a noticeable part of the benefit dollar. Often it was not even a standard component of the benefit. The trend toward inclusion of a prescription drug benefit as part of a managed care plan's benefit package, however, has created an environment for pharmaceutical services that has evolved from health maintenance organizations (HMOs) to self-insured employers and indemnity insurance plans.

In tandem with this desire to include drug coverage as a benefit has been the growing number of medications available to improve the quality and quantity of life. As with all components of health care, the drug costs associated with acute treatment and maintenance therapy increase annually. Throughout the entire health care industry, prescription costs are placing a financial stress on payers and budget managers of

Henry F. Blissenbach is President of Diversified Pharmaceutical Services (DPS), a wholly owned subsidiary company of United HealthCare corporation in Minneapolis, Minnesota. DPS maintains a leadership position in the management of prescription drug programs for both United HealthCare and non–United HealthCare health maintenance organizations and employer groups, and comprises more than 5 million members. Dr. Blissenbach also holds an academic appointment at the University of Minnesota College of Pharmacy.

health care plans. To the individual who has health care coverage and a prescription drug benefit as part of that coverage, medications are considered part of that to which they are entitled. The economics of a prescription drug benefit, however, require continued assessment of the appropriateness and necessity of therapeutic expenditures and subsequent aggressive, and sometimes controversial, interventions to manage cost.

The challenge to an appropriate pharmaceutical management program is to control costs without adversely affecting the quality of care and, equally important, providers' and recipients' perceptions of the quality of care. To decrease, cut back, not cover, or omit something previously perceived as a benefit is not well accepted by plan members. Additionally, providers often perceive these same changes as a threat to their independence to practice medicine or pharmacy.

Managing a pharmaceutical benefit requires an understanding of the components of that benefit. When we contract with members of our managed care organizations to provide a quality drug benefit, we mean that we will allow physicians to prescribe medicines that will either cure acute illness or increase the quantity and improve the quality of life of individuals with chronic illness. Our responsibility is to contain the cost of these medicines without depriving individuals of necessary medicines.

COST OF DRUGS

Are drug costs too high? Certainly the percentage of the total health care expenditure that pharmaceuticals represent is a highly scrutinized area of economic concern to the public, the payers, and the policy makers. The pharmaceutical industry as a whole, including the manufacturers, wholesalers, and dispensers of the product, has been widely criticized because drug products are perceived to be expensive without adequate evidence of cost effectiveness. Yet, as Dr P. Roy Vagelos, chairperson and chief executive officer at Merck and Company, states, "even if each of the medicines that may eventually be found to prevent or treat diseases become tremendous commercial successes and generate one billion dollars a year in sales, patient cost for the medicines would be far less than the cost of the diseases."[1(p1080)]

The producer price index (PPI) and the consumer price index (CPI) are the two barometers typically used to measure price changes over time. Both have been quoted frequently over the past several years to demonstrate escalating pharmaceutical costs. The PPI measures change over time of the prices received by manufacturers, suppliers, or producers of products. Although the PPI for all prescription products grew 78.3% between 1981 and 1986, in recent years the percentage increase has fallen below the 10.1% per year average between 1981 and 1986 to approximately 9.0%.

The CPI measures the average change in retail prices paid by consumers for the product. The CPI further differentiates drug products according to their product type. Prescription drugs are reflected in the CPI-Rx. Between 1981 and 1986, this component increased by almost 80.0%, an average rate of 10.2%. As with the PPI, the CPI-Rx average dropped during subsequent years. After a slight increase in 1989 to 9.5%, the CPI-Rx has maintained at about 9.0%.

What does this mean in terms of overall cost to the managed care organization when providing a drug benefit program? As Table 14-1

shows, since 1988, when drug expenditures accounted for approximately 6% of the premium, drug costs have accounted for approximately 10% of operating expenses. Since that time, drug costs as a percentage of operating expenses have continued to run higher than drug expenditures as a percentage of premium. In other words, managed care organizations have seemingly been reluctant to charge the premium payer an amount equivalent to the percentage of operating expense that the drug benefit consumes. Hence for most managed care organizations offering a pharmacy benefit, the drug benefit program has served as somewhat of a loss leader.

As we will see throughout this chapter, it is becoming more important to manage the cost of the pharmaceutical benefit than to save money. If managed care organizations choose to continue to operate at a loss for the drug benefit program, managing the amounts of these losses becomes paramount.

THE PHARMACY BENEFIT

Before we discuss policies, procedures, and services necessary to ensure successful management of the pharmacy benefit, we need to review

Table 14-1 Drug Expenditures as Percentage of Premium and Operating Expenses

			Type of Managed Care Organization		
Year	Total	Staff	Network	Individual Practice Association	Group
Percentage of Premium					
1988	6.0	3.4	5.4	6.9	6.8
1989	5.5	4.0	5.5	5.7	5.9
1990	6.2	5.1	6.2	6.3	6.9
1991	7.1	5.9	7.9	7.1	6.8
Percentage of Operating Expenses					
1988	10.0	5.0	12.0	11.0	15.0
1989	10.0	5.0	10.0	11.0	10.0
1990	9.0	6.0	10.0	9.0	11.0
1991	11.0	9.0	10.0	11.0	10.0

Source: Marion Merrell Dow Digest 1991.

what a managed care pharmacy benefit includes. Each member of a managed care organization that offers a prescription drug benefit can receive prescriptions as a covered benefit as long as the following criteria ordinarily are met:

- The individual must be eligible for coverage by the managed care organization. An eligible member is the primary card holder or dependent of the card holder. The eligible member or employee usually must present identification designating that he or she is a member of that managed care organization.

- In some cases, the prescription must be written by a contracted prescriber (ie, an eligible prescriber on record with the HMO). When the managed care organization closes its physician prescriber list and requires prescriptions to be written only by contracted physicians, the pharmacist must determine eligibility.

- Prescriptions for over-the-counter medications are ordinarily not covered; only prescriptions that are legend will be covered. A legend drug is one labeled "Caution: Federal law prohibits dispensing without a prescription." Even if the medication is a legend drug, however, that does not necessarily mean that it is covered. Many legend medications are not covered. Additionally, some managed care organizations require specific guidelines to be followed and criteria met before authorization to fill the prescription is rendered.

- Prescriptions must be filled at designated pharmacies; these are drug stores that have a contractual agreement with the managed care organization. The covered member cannot take the prescription into any drug store to have it filled but must remain within the network.

- Medications eligible for coverage by the managed care organization must be contained in the HMO's drug formulary.

- If the medication is available generically, it will be reimbursed at a generic rate and probably will be dispensed as a generic equivalent. Almost always, the member has the option of paying the difference between the generic and the branded cost.

- For the member to receive the prescription, a deductible or copay is usually required. Members are expected to pay a portion of the cost of their prescriptions.

CERTIFICATE OF COVERAGE

The pharmacy benefit is typically defined in a document called the certificate of coverage or certificate of benefits that the HMO provides to the member to describe his or her covered health care benefits. Before any cost management or cost containment procedures can be implemented, the benefit certificate must have language to allow these procedures. Once benefit language changes are in place, these need to be communicated and explained to members and to providers. This entire process often takes considerable time for approval and implementation. Many cost management efforts can be accomplished without changes being required in the certificate of coverage, however.

The certificate typically addresses the fact that medications are eligible for coverage if they meet certain criteria and are medically necessary and appropriate for treatment of the illness. Generally, the treatment must also be consistent with medical standards of the community and prevent the patient's condition from worsening. The fact that a provider recommends a certain medication or service does not necessarily mean that the service is eligible for coverage under the contract.

Typically excluded from pharmacy benefit programs are services or prescription drugs that the managed care organization determines to be experimental or unproven, services or prescription drugs that are not generally accepted by the medical community as a standard of care, and others. Typical exclusions include anorexant drugs, cosmetic medications, and vitamins. All managed care organizations allow the member an appeal process should there be a disagreement with a coverage decision.

Do therapeutic qualifications alone automatically qualify a drug for coverage? Covered drug decisions can also be based on a determination that an individual's life will be better in terms of quantity or quality. In other words, quality and outcome qualifications can be included when coverage of a medication is determined.

MANAGED HEALTH CARE AND THE PHARMACY BENEFIT

When one refers to a prescription drug benefit, ordinarily the implication is that someone other than the recipient is paying for the benefit. In other words, the receiver of the service is not the payer for the prescription. Although there are still a significant number of individuals who pay for their prescriptions out of their own pocket, the largest segment of these is represented by the over 60 retired community. The percentage of the population that has partial or total prescription drug coverage is increasing yearly, however.

How the Benefit Is Received

There are several ways that prescription services are obtained, and each of these has its own characteristic method of payment.

Recipient of Service Pays Entire Cost of Prescription

Until recently, this was the most common way that prescriptions were obtained. The recipient would call or visit the physician, the physician would write a prescription, and the recipient would take the prescription to a drug store, have it filled, and pay the cost of the product plus the service. Competition then entered the pharmacy marketplace, driving some of the product and service fees downward and somewhat decreasing prescription costs.

Partial Pay for Both Recipient and Third Party

Partial payment plans for drug benefit programs usually require an identification card designating eligibility. These programs are further classified as managed or unmanaged programs. The managed card program traditionally has been associated with HMOs. More recently, for

quality and cost reasons, self-insured employers and even indemnity insurance plans with prescription drug riders are moving from unmanaged to managed card programs.

Prescription drug benefit programs with a partial payment requirement on the part of the recipient are increasing in popularity, and variations in the partial pay amount are significant factors in enabling the payer to manage the drug benefit cost. The common variations are as follows:

1. *Copayments*—typically these are handled at the point of service. This mechanism requires a designated dollar amount in exchange for the product or service. In other words, a prescription is presented at the pharmacy, and upon delivery of the prescription to the recipient, the recipient pays a copayment amount. Sometimes the copayment is the same for a branded or generic, formulary or nonformulary prescription; other times there is a higher copay for branded than generic drugs. The copayment may vary from $3.00 to $20.00 per prescription, with lower copays being more common.

2. *Deductibles*—typically these are associated with indemnity insurance plans and sometimes with self-insured employer groups. They are gaining popularity in HMOs and preferred provider organizations (PPOs), particularly now that calculation and notification of up-to-date deductibles via on-line point-of-service claims processing systems are common. The prescription deductible, like any other medical service deductible, requires a designated out-of-pocket expenditure before the pharmacy benefit coverage comes into effect. Although the deductible should be approximately 25% to 35% of the annual drug cost, because these are prospectively determined amounts they most often are underestimated and rarely reach an appropriate percentage of partial payment. In the past, insurers and other payers have gambled that recipients would "shoe" box the receipt for services

and would not file a claim for the eligible amount. With the increasing cost of prescription drugs, the decreasing comparative percentage of salary increases compared to prescription cost increases, and the ease of record keeping via on-line point-of-service claims processing systems, however, the shoe box effect is becoming less and less apparent.

3. *Coinsurance*—this is most common with indemnity insurance plans. Each time the benefit is used, a designated percentage is applied to the total cost of the prescription. In other words, a drug benefit plan with 20% coinsurance would require the recipient to pay 20% of the cost of the prescription each time it is obtained. Again, because they once relied on the shoe box effect, indemnity insurance plans are finding that unmanaged drug benefit riders with coinsurance applications are experiencing high costs.

Recipient Has No Partial Payment: Third Party Pays All

This method of payment typically is associated with state and federally financed programs. In these Medicaid type programs, the recipient is not required to pay out of pocket any part of the drug benefit. There are a few exceptions to this. Some states have initiated minimal copayments ($0.25 to $1.00) on the part of the Medicaid recipient. Government funded programs are typically managed by legislative regulations, and special interest groups have made managing a drug benefit system for state Medicaid programs difficult at best. Provider reimbursement fees are usually legislated, and discounts off the average wholesale price (AWP) of the product are determined by Congress. Because federal and state funded programs have been experiencing higher drug expenditures than the private sector, however, both levels of government are requiring more management applications to these programs.

Components of a Pharmacy Benefit

A prescription drug benefit has several components. These components depend on whether the benefit is unmanaged or managed. An unmanaged program is simple to facilitate and, with minor exceptions, allows the eligible recipient to have prescriptions filled, with the pharmacy collecting the designated copay, deductible, or coinsurance.

A well-managed prescription drug benefit, on the other hand, can be complex and includes the following characteristics:

- appropriate benefit design
- point-of-service claims adjudication and processing
- a contracted and discounted pharmacy network
- an aggressive generic reimbursement program
- a cost-effective drug formulary program
- discounts from manufacturers via volume purchase or rebate programs
- financial and utilization management reporting
- budgeting appropriateness based on accurate information

THE PROVIDERS

Staff Model or Closed Panel Health Maintenance Organization

This type of HMO often employs its own pharmacist and owns its own in-house pharmacies. The HMO assumes all the risk for the prescription drug service and is the oldest form of prepaid pharmaceutical services in the country. The HMO-employed pharmacists dispense medications to plan members at HMO-owned pharmacies. The primary advantages of a staff model HMO prescription benefit are as follows:

- The HMO saves administration cost because there are no claims processed for reimbursement.
- Program changes (eg, drug formularies, copayment) are made easily because all affected providers are employed by the HMO.
- The HMO can take advantage of volume purchasing because of a large in-house prescription volume.

There are also some disadvantages:

- This system requires a considerable capital investment by the HMO to provide pharmacy space, drug inventory, and staff.
- Lack of evening and after-hours emergency service and convenient accessibility often creates problems for plan subscribers.
- Difficulty in establishing pharmacist-patient relationships is often experienced.

Some staff model HMOs also agree to cover over-the-counter (nonprescription) medications.

Independent Practice Association or Open Panel Health Maintenance Organization

The base of pharmacy benefit programs in independent practice associations (IPAs) and open panel HMOs is contracted provider networks. Pharmacies are not owned, nor is the pharmacist's salary paid by the HMO. Instead, these are established community pharmacies, freestanding from the HMO. Pharmacy participation in the limited pharmacy network is, for the most part, determined by the HMO.

Advantages include the following:

- Pharmacies are conveniently located for patient/member accessibility.
- The HMO can provide pharmaceutical benefits without a considerable investment in facility space, drug inventory, and pharmacy staff.
- The pharmacy network can expand easily as growth requirements emerge.
- The HMO can take advantage of competition in the marketplace to generate discounts.

There are also disadvantages:

- Administrative expenses increase as a result of claims processing and reimbursement.
- This decentralization of pharmaceutical services makes it more difficult to implement program, policy, and procedural changes.

- Criteria are necessary for selection of participating pharmacies to ensure nonviolation of existing laws.
- Policies regarding reimbursement for pharmacy services must be determined and established.

Preferred Provider Organization

This benefit may look like a traditional HMO benefit with an IPA flair because there is a pharmacy network that is typically contracted and limited. A PPO benefit may also resemble an indemnity insurance benefit if it is not tightly managed, although this is losing favor. Most PPOs have not been able to manage their pharmaceutical costs as well as the HMOs, primarily because PPOs tend to be more provider sensitive and have been reluctant to implement aggressive cost-management applications as have the HMOs.

Indemnity Insurance Plan

Typically unmanaged, these may utilize a prescription card program within a relatively large pharmacy network. Under this mode, all pharmacies located in the geographic service area are generally afforded the opportunity to provide pharmacy services to the indemnity insurance subscriber. Ordinarily, these operate under a pay and submit approach with little or no benefit restrictions. Mail-order pharmacy is a variable percentage of the cost. Some indemnity plans function in a major medical approach, in which the subscribers pay out of pocket and then submit claims to the insurance plan for reimbursement (after deductible and coinsurance).

Advantages of this program include the following:

- Card programs deliver some level of control over ingredient cost and dispensing fee.
- Such programs maintain a strong freedom of choice concept, preserving longstanding pharmacist-patient relationships.
- Subscribers are not forced to drive considerable distances to have their pharmaceutical needs fulfilled.

- Mail-order programs achieve good control of ingredient cost and dispensing fee and are convenient for members on long-term medications.

The following are some disadvantages:

- As one might expect, the costs associated with operating an open pharmacy network are much greater than those of the other two alternatives.
- Plans that use card programs must print and distribute administration manuals, participating pharmacy agreements, claims reimbursement forms, and the like, all of which contribute to total administrative cost.
- Such plans are unable to take advantage of competition in the marketplace to drive significantly discounted fees.
- Mail-order programs may result in waste when a prescription is changed in mid-course or when a member loses eligibility shortly after receiving a 90-day supply.

Self-Insured Benefits

The advantages and disadvantages are similar to those for indemnity insurance.

Government/Medicaid Programs

These utilize contracted pharmacy networks and have the same advantages and disadvantages discussed above. They are usually card and point-of-service programs and are typically unmanaged.

DETERMINING PHARMACEUTICAL BENEFIT COSTS

How does one determine the true cost of a pharmaceutical benefit? How should that benefit be priced? What is its overall value? How does your cost compare to that of other managed care organizations and competitors? Trying to provide a pharmacy benefit program without knowing the answers to these questions puts managers at a distinct disadvantage.

Before management approaches can be initiated to control pharmaceutical expenditures, it is necessary that managed care understand the cost

of that product and the degree of responsibility that each of the components of that cost has to the overall bottom line.

The cost of pharmacy benefit can be determined by applying the following formula:

$$\text{Total drug cost} =$$
$$(\text{ingredient cost} + \text{dispensing fee} - \text{copay})$$
$$\times \text{number of prescriptions}$$

Total drug costs can be calculated either as a per member per month (PMPM) or per member per year (PMPY) expenditure. The actual prescription cost is represented by the values in parentheses (ingredient cost + dispensing fee–copay). If the intent is to decrease overall pharmacy benefit expenditures, we need to determine the percentages that each component represents. Although the prescription cost is often the cost indicator, PMPM costs are a more accurate indicator. An example is illustrated in Exhibit 14-1.

The next step is to determine high or low status and to react accordingly. As you can see by the above formula, there are several ways to reduce or control the PMPM cost:

- *Reduce ingredient cost*—this is accomplished by maximizing generic substitution, reimbursing for generics only according to a maximum allowable cost (MAC) list, implementing a drug formulary, and using volume purchase (rebate) contracting.
- *Decrease dispensing fees*—take advantage of the competition in the marketplace to ensure the lowest acceptable dispensing fee.
- *Increase copays*—increase the member's (or subscriber's) out-of-pocket responsibil-

Exhibit 14-1 Illustration of PMPM Drug Cost

Assume:
  Ingredient cost = $18.00
  Dispensing fee = $2.50
  Copay = $7.00
  Number of prescriptions = 0.6 PMPM

Then:
  PMPM drug cost = ($18.00 + $2.50 − $7.00) × 0.6
               = $9.30

ity for a portion of the drug benefit. This can act as a disincentive for utilizing the drug benefit.

- *Decrease the number of prescriptions*—the total number of prescriptions written by physicians multiplies the prescription cost. Outlier prescribers, once identified, can be evaluated for cost effectiveness and notified if appropriate.

MANAGING THE PHARMACY BENEFIT

Adequately and appropriately managing a pharmacy benefit consists of two integral pieces: management of the cost and management of the quality of that benefit. Successful pharmacy benefit management applications have proven that drug costs can be managed without adversely affecting quality of care.

Benefit Design

The manner in which the pharmacy benefit is designed determines how the pharmacy benefit works. Simply stated, the benefit identifies for both the member and the provider the terms and extent of the coverage. All determinants of coverage hinge on the benefit design. The actual benefit design depends on several factors: competition, government regulations and requirements, union or employer specifications, dollars available, and the like. The real art of prescription benefit design is choosing where to save money and where compromises are possible. The benefit design should define prescription medications, describe refill restrictions if any, list products or services excluded from the benefit, state payment responsibilities of the member, specify limits on the amount of medications allowed with each transaction, and identify approved prescribers and providers. Also, generic and formulary requirements as well as allowances for investigational or experimental medications should be listed.

Claims Adjudication

Once the benefit design has been finalized, a process must be implemented to reimburse for benefit coverage. Whether the pharmacist adjudicates the claim electronically or a claims processor at the plan performs this task, this procedure includes the following:

- verification of eligibility on the basis of enrollment information provided by the payer
- verification of coverage on the basis of the benefit design of the group
- verification of copay
- verification of reimbursement amount to the pharmacy in accordance with prearranged or contracted specifics

Enrollment Information/Eligibility Verification

Of utmost importance is the verification of eligibility before a claim is paid. Until recently, eligibility verification at the point of sale was not required or even possible. In fact, it was not unusual for many plans to pay pharmacy claims without having adequate eligibility or enrollment information to determine whether the submitted claim was eligible for reimbursement. Hand in hand with member eligibility goes prescriber (ie, physician) eligibility. Although still not the standard, a requirement to determine prescriber eligibility and the entering of a prescriber identification number as part of the claims processing are important parts of managing pharmaceutical costs.

Eligibility verification is accomplished simply: The member presents an eligibility card, and the provider verifies the member as eligible. Although some plans use printed eligibility lists, more and more pharmacies are moving to online point-of-service eligibility verification and claims processing.

Electronic Claims Adjudication

Not so long ago, all pharmacy claims were submitted on paper. The primary disadvantage was that, although the recipient of the prescription could present an identification card indicating eligibility for coverage, often eligibility had terminated without adequate notification to the provider; or the pharmacist would have a claim returned without payment with a designated ineligible reason; or incorrect payment was received by the pharmacist; or the wrong amount of copayment was collected. All these increased the frustration level of the pharmacist and often put members at odds with the pharmacist in terms of who owes money to whom.

Electronic claims processing eliminates all these and allows for the point-of-service coordination of benefit services such as deductible, copayment, and coverage limits. When the pharmacist enters the prescription on line, that pharmacist receives up-to-date eligibility status and knows that acceptance by the on-line system ensures payment. Additionally, the delay in receiving payment for the prescription is decreased significantly, and rejected claims are eliminated.

Interestingly, the driving force behind point-of-service eligibility systems has not been the pharmacist but the payer.[2] Cost-containment pressures are forcing health care plans to take a hard look at the cost of paying for bad claims. Most payers are including a point-of-service requirement as part of pharmacy network contracting.

Pharmacy Provider Networks

Limitations on the number of pharmacies to provide services for enrolled members are typical of managed care plans. Like hospital and physician networks, pharmacist networks have been limited to provide a network exchanging volume for price. Limiting the pharmacy network allows the HMO to accomplish two objectives: lower dispensing fees and improved compliance with policies and procedures. In most large cities, the available pharmacy network is generally larger than necessary to fill the prescriptions of the plan's membership. Managed care organizations will take advantage of that competitive marketplace to obtain discounts. Reimbursement is a function of supply and demand.

Part of the pharmacy benefit cost management process is an analytical evaluation of the current pharmacy network. According to the *Marion Merrell Dow Digest*,[3] all model types of HMOs increased their reliance on contracted pharmacies in 1990. Only 11% of HMOs utilize in-house pharmacies to fill prescriptions, 74% use contracted pharmacies, and 14% use a com-

bination of in-house and contracted pharmacies. More HMOs use a combination of chain and independent drugstores, and there has been a yearly increase in the use of drugstore chains.

For the contractual arrangement to be successful, the payer must be willing to restrict covered members' access to pharmacies. When this happens, there may be an initial negative reaction. If the plan is large enough, one can also expect the local pharmacist associations to organize against the plan's decision. When a plan is deciding to decrease the pharmacy network, the negative reaction should be weighed carefully against the benefit. The standard within the managed care industry, however, is to provide the pharmacy benefit through a restricted pharmacy network.

Mail-order pharmacy seems to be increasing in popularity nationally, although its popularity within managed care organizations, particularly HMOs, is questionable. Employers offering a self-insured pharmacy benefit have offered mail order usually as an option. This has also been an especially popular method for retirees to receive prescriptions at a discounted rate. Those managed care organizations offering mail order as a component of the pharmacy benefit should require the mail-order dispenser to follow the same policies and procedures as the rest of the pharmacy provider network. Formularies, MAC reimbursement, eligibility verification, copay collections, and all other procedures must be followed. Usually, the mail-order companies are willing to compete even more aggressively than the members of the pharmacy network.

The final type of prescription vendor is the physician dispenser. Several companies offer repackaging services to physicians' offices as part of a system to dispense prescriptions. Some managed care organizations allow physician dispensers as part of the pharmacy benefit system, but the physician must accept the same discounted reimbursement as the rest of the pharmacy network. This includes a percentage discount from the AWP of the product and the discounted dispensing fee. Physician dispensers primarily dispense short-term medications and usually have little or no refill capabilities. The popularity of this system in HMOs is low, and usually there is little interest on the part of the physician to fill prescriptions for third-party payers.

Ingredient Cost

There are several approaches to managing this significant cost portion of the equation. The ingredient is the product itself, that is, the tablet, capsule, liquid, or syrup. There are multiple approaches to managing ingredient cost; each method is dependent on the design of the drug benefit.

Generic Drug Policy

When the patent expires on a previously brand only medication, almost always other manufacturers competitively distribute the same drug. The quality indicators of a generic program are covered later in this chapter; the advantage to this is that the generic brand of the medication is significantly less costly than the branded medication. Almost two thirds of HMOs require use of generics,[3] and approximately 40% of HMO prescriptions are filled with generic drugs. The average generic cost is anywhere from 40% to 70% less than the equivalent branded product cost.

The components of an aggressive generic program include generic reimbursement according to a MAC reimbursement rate. Because there are multiple manufacturers of generic medications, each pricing at different AWPs, and because most pharmacies participate in some form of purchasing group arrangement, the difficulty in identifying the true average price of a generic medication has created the MAC reimbursement process. This process allows the payer to set a price for a specific generic medication and indicates to the pharmacist the maximum amount that will be reimbursed as the ingredient cost. The determination of the MAC is highly technical and work intensive.

Remember that generic utilization numbers can be misleading. An HMO could have an extremely high generic utilization rate and yet not maximize generic cost savings. This is exactly what happens when a MAC list is not the reimbursement policy.

If exceptions are included in the benefit design that allow the pharmacist to be reimbursed for prescriptions at other than the MAC, benefits costs will increase. These exceptions are a benefit design allowing the physician and/or member to request the branded product at the expense of the plan. Commonly called a dispense-as-written (DAW) policy, this request may be generated by the physician by writing "dispense as written" on the prescription. It may also be generated by a verbal request on the part of the member to receive the branded product rather than the generic. This will decrease the number of prescriptions dispensed generically and will cause a significant increase in the average ingredient cost. A well-managed pharmacy benefit program allows for member payment of the difference between the generic and the branded product should either the physician or the member request this option. Anything short of this will unnecessarily cost the plan money.

Average Wholesale Price Discounts

The AWP of a medication implies that it is the purchase price of the medication or ingredient from a drug wholesaler. Little is more confusing or more difficult to determine than the purchase price of a medication. Hence the claims processor or the third-party payer utilizes an independent source, or pricing vendor, to determine the AWP of the medication. This AWP reference has become the standard of payment for the ingredient, and this reference source is usually part of the pharmacy contract.

To complicate the issue further, there are often discrepancies between the actual purchase price of the ingredient by the pharmacy and the designated AWP per the pricing source. Like sticker prices on automobiles, the reference source purchase price and the actual purchase price are typically different. Hence a negotiated discount off the referenced AWP is a standard part of the pharmacy contract. This discount is often more important to the pharmacist than the dispensing fee because the AWP of the ingredient will continue to inflate over time whereas the dispensing fee is generally the same over time. The current marketplace allows the AWP discount for branded products to be in the 10% to 15% range. The differential factor is the competition within the marketplace. The AWP discount for generic drugs is significantly higher (estimated to be in the 40% to 60% range). Managers should not concentrate on AWP discounts for generics but rather should utilize a MAC rate.

Drug Formularies

The decision to require a drug formulary in a managed care environment is one that mandates careful planning. More and more HMOs are realizing the value of the drug formulary in managing costs and are moving toward aggressive formulary management. More HMOs are using formularies than ever before.[3]

A drug formulary is best defined as a dynamic, comprehensive list of drugs designed to direct physicians to prescribe the most cost-effective medications. The list is organized by therapeutic class; the selection criteria for the drugs on the formulary are primarily patient care and secondarily cost.

A drug formulary must meet three criteria to be successful:

1. It must reflect the practice of medicine in the community. Attempting to restrict physicians from using medications that have become a standard of practice in the community will be a difficult endeavor indeed.

2. It must be responsive to the therapeutic needs of the physicians. If physicians are not able to find medications that are necessary to treat patients and are continually requesting exceptions to the formulary, the effort to enforce a formulary will serve neither the physicians nor patients.

3. It must be representative of cost-effective therapy. This is where most formularies that are nothing more than drug lists fall short. All drug formularies provide community standards and therapeutic necessities. The true differentiating criterion amongst formularies, however, is the ability to ensure community standards in a cost-effective manner.

When a drug formulary is used in an appropriate manner, quality of care is improved. Furthermore, by moving toward a closed or mandatory

status and maximizing volume purchase contracts, a drug formulary can save upward of 10% or more on the pharmaceutical benefit cost.

The formulary development process is extremely important to the success of a formulary system. Educating physicians that the drug formulary is coming ensures implementation without undue delay. A simple statement in the physician newsletter that the managed care organization or HMO has decided, via its medical staff advisory committee, to implement the drug formulary is useful.

A formulary committee or pharmacy and therapeutics committee comprising physicians, clinical pharmacists, and representatives from the administrative offices of the health plan is necessary to give adequate documentation to the drug formulary process. Certain physician specialties are a must for this committee, including family practice, internal medicine, pediatrics, and gynecology. These physicians prescribe the majority of the medications for the members of health plans and thus deserve the largest representation on the committee. Often, for various reasons, other specialty areas are represented (eg, psychiatry, dermatology, and surgery). Usually the internal medicine representatives on the committee have subspecialty areas for which input can be provided. In situations where there is no expertise on the committee (eg, infectious disease, rheumatology, cardiology, and so forth), those specialists can be asked to attend a subsequent meeting or to attend on an ad hoc basis. Maximum success can be ensured if the formulary is developed at the local level.

A written protocol addressing the process to be used for additions to the drug formulary is beneficial. One of the more difficult aspects of managing a drug formulary system is the fact that addition requests usually outnumber deletions. Attention needs to be paid continually to the addition/deletion ratio.

After the formulary document has been approved, it is ready to be sent to the providers and promoted as the cost-effective, quality document that it is intended to be. Directions explaining how to use the document need to be included. The document should be formatted to be as simple and easy to follow as possible; also, the way that the formulary is organized on the front end will be the way that it carries on for history. There needs to be an index to which providers can turn to find immediate formulary information and a therapeutic categorization that facilitates identification of drugs available for certain disease entities.

The promotion of the formulary also needs to include information about what happens if providers do not follow the formulary. This can be part of the endorsement on the front end, simply stating that there will be a monitoring process in place that will identify physicians who are continually not complying with the drug formulary, that these physicians will be contacted if they do not follow the formulary, and that consistent outliers (without justification) will be dealt with.

Drug formularies in the staff model HMOs are generally followed without question. In the IPA model HMO, however, providers are typically private practice physicians and pharmacists who see the formulary as a hindrance or constraint on their ability to practice their profession. Furthermore, the providers may participate with multiple plans, each with a slightly different formulary. Therefore, the plan should expect provider pharmacies to call physicians about nonformulary medications, and the physicians should follow the advice of the pharmacist when they are called in terms of changing to a formulary drug.

Last comes the question of assessing the success of the formulary. This is easier if you determine the percentage of prescriptions that are written in compliance with the formulary than if you apply financials to that formulary in a retrospective process. If cost-effective guidelines were followed in developing the drug formulary, however, then the logical assumption is that the higher the formulary compliance, the more cost effective the drug formulary.

With respect to compliance in those environments where there is a voluntary formulary, a compliance rate of greater than 95% should be expected. In an open formulary environment, however, a high compliance rate does not necessarily mean cost effectiveness. Obviously, the easiest way to obtain 100% compliance is to put all medications on the formulary. A mandatory

closed formulary with high compliance will achieve the greatest savings.

The institution of a drug formulary system also requires notification of the members of the plan that their medications will now be required to be prescribed per a drug formulary. Often, if this is a new policy, a period of grandfathering can be put in place so that individuals who are stabilized on a particular medication that will no longer be a part of the drug formulary can continue to use that medication. It is important to understand that the intent of the drug formulary is not to restrict medications from individuals who need them but rather to change physician prescribing behavior to the most cost-effective therapeutics.

Volume Purchasing and Rebates

The fourth mechanism in managing ingredient cost is volume purchase contracting, commonly called rebates. This is the mechanism by which the pharmaceutical manufacturer agrees to a volume-driven discount contract in exchange for formulary considerations. Most pharmaceutical companies have formed a managed care department to understand and interface with managed care organizations. Many companies have contractual relations with HMOs already and share utilization of their products. Although a couple of the manufacturers have ignored or fought the HMOs' attempts to manage cost, the gamble that their freedom of product choice philosophy will outlast cost containment is slowly deteriorating. The necessity for managed care organizations and the pharmaceutical industry to work as allies is becoming more obvious. Both industries have the pharmaceutical product as their focal point, and both have much to gain by cooperative efforts in proving the value of their product.

Why should pharmaceutical companies agree to contract with managed care organizations? Why should they discount their products? There are a number of important reasons.

- It often is the only way the managed care organization will accept the company's product on the drug formulary. Most medications newly marketed today are therapeutically equivalent to a product currently in existence and probably already on the formulary.

- The plan in essence becomes an extension of the industry sales force. Because the product has been given formulary status, it serves as an endorsement for the product.

- Once an established relationship exists, the plan will preferentially review newly marketed products in a way that ensures the partner company the greatest opportunity for inclusion on the formulary.

- Most closed panel plans will cooperate with the partner company to facilitate local representatives' accessibility to providers, at least for those products that are already on the formulary. The ability to see physicians and pharmacists is essential for pharmaceutical sales representatives.

- Formulary decisions provide a spillover effect; that is, physicians will tend to prescribe formulary products for all their patients, not just those belonging to the HMO.

QUANTITATIVE DRUG UTILIZATION REVIEW

An integral part of managing pharmaceutical costs is the development of drug utilization review (DUR) programs. DUR and drug utilization evaluation programs offer the prospect of saving money both by restraining the use of unnecessary or inappropriate drugs and by preventing the adverse effects of misused medications.[4] DUR programs assess the appropriateness, safety, and efficacy of drug use. Under the heading of utilization review, we have tended to blend together cost and quality considerations in managing pharmacy benefits. Realistically, the emphasis has been on the cost side; there are various reasons for this, including convenient access to cost data and the completeness of those data. Because plans are effectively managing the cost aspects of cost utilization, the demand for proof that the therapeutics/quality of care considerations are not being affected by these cost considerations continues to arise. Hence it is best to separate the DUR process into quantita-

tive and qualitative elements. Quality is discussed later in this chapter. Realistically, quantitative DUR answers the questions "How costly? How often? For whom? By whom?" The properties of quantitative DUR are as follows:

- It describes patterns of drug utilization and cost.
- It quantitates drug utilization and cost.
- It identifies areas and categories to be used for qualitative drug utilization review.
- It identifies areas for education.
- It is not based on any predetermined criteria for standards.
- It can be used to describe the quality of drug use.

In essence, quantitative DUR selects the therapies to be reviewed. Data are collected, and those data are analyzed and reported. Certain management and educational applications are then put into effect. To determine the significance of the quantitative information, we can use a comparative analysis when looking at our results. In other words, for each of the therapeutic categories indicated, one compares data with national utilization data in that therapeutic category to determine whether utilization findings are significant outliers.

Success with any program of DUR demands a management information system capable of providing information. The ability to tie in all components of the information, not just pharmacy, to analyze the entire picture will ensure therapeutically cost-beneficial decisions. Differences in therapeutic utilization are driven by various factors, and it should not be inferred that inappropriate utilization is always the cause. Both local and national dynamics need to be considered before assumptions and action plans are made.

AUDITS

Often receiving less attention within the managed care pharmacy benefit than other more common cost management applications, the auditing process is extremely important. The auditing function is performed essentially for fraud and abuse detection. Fraud can be perpetrated by the member as well as by the provider. Reports focusing on the following should ensure that reasonable attempts to identify fraud are in place:

- generic utilization by pharmacy
- number of prescriptions dispensed costing more than $100.00 per prescription
- number of prescriptions dispensed indicating dispense as written.

Although abuse generally is unintentional, sometimes it is not. From a quality of care standpoint, and certainly from a cost management perspective, providers and members abusing the system need to be identified and dealt with. Thanks to today's on-line electronic claims processing systems, abuse is becoming increasingly difficult to commit . The requirement on the part of most managed care organizations for pharmacies to have the on-line capability of checking for duplicate prescriptions, prescriptions filled too soon, and multiple providers is becoming the norm.

An additional audit process that needs to be implemented is one to ensure the integrity of the volume purchase or rebate contracting program. The pharmaceutical industry is aware of the possibility of fraud on the part of the provider and the potential for paying rebates for medications that are not dispensed. The successful total audit program that the plan must have in place should include determination of fraud or abuse by providers and members and protection when pharmaceutical industry rebate contracts exist.

MANAGEMENT OF QUALITY

Quantitative DUR deals with generics, formularies, dispensing fees, and other efforts to ensure cost-effective prescription drug benefits. One necessity is the ability to reduce pharmacy costs without compromising quality. Accomplishing this requires an efficient and reliable data system, quality assurance and utilization review processes, and assessment according to criteria standards.

Defining quality has always been difficult. Most often it is a subjective rather than objective measure. The necessity to ensure the provision of safe and effective drug therapy to health plan members is a focal point of managed care. A structured program with continuous collection and analysis of information, in conjunction with authority to compare this information against a previously established standard, ensures the quality of the pharmaceutical benefit program. With the majority of the emphasis today seemingly on cost, those managed care organizations successfully managing cost do so by a process focusing on the quality of care rather than solely on cost management.

Therapeutics

Drug Formulary

A well-managed drug formulary process can ensure the quality of the drug formulary document. Over and above any cost considerations in the drug formulary decision is the comparable therapeutic advantage of a product in terms of its cost. This review process includes the following:

- *Product therapeutic review*—the comparative review of the therapeutic advantages of one product over another (ie, the indications, the uniqueness, and the value of this product compared to the therapeutic alternatives available to physicians). Those drugs offering little or no therapeutic advantage are rejected despite their inexpensiveness.
- *Pharmaceutics*—the characteristics of the drug in terms of its absorption and metabolism. The therapeutic advantage of rapidly attaining short- or long-acting blood levels rather than fast onset needs to be determined. Once-a-day therapy, which is typically more expensive, compared to multiple daily dosing is a part of the therapeutic evaluation. If, in fact, dosing several times throughout the day will not affect the quality of the care, this determination can then be part of the cost containment strategy.
- *Side effects/adverse effects*—determining a product's profile in comparison with another with regard to the likelihood of adverse effects. Patient tolerance or intolerance to the medication means that

compliance will be questionable. The drug formulary should assure the prescriber that the adverse effect profile of this medication has been considered and that a determination of appropriateness for drug formulary status has been attained. These types of formulary assessments are relatively easy to make, and the literature information comparing these products is readily available.

Step Therapy

A mechanism that is often employed with success within staff model HMOs but is more difficult to institute in IPA models is step therapy. Step therapy refers to the steps that a physician is encouraged to follow when prescribing medications to treat a specific illness. Step therapy for any disease for which step criteria have been initiated implies that, unless the treatment modality is part of step 1, it should not be instituted without justification. As an example, step 1 for hypertension could be salt restriction, weight reduction, and exercise. If this fails to lower blood pressure, step 2 could be choosing any medication within the therapeutic categories of thiazide diuretics, calcium channel blockers, angiotensin converting enzyme inhibitors, or β blockers. If these fail, step 3 would be the addition of another drug from the step 2 category, and step 4 could be the introduction of medication choices from other therapeutic categories.

Step therapy typically is designed according to nationally or community accepted criteria, often developed by the National Standards Committee on Therapeutic Modalities. These step therapies can also be adapted institutionally and often become a standard of practice for the community. The difficult political aspect of step therapies is that physicians often interpret them as dictatorial in terms of their freedom to practice medicine. Claiming that individualization of patient care often runs counter to step therapy, some physicians will refuse to follow or even acknowledge step therapy but rather will insist on practicing medicine according to the standards and guidelines with which they are more familiar. Step therapy will probably be incorporated into prescribing according to outcome criteria in the near future.

Community Standards

Like step therapies, community standards imply an identifiable standard by which prescribers are to prescribe. Unlike step therapy, however, community standards are often more subjective that objective. It is difficult to determine how one establishes a community standard. They may well be determined according to accumulated data, which essentially means that community standards are similar to the community norm, or they could be determined by a representative group of specialists in a particular area who blatantly state that treating a medical problem in a manner different from their recommended way does not meet an acceptable standard of care.

Ensuring the quality of a managed pharmacy benefit program requires attention to community standards. Possibly more from a feasibility and dependability perspective, utilizing expertise in the community to determine standards allows the HMO to defend its decisions. Many physicians and attorneys discourage the use of prescribing according to community standards. They point out the lack of organization in determining these standards and the potential inappropriateness of this method. Nonetheless, the practice of medicine according to community standards utilizes patterns within the community known to be credible.

Outcomes Management

According to Paul Ellwood, founder of the Excelsior, Minnesota–based managed care research firm InterStudy, outcomes management is defined as "a tool to use in the everyday management of managed care organizations. It would measure and compare the impact of ordinary medical care on the patient's quality of life."[5]

Undoubtedly, outcome information will be part of both cost management and quality of care programs within the managed care organization. Decisions will be easier, and much more defensible, with enhanced credibility if they are based on outcomes. The public will be better assured that the quality of the pharmacy benefit not only is safe and effective but will result in a more positive outcome. To date, little is known about how expenditures for pharmaceutical therapeutic agents can positively affect health care outcomes compared to other treatments. As we accumulate the necessary information, the data are analyzed and the results disseminated.

We can anticipate that the results will show the pharmaceutical logic of interventions that improve both cost and the outcomes of health care. As new medications emerge, the value of the outcome will be weighed against the cost of the therapy. Reimbursement for new and expensive agents may be denied unless the quality of therapeutics based on outcome has been demonstrated. Justification for coverage of high-cost drugs will be an increasingly difficult and data-intensive task but will ensure quality of care.

Patient/Member Expectations of the Pharmacy Provider

The primary expectation of the members of the HMO is that, when they present a prescription to the pharmacist, the prescription is filled accurately and is indicated as a treatment modality for the problem with which they presented to their physician. Although they are not directly involved with the quality assurance associated with ensuring that expectations are met, they believe there is a process in place by which the quality of that service is protected. Unlike the situation with physicians, however, where credentialing is a standard dictating whether one is an eligible participant in the health plan, the pharmacies rather than the pharmacists are credentialed. The credentialing of the pharmacist is left to the regulatory agencies appointed by the state to ensure the competency of the practitioner pharmacist.

Along those same lines, the assurance of the quality of the pharmacy is also often overseen by a state regulatory agency. Within the pharmacy practice acts of each state, specific qualifications are described for a pharmacy to meet the licensing requirements. Some plans have elected to go beyond this, requiring certain quality of care enhancements such as to-the-door delivery services, 24-hour service, and on-line utilization review programs. Each of these enhancements forces the plan to walk a tighter line between

deeply discounting a pharmacy network and increasing the services required by the pharmacist and at the pharmacy. The best indicators of lack of quality in pharmacy services are obtained by audits, as addressed earlier in this chapter, and by encouraging member feedback concerning service at the participating pharmacy.

Health Maintenance Organization Expectations of the Pharmacy Provider

Like the member, the plan expects the pharmacist to dispense the prescription accurately and in a cost-effective manner. Additionally, the plan requires the pharmacist to follow all aspects of the contract between the plan and the pharmacy. In other words, all policies and procedures addressed in the pharmacy contract must be adhered to.

The plan also often expects the pharmacy to participate in a utilization review program, audit processes, and other services of value to the plan. If this is the case, the plan will have expectations of the pharmacy beyond the normal dispensing of prescriptions in a quality manner in exchange for an agreed-upon reimbursement rate.

Point-of-Service Review

The increasing popularity of point-of-service claims adjudication indicates the likelihood of an increase in on-line utilization review. One does not have to think too far down the line to imagine a situation where a prescription will be entered into an on-line claims adjudication system, the reason for the medical intervention will be checked via compatible information systems, and the appropriateness of the medication prescribed for that medical intervention will be analyzed. Currently, on-line point-of-service systems at the least ensure checking for drug-drug interactions; checking for food-drug interactions; checking for age, sex, and pregnancy interactions; checking for therapeutic duplication; and checking for allergies.

Without any doubt, the value of an on-line claims adjudication system to both the HMO and the provider has significantly increased the likelihood of utilization of this type of system. This system also significantly increases the quality assurance possibilities within that system, however. Any HMO that is not approaching 100% on-line electronic claims processing will be sorely lacking in quality assurance.

QUALITATIVE DRUG UTILIZATION REVIEW

Earlier in this chapter we addressed the quantitative aspects of DUR. This is the aspect of utilization review associated with cost containment. The other aspect is qualitative DUR. The properties of qualitative DUR are the following:

- criteria/standard–based processing
- determination of the appropriateness of drug therapy prescribing and dispensing
- direct relationship of information generated to the quality of patient care

In starting the process of qualitative DUR, objectives need to be identified and stated. Criteria need to be created that define quality and standards for measurement. Data are then collected and analyzed. When there is failure to meet criteria, causes are identified. Subsequently an intervention takes place, and there may well be a reassessment of the results of that intervention. If necessary, the original objectives are modified. There is then documentation and dissemination of the DUR process and results.

As an example, consider a drug interaction. The objective is to perform concurrent DUR of a drug interaction and to inform pharmacies and prescribers of the presence of such interaction. By using criteria defining quality standards, one collects the information to identify patients who are receiving the drug in combination and then notifies physicians who have prescribed this drug, informing them of the problem. Last, one monitors the results and then documents and disseminates this information.

Qualitative utilization review can be directed at the member, physician, or pharmacy. Each can be performed prospectively, concurrently, or retrospectively. Today, the approach usually is essentially retrospective, primarily because of the lack of sophistication of on-line electronic point-of-service systems in providing the necessary information to do concurrent utilization and because the majority of the data currently are in a retrospective format.

The following are the elements necessary to provide a qualitative DUR program:[4]

- electronic point-of-sale review of drug therapy to alert the dispensing pharmacists of a potential problem
- retrospective data analysis (patient, prescriber, or pharmacy specific) to identify and evaluate concerns
- clinically based screening criteria that use decision-tree analysis
- evaluation of drug therapy for specific targeted populations
- definition of mechanisms for intervention and follow-up to identify problems
- definition of mechanisms to assess the impact of intervention
- integration of DUR with other databases providing medical diagnosis and financial cost

There are definitely some challenges to a quality-driven DUR program. If we are going to utilize successfully the combination of quantitative and qualitative review to provide a safe and cost-effective pharmacy benefit program to members, the following must be addressed:

- Technology needs to be available to a plan-performed qualitative DUR, both concurrently and prospectively.
- We need to move from case review analysis to drug therapy process intervention.
- We spend too much time analyzing cases; our movement to an action plan is often too slow.
- Currently the patient and pharmacist are at the center of concurrent DUR intervention and managed care environments. The prescriber must be brought into the loop.
- We need to develop patient outcome-driven DURs. Outcome is the next logical step from quality assurance. Realistically,

it is difficult to make cost-effective determinations without knowing outcomes.

MEASUREMENT OF SUCCESS

The successful management of a pharmacy benefit program can be determined from two aspects: the overall ability to manage the cost of that program, and the dependability of the quality.

First, with regard to cost management, as a manager of a pharmacy benefit program your requirements to manage costs are based on your ability to maintain pharmaceutical expenditures within a predetermined budget. Without any doubt, the emphasis is not only on managing costs but on containing costs. Your cost containment programs drive the budget each year. A portion of the pharmaceutical expenditure, the manufacturer's cost, is becoming more predictable. The utilization factor, that is, the shifting in utilization trends from less expensive to more expensive therapeutics to treat the same illnesses, is becoming more difficult to predict. You can consider that you are practicing successful cost management, or cost containment, if in fact you continue under budget in a pharmacy benefit as well as maintain pharmaceutical indicator costs (PMPM, ingredient costs, and prescription costs) at or under the national average for a managed care organization similar to yours. Anything less than this should be considered an inability to manage appropriately and should give the plan manager an incentive to find management support for the pharmacy benefit program.

Quality is a much more difficult parameter by which to measure success. Certainly, the DUR programs addressed earlier in this chapter will help and, if followed, will provide the documentation for any internal or external agency requiring it. Because quality is often such a subjective entity, however, the development of subjective criteria to determine quality is helpful. A successful quality-run program can be based on the results of these subjective criteria. Again, utilizing the averages or norms found in similar plans for member utilization, beyond the cost of the service, will help ensure and document a successful quality of care–driven pharmacy benefit

program. Simply taking the information available, via a retrospective information system, and applying this information against comparable information and then documenting action taken to investigate, and change if necessary, inappropriateness in the pharmacy benefit will ensure that successful quality.

PHARMACY BENEFIT MANAGEMENT: NEXT PHASE

This chapter has attempted to point out the future of pharmacy benefit programs. Essentially, pharmacy programs can be divided into three specific areas, each of which is going to have significant application to success and even to the continuance of coverage of prescription drugs in the future.

We Will Be Paying More Attention to Truly Managing Costs, Not Cost Shifting

In the past few years, we have made many successful applications to managing the pharmacy benefit cost profile. We have moved to an on-line claims and adjudication system, we have increased significantly the utilization of generics, we pay pharmacists according to a MAC schedule for generic medication, we have instituted drug formularies, we have successfully negotiated discounts from the pharmaceutical manufacturers, and we have discounted our pharmacy networks. Even so, drug costs continue to increase at percentages that are considered inappropriate. The reason is, quite simply, cost shifting. As an example, the increase in the therapeutic categories in numbers of drugs within a category is staggering. One only needs to look at the nonsteroidal anti-inflammatory drug category, the angiotensin-converting enzyme category, or the cephalosporin category to realize that the number of medications available to treat the same medical problems reads like a menu in a restaurant.

Statistics indicate that with each new therapeutic entity within the category the utilization does not just divide between the group but actually increases. In other words, with each new drug that is marketed within the therapeutic category, utilization of medications within that therapeutic category increases manyfold. We can no longer continue to add therapeutic entities of all kinds to our drug formularies. Medications that offer no therapeutic benefit will not be allowed formulary status, and as the utilization creep begins to emerge criteria will be developed by which the medication will be covered.

Prior Authorization Will Increase; Usual and Customary Prescribing Will Become a Thing of the Past

As medication types, medication capabilities, and medication expenses all increase, the only response to managing the utilization of these medications is by the prior authorization process. Many drugs today, all of which are presumably better than previously available medications to treat similar medical problems, do not need the formulary or nonformulary status. In other words, many of these drugs now fit into a formulary-if category. Too many medications are valuable for a certain population, and our current system of a product being either covered or not covered no longer applies. Hence there is a need for a prior authorization process for many of these medications.

To make the prior authorization process feasible, from both an administrative and a compliance standpoint, we must be able to develop an acceptable and easy system. On a local level, this means accessibility to HMO case managers to ensure the appropriate application of the prior authorization process. On a national scope, this means telephone access by toll-free numbers to centrally located case managers. In both cases, the cooperation of the provider, including the pharmacist and physician, is a must. We will not

be able to continue the same covered yes–covered no approach that we currently have.

Outcomes Information Will Be Used To Make Decisions

Adequate resources will be available to develop sound outcome methodologies and variable environments. Large-scale measurement of health outcomes, with feedback to all decision makers, will help ensure that quality is maintained and costs are managed. Drug costs are increasing at a faster rate than other health care costs, and these inflationary trends are not compatible with the continuance of coverage for a pharmacy benefit service. Therapeutic decisions in our managed care environment will be based on results of both local managed care organization and national, often federally funded outcomes information.

CONCLUSION

The purchasers of the managed care benefit seek both quality and price. Expectations run high, and pressure is tremendous to keep the costs at a minimum while meeting these high expectations. Reimbursement for services continues to be a focal point of disagreement between the managed care organization and the provider. The pharmaceutical industry is experiencing for the first time hands-on intervention by the federal government into their pricing policies. The past years have noted significant efforts to manage the costs of the pharmacy benefit. DUR, subsequent outcome results, action plans, and implementation of these action plans will dictate the future.

REFERENCES

1. Vagelos PR. Are prescription drug prices high? *Science.* 1991;252:1080–1084.
2. Part 1: the new claims systems. *Drug Top.* February 1988.
3. *Marion Merrell Dow Managed Care Digest, HMO Edition.* 1991.
4. Atlas R. Editorial. *Drug Benefit Trends.* 1992;4:3.
5. Marcinko T. Outcomes management: medicine under the microscope. *Managed Care Insights.* 1990;3:2–4.

Chapter 15

Quality Management

Michael Pine and Peter R. Kongstvedt

Consumers of health care who have unlimited free choice in the marketplace are at liberty to define quality of care in their own terms and to select or reject caregivers at their discretion. In contrast, under managed care a third party limits the members' options. Establishment of a network of exclusive or preferred providers influences or restricts the members' choice of providers, and policies for payment or reimbursement affect or control the volume and nature of care provided. An organization that has the power to narrow the consumer's range of choices has an obligation to ensure that the choices it makes on the consumer's behalf result in care that is of average quality or, preferably, better. Thus the managed care organization has a responsibility for quality assurance and management.

To understand the dimensions of this task, it is important to appreciate the broad range of services encompassed by this activity. In a moderately large open panel plan, it is not unusual to have contracts with 300 to 400 primary care providers, 1,000 to 2,000 specialists, 10 to 25 hospi-

tals, and numerous other providers such as nonphysician professionals (eg, psychologists, podiatrists, and optometrists) and institutions (eg, pharmacies, home care providers, and skilled nursing facilities). Each type of provider may be subject to the same basic concepts of quality management, but in a way that may be unique to that provider.

It is important to manage the delivery system as a system and not get obsessed with any one element of it. A comprehensive program helps ensure balance and perspective, so that even the more important aspects of health care do not prevent attention to others that also are essential but may appear less urgent or more difficult to address. Practical limitations of personnel, time, money, and expertise may limit an organization's ability to implement all the quality management activities that would be ideal, but a strong and comprehensive program is still a reasonable goal.

There are a variety of approaches to managing and ensuring quality in a managed care plan. These approaches are quite compatible and complementary, although they may appear to be only distantly related. To illustrate such approaches, this chapter will discuss quality management under two broad concepts: classic quality management (sometimes referred to as

---

Michael Pine is President of Michael Pine and Associates, a Chicago-based consulting firm that assists purchasers, providers, and other concerned organizations throughout the nation to measure and improve the quality of health care.

quality assurance) and new directions in quality management.

CLASSIC QUALITY MANAGEMENT

Traditionally, quality assessment in health care has concentrated on three dimensions: structure, process, and outcome. This has formed the basis for quality management programs for most managed care plans and continues to be a necessary and useful activity. The concepts of structure, process, and outcome may be applied to any professional or institutional provider that contracts with a managed care organization for health care delivery. The methods and standards applicable to one type of provider may not be appropriate for another. For example, credentialing criteria for primary care physicians would not be the same as those for an ambulance service, and a guideline for treatment of hypertension will have little relevance to orthopedic care.

Any aspect of quality may be examined with this paradigm. For example, access to care may be viewed as a structure issue (eg, are emergency services provided, what is the provider's capacity, and so forth), an issue of process (eg, what is the response to an emergency call, how are admission decisions made, and so forth), and an outcome issue (eg, are members satisfied with emergency services, how many beneficiaries require admission to a hospital for conditions that may be avoided with good outpatient care, and so forth). Further discussion of classic quality management follows.

Structure Studies

Structural requirements encompass minimal and widely accepted standards intended to ensure a safe environment, competent professionals, proper organizational structure, and adequate record keeping. Many such requirements are delineated in federal, state, and local regulations that govern licensing and mandate periodic review and reporting mechanisms (see Chapters 34 and 35). Compliance with all these regulations is necessary for the provision of good care,

although they are not sufficient to guarantee it.

Because conformance with structural requirements is relatively easy to document, accrediting and regulatory bodies have traditionally placed great emphasis on them. This tradition has been perpetuated by the many requests for proposal (RFPs) that are used to select managed care organizations to participate in benefits plans. Therefore, it is important that a managed care organization be able to document satisfactorily that its professionals are properly credentialed (see Chapters 4 and 5), that it has clear organizational lines and the proper committees and governance (see Chapter 3), and that it complies with safety regulations and other requirements specified by accrediting organizations and potential customers (see Chapters 21, 34, and 35).

Specific requirements and forms of documentation needed may vary from year to year. Accrediting bodies and corporate benefits managers usually have guidelines, checklists, or other explanatory materials that have been prepared to assist providers in meeting their requirements and documenting compliance.

Although compliance with a basic core of structural requirements clearly is important, it would be a mistake to infer that such compliance can either determine or ensure quality. Using a checklist of licensing, regulatory, and credentialing requirements to assess quality of care is rather like evaluating the performance of an automobile by using a checklist to verify that the car has an engine, brakes, headlights, four wheels with tires, a steering wheel, a gas tank, a windshield with wipers, and an exhaust system. These are all essential features in an automobile, and no one would purchase a vehicle that lacked any one. Nevertheless, their mere presence is insufficient evidence that an automobile will perform to anyone's satisfaction.

Process Studies: Case Audits and Peer Review

Traditional quality assurance programs monitor conformity to standard processes of care by conducting case audits (occasionally referred to as medical care evaluations) and peer review.

Audits may be triggered by a rash of undesirable outcomes or may rotate among topics of interest according to some predetermined plan (eg, disease of the month or procedure of the month).

In a routine audit, the quality management committee first approves the standards against which medical records will be reviewed; this is a sort of Twenty Questions, preferably one that uses branched-chain algorithms. These standards may have been developed by the plan, or the plan may use standards developed by professional organizations and published in the medical literature. For each provider of interest, a sample of cases that meet the criteria for review is then selected for study (eg, 20 of each primary care physician's most recent cases of hypertension). A nurse reviewer goes to the physician's office (or to the medical records department in the case of a closed panel plan or hospital) at an agreed-upon time and screens the medical records for each case, looking for deviations from standard practice. It is not uncommon in open panel plans to audit only a portion of the provider network during any given study; limitations in time and resources prevent visits to every provider every month.

During the review of the medical record, deviations from standards are noted, and data about compliance with standards are collected for each physician studied. The nurse reviewer may then have an exit interview with the physician to report the findings. The data are collated and results analyzed for the entire plan and for each physician individually. Desired changes are communicated to the entire provider panel and to individual physicians as appropriate. The study is repeated later on to determine whether required changes were made. If serious and flagrant quality problems are identified, the medical director may have to take preemptive action (see Chapter 9).

As part of most process studies, outcome for the sentinel condition is noted as well (eg, was hypertension controlled and were side effects minimized). In many systems, cases with adverse outcomes or gross noncompliance with process standards may be flagged for further examination and discussion by professional peers

of the practicing physicians under scrutiny. The goal of peer review in quality assurance is to find and correct practices that do not conform to standard policy.

The effect of peer review often has been to single out individual practitioners as bad doctors and to censure their performance in the possibly mistaken belief that the bad results were directly related to the physicians' errors or neglect. At the opposite extreme, peer reviewers may be hesitant to second-guess a colleague or to pass any judgment in the fear that they may someday be on the other end of the inquiry. Management of the peer review process therefore requires great skill on the part of the medical director or quality management committee chairperson.

In health care, process studies and peer review encourage conformity to standards created by experts whose notions of quality may become outdated within a few years, given the swift evolution of medical knowledge. Most physicians who have been out of medical school two decades or more can think of therapies they were taught to use that, if administered today, would be considered malpractice. Insistence on conformity to standards, although useful for examining the performance of providers, may also promote blindness to opportunities for improvement.

Peer review has the potential to trigger time-consuming investigations and efforts to solve inconsequential or nonexistent problems. For example, the cases marked for review generally are those with adverse outcomes. Similar cases that were managed in exactly the same way may have escaped notice, however, because they were concluded successfully. What appears to be a problem may instead be the result of a random or rare combination of events that would be unlikely to happen again. Similarly, cases chosen for examination may not represent physicians' typical caseloads, management styles, or qualities of performance. Directing attention to atypical situations is inefficient and may distract both clinicians and managers from the identification and correction of conditions that breed errors in the system of health care delivery. Even so, a plan does have an obligation to review cases where the probability of poor care is high.

Procedural Standards

Some third-party payers may specify particular policies and procedures that they want their managed care organizations to follow. For example, they might require that immunizations be completed on all pediatric patients or that mammograms be given annually to women older than age 40. It is reasonable to expect that care rendered to members will meet such standards, and when procedural standards are among the expectations of purchasers it is important that the quality management program be able to produce evidence that they are being met.

If and when these policies are not followed, it should be possible to provide either good reasons for the exceptions or documentation of steps being taken to improve the degree of adherence to standard procedures. Although an organization that lacks procedural standards may be at a disadvantage, it is far worse in the eyes of corporate clients to have standards that are ignored.

As quality management tools, procedural standards have major limitations. Although many are appropriate, many of them are somewhat arbitrary and do not always have adequate scientific justification. They change frequently, and occasionally the new standards are diametrically opposed to the former standards. Nevertheless, providers should understand the attractiveness to potential purchasing groups of currently fashionable preventive screens such as cholesterol checks and Pap smears. (For a more rational approach to developing procedural monitors, see the section below on protocols and flow charts.)

Outcome Studies

Outcome studies are necessary to determine what has actually happened to patients who receive care. A full discussion of outcome as it applies to the broad membership base is discussed in the second portion of this chapter. The search and destroy method of outcomes management should be mentioned here, however.

Most managed care plans have systems in place to look for potentially adverse events. Often in conjunction with utilization management,

surveillance is conducted to detect sentinel events that may indicate inadequate or poor care. When these events are detected, the quality management department is alerted to review the medical record. Exhibit 15-1 illustrates examples of events that, when detected by the utilization management nurses, would trigger an audit.

Certain inpatient admissions may result from poor outpatient care. To find such cases, certain inpatient diagnoses may be identified as possible indicators of inadequate or improper outpatient care that would necessitate admission to the hospital. Exhibit 15-2 illustrates examples of such diagnoses.

This activity may not always be worth the effort, but if the claims system reveals a statistically significant number of such diagnoses linked to a single provider, there may be more cause for investigation. This analysis requires relating these admissions to the size and nature of the panel of patients treated by a physician. The subject of risk adjustment and rates is discussed in the section New Directions in Quality Management and in the discussion of practice profiling in Chapter 16.

Service Quality

Managed care organizations do not treat disease only; they treat people with and without disease. People have needs other than diagnosis and therapy. Among the issues that concern them are access to care, time spent in the waiting room, time to referral, amenities, courtesy, adequate explanations, patient education, and so forth. Many of these factors lend themselves to objective measures. Therefore, monitoring them is essential to establishing the perception of a high-quality program. How the resulting data can serve as important adjuncts in the process of quality improvement will be discussed in the second half of this chapter.

Member Satisfaction

Effective quality management must be concerned with the organization's achievements as well as with its activities. A classic indicator of

Exhibit 15-1 Examples of Events among Hospitalized Patients That May Indicate Inadequate Quality of Care

Adequacy of discharge planning
- No documented plan for appropriate follow-up care or discharge planning as necessary, with consideration of physical, emotional, and mental status/needs at the time of discharge

Medical stability of the patient at discharge
- Blood pressure on day before or day of discharge: systolic, < 85 mmHg or > 180 mmHg; diastolic, < 50 mmHg or > 110 mmHg
- Oral temperature on day before or day of discharge > 101°F (rectal, > 102°F)
- Pulse < 50 beat/min (or < 45 beat/min if patient is on a β blocker) or > 120 beat/min within 24 hours of discharge
- Abnormal results of diagnostic services not addressed or explained in the medical record
- Intravenous fluids or drugs on the day of discharge (excludes the ones that keep veins open [KVOs], antibiotics, chemotherapy, or total parenteral nutrition)
- Purulent or bloody drainage of postoperative wound within 24 hours before discharge

Deaths
- During or after elective surgery
- After return to intensive care unit, coronary care, or special care unit within 24 hours of being transferred out
- Other unexpected death

Nosocomial infections
- Temperature increase of more than 2°F more than 72 hours from admission
- Indication of infection after an invasive procedure (eg, suctioning, catheter insertion, tube feedings, surgery)

Unscheduled return to surgery within same admission for same condition as previous surgery or to correct operative problem (excludes staged procedures)

Trauma suffered in the hospital
- Unplanned removal or repair of a normal organ (ie, removal or repair not addressed in operative consent)
- Fall with injury or untoward effect (including but not limited to fracture, dislocation, concussion, laceration)
- Life-threatening complications of anesthesia
- Life-threatening transfusion error or reaction
- Hospital-acquired decubitus ulcer
- Care resulting in serious or life-threatening complications not related to admitting signs and symptoms, including but not limited to neurologic, endocrine, cardiovascular, renal, or respiratory body systems (eg, resulting in dialysis, unplanned transfer to special care unit, lengthened hospital stay)
- Major adverse drug reaction or medication error with serious potential for harm or resulting in special measures to correct (eg, intubation, cardiopulmonary resuscitation, gastric lavage), including but not limited to the following:
  1. Incorrect antibiotic ordered by physician (eg, inconsistent with diagnostic studies or patient's history of drug allergy)
  2. No diagnostic studies to confirm which drug is correct to administer (eg, culture and sensitivity)
  3. Serum drug levels not measured as needed
  4. Diagnostic studies or other measures for side effects not performed as needed (eg, blood urea nitrogen, creatinine, intake and output)

Source: Health Care Financing Administration, 1986.

Exhibit 15-2 Examples of Inpatient Diagnoses That May Indicate Inadequate or Improper Outpatient Care

- Cellulitis (extremities)
- Dehydration of child with severe diarrhea (younger than 2 years)
- Diabetic coma–ketoacidosis
- Essential hypertension
- Gangrene (angiosclerotic, extremities)
- Hemorrhage secondary to anticoagulant therapy
- Hypokalemia secondary to potassium-depleting diuretic
- Low–birth weight infant (premature, less than 2,500 g)
- Malunion or nonunion of fracture (extremities)
- Perforated or hemorrhaging ulcer (duodenal, gastric)
- Pregnancy-induced hypertension (pre-eclampsia, eclampsia, toxemia)
- Pulmonary embolism (admitting diagnosis)
- Readmission of same condition within 14 days
- Ruptured appendix
- Septicemia (admitting diagnosis)
- Status asthmaticus
- Urinary tract infection (bacteria, pyuria)

Courtesy of Blue Cross and Blue Shield Association, Chicago, Illinois.

achievement is member satisfaction. Although most managed care plans now perform member surveys, anecdotal information has in the past been the basis for most of this information. Customarily, complaints and adverse publicity have prompted internal investigations, and complimentary letters from members and words of appreciation have been widely distributed.

The opinions of members, because they are customers, surely are important. Relying on voluntary anecdotes for an assessment of performance, however, is like evaluating a product solely by the opinions of friends. It may be better than no information at all, but one should not believe that the conclusions are objective or reliable. Each person may have different criteria for quality and different ways of assessing whether those criteria have been met. Similarly, providers of health care have no way of knowing whether patients who volunteer their positive or negative opinions are at all representative of the entire population served. Because of such inadequacies, anecdotal information has been replaced at most plans by specific surveys of member satisfaction. If administered and scored properly, these can be valuable clues to the perceptions of the population served.

Obvious though it may appear, it is important to keep in mind that potential insights from any questionnaire are limited by the questions asked (and the choice of words as well). Knowing the percentage of patients who liked the food in the hospital or who thought the nurses were friendly and the billing personnel were courteous is useful in maintaining and improving good public relations. It may be more germane to patients' priorities, however, to determine the extent to which patients believe they were treated courteously, their privacy was respected, their individual needs or preferences were accommodated, and so forth.

Even these factors do not address whether the members' goals of care were accomplished. To illustrate, the reader may recall answering a questionnaire from an automobile dealer's service center in which all the questions concerned courtesy and formalities but there was no opportunity to indicate whether the car functioned properly after servicing. Efforts are underway currently to move member surveys closer to the heart of the matter by researching the extent to which members' perceptions of their own health status are accurate. On the basis of the findings, questionnaires will be modified or new ones created to maximize the members' potential as a source of information about the quality of care.

Risk Management

Efforts to examine the processes and outcomes of care have become formalized in classic programs of quality assurance, utilization review, and risk management. Ideally, risk management should be concerned with identifying and eliminating potential risks. In the reality of everyday crises, however, its function has been to minimize undesirable consequences of already identified adverse occurrences through legal and public relations means. For this reason, risk management sometimes has been characterized as damage control: an attempt to remedy the effects of internal failures before they can become external embarrassments. Risk management activity that arises in response to a suboptimal outcome is reactive rather than proactive. As such, although its contribution to reducing legal and marketing exposure is clear, its contribution to quality assurance is too little and too late.

NEW DIRECTIONS IN QUALITY MANAGEMENT

Classic quality management remains an important part of any plan's quality management program. Regulatory agencies require it, and the marketplace clearly demands it. In large open panel managed care plans, whether primary care case managing models or preferred provider organizations, the plan may have practical limitations on the amount of intervention it can carry out. Most managed care plans do not themselves provide health care but rather depend on contracted providers and hospitals to do so. Surveillance of quality that includes standards for provider performance, data feedback, and interventions as necessary is compatible with the broad scope required of these quality programs.

Nonetheless, many providers and some health plans are moving beyond classic quality management. They feel that the limitations and flaws of classic quality assurance do not necessarily lead to genuine and continuous improvements in quality. Closed panel plans and organized medical groups, because they provide health care directly, are in an ideal position to undertake the tasks necessary to move into the next generation of quality management. Plans that do not provide direct care can still take advantage of new techniques but must work through their contracted providers and hospitals in the undertaking.

Effective quality management is both a continuous and a systematic endeavor. Instead of centering on crises, wrongdoing by individuals, and conformity to correct processes established by experts, quality management should engage everyone in the organization in continuous efforts to raise the organization's level of performance. There is more to this than "Let's all try harder." Systems that do not work seldom fail through lack of earnest effort. More often, they are unduly complex or miss the point altogether.

The concept of continuous improvement has been successfully applied in general business management for years, and this concept of quality management can and should be applied to the business operations of the plan. Likewise, continuous improvement is a concept that can and should be applied to health care delivery.

Emphasis on Systems

Systematic quality management emphasizes the performance of the entire organization and of teams within it. This is not to overlook individual effort and expertise or to deny that someone can be a weak link in the organizational chain. Rather, it encourages groups to function in a way that maximizes individual strengths and compensates for individual weaknesses. This occurs naturally in organizational systems that are functioning well (ie, that achieve their goals).

The first step in developing a systematic quality monitoring program is to identify and define the organization's goals. What is the mission of this managed care organization? What can the group do that could not be done by its individual members? What are the specific objectives that the organization hopes to accomplish? What is its notion of success? The answers to these questions will determine what the organization means by quality. Before deciding how to measure, one must know what to measure and why.

Not just one but several qualities generally will emerge as important. Arriving at a consensus on this issue is of critical importance because organizations cannot achieve without teamwork. A group that does not have a set of commonly agreed-upon goals is like a rowing crew in which each crew member is aiming for a different destination. All must agree on where they are going before they can make any headway or monitor their progress in reaching their destination.

To serve as a basis for quality management, grandiose, overarching goals must be clearly defined and subdivided into segments that can be understood as attainable. For example, providing cost-effective care sounds wonderful, but what does it really mean? Does everyone define the term the same way? Can it be translated into dollars, profit margins, low complication rates, a combination of these, or something else? Each department in the organization may need to identify and define its own secondary and tertiary goals and explain how their fulfillment would contribute to the primary goals of the entire organization.

The second step is to translate goals into measures of success. How will the organization or department know if a goal has been achieved? What is being done currently to accomplish each goal? In answering these questions, it is important to be specific. What are the critical or essential steps in each process? This is important to know because an organization that does not know what it is doing probably is not doing the right things or doing them very well.

Protocols and Flow Charts

It may be helpful in visualizing or understanding current processes to make a flow chart of major activities. A flow chart of steps in clinical care is often called a protocol. (Algorithms, clinical pathways, and parameters, whether in chart or outline form, are essentially similar; the term *protocols* has been favored for this discussion.) A clinical protocol should support achievement of a medical goal such as early detection of breast cancer or alleviation of symptoms of angina pectoris. An administrative flow chart should support achievement of a managerial goal such as moving patients to a point of treatment with a minimum of waiting time or avoiding adverse consequences of known drug interactions. (As in the latter example, it sometimes may be difficult to designate a flow chart or protocol as clinical or administrative because both types of activities are closely intertwined in the care of members.) If a process cannot be related directly or indirectly to any organizational goal, then its usefulness should be questioned seriously.

On each flow chart or protocol, it should be possible to identify critical junctures at which the process either goes forward smoothly or breaks down. These may be points of transition, of interaction with another group, or of pivotal decisions. These critical junctures should be divided into actions (ie, intermediate outcomes) that can be measured quantitatively. Here are some examples:

- Ninety percent of patients moved from point A to point B within 15 minutes.
- In 97% of applicable cases, physicians were advised that newly prescribed medications had potential for interaction with medications currently prescribed.
- Sixty percent of patients with suspected angina were scheduled for exercise testing within 2 weeks of examination.

Data can be collected to determine the extent to which objectives are being met and current outcomes of care such as mortality rates, complication rates, and lengths of hospitalization. Data are collected first to assess initial performance. This provides insights about what is actually happening rather than what managers have directed and supervisors think is occurring. The initial assessments serve two functions: disclosure of areas that offer opportunities for im-

provement and benchmarks for future evaluations.

Outcomes Measurement

The following are some basic principles for using data to measure outcomes of care:

1. Data must be collected on large numbers of individual patients. As discussed previously, when just a few cases are analyzed, the data may reflect rare or unusual events rather than frequent occurrences.

2. Data must be clearly defined and must be collected in a uniform fashion. Data cannot be compared reliably when measurements are not taken in the same way, at the same point in diagnosis or treatment, and so forth.

3. Data must be adjusted for patients' characteristics (risk factors) that affect outcomes but are beyond providers' control. Risk adjustment should be closely related to the outcome being measured. For instance, factors that would place a patient at high risk for a sudden heart attack would not all be the same as risk factors for frequent outpatient visits. Risk factors for disability are different from those for mortality.

5. Actual performance should be compared with predicted or expected values. Expected values should incorporate risk adjustment and may be calculated on the basis of rates or averages for similar groups (eg, national averages for hospitals treating Medicare patients, averages for a state or community, averages for all providers in a network, and averages for a group's performance in the past).

6. Some measure of statistical probability should be included in the analysis, if possible, to avoid conclusions based on differences that were likely to be due to chance alone.

Relationship between Process and Outcomes

Combining analyses of clinical outcomes and clinical and managerial processes is particularly useful for understanding how an organization's activities affect the results it gets. There should be a direct relationship between processes of care and outcomes of care. Less than optimal outcomes have their roots in inappropriate or poorly implemented processes. When the process is changed or improved, the outcome should be better (unless the change is not really an improvement). In contrast, some processes may be found to contribute little or nothing to the outcome or achievement of the primary goal of the process. A process is not worth doing for its own sake. Unless it makes a measurable contribution to the goal, it probably is wasteful and should be abandoned.

Known performance serves as a baseline for future monitoring and a foundation from which to search for ways to improve. Flow charts and protocols are used as ways to describe processes, not to codify them. They can clarify how things are being done currently, and they are useful in describing and communicating proposed changes. It should be recognized that, in clinical processes particularly, decisions about patients often are made or altered midway during a procedure or course of treatment. Patients have individual differences, and the course of disease may be dynamic or at times unexpected. Therefore, professional judgment cannot be reduced to formulas. For this reason, clinical protocols are descriptions rather than prescriptions and should be subject to continual re-examination and revision.

When this form of quality management is followed, goals and standards are not arbitrary or based on the changing opinions of experts but are rooted in reality because they are derived from actual performance. Expectations are calculated objectively on the basis of performance that has been achieved already by fallible human organizations with current technology. Therefore, they are neither unrealistically high nor meaninglessly low.

Two pitfalls in quality monitoring are false positives (ie, finding errors where there are none or identifying problems that do not really exist) and false negatives (ie, failing to find problems or overlooking errors). Peer review has a strong tendency toward the former, and data-centered quality management as just described must guard against the latter. Systematic attention both to process and to outcomes should minimize these problems. Errors or problems that might be overlooked will be reflected either in failure to meet objectives at critical junctures or in poor outcomes and failure to meet major goals.

This is another reason why quality management should be continuous as well as systematic. When everyone in the organization agrees on its goals, recognizes an obligation to work as a team in meeting them effectively and efficiently, and participates in the collection of data to monitor progress, there should be few surprises. An ongoing process of quality improvement can be incorporated into the organization's daily routine, eliminating most needs for fire extinguishing, crisis responses to adverse occurrences, and the flurry of activity that precedes inspections for accreditation and licensure.

CONCLUSION

Systematic and continuous quality management is at once easier and more difficult than what has been done by most institutions in the past. It is more difficult in that it requires time, skill, and hard work to lay the foundation: achieving consensus on goals, examining processes, identifying critical junctures, defining objectives in terms that can be measured objectively, collecting and analyzing data on outcomes, comparing the results with past performance or objective standards, drawing inferences to make recommendations for improvement, and implementing proposed improvements.

Once the foundation has been laid, however, quality management becomes easier. When goals are agreed upon and understood, people work at cross-purposes less often. Quality becomes everyone's concern, not just the burdensome responsibility of a single person or group within the organization. Objective quality monitoring breeds satisfaction rather than defensiveness and fear because progress toward commonly agreed-upon goals can be charted and easily observed. Opportunities for improvement become group challenges rather than personal failures. Finally, quality management becomes easier because it is a style of operation akin to preventive maintenance. Instead of waiting for breakdowns, it anticipates and averts potential problems before serious, costly malfunctions occur. Although this would be an advantage almost anywhere, it offers special dividends to organizations entrusted with caring for human lives.

SUGGESTED READING

Coopers & Lybrand and Michael Pine and Associates. *Guide to Designing and Implementing a Value-Centered Benefits Plan for Employee Health Care*. Solon, OH: Center for Policy Studies and Health Action Council of Northeast Ohio;1992.

Couch JB. *Health Care Quality Management for the 21st Century*. Tampa, FL; American College of Physician Executives; 1991.

Donabedian A. *Explorations in Quality Assessment and Monitoring* (3 vols). Ann Arbor; MI: Health Administration Press; 1982.

Foster R. *Innovation: The Attacker's Advantage*. New York: Summit; 1986.

Goldfield N, Nash DB. *Providing Quality Care: The Challenge to Clinicians*. Philadelphia: American College of Physicians; 1989.

Goldfield N, Pine M, Pine J. *Measuring and Managing Health Care Quality: Procedures, Techniques, and Protocols*. Gaithersburg, MD: Aspen; 1991.

Hughes E, ed. *Perspectives on Quality in American Health Care*. Washington, DC: McGraw-Hill Health Care Information Center; 1988.

Walton M. *The Deming Management Method*. New York: Doss, Mead & Co; 1986.

Chapter 16

Use of Data and Reports in Medical Management

Peter R. Kongstvedt

This chapter should be read in the context of your plan's specific needs and in conjunction with the information presented in other chapters. It is the intention of this chapter not to be highly redundant and review all the possible reports that may be produced by your plan's management information system (MIS) but rather to concentrate on those reports specific to utilization and medical management that will help medical directors carry out their job. Clearly, the need for these types of reports will be influenced by the configuration of your plan and the types of controls and incentives in place. Not all the reports discussed in this chapter will be helpful, and there will certainly be situations where there are necessary utilization reports that are not discussed here. It is up to the medical director to decide what reports are necessary, and it is up to the director of MIS to provide them.

One common problem is overkill with detail. Judging by the stacks of greenbar computer paper printouts that are seen holding up the ceiling, reports in some plans must be valued by weight. It is easy to believe that the more data and detail the better. When that happens, you get the classic problem of not seeing the forest for the trees, with the manager spending more time grinding through reports than managing. Computers are wonderful tools, but they can smother you with data. Know what to ask for and when to ask for it.

GENERAL REQUIREMENTS FOR USING DATA TO MANAGE THE HEALTH CARE DELIVERY SYSTEM

To use data at all for managing health care costs, certain basic requirements must be met. First, the data must have integrity. Data must be consistent and mean the same thing from provider to provider. This occasionally may mean having to change or otherwise modify data to force conformance of meaning.

Data must also be valid: They must actually mean what you think they mean. Diagnostic coding is particularly problematic when one is analyzing data from physician outpatient reports. Because diagnostic coding is not important in determining what a physician is paid (except for those claims systems that match diagnostic code to procedure code), there is a great deal of laxity in coding. Even when there is greater attention to diagnostic coding, the reason for the visit may or may not be related to everything that gets done (eg, a patient is seen with the diagnosis of hypertension but also gets a hearing test), or the diagnostic code may not be the same as the underlying disease (eg, a patient is seen for an upper respiratory infection, but the relevant diagnosis is emphysema).

Procedure coding tends to be more accurate because there is a direct relationship between what a provider codes as having been performed and what the provider gets paid (except in capitated systems). Although that does not rule out fraud or common upcoding, even knowing that is helpful in profiling.

The measures must be meaningful. It is of no value (other than academic) to measure things that have no real impact on the plan's ability to manage the system. Even worse, there is potential harm in producing reports that purport to mean one thing but really mean another.

The sample size must be adequate. Measuring encounters or referral statistics by physician is of little value if a physician has only 20 members in the panel. Even large databases may fall prey to this problem if the claims and clinical data are spread over too large a provider base, so that there are insufficient data for any given provider.

The data must encompass an adequate time period. Simple snapshots in time do not reveal the true picture. This is particularly important when one is looking at total health care resource consumption of patients. This is even more important when one is trying to determine whether a provider's behavior is consistent.

ROUTINE AND AD HOC REPORTS

To manage information wisely, you need to decide which reports you will want on a routine basis and which reports you will want to call on an ad hoc or an as needed basis. For example, in a stable open panel plan, it is unnecessary for the medical director to receive a monthly report listing the recruiting activity or membership for each participating physician. That information, if it is needed, could be provided once per quarter. On the other hand, the medical director will usually want a hospital report on a daily basis.

The basic rule of thumb is to ask for routine reports for those functions that require constant management and will provide sufficient data to spot trends and aberrations. Routine reports should allow you to decide when to focus on

specific areas for further investigation. For example, watching the trend in referral costs could reveal an upswing that would result in your requesting detail about utilization by specialty. That in turn could lead to a need to look at utilization by individual providers in a single specialty. Save the highly detailed reports for infrequent intervals or ad hoc requests. Time spent deciphering cryptic reports is time spent not managing.

FORMAT

How reports are formatted is a matter of taste and the MIS department's ability to produce the requested format. The easiest type of report for MIS to produce is one that tabulates columns of numbers. That is also usually the type most deadly to a busy manager. An already overburdened medical director has better things to do than sift through 20 pages of printout looking at raw numbers of referrals for each physician to get an idea of the referral rate.

The best types of report formats for senior plan managers usually are ones that can fit onto one or two 8" × 11" sheets of paper. Those reports should summarize the important data, indicate the outliers and deviations from the norm (or from preset standards), and indicate whether the manager will need to seek more detail. If managers need the raw data, they can always ask for them. For example, a two-page report giving the overall referral rate for the plan and the annualized referral rate per 1,000 members per year for each primary care physician (PCP) for the month and the year to date may be sufficient by itself. If there are PCPs who are grossly over the norm, the medical director can then ask for the detail behind the report.

Graphic reports are especially useful for conveying large amounts of information quickly to busy managers. This is particularly true when one is presenting data to managers and providers who are not used to looking at reports. Unfortunately, most mainframe computer systems are not set up to produce graphic reports, so that data must be entered (or downloaded and then imported) into a personal computer before the graphs can be produced. This is a cumbersome process and not amenable to mass production. It is anticipated that, as computers and software become more sophisticated and interlinked, production of graphic reports will become more common.

Further discussion of what types of summary reports may be useful follows. The message here is that reports for busy managers should be concise, readable, and easily interpreted and allow the manager to request further detail as needed.

FOCUS

Reports may be focused in a variety of ways to reveal useful information. For example, the overall admission rate for the plan may be normal, but a report focusing on where the patients are admitted may reveal that most of the admissions are to nonparticipating hospitals. What follows is a general guide to the different ways in which data can be focused.

Plan Average

Plan average simply looks at the average performance for the entire plan. It is useful in that it will relate closely to the plan's financial performance. For example, if the plan is over budget in medical expense, a plan average report that reveals hospital admissions to be greatly over budget will allow management to focus on that first. It also allows for comparative data between plans that may have somewhat different types of arrangements for the delivery of care.

It is limited because it is relatively insensitive to specific causes of problems. That can be an advantage in some circumstances, however. In plans that manage by trying to keep performance clustered around a norm, that norm can sometimes be one of mediocrity. If the plan average reports and the provider-specific reports tie closely (ie, there are no real outliers in performance), and if the plan is not doing as well as it should, then it is clear that there is a general problem of attitude or skills in the managers themselves and not a problem with a few recalcitrant providers or hospitals.

Plan average reports are frequently required by regulatory agencies and are also useful for reporting the overall performance of the plan to participating physicians and corporate parents. Plan average reports also function as the backdrop against which other reports are viewed.

Health Center, Individual Practice Association, or Geographically Related Center

The purpose of this focus is to provide midlevel managers with data for their own areas of responsibility. In many plans, especially large or geographically diverse ones, it is common to divide up responsibility into manageable units. The problem of span of control in large or diverse plans can be a very real one. In closed panels this often refers to a health center or a small number of geographically related health centers. In open panels, this usually refers to discrete multiple individual practice associations (IPAs) or subunits within the overall health plan or to geographically divided territories.

Individual Physician

Most managed care plans produce reports that focus on individual physicians. This may refer to PCPs who are functioning as gatekeepers or care coordinators but may apply equally to open access health maintenance organizations (HMOs) or preferred provider organizations (PPOs). Virtually all the types of utilization reports discussed later in this chapter are amenable to focusing on individual physicians.

Physicians become understandably paranoid about the plethora of reports that are produced about them. They feel that they are being judged by machines or by standards that fail to take into account any extenuating circumstances and that their fate will be decided on the basis of sterile reports. In truth, it is the ability to report the behavior of individual physicians that provides managed care plans with their most powerful tool and physicians with their greatest source of both concern and potential help.

Care must be taken when one is using physician-specific reports. The medical director must look behind the data of the report for the reasons for the reported performance. This is not to say that any behavior should be rationalized, and physicians are as adept as anybody in arguing that they are different and should not be held to the same standards as anyone else. Rather, this is to say that individual physician performance reports need to be used intelligently and properly.

Service or Vendor Type

This type of report refers to the entity delivering the service (eg, a hospital or a type of referral specialist). Focusing reports on those delivering the service (also referred to as vendors) will be of great value when one is negotiating contracts and will allow for improved utilization control. These types of reports also help focus on areas where attention should be paid. Remember Sutton's Law: Go where the money is!

Employer Group

This tracks utilization by enrolled group. For those plans that are allowed to experience rate (refer to Chapter 26 for a discussion of rating), this will be necessary to develop the actual cost experience. Even for those plans that must community rate, these data will tell you whether you have a problem with that group that may need to be addressed. Also, as discussed in Chapter 23, some large employers are demanding such data as a requisite for offering your plan to their employees.

HOSPITAL UTILIZATION REPORTS

Routine hospital utilization management reports may be divided into two categories: the daily log and monthly summaries. Many plans now automate their utilization management systems (see Chapter 10). In addition to producing reports as discussed below, these systems allow for on-line access to far more information than would be practical on a printed report. Nevertheless, printed reports regarding hospital utilization remain useful to medical managers, who may review them in a manner and time not possible if they were required to stare at a computer terminal.

Daily Log

It is almost a requirement for a managed care plan to produce a daily hospital log. This document serves as a working tool for the utilization management nurse and the medical director in controlling institutional utilization. Its design should be directed toward providing the necessary information to manage cases actively that are current or prospective. Data should be sorted and printed by whatever management criteria make sense. For example, you may wish to print each hospital's census separately so that the utilization review nurse can take it when making hospital rounds. In plans where associate medical directors will have primary responsibility, you may want to print the log so that it sorts by geographic region, IPA, or health center.

Useful information for any daily log includes elements illustrated in Exhibit 16-1. Information on a daily log that is also useful in most types of health plans is illustrated in Exhibit 16-2.

Monthly Summary

A monthly summary report of hospital utilization should also be produced. This differs somewhat from the daily log because it is used to identify patterns for overall management rather than to serve as a mechanism for performing

---

Exhibit 16-1 Minimum Data Elements for a Daily Hospital Log

- Current census
  —Name of patient
  —Hospital
  —Diagnosis and procedures
  —PCP
  —Admitting physician
  —Consultants or specialists
  —Admission date
  —Length of stay to date
  —Free text narrative with clinical information
  —In-network compared to out-of-network status
- Hospital statistics
  —Days per 1,000 today
  —Days per 1,000 month to date
- Prospective admits and outpatient surgeries

Exhibit 16-2 Additional Useful Data Elements for a Daily Hospital Log

- Service type (as part of current census)
  —Medicine
  —Surgery
  —Pediatrics
  —Gynecologic surgery
  —Obstetrics
  —Mental health
  —Chemical dependency
  —Intensive care unit/cardiac care unit
  —Neonatal intensive care unit
  —Rehabilitation
  —Outpatient surgery
- Estimated length of stay or maximum length of stay
- Admissions and discharges today and month to date
- Authorization or denial status
- Catastrophic case report

concurrent utilization review. A monthly report might include the data illustrated in Exhibit 16-3 for both the month ended and the year to date.

Exhibit 16-3 Sample Data Elements for a Monthly Summary of Hospital Utilization

- Plan statistics
  —Days per 1,000
  —Admissions per 1,000
  —Average length of stay
  —Average per diem cost
  —Average per case (per admission) cost
- Hospital- and provider-specific statistics
  —Days per 1,000
  —Admissions per 1,000
  —Average length of stay
  —Average per diem cost
  —Average per case (per admission) cost
- Statistics by service type (see Exhibit 16-2)
  —Days per 1,000
  —Admissions per 1,000
  —Average length of stay
  —Average per diem cost
  —Average per case (per admission) cost
- Retrospective authorizations
- Pended cases for review
- In-network compared to out-of-network statistics
- Number and percentage of denied days

OUTPATIENT UTILIZATION

Although daily reports are necessary for controlling hospital utilization, in only the most tightly managed health plans will that be necessary for controlling outpatient utilization. In general, outpatient utilization control is usually best done by using monthly reports, both routine and ad hoc. Reports should include data both for the month ended and for the year to date. Data may also be reported by month on a 12-month rolling basis. Data for such reports might include elements as illustrated in Exhibit 16-4.

As has been mentioned earlier, once you decide on the routine reports, you can use those to decide what reports to request on an ad hoc basis. For example, if total expenses for cardiology appear to be high, you could investigate further by requesting reports that show who is ordering the referrals, what ancillary testing is being done, who the specialists are that are seeing the patients and how much are they charging, and so forth.

Exhibit 16-4 Sample Data for a Monthly Summary of Outpatient Utilization

- Primary care encounter rates
  —Visits per day (closed panels only)
  —Visits per member per year (annualized)
  —Percentage of new visits
  —Revisit interval rates (to look for churning)
- Laboratory utilization per visit
- X-ray utilization per visit
- Prescriptions
  —Prescriptions per visit or prescriptions per member per year
  —Average cost per prescription
  —Percentage generic
- Referral utilization
  —Referral rate per 100 primary care visits or per 1,000 members per year
  —Comparison of PCP referral rate to peer group
  —Initial referrals only compared to total referral visits
  —Cost per referral by PCP, plan average, and specialty
  —Number of visits and cost by specialty
       Average cost per visit
       Per member per month cost by specialty

Open access systems, or systems that do not use a primary care gatekeeper model, present special problems in monitoring utilization. In a PPO or managed care indemnity plan, there will be no physician-specific membership base to use as a denominator. In HMOs that allow open access to specialists or allow specialists to self-authorize revisits or secondarily to authorize referrals to other specialists, there will be no way to measure specialist utilization against a fixed membership base (the base is only for the PCPs, not the specialists).

In these situations, you must be willing to accept less precise methods of measuring utilization of referral services and specialist utilization. Reports should focus on those areas under control of the specialist as well as primary care. Examples of such data elements are illustrated in Exhibit 16-5.

Exhibit 16-5 Sample Data for an Open Access Model Plan

Outpatient Services
- Average number of visits per member per year
- Average number of visits per member per year to each specialty
- Diagnostic utilization per visit
  —Laboratory
  —Radiology and imaging
  —Other
- Average cost per visit
- Procedures per 1,000 visits per year (annualized)
  —Aggregate
  —By procedure for top 10 by specialty type
  —By individual specialist
- Average cost per episode (as defined for each sentinel diagnosis) over a defined time period, including charges not directly billed by provider

Inpatient Services
- Average total cost per case, including charges not billed by provider, for hospitalized cases
- Average length of stay for defined procedures
- Average rate of performance of a procedure, such as:
  —Cesarean section rate
  —Hysterectomy rate
  —Transurethral prostatectomy rate
- Readmission rate or complication rate
- Use of resources before and after the hospitalization

PROVIDER PROFILING

Closely related to all the issues discussed in this chapter is provider profiling. Profiling means the collection, collation, and analysis of data to develop provider-specific profiles. Such profiles have a variety of uses, but the most important ones are recruiting providers into the network and choosing which providers may not (or are not) the right fit with the plan's managed care philosophy and goals. Other uses include determining specialists to whom the plan will send certain types of cases, producing provider feedback reports to help the providers modify their own behavior, detecting fraud and abuse, determining how to focus the utilization management program, supporting performance-based reimbursement systems, and performing economic modeling.

The initial focus of many physician-profiling activities has been inpatient care. A hospital case is usually definable (except for cases that are transferred or readmitted), and the physicians delivering care are usually identifiable. The cost of inpatient care has also led to this focus. Recent activity has shifted to consider outpatient care as well, recognizing that care occurs across a continuum rather than in isolated episodes.

Many provider profiling systems simply look at the behavior of the provider against certain norms. Comparison against norms is certainly necessary, but it is fraught with difficulties. The chief difficulty is defining the norm, but an attendant difficulty is choosing what to look at. Most profiling activities focus solely on the actions of the provider. It is better to attempt to examine provider behavior from the standpoint of total health care resource consumption and outcome, including resources not directly delivered or billed by the provider, and to look at true episodes of care as opposed to single visits.

Episodes of Care

Episodes of care are defined as time-related intervals that have meaning to the behavior you are trying to measure. Episodes may vary considerably both by clinical condition and by the provider type that is being measured. In the case of obstetrics, obvious measures such as cesarean section rate and average length of stay are important but will not reveal the full picture. Looking at the entire prenatal and postnatal episode may reveal significant differences in the use of ultrasound and other diagnostics or perhaps a great deal of unbundled claims during the prenatal period. In the case of medical conditions, the episode may extend over the course of years.

Related to the issue of episode is the problem of identifying which provider is actually responsible for care. As an example, an internist may be responsible for the care of a diabetic but may have little responsibility for managing that patient's broken leg other than to refer the patient to a cost-effective orthopedist. This issue is especially difficult regarding hospitalized patients. It is not uncommon for the admitting physician not to be the attending physician, especially when surgery is involved.

The hallmark of episode definition is the ability to link up all the health care resources into a defined event. This may mean diagnostic services (eg, laboratory or imaging), therapeutic services (eg, physical therapy), consultations, outpatient visits, and inpatient visits. In other words, it must be a patient-based analysis rather than a provider-based one; the analysis of the behavior of providers is a product of examining what happens to their patients.

Problems with Provider Profiling

There are certain problems inherent with provider profiling. All these problems are resolvable, but medical managers need to be aware of them before embarking on profiling.

It is not always clear what specialty a physician really is. Most plans have provider files that indicate what specialty type a physician has self-indicated, but it is surprising how often that information does not match up with specialty indicators in the claims file. Even when it does, there is no guarantee that the initial credentialing was done accurately, and even when it was done accurately there is no guarantee that the provider actually makes a living at that specialty.

The problem of provider specialty definition is particularly acute when one is looking at primary care. Many board-certified specialists ac-

tually spend a considerable amount of time performing primary care, whereas others spend the majority of their time practicing true specialty medicine. This has great implications for how a plan will evaluate performance of specialists as well as PCPs. A related issue is in determining which physicians will be considered specialists at all because the plan may not want to send referrals to a specialist who is not particularly active in his or her designated specialty.

Even when the issue of specialty definition is resolved, there remains the problem that no two practices are exactly alike. As an example, either general internists perform flexible sigmoidoscopies or they do not. If one looks only at charge patterns, the internist who performs the procedure will look more expensive compared to the internist who does not, but that analysis will fail to pick up the fact that the internist who does not perform flexible sigmoidoscopies instead refers them all to a gastroenterologist who charges more than the first internist (of course the first internist could be overutilizing the procedure, but that is a separate part of the analysis).

Practices also may have differences in the age and sex make-up of their patient panel. Geographic differences may also account for utilization variations. These must be factored into any profiling report.

Case mix and severity are always issues of contention when one is profiling providers: Providers with costly profiles will always complain that they have the sickest patients. When you are performing profiling, the issue of severity must somehow be accounted for. Techniques for doing so include severity of illness indicators (most useful in hospital care), statistical manipulation such as trimming in outlier cases (ie, if only a few cases are outliers, one brings those cases back to the mean), and looking at the degree to which a physician is truly a specialist and his or her mix of routine and complex cases.

The next issue is the problem of providers who behave as though they are in a group but are not legally connected and do not appear as a group in the plan's provider file. An example would be two physicians who share an office, share call, and see each other's patients but who have different tax numbers and billing services.

The reason that this is important in managed care is that, if the plan contracts with one but not the other, the member may wind up seeing the nonparticipating physician and be subject to balance billing. Even if the physicians agree not to balance bill, the plan still may not actually want the other physician in the network, even on an occasional basis.

Related to the above is the ability to detect linkages between practices and ancillary services. Examples include orthopedists who own physical therapy practices and neurologists who have a proprietary interest in a magnetic resonance imaging center. This issue is discussed in Chapters 11 and 12.

Incorporation of Other Data

Many plans incorporate other data into a provider profile analysis. Claims data are enormously useful, but there are additional sources of data as well. Credentialing data (see Chapters 4 and 5) may be automated and referenced. Data from member services (see Chapter 19) such as complaints, transfer rates, or administrative problems may be incorporated. Data from the quality management program (see Chapter 15) or formal performance review programs (see Chapter 18) may likewise be added to practice profiling.

FEEDBACK

Medical management reports need not be confined to plan managers. As mentioned in several chapters in this book, feedback to providers is a useful adjunct to other medical management activities. Feedback to providers must be clear, easy to understand, and accurate.

Feedback should be meaningful and useful to both parties, not just the plan or the provider. When feedback reports are clearly linked with performance expectations, and when such reports can help a provider alter a behavior in a positive way (which will in turn benefit that provider), then feedback may be successful.

Providers will alter their behavior in response to feedback for a variety of reasons. Natural competitiveness and peer pressure may exert influence. More important, the opportunity to increase market share and to improve their revenue will be a powerful reason to respond to feedback. Fear of possible adverse actions by the plan may also play a role if a provider is a clear outlier and if feedback provides a concrete measure of expectation by the plan.

Hospitals may benefit from feedback reports as well. Hospitals are providers in their own right, even though the physicians on staff give the orders. Nevertheless, hospitals have their own policies and procedures that influence how care is rendered, and hospitals certainly have their own billing practices. Hospitals can also have a strong role in influencing the practice behavior of the physicians on staff and can work effectively with managed care plans to effect changes.

CONCLUSION

Utilization reports are powerful and absolutely necessary tools for managers of health plans. Routine reports need to be simple to read and compact and to provide only those data required generally to manage the plan. They need to provide managers with sufficient information to order ad hoc detail reports required to solve specific problems that were flagged by the routine reports. Provider profiling is taking on an ever greater role in managed care but remains a complex area. Data overload is a frequent and deadly problem in managed care, but intelligent use of reports should prevent that from occurring.

SUGGESTED READING

Betty WR, Hendricks HK, Ruchlin HS, Braham RL. Physician practice profiles: a valuable information system for HMOs. *Medical Group Management*. 1990;37:68–75.

Braham RL, Ruchlin HS. Physician practice profiles: a case study of the use of audit and feedback in an ambulatory care group practice. *HCMR*. 1987;12:11–16.

Doubilet P, Weinstein MC, McNeil BJ. Use and misuse of the term "cost effective" in medicine. *N Engl J Med.* 1986;314:253–256.

Eisenberg JM. Clinical economics: a guide to the economic analysis of clinical practices. *JAMA.* 1989;262:2879–2886.

Harris JS. Watching the numbers: basic data for health care management. *J Occup Med.* 1991;33:275–278.

Hughes RG, Lee DE. Using data describing physician inpatient practice patterns: issues and opportunities. *Health Care Manag Rev.* 1991;16:33–40.

Physician Payment Review Commission. *Physician Payment Review Commission Conference on Profiling.* Washington, DC: Physician Payment Review Commission; 1992.

Chapter 17

Authorization Systems

Peter R. Kongstvedt

One of the definitive elements in managed health care is the presence of an authorization system. This may be as simple as precertification of elective hospitalizations in an indemnity plan or preferred provider organization (PPO) or as complex as mandatory authorization for all nonprimary care services in a health maintenance organization (HMO). It is the authorization system that provides a key element of management in the delivery of medical services.

There are multiple reasons for an authorization system. One is to allow the medical management function of the plan to review a case for medical necessity. A second reason is to channel care to the most appropriate location (eg, the outpatient setting or to a participating specialist rather than a nonparticipating one). Third, the authorization system may be used to provide timely information to the concurrent utilization review system and to large case management. Fourth, the system may help finance to estimate the accruals for medical expenditures each month (see Chapter 25).

DEFINITION OF SERVICES REQUIRING AUTHORIZATION

The first requirement in an authorization system is to define what will require authorization and what will not. This is obviously tied to the benefits design and is part of full and fair disclosure marketing requirements in that, if services require authorization, your plan must make that clear in its marketing literature.

There are no systems that require authorization for primary care services. PPOs and HMOs require members to use providers on their panels, and most HMOs require members to choose a single primary care physician (PCP) to coordinate care, but this does not require an authorization. Defining what constitutes primary care services is another issue and is addressed in Chapters 4 and 5.

The real issue is determining what nonprimary care services will require authorization. In a tightly controlled system, such as most HMOs, all services not rendered by the PCP require authorization. In other words, any service from a referral specialist, any hospitalization, any procedure, and so forth requires specific authorization, although there may be certain exceptions such as an optometry visit or a routine Pap smear from a gynecologist. In less tightly controlled systems, such as many PPOs and most indemnity plans, the requirements are less stringent. In those cases, it is common for authorization only to be required for elective hospitalizations and procedures, both inpatient and outpatient.

The tighter the authorization system, the greater the plan's ability to manage utilization. An authorization system per se will not automatically control utilization, although one could expect some sentinel effect. It is the management behind the system that will determine its ultimate effectiveness. If the medical director is unable or unwilling to deal with poor utilization behavior, an authorization system will have only a marginal effect. If the claims department is unable to back up the authorization system, it will quickly be subverted as members and providers learn that it is little more than a burdensome sham.

In any plan there will be times when a member is unable to obtain prior authorization. This is usually due to an emergency or to an urgent problem that occurs out of area. In those cases, the plan must make provision for the retrospective review of the case to determine whether authorization may be granted after the fact. Certain rules may also be defined regarding the member's obligation in those circumstances (eg, notification within 24 hours of the emergency). Be careful that such requirements do not allow for automatic authorization if the plan is notified within 24 hours but only for automatic review of the case to determine medical necessity.

DEFINITION OF WHO CAN AUTHORIZE SERVICES

The next requirement of an authorization system is to define who has the ability to authorize services and to what extent. This will vary considerably depending on the type of plan and the degree to which it will be medically managed.

In PPOs that are tightly controlled, there may be a requirement for PCP authorization. In loosely controlled PPOs and in managed indemnity plans, there is usually only a requirement for authorization for elective hospitalizations and procedures, but that authorization comes from plan personnel and not from the PCP or any other physician.

For example, if a participating surgeon wishes to admit a patient for surgery, the surgeon first calls a central telephone number and speaks with a plan representative, usually a nurse. That rep-

resentative then asks a number of questions about the patient's condition, and if predetermined criteria are met, and after the member's eligibility is confirmed (if the plan has that capability), an authorization is issued. In most cases, the surgery must take place on the day of admission, and certain procedures may only be done on an outpatient basis.

It is common practice in HMOs to require that most or all medical services be authorized by the member's PCP. Even then, however, there can be some dispute. For example, if a PCP authorizes a member to see a referral specialist, does that specialist have the ability to authorize tests, surgery, or another referral to himself or herself or to another specialist? Does a PCP require authorization to hospitalize one of his or her own patients?

A relatively common exception to this practice is in the area of mental health and substance abuse (MH/SA). As discussed in detail in Chapter 13, MH/SA services are unique and often lend themselves better to other methods of authorization. Plans or even the accounts themselves may carve out MH/SA from the basic health plan and treat it as a standalone function.

Another exception to the PCP-only concept occurs in HMOs that allow specialists to contact the plan directly about hospitalizations. In these cases, the referral to the specialist must have been made by the PCP in the first place, but the specialist may determine that hospitalization is required and obtain authorization directly from the plan's medical management department. Plans that operate this way generally do so because the PCPs have no real involvement in hospital cases anyway and because there is no utility in involving them in that decision.

In any type of managed care plan, there may be services that will require specific authorization from the plan's medical director. This is usually the case for expensive procedures such as transplants and for controversial procedures that may be considered experimental or of limited value except in particular circumstances. This is even more necessary when the plan has negotiated a special arrangement for high-cost services. The authorization system not only serves to review the medical necessity of the service but ensures that the care will be delivered at an institution that has contracted with the plan.

As mentioned above, the tighter the authorization system, the better the plan's ability to manage the care. For optimal control, only the PCP should be able to authorize services, and that pertains to all services except those that specifically require the approval of the plan's medical director or MH/SA services in those plans that have carved out that piece. In other words, even if a member is referred to a specialist, only the PCP can actually authorize any further services such as diagnostic tests, rereferral, or a procedure. This is the tightest form of a gatekeeper or case-coordinator model. As discussed below, this requires the use of unique authorization numbers that tie to specific bills, and the claims department must be able to back that up. As one backs away from that degree of tight control, utilization will tend to increase.

CLAIMS PAYMENT

A managed care health plan does not exist as an absolute dictator; you cannot issue blindfolds and cigarettes to members who fail to obtain authorization for services. The only recourse a plan has is to deny full payment for services that have not been authorized. This pertains equally to services obtained from nonparticipating providers (professionals or institutions) and to services obtained without required prior authorization.

In an HMO, payment can be completely denied for services that were not authorized. Point of service (POS) is unique and is discussed below. In most PPOs and in indemnity plans, if a service is not authorized but is considered a covered benefit, payment may not be denied, but the amount paid may be significantly reduced. For example, a plan pays 90% of charges for authorized services but only 50% of charges for nonauthorized services or perhaps imposes a flat dollar amount penalty for failure to obtain authorization.

In certain cases, a plan may deny any payment for a portion of the bill but will pay the rest. For example, if a patient is admitted the day before surgery even though same-day admission was required, the plan may not pay the charges (both hospital and physician) related to that first day but will pay charges for the remaining days.

In a PPO where a contractual relationship exists between the provider and the plan, the penalty may fall solely on the provider, who may not balance bill the member for the amount of the penalty. In the case of an indemnity plan (or a PPO in which the member received services from a nonparticipating provider), the penalty falls on the member, who must then pay more out of pocket.

Point of Service

POS is a special challenge for authorization systems and claims management (see Chapter 20). It is necessary to define what is covered as an authorized service and what is not because services that are not authorized will still be paid, albeit at the lower out-of-network level of benefits. Because POS is sold with the expressed intent that members will use out-of-network services, it is not always clear how a service was or was not authorized.

Common examples of this issue are illustrated as follows. If a PCP makes a referral to a specialist for one visit and the member returns for a follow-up, was that authorized? If a PCP authorizes three visits but the member goes four times, does the fourth visit cascade out to an out-of-network level of benefits? If a PCP refers to a specialist and the specialist determines that admission is necessary but the member is admitted to a nonparticipating hospital, is that authorized? What if the member is admitted to a participating hospital but is cared for by a mix of participating and nonparticipating physicians? What if a member is referred to a participating specialist who performs laboratory and radiology testing (even though the plan has capitated for such services); is the visit authorized but not the testing? What if the member claims that he or she had no choice in the matter?

The list of what if's is a long one. Most plans strive to identify an episode of care (eg, a hospitalization or a referral) and to remain consistent within that episode. For example, the testing by the specialist referenced above would be denied and the specialist prohibited from balance billing, or an entire hospitalization would be considered either in network or out of network. In any case, the plan must develop policies and procedures for defining when a service is to be considered authorized (and when it is considered in network in the case of hospital services that require precertification in any event) and when it is not.

CATEGORIES OF AUTHORIZATION

Authorizations may be classified into six types:

1. prospective
2. concurrent
3. retrospective
4. pended (for review)
5. denial (no authorization)
6. subauthorization

There is value in categorizing authorization types. By examining how authorizations are actually generated in your plan, you will be able to identify areas of weakness in your system. For example, if you feel that all elective admissions are receiving prospective authorization and discover that in fact most are being authorized either concurrently or, worse yet, retrospectively, you will know that you are not able to intervene effectively in managing hospital cases because you do not know about them in a timely manner. A brief description of the authorization categories follows.

Prospective

Sometimes referred to as precertification, this type of authorization is issued before any service is rendered. This is commonly used in plans that require prior authorization for elective services. The more prospective the authorization, the more time the medical director has to intervene if necessary, the greater the ability to direct care to the most appropriate setting or provider, and the more current your knowledge regarding utilization trends.

Inexperienced plan managers tend to believe that all authorizations are prospective. That na-

ive belief can lead to a real shock when the manager of a troubled plan learns that most claims are actually being paid on the basis of other types of authorizations that were not correctly categorized. This is discussed further below.

Concurrent

A concurrent authorization is generated at the time the service is rendered. For example, the utilization review nurse discovers that a patient is being admitted to the hospital that day. An authorization is generated, but by the nurse and not by the PCP. Another example is an urgent service that cannot wait for review, such as setting a broken leg. In that case, the PCP may contact the plan, but the referral is made at the same time.

Concurrent authorizations allow for timely data gathering and the potential for affecting the outcome, but they do not allow the plan medical managers to intervene in the initial decision to render services. This may result in care being inappropriately delivered or delivered in a setting that is not cost effective, but it also may result in the plan's being able to alter the course of care in a more cost-effective direction even though care has already commenced.

Retrospective

As the term indicates, retrospective authorizations take place after the fact. For example, a patient is admitted, has surgery, and is discharged, and then the plan finds out. On the surface, it appears that any service rendered without authorization would have payment denied or reduced, but there will be circumstances when the plan will genuinely agree to authorize services after the fact. For example, if a member is involved in a serious automobile accident or has a heart attack while traveling in another state, there is a clear need for care and the plan could not deny that need.

Inexperienced managers often believe not only that most authorizations are prospective but that, except for emergency cases, there are few retrospective authorizations. Unfortunately, there are circumstances when there may be a high volume of retrospective authorizations. This commonly occurs when the PCPs or participating providers fail to cooperate with the authorization system. A claim comes in cold (ie, without an authorization), and the plan must create one after the fact if it finds out that the service was really meant to be authorized. The plan cannot punish the member because it was really the fault of the PCP, so that claim gets paid.

Most plans have a no balance billing clause in their provider contracts (see Chapter 36) and may elect not to pay claims that have not been prospectively authorized, forcing the non-compliant providers to write off the expense. That will certainly get their attention, but it comes at some cost in provider relations. Even so, sometimes it becomes necessary if discussions and education attempts fail.

If the plan's systems allow an authorization to be classified as prospective or concurrent regardless of when it is created relative to the delivery of the service, it is a sure thing that retrospective authorizations will occur but not be labeled retrospective; for example, the PCP or specialist will say "I really meant to authorize that" or "It's in the mail" and call the authorization concurrent. Another possibility is that claims clerks may be creating retrospective authorizations on the basis of the belief that the claim was linked to another authorized claim (see below).

In a tightly managed plan the ability to create a retrospective authorization is strictly limited to the medical director or utilization management department, the ability to create prospective authorizations does not exist once the service has actually been rendered, and concurrent authorizations cannot be created after 24 hours have passed since the service was rendered.

Pended (For Review)

Pended is a claims term that refers to a state of authorization purgatory. In this situation, it is not known whether an authorization will be issued, and the case has been pended for review. This refers to medical review (for medical necessity, such as an emergency department claim) or to administrative review. As noted above, if a plan is having problems getting the PCPs or partici-

pating providers to cooperate with the authorization system, there will be a significant number of pended claims that ultimately lead to retrospective authorizations.

Denial

Denial refers to the certainty that there will be no authorization forthcoming. As has been discussed, you cannot assume that every claim coming into the plan without an associated authorization will be denied because there are reasons that an unauthorized claim may be paid.

Subauthorization

This is a special category that allows one authorization to hitchhike on another. This is most common for hospital-based professional services. For example, a single authorization may be issued for a hospitalization, and that authorization is used to cover anesthesia, pathology, radiology, or even a surgeon's or consultant's fees.

In some plans, an authorization to a referral specialist may be used to authorize diagnostic and therapeutic services ordered by that specialist. Great care must be taken to control this. If not, the phenomenon of linking will occur.

Linking refers to claims clerks linking unauthorized services to authorized ones and creating subauthorizations to do so. For example, a referral to a specialist is authorized, and a claim is received not only for the specialist's fees but for some expensive procedure or test as well, or a bill is received for 10 visits even though the PCP intended to authorize only 1. The claims clerk (who is probably being judged on how many claims he or she can process per hour) may then inappropriately link all the bills to the originally authorized service through the creation of subauthorizations, thereby increasing the costs to the plan.

STAFFING

Plan personnel required to implement properly an authorization system are the medical director, an authorization system coordinator (whatever that person's actual title), and the utilization review nurses. Various clerks and telephone operators will also be required; the number of these depends on the size of the plan and the scope of the system.

The medical director has three primary roles. The first is to interact with the plan's PCPs to ensure cooperation with the authorization system. Second, the medical director is responsible for medical review of pended claims. That does not mean that the medical director will have to review every claim personally, but that it is ultimately the medical director's responsibility. In some instances the case will be reviewed by the member's PCP; in others it will be more appropriate for a nurse reviewer or even the medical director (or designate) to perform the primary review. Third, the medical director will sometimes have interactions with members when payment of a claim is denied. Although the claims department usually sends the denial letters and responds to enquiries, it is common for members to demand a review of the denied claim on the basis of medical necessity or a belief that the PCP really authorized the service. In those cases, the medical director will often be involved.

The authorization system needs a coordinator to make sure that all the pieces fit together. Whether that responsibility falls to the claims department, the utilization department, the medical director's office, or general management is a local choice. In a small plan, the role of coordinator usually falls to a manager with other duties as well, but as the plan grows it is best to dedicate that function.

The coordinator's primary purpose is to track the authorization system at all its points. All systems can break down, and the coordinator must keep track of where the system is performing suboptimally and take steps to correct it. In some cases that will require the intervention of others because an authorization system has ramifications in the PCP's office, the hospitals, the utilization review department, the claims department, member services, and finance. If no one is in charge of maintaining the authorization system, people will tend to deny their responsibilities in making it work.

Some thought must be given to the relationship of the authorization system to the utilization review coordinators. Specifically, how much can the utilization review coordinator authorize? It makes sense to allow some ability to create authorizations, especially subauthorizations for hospital services, but you must decide whether you will allow the utilization review coordinators to create primary authorizations, particularly for hospital cases and for large case management (see Chapter 10).

COMMON DATA ELEMENTS

The needs of your plan will dictate what data elements you actually capture. In some plans, the management information system will be able automatically to provide some of this information, so you would not have to capture it at the time the authorization is created. The data elements that are commonly captured in authorization systems are illustrated in Exhibit 17-1.

In systems where there are clinical requirements for authorization, the system then must determine what the requirements are on the basis of the diagnosis. For example, if your plan has preset criteria for authorization for cataract surgery, those requirements may be reviewed with the physician calling in for authorization. The same issue applies to mandatory outpatient surgery: If admission is being requested, the procedure may be compared to an outpatient surgery list to determine whether the physician needs to justify an exception. Such reviews should only be done by medically trained personnel, usually nurses. In the case of disagreements with the requesting physician, the medical director must be able to contact the physician at that time or as soon as possible.

If an authorization is made, the system also must be able to generate and link an authorization number or identifier to the data, so that every authorization will be unique. In tightly controlled plans, any claim must be accompanied by that unique authorization number to be processed.

METHODS OF DATA CAPTURE AND AUTHORIZATION ISSUANCE

There are three main methods of interacting with an authorization system: paper based, telephone based, and electronic.

Exhibit 17-1 Data Elements Commonly Captured in an Authorization System

- Member's name
- Member's birth date
- Member's plan ID number
- Eligibility status
  - —Commercial group number
  - —Line of business (eg, HMO, POS, Medicare, conversion, private or self-pay)
  - —Benefits code for particular service (eg, noncovered, partial coverage, limited benefit, full coverage)
- PCP
- Referral provider
  - —Name
  - —Specialty
- Outpatient data elements
  - —Referral or service date
  - —Diagnosis (*International Classification of Disease*—9th Edition, Clinical Modification [ICD-CM9], free text)
  - —Number of visits authorized
  - —Specific procedures authorized (*Current Procedural Terminology*—4th Edition [CPT-4], free text)
- Inpatient data elements
  - —Name of institution
  - —Admitting physician
  - —Admission or service date
  - —Diagnosis (ICD-9, diagnosis-related group, free text)
  - —Discharge date
- Subauthorizations (if allowed or required)
  - —Hospital-based professionals
  - —Other specialists
  - —Other procedures or studies

data into its system. Claims submitted to the plan may or may not require a copy of the authorization form, depending on your choice.

The advantages of paper-based systems are as follows. They are less labor intensive than telephone-based systems and therefore require less overhead for the plan. Although electronic systems are even more labor efficient, electronic systems require a higher level of sophistication and support than paper-based systems. Data entry can be done in batch mode because there is little need for real-time interaction. They also tend to be more acceptable to physicians because they are less intrusive regarding clinical decision making, run less risk of violating patient confidentiality, and do not have the problem of busy signals or a physician's being placed on hold during a busy day in the office.

The main disadvantage of paper-based systems is that there is less opportunity to intervene at the time the authorization is made. Once an authorization is issued, it is nearly impossible to reverse it. You may be able to alter future behavior, but neither physician nor member will easily accept an after-the-fact reversal of an authorization. Another disadvantage is that it may increase the administrative burden on the physician, particularly if he or she is participating in multiple plans, each with its own complicated set of forms. Paper authorizations can also get lost in the mail (or mail room) and lend themselves to data entry errors (eg, digit transpositions).

Paper-Based Authorization Systems

Paper-based systems generally work in plans that allow the PCP to authorize the service. If plan preapproval is necessary before an authorization is issued (except for infrequent services such as transplants), a paper-based system will not be responsive enough. If, however, the PCP has the authority to authorize services, a paper-based system will be adequate.

This type of system depends on the PCP (or other authorizing provider) to fill out an authorization form, which may be used as a referral or admission form as well. A copy of the form is sent to the plan, which enters the authorization

Telephone-Based Authorization Systems

Telephone-based systems rely on the PCP or office staff to call a central number and give the information over the phone. If clinical review is required, it is done at that time. Telephone-based systems have the built-in potential of clogging up and leading to poor service. If the system is unresponsive, or if PCPs get frequent busy signals or are put on hold, they will stop calling. The investment in a responsive telephone-based system will be paid back in a reduction of pended claims and retrospective authorizations.

Collecting the data and issuing an authorization number may be done either manually or by an automated system. It is rare for a health plan not to use computers for claims payment, although a new start-up plan could certainly perform this function manually for a while. Because authorization is linked to claims payment, there must be an interface between the two systems.

One approach is to collect all the data on manual logs and then enter them into the claims system through batch processing. Another approach is to automate the entire process. If you have systems capabilities to do so, you may wish to have your authorization clerks or nurses enter the data directly into the computer. Be aware, though, that computer systems can delay you with slow screens, complicated menus and entry screens, down time, training problems, and a host of other problems. Some computer systems are made for batch entry, making real-time entry too inefficient. In those situations, you may wish to use a manual log for data capture and authorization issuance until your automated system is well tested. You should also be able to use a manual system as a back-up on a moment's notice.

The advantages of telephone-based systems are that they can be more responsive and timely, have greater potential for directing care to the appropriate location and provider, and have the potential of reducing the administrative burden on the PCP's office staff. The disadvantages are that they increase the administrative burden on the plan and, if not run efficiently, can generate great ill will with the PCPs.

Electronic Authorization Systems

Electronic authorization systems are not as common as paper- or telephone-based systems, but their popularity is growing. Electronic-based systems require participating physicians and hospitals to interface electronically with the plan, usually through a personal computer or a dumb terminal in the office. Generally, electronic communications with providers focuses on claims submission and payment, but authorizations are equally possible.

Electronic authorizations may be nothing more than an electronic form that the provider completes on line and transmits to the plan. The

authorization system may be more complex, editing fields to ensure that the referral or admission is to a participating provider and requiring key data elements to be provided. An electronic authorization system may also provide automatic information transfer (eg, member status and demographics). It is also possible for an electronic system to gather clinical information and to compare that to protocols before processing the authorization, but currently that is more conjecture than fact.

Electronic systems generally enter the authorization data directly (or via electronic batch entry) into the management information system, so that the need for personnel to enter data is reduced. Such systems require a high level of expertise by the plan and a certain level of sophistication by the providers themselves.

AUTHORIZATION SYSTEM REPORTS

The reports needed from an authorization system will depend on the complexity of the system and your management needs. Obviously, the one absolutely necessary report function is linking incoming claims to authorized services. That function is addressed in Chapter 20 as well as here.

Hospital logs and reports are discussed in greater detail in Chapter 16. The authorization system should be able to print out a report indicating prospective admissions and procedures, current admissions and procedures, and retrospectively authorized cases. Cases pended for review should also be reported, with data indicating when the claim was received, when it was reviewed, and its current status.

Outpatient reports are also discussed in greater detail in Chapter 16. Reports from the authorization system could include summaries of authorizations by type for each PCP expressed as ratios, for example, total authorizations per 100 encounters per PCP or per 1,000 members per year (annualized), with a breakdown of prospective compared to concurrent compared to retrospective, and so forth. Authorization types may also be expressed as a percentage of the total number of authorizations for that PCP. For example, the total authorization rate may be 8 per 100 encounters per PCP with 50% prospective, 40% concurrent, 6% retrospective, and 4% pended (if it is denied, it is not an authorization, although it is still quite useful to report denial statistics by provider as well).

A valuable report is a comparison of authorization types to paid claims. This is basically looking at the percentage of claims that have been authorized prospectively, concurrently, and so forth. This is valuable in determining your ability to capture the data in a timely fashion. It will be inversely proportional to your plan's rate of incurred but not reported claims (IBNRs).

These reports will allow you to identify noncompliant providers or providers who comply but not in a timely fashion. The medical director will be able to focus on those providers who either do not obtain authorizations or who do so in a way that does not allow for active medical management by the medical director (if that is needed). These reports, along with a report on the number and nature of open authorizations (ie, authorizations for services for which a claim has not yet been received), will also allow the finance department to calculate more accurately the accruals and IBNR factor for the plan, reducing the chances of nasty surprises later.

CONCLUSION

An effective authorization system is a requirement of any managed care plan. Whether that system is all encompassing or pertains only to certain types of services is dependent on the type of plan. Key elements to address are what services require authorization, who has the ability to authorize, whether secondary plan approval is required, what data will be captured, how they will be captured, and how they will be used.

Chapter 18

Formal Physician Performance Evaluations

Peter R. Kongstvedt

Practicing physicians, unlike physicians in managerial or administrative roles, are seldom subjected to formal performance evaluations. The emotional distaste that physicians, including physician managers, have for formally and openly evaluating their colleagues' performance is great indeed. For that reason, raises and bonus payments tend to be either across the board or based on some single objective standard such as productivity or utilization.

In managed care it is difficult to use any single criterion or small set of criteria for judging performance. As is discussed below, it is relatively easy to game a system that has only a few elements, and that can lead to problems.

There is no inherent reason why a practicing physician's performance cannot be evaluated in a manner similar to that of any senior manager. Granted, the criteria for evaluation will be substantially different, but a physician is still a man-

The author wishes to thank the following individuals for conceptual contributions to this topic in prior years: for closed panels, Jacob Lazorovic, MD, and Carl Mankowitz, MD, and especially as referenced in this chapter, Richard Cooper, MD; and for open panels, Gordon Church, David Ward, Pamela Shorter, Tim O'Hare, and Lawrence Dotin, MD.

ager. Physicians manage the health care of their patients, they manage the economic resources of the plan, and they manage their own productivity and performance. The purpose of this chapter is to explore the ways in which physician performance may be formally reviewed and how such reviews may be structured.

CLOSED PANELS COMPARED TO OPEN PANELS

Obviously, there are significant differences between closed and open panels that affect formal physician performance evaluations. In closed panels it is easier to observe behavior, and a greater reliance on subjective evaluations is possible. Closed panels also frequently include both primary care physicians (PCPs) and consultants, both of whom may authorize services and may care for a regular panel of patients. Formal performance evaluations in closed panel managed care plans, similar to what is discussed in this chapter, have been in use for many years.[1]

In open panels, the issues may be confused by existing risk/bonus systems in the private practice setting that often reward physicians strictly on the basis of utilization or productivity. Such systems generally place a greater reliance on objective measures. Further, open panels tend to focus more on PCPs rather than on both PCPs and consultants. It is certainly possible to construct an open panel performance evaluation program for consultants as well as PCPs, and the principles will be the same. This chapter focuses on PCPs, looks at both types of systems, and makes suggestions for methods that may work in one or the other. Although most performance evaluation systems have been applied to PCP managing plans (ie, gatekeeper plans), it is also possible to apply them to preferred provider organizations.[2]

THE VALUE OF FORMAL PERFORMANCE EVALUATIONS

Beyond the intellectual challenge, there are some practical uses for formal performance evaluations. What follows are examples for closed panels, open panels, or both.

Annual Compensation Adjustments in Closed Panels

Formal performance evaluations are quite useful in groups that use merit raises to adjust annual compensation. If a group uses strict percentage raises, or perhaps tails off the percentage after time but still handles raises in an across the board manner, adding an element of merit to the process of getting a raise can help reward the types of behavior one wishes to encourage.

Few physicians will argue that there are various levels of contributions from the closed panel medical staff. In a private fee-for-service practice, the less you collect, the less money you get. In a managed care setting, the criteria are not all that clear, and there is no built-in reward structure for superior performance. Formal evaluations provide that structure.

In prepaid groups where the idea of performance-based compensation may be too volatile to implement fully, it is possible to combine an element of across the board raise with a performance-based raise. For example, if a plan has budgeted a 6% increase in physicians' base sal-

ary, one could allocate 3% for an across the board (or cost of living) raise, and the remaining 3% would be based on performance.

Bonus Distribution in Open or Closed Panels

In open panels, year-end payouts from withhold or risk-sharing pools are usually based strictly on utilization, either individual or aggregate. It is possible for an open panel plan to budget for a bonus or to use some profit or withhold for incentive compensation (IC) payments based on performance evaluations.[3,4] This allows the plan to reward individual performance by some physicians that goes beyond low utilization.

Behavior Modification

Certainly the purpose of any system that has an impact on compensation is geared toward modifying behavior. Even if you have chosen not to use a formal evaluation process for adjusting compensation or bonus distribution, however, or in those years when there is no bonus to distribute, there remains merit in its use. Most professionals are motivated to do a good job simply for its own sake but often lack sufficient feedback. A formal system for performance evaluations is designed to provide such feedback.

Because frequent feedback about performance has a more significant impact than an annual review, it is generally desirable to provide such feedback on a quarterly or semiannual basis unless constraints in data processing, personnel, or money require that feedback be given only annually.

Required Feedback

Medical managers are no different from non-medical managers when it comes to not wanting to do performance reviews. The main difference is that most medical managers get away with not having to do them, at least in a meaningful way. The dangers of not conducting performance reviews are these: If physicians are being judged but the results of that judgment are not fed back properly, an atmosphere of distrust can occur.

Even worse, performance ends up not actually being judged at all, and the medical manager has no idea how to improve a situation once it has become a problem. Worst of all, a manager ends up having to discipline a physician, and the physician retorts that he or she had never been told before that his or her performance was substandard.

For these reasons, it is valuable to have in place a system that forces plan management to conduct performance evaluations on a regular basis. When the duty is inescapable, it will be carried out. In fact, it is also possible for part of the medical director's own bonus to be contingent upon performing the reviews.

Documentation of Substandard Performance

Documenting and tracking substandard performance is also one of the elements of formal performance evaluation. Beyond the issues of discipline and sanctions (see Chapters 9 and 38), there will certainly be instances where performance is not so poor as to warrant immediate termination or probation but where improvement is clearly required. The formal performance evaluation is an excellent vehicle for documenting needed improvements as well. This is useful not only for the time period at hand but for providing a documented history if an action is required at a later date. In open panels, this documentation, in conjunction with utilization results, also allows management to identify and clearly rank priorities as to which physicians need increased attention.

PROBLEMS WITH FORMAL EVALUATIONS

Evaluating physician performance is unique in managed health care. As mentioned earlier, traditional fee-for-service has a straightforward reward system: The more you collect, the more you are rewarded. Because that often works in opposition to the goals of managed care, different criteria are necessary.

At first, it would appear that simply reversing the economic reward would work. In other words, the less physicians utilize services, the

more money they get. That, in fact, is the way many capitation schemes work in open panels. Unfortunately, that method not only fails to take into account certain behaviors that have no direct impact on utilization (such as member satisfaction, participation with the quality management program, or compliance with administrative procedures) but may also be subject to inappropriate manipulation.

Objective Criteria

The use of strictly objective criteria has significant drawbacks. Examples of strictly objective criteria include utilization rates (eg, hospital rates, referral rates, and ancillary testing), overall medical cost [eg, per member per month (PMPM) cost], productivity (eg, visits per day), and so forth. The major problem with strictly objective criteria is that they can be gamed. The two major games played with objective criteria are (1) churning and (2) buffing and turfing.

Churning is the major complaint against fee-for-service medicine but can be equally prevalent in some managed care environments. Churning is simply increasing the revisit rate of existing patients more than is medically necessary. If a closed panel has a reward system that has an emphasis on productivity, an element of churning could creep in. For example, it is just as easy to schedule a hypertension recheck in 4 weeks as 8 weeks. Further, a revisit is a lot easier than a new patient, so the temptation can occur to see many revisits rather than allow the time for lengthy visits from new patients.

Buffing and turfing can occur in any plan with an undue emphasis on utilization and when the compensation and reward structure for physicians is heavily weighted toward individual physicians having low utilization profiles. Buffing and turfing refers to a physician's culling sick patients out of the practice to make the utilization profiles look better. Buffing refers to a physician's making this practice appear (to the plan) to be justifiable, and turfing refers to transferring the sickest patients to other physicians for care in order to look like a low-utilizing provider.

This problem is not to be confused with the common excuse for failing to control utilization, the excuse of "But I've got all the sick patients!" It is up to the medical director to determine whether there is validity to that. Buffing and turfing refer specifically to physicians trying to dump their high-cost patients on other physicians.

Subjective Criteria

Strictly subjective criteria are just as problematic as strictly objective criteria. Examples of strictly subjective criteria can include judgments about attitude, professionalism, demeanor, and the like. The principal problems with subjective criteria are the variability of interpretation and charges of favoritism and bias.

The very nature of subjective criteria demands variability in interpretation. Although a subjective category may be defined, performance in that category will be judged on the basis of the evaluator's opinion rather than on a set of numbers. This is certainly legitimate because presumably the manager making the judgment has a reasonably good idea of what he or she wants to see. It is still true, however, that different managers may judge the same behavior in different ways.

Charges of favoritism and bias are much more serious. If strictly subjective criteria are used, and if a negative evaluation is given to a physician, the manager may find that the physician does not accept the results, and charges of favoritism or bias may ensue. This can be of great concern if disciplinary actions are necessary and could theoretically lead to legal action against a plan.

CATEGORIES FOR EVALUATION OF PHYSICIAN PERFORMANCE

As we have seen, the use of strictly objective or subjective criteria can cause problems. It is therefore more useful to use both types of evaluation criteria in assessing physician performance. There are clearly objective items that can be measured and evaluated, items that a medical manager will consider important, such as utilization or productivity. The same is true for subjective measures such as participation, attitude, and

so forth. The real issue is to combine objective with subjective in such a way as to avoid as much as possible the disincentive aspects of concentrating too heavily on any one category. It is unlikely that any plan will use all categories discussed; rather, plan management will choose what is important to the plan's particular situation.

Categories for Evaluation in Closed Panels

This section discusses 11 suggested categories for evaluation of physician performance in closed panels. These categories are listed in Exhibit 18-1 and are discussed below.

In any individual plan, certain categories will have more or less importance, and there are surely categories that are not even mentioned here. Unlike open panels, where utilization results may have a direct economic impact on a physician, in many closed panels a physician's utilization-based performance will require increased attention during this process.

It is important that the physicians in the group buy in to the process, and not feel that it is being forced upon them. It is up to plan management to decide what behavior it wishes to motivate and then to present the concept to the practicing physicians. Allowing the physicians to have input into developing the criteria against which their performance will be judged is crucial to gaining acceptance and cooperation with the program.

What follows are areas that one may wish to consider for evaluation of closed panel physi-

---

Exhibit 18-1 Categories for Closed Panel Physician Evaluation

- Productivity
- Medical charting
- Dependability
- After-hours call duty
- Medical knowledge
- Management of patient care
- Management of outside resources
- Patient relations
- Staff relations
- Attitude and leadership
- Participation

cian performance. A general idea of how the category is defined is also given, although before using these categories one would want to define more specifically just what aspects of behavior would be evaluated.

Productivity

This category looks at volume of work and efficiency. Whatever standard a plan sets, such as number of visits per week, hours worked, and so forth, would be used as judgment criteria. One could add an element of time management as well. Productivity is discussed in Chapter 4.

Medical Charting

This would evaluate a physician's outpatient charts for legibility, timeliness, thoroughness, and compliance with whatever system is being used (eg, chart format, face sheets, medication sheets, and so forth).

Dependability

This category would include arriving on time for work, sticking to the schedule, and complying with administrative aspects of the plan, such as properly using the forms.

After-Hours Call Duty

This category looks at responsiveness, appropriate use of emergency medical resources, proper documentation, ensuring continuity of care through follow-ups or transfer of care to the appropriate primary physician, and any other aspects of care delivered through the after-hours on-call mechanism.

Medical Knowledge

This evaluates the level of medical knowledge, amount of technical skills, evidence of proper medical judgment, awareness of limitations in skills and knowledge, and appropriate use of continuing medical education opportunities.

Management of Patient Care

Closely related to the category of medical knowledge, this category looks at how the basic medical skills are translated into action and how that relates to cost effectiveness. This category would include both outpatient and inpatient care.

Examples would include logical and efficient plans for diagnosis and treatment, proper discharge planning, appropriate follow-up intervals, and so forth. The common thread is how patient care is handled by the physician being evaluated rather than by a consultant.

Management of Outside Resources

This category looks at a physician's use of outside resources, including consultants and ancillary services, both diagnostic and therapeutic. Evaluations of appropriateness, cost-effective use, and maintenance of continuity would be made.

Patient Relations

This category looks at a physician's ability to communicate effectively with patients, the quality of patient relations, and any concerns regarding member satisfaction.

Staff Relations

This looks at a physician's ability to communicate and cooperate with other members of the medical staff, including a physician's working relationship with support staff.

Attitude and Leadership

Attitude looks at a physician's enthusiasm, interest, commitment, flexibility, responsiveness, and so forth. Although essentially this is a measure of positive attitude, one may wish to add those specifics about what is considered most important in judging attitude. Leadership refers to a physician's ability to train others and to motivate and lead as well as to his or her decision and communication skills in nonmedical matters.

Participation

Closely related to attitude, participation refers specifically to participation in plan committees and meetings. This looks at attendance, contribution, and initiative in taking responsibility.

Categories for Evaluation in Open Panels

This section discusses nine possible categories for formal performance evaluation in open panels; again, this list is not exhaustive, and a plan would not necessarily use all the catagories. These categories are much more objective than subjective, in keeping with the management structure of open panels. They are listed in Exhibit 18-2 and are discussed below.

Unlike the traditional method in open panels of rewarding physicians for low utilization, these categories allow the manager to recognize utilization that may be too low (for reasons of poor management or simple luck) and to take that into account. In other words, the best evaluation for certain categories (eg, productivity, referral utilization, and hospital utilization) could be for performance around a norm rather than the lowest utilization. Performance could also be evaluated completely external to utilization results if that is desirable. Practice profiling based on claims data is discussed in Chapter 16.

Productivity

Productivity is generally measured as office visits per member per year (PMPY). Too low a number (eg, fewer than 1.5 visits PMPY) could indicate either good luck or denied access. Too high a number (eg, more than 5) could indicate either bad luck or inefficient case management.

Referral Utilization

One could look at referrals PMPY, total referral costs PMPY, or both, or other common measures of referral utilization. Values that are either too low (eg, fewer than 0.5 referrals PMPY or less than $30 PMPY) or too high (eg, more than 3 referrals PMPY or more than $100

Exhibit 18-2 Categories for Open Panel Physician Evaluation

- Productivity
- Referral utilization
- Hospital utilization
- Ancillary utilization
- Cooperation with pre-certification and authorization requirements
- Compliance with use of the plan network
- Cooperation with plan policies and procedures
- Participation with and results of quality management
- Patient relations and member satisfaction

PMPY) would have the same ramifications as noted above.

Hospital Utilization

This could measure days per 1,000 (annualized) or could be subdivided to look at the admission rate and the average length of stay. Again, values that are either too high or too low would have possible implications.

Ancillary Utilization

This category would measure the physician's use of laboratory, radiology, pharmacy, or whatever ancillary service the plan wished to observe.

Cooperation with Precertification and Authorization Requirements

This measures the physician's compliance with the plan's requirements for precertification and authorization of services and is measured as a percentage. For example, 88% of admissions for a physician are precertified, and 95% of referrals are prospectively authorized. There is no value that can be too low; the scale is linear rather than bell shaped.

Compliance with Use of the Plan Network

This measures a physician's use of the plan network, both consultant and hospital. The more a physician uses nonparticipating providers, the worse the compliance. A certain amount of background noise (eg, from out of area emergencies) is to be expected, especially with point-of-service plans.

Cooperation with Plan Policies and Procedures

Beyond the policies and procedures for precertification and authorization, this measures compliance with encounter tracking, participation in meetings and committees, fee structures, and so forth. This measure may be somewhat subjective.

Participation with and Results of Quality Management

This would look at a physician's cooperation with the quality management (QM) program and the results of actual audits. Failure to cooperate would result in either no points or a negative score or evaluation. Standards of care for such things as health maintenance or common problems (eg, hypertension) would be evaluated, and a cumulative score would be developed. For example, 85% compliance with standards for a particular audit would yield a result equal to 85% of the maximum possible score.

Patient Relations and Member Satisfaction

These data are obtained from member services reports (see Chapter 19). Evaluations could include the rate at which members transfer out of the practice, the rate at which the physician asks to remove members from the practice, and complaints or grievances about the physician. Other data might include the results of waiting time studies and appointment availability.

Another source for member satisfaction data are member surveys. Periodic mail or telephone surveys with a well-designed survey instrument can yield valuable information about patient satisfaction and perceived quality of service.

MEASURING THE CATEGORIES AND PRODUCING A RESULT

Although you may wish to use the above categories simply for discussion, there is utility in quantifying the results of the evaluation. For example, if you are using a formal evaluation system for allocating bonus payments, it is extremely useful to have the results of the evaluation tie directly to the amount of money that is paid out.

To facilitate measurement, it is sometimes helpful, although not required, to assign relative weights to each category. These weights would reflect the importance of that category in the overall scheme of things. For example, you may decide that medical charting is less important than cost-effective use of resources.

Regardless of whether you use a weighting factor, it is quite helpful to translate the evaluation of performance in each category into a numeric value or score. For example, you may use a scale of 1 to 5 or 1 to 10. The better the performance in that category, the higher the number.

For categories in which the result depends on achieving a norm, a bell-shaped curve could be used. For example, if PCP encounters are expected to be 3.5 visits PMPY, then 5 points could be awarded for visits of 3.0 to 4.0 visits PMPY, 3 points for 1.5 to 2.9 or 4.1 to 5.0 visits PMPY, 2 points for 0.5 to 1.4 or 5.1 to 6.0 visits PMPY, and so forth.

If you are using weighting factors, you would then multiply the score by the weight to achieve a numeric result. For example, if a score of 5 is given and the weight is also 5, the score would be 25.

The last step is to tabulate the results. For example, if you were using an evaluation system with 11 categories, a scale of 1 to 5, and no weighting factor, the highest possible result or score would be 55.

If you are using an evaluation system for allocating bonus or adjusting annual base compensation, the numeric result would be used to calculate the amount of payout as described below.

Closed Panel Example

The following example will illustrate the use of a formal evaluation system for allocation of bonuses in a small group. Assume that there are five full-time physicians eligible to participate in a year-end bonus equal to $40,000. First add up all the points for all the physicians. Assuming a system with 11 categories, a scale of 1 to 5, and no weighting factor, you might find that the scores of the physicians are 50, 45, 40, 51, and 39. The total number of points then is the sum of these five scores, or 225. The first physician receives 50/225 of the $40,000, or $8,889 (rounded); the second physician receives 45/225 of the total amount of available bonus, or $8,000; the third receives $7,111; the fourth receives $9,067; and the fifth, who had the poorest evaluation, receives $6,933.

Open Panel Example

How complex one makes an IC program will be dependant on the plan's goals for the program, the level of sophistication in the physician panel, the size of the panel to be covered under the program, and the amount of money available for IC. Some plans pay IC from utilization-based risk pools (such as referral or institutional; see Chapter 6); other plans budget IC as a separate line item independent of utilization. In open panels, it is also quite useful to look at both behavior and the size of the membership base a physician is responsible for, with greater potential rewards going not only to those physicians who demonstrate desired behavior but to those whose panel size is large.

In a small, stable, and sophisticated individual practice association, one may use all the above mentioned categories for evaluation. In a large and heterogeneous direct contract model open panel, the focus may be more narrow. The following examples illustrate some different ways to approach an open panel.

Many physicians in private fee-for-service practice complain about the administrative burden placed on them by managed care. That complaint is partially legitimate, although if utilization is controlled the economic reward should offset the hassle factor. Nevertheless, one may agree to compensate through IC for those items that are important to the plan but do not necessarily result in a direct utilization-based economic reward (eg, QM, compliance with administrative procedures, and member satisfaction). In this example, payment of performance-based IC is not influenced by utilization results or the status of any utilization-based risk/bonus pool. The incentive compensation is funded on a PMPM basis and as a distinct line item. Points are assigned for each category, and a minimum score (say 50% of the total possible points) must be achieved for the physician to participate in the IC program.

In this example, assume that there are 180 PCPs in a direct contract open panel health maintenance organization (HMO). Because of problems with member satisfaction, it is decided to pay out IC based 40% on member satisfaction and 30% each on compliance with administrative procedures and QM. For simplicity's sake, assume that that translates to 40 possible points for member satisfaction and 30 possible points each for compliance and QM. Funding is at

$0.30 PMPM, and there are 60,000 members in the HMO, so there is $216,000 potentially available (60,000 × 12 × $0.30) at year end.

Member satisfaction is measured by telephone surveys of members who have seen the PCP in the past 6 months, transfer rates out of the practice, and member complaints and concerns.

Compliance with administrative procedures is measured by looking at compliance with precertification requirements (measured as a percentage of hospital admissions and outpatient surgeries that are precertified), encounter form submission (measured against a statistical average, 3.2 visits PMPY, for example), and compliance with the referral authorization system (measured by timeliness and completion of the referral authorization form and use of participating providers).

QM is measured by compliance with standards of care set by the QM committee for both routine health maintenance and disease-specific process audits. For example, a set number of charts are audited for a fixed set of criteria; if the PCP meets the criteria 90% of the time, then the score would be 90% of the maximum number of possible points. If a PCP refuses to participate in the QM program, or if the PCP has been sanctioned by the QM committee, no participation in the IC program is allowed.

The plan may choose to pay out IC only on the basis of the PMPM allocation to any individual PCP, or it may choose to pay out the entire IC pool but only to those PCPs who are eligible to participate. In other words, if half the network qualifies, the plan must choose whether to pay out only half the IC pool (based on the assumption that PCPs who fail to qualify increase the overhead cost to the plan because of their poor habits) or to pay out the entire pool but only to half the network.

In the case of only paying out an individual PCP's IC allocation, the plan simply pays out the individual PCP's PMPM allocation times the total member months for a qualifying physician times the percentage of the maximum score received. For example, assume that a single PCP has 700 members and has achieved a rating of 85% on member satisfaction, 75% on compliance, and 80% on QM. The calculation would then be ($0.30 × 700 × 12) × [(0.4 × 0.85) + (0.3 × 0.75) + (0.3 × 0.8)] = $2,028.60.

In the situation where the entire IC fund is to be paid out to qualifying PCPs, the following calculations illustrate disbursement of IC. First, membership must be factored into the score. One simple method is to multiply the score by the membership base the PCP covers; for example, if a PCP has achieved results as noted above, the total score would be (700 × 12) × [(0.4 × 0.85) + (0.3 × 0.75) + (0.3 × 0.8)] = 6,762. Next, the entire IC fund must be divided by the total number of available points to assign a value to each point; for example, if 70 PCPs qualified to participate and the aggregate point value of those 70 PCPs is 444,500, then each point is worth ($216,000/444,500) = $0.486. Last, each PCP has his or her individual total points multiplied by the point value; in our example that would be (6,762 × $0.486) = $3,286.33.

Some managers feel that, if a PCP has already received a substantial bonus from the utilization risk/bonus pools (in a capitated system), then IC should be reduced, and they therefore include a negative factor for bonus already received. In that way, the IC program preferentially rewards PCPs who were good case managers but who experienced more than their share of bad luck in terms of adverse selection.

CONCLUSION

Most managed care products have similar benefit designs. As the industry matures, the plans that survive will no doubt be those that motivate health care providers to provide cost-efficient service. As efficiencies standardize across plans, price competition may intensify and create a marketplace where plans can only distinguish themselves on service. Performance evaluation in health care, therefore, should reward cost efficiency and high-quality service.

Formal evaluations of physician performance can and should be made in a managed care plan. Professional behavior may be evaluated with a combination of objective and subjective criteria. Excessive emphasis on any one area must be avoided to prevent inappropriate manipulation of the system. The managerial goals may be translated into certain types of behavior that should be motivated. Even in the absence of monetary rewards associated with an evaluation system, feedback regarding behavior is still a useful tool for a medical director.

REFERENCES

1. Cooper RM. Formal physician performance evaluations. *J Ambulatory Care Manage*. 1980;3:19–33.

2. McGuirk-Porell M, Goldberg GA, Goldin D, et al. A performance-based quality evaluation system for preferred provider organizations. *Qual Rev Bull*. November 1991;365–373.

3. Schlackman N. Integrating quality assessment and phy-

sician incentive payment. *Qual Rev Bull*. August 1989: 234–237.

4. Beloff J. AV-Med Health Plan of Florida: the physician incentive bonus plan based on quality of care. In: Boland P, ed. *Making Managed Healthcare Work: A Practical Guide to Strategies and Solutions*. New York: McGraw-Hill; 1991:322–330.

Part IV

General Management and Marketing

We could manage this matter to a T.

Sterne
Tristram Shandy, bk. II, ch. 5, 1760.

Chapter 19

Member Services and Consumer Affairs

Peter R. Kongstvedt

All managed health care plans need a member services, customer services, or consumer affairs function. For purposes of discussion, the term *member services* will be used synonymously with the terms *customer services* and *consumer affairs*. Member services are not to be confused with membership services; the latter term is sometimes used to describe the operational area responsible for processing enrollment applications and sending out membership cards and evidence of coverage documents. Member services, in the context of this chapter, refers to the department responsible for helping members with any problems, handling member grievances and complaints, tracking and reporting patterns of problems encountered, and enhancing the relationship between the members of the plan and the plan itself.

Managed care plans are far more complicated than simple indemnity insurance plans (as though those are simple!): Members are required to choose a primary care physician (PCP), to follow rules for accessing health care (eg, obtaining an authorization from their PCP for referral services), to understand complex benefits structures, and so forth. Health maintenance organizations (HMOs) are complicated enough; point-of-service (POS) plans are even more complicated and have different levels of coverage depending on how the member accessed services (intentionally or not). See Chapter 2 for a description of these types of plans.

The central point is that plans that restrict access to care through the use of a provider panel and an authorization system need to have a system to help members use the plan, a system to monitor and track the nature of member contacts, and a mechanism for members to express dissatisfaction with their care because members have less ability simply to change providers. Likewise, plans that have the ability to deny or reduce coverage for nonauthorized services need a mechanism for members to seek review of claims that have been denied or covered at a lower than expected level of benefits.

TRAINING AND STAFFING

The amount of training required of member services representatives before they are allowed to interact with members varies from plan to plan. It is common for large and complicated plans to require new representatives to spend 2 to 3 months in training before they begin actually interfacing with members, and even then the first few weeks are monitored by the supervisor.

Smaller or less complicated plans generally require less training. It is a clear mistake to skimp on training because how the member services representative performs will have a direct impact on member satisfaction and perhaps on the legal risk profile of the plan.

Staffing this department is a function of both the scope of responsibilities of the representatives and the complexity of the plan. For highly complex plans with significant growth, complicated products such as POS, and active outreach (discussed below), staffing ratios may be as generous as 1 representative for every 3,500 members. Plans with benefits designs that are simpler and more consistent, that have stable membership levels, and generally have good service levels may staff at a ratio of 1 representative for every 7,500 members.

It is common in large plans to organize the department into dedicated service units. Such units are responsible for a limited number of accounts, particularly if those accounts are large. In that way, the representatives working in the unit are better able to be familiar with a limited set of benefits issues, to gain knowledge about particular problems unique to an account, and to be more responsive to the accounts. Dedicated service units are sometimes required by large employers before you can obtain their business.

PERFORMANCE STANDARDS

Member services departments generally have responsiveness requirements as part of their performance standards. Such standards generally revolve around a few simple measures. Telephone responsiveness is usually measured by how many times the telephone rings on average, or the elapsed time (in seconds) before it is answered by a representative, and what percentage of calls are abandoned before they are ever answered.

Timeliness of response is also measured against standards. This is done by tracking the percentage of calls that are resolved on the spot (ie, no follow-up is required; for example, 80% of calls require no follow-up). For problems or questions that require follow-up, there are usually standards for how long that takes (eg, 90% of outstanding inquiries or problems are resolved within 14 days and 98% within 28 days). Similar standards apply to written correspondence.

Individual service representatives are usually monitored for both productivity and quality. Productivity may be measured by tracking the number of contacts per day or per hour, the length of time each contact takes to complete, and the percentage of contacts that are resolved on the first call. Quality is usually monitored through silent monitoring of the calls themselves. This refers to the supervisor or manager listening to random calls for each service representative and then making a qualitative judgment about how well the service representative handled the call. It is not enough to take and give information when a member has a problem or complaint; the representative must apply communication techniques developed for customer service in order to be optimally effective.[1]

SERVICE AND HELP

Member services is responsible for helping members use the plan. New members commonly have less than complete (or even no) understanding of how the plan operates, how to access care, how to obtain authorization for specialty services (in a PCP case manager type plan), and so forth. These are services to members as opposed to complaint and concern resolution, which is discussed later.

Primary Care Physician Selection

In plans that use PCPs to access care, member services will frequently be called on to help members select a PCP. This may occur because the member failed to select a PCP in the first place, particularly in a POS plan in which the member has no intention of using the HMO part of the plan. Even in POS, it is best to require the member to select a PCP because it is not known whether the member will change his or her mind later and because the plan really does want to encourage the member to use the managed care system.

Another reason that a member may need to select a new PCP is if a participating PCP leaves the network for any reason, or if the PCP's practice closes because it is full but that information did not get into the most recent provider directory. One other common reason for change is that the member and the PCP simply were not the right match for each other, and the member is requesting a change to another PCP. This often occurs when a member is new to the system, and it occurs particularly often when managed care is installed as a replacement for all other insurance (as with most POS plans), thus requiring new members who never wanted to go into a managed care plan to select a PCP.

In any event, member services is generally responsible for helping the members with this problem. Many plans have more information about PCPs available on line to the member services representative than is available in the directory, and representatives may be able to help the member select a PCP on the basis of special information such as languages spoken, training, hours available, and so forth.

Identification Cards

Although this chapter does not address the basic issues of entering enrollment information and issuing identification cards, it is inevitable that some members will have problems with their cards, and then member services will need to resolve those problems. Common problems include lost cards, cards that were sent to the wrong address, incorrect information on the card, and changes required because of change of status (eg, the subscriber got married).

Outreach

An outreach program can be of great benefit in preventing member complaints and problems. An outreach program is one that proactively contacts new members and discusses the way the plan works. By reaching out and letting members know how the authorization system works, how to obtain services, what the benefits are, and so forth, the plan can reduce confusion. This also gives the member a chance to ask questions

about the plan, especially when those questions do not come up until the member has heard about the plan from the outreach personnel.

Many plans accomplish an outreach program by carefully scripting the contact. Development of scripts allows the plan to use lesser trained personnel to carry out the program; when questions arise that are not easily answered from the script, or when problems are identified, the member may be transferred to an experienced member services representative. Outreach is most effective when carried out during both daytime and early evening hours to ensure that contact is made.

Outreach is especially useful when the plan undergoes a large enrollment surge. The level of problems that members experience with a managed care plan is generally highest during the initial period of enrollment (because new members are still unfamiliar with the way the plan operates), and outreach can help ameliorate that issue. The sooner the members understand how to access the system, the sooner the burden on the plan to deal with complaints and grievances will diminish.

MEMBER COMPLAINTS AND GRIEVANCES

Complaints Compared to Grievances

Complaints by members may be generally defined as problems that members bring to the attention of the plan; they differ from grievances in that grievances are formal complaints, formally demanding resolution by the plan. Complaints that are not resolved to the satisfaction of the member may evolve into formal grievances. It is clearly in the best interest of the plan to try and resolve complaints before they become formal grievances because there are greater legal implications and member satisfaction issues involved with grievances.

Resolution of complaints is usually informal, although the plan should have a clear policy for investigating complaints and responding to members. Despite the informal nature of complaint resolution, it is extremely important for the member services department, or in fact any staff member, to document carefully every contact with a member when the member expresses any dissatisfaction. For complaints, the member services representative should keep a log of even casual telephone calls from members as well as notes of any conversations with members while he or she is trying to resolve complaints. Concise and thorough records may prove quite valuable if the complaint turns into a formal grievance. Such documentation also helps in data analysis, as discussed later in this chapter.

Grievance resolution is distinctly formal. State and federal regulations require HMOs to have clearly delineated member grievance procedures, to inform members of those procedures, and to abide by them. Clearly defined grievance and appeals procedures are usually required in insurance and self-funded plans as well. As a general rule, members may be contractually prohibited from filing a lawsuit over benefits denial until they have gone through the plan's grievance procedure. Conversely, if a plan fails to inform a member of grievance rights or fails to abide by the grievance procedure, the plan has a real potential for liability. Suggested steps in formal grievance resolution follow later in this chapter.

Claims Problems Compared to Service Problems

Member complaints and grievances fall into two basic categories: claims problems and service problems. Service problems fall into two basic categories as well: medical service and administrative service.

Claims Problems

Claims problems generally occur when the member seeks coverage for a service that is not covered under the schedule of benefits or is not considered medically necessary or when the member had services rendered without authorization and the plan denied or reduced coverage.

In the first two situations, the plan must rely on both the schedule of benefits and determinations of medical necessity. In the case of denial or reduction in payment of claims already incurred, the issue of plan policy and procedure is

also present because this situation arises from cold claims received without prior PCP authorization.

For prospective denial or reduction of coverage, the plan should respond to the member with the exact contractual language upon which it bases its denial of coverage. There also needs to be a mechanism in place for second opinions by the medical director or designee in those cases where there is a dispute over medical necessity. The medical director must be careful not to confuse these two issues: There may be times when a service can be considered medically necessary but the plan does not cover it under the schedule of benefits.

Cases involving denial or reduction in coverage for services already incurred are a bit more complex. The claims department of the plan will receive a claim without an authorization for services. As discussed in detail in Chapter 20, the plan must have clear policies and procedures for processing such claims. In the case of an HMO without any benefits for out-of-network services, the plan may pend or hold the claims to investigate whether an authorization actually does exist (or should have been given). If an authorization for services ultimately is given, the claim is paid; if no authorization is forthcoming, the claim is denied. The plan may occasionally wish to pay the claim even without an authorization in certain circumstances, such as a genuine emergency, an urgent problem out of the area, or a first offense of a new member.

In POS plans an unauthorized claim is not denied (assuming it is covered under the schedule of benefits), but the coverage is substantially reduced. As discussed in Chapters 11 and 20, it is not always clear when a service was actually authorized and when the member chose to self-refer. The plan must have very clear policies to deal with these claims because it is impractical to pend every unauthorized claim, since POS is predicated on a certain level of out-of-network use.

In those instances where the claim is ultimately denied or coverage is reduced, members need an appeal mechanism. It is conceivable that the plan's claims payment policies will not envision every contingency, that the claims investigation mechanism will not always be accurate, or that there may be mitigating circumstances involved. There may be a genuine conflict of opinion over whether the member followed plan policies or over issues such as medical necessity. In the case of denial of a claim, the member needs to be informed of appeal rights; whether such information is required when one is processing POS claims is not clear, but most plans do not do so under the assumption that unauthorized claims are a result of voluntary self-referral by the member and that coverage has not been denied but only paid at the out-of-network level.

Service Problems

Service problems include medical service and administrative service problems. Medical service problems could include a member's inability to get an appointment, rude treatment, lack of physicians located near where the member lives, difficulty getting a needed referral (difficult at least in the opinion of the member), and, most serious, problems with quality of care. Administrative problems could include incorrect identification cards, not getting a card at all, poor responsiveness to previous inquiries, not answering the telephone, lack of documentation or education materials, and so forth.

Member services personnel need to investigate service complaints and to get a response to the member. When the complaint alleges quality of care problems, the medical director needs to be notified. If investigation reveals a genuine quality of care problem, the matter requires referral to the quality assurance committee or peer review committee (see Chapter 15). In most cases, the real problem may be one of communication or of a member demanding a service that the physician feels is unnecessary. In those cases, the member services personnel need to communicate back to the member the results of the investigation or to clarify plan policy regarding coverage.

In all cases of service problems, the key to success is communication. If member services communicates clearly and promptly to all parties, many problems can be cleared up. Such communication must not be confrontational or accusatory. It is important for member services always to keep in mind that there are at least two ways of looking at any one situation and that there is rarely a clear-cut right or wrong.

FORMAL GRIEVANCE PROCEDURE

As indicated earlier, plans (HMOs at least) are required to have a formal grievance procedure, and the responsibility for implementing it falls to the member services department. State regulations [and federal regulations for federally qualified HMOs and competitive medical plans (CMPs)] often spell out the minimum requirements for the procedure. Such requirements may include timeliness of response, who will review the grievance, what recourse the member has, and so forth. Plans are also usually allowed to have a limitation on how long a member has to file a grievance; for example, if a member fails to file a grievance within 90 days after the problem arises, he or she may lose the right under the plan's grievance procedure to file. Such restrictions may not ultimately prevent lawsuits, but they probably serve to strengthen the plan's position.

Each plan must review applicable state and federal regulations to develop its grievance procedure; the procedure should also be reviewed by the plan's legal counsel to evaluate its utility as a risk management function. A general outline of a suggested grievance procedure follows.

Filing of Formal Grievance

Assuming that the plan has been unable satisfactorily to resolve a member complaint, the member must be informed of and afforded the opportunity to file a formal grievance. This is usually done with a form specific to that purpose. The form usually asks for essential information (eg, name, membership number, parties involved, and so forth) and a narrative of the problem. The form may also contain space for tracking the grievance and responses by other parties.

Investigation of Grievance

Between the time period that begins when the form is received and ends when the plan responds, the grievance needs to be investigated.

This may include further interviews with the member, interviews with or written responses from other parties, and any other pertinent information. The time period may be set by law or may be set by the plan, but it should not exceed some reasonable period (eg, 60 days). At the end of that time period, the plan responds to the member with its findings and resolution. The response includes the requirements for the member to respond back to the plan if the resolution is not satisfactory.

Appeal

If the member's grievance is not resolved to his or her satisfaction, the member has the right to appeal. This appeal may involve having the case reviewed by a senior officer of the company or by an outside reviewer. This first appeal is usually done without any formal hearings or testimony but rather is based on the material submitted for review by both the plan and the member. Again, the plan usually sets a reasonable time period for requesting the appeal (eg, 30 days) and a reasonable time period for the review to occur (eg, 30 days).

Formal Hearing

If the plan's response is still not satisfactory to the member, some plans afford the member a right to request a formal hearing. There is usually a time limitation set (eg, 15 working days) during which the member must request the hearing or forfeit the right to a hearing. If the plan has a formal hearing right, then once the plan receives a request for a formal hearing the plan has an obligation to respond in a timely manner (eg, 15 working days). The response is notification of when and where the hearing will take place. The hearing should be scheduled within a reasonable time period (eg, 15 working days).

The purpose of a formal hearing is to afford the member a chance to present his or her case in person to an unbiased individual or a panel of unbiased individuals. To that end, the hearing officer or the voting members of the hearing panel should not have participated in the earlier decisions; plan managers who have been involved before will surely participate, but not as the hearing officer or as voting members. If a single hearing officer is used, that individual should be the board chairperson, the president of the corporation, or an independent person capable of understanding the issues (eg, an attorney specializing in health care).

It is more common to use a panel for formal hearings. Panels may be made up of board members, providers (who are not involved with the member on a professional basis), lay members of the plan, or managers from the plan who do not participate in member services issues except for grievances. It is best to use a panel size of odd numbers, preferably five or seven, to prevent ties. There should be a panel chairperson to function as the hearing officer.

The hearing provides the member the opportunity to present the grievance and any pertinent information. The plan does likewise, usually by having the member services representative present the plan's case. The executive director and medical director may likewise present testimony.

It is a very bad idea to ask the member's provider to appear at the hearing in those cases where the provider has been involved in the grievance. This carries the potential of disrupting the physician-patient relationship and of placing the provider in a no-win situation, and it can have implications for future legal action against the provider or plan. Any information from the provider should be presented by the medical director.

A resolution of the grievance is rarely given to the member at the close of the hearing. When the hearing is over, the member is told that he or she will be informed of the results within a set time period (eg, 15 working days). After the member and staff have left, the voting members of the panel discuss the case and reach a resolution. That resolution is communicated in writing to the member and any other pertinent parties, along with the statement that the member has the right of further appeal to arbitration or the government agency, as appropriate.

Arbitration

In some states, arbitration is allowed. This may occur before or after appeal to the state agency. In those states where arbitration is allowed, and if the plan wishes to pursue it (or if it is required), the plan would comply with the regulations regarding arbitration in terms of selection of the arbitrator(s) and form of the hearing.

Appeal to Government Agencies

In all cases, if the member is not satisfied with the results of the formal hearing, he or she has the right to appeal to the appropriate government agency.

Usually, most members are commercial members; that is, they are members who are neither federal employees nor beneficiaries of entitlement programs but who enroll through a private company or are employees of state or municipal government. For commercial members, the state insurance department has jurisdiction. In cases where the grievance involves quality of care, the health department may have jurisdiction.

Federal employees, or those who are covered under the Office of Personnel Management (OPM), have the right of appeal to OPM. OPM specifically reserves the right in its contract with health plans to resolve and rule on grievances by members who are federal employees. Members who are covered under entitlement programs (Medicare and Medicaid) have the right to appeal to the respective government agency; for Medicare that means the Health Care Financing Administration, and for Medicaid that refers to the state's human services (or welfare) department.

Lawsuits

Although not a part of a plan's grievance procedure, the last legal remedy for a disgruntled member is legal action. If the plan carefully follows its grievance procedure, the chances of a successful lawsuit against it are small. If the plan fails to follow proper policy and procedure, the chances become pretty high.

DATA COLLECTION AND ANALYSIS

The member services department should be responsible for collecting, collating, and analyz-

ing data. Data may be considered in two broad categories: data regarding general levels of satisfaction and dissatisfaction, and data regarding medical and administrative problems.

Satisfaction Data

Satisfaction data may include surveys of current members, disenrollment surveys, telephone response time and waiting time studies (these may be done in conjunction with the quality management department, but they are essentially patient satisfaction studies), and surveys of clients and accounts (although marketing rather than member services may perform many of these studies).

Member surveys are particularly useful when done properly. Even when a managed care plan is the sole carrier in an account (eg, a replacement POS plan), surveys help the plan evaluate service levels and ascertain what issues are important to the members. Surveys may be focused on a few issues that the plan wants to study, or they may be broad and comprehensive.[2]

In an environment where members have multiple choices for their health care coverage, member surveys will be geared toward issues that influence enrollment choices. It is easier and less expensive to retain a member than it is to sell a new one. Of special importance are those members who do not heavily utilize medical services because their premiums pay for the expenses of high utilizers and because such members tend to disenroll more often than members who utilize services heavily.[3] Surveys designed to analyze what makes those low-utilizing members leave or stay (or join in the first place) can lead to the development of targeted member retention programs. Some plans develop direct mail campaigns that include giveaways or promote services available to low utilizers (eg, health promotion) to have those members place a sense of value on their membership in the plan.

Medical and Administrative Problems

Problems that are brought to the plan's attention not only require resolution but need to be analyzed to look for trends. If a problem is sporadic or random, there may be little required other than helping the individual member as needed. If problems are widespread or stem from something that is likely to cause continual problems, then the plan must act to resolve the problems at the source. Such resolution may mean changing a policy or procedure, improving education materials to the members, dealing with a difficult provider, or any number of events. The point is that plan management will not know of chronic problems if the data are not analyzed.

Many plans now automate their member services tracking systems. Such automation not only serves to help member services track and manage individual problems but also serves as a method to collect and collate data. Each member contact with the plan is entered into the computerized tracking system and assigned a category (or multiple categories if necessary); issues involving providers are generally tracked not only by category but by provider as well. Repeat or follow-up calls are also tracked but usually still count as only one problem or enquiry.

Producing regular reports summarizing frequency of each category, as well as frequency of problems or complaints by provider (along with monitoring of the rate at which members transfer out of a provider's practice) allows management to focus attention appropriately. An example of the types of categories that a plan may track is given in Exhibit 19-1. This example applies primarily to HMOs or POS plans and is by no means exhaustive; conversely, it is unlikely that a plan would use all of these categories.

PROACTIVE APPROACHES TO MEMBER SERVICES

Most member services departments become complaint departments. When that happens, the plan not only loses a valuable source of member satisfaction but runs the risk of burning out the personnel in the department. It is emotionally draining to listen to complaints all day. Even the satisfaction of successfully resolving the majority of complaints can be inadequate if there is nothing else the plan is doing to address satisfaction. In addition to analyzing the sources of dissatisfaction and complaints to resolve the problems at the source, the plan might consider the following suggestions.

Member Suggestions and Recommendations

Soliciting member suggestions and recommendations can be valuable. This may be done along with member surveys, or the plan may solicit suggestions through response cards in physicians' offices or in the member newsletter. There are times when the members will have ways of viewing the plan that provide valuable insight to managers. Although not all the sug-

---

Exhibit 19-1 Examples of Categories for a Member Contact Tracking System

Enrollment Issues
- Selecting a PCP
  —Practice closed
  —Never selected
  —Special needs
- Changing PCP
  —Dissatisfied with PCP
  —PCP no longer participating with plan
  —Geographic reasons
- Identification card(s)
  —Never received
  —Errors on card
  —Change in information
  —Lost card
- Change in enrollment status
  —New dependent
  —Delete dependent

—Student of disabled dependent verification
- Change in address
  —Subscriber
  —Dependent(s)
- Need evidence of coverage or other documentation
- Need new directory of providers

Benefits Issues
- Questions
  —Physician services
    Primary care
    Specialty care
  —Hospital or institutional services
  —Emergency services
  —Ancillary services
    Pharmacy
    Other

Exhibit 19-1 continued

—POS benefits questions
- Complaints
  —Copayment or coinsurance levels
  —Limitations on coverage
  —Did not know benefits levels

Claims Issues
- In-network
  —Claims denied (HMO)
  —Claim paid at lower level of benefits (POS)
  —Unpaid claim
    Provider submitted
    Member submitted
  —Received bill from provider
  —Coordination of benefits
  —Subrogation/other party liability
- Out-of-network
  —Claims denied (HMO)
  —Claim paid at lower level of benefits (POS)
  —Unpaid claim
    Provider submitted
    Member submitted
  —Received bill from provider
  —Coordination of benefits
  —Subrogation/other party liability

Plan Policies and Procedures
- Authorization system for specialty care
- Precertification system for institutional care
- Second opinion procedures
- Copayments and coinsurance
- Unable to understand printed materials or instructions
- Complaint and grievance procedures

Plan Administration
- Personnel rude or unhelpful
- Incorrect or inappropriate information given
- Telephone responsiveness problems
  —On hold
  —Unanswered calls
  —Call not returned
- Complaints or grievances not addressed satisfactorily

Access to Care
- Unable to get an appointment
- Too long before appointment scheduled

- Office hours not convenient
- Waiting time too long in office
- Problems accessing care after hours
- Too far to travel to get care
- No public transportation
- Calls not returned

Physician Issues
- Unpleasant or rude behavior
- Unprofessional or inappropriate behavior
- Does not spend adequate time with member
- Does not provide adequate information
  —Medical
  —Financial
  —Administrative (eg, referral process)
- Lack of compliance with use of plan network
- Lack of compliance with authorization policies
- Does not speak member's language
- Speaks negatively about the plan

Perceived Appropriateness and Quality of Care
- Delayed treatment
- Inappropriate denial of treatment
- Inappropriate denial of referral
- Unnecessary treatment
- Incorrect diagnosis or treatment
- Lack of follow-up
  —Physician visit
  —Diagnostic tests

Medical Office Facility Issues
- Lack of privacy
- Unclean or unpleasant
- Unsafe or ill equipped
- Lack of adequate parking

Institutional Care Issues
- Perceived poor care in hospital
- Discharged too soon
- Hospital or facility staff behavior
  —Rude or unpleasant behavior
  —Unprofessional or inappropriate behavior
  —Speaks negatively about plan
- Unclean or unpleasant
- Unsafe or ill equipped
- Problems with admission or discharge process
- Other administrative errors

gestions may be practical, they may at least illuminate trouble spots that need attention of some sort.

Affiliations with Health Clubs and Health Promotion Activities

Managed care plans frequently develop affiliations with health clubs and other types of health-related organizations. This serves to underscore the emphasis on prevention and health maintenance, allows for differentiation with competitors, and provides value-added service to the member. Access to or sponsorship of various health promotion activities falls into the same category.

A special type of health promotion is the provision of health advice from nurses available on the telephone. This is not meant to replace physician advice but rather as a supplement. Advice may range from helping a member deal with a minor illness to explaining and educating about surgical procedures. This may be done in tandem with distribution of self-help medical books and other health-promotion literature.

Some closed panel plans are providing this type of service to a remarkable degree. These plans have well-designed education materials such as interactive videos, literature, and personal education. For certain types of procedures such as transurethral prostatectomy, the member must participate in an interactive video before making a choice regarding this elective procedure. Some open panel plans are also providing such services either through their own personnel or through contracts with outside firms.

CONCLUSION

Member services are a requirement of any managed care plan. The primary responsibility of member services is to help members resolve any problems or questions they may have. Member services must also track and analyze member problems and complaints so that management can act to correct problems at the source. Mechanisms to resolve complaints and grievances not only are required by law but make good business sense. Plan management should not be satisfied with a reactive member services function but should take a proactive approach as well.

REFERENCES

1. Bell CR, Zemke R. Service breakdown: the road to recovery. *Manag Rev.* 1987;76:32–35.
2. Group Health Association of America. *GHAA's Consumer Satisfaction Survey.* Washington, DC: Group Health Association of America; 1992.
3. Wrightson W, Genuardi J, Stephens S. Demographic and utilization characteristics of HMO disenrollees. *GHAA J.* Summer 1987:23–42.

Chapter 20

Claims and Benefits Administration

Elizabeth Brennfleck Pascuzzi

The claims department of a managed care organization is the pivotal point upon which the financial health of the organization turns. All the health plan's operational aspects converge in this department to enable the claims staff to adjudicate claims on the basis of eligibility, coverage, authorization, and payment terms and in consideration of other party liability. The success of the claims department has a profound impact on the health plan's ability to retain and attract new members, negotiate advantageous contracts with providers, and meet bottom line goals.

To serve this end, the claims department must be well organized with a well-trained staff that can refer to up-to-date documentation and has solid lines of accountability. It is a wise claims manager who understands the critical role the claims department plays in the plan and who coordinates all goals and activities to carrying out that critical role successfully.

This chapter will examine the pertinent issues involved in managing a successful claims operation. It is organized under four headings: management issues, organization issues, communication issues, and finance issues. We will also examine the qualities that a successful claims manager must possess to motivate staff and control the process.

MANAGEMENT ISSUES

Management issues are those that the department head and other supervisory staff are responsible for mastering. The more successfully these concepts are put into practice, the more successful the claims department.

Mission Statement

Just as every business organization needs a mission statement to guide its policies and practices, so does a claims department need such a statement to give the staff direction. The mission statement answers the question, "Why are we here?" One's first response may be, "We are here to process claims" or, more elaborately stated, "We are here to process 90% of all claims within 10 days of receipt at a 97% accuracy rate."

Elizabeth Brennfleck Pascuzzi, an experienced indemnity and managed care claims manager, is Principal of Pascuzzi & Associates, a managed care consulting firm specializing in managed care operations as well as documentation/training. She is currently developing computer-based training programs for the managed care industry.

The claims manager who sees this as the sole mission statement, however, is missing something significant. It is a perceptive claims manager who sees the department's true mission as being service to the managed care organization, its members, and its providers. Processing claims within a specified period of time and at a certain accuracy rate is a means to an end, not an end in itself. The sample mission statement in Exhibit 20-1 describes the goal and then the means of attaining the goal.

By thinking of itself as a service department as opposed to a processing department, the claims staff will be more cognizant of the consequences of its actions because the human element is injected into the process. Staff members will understand that they are not just moving paper; they are serving members, providers, and the plan itself. They will also understand that serious claims processing problems have serious implications throughout the organization. The responsible claims manager continually reminds staff that "We are a service department" to reinforce the department's real mission.

Production Standards

Production standards are a definition of what the staff must accomplish to fulfill its mission. Production standards also supply a motivating force which inspires the processor to meet at least the minimum standard for the day or week. Such a motivating force can include an incentive system that rewards high producers with something of value.

Exhibit 20-1 Sample Mission Statement

The claims department is a professional group that processes claims and determines benefits for plan members. Our mission is to enhance the plan's profitability and member satisfaction through prompt, accurate, and consistent adjudication of claims while applying industry standard cost-saving measures. We accomplish this by processing 90% of claims within 10 days of receipt at a minimum of 97% accuracy.

Above all else, production standards must be fair and must be perceived as being fair. Fairness is determined by how the processed claims are counted and by how the difficulty level of processing a claim is factored into the production standard.

The key to establishing realistic production standards is in collecting and analyzing production statistics. For example:

- Begin by determining a benchmark (eg, 100 claims per day) for a test period (eg, 12 weeks).
- Design a tick sheet that the adjudicators must complete each day.
- Count everything: paid claims, denied claims, pended claims, pended claims that are unpended and finalized, adjustments, corrections, and so forth.
- Identify types of claims handled: hospital, radiology, referral specialist, primary care physician (PCP), and the like.
- Identify time spent processing as well as system down time, meeting time, break time, and the like.
- Total the number of claims handled and the processing time to calculate the number of claims processed per week and per hour; compute an average.

The savvy claims manager does not merely count claims, however. That manager is out of the office, coaching staff to strive for a level of excellence and looking for barriers that prevent processors from achieving the benchmark standard, barriers such as gaps in training, insufficient documentation, inefficient work flow, and even poor lighting or a desk too close to the break area. That claims manager is also counseling processors who fall below the benchmark to ensure that they understand their job responsibilities.

The sharp claims manager is also evaluating claim complexity. Generally speaking, an inpatient claim is more complex than an office visit claim; a surgery claim is more complex than a radiology claim. If one processor adjudicates 150 radiology and office visit claims in a day and another processor adjudicates 75 inpatient hospital claims, who is more productive?

This question can only be answered in light of the participating providers' contracts. If the provider is capitated or the payment terms can be captured in the computer system to determine payment automatically, the difficulty level is reduced. But if the adjudicator must calculate the payment off line, the process becomes more time consuming. This additional processing time must be factored into the productivity standard.

While one is going through this process, current claim receipts must also be evaluated. If staff members perform at this initial minimum level, are they processing enough claims to meet the current receipts? If not, how much more must be produced? If a few more claims per processor per day are required, this can be accomplished through extra encouragement or some rearrangement of responsibilities. If the number of additional processed claims far exceeds the maximum number of claims the staff can handle, however, more staff may be needed. Requesting more staff, though, always requires a demonstration that the current staff is as productive as possible.

Quality Standards

An equally important standard for the claims manager to set is a quality standard. It is of no use at all to process a multitude of claims if half of them are wrong. In fact, poor quality can damage the department more than a low productivity level.

There are three objectives to a quality review program:

1. to establish an objective measure of success for the department as a whole as well as an objective evaluation of each claim adjudicator's quality of work
2. to identify gaps in a claim adjudicator's knowledge and/or training
3. to discover discrepancies in information from other departments (ie, new provider fee schedules, changes in benefits, and so forth) in addition to identifying processing problems in the software

Establishing a quality standard is easy: 100% accuracy is the goal. But is this realistic? Before

that question is answered, consider what less than 100% quality really means.

If a department is operating at 97% accuracy, this means that 3% of processed claims are incorrect; 3% of 5,000 processed claims in a week computes to 150 incorrect claims. At the other end of these incorrect claims are, at the very least, annoyed members or providers who are now burdened with the problem of contacting their customer service representatives to resolve the issue. It could also be a member who cannot afford to have his or her next prescription filled because he or she was shortchanged $50 on the current prescription claim. Or it may be a provider who refuses to see any more plan members because the latest error is one of a long line of errors. In extreme cases, poor quality of claim payments may even potentially compromise the quality of medical care, and that is definitely unacceptable.

Less dramatically, most incorrect claim payments generate a telephone call to member services or provider relations (sometimes to marketing). The 150 claims in error now pose staffing considerations for these departments as well. Additionally, 150 adjustments must now be made in the claims department, where at least one processor, perhaps two, is needed for a full day. This means that new claims are delayed while the adjustments are completed. The implications of that 97% accuracy rate are very far reaching!

Now consider if processed claims equal 10,000 each week. A 3% error rate equals 300 problem claims with their corresponding members and providers annoyed, inconvenienced, or worse. Those 300 claims needing adjustments now require at least two if not three adjudicators to adjust while that many new claims are left to wait. A higher error rate and/or a higher number of processed claims compounds a quality problem dramatically.

In a managed care setting, the quality goal should be 100%, with the minimum quality standard being set at 97% accuracy at the very least. Anything less results in serious staffing issues for claims as well as other service departments. Claims processors should not see a 97% quality standard as an end in itself; it is only a minimum.

How is this quality standard determined? Each claims department should be staffed with at least one person whose primary responsibility is quality review. Typically, a formal quality review program involves a weekly review of a fixed number of randomly selected processed claims for each adjudicator. Some computer systems can perform the random selection automatically. Otherwise, the quality reviewer must use a formula (eg, every sixth claim in a batch, up to four claims) to select claims for review. The formula should be changed each week so that there is no chance for adjudicators to arrange claims to their advantage. The same number of claims must be reviewed for each adjudicator.

The review should go beyond the claims processing screen to include a review of the eligibility file, the authorization file, and the coordination of benefits (COB) file to be sure that these aspects were also handled appropriately. Every error should be highlighted on the claim and documented in the adjudicator's personal quality review log.

All errors are not equally serious. It is therefore important to assign an error weight to each type of error that could be made. The error weight is a judgment made by the claims manager considering the effect that error has on the member, the provider, and the plan. The quality reviewer may also exercise some judgment during the review process as long as those judgments are consistently applied.

The quality reviewer must perform his or her duties in a scrupulously fair manner. Any perception of favoritism, no matter how well meaning, will cast the entire program under suspicion among the adjudicators. An appeals process should be established so that any adjudicator can question an error charged to a claim and have that error removed from the adjudicator's score if he or she is not to blame.

Evaluating processed claims for quality is only half the story, however. Total quality management, if it is to be achieved, must apply to the entire process. With its goal as zero defects, total quality management is an attempt to reduce claim errors by reviewing the process as well as the end result. If quality inspections are done throughout the production line, the end result is a higher quality rate. Figure 20-1 illustrates the financial advantage of preventing errors.

Motivation

After production and quality standards are established, the next challenge is to motivate the staff to achieve them. One of the single most effective motivating methods is a promotion. A farsighted claims manager is one who has established a career path within the department so that there is true incentive for the adjudicators to stay, achieve, and ultimately be rewarded. The larger the claims operation, the more opportunity exists for creating positions such as senior level specialists, team leaders, trainers, and so forth. But even in small operations, establishing three salary grades or levels of adjudicators (entry, intermediate, and senior) can work very well.

The adjudicators must be informed at the outset as to what is required to be promoted in terms of productivity, quality, attendance, and willingness to take on additional responsibility, especially when moving to the senior level. Length

For every $1 spent to prevent errors, you will spend $10 to detect and $100 to correct.

Figure 20-1 The cost of poor quality. *Source:* Organizational Dynamics, Inc, Burlington, Massachusetts. Reprinted with permission. All rights reserved.

of service should not be a factor if the other criteria are not met. There should be a fixed time period (6 months to 1 year), in which the adjudicator moves from entry level to intermediate level. If the adjudicator cannot perform above an entry level at this cutoff point, the disciplinary process should take over.

Another key to motivating employees is to develop a team mentality. Indeed, the entire claims operation must be pulling in the same direction to fulfill its mission. Each employee must feel like a valued member of the team. The sensitive claims manager makes sure that each person understands his or her role in the process and how he or she contributes to the team's success. The clerk who opens and date stamps the mail performs as necessary a function as the top quality adjudicator and should be made to realize that.

Although many managers think that cash is the only true motivating force, many human resource studies have demonstrated that employees identify recognition of a job well done as a major motivating force. Recognition can come in many forms, from the claims manager making rounds through the department each morning congratulating those who achieved or exceeded production goals the day before, to having staff recognition lunches complete with awards for most improved staff member or best overall quality.

Training

Regardless of motivating techniques, production and quality standards will not be met easily, if at all, by those who are not properly trained. There is no substitute for an organized, well-paced, and documented training program conducted by a training specialist.

Training must be built concept upon concept, complexity upon complexity, according to a coherent plan that provides some classroom time but allows the trainee on-the-job practice. Such a program provides consistency in approach and delivery and ensures that all topics are covered.

Alternatively, having existing adjudicators sit with new hires at the computer terminal demonstrating how data are entered into the system poses many problems:

- The new hire absorbs the training adjudicator's bad habits or shortcuts.
- The new hire has little opportunity to understand the reasons behind the tasks being taught (the why behind the how).
- The new hire must rely on an adjudicator who may not be the best communicator.
- The new hire requires a great deal of time and energy, which takes away production time from the experienced adjudicator.

If many different adjudicators are involved in this approach, trainees are bound to have gaps in their knowledge and skills. As a result, they will spend precious production time asking questions, doing research, or, worse, making mistakes.

Evaluations

Good evaluations are based on measurable and verifiable data. Fortunately, most work in a claims department can be quantified and measured against established production and quality standards, which means that personal bias is largely removed from the evaluation process. The key to making this work well is twofold: keeping accurate records and continually advising employees of their standing. A weekly score card must be maintained for each adjudicator to record production and quality scores. The results should be shared with the adjudicator so that there are no surprises at the time of the annual review. If there are, the fault is with the manager, who has failed to alert an adjudicator of production or quality problems.

Coupled with the identification of problems is the need to identify solutions. If quality is a problem, retraining may be in order. If production is a problem, moving the employee to a quieter work space may help. If coaching and counseling (all well documented) are not solving the problem, then a well-defined disciplinary process should take over. A judicious claims manager is one who is not reluctant to dismiss an employee for cause because of the assumption that it will take too long to train a new one, or that some production is better than no production. The resources needed to support a poor-quality employee are greater than those required to train a new employee. Additionally, employees must understand that standards are essential and that, if the minimum standard cannot be met, the employee cannot stay.

On a more positive note, salary incentives and other rewards can be linked to evaluation standards. A percentage increase in salary or an actual dollar amount can be tied to the various levels of achievement for production and quality.

Staffing

To fulfill its mission, the claims department must be adequately staffed to process its average number of weekly claim receipts. There are two categories of tasks the staff must perform to accomplish this: production and support.

Production tasks involve all those steps that move claims from the mailroom through the adjudication process until checks and/or letters are mailed to the member and/or provider. Support tasks are those needed to support the production team and to coordinate claims issues with other departments. If a claims department is a regional or corporate operation, support involves coordinating activities with the plans themselves.

The staffing required to sustain production and support is illustrated in the staffing model in Figure 20-2. A distinction is made between production and support by having a supervisor in charge of each area. These are separate and distinct modes of operation, but both are equally important to the claims department as a whole. Neither aspect can be emphasized at the expense of the other.

Production Staff

Entry level production employees are clerks. The primary goal of the clerical staff is to aid productivity by handling claims at the beginning and at the end of the process in an orderly manner and by performing certain investigative chores to assist the adjudicators. The number

and functions of clerical personnel are largely dependent on:

- the functionality of the claims processing system
- how new mail is received and distributed in the plan (or at the corporate or regional office)
- whether new mail is microfilmed
- which department has the responsibility for mailing checks

Exhibit 20-2 displays some of the tasks usually performed by clerical staff. Those items marked with an asterisk (*) are functions that may be performed in other departments. If so, the claims manager must still be sure that these tasks are completed in a timely manner because they affect the claims department's mission.

The other part of the production team is, of course, the adjudicator. A key question, though, is how many. Some managed care plans such as health maintenance organizations (HMOs) use a rule of thumb of hiring one adjudicator for every 8,000 to 10,000 members. Although this can be a guide, the actual number required depends on the volume and type of claim receipts. Significant spikes in receipts or dips in productivity due to circumstances beyond control can be handled with overtime. Overtime should not be an alternative to adequate staffing, however. How the claims manager answers the questions in Exhibit

---

Exhibit 20-2 Examples of Clerical Tasks

- Open, date stamp, and count mail receipts*
- Prepare mail for micrographics/perform micrographics
- Sort claims
- Review and/or batch claims on system, screening out claims with incomplete information or with member or provider not on file
- Batch claims for adjudicator
- Investigate members or providers not on file
- File processed claims
- Retrieve filed claims for correction or adjustment
- Fold, stuff, and mail claim checks and letters*

*Tasks may be performed by another department

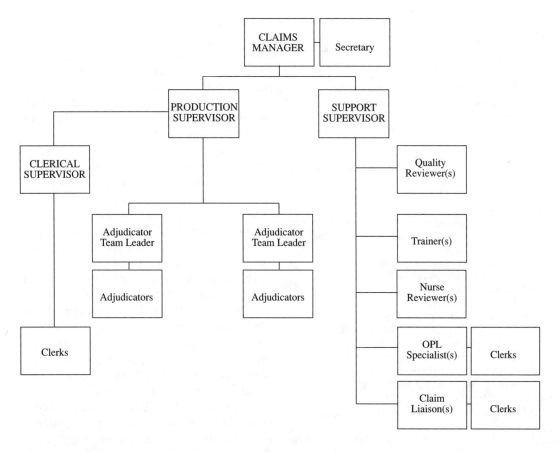

Figure 20-2 Claims department staffing model. OPL— other party liability.

20-3 will help determine the number of adjudicators because all these variables affect productivity.

The total number of adjudicators will, in turn, determine the number of supervisory personnel required. Generally speaking, a first line supervisor's span of control should be 8 to 12 adjudicators. This span could be increased by adding an additional staff level of team leaders. Teams can be organized according to line of business (eg, HMO only members and point of service members, or by large accounts), according to plans in a regional or corporate office, according to claim types (hospital team, PCP team, referral specialist team, emergency claim team, and the like), according to specific providers, and so forth.

A team leader's roles are to keep the process moving according to the plan's policies and pro-

cedures and to provide technical assistance in terms of coverage, contract terms, and system use (ie, to be the technical expert). True supervisory functions (hiring, discipline, and evaluations) are still retained by the supervisor.

Support Staff

The other side of the department is designed to provide support not only to the production side but to other departments within the plan. Support positions are the senior level positions ideally filled by promoting from within. A larger operation can probably support one or more quality reviewers as well as a trainer. A smaller department could combine these functions in one person. Other support personnel include one or more nurse reviewers, an other party liability specialist (with attendant staff), and two or more claims liaisons. Quality and production (or turn-

Exhibit 20-3 Production Variables That Have an Impact on Staffing

---

- Do PCPs submit claims for payment?
- How are capitated providers handled? Do they still submit invoices to be recorded in the system?
- What is the nature of the hospital contracts? Are they all per diem arrangements, where only one or two line items need to be entered for adjudication, or are multiple line items required?
- Are hospital-based physician charges unbundled? That is, will a single episode of hospital care (inpatient or outpatient) generate multiple claim submissions?
- How is the prescription drug benefit administered? Do members submit prescription receipts for reimbursement?
- How many different types of plans are being administered? HMO only? HMO and preferred provider organization? Point of Service plan? Any Medicare risk programs?
- Are all claims processed with the same software? For example, are point of service claims processed on different systems depending on in-network versus out-of-network status?
- How much off-line work must be done by the adjudicator to determine benefits and/or calculate payments?

---

around) standards must be established for each function.

The quality reviewer reviews processed claims for compliance with benefits and the plan's policies and procedures and compiles statistical reports for individual adjudicators and the department as a whole. The quality reviewer also advises on retraining issues and reports on trends or problems that may require new or restated policies. Important qualifications include being detail oriented, being able to keep meticulous records, and being knowledgeable about the system, the benefits, and the plan's administrative practices.

The trainer is responsible for training and testing all new hires as well as retraining and cross-training experienced employees. Another key responsibility is producing and updating training materials. Important qualifications include a keen desire to see others succeed, excellent communication skills (speaking, listening, and writing), and a thorough knowledge of the system, the benefits, and the plan's administrative practices.

The nurse reviewer serves a very valuable function that directly affects the bottom line. This individual reviews claims where substantial savings can be realized over and above the provider contract terms, such as surgery claims (including those involving an assistant surgeon or multiple procedures), physical and other types of therapy claims, and suspected unbundled, inappropriate, or medically unnecessary claims. The nurse reviewer can also negotiate large dollar claims from nonparticipating providers and work with the staff in general to raise consciousness regarding the kinds of claim situations to question. Important qualifications, in addition to nursing experience, include excellent analytic and communication skills.

The other party liability specialist performs a function that also has a direct impact on the bottom line by investigating and resolving claims where another party is primarily liable. This function may be served by several staff members, including clerical personnel if tasks must be done manually. The other party liability specialist must be available to train other plan personnel as well as PCPs about the savings that can be realized with their support and cooperation. Key qualifications include an investigative nature and excellent analytic, organization, communication, and record-keeping skills. Incentive compensation may be considered for these salaried positions.

The claims liaison function may also be served by several staff members, including clerical personnel as needed. The claims liaisons are those individuals assigned to specific departments (or plans in a regional or corporate office) to resolve complaints, errors, problems, and concerns. They must keep logs of all activity (manually if not electronically; see Chapter 19) and are subject to turnaround and quality standards. Important qualifications include excellent organization skills and the ability to resolve problems or negotiate solutions quickly. Above all, they must be able to keep a sense of humor and perspective in a stressful position.

This staffing plan assumes that claims-related telephone inquiries or complaints are initially fielded by member services or provider relations personnel. If the responsibility of handling claims calls lies within the claims department, however, a separate unit must be created for this activity. Never, never mix production duty and telephone duty. An adjudicator cannot answer the telephone and process claims at the same time.

Reports

The astute claims manager commissions a variety of reports to provide a statistical picture of how the department is operating. Because the work in claims is so data intensive, virtually everything is measurable and reportable.

Exhibit 20-4 shows the kind of data that should be reported each week. Most automated systems can produce some of these reports. A personal computer program can be used to produce others. As a last resort, there is always accounting ledger paper and a calculator.

These reports are not meant exclusively for management use. They should be shared with all staff members so that they can see how well they are serving the department's mission.

ORGANIZATION ISSUES

Organization issues are those that have an impact on the department's productivity and quality. Working out these issues inside the department as well as with other departments will influence the successful implementation of the claims department's mission.

Work Flow

Claims must physically move through the department from one level of expertise to the next and, when finalized, be filed in an orderly fashion. Many larger claims processing operations have established electronic claims submissions, which reduce the paper chase to a minimum. Many managed care operations, however, must find a way to dominate the paper rather than let it bury them. It takes little time for the process to careen out of control.

Figure 20-3 displays a simplified work flow. Every claims department should prepare such a graphic, but one that itemizes every step taken to process a claim. This is a useful exercise because it illuminates the process in a visual manner designed not only to display the path that a claim takes but also to display the relationship among the various steps. A visual representation can help weed out the duplicate steps and combine certain steps to simplify the process. There are several software products on the market that allow even a novice user to construct flow charts on a personal computer, or one can purchase a flow chart template in an art or business supply store to draw a flow chart with paper and pencil.

Clerical Preparation

Ample space must be allotted to opening, date stamping, counting, and sorting new mail daily. Keeping order in this part of the operation is vital to achieving turnaround goals. These tasks

---

Exhibit 20-4 Example of Topics for Weekly Reports

Turnaround Time
- Oldest claim on hand
- Percentage resolved within 14 days
- Percentage resolved within 30 days
- Percentage resolved within 60 days
- Percentage resolved within 90 days

Backlog
- Week's work on hand
- Pending, in system
- Pending, not in system

Quality
- Percentage accuracy rate
- Percentage claims-related customer complaints
- Number of claims adjusted

Production
- Department production
- Individual production
- Improvement
- Resolution rate

Budget
- Cost per claim (by product)
- Claims employees per 1,000 enrollees

Dollars Saved
- Coordination of benefits
- Recovery
- Medical reviews
- Audit results

Source: Reprinted with permission from GHAA Conference Materials, "Managing Claims in Managed Care," August 28–30, 1988, Group Health Association of America, Inc.

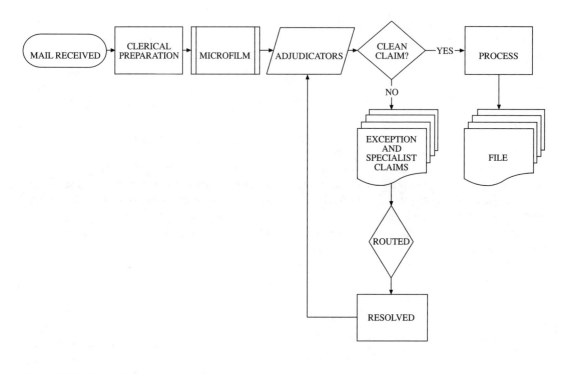

Figure 20-3 Claims department work flow model.

Microfilming

Many claims operations have claims microfilmed either in house or by an outside vendor. Microfilming claims can be advantageous because it virtually eliminates the need for a provider to resubmit a lost claim and reduces the amount of paper that must be stored. The disadvantage is that it adds another process to handling claims. Even if an outside vendor performs this service, the claims staff must still prepare the claims for filming, removing staples, perhaps affixing numbers, counting, batching, and boxing.

The key to a successful microfilming operation is being able easily to find the claim again on the microfilm reader. This is contingent on the unique identifying number attached to each claim. Ideally, the date of receipt will be imbedded in this number and will be the claim identifi-

will vary if the department decides to microfilm its claims. For example, if claims are microfilmed off site, the microfilm vendor may date stamp and count claims as part of its service.

cation number entered into the computer system.

The checklists in Exhibits 20-5 and 20-6 are decision-making tools useful in evaluating the options of performing the microfilm operation in house or using an outside vendor.

Some large organizations now use electronic imaging and storage rather than microfilming. Electronic imaging requires the ability to scan documents (which requires preparation and a certain amount of standardization) and to retrieve them later for either electronic presentation (eg, in an image window on an adjudicator's terminal) or, more commonly, printing. Electronic storage is potentially more efficient than other forms but requires adequate volume to be economically feasible and has higher technical sophistication and software maintenance requirements.

Sorting Claims

Another front-end clerical task is sorting and batching claims for the adjudicators. The first major sort should be among types of business: HMO, preferred provider organization, point of

Exhibit 20-5 In-House Microfilming Evaluation Questions

- How much does the equipment cost? (examine lease and purchase arrangements)
- Is the reader a separate piece of equipment?
- What is the cost per claim page?
- How much space does the equipment require?
- How easy is it to operate? to learn to operate?
- What safety precautions must be observed?
- How is the film developed for reading?
- Can the reader print hard copies easily? What is the quality level?
- Are there any hazardous chemicals involved?
- What is the service agreement?
- Are there any warranties?
- Can the equipment date stamp, assign a number, and count the number of claims?
- How are multiple-page claims handled?

service, or indemnity. In fact, this sort can be aided by giving HMO providers a mailing address with one box or suite number and all others another box or suite number, so that the initial sort can be done in the mailroom or, better yet, by the Post Office.

Further sorts can be done by type of claim: hospital, radiology/laboratory, referral specialist, PCP, prescription drug, and so forth. This sort assumes various levels of complexity on one hand as well as training and skill on the other. For example, PCP claims, usually office visits that do not require a referral, can be designated

Exhibit 20-6 Outside Vendor Microfilming Evaluation Questions

- How is the service priced?
- What is the cost of the reader?
- What is the cost per claim page?
- What are pick-up and delivery schedules? Are they guaranteed?
- How close is the vendor's site to the claim operation?
- Can the reader print hard copies easily? What is the quality level?
- What is the service agreement on the reader?
- Are there any warranties on the reader?
- Can the equipment date stamp, assign a number, and count the number of claims?
- How are multiple-page claims handled?

as entry level claims. Likewise, radiology and laboratory claims, although they usually require a referral, can be designated as the next level of claim complexity. Referral specialist and hospital claims require the most skill and should be assigned to intermediate or senior level adjudicators.

Claims are further sorted by provider within these categories. The provider often assists in this process by sending a large quantity of claims at the same time. Keeping these together, in date of receipt order, will aid production, especially if specific contract terms must be manually referenced or calculated.

Once sorted, claims should be bundled into reasonably sized batches, usually the amount that an adjudicator can process in 1 day. The bundled claims are then moved to a holding area and placed in date of receipt order, waiting to be assigned to the appropriate adjudicators.

Assigning Claims to Adjudicators

In some claims departments, adjudicators pick up their claims themselves as they finish with the previous batch. A recommended approach, however, is having the supervisory staff assign work daily in date of receipt order.

At the beginning of each workday (or shift, if applicable), claims management must evaluate the state of the backlog of work and determine how best to meet the day's goals. By assigning work to the adjudicators, the backlog is truly managed. Management can also ensure a fair distribution of work so that production goals can be achieved.

Exception Claims

Clerical staff tasks should also involve certain investigative chores to resolve problems when a member or provider cannot be identified in the system or if a diagnosis or procedure code is missing or illegible. How these claim problems are identified and routed to the clerical staff often depends on the computer software.

Some processing systems are structured so that all claims are initially entered into the system, batched, and forwarded onto the adjudicator level. The disadvantage of this type of operation is that the claim paper is handled at least twice before it has a chance of being finalized. The advantages, however, are that problem claims can be identified almost upon receipt and the problem resolved before the adjudicator receives the claim and that such a structure allows for a more conservative approach to financial accruals (see Chapter 25).

The alternative approach is to have claims initially entered into the system by the claims adjudicators, who will kick out those items that cannot be processed because of missing data. In any event, it is not acceptable to allow claims to accumulate unentered into the system. There must be some method of entering claims into inventory upon receipt and accruing a liability even if the ultimate claim liability is not yet known.

Even if claims are prescreened, adjudicators will always identify some claims that require further investigation. This is especially true of claims for which there is no corresponding authorization. An efficiently run department is one where claims that cannot be finalized are routed to specific personnel who are responsible for the timely resolution of the problem. A major pitfall of most claims operations are its exception claims, which can languish in a pending status indefinitely when accountability is ill defined. Unlike wine, claims do not improve with age.

Specialist Level Claims

Certain claims should be routed to specialists for skilled handling. Examples of such specialized review are as follows:

- Nurse reviewer: surgery claims (including assistant surgeon and multiple procedures), physical therapy, emergency room; anything else that requires medical training
- Other party liability specialist: any claim with other party liability potential
- Team leader: any claim that poses a serious question to the adjudicator regarding coverage, contract terms, authorization, or system problems

- Supervisor: any claim over defined dollar limits (eg, payment exceeds $5,000) for higher level approval; high dollar claims can be defined in increments requiring successive approval levels (claims manager, chief financial officer, or chief executive officer).

Emergency claims are a special category that requires certain plan decisions. Examples of such decisions include the following:

- Must members notify the plan only in advance of emergency care or within 48 hours of such care?
- If no prior authorization exists, is the claim denied outright or pended for further investigation?
- If pended, which department is accountable for gathering statements from the patient and provider? How many follow-up requests should be made?
- Can medical management define criteria to be applied by the adjudicators to process emergency claims without further investigation (eg, heart attack, loss of consciousness, fractures, lacerations, and so forth.)?

Emergency claim investigations can be paper and labor intensive. But because this is an area of potential member abuse, it behooves a plan to develop policies and procedures to expedite the process, protect the plan's interests, and provide coverage to the member.

Finalization

At the end of the process, all finalized claims must be filed for easy retrieval. If the department microfilms claims, the on-site storage can be brief, just long enough to perform quality review audits. If not microfilmed, it is necessary to keep claims at least 12 months on site to respond to member and provider inquiries and appeals. Dead storage must also be adequately maintained to provide easy retrieval. An outside vendor for such storage may be worth investigating, especially if it can provide 24-hour retrieval time.

Another end process activity is mailing checks and letters. In larger plans, this function may be handled by a distribution department. If the claims department is responsible, however, adequate space must be allotted, complete with the necessary tools (decolator, envelopes, folding machine, and postage meter). The computer system should be programmed to produce checks, remittance reports, and address labels in the same provider name order to expedite the process.

Denial letters and explanation of benefits (for indemnity benefits) also must be mailed to members. System programming should be set up to produce these items for window envelopes.

Checks and letters should be produced according to a published schedule. Any delays must be reported to customer service personnel so that they may advise callers as to when payment or denial can be expected.

COMMUNICATION ISSUES

Communication issues are those that have an impact on the department's ability to function as a viable entity within the plan. The claims department does not operate in a vacuum. Communication lines must be established with virtually every other department within the plan. Communications in general are ideally managed by assigning claims department liaisons to specific personnel in other departments who will handle problems, requests, questions, and concerns. Logs (manual or electronic) must be kept to ensure prompt turnaround time and quality resolution. The discerning claims manager also makes a point of building his or her own bridges to other department heads to fulfill the department's mission of service. These links are discussed by department.

Customer or Member Services

Requests for priority handling of claims as well as appeals will come from members through member services (see Chapter 19). The claims department must design forms and establish procedures for expediting important claim requests and for returning items to member services if information is incomplete or if a request is invalid.

Information must also flow from the claims department in terms of changes in processing procedures. Probably the most significant communication device a claims adjudicator can use is the internal comment field on the claims processing screen to explain further how a claim is processed. Beyond this, regularly scheduled meetings with customer service representatives will serve to bring problems to the surface and provide an opportunity to close communication gaps.

Provider Relations

Requests for priority handling of claims and appeals will come from providers through provider relations. In addition to procedures for handling these, a mechanism must also be established for provider relations personnel to inform the claims department of any changes in provider contracts. Frequently, the claims department is informed of changes in provider contracts after the effective date, sometimes months after. In reality, provider negotiations often result in a backdated effective date. But the vigilant claims manager makes every attempt to determine what negotiations are ongoing and what the outcome is likely to be, making plans to absorb any new or changed contracts, especially if retroactive adjustments are required.

Marketing

Complaints from members are often funneled through the employer and ultimately through the marketing department. Again, forms and procedures must be established not only to resolve these issues but to provide feedback to marketing and the employer. Additionally, marketing is usually the source of information concerning changes in the plan's coverage and projections of future membership. The claims manager must be tuned into anticipated changes because they will affect staffing and adjudication decisions.

Utilization Management

No other department is as important to communicate with than utilization management (UM) because the decisions made in UM have a direct impact on adjudication decisions (see Chapters 10 and 11). Assuming an electronic link exists between UM and claims, an analysis must be made of UM records to ensure that the data recorded are complete and clearly stated. A determination must also be made by the plan as to what an authorization record actually communicates (ie, what specific claims can be linked to a single authorization). This is often referred to as subauthorization, which allows the claims adjudicator to pay several related claims with a single authorization record. The subauthorization process, however, must be well defined and approved by medical management. See an example in Table 20-1.

Finance

Communication with finance/accounting revolves around such issues as returned checks, refund checks, stop payments, reinsurance, check signing, and claim audits. Forms and procedures are needed to define precisely the steps to be taken, especially where live checks are concerned. Auditors will be particularly interested in seeing that there is virtually no risk of fraud or abuse concerning these matters.

Management Information Systems or Data Processing

The primary advantage of good communications with management information system (MIS) personnel is more efficient use of the system. Every effort must be made to discover and utilize all system processing functions and to enhance them continually. MIS may also offer personal computer support for producing reports that cannot be generated from the mainframe.

Claims Department

Finally, communication within the claims department is of equal importance. Regularly scheduled staff meetings to bring everyone up to date as well as to resolve questions and concerns are vital. In a large operation, a department newsletter can provide important business information in addition to personal data such as upcoming birthdays, anniversaries, prizes for productivity and quality, and so forth.

DOCUMENTATION

"But where is it written down?" This is one of the most often repeated questions in a managed care organization, especially among new employees. Indeed, how are new employees trained, how are existing employees cross-trained, how are evaluations defended, and how are adjudication decisions consistently made

Table 20-1 Authorization Decisions for Claim Adjudication

Claim Type	Type of Authorization				
	Inpatient	Outpatient Surgery	Outpatient	Referral	Emergency
Hospital facility	Pay	Pay	Pay	SAR	Pay
Hospital-based radiology	Pay	Pay	Pay	SAR	Pay
Hospital-based pathology	Pay	Pay	Pay	SAR	Pay
Hospital-based anesthesia	Pay	Pay	N/A	SAR	Pay
Hospital-based ER physician	N/A	N/A	N/A	N/A	Pay
Ambulance	SAR	SAR	SAR	SAR	SAR
Referral physician	SAR	Pay	SAR	Pay	SAR
Laboratory	N/A	N/A	N/A	SAR	N/A
Radiology	N/A	N/A	N/A	SAR	N/A
Durable medical expense	SAR	SAR	SAR	SAR	SAR

Note: Abbreviations: SAR, separate authorization required; N/A, not applicable.

without good documentation? Thorough, concise, and well-organized documentation is a vital component of a well-managed claims department.

Training Manual

There is no substitute for a training manual for new employees. Even veteran staff can benefit from periodic review of training materials. The training manual should consist of:

- background information about the plan and managed care concepts in general
- descriptions of the functions of other departments, especially UM, provider relations, and member services
- discussion of authorization and other party liability concepts
- detailed benefits review
- processing system tutorial

Even though processing software is becoming more sophisticated and is automating more adjudication decisions, a department that relies only on its system and not on its staff is doomed to mediocrity. Well-trained claims adjudicators will not only be more productive of high-quality work but will also be able to detect opportunities that will have a positive impact on the bottom line: other party liability, inappropriate unbundling, improper billing practices, and the like.

Training manuals can be designed to be self-study or to be used with a trainer. To be continually effective, however, the manual must be kept up to date. One word of caution: User manuals provided by software vendors are not good training manuals. They can provide a good foundation, but they will never be specific to the plan's operations.

Quick Reference

Most processing systems use various codes to indicate everything from provider type to processing disposition. These codes and other data such as provider contract terms should be at the adjudicators' fingertips for increased productivity and accuracy. This is especially important if provider terms must be calculated manually. Often adjudicators will have handwritten notes posted all over the work station for quick reminders. The fundamental problem with this approach is that the notes are not always accurate, complete, or applied consistently by all adjudicators. A quick reference volume packaged in an easel display binder or available through electronic pop-up windows, and kept current, is vital to achieving the zero defect quality goal.

Policies and Procedures Manual

The training manual and the quick reference volume must be limited in scope and size to be effective, and as a consequence many details cannot be included. The policies and procedures manual fills this void. As its name implies, this manual comprises specific policy statements complete with step-by-step procedures to administer the policies.

Although this manual can function well within the claims department, it is advisable that all operational department heads agree to produce a complete operations policies and procedures manual. This is especially useful when one is documenting procedures that cross department lines. The main purpose of the policies and procedures manual is to document accountability (ie, who is responsible for carrying out policy decisions).

Benefits Interpretation/Medical Policy Manual

One key to member and provider satisfaction is the consistent application of benefits. This can be enhanced by documenting plan policy decisions as they affect benefits administration. For example, the specific coverage for prosthetics may be limited to surgical implants only; if so, the benefits interpretation manual can specify exactly what this entails, including procedure codes. One approach to constructing this type of manual is to take the various coverage headings from the schedule of benefits as topics for the manual. This is especially useful for the noncovered items because they should be identified by current procedural terminology (CPT) procedure codes. Medical management must be involved in the development of this manual.

FINANCE ISSUES

Finance issues are those that have a direct impact on the profitability of the plan. Mastering these concepts will enable the claims department to seize opportunities to conserve the plan's funds while still providing the maximum benefit to the member.

Other Party Liability

No other activity can directly affect the plan's bottom line as well as identifying monies to be saved or recovered from other party liability. There are four components to consider: COB, workers' compensation, automobile insurance, and subrogation. The success of these programs, however, depends on how many departments outside claims are actively gathering information and supporting the programs.

The claims department staff responsible for these activities should keep extensive records of savings and recoveries split among the various components discussed below. It is amazing to see how quickly savings and recoveries grow.

Coordination of Benefits

The beauty of a successful COB program is that it gives the claims department the opportunity to earn money for the plan rather than spend it. Considering that a plan can save or recover $5 or more per member per month, any dollars spent on staff salaries and other expenses to make the program viable are easily recovered. The key to a successful COB program is data. There must be a way to collect other health insurance information from the member and have it available to the adjudicator as claims are processed.

In traditional insurance environments, covered individuals are usually required to submit a completed claim form at least once a year identifying other coverage, if any. If medical invoices are submitted without a claim form, such invoices are pended until the insured submits COB information.

In a managed care environment, however, members are usually not required to submit claim forms. Therefore, plan personnel must be creative in securing COB data. One popular mechanism is to include a postpaid COB questionnaire in the member newsletter at least once per year. Prizes can even be offered as an incentive; for example, a drawing can be made from all completed questionnaires for something of value. The expenses related to this endeavor can often be recouped in just one COB claim!

Other methods of collecting data include requiring the PCPs to ask for COB data at least once per year when the patient visits, requiring UM personnel to ask hospital admissions for other insurance information, and coaching member services to ask routinely for COB information as they converse with members. If a plan has an outreach program for new members (see Chapter 19), COB questions should be part of the script.

All these data must be recorded in the processing system so that adjudicators can be alerted to COB potential as they are processing claims. Most processing systems integrate COB data with claims processing. If this cannot be done, the process becomes much more challenging but still viable.

Even without COB data recorded for the member, the claims adjudicator must be alert to COB clues found on submitted invoices. Both the standard HCFA 1500 (for professional) and UB82 (for institutional) claim forms have designated spaces for the provider to record other insurance information. Absent these data, any amount already paid toward the total charges should be questioned because another carrier probably made such a payment. The adjudicator should also be alert to any COB data captured on the authorization record.

With the help of medical management, the claims adjudicator can be advised of certain diagnosis and procedure codes that have other insurance potential. Chief among these is dialysis treatment, where Medicare is primary under strictly defined conditions.

One fundamental decision the plan must make is how to administer COB once the potential is identified. If the member's primary coverage is another carrier, the plan may opt to deny any benefits until it is advised of what the primary carrier paid; this is often referred to as pursue and pay. Some plans are uncomfortable with this approach because it places the responsibility on the member to supply the data. Alternatively, the plan can pay the claim (assuming all other payment criteria are met) and then contact the other carrier directly by telephone or by the industry standard coverage inquiry form (CIF) for a benefits determination. The plan then may recover funds directly from the other insurance carrier; this is often referred to as pay and pursue.

The plan is better off financially if it does not pay initially because recovery is never guaranteed. This approach must be weighed against member satisfaction issues and potential legal issues, however, if an accusation can be made of bad faith claims processing. This risk can be substantially reduced with well-documented COB policies and procedures and consistent turnaround times.

Workers' Compensation and Automobile Insurance

Claims resulting from accidental injury should be questioned for potential workers' compensation or automobile insurance liability. PCPs and referral specialists should be counseled on the advantages of alerting the plan of any patient with a work-related or automobile-related injury. Claims adjudicators can also be trained to look beyond the fractures to other medical episodes that can possibly be linked to occupation: heart attacks for fire fighters, lung disease for mill workers, auto accident injuries for truck drivers, even hand injuries for computer operators. Some of these may be disputed, but they are all worth pursuing. The adjudicator may also have access to an emergency room report, nursing notes, or an operative report that may shed light on the liability issue. The topic of workers' compensation is discussed fully in Chapter 33.

Every state has its own laws governing workers' compensation and automobile insurance and how expenses for injuries are coordinated, if at all, with the patient's medical coverage. If a case is recognized by all parties as a workers'

compensation or an automobile insurance liability at the outset, the plan may be able to deny any associated claims upon receipt. If the liability is disputed, however, the plan will probably have to pay the charges and continue to follow the case until a determination is made. If other party liability is confirmed, the plan can recover directly from the workers' compensation or automobile insurance carrier without inconveniencing the member.

Subrogation

A subrogation clause, if it exists in the member's schedule of benefits, gives the plan the right to recover any damages the member may receive from a third party found responsible for injury to offset the medical expenses incurred. Such cases can be identified by ascertaining the cause of a member's injuries and then investigating potential subrogation situations. The member usually is unfamiliar with this clause, and some can be uncooperative. Every effort, however, should be made to recover expenses that a third party has agreed to settle financially. It may be necessary to work with the member's or third party's legal counsel, who will recover the funds for a percentage.

Carefully drawn guidelines must be developed with the plan's senior management and legal counsel to govern this process and set a cap to the percentage that the plan is willing to forfeit. Although the plan may not fully recover its expenses because of attorneys' fees, any amount that is recoverable is usually worthwhile.

Reinsurance

Most plans have reinsurance contracts, which help defray the costs of catastrophic claims. The responsibility of filing a reinsurance claim is often assigned to finance personnel. The claims manager, however, should be aware of the reinsurance contract provisions because there may be a need to advise finance of potential claim situations. The reinsurance contract usually has a large deductible, perhaps $50,000, but the reinsurance carrier may require notification of a potential case when charges paid exceed half the reinsurance deductible. Even if this is not required, it is a sound practice to set such a limit, which flags any member whose claim payments exceed that amount. This procedure will alert all concerned to follow the case closely so that the reinsurance claim can be filed at the appropriate time.

Policies and procedures should be governed by the reinsurance contract, which will specify the deductible amount, whether the deductible is annual or lifetime, and any limitation of charges that can be included. For example, the reinsurance contract may apply only to inpatient hospital charges. Accountability in both claims and finance should be assigned to specific personnel for prompt and accurate administration.

Fraud and Abuse

Fraud and abuse, internal and external, are two of the ugliest situations in claims administration, but they are a reality that the wary claims manager faces. Adequate controls for security and administrative procedures will provide a large measure of protection as well as grounds for disciplinary action.

Internally, the plan must be protected from any attempted circumvention of policies and procedures for personal gain. Security within the processing system must be strictly enforced with unique and confidential passwords for every adjudicator who has the ability to generate payments. Limitations on dollars payable can be placed on new hires until a probationary period is satisfied.

There are three additional areas where security should be tight: authorization data entry, provider record establishment, and check production/signing.

The authorization record acts as a purchase order for an adjudicator to link to a claim for payment. The ability to cut a purchase order should never be coupled with the ability to cut a check; in other words, the system authority to add, change, or delete authorization records should not be assigned to anyone in the claims department.

Accountability for maintaining provider records in the system must be also assigned to staff outside the claims department. Provider records must be created according to prescribed procedures that ensure that only authentic practitioners and facilities, with valid tax identification numbers, are added to the system for payment. Any changes in name, address, or tax identification should be submitted on the provider's stationery and never taken over the telephone. The full name of the provider should be entered in the provider record. Abbreviations due to field length should be made according to established conventions designed to prevent duplicating records. For example, university hospitals should always be abbreviated in the same way (eg, Univ of ____). If some are entered "Univ." and others "U of," the alphabetical listing will be distorted, resulting in duplication of records and incorrect selection by adjudicators.

The credentialing process and other mechanisms within the provider relations department will usually be sufficient to protect the plan from problems with participating providers. Extra care, however, must be taken with nonparticipating providers to ensure that they are genuine entities. Only valid claim forms complete with signatures and tax identification numbers should be used to establish a nonparticipating provider record unless otherwise approved by medical management.

The check production and signing authority should be governed by finance. Any type of signature mechanism must be secured by lock and limited access. Certain high dollar claim checks should also require an additional live signature by a plan officer. Manual checks (those issued outside the normal check run) should be held to an absolute minimum, with approval for issuing such a check being given by the chief financial officer or controller.

Aside from fraud, the conscientious claim manager must also be concerned about the abuse of confidentiality. Medical claims contain the most personal information of virtually any computerized records in contemporary society. Especially with such explosive issues as abortion and acquired immunodeficiency syndrome, the claims manager must be assured that staff will honor the privacy of the plan's members, especially when an adjudicator sees a claim for a friend, relative, or neighbor. Every plan employee should be required to sign a statement promising to uphold confidentiality, knowing the penalty for a breach in confidentiality to be immediate dismissal.

If the claims department processes claims for the plan itself, extra precautions should be taken to ensure the privacy of fellow employees and their families. Some plans restrict certain employee claims (eg, for psychiatry) to one or two higher level claims staff members. MIS may be able to assign confidential member numbers to handle these particularly sensitive claims. Other plans choose to restrict all employee claims. In this case, MIS can limit access to the plan's group records to designated individuals. In either case, procedures must be strictly defined so that restricted handling is ensured from the mailroom to the check-writing process.

Externally, fraud and abuse come in the form of claims with inflated or inappropriate charges. Although it is difficult to prove fraud on the part of a provider, it is necessary to be ever vigilant.

Criteria must be defined to audit any hospital claim (not paid on per diem or per case terms) over a certain limit (eg, $10,000) where more than 50% of the charges are for other than room and board. The object is to verify that all charges are legitimate and ordered by a physician. There are at least two national firms who specialize in hospital audits, having established relationships with hospitals nationwide and solid reputations for service and savings. Alternatively, a plan may be able to arrange to have a skilled nurse reviewer perform such audits at local hospitals and avoid the fees charged by outside firms. In either case, audits are worth performing on high dollar invoices where hundreds or thousands of dollars can be saved.

Code Explosion

Abuse on physician claims has to do with the relation between the services provided to the patient and those that are billed. Claims operations nationwide have recognized a trend among physicians to file claims with upcoded, unbundled, mutually exclusive, or otherwise inappropriate charges. Whether these are attempts deliberately to game the system or clerical errors, the prudent claims manager must institute procedures for protecting the plan against manipulative practices. Exhibit 20-7 shows the types of charges which can be "gamed" and which should be audited.

At a minimum, all surgery claims should be reviewed by the nurse reviewer for unbundling of procedures as well as for assistant surgery charges and charges for multiple procedures. Claim history should be examined to ensure that hospital and office visits are incorporated into the surgery fee, except for the initial diagnostic visit.

Claims adjudicators can be instructed to review all initial office visits in light of the patient's claim history to ensure that only one initial office visit to a practice is allowed. Retrospective analysis of claim payments may reveal disturbing billing practices among certain specialists (or even PCPs) in which all patients are routinely given the same battery of diagnostic tests, which may be medically unnecessary. The watchful claims manager develops a working protocol with the plan's medical management to analyze areas of potential abuse and corresponding strategies to reduce the plan's expense. This issue is addressed in Chapter 16.

There is a limit, however, to the amount of upcoding that can be discovered by alert adjudicators. To that end, several software products have been developed that can operate independently or be integrated with the claims processing software to flag potential code problems and offer more appropriate coding alternatives. Having claims automatically adjusted to the correct

---

Exhibit 20-7 Examples of Physician Claims To Audit

- Obsolete or inappropriate codes
- Experimental procedures
- Assistant surgery
- Separate procedures
- Surgical global fee
- Visit frequency
- Radiology unbundled
- Secondary procedure management
- Chemistry laboratory unbundled
- Surgery unbundled
- Cosmetic procedures

coding reduces the number of claims being pended and routed, thereby increasing the productivity of the department. With savings potential both in productivity and in dollars, these systems are well worth investigating.

Refund and Return Checks

Procedures must be established to deposit all refund checks and to invalidate all returned checks immediately upon receipt. Adjustments may be a three-way responsibility among claims, provider relations, and accounting personnel, or they may be limited to a single senior adjustor. Regardless, well-defined policies and procedures will protect the plan financially and will expedite the adjustment, especially if a claim is paid in error.

CONCLUSION

Throughout this chapter, many adjectives have been used to describe a successful claims manager: *wary, judicious, conscientious, discerning, prudent, astute, vigilant,* and *wise.* Indeed, a claims manager must be all these, juggling people, paper, and systems to deliver results. But when it all works well, that claims manager is satisfied, having truly been of service to the plan, the providers, and the members.

SUGGESTED READING

Aetna heads up fraud squad. *HMO Manag Lett.* November 7, 1988:7–8.

Begole C. How to get the productivity edge. *Working Woman.* May 1991:47–60.

Brant O. From mini to mainframe: how one HMO made the leap. *Comput Healthcare.* September 1990:26–28.

Capp Care aggregates claims data to control MD volume of services. *Manag Care Rep.* April 16, 1990:7.

Cave DG, Tucker LJ. 10 facts about point-of-service plans. *HRMagazine.* September 1991:41–46.

Griffith RF, Fernow LC. Stopping big buck claim errors. *Bus Health.* March 1989:37.

Kienle KW. Clamping down on code creep. *Best Rev.* January 1991:56–77.

Mullen P. Prudential preps electronic claims verification. *HealthWeek.* December 17, 1990:9.

Politzer B. Claims of excellence. *HMO Mag.* November-December 1991:38–44.

PPOs move, but don't rush, toward implementing RBRVS. *PPO Lett.* January 13, 1992:6–8.

Thorpe B. Marriott's nationwide managed care benefits program—a case study. *Fed Am Health Syst Rev.* May-June 1989:36–38.

Wojcik J. Containing health costs. *Bus Insur.* February 18, 1991:3–6.

Workers' comp costs can be lowered through aggressive claim management. *Manag Care Outlook.* May 11, 1990:5–6.

Chapter 21

Outside Accreditation of Managed Care Plans

Margaret E. O'Kane

With the increasing prominence of managed care in today's health care market has come a concern on the part of purchasers, regulators, and consumers that the quality of care not be harmed by these new organizational arrangements. Responding to these pressures are three accreditation organizations, each of which specializes in a different organizational type of managed care organization (MCO). The various organizational types and the quality issues associated with each type are described in detail below.

All the accrediting bodies were developed with the purpose of responding to external demands for accountability. For health maintenance organizations (HMOs), the oldest organizational form, the intent of the new accreditation program is to rationalize what has become a maze of different customer and regulatory re-

quirements, including federal qualification, Medicare certification, review by peer organizations, Medicaid quality review, and state licensure review; often the effort extends to responding to numerous requests for proposals and even external review teams for individual corporate clients.

Preferred provider organizations (PPOs) and utilization review (UR) firms, the newer organizational forms, have attempted, by establishing their accreditation programs, to head off incipient regulatory initiatives in many states and also to respond to the demands of their customers for assurances about the integrity of their functions.

As discussed below, there are important differences among the accreditation programs that reflect to some degree the differences among the organizations that are the focus of their review process.

For the Utilization Review Accreditation Commission (URAC), because it was established largely to respond to provider concerns, the major emphasis of the process is reducing the hassle factor and creating a degree of uniformity among UR processes. For the American Accreditation Program, Inc (AAPI), the major emphasis of the process is to reduce risk and liability for the purchaser of services as well as

---

Margaret E. O'Kane is the President of the National Committee for Quality Assurance (NCQA). NCQA is an external quality review organization for health maintenance organizations. Previously, Ms. O'Kane served as the Director of Quality Management for the Group Health Association, a staff model HMO with approximately 150,000 members. Before that she was Director of the Medical Directors Division for the Group Health Association of America.

to assess the value of a particular PPO. For the National Committee for Quality Assurance (NCQA), the major emphasis is on the quality of care and service that the organization delivers to its enrollees and on the mechanisms that the organization has established to improve continuously its quality.

There are two other organizations that do accredit some MCOs. The Joint Commission on Accreditation of Healthcare Organizations does accredit some group and staff model HMOs under its ambulatory care accreditation program. The Accreditation Association for Ambulatory Health Care also accredits HMOs under its ambulatory care accreditation program. Because neither of these programs is specifically designed to deal with MCOs, however, they are not within the scope of this chapter.

TYPES OF MANAGED CARE

The simplest type of MCO is the UR firm. UR firms typically do not include a defined delivery system. Most often, the UR function is performed by these firms on behalf of purchasers of health care to manage health care costs for individuals who have traditional indemnity health insurance. PPOs, prepaid MCOs, and HMOs sometimes contract with UR firms to perform this function, although most frequently these organizations perform UR functions themselves.

A PPO is an insurance arrangement wherein patients are encouraged through financial incentives (lower copayments and deductibles) to use a defined network of providers. Typically the preferred providers are selected on the basis of the ability of the insurer to receive discounted fees or the insurer's assessment that the preferred providers provide more cost-effective care. PPOs often have a UR function that applies both to the preferred providers and to care received outside the defined network, which is essentially indemnity insurance.

The most comprehensive form of managed care is the HMO. An HMO or prepaid MCO is an organized prepaid health care system that is responsible for the provision of comprehensive health services to an enrolled population in re-

turn for a predetermined capitation payment. The prepaid MCO includes a defined delivery system that serves a defined population with a defined set of benefits. Prepaid MCO primary care physicians often are either capitated (ie, they receive a fixed monthly payment for providing services to specific enrollees), salaried, paid on a fee-for-service basis with a withhold, or paid on some other type of performance-based reimbursement (see Chapters 4 and 6 for detailed discussions of physician reimbursement). These payment arrangements, which were developed with the expressed intention of giving financial incentives to manage resources effectively, have led many critics of the HMO concept to argue that they provide an incentive to underserve.

The prepaid MCO usually also has a defined network of specialists, who may be paid on a capitated, salaried, discounted fee-for-service, or other basis (see Chapter 7 for a detailed discussion of specialist reimbursement). Prepaid MCO members usually may receive services only from contracting providers. Together with the financial incentives, it is this lock-in feature of prepaid MCOs that has led regulators and policy makers to require active quality assurance programs for prepaid MCOs as a condition of licensure (see Chapter 34) or federal qualification (see Chapter 35).

Although it is possible to conceptualize these pure forms of MCOs, the reality is increasingly more complex. The boundaries among types have become blurred, and there is a great variety of hybrid forms of MCOs. Just as there has been a blurring of the boundaries of types of MCOs, prepaid MCOs have also become increasingly hybridized as, for example, a staff model develops an independent practice association (IPA) network or a point-of-service product.

The point-of-service HMO product is essentially a hybrid of the HMO and the PPO in which the HMO forms the preferred provider network but the patient may go outside the HMO and still be insured through an indemnity wraparound (with higher copayments and deductibles). As suggested by the name, at the point of service the patient may decide whether he or she will seek services inside or outside the defined network.

The main types of MCOs may be viewed as points along a continuum of medical management. At one end of the continuum, the UR firm does not seek to define a delivery system or to ensure most aspects of quality. Its focus is on cost containment. For the most part, its approach to quality management addresses only one of the many complex components that determine clinical quality: elimination of unnecessary services.

When effective, UR helps prevent services from being delivered that are inappropriate in the sense that they are not medically necessary. Sometimes this results in positive gains in the quality of care, as when patients avoid the risk of unnecessary or ineffective procedures such as unwarranted hysterectomies or carotid endarterectomies. But because the pure UR firm by definition has no control over who provides medical services, it cannot credential providers; it also cannot monitor for underutilization, misdiagnosis, incompetent use of the right treatment, or use of the wrong medical treatment, all of which are important threats to quality.

Moving along the continuum, PPOs can achieve more medical management than UR firms. Because there is a defined system of preferred providers, the plan has the opportunity to select providers who meet certain defined criteria of quality as well as of price or economical practice style. Because it is not possible to link patients to a given physician within the PPO, however (patients do not select a single gatekeeper type physician), it is not easy or common to perform systematic evaluations of the quality of care across providers.

Prepaid MCOs or HMOs offer the most opportunity for medical management by ensuring that many of the complex issues that have an impact on the quality of care in the system are addressed. Like the PPO, the prepaid MCO can establish quality standards for entry into its provider network through its credentialing process. Because there is a defined system of providers within which patients must seek care, it is also possible to evaluate the quality of care by applying defined criteria. When problems occur within the delivery system, it is possible to seek the roots of those problems within the system and to implement actions for improvement. An-

other implication of the defined system of providers is that the HMO has greater potential exposure to legal liability for the performance of providers in its system and thus has additional incentives to develop management processes and oversight systems.

QUALITY ASSURANCE SYSTEMS IN MANAGED CARE ORGANIZATIONS

As noted in the preceding discussion, there is a range of possible strategies for quality assurance in the various types of MCOs. In the following discussion, we will discuss some techniques of quality assurance that are theoretically possible, given the attributes of the delivery system. Quality management is also addressed in Chapter 15.

The reader should be aware that there is wide variation in quality assurance activities even within similar types of organizations. Thus, although it is theoretically possible for a PPO to have more control over the quality of care received by its enrollees than a UR firm can achieve for the populations that it services, if the PPO has few or inadequate mechanisms to ensure the quality of its provider network, the quality will be no better than that of unmanaged care. Worse, if the preferred providers were selected on the basis of price alone, it is possible that they may be lower in quality than the general run of providers in an area.

Although there is somewhat more homogeneity among prepaid MCOs or HMOs because of federal and state regulatory requirements, the degree of attention to quality assurance varies widely in that sector of managed care as well. State requirements and enforcement mechanisms are uneven, and HMOs do not need to meet federal requirements to do business.

Quality assurance activities of the UR firm can be geared to ensuring that the system is effective in terms of avoiding unnecessary services, that it does not prevent or delay unacceptably the provision of services that are necessary, and that providers and patients are satisfied. To these ends, firms may use such mechanisms as telephone and documentation monitoring of performance of UR nurses, review of denied cases,

monitoring of readmissions as a possible outcome of premature discharge, and surveys of
member and provider satisfaction. Because there
is currently little regulation of UR, these organizations may or may not have these quality assurance mechanisms in place.

As noted in the discussion above, because
PPOs have a defined set of hospital and/or physician providers, it is possible for them to use
quality as a criterion for participation. With regard to physicians, this can range from minimal
credentialing, including proof of licensure and
hospital privileges, to more selective criteria
such as board certification or demonstrated compliance with defined clinical quality standards.
Again, there are few regulatory mechanisms for
PPOs, and there is little information available
either about what proportion of PPOs have quality assurance programs or about the efficacy of
those programs that do exist.

In this section, we will describe some of the
prevalent types of quality assurance that currently exist in the managed care sector. Because
there is much new and exciting technologic development taking place, and because purchasers
of health care are demanding that managed care
systems assume more accountability for the
quality of their systems, quality assurance is a
rapidly evolving and increasingly important aspect of managed care systems. Although it is not
possible to detail here all the types of quality assurance mechanisms that are currently being
used in managed care systems, what follows is a
description of quality assurance activities that
are frequently in use today.

Credentialing and Recertification Systems

As previously noted, one of the advantages of
a defined delivery system is the ability to ensure
that only high-quality providers participate in
the system. Prepaid managed care systems and
PPOs are able to evaluate the qualifications, if
not the actual performance (with a few notable
exceptions), of the physicians they hire, contract
with, or designate as preferred when there is a
systematic and thorough application and
credentialing process. Other providers (eg, hospital and home health agencies) that contract
with or are part of a preferred system should un-

dergo some kind of credentialing or quality systems review as well.

The initial physician credentialing process
generally includes verification of licensure,
Drug Enforcement Agency (DEA) certification,
graduation from medical school and residency
program, and board certification. Staff and
group model prepaid MCOs will generally review work history in depth, including evaluation
of references. There is generally an extensive interview process before a physician is hired, and
there may be an initial probationary period before the physician achieves permanent status
with the medical group or the staff of the MCO.

IPA models and PPOs may not review work
history in detail because they generally contract
with independent practitioners. Many plans also
review professional liability claims history.
Hospital privileges in good standing are generally a prerequisite for physicians who wish to
contract with IPAs.

Prepaid MCOs increasingly request information about potential hires or contractor physicians from the National Practitioner Data Bank.

Many IPA model MCOs also conduct a review of the private practitioner's office before
signing a contract. Besides allowing the plan to
ensure that the office meets basic standards of
safety, cleanliness, comfort, and patient privacy,
this review also offers the opportunity for the
plan to ensure that there are adequate medical
record systems and sufficient appointments
available for the new enrollees it hopes to send
to the office.

Perhaps even more important than the initial
credentialing process is the process of performance review and recertification that managed
systems conduct periodically, usually every 2
years. Besides the review of the structural credentials which is repeated from the initial
credentialing process, this recertification allows
for the review of the actual performance of the
practitioner, including information from member satisfaction surveys, results of quality reviews, and review of utilization patterns and
member complaints.

Although credentialing has not always been a
high priority activity in every MCO, it has become increasingly important both because of the
interest of purchasers in strong credentialing

systems and because the courts have increasingly held that managed care systems, because they do define a delivery system, have a responsibility to try to ensure the quality of that system (see Chapter 38). Further discussion of credentialing is found in Chapter 4 (for closed panel plans) and Chapter 5 (for open panel plans).

Establishment of Standards for Medical Records and Monitoring of Compliance with Standards

One common quality improvement technique that has become increasingly widespread among MCOs is the review of documentation in medical records against a set of standards. Although these studies have been widespread among staff and group model MCOs for years, they have only recently begun to be widely used in IPA model organizations, where the challenge is often greater because of the multiplicity of charting styles among independent practitioners.

Sentinel/Adverse Event Monitoring

One methodology that has been used quite frequently by prepaid plans is the investigation of adverse events. Originally introduced in hospital risk management programs as generic occurrence screening, the method has intuitive appeal because it deals with defined events and because it avoids many technical issues of case finding.

The review methodology identifies a list of sentinel or adverse events that may indicate that there was a problem with the care provided before the event. The original examples from hospitals include events such as unplanned transfer to the intensive care unit, unplanned return to surgery on the same admission, and surgery and myocardial infarction on the same admission. Typically the case that is identified by the generic screen is subjected to peer review, and the reviewing physician renders an opinion as to whether the adverse event resulted from a problem with the quality of care.

The system has been adapted for use in managed care quality assurance programs. Although

some MCOs use the generic hospital screens to monitor the quality of their hospital care, many use a different set of screens that were intended to identify potential deficits in the quality of ambulatory care that may have caused the hospital admission. Some examples include ruptured appendix, complications of diabetes, and late-stage breast cancer. Examples of both types of screens are found in Chapter 15 (Exhibits 15-1 and 15-2).

Establishment of Practice Guidelines and Evaluation of Performance against Guidelines

A technique that has great appeal in that it sets out expectations in advance is the measurement of performance against criteria that are linked to generally accepted practice guidelines. Thus a plan may study immunizations in children to determine, for example, the proportion of children who are up to date for measles, mumps, and rubella immunizations. Likewise, the plan may study the proportion of women older than 50 years who received a mammogram in the past year. An important limitation of this technique is the shortage of generally accepted practice guidelines. Currently, there are widely accepted guidelines for preventive services, for many pediatric services, and for many services in obstetrics/gynecology.

There is much activity in the development of practice guidelines by the American Medical Association, many specialty societies, and the federal government, however, and there is a general expectation that more will emerge over the next 5 to 10 years.

This type of monitoring has the advantage of allowing assessment of system performance with the goal of overall improvement. Interestingly enough, the widespread use of practice guidelines originated with UR under the rubric of UR criteria. For the first time, UR criteria were used for preauthorization of certain surgical procedures by all forms of managed care. This process introduced to the general American health care system the notion that there are generally accepted decision rules that can be applied to the practice of medicine.

Monitoring of Outcomes of Selected Services

As discussed above, monitoring of the outcomes of care—the effect on the health status and well-being of patients—is an important way of assessing system performance. Outcome measurement has some important shortcomings and usually needs to be supplemented by detailed review of the process of care to work systematically for quality improvement. An additional complicating factor for MCOs is that they may not have a large enough population base of enrollment to perform meaningful analyses of specific conditions. Nevertheless, some large systems have been able to conduct extremely valuable analyses of the outcomes of their care in such areas of medicine as prenatal care and cancer screening, and they have been able to demonstrate improvement in performance after new interventions have been put in place.

Member Satisfaction Surveys

Another widely used quality improvement technique is the member satisfaction survey. Although most prepaid MCOs conduct a survey of general member satisfaction, there are also a number of organizations that have developed specialized satisfaction surveys to focus on more specific aspects of care in their systems. Some MCOs now conduct surveys with a large enough sample size to allow analysis at the individual primary care physician level. In some cases, the member satisfaction score is used to adjust the physician's reimbursement (see Chapter 18). One large staff model prepaid MCO conducts "How was your visit?" surveys, wherein all the patients seeing a given physician within a given week are surveyed at the end of their visit. The results are used to provide detailed feedback to the physicians. Other organizations have used patient satisfaction surveys to assess hospital and specialty care.

Evaluation of Adequacy of Follow-Up Care

Risk management case files are replete with cases of patients who were harmed because of the failure to follow up on abnormal tests, radiographs, or symptoms. Most often, these failures

result not from the error of any particular individual but from a failure of the system, such as a laboratory slip that never got filed or was filed before the abnormal result was noted and the next step taken, or a patient who was not at home to receive a phone call to schedule follow-up care and then was lost to the system. Although these events are no more likely to occur in managed care systems than elsewhere in the delivery systems, managed care systems are in a better position to improve their processes because they have some degree of control over an entire delivery system.

Control over the Delivery System

The degree of control that an MCO exerts over its delivery system will vary depending upon factors such as the ownership, degree of integration, and local market conditions. Likewise, the ability of the MCO to influence its enrollees' behavior varies with the nature of the insurance arrangement. Depending on the specific situation, quality improvement can be achieved through one or a combination of strategies such as internal quality improvement, cooperation, education, market influence, and decontracting. Nevertheless, the prepaid MCO has a degree of control over all the components of the provider system and its enrollees that is unmatched in the other types of MCOs. The prepaid MCO has the greatest potential impact on quality both in terms of ability to deliver high-quality care and in terms of ability to compromise on quality. For this reason, expectations for quality assurance activity have been greater for prepaid MCOs than they have been for the other forms of managed care.

ADMINISTRATIVE ISSUES RELATED TO MANAGED CARE ORGANIZATIONS

The impetus for the development of national accreditation programs for MCOs came, in part, from concerns about the administrative burden these systems may impose on individual physicians and hospitals. *Administrative burden* is a term that has traditionally been used to refer to the preparation of claims and related information needed for a provider to obtain reimbursement for services. With the advent of precertification (ie, requirements imposed by payers that certain services be approved in advance), UR activities now constitute an increasing proportion of administrative burden. Quality assurance and improvement programs also impose administrative burden, such as special data collection efforts, the retrieval of medical charts for retrospective review, and requirements to participate in quality assurance committees and projects. But to date, the burden associated with UR has been far more extensive than that associated with quality review.

Different approaches to UR impose different degrees of administrative burden on physicians and hospitals. Prospective UR generally refers to the prior approval of certain surgical procedures and may involve both ambulatory and inpatient surgery. Concurrent review generally takes place during an approved hospitalization; authorization has been given for a specified period of time, and any additional days of stay require a second approval. Retrospective review, used extensively in both quality review and UR, involves the analysis of the appropriateness of care after it has been provided.

Prospective and concurrent reviews are far more intrusive than retrospective review and have the potential, under certain circumstances, of disrupting the physician/patient relationship. Under prospective and concurrent review, the attending physician's judgment may be brought into question in full view of the patient. In addition, both physician and patient may become involved in lengthy appeals processes in the event that a procedure or continued hospital stay is denied. Prospective and concurrent review processes do afford some financial protection to patients in that the patient and provider are put on notice before the provision of services that the costs of those services will not be covered by insurance. Under retrospective UR, a patient with indemnity coverage might be held financially accountable for services provided but judged to be medically unnecessary after the fact.

In general, the type and extent of administrative burden imposed on individual physicians and hospitals depends on two factors: the type of

MCO involved, and the number of MCOs involved.

DEVELOPMENT OF ACCREDITATION PROGRAMS FOR MANAGED CARE

As already discussed, there were some common reasons for the development of accreditation programs for the three dominant forms of managed care: the desire to be accountable to external customers; the desire to avoid or provide an alternative to burdensome, state-specific regulatory processes; and the desire to respond to allegations of poor quality from various provider groups. For the three different sectors of managed care, the evolution and the dominant impetus were different, and these differences are reflected to a large degree in the governances of the organizations, in the focus of their review process, and in the actual operation of the process.

ACCREDITATION OF UTILIZATION REVIEW

The leading accreditation organization for UR is URAC.

History and Governance

URAC was established in December 1990 and was developed out of an initiative led by the American Managed Care and Review Association (AMCRA), a trade association for UR firms, PPOs, and HMOs, to address providers' concerns and frustration with the diversity of UR procedures and with the growing impact of UR on physicians and hospitals. As a result of this provider frustration, legislative initiatives were underway in a number of states to pass legislation that, according to advocates of managed care, would severely limit the impact of UR in some instances, and make it impossible to conduct UR in others. The URAC accreditation process was developed to be an alternative to state regulation that would nevertheless introduce more consistency into the UR process.

URAC's board of directors includes representatives from the American Medical Association, the American Hospital Association, the American Nurses' Association, the American Psychiatric Association, the Washington Business Group on Health, the National Association of Insurance Commissioners, the National Association of Manufacturers, the United Auto Workers Union, AMCRA, the American Medical Peer Review Association, the Blue Cross and Blue Shield Association, and the Health Insurance Association of America.

Goals of the Utilization Review Accreditation Commission

As stated in URAC's promotional materials, URAC's goal is "to continually improve the quality and efficiency of the interaction between the UR industry and the providers, payors, and purchasers of health care." The URAC accreditation process is specifically designed to reduce the hassle factor for providers, and the standards are not designed to evaluate the adequacy of UR criteria and protocols.

URAC standards are designed to foster this goal and:

- to encourage consistency in the procedures for interaction between UR organizations and providers, payors, and consumers of health care
- to establish UR standards that cause minimum disruption to the health care delivery system
- to establish standards for the procedures used to certify medical services and to process appeals of certification determination
- to provide the basis for an efficient process of credentialing and accrediting UR organizations
- to provide consistent standards and an accreditation mechanism that can be applied efficiently nationwide for those states that choose to regulate UR organizations

Utilization Review Accreditation Commission Standards

The following is a synopsis of the URAC standards.[1]

Applicability

The URAC standards apply to prospective and concurrent UR for inpatient admissions to hospitals and other inpatient facilities as well as to outpatient admissions to surgical facilities.

Responsibility for Obtaining Certification

The standards specify that a UR organization shall allow any licensed hospital, physician, or responsible patient representative, including a family member, to assist in fulfilling that responsibility.

Information upon which Utilization Review Is Conducted

This standard specifies that UR organizations shall collect only the information necessary to certify the admission, procedure or treatment, and length of stay. The standard stipulates that the UR organization shall not routinely request copies of medical records on all patients reviewed but only when a difficulty develops in certifying the medical necessity or appropriateness of the admission or extension of stay. In such cases, only the pertinent sections of the records are to be requested. The standard specifies that UR organizations may request copies of medical records retrospectively for purposes such as auditing the services provided, quality assurance, and evaluation of compliance with the terms of the health benefit plan or UR provisions. In most cases, the standard states that health care providers should be reimbursed for copying costs.

This standard also specifies the maximum data elements that can be required by the UR organization, including categories of information such as patient, enrollee, attending physician/ provider, diagnosis/treatment, clinical status, and facility, and information necessary for concurrent review, such as additional days/services proposed with reasons for extension. For admissions to facilities other than acute medical/surgical hospitals, added information may be required about history of present illness, patient treatment plan and goals, prognosis, staff qualifications, and 24-hour availability of staff. The standard does allow for additional information to be requested for such specific review functions as discharge planning or catastrophic case management. Second opinion information may also be required. The standard also allows for additional information to be requested where there is significant lack of agreement between the UR organization and the health care provider regarding the appropriateness of certification during the review or appeal process.

Procedures for Review Determinations

The standards require that reviews be conducted in a timely manner. For most cases, certification determinations are to be made within 2 working days of receipt of the necessary information about a proposed admission or service. The UR organization may require a discussion with the attending physician or a completed second opinion review.

The standards stipulate that the UR organization may review ongoing inpatient stays but may not conduct daily review of all such stays.

The standard also specifies that the organization must have in place procedures for providing notification of its determinations. There is considerable detail concerning the required contents of these procedures. The UR organization is also required to have procedures to address the failure of a health care provider, patient, or their representative to provide the necessary information for review.

Appeals of Determinations Not To Certify

The standard specifies that the right to appeal shall be available to the patient or enrollee and to the attending physician. The standard also defines minimum elements of the appeals process, including provision for an expedited appeals process. Other requirements include notification by the UR organization to the patient or enrollee, provider, and claims administrator no later than 60 days after receiving the required documentation on the appeal; provision for review of the original decision not to certify by a physician who did not make the original decision not to certify; and the opportunity for the attending physician who has been unsuccessful in an attempt to reverse a determination not to certify to be provided the clinical basis for that determination upon request.

The standard also states that, in cases where an appeal to reverse a determination not to certify for clinical reasons is unsuccessful, the UR organization should ensure that a physician in the same or a similar general specialty as typically manages the medical condition, procedure, or treatment under discussion be reasonably available to review the case as mutually deemed appropriate.

Confidentiality

UR organizations are required to have written procedures including certain minimum elements. The standard stipulates that summary data shall not be considered confidential if they do not provide sufficient information to allow identification of individual patients.

Staff and Program Requirements

The standard requires that UR staff be properly trained, qualified, supervised, and supported by written clinical criteria and review procedures. Review criteria and procedures are to be established with appropriate involvement from physicians and periodically evaluated and updated. The standard requires that a physician review all decisions not to certify for clinical reasons and utilize, as needed and available, specialists who are board certified or board eligible and working toward certification.

The standards require written documentation of an active quality assessment program.

Accessibility and On-Site Review Procedures

The standards specify requirements for accessibility, including a toll-free telephone line that must be available from 9:00 AM to 4:00 PM in the provider's local time zone. There are detailed requirements for the conduct of on-site hospital reviews.

Review Process

The URAC accreditation process begins with a desktop review of a detailed application.[2] The reviewer then verifies the answers on the application telephonically. If the applicant did not pass the telephonic review, a letter is sent to the applicant notifying him or her of this. At this time, the applicant is given 90 days to correct the deficiency. An extension of the 90-day period can be granted for an additional 90 days if a request is made in writing to the accreditation committee.

If URAC staff are unable to verify information telephonically, or if they cannot interpret the information that is given telephonically, they will ask for a recommendation from the accreditation committee. The accreditation committee will recommend either an on-site inspection by URAC staff, for which the applicant organization will pay expenses, or a nonaccreditation decision (which will be made by the executive committee of the URAC board of directors).

If the organization meets the minimum criteria for accreditation, the reviewer's recommendation is forwarded to the accreditation committee, which reviews the information with all organizational identifiers deleted. If the accreditation committee decides to recommend accreditation, the application is sent to the executive committee of the board of directors for final approval. Accreditation is granted for a two-year period.

Copies of the URAC standards and application materials can be obtained by writing to URAC, 1227 25th Street NW, Suite 620, Washington, DC 20037.

PREFERRED PROVIDER ACCREDITATION

The leading accreditation organization for PPOs is the American Accreditation Program, Inc (AAPI).

Established in May 1989 by the American Association of Preferred Provider Organizations and MedStrategies, Inc, a PPO development consulting firm, AAPI was founded "to develop, field test, and demonstrate the value of a PPO accreditation program."[3(p22)] MedStrategies currently handles the marketing and administration of the process.

According to AAPI promotional materials, the AAPI accreditation process focuses on the following areas:

- *Managed care network*—This part of the accreditation process reviews the scope and

stability of the provider network, how out-of-panel referrals are controlled, and how patient access is handled.

- *Provider selection*—The review process examines the objective criteria used in the selection of providers of each type, the consistency of application of the criteria, and verification of data submitted by potential providers and establishes that there is a periodic credentialing and recredentialing process.

- *Payment methods and levels*—The review team reviews payment levels (and decides whether they are competitive and equitable), the flexibility of the PPO in responding to purchasers' needs, how the reimbursement level fosters incentives for efficient provider behavior, and how fee increases are monitored and controlled.

- *Utilization management*—This part of the review assesses the comprehensiveness and effectiveness of utilization management activity, the training and experience of program staff, the standards or criteria used by the program, and the degree of integration of utilization management data and analysis with the PPO's management information system.

- *Quality assessment*—The process reviews the comprehensiveness of the quality assessment program, training and experience of staff, what quality data are generated, the effectiveness of the program in identifying and correcting quality problems, and whether quality assessment data are used in provider credentialing.

- *Management/administrative capabilities*—The team assesses such factors as the PPO's organizational structure, the experience of management and supporting staff, management information systems, how the PPO is marketed, and the content and scope of the patient and provider relations programs.

- *Legal structure*—The team assesses the legal structure of the PPO, evaluates its provider and purchaser contracts, reviews the organization's litigation history, and examines the adequacy of arrangements for due process. The team also examines how anti-trust issues are handled.

- *Financial stability*—The accreditation process evaluates the PPO's past and current financial stability through review of its financial statements, the budget process, and accounting controls. A determination of the adequacy of the organization's reserves and insurance coverage is also made.

Because the AAPI does not publish its standards, it is not possible to ascertain exactly how compliance with these standards is assessed.

The Review Process

AAPI's accreditation process has three steps:

1. The PPO completes a 100-page questionnaire that covers the eight accreditation components.
2. The questionnaire is reviewed by AAPI's primary accreditation team, which consists of a PPO administrator, a physician, and an attorney.
3. A team of PPO professionals with specific expertise in medicine, law, finance, UR, management information systems, and administration conducts a site visit.

The purpose of the site visit is to verify questionnaire answers, gather additional information, examine records, and interview PPO staff. The site visit typically lasts 2 days. In each of the eight accreditation areas, AAPI gives the PPO a numeric grade based on a 100-point total. Each component is also rated by level (levels I, II, and III). The higher the level, the greater the PPO's degree of complexity and sophistication.

Accreditation decisions are made by the site visit teams. AAPI does not currently have a board of directors.

Types of Accreditation

AAPI grants full accreditation to PPOs that meet established standards in each of the eight component areas. Full accreditation is effective for 2 years. Provisional accreditation is granted for 6 months if a PPO meets five of the standards. If the deficiencies are met within the 6-month period, the PPO is fully accredited. If they are not met, the PPO is denied accreditation.

ACCREDITATION OF HEALTH MAINTENANCE ORGANIZATIONS OR PREPAID MANAGED CARE SYSTEMS

NCQA accredits prepaid MCOs and HMOs, including traditional staff and group model HMOs, network and IPA model HMOs, mixed models, and open-ended HMOs or point-of-service products.

Eligible organizations must provide comprehensive health care services to enrolled members through a defined benefit package in both ambulatory and inpatient settings, have been in operation and actively caring for members for at least 18 months, have an active quality management system, and have access to essential clinical information about their patients.

History

NCQA was established in 1979 by the Group Health Association of America (GHAA) and the American Association of Foundations for Medical Care (now AMCRA), the trade associations for HMOs. Original NCQA governance was by the HMO industry.

In 1987, HMO industry leaders, believing that NCQA provided a good base for external quality review, studied a broader role for NCQA and began a process to spin NCQA off from the trade associations and make it independent, a recognized prerequisite for its credibility. As part of that process, the board was restructured to empower users.

In 1988 meetings funded by the Robert Wood Johnson Foundation (RWJ), NCQA began exploring with purchaser community leaders their interest in, and evaluation of, NCQA's potential usefulness as an independent external review organization. The group of purchaser representatives—benefits managers from Fortune 500 companies who were at the leading edge of external quality assessment—gave a resounding mandate for NCQA to go forward.

In late 1989, RWJ awarded NCQA a grant to develop as an independent entity. As evidence of industry support, the grant required that matching monies be raised from the managed care industry. Industry contributions demonstrated support, and NCQA was officially launched in March 1990.

Reviewers

NCQA review teams typically consist of an administrative reviewer and two or more physician reviewers. Administrative reviewers are nonphysician clinicians or quality assurance experts with extensive experience in quality assurance in managed care. Physician reviewers are medical directors or directors of quality management from MCOs.

Areas of Review

Quality Assurance

The first and most intensive area of NCQA review is an organization's own internal quality control systems. To meet NCQA standards, an organization must have a well-organized, comprehensive quality assurance program accountable to its highest organizational levels. The program's scope and content must be broad, covering the full spectrum of services included in its delivery system; the program should focus on important aspects of care and service and address clinical issues with major impact on the health status of the enrolled population.

Quality assurance must be coordinated with other management activity. Contracts with physicians and other health care providers must be explicit about the need to cooperate with the plan's own quality activities or about the contractor's delegation of quality assurance responsibilities. An organization must actively monitor any delegated quality assurance activity.

Finally, and most important, an organization must be able to demonstrate program effectiveness in improving its quality of care and service.

NCQA establishes compliance with its standards by thorough review of an organization's quality assurance program description and related policies and procedures, quality assurance studies, projects and monitoring activities, quality assurance and governing body minutes, interviews with key staff, tracking of issues uncovered by the quality assurance system to ensure resolution, and documented evidence of quality improvement.

Credentialing

The review process includes a thorough review of an organization's credentialing system. NCQA requires that the MCO conduct primary verification of such credentialing information as licensure, malpractice history, good standing of hospital privileges, DEA certification, and so forth. Additionally, for IPA model organizations, NCQA requires the MCO to conduct a structured review of primary care physician offices before contracting.

An important part of ensuring delivery system integrity is periodic recertification or reappointment of providers. Aside from reverifying the paper credentials, NCQA requires a periodic performance appraisal to include information from quality assurance activity, risk and utilization management, member complaints, and member satisfaction surveys. Organizations delegating credentialing responsibility retain responsibility for ensuring that it meets NCQA standards.

Compliance with credentialing standards is ascertained by reviewing an organization's credentialing policies and procedures, sampling individual provider files, conducting interviews with relevant staff, and tracking issues identified through the complaint system or quality assurance findings.

Utilization Management

Utilization management, a keystone of effective managed care, is an important determinant of both the cost and the quality of an MCO. NCQA standards for utilization management seek to establish that an organization has an organized system for utilization management, that review decisions are made by qualified medical professionals, that the organization has written utilization management protocols based on reasonable scientific evidence, that there are adequate appeals mechanisms for physicians and for patients, that decisions and appeals are processed in a timely manner, and that the utilization management system monitors for underutilization as well as overutilization. An organization must actively monitor any delegation of utilization management.

The process includes review of utilization reports, committee minutes, individual chron files, as well as interviews with relevant staff.

Member Rights and Responsibilities

To meet NCQA standards, an organization must have written policies that recognize such member rights as voicing grievances and receiving information regarding the organization, its services, and its practitioners. These written policies must also address such member responsibilities as providing information needed by the professional staff and following practitioners' instructions and guidelines.

NCQA requires an organization to have a system for resolving members' complaints and grievances, to aggregate and analyze complaint and grievance data, and to use the information for quality improvement.

NCQA standards require communication to members of certain types of information about how the health plan works, including the organization's policies on referrals for specialty care; provisions for after-hours and emergency coverage; covered benefits; charges to patients; procedures for notifying patients about terminations or changes in benefits, services, or delivery sites; procedures for appealing decisions regarding coverage, benefits, or relationship to the organization; disenrollment procedures; and complaint and grievance procedures. The standards require that member information be written in readable prose and be available in the languages of the major population groups served.

Organizations must have mechanisms ensuring confidentiality of specified patient information and records.

Finally, an organization must have mechanisms to protect and enhance member satisfaction with its services, including member satisfaction surveys, studies of reasons for disenrollments, and evidence that the organization uses this information to improve its quality of service.

Preventive Health Services

HMOs have traditionally prided themselves on their commitment to preventive health services. Moreover, because they serve defined populations, they are in a better position than the fee-for-service system to ensure that preventive services are used appropriately. NCQA preventive services standards require adoption of specifications (clinical policies or practice guidelines) for the use of preventive services, communication of this information to providers and patients, and yearly measurement of performance in the delivery of two such services chosen from a list developed by NCQA. These results are audited by NCQA.

In its next development stage, NCQA will develop a common measurement system for this important dimension of clinical performance. Work is already underway to specify common definitions and to develop data collection instruments to assist plans in calculating mammography and immunization rates.

Medical Records

NCQA supplements management systems review with a sample of ambulatory records to assess both the quality of documentation and the quality of care. NCQA physician reviewers, guided by a 21-item medical record review form, assess the adequacy of diagnosis, the appropriateness and continuity of care, and the use of preventive services.

Review Process

At the time of application, the applicant organization fills out a preliminary information form, which contains detailed descriptions of the plan's delivery system, including information about delegated quality assurance, utilization management, and credentialing activity. NCQA uses this information to determine the size and composition of the review team and the duration of the on-site review, both of which are used to determine the price of the review. Before the review, the applicant organization fills out a detailed preassessment information form, which contains information regarding the plan's compliance with each of the accreditation areas.

The on-site review typically lasts 3 days and includes extensive review of documentation such as minutes of quality assurance committee and board meetings; policies and procedures relating to various areas of the standards; provider contracts; quality assurance studies, reports, and case files; utilization management review criteria, reports, and files; credentialing files; complaint and grievance files; and member satisfaction and disenrollment surveys. Interviews are conducted with the chief executive officer; the medical director; the directors of quality assurance, utilization management, provider relations, and member services; members of the quality assurance committee; a member of the board of directors; and participating physicians. The review team reviews for evidence of compliance with each of the NCQA standards and presents a summary of its findings of fact at the end of the site visit. A member of the review team prepares a report that is submitted to NCQA.

The report is reviewed by the NCQA staff and the NCQA review oversight committee. The review oversight committee makes compliance determinations for each of the NCQA standards as well as for the overall accreditation decision.

Accreditation Decisions

Plans that substantially meet the NCQA standards receive full accreditation, which lasts for a period of 3 years. If there are areas of deficiency that are remediable within 90 days, the plan is granted accreditation with recommendations. Upon submission of evidence that the areas of deficiency have been corrected, the plan is granted full accreditation. Depending upon the nature of the deficiency, a site visit may be warranted.

Plans that have more significant areas of noncompliance but are still in substantial compliance with most of the standards (and where the areas of deficiency are remediable within 1 year) are awarded provisional accreditation. Plans receive provisional accreditation for a period of 15 months and are rereviewed for the areas of deficiency 3 months before the expiration of the provisional accreditation. Plans that correct the areas of deficiency receive full accreditation for a period of 21 months. Accreditation lapses for provisionally accredited plans that fail to correct the areas of deficiency. Plans that fail to meet the NCQA standards are denied accreditation.

Copies of the NCQA accreditation standards and application materials can be obtained by contacting NCQA, 1350 New York Avenue, Suite 700, Washington, DC 20005 (202/628-5788; FAX, 202/628-0344).

CONCLUSION

This chapter presented a summary of the three organizations that currently accredit MCOs. Like the organizations that they review, the three organizations vary in their goals and in their approach to external review.

Although they vary considerably in their approach, all hold the potential for rationalizing and consolidating current external review processes (state, federal, and individual purchasers) that are sometimes duplicative, contradictory in their requirements, and in some cases harmful in their impact on managed care programs. Ultimately, however, their effectiveness must be judged in terms of their ability to improve the quality of care and service that MCOs provide to their customers.

REFERENCES

1. Utilization Review Accreditation Commission (URAC). *Standards.* Washington, DC: URAC; 1991.
2. Utilization Review Accreditation Commission (URAC). *Accreditation Process.* Washington, DC: URAC; 1991.
3. Bell NN. The AAPI accreditation program. *Med Interface.* April 1991:22–27.

Chapter 22

Common Operational Problems in Managed Health Care Plans

Peter R. Kongstvedt

As in most enterprises, managed health care plans are prone to problems that are common to their own industry. The most common problem for start-up plans is inability to gain market share. That problem, languishing in the market, is not addressed in this chapter. The reader is referred to Chapter 24 for an in-depth discussion of marketing issues, including common pitfalls and problems. The focus of this chapter is operational problems rather than the problems of gaining membership.

Whether a problem occurs and how serious that problem is will depend on a variety of factors. None of the problems and common mistakes that are discussed in this chapter occurs in a vacuum. Certain problems will be exacerbated by the presence of other, concurrent problems. In some types of plans the relative dangers will be far less than in others. The purpose of this chapter is to discuss these common problems and mistakes so as to help make a manager aware of them. Early detection could prevent severe damage to the plan.

Not all these problems would be found in the same plan at the same time, and rarely will only one problem exist at a time. In general, troubled health plans will have problems in logical combinations. For example, if significant problems are occurring with expenses that are incurred but not reported (IBNRs), it is likely that the plan will also be having problems with claims processing and inaccurate utilization reports as well.

In some cases, the problems discussed in this chapter will be serious only in plans that assume full financial risk [ie, health maintenance organizations (HMOs), full risk-bearing preferred provider organizations (PPOs), and individual practice organizations (IPAs) that take full responsibility for enrolling members, collecting premiums, paying providers, and so forth]. Other problems, especially those that relate to medical management, may be found in organizations that accept limited risk as well as organizations accepting full risk (eg, medical groups, contracting IPAs within an HMO, or any other organization responsible for delivering medical services).

Regardless of how a particular organization is configured, it is worthwhile understanding the potential common problems that any health plan can encounter. This may allow you to see if a plan is running into trouble, even if you yourself do not have responsibility for that particular area of management. It will also allow you to analyze better the competition and develop strategies for success. What follows are brief descriptions of some common problems.

UNDERCAPITALIZATION OF NEW PLANS

A classic problem in business, undercapitalization is just as troublesome for health plans as for any other business. Losses can mount more quickly than anticipated, and if the pricing strategy was too low, losses can continue for quite some time. With preoperational expenses ranging from $500,000 to well over $1,000,000 and budgeted losses in the first year often doubling the preoperational expenses, getting to break-even status can be costly. The best way to handle this is to prevent it by using an experienced actuary or financial consultant to estimate losses before break even and to do so under a number of different scenarios.

Once a plan is operational, if it is undercapitalized and not amenable to fast repairs (eg, sharp reductions in administrative cost or medical cost, or rapid increases in premium revenue), there are a limited number of responses available to management. One response is to try to get the providers to assume the expenses, perhaps through mandatory fee reductions or promissory notes. The other routes involve obtaining money from outside sources, either as debt or by selling equity. In any of these cases, you are obviously dealing from a position of weakness and will usually pay the price of failing to obtain adequate capital before commencement of operations. Failing even that, the plan may wind up in a forced merger with a healthy plan, in receivership to creditors, seized by the state insurance department, or having to declare bankruptcy or even fold. All these last options may be considered career-limiting moves on the part of management.

PREDATORY PRICING OR LOW-BALLING

This refers to premium rates that are intentionally well below the actual cost of delivering care. This is usually found in start-up plans, although a mature plan may low-ball to preserve or rapidly gain market share in response to a competitor's rates. Price undercutting is a venerable tradition in a capitalistic system and has great utility in enhancing one's competitive stance. Buying market share is not necessarily a mistake under all circumstances, but it is a dangerous strategy that must be undertaken with great care.

There is a crusty old cliché in business that goes: "You can't buy widgets for a dollar, sell them for eighty cents, and make it up on volume." This is even more true in managed health care than in manufacturing. The manufacturer may hope to sell a service contract with the widget and recoup the loss or raise the price of widgets after a few months. In a health plan, all you sell is service; there are no benefits riders that will make up for a grossly underbid base premium. Further, once you sign up a group for a set premium rate, you usually have to live with that rate for at least a year. Even in accounts in which the plan is not bearing financial risk for medical expenses (such as an administrative services only account), the plan may suffer a financial penalty if it has guaranteed medical expense trends, and it will doubtless suffer a tarnished reputation for effective management, veracity, or both.

The purpose of low-balling is to drive enrollment up and buy market share. If you low-ball a rate so that you lose $5 per member per month (PMPM), and if you succeed in increasing enrollment by 5,000 members, you have succeeded in increasing your losses to $5,000 \times \$5$ PMPM, or $25,000 per month, or $300,000 per year. You cannot make it up on volume.

Occasionally, managers may low-ball primarily to cover high overhead costs (in other words, to get some cash flowing in) rather than as an attempt to get market dominance. In those cases, the losses from the fixed overhead are in fact attenuated by the premium revenue brought in, at least initially, even though the medical loss ratio is unacceptably high. Low-balling may provide a short-term fix for highly leveraged plans such as closed panels, but the long-term result is the same: As enrollment increases, the overhead required to provide service increases as well, leading to a continuing loss situation that may become more severe than anticipated.

In addition to sustained losses, low-balling is a market strategy that appeals to the most price-sensitive consumers. That can be a set-up for a raid by a competitor who low-balls the rates even further. Unless another strategy is available, the plan could then end up in a price war and never recoup its losses.

None of this is to say that a plan may not have to hold rates down or even lower them for competitive reasons. This is to say that low-balling should never be the only competitive strategy. It should really be used only as an adjunct to a longer-range strategy, and even then only with caution. Far too many plans have found that their pockets were not as deep as they thought or that they underestimated how deep those pockets would need to be.

A common and critical mistake by plan managers facing price competition is to lower the rates to unrealistic levels and simply budget expenses lower, usually medical expenses. Unless there is a clear and believable strategy for lowering those expenses, the savings will not materialize. It is not enough to order the medical director to harass the physicians and get costs down; there needs to be a more cogent plan for reducing expenses. Sadly, a manager under pressure frequently indulges in a combination of magical thinking and rule by decree. In other words, by decreeing that expenses must be reduced, the other managers will magically figure out how to do that despite not having succeeded the previous year. The lesson here is that, if the rates are intentionally lowered, managers had better figure out specifically how they are going to reduce expenses in each category. If they cannot come up with a clear plan for each category, they should budget the loss.

Assuming that the decision has been made to try to recover some of the losses, the main question is whether to raise the rates in one breathtaking rate hike or to phase it in over a number of years. That decision must be made by analyzing the plan's financial resources, the market conditions, the clients' willingness to put up with a rate hike, the danger of losing significant enrollment in that group (which may or may not be a bad thing, depending on the degree of losses you are sustaining in the group; in turn this may lead to adverse selection, which is discussed below), and the plan's ability to control expenses. Of course, if the situation is bad enough, the state insurance commissioner may wind up making the decision unilaterally.

OVERPRICING

The antipode of low-balling, overpricing simply refers to rates that are unacceptably high in the marketplace. This is usually found in mature plans, but occasionally it occurs in new plans that anticipate high costs or that have incurred unusually high preoperational expenses. There are five primary reasons for overpricing:

1. a panic response to previous low-balling
2. excessive overhead
3. failure to control utilization properly
4. adverse selection
5. avarice

The fifth reason, avarice, is obvious and will not be addressed in this chapter except to note that the competitive marketplace may help hold down excessive prices that are based on greed.

A panic response to previous low-balling is not unusual. As losses mount, plan management feels unable to weather the losses and tries to make up the revenue quickly. This is particularly true when a plan is being pressured by investors or regulators or when the plan's financial reserves are projected to be dangerously low. If the low-balling strategy has driven out competition (not a likely event), exorbitant rate hikes may occur simply as a natural course.

Excessive overhead may also lead to overpricing. If plan management is unable to improve efficiency, the price must be paid. Excessive overhead may occur in any plan. It occurs in new starts when required administrative support has been estimated on the basis of enrollment projections that fail to materialize. In mature plans, excessive overhead usually is traced to a combination of internal politics, or turf battles, and management's unwillingness or inability to explore new methods of managing the plan.

Excessive medical expense is the most common reason for overpricing. It is far easier to raise prices than to deal with the causes of overutilization. The usual rationalization goes something like this: "The reason we have the highest rates is that we have the best physicians, and so we have the sickest patients. It's all adverse selection!" In these cases, the plan has often marketed benefits comparable to or better than those of competing HMOs and has assumed utilization rates similar to those of tightly run HMOs (after all, if you call yourself an HMO, you should perform like one, right?) but has imposed fewer controls on physicians and hospitals. Rather than impose restrictions and tighten management, administrators indulge in the common fantasy that they are doing the best they can and it is all the fault of external events.

Bear in mind, however, that excessively high rates can lead to adverse selection. This is especially true when an account allows more than one health plan to market to employees, in contrast to a total replacement account, where no competing health plans are allowed to market. In a multiple-choice environment, if the plan becomes too expensive for most people only those facing high medical costs will choose to enroll because the plan's premiums are still less than the coinsurance and deductibles they would face with the competition. A related phenomenon has been a classic problem with indemnity insurance when multiple HMOs are offered: Despite high premium rates in the indemnity plan, individuals with high medical costs and an affinity with a provider not in the managed care plan will enroll at almost any premium cost.

UNREALISTIC PROJECTIONS

Any and all categories of revenue and expense are subject to unrealistic projections and expectations, but two stand out: overprojecting enrollment and underprojecting medical expenses.

In new plans, it is common to overestimate enrollment. The reasons are probably a combination of high optimism, inexperience of the marketing director, failure to correctly forecast and reforecast enrollment on an account-specific basis, and an unrealistic start date. Unless the marketing director is a seasoned veteran, the forecast may include accounts considered sold that were only being polite, a factor may be added for new business even when the source and probability of that business are in doubt, or a standard penetration factor may be used that fails to address competitiveness in the account. If the plan does not go operational when antici-

pated, or if the delivery system is weaker than the anticipated delivery system used to forecast enrollment, significant negative variations in projected growth can occur.

Certainly unanticipated events can blindside even the most experienced marketing director. Competing or invading plans may spark a price war, or a regulator may delay certification for unexpected reasons. For all these reasons, the best marketing projections are conservative ones. Some executive directors feel that enrollment projections should always be high to motivate the director of marketing through his or her bonus. Unfortunately, enrollment projections drive financial projections, so care must be taken, especially in new plans.

Underprojecting medical expenses, or overestimating ability to control utilization, is equally common in new plans. As has been mentioned earlier, naive managers sometimes assume that if they call themselves an HMO or a PPO and put some rudimentary controls in place they will have the same results as an experienced and successful plan. If the medical director is inexperienced, or if the physicians in the panel are not used to tight medical management, it is unlikely that good utilization results will occur, unless by good luck.

Luck can also be bad. During the early stages of a plan's life, enrollment will be small enough so that a few bad cases can have an excessive impact on expenses. A common and critical mistake for new plan managers to make is to project utilization as though there will be few serious cases. When the cases occur, management keeps factoring out the cost of caring for those sick patients and measures utilization on the basis of the remaining members. Clearly, if one factors out sick patients, utilization will always look reasonable. This mistake can be partially offset by purchasing adequate reinsurance, but that comes at a cost.

UNCONTROLLED GROWTH

Rapid growth is usually greeted with applause. In fact, many readers of this book may be saying to themselves, "I wish we had such problems," but rapid growth is not always a good thing (dandelions come to mind). Certainly growth is a necessary ingredient to long-term success, but if growth is too rapid it can lead to problems that are long in resolving.

Closely related to the problem of overextended management, the problem of uncontrolled growth is a bit more generalized: rapid growth not only may quickly outstrip the ability of the plan's managers to keep up but may outstrip the system's capabilities as well. Dysfunctional patterns can set in, such as referral patterns or utilization behaviors that are more difficult to change after the fact than if they were addressed early on. Because the systems and management capabilities in the plan may now be inadequate, the developing problems will not be picked up until they are serious.

Rapid growth also means rapid expansions in the delivery system. The same attention paid to recruiting and credentialing in the development stages may not be present, and there may be little or no time spent properly orienting new providers to the plan's policies and procedures. That ultimately leads not only to inefficient practice patterns but to frustration on the part of those new providers.

Conversely, rapid growth can lead to saturation of the delivery system before there is adequate recruiting to take up the volume. This becomes especially problematic when practices begin to close more quickly than directory printing can accommodate, and new groups are enrolled with inaccurate directories of providers (or directories are distributed with addendums falling out onto the floor). In many cases, the physician practices will decide to close before they even notify the plan, and new members are signed up for those practices only to be turned away when calling for an appointment.

Service erosion is common when growth has been too rapid. Identification cards are not produced on time (or are produced inaccurately), claims are not paid properly, telephone calls to the plan are not answered in a timely or quality manner, evidence of coverage statements are not sent out on time, inadequate information is given to new members, and so forth. Poor service leads to a vicious cycle of ever escalating problems resulting in a poor reputation that takes a long time to recover from.

Last, rapid growth may lead to inadequate reserves. If reserves were adequate for a small plan, utilization in a plan suddenly grown large may take those reserves down to a dangerously low level. A plan's ability to withstand the cyclic nature of the insurance business, or just a run of bad luck, is directly tied to the amount of reserves available.

One approach to the problem of rapid growth is to limit increases in enrollment through decreased offerings and marketing. This has been done by a few plans in the past and is a viable approach. The risk to this is that your competition may pick up the members, and you will never catch up. For that reason, most plan managers are reluctant to turn off the tap unless it is a critical situation.

It is preferable to have plans for dealing with rapid growth before your back is against the wall. Plan for expansion of the plan's information and computer systems. Groom potential candidates for managerial promotion; you may even consider delegating certain responsibilities before such delegation is required. Some amount of physician recruiting activity should always be occurring, especially in areas without a great deal of capacity, although the rate of actual contracting needs to be coordinated with projected enrollment increases. Careful attention to staffing levels and training lead times in service areas such as claims and member services will help a great deal, although if projected enrollment does not occur the overhead to the plan can become crushing.

OVEREXTENDED MANAGEMENT

What may have been appropriate or even generous staffing at the start-up stage can become understaffing after significant growth, especially if that growth has been rapid. The problem is more complex than the number of management bodies available; it is really one of span of control and experience of managers.

It is not uncommon in any industry for management requirements to change over time. Frequently, the methods used by the pioneers become dysfunctional as plans reach significant size. Tight control concentrated in a few managers, overreliance on central decision making, heavy hands-on involvement by senior managers, and so forth all can lead to paralysis and calcification as a plan becomes large and complex. The few managers with the control are unable to keep up with all the necessary details and demands of running operations, and failure to delegate properly prevents the plan from recruiting and retaining talented second level managers.

As a plan grows, its ability to change and adapt to the competitive environment becomes diminished. All the details necessary for proper operations become overwhelming. If senior managers are personally responsible for all these details, they may be unable to keep up, and things will get missed. Change becomes even less likely when overloaded managers cannot handle the prospect of having to learn yet another set of management skills while still having to use the old ones. This becomes demoralizing to subordinates and providers when plan management is seen as unresponsive, inattentive, or both.

A full discussion of appropriate delegation of authority and responsibility is beyond the scope of this chapter. Here it is sufficient to point out the dangers inherent in failing to create proper tiers of management as a plan grows. This is not to imply that senior managers should insulate themselves from the operations of the plan, overdelegate, or drive up administrative costs for no good reason. Rather, this is to emphasize that health plans are complex organizations, and nobody can do it all.

IMPROPER INCURRED BUT NOT REPORTED CALCULATIONS AND ACCRUAL METHODS

As discussed in Chapter 25, the calculation and booking of liabilities in managed care plans is different from that found in most other industries. There have been quite a few health plans where accruals were based on the bills that came in the mail that month or on historical data only. A health plan that is standing risk for medical services must estimate accurately the cost of those services and accrue for them. If the costs are simply booked as they come in, disaster is certain.

The usual culprit here is failure to accrue properly for expenses that are IBNR. With data from lag studies and the plan's information system (ie, the authorization and encounter data systems) as well as prior experience, sufficient accruals must be made each month for all expenses, regardless of whether the bills came in or not. Calculation of proper accruals and IBNRs becomes especially difficult in plans that are experiencing rapid growth. If the plan fails to perform the lag studies, the problem can be compounded. For all the reasons discussed earlier, a rapidly growing plan will have a diminished capacity to capture data accurately and will have lessened efficacy of utilization controls. Rapid growth should always lead management to consider boosting IBNRs.

In plans that have failed to accrue properly for expenses, actual expenses may exceed accruals as early as the first 6 months. The malignant feature of this problem is that it can go inexorably on for another 6 months or even more, especially if the plan is experiencing a claims processing problem, as most plans undergoing rapid growth do. Each month's accruals have to be adjusted for expenses related to past months, and financial performance suffers not only for performance to date but for past periods as well. The plan cannot stop the financial hemorrhage quickly because the expenses were already incurred and will keep rolling in. Monthly performance gets muddied up with adjustments for prior performance, and managers find themselves chasing their tails. This problem becomes intensified if the plan is generating inadequate premium revenue either through intentional low-balling or through faulty rate calculations.

This problem has accounted for a disproportionate number of health plan failures. It does not occur as an isolated problem and is usually accompanied by serious claims processing problems and inadequate controls on utilization. Failure to accrue properly is the equivalent of failure to diagnose cancer; like many forms of cancer, it is preventable or curable with vigilance and early detection.

FAILURE TO RECONCILE ACCOUNTS RECEIVABLE AND MEMBERSHIP

Typical managed care plans have considerable changes occurring in membership each month. When the plan is standing risk for medical expenses, capitates providers, capitates administration fees, books some accruals based on PMPM historical cost, and so forth, it is vital to have as accurate a reconciliation of membership as possible. Most importantly, accounts receivable are directly tied to membership and billing.

It is common for plans to have difficulty with this activity. In some accounts (eg, the federal employee health benefit program), the account is chronically late in providing accurate enrollment information. In other cases, the plan receives information from an account but never properly reconciles it every month because it is such a labor-intensive process. In any case, if the plan pays medical expenses for members who are no longer eligible or fails to collect premiums for members who are newly enrolled, losses are sure to follow. Even more devastating is the need to make a huge downward adjustment on the balance sheet to write off an uncollectible receivable.

FAILURE TO USE UNDERWRITING CRITERIA

As this book is being written, the topic of small group market reform is being actively debated both at the federal level and in many states. Such reforms would sharply limit the degree to which a plan may medically underwrite accounts. That is, plans would not be able to turn down any valid group for coverage because of medical conditions, although the plan may be able to use such information in premium rate development. Although none of these reforms has been enacted as this book is being written, it is expected that they will soon occur.

Even in the face of market reform, underwriting has a place, and in the desire to grow, proper underwriting guidelines may be neglected. This is most likely to occur in a new plan trying to grow, but it can occur in any plan where marketing representatives and managers are inadequately supervised at the same time that they are being pressured to produce growth. Proper information must be obtained and acted upon both to determine what product to offer (or even whether the group qualifies for coverage under any circumstances) and to determine proper premium rates.

A related issue is the actual sales effort when the plan is offered in an account with multiple other carriers or plans competing to enroll employees. Marketing managed care in this setting is essentially retail selling. Unlike underwriting when the plan is the sole carrier, one cannot look at the entire group and accurately assess the actuarial risk because it is possible to enroll only those members who have high medical needs. In other words, the possibility of adverse selection occurring within a group is very real. This is a particular problem in a highly competitive market, where the pressure on the marketing department is high. If the sales representative is on a pure commission basis, the pressure may be overwhelming. If emphasis is placed on the ease of access to high-cost specialists and hospitals, and if any restrictions to that access are downplayed, it can lead to adverse selection within an otherwise normal risk group.

FAILURE OF MANAGEMENT TO UNDERSTAND REPORTS

Difficult as it may be to believe, managers may not always understand how reports are developed and written. A report may be labeled as one thing, but the data that are put into the report are really something else. For example, there may be a report that gives the rate of disenrollment from the plan. Depending on how the management information system department inputs the data or how the computer was programmed, the disenrollment rate may include any member who changes status (eg, goes from single to family) or coverage (eg, changes jobs but continues with the plan under the new group). If that is the case, the disenrollment rate will be spuriously high. Failure to understand the meaning behind the disenrollment rate can lead to inaccurate forecasting and budgeting. Failure to understand the data elements in medical management and utilization reports is obviously far more serious.

To prevent this, senior management should be involved in developing the formats of reports and deciding what data will be used. The decisions about how to collect data and how to input them should not be made solely by the management information system department. In the event that the plan has experienced changeover in managers, it is important for the new manager not to assume anything and to ask explicitly what data go into each report. This last may seem embarrassing to a manager, but that type of compulsive behavior could prevent a serious mistake in the future.

FAILURE TO TRACK CORRECTLY MEDICAL COSTS AND UTILIZATION

This is a special subset of the problem just discussed, that of failure of management to understand reports. The problem of tracking medical expenses and utilization is so important that it merits brief discussion by itself.

As growing plans develop problems with operations (the authorization system, claims, or data gathering in general), medical expense and utilization reports frequently suffer. If the plan is accruing for IBNRs based on historical data because current data are inaccurate, expenses may be allocated to categories primarily because that is where the expenses have been found before. For example, if a plan historically has had high costs in orthopedics, and if the data system is unable reliably to provide current utilization data, finance may accrue expenses to orthopedics even if the medical director has been able to reduce costs in that area. It may take 6 months for the data to come through the system that show a reduction in orthopedics expenses, but by that time the medical director has resigned in frustration.

Another example would be a plan that has an authorization system for referrals but that system allows for subauthorizations, automatic authorization of return visits, and self-referral. Because of the loose nature of the system, the finance department cannot rely on it when calculating accruals. If there is a concomitant problem with claims processing, then there will be no timely and accurate data about utilization. In that case, finance will calculate accruals by using lag studies and best guess numbers and will assign the expenses where they fell as the claims were processed. In this way, high expenses may really be reflective of a combination of two things: what was happening in utilization some time back, and what type of claims were processed that month.

If the calculation of these numbers is sufficiently removed from senior management, and if the medical director does not know how the numbers are derived, tremendous efforts may be expended in dealing with problems that are neither timely nor high priority. As mentioned in Chapter 15 (on quality management), a plan's ability to implement continuous quality improvement in its business operations will be hampered if efforts are wasted trying to solve problems that are not indicative of the true problems facing management.

Closely related is the problem of not properly tracking utilization. For example, if a plan has an authorization system for referrals that tracks initial referrals from the primary care physician but fails to track adequately subauthorizations, self-referrals, and repeat visits, the referral rate may be grossly inaccurate. Another example would be a plan that is able to report high rates of utilization but is unable to provide the detail about who is responsible.

In a perverse twist, in those cases where data are presented in an inaccurate or inadequate form but the medical director understands why that is so, a false sense of complacency can develop. For example, if a hospital utilization report consistently and inaccurately reports high utilization for a certain physician (perhaps because that physician represents a three-physician group), the medical director may continually make adjustments when reviewing the report and fail to recognize a genuine increase in utilization.

FAILURE TO EDUCATE AND RE-EDUCATE PROVIDERS

An all too common sin of omission is the failure properly to educate providers. As discussed in Chapters 4 and 5, proper orientation of new providers and office staff is an important success factor. All too often the providers are simply given a procedure manual and a metaphorical kiss on the cheek. Even in those situations where proper orientation has taken place, it is unlikely that the information will stick unless there are already a large number of patients coming in through the plan. This is even more of a problem when there are a number of competing health plans, each with its own unique way of doing things.

Just as important as the initial orientation is a program of continuing education in the procedures and policies of the plan. Regular maintenance of the knowledge base of the providers and their office staff will help prevent problems caused solely by lack of communication.

Examples of this problem abound in most open panels. Physicians may fail to use properly the authorization system, may provide or promise benefits that the plan does not cover, may allow open-ended authorizations to specialists, and so forth. Although none of these occurrences is dangerous in itself, they all can be additive. In a large plan, failure to communicate properly with providers can lead rapidly to a loss of control. Far more energy is spent trying to repair damage than would have been spent in maintenance.

FAILURE TO DEAL WITH DIFFICULT OR NONCOMPLIANT PROVIDERS

Perhaps the most difficult of all the tasks of a medical director is dealing with difficult and noncompliant physicians. The same task applies to nonphysician providers, but that is generally easier for most medical directors. Because dealing with difficult physicians is so onerous to physician managers, they tend to avoid it or at least procrastinate. Assuming that the plan is reasonably well run and not subject to a justified physician mutiny, difficult physicians, like difficult patients, make up only a tiny minority of the total panel but consume an inordinate amount of managerial energy. Failure to deal with such physicians has both direct and indirect ramifications.

The direct result of failing to deal with an uncooperative physician is the expense associated with that physician's utilization of resources. This problem is obvious, although easy to rationalize away ("Well, maybe they have sicker patients"). If the physician's utilization behavior really is a problem, it may be worthwhile to calculate in whole dollars the cost of that overutilization.

The indirect results are less obvious. The most important is the effect on members. If the physician has a truly bad attitude, that will be transmitted to members. For example, the physician may tell members that they need services but the plan will not allow it. A little bit of this "blame the bogeyman" behavior can be tolerated and understood, but if it becomes chronic, the plan can find itself fighting off unwarranted attacks by members and employee benefits managers. Other indirect effects include promoting a poor attitude among the other physicians and lowering the morale of the plan staff who have to deal with that particular physician.

The most frequent objection to dealing with difficult physicians is that the plan needs them because they are so prestigious or popular. In many cases, that physician also has a large number of members, and there are fears that if the physician leaves or is kicked out the plan will lose membership. It is up to plan management to determine whether the plan is worse off with or without the physician. Do not let numbers of members alone make that determination (remember, if you are losing on each member, you cannot make it up on volume). Regarding the issue of prestige, it is far worse to have that physician bad mouthing your plan directly to the members than it is to have him or her deriding you in the hospital lounge (where he or she is probably doing it anyway). You may also find that the members stick with the plan and agree to change physicians.

If education and personal appeals fail to effect the needed change, you must take action. Failure to take action is the mark of weak and ineffectual management.

CONCLUSION

This chapter presents some of the common problems that can occur in managed care plans. There are few plans in existence today that have not experienced at least a few of these difficulties at some point. The list is not exhaustive, and there are certainly many other difficulties that a plan can experience. The important point is to recognize that managed care plans do indeed develop predictable problems and to be ever vigilant for their emergence.

Chapter 23

The Employer's View of Managed Health Care: From a Passive to an Aggressive Role

Allison A. Alkire and Sidney W. Stolz

Over the years, the term *managed care* has meant different things to different people. For some, it conjures up an image of medical clinics, restricted access to care, and a loss of autonomy. For others, managed care is a continuum ranging from the fairly low-level interference imposed by second surgical opinion plans to the tightly controlled environment under staff model health maintenance organizations (HMOs). Still others see it as an opportunity for employers truly to manage their health benefit expenditures and for employees to take more responsibility for their health care.

But despite differing views and experience, there is little doubt that managed care is the direction of the future. Many employers have already embraced it in a variety of forms. And despite fairly dramatic development in a relatively short time, managed care continues to grow, change, and mature, albeit in somewhat awkward fashion. This chapter focuses on how the employer's role in managed care has evolved, moving from a passive stance to more aggressive, hands-on management of company-sponsored health care plans.

HEALTH MAINTENANCE ORGANIZATIONS: THE EARLY YEARS

In the early 1970s, managed care was essentially limited to, and defined by, HMOs. A dramatic boost provided by Congress is largely responsible. HMOs first appeared in the 1940s but failed to spread beyond California and parts of the Midwest until lawmakers passed the Health Maintenance Organization Act of 1973 (PL 93-222). The Act promised financial support to HMOs that offered a minimum level of benefits to enrollees, charged premiums based on communitywide health care costs, and met certain other criteria for federal qualification.

Most important, the new law gave federally qualified HMOs the right to mandate employers, a critical factor in ensuring enrollment growth. Mandating meant that employers who had heretofore failed to recognize the potential of HMOs in providing comprehensive medical care at a reasonable cost (including preventive, acute, and chronic care) could now be forced to offer

Sidney W. Stolz is a Principal at Towers Perrin, an international actuarial, benefits, and compensation consulting firm. Based in the firm's Washington, DC, office, he specializes in health care and managed care issues and works with employers nationwide. Allison A. Alkire is a researcher specializing in health care and managed care in Towers Perrin's Valhalla, NY, office.

them alongside traditional fee-for-service medical plans. A full discussion of federal qualification is found in Chapter 35.

Federal financial support, coupled with employer mandates, clearly enabled some HMOs to develop faster than they might have otherwise. But expanded enrollments were not accompanied by a philosophic change among employers; in other words, the growth of HMOs did not necessarily mean that employers had embraced the concept of managed care. In fact, at the same time employers were adding HMOs to their health care programs, many began to pursue other means of cost control.

MANAGED INDEMNITY PLANS

The HMO Act was widely acknowledged as a government effort to help bring health care costs under control, and its passage coincided with the beginning of an intensified cost control effort in the private sector. Health benefit costs rose steadily throughout the 1960s but began to skyrocket in the early 1970s. So employers entered an era of cost containment in which, it would seem, HMOs could have played a valuable role. Nonetheless, early private sector strategies aimed to control costs while working within the traditional fee-for-service environment.

Surgical Second Opinions

One of the first tactics to emerge was introduced in the early 1970s by Dr. Eugene McCarthy of Cornell University Medical Center in conjunction with the United Store Workers. Dr. McCarthy believed that a minority of physicians were responsible for performing an excessive number of surgical procedures. He suggested that benefit plans should require a second opinion before reimbursing certain surgical procedures to stem the increasing frequency of surgeries and thereby reduce or eliminate corresponding physician and hospital expenses.

This requirement remained fairly common in fee-for-service plans until the early 1980s, when program evaluations began to indicate that the cost of second opinions equaled or exceeded the savings they generated, particularly because second opinions confirmed the need for the vast majority of procedures. Focused reviews targeting high-cost procedures replaced the early second opinion programs and probably played a role in the emergence of a new player, the utilization review vendor.

Utilization Review

As medical science developed throughout the 1970s and 1980s, experts began to examine and question treatment patterns that had long been part of mainstream medicine. As a result, clinical indicators to guide the provision of medical, surgical, and, more recently, pharmacologic care began to emerge through consensus building in the industry.

Recognizing that fee-for-service medicine gave providers an incentive to overtreat, the founders of utilization review organizations began using these indicators to evaluate the appropriateness of treatment plans before any costs were incurred. Employers expected that the resulting preadmission certification, concurrent review, and case management programs would further reduce or eliminate unnecessary costs, and improve the quality of care, by ensuring that patients received only the appropriate treatment. In the process, both patients and providers would become better educated about health care.

Plan Design

Even while incorporating changes such as these in their health plans, employers continued to use the time-honored strategies of plan design and employee cost sharing to control company costs. Deductibles and out-of-pocket limits rose steadily, and employees became responsible for more and more of their health care premiums, particularly for dependent coverage (Figures 23-1 and 23-2).

EMPLOYERS CONFRONT THE DELIVERY SYSTEM

Despite employer efforts to control health care utilization and their own share of the costs, overall health care cost inflation continued un-

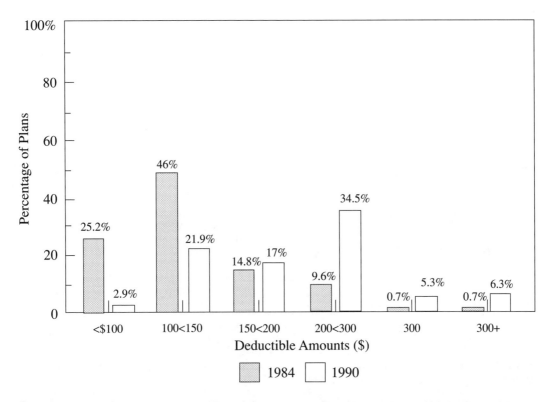

Figure 23-1 Individual deductibles under comprehensive indemnity plans, 1984 and 1990. Courtesy of Towers Perrin, New York, NY.

checked, with total expenditures nationwide exceeding 10% of the gross national product (GNP) in 1982 and 11% of the GNP by 1988 (Figure 23-3). Perhaps as a result of frustration or of a growing sense of the perverse incentives at work in the US health care delivery system, employer strategies in the middle to late 1980s began more directly to target the system itself.

Preferred Provider Organizations

HMOs enjoyed significant enrollment growth throughout the 1980s, but their market share did not stand unchallenged. Still reluctant to forgo the flexibility and provider choice features inherent in fee-for-service medicine, employers experimented with yet another alternative to HMOs: the preferred provider organization (PPO). PPOs grew tremendously beginning in 1983, as shown in Figure 23-4.

PPOs are essentially networks of physicians who contract to provide medical care at dis-

counted fees or who accept maximum fee schedules that are usually set below usual and customary rates. Although early projections anticipated that PPOs would achieve savings of 15% or more for employers, several key factors undermined their success.

Early PPOs did not include utilization controls in their physician contracts. As a result, participating physicians often provided additional services to make up for lower fees per service. In addition, employees were given financial incentives (eg, 100% reimbursement or waiver of the deductible) to use discounted providers, and the cost of these incentives often offset savings. Another factor was that, to provide the freedom of choice that employees desired, PPOs frequently contracted with a majority of the physicians in a community. This strategy made it difficult to guarantee physicians enough additional patient volume to make discounted fees worth their while. Without control over a substantial amount of the provider's patient vol-

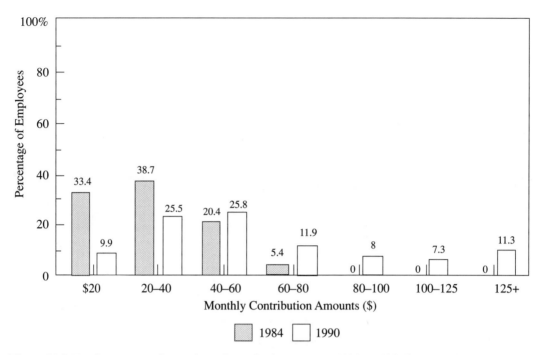

Figure 23-2 Family coverage: Comparison of contribution amounts, 1984 to 1990. Courtesy of Towers Perrin, New York, NY.

ume, PPOs had difficulty persuading physicians to comply with cost controls such as utilization review. And it soon became apparent that such controls would be essential if PPOs were to remain price competitive.

Health Maintenance Organization Consolidation

By the late 1980s, it was becoming clear that unmanaged PPOs did not have the firepower necessary to provide long-term, comprehensive cost control. At about the same time, employers began to realize that they could get more mileage out of their HMOs, and reduce administrative expenses, by consolidating their offerings.

As might have been expected, years of dealing passively with HMOs led to multiple offerings in multiple locations, a structure that achieved minimal enrollment and generated more costs than could be offset by savings. Compounding the problem, indemnity plan costs increased at disproportionately rapid rates

when younger, healthier employees chose HMO coverage and the high utilizers remained in the indemnity plan.

Finally, the common practice of calculating HMO premiums to shadow indemnity plan premiums (ie, setting rates just enough below the indemnity plan to attract enrollees) reduced the savings potential of HMOs and provided little incentive for competition among them.

In response to these problems, employers embarked on the path to HMO consolidation. In general, they intended to reduce the number of HMOs offered and to use the enrollment leverage they gained among the winners to accomplish more effective cost control overall. A number of management techniques surfaced as part of this new, aggressive strategy.

Most important, employers intensified their demands for utilization data from HMOs and argued that premiums should reflect actual results for the employee population rather than the higher community rates the HMOs charged. Non–federally qualified HMOs had the flexibil-

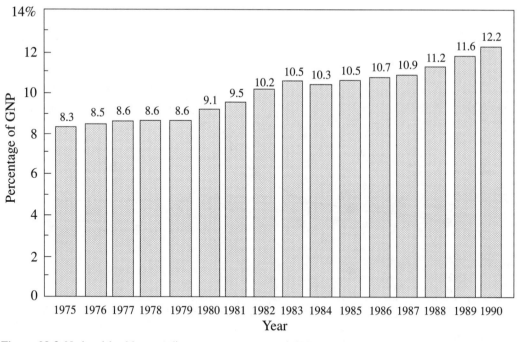

Figure 23-3 National health expenditure as a percentage of GNP, 1975 to 1990. *Source:* Data from HIAA Source Book of Health Insurance Data 1991.

ity to experience rate their plans, and many agreed to do so. Meanwhile, federally qualified HMOs achieved some degree of rating flexibility through the 1988 amendments to the HMO Act.

The amendments also phased out the employer mandate provision effective in 1995, so that HMOs would soon be competing head to head with indemnity plans and other managed care programs for employer business. And although most HMOs abandoned federal qualification well before 1988, the amendments clearly marked the end of a significant chapter in HMO development and encouraged them to become more aggressive in the marketplace.

POINT-OF-SERVICE MANAGED CARE EMERGES

From the employer perspective, the lingering sticky wicket of HMO coverage was lock-in enrollment. Employees resisted the inflexibility of annual enrollments and did not want to sacrifice

benefits completely when using nonparticipating physicians or hospitals. In 1987, one employer took a high-profile approach to tackling these issues.

Aiming to develop a long-term cost control strategy in the face of substantial retiree health care liabilities (soon to be reported on company financial statements as required by the Financial Accounting Standards Board), Allied-Signal negotiated with CIGNA, a national insurance company, to use the insurer's HMO network to deliver health care to all Allied employees wherever the HMOs were available. The new wrinkle was that employees could decide, at the point of service (POS), whether they wanted to be treated by an HMO physician or not. In either case, CIGNA would cover the expense, albeit at differing levels of benefits. This was one of the early, and certainly among the most visible, new generation managed care programs now known as POS plans.

To encourage use of CIGNA's provider networks, Allied required employees to select a pri-

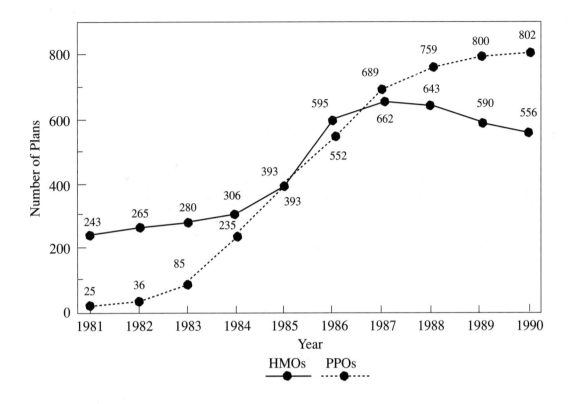

Figure 23-4 Prevalence of HMOs and PPOs, 1981 to 1990. *Sources:* Data from *Interstudy Edge, Decade in Review 1980–1990;* AMCRA Directory & Industry Report 1990.

mary care physician at the time of enrollment and imposed significant reimbursement differentials between in- and out-of-network services (ie, no deductible or coinsurance for in-network care and deductibles of 1% of pay for individuals and 4% of pay for families, along with 80% coinsurance, for out-of-network care).

Another significant component of the health care connection program was CIGNA's guarantee that Allied would experience a low rate of annual cost increase over the 3-year period of the contract. Despite the fact that the financial results of this pioneering program would prove to be less favorable for CIGNA than for Allied, it did not take long for other major carriers to develop and market similar products.

Point of Service and Employer Expectations

Once they began dealing more directly with managed care organizations, employers began to develop certain expectations for results. These expectations were refined even further when POS plans emerged. Generally, employers are now interested in choice (provider access), cost effectiveness (provider discounts and risk sharing), and quality in the delivery of health care.

POS plans employ several key components geared to meet these expectations. Most important, financial risk sharing among all parties—network manager, employer, providers, and employees—drives the system. In addition, a primary care physician serves as medical manager, controlling and monitoring all care delivered to the employee or family members, including hospital and specialty care. Finally, the network manager (a role initially filled by insurance carriers but now including other entities, such as HMOs) generally takes responsibility for quality of care, network development and maintenance, claims processing, client reporting, and other relevant services.

What Makes Point of Service Work

One critical characteristic of POS plans is their ability to combine access to care with effective cost control by using PPO-like elements of choice with HMO-like cost management features that satisfy both employers and employees. This combination does, in fact, seem to work. Ninety-one percent of employers with network-based managed care who participated in a Towers Perrin phone survey in early 1992 believe that managed care is meeting company objectives, and 73% said their employees are as satisfied or more satisfied with their benefits than before.[1]

Most survey participants have POS plans under which employees select a primary care physician when they enroll. Having the option to go out of network if they choose to, however, may make employees more amenable to trying the network. Nevertheless, plan design encourages employees to use network providers by applying deductibles, relatively higher coinsurance, and out-of-pocket limits to services received outside the network; only copayments and limited coinsurance are required in network. For example, Towers Perrin's database of POS plans (as of December 1991) showed that 42% of in-network plans required deductibles compared with 98% of out-of-network plans. Among in-network plans, 95% had copayments compared with only 11% of out-of-network plans. Coinsurance differences are illustrated in Figure 23-5.

Network managers also understand the need to ensure substantial patient steerage to encourage provider participation. Moreover, they recognize that steerage should increase over time, so that physicians will continue to negotiate their fees. Optimally, networks would like to account for 20% to 30% of a physician's patient base, enough to provide significant leverage but not enough to suffer if the physician should decide to drop out of the network.

Increasing Employer Involvement

By far the most interesting development associated with POS is the degree to which employer participation has increased. Employers did little actively to encourage the use of HMOs and PPOs, essentially insulating themselves from day-to-day health care delivery. By contrast, risk sharing and the fact that employees must choose to use the network if POS plans are to realize expected savings have encouraged employers to play an active role in network selection. For example, in-depth, on-site evaluations have become a principal part of the network selection process. These hands-on techniques help educate employers about the inner workings of the network organization, establish a rapport between the parties, and clarify the employer's objectives for network management.

In addition, employers are developing specific criteria and standards that serve as benchmarks for measuring network capabilities. Network management, provider network development and maintenance, medical management, quality assurance, member services, financial performance, and information systems are all closely examined by employers before a selection is made. Table 23-1 briefly notes key network characteristics that are subject to scrutiny along with the fundamental question to be answered about each.

Employer familiarity with and monitoring of network operations also play critical roles in keeping the network on its toes. Performance guarantees, for example, have emerged as a tool for ensuring that the networks meet mutually agreed-upon objectives. Here, network managers guarantee, against penalties and bonuses, the qualitative elements of performance such as service, levels of employee satisfaction, performance against desired medical outcomes, and responsiveness to an employer's special needs for network or service customization. Performance guarantees also provide a mechanism for an annual review of program objectives, and they ensure that measurement criteria evolve along with medical and systems innovations.

The Future of Point of Service

POS is a good way to introduce employees to the concept of managed care and is a strong, effective strategy in the current health care environment. It is not, however, likely to be the last

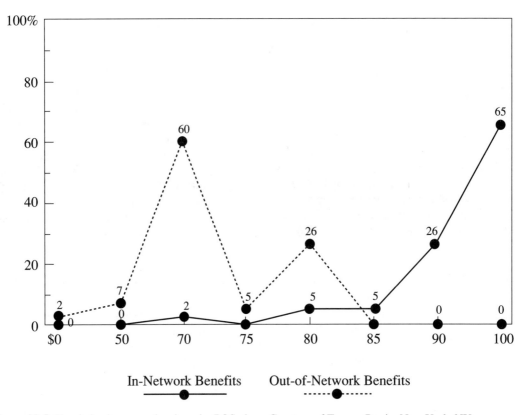

Figure 23-5 Hospital coinsurance levels under POS plans. Courtesy of Towers Perrin, New York, NY.

frontier of managed care. Instead, POS may provide a transition to true managed care: the HMOs that were so unpopular only a few decades ago. Managers are already looking at tightening their provider networks, which will make even non–HMO-based networks more like HMOs than ever before.

Notably, some HMOs are moving in the opposite direction. About half of all HMOs are already offering their own POS (or open-ended) products to attract employees. Although they are doing so to retain and expand their market share, they do run the risk of eroding the comparatively effective cost control that was their strength for years.

Meanwhile, employees have willingly embraced managed care, as evidenced by Towers Perrin's telephone survey of employers (cited above) and corroborated by its earlier survey of plan participants.[2] If in-network utilization continues to increase and networks are held to the quality standards that keep employees happy

with the care they receive, employers will be less reluctant to offer network-only benefits. And as more and more claims are covered in the networks, it may become possible for employers to provide only catastrophic benefits out of network.

SUPPLEMENTAL NETWORKS

If managed care networks are to continue to meet employee and company needs, they may have to take on different forms and involve new players. One reason is that the major carriers have pretty well penetrated their first-tier market areas and are slowing network expansion, except as new enrollments in those areas demand. In addition, many rural areas do not have networks available to them, leaving some employees ineligible for network coverage. This might not be a problem if there were sufficient competition among providers in these areas to keep costs under control and to ensure quality. Employers are

Table 23-1 Network Evaluation Concerns

Characteristic	Fundamental Questions
Provider network	Is the network constructed and managed in such a way that the majority of providers prove sound, efficient, and effective over time?
Quality of care	Has the network implemented its written plans for identifying and correcting quality problems?
Customer service	Does the network treat members as people instead of transactions?
Medical management	Does the network have the approach, expertise, resources, and willingness to control the utilization of all significant services over time?
Network management and information systems	Does the network have a well-organized, qualified, and coordinated management team that effectively implements policy, utilizes the system, and maintains key relationships?
Financial performance	Regardless of the magnitude of corporate support, does the network's performance reflect effective management direction and control?

Source: Courtesy of Towers Perrin, New York, NY.

beginning to see that these pockets of the country require cost control, however, and that the quality of care delivered to their employees could be improved in some cases.

Filling the Coverage Gaps

For employers with multiple locations who find it difficult to cover 100% of their employees under a single network, one approach to filling the coverage gaps is to supplement the main network with local HMOs or PPOs where available. Others, satisfied with the aggregate cost control they can achieve by covering the majority of their employees with networks, will not concern themselves about the balance.

Still others, however, have expressed interest in developing direct relationships with local providers to achieve cost and quality control. Direct contracting with providers brings with it a multitude of concerns, most of which can be addressed, but all of which must be given thorough consideration before an employer takes this route. Some of these concerns are highlighted in Exhibit 23-1.

Employers Take Control

Direct contracting is the ultimate step in an employer's progression from a passive to an aggressive role in managing health care. POS does allow employers to evaluate and compare how network managers select, contract with, and oversee providers of health care and then to se-

lect the manager they believe does these jobs in a manner most likely to meet the company's objectives.

Direct contracting goes a step further, putting the employer in control of the provider selection process and letting the company determine the basis for contracting. And although most employers retain outside parties to conduct provider negotiations, many of those negotiators assert that the employer's presence at and participation in negotiations can be critical to their success. As a practical matter, employers want to stay somewhat distanced from the day-to-day operations of a network, even one they

Exhibit 23-1 Direct Contracting Concerns

How will prospective network providers be identified in a community?

Who will be responsible for provider credentialing?

What will be the basis of provider fee negotiations?

Will performance guarantees be negotiated? Who will be responsible for conducting the negotiations?

How and by whom will management reports be generated?

Who will be responsible for quality assurance, and how can necessary corrections or improvements be ensured?

Will the directly contracted network provide benefits and services consistent with other networks in use (if applicable)?

Where will customer services be provided?

Source: Courtesy of Towers Perrin, New York, NY.

have worked to create. This is simply because employers are not in the business of hands-on health care delivery and are best advised to limit potential liability and excessive costs by leaving this role to the professionals. Consequently, in direct contracting situations an employer may want to employ a manager to run the network. The selection process in this situation should be competitive, should be based on clearly defined objectives for the network, and should set parameters within which the network manager will have to operate.

MICRO-MANAGED CARE

One of the areas in which employers could choose to take the direct contracting approach is micro-managed care. Mental health and substance abuse, prescription drugs, or medical care specialties such as cardiac care are areas where micro-managed care can be effective.

As employers have become more involved in health care cost management, they have used claims and utilization data to identify areas of particularly high cost or frequency in their own populations, developing specific strategies to target these problems. For example, mental health and substance abuse costs generally run at about 15% of total claims cost but can be as high as 50%.

To address such needs, specialty networks are available to cover a broad range of services from employee assistance counseling to long-term therapy, crisis intervention, and hospitalization. The gatekeeper role has become common in this arena. There may be situations, however, where an employer could appropriately establish direct relationships, for example, with a local drug testing service, to meet specific program or policy objectives. Mental health and substance abuse services are discussed in detail in Chapter 13.

Similarly, although prescription drug plans and their related provider networks have become common over the years, some employers have looked into more exclusive arrangements in which these services are provided on site. And in this sense, the evolution of drug plans is another example of lessening employer passivity.

When drug card programs first started, for example, it was not uncommon for employer plans simply to pay all costs in excess of the copayment. These plans obviously failed to control costs, and despite averaging only 10% to 12% of total benefit costs, prescription drug costs have been rising two or three times as fast as costs for general medical care. As a result, employers have been encouraged to pressure the market to develop strategies that parallel solutions elsewhere in the medical arena. Among the outgrowths of this effort are drug utilization review programs and more aggressive pricing methodologies. Pharmacy programs are discussed in detail in Chapter 14.

CONCLUSION

Employer concern with rising health care costs has led to a variety of strategies over the years. Initially reluctant to forgo the advantages of fee-for-service indemnity plans, employers encouraged providers and third-party administrators to develop cost controls that would work within that environment. And although a short-sighted view of the potential for HMOs to provide long-term cost control deferred employer savings, imposing managed care prematurely might have caused disastrous employee relations problems and prevented managed care from achieving the success it enjoys today.

The progression from relative disinterest in lock-in HMOs to PPOs and then POS and supplemental direct contracting may, in the long run, bring employers back to lock-in HMOs. In the interim, employers will have learned enough about health care delivery that they can be confident in their ability to shape policy and practice in this area. The learning process has also brought refinements and enhancements that put the private sector today in better position to control cost, quality, and delivery of health care.

REFERENCES

1. Towers Perrin. *Managed Care: Employer Perspectives 1992.* New York: Towers Perrin; 1992.

2. Towers Perrin. *Managed Care: The Employee Perspective.* New York: Towers Perrin; 1991.

Chapter 24

Marketing Managed Health Care Plans

John P. Anton

Marketing is key to a managed care organization's expansion and member/customer retention. It seeks to determine existing and changing market demand, to help the managed care organization meet that demand, and to persuade current and prospective members and customers that the organization best meets their needs.

In doing so, members of the marketing staff must be ambassadors who can convince people in other parts of the managed care organization to support the marketing effort. They must have diplomatic and negotiating skills that enable them to improve or maintain their position in tense situations, turning possible adversarial situations into agreements. Finally, the marketing staff must possess and exercise investigative skills so that they can uncover hidden information, analyze it, and use it to develop marketing strategies.

John P. Anton is Vice President of National Marketing for the CIGNA Employee Benefits Companies. Before joining CIGNA, he was Vice President and Executive Director of Georgia Medical Plan, an Atlanta health maintenance organization. Earlier, he was responsible for Medicare and Medicaid contracts for the Health Care Financing Administration's Southeast Region, coming to that position from The Traveler's Companies, where he was a claims manager for more than 9 years.

This chapter will discuss how to develop information to help sell your plan and compete successfully. It will then discuss product and marketing diversification, prospecting, marketing communications, sales promotions, the marketing staff, and client retention.

MARKET RESEARCH

The goal of market research is to enable a managed care organization to survive and grow. Market research identifies markets and submarkets by such variables as geographic area, industry type, case size, and competitor. It enables the managed care organization to determine what that particular market wants, the factors that influence its choices, and how the market or its demands and needs may change in the future. The managed care organization that does not know its market or does not respond to market interests or demands is living on borrowed time.

Benefits

Market research can help you determine whether a market is viable for your organization and can keep you from wasting your marketing efforts. For example, market research may reveal that a particular city, industry, or number of prospective companies has a consistent history of rejecting managed care. It may tell you that a market is shrinking because of industry turndowns, company relocations, or closings. It may show that a market is saturated or alert you to client and prospect moves to reduce the number of managed care organizations offered to employees.

On the other hand, market research may reveal opportunities such as an emerging receptiveness to managed care, unserved areas, a company's pending decision to move to or start a new operation in your area, or increasing interest in a particular market niche (eg, mental health and substance abuse or vision care services).

Market research may indicate the approaches you can take to market the plan. For example, it can help you determine whether the health care business in the community allows direct selling or whether you will have to sell through an established broker or respond to consultants' requests for proposals on behalf of an employer. You can also use market research to tell you which brokers control which accounts.

You may find that market research can even help you with specific client approaches. Having a sense of a prospect's specific needs can help your organization present its potentially unique value to a prospect [eg, "We operate health maintenance organizations (HMOs) in the three Texas cities where you have operations, and we have preferred provider organizations (PPOs) that can serve your Oklahoma City and St. Louis employees"].

Competitive intelligence, a specialty area of market research, helps you identify your competition and its strengths. It may reveal a tough-to-break lock on the market by a formidable competitor, or it may reveal a competitor's weaknesses, such as member dissatisfaction with the time it takes to get an appointment with a physician or a lack of providers close to where members live. Competitive intelligence may provide early warning of a competitor's activities, such as an acquisition, that may result in a temporary disruption for its clients. While the competition fumbles the ball, you can move in.

Market research can give you important data for plan design and pricing. You can learn about an area's demographics, income, and average health care costs. Research may alert you to health care outliers, which represent an uncommonly high rate of certain treatments that may indicate overutilization or costly overtreatment. Research can tell you about a market's potential or special needs. For example, you may find that an area has a greater than average need for pediatricians or for clinics with a bilingual staff.

But market research is not only a tool for new business prospecting. Your consumer research and member surveys can help you retain clients by keeping tabs on what they most appreciate and what they dislike. In turn, you may be able to enjoy a double benefit of market research by recycling your research and survey results as a marketing tool. For example, if the results are impressive, tell clients and prospects the results of your member satisfaction surveys.

Market Research Resources

Your market research needs and resources will determine your choice of research methodology. For example, you would not use a focus group to identify a community's demographics. Your budget, staff, and skills also will affect whether you can or cannot employ an outside organization to conduct market research for you.

You can gather a considerable amount of market information for relatively little cost and moderate time investment. The US Department of Labor's Bureau of Labor Statistics (BLS) conducts extensive surveys. The results it publishes sometimes break down findings by region or even standard metropolitan statistical areas, as does the Department of Commerce's Bureau of the Census.

Your local, state, or university library may have some BLS or Census documents and be able to provide you with guidance, as may your local or state Chamber of Commerce. They can probably also point you to other useful surveys conducted by nonfederal agencies.

Several of the large benefits consulting organizations conduct their own national surveys on managed care topics and provide the published results for anywhere from $25 to a few hundred dollars. Dunn & Bradstreet, which has sales offices around the country, may be able to conduct specialized research on your organization's behalf, obtaining information about local employers by sales, industry, and size of employer; information about their insurance programs; and names of such key contacts as company chief executive officers, chief financial officers, benefits managers, and human resource directors.

The major polling organizations, such as Louis Harris and Associates, the Roper Organization, Gallup & Robinson, and Yankelovich Clancy Shulman, as well as smaller polling and research organizations often conduct market research for health care organizations, as do the major benefits consulting organizations. But be a careful shopper because prices can vary tremendously.

A growing number of university libraries now offer fee-based information services, where library staff conduct research for client projects. A clipping service may also be helpful in alerting you to trends and developments among local or national employers.

Informal Market Research

Some of the most productive research you can undertake will be less scientific and methodical in approach. You probably already conduct informal market research. Whenever you build a relationship with brokers or employers, you develop resources that can provide you with information you cannot obtain otherwise.

One highly effective method that managed care organizations use to build their informal information bases is organizing luncheon or breakfast programs with groups of brokers, consultants, and employers to discuss benefits or health care issues. It is a far less expensive research approach than organizing a focus group, and it also builds goodwill.

You may get a pleasant surprise when you find how willing the different segments of the benefits community are to participate in these discussions. For example, brokers often will talk freely about what sells and what does not. But these programs also serve them well: They learn about your organization, which helps put them in a better position to serve their clients; they know their feedback will help make you serve

their clients better; their discussions help them reinforce their control over their accounts; and they learn from other brokers.

Community organizations can also serve as launchpads for you to establish employer relationships, as will any opportunities for involvement in health care coalitions. They give you the chance to listen to what the organized business community is saying and what people in the community are complaining and talking about. In looking for ways to meet local employers, look also to your board members for referrals to people they know.

Your informal market research may be particularly helpful in evaluating subtle differences in market wants. Every product has the potential to meet more than one market need. Just as automobiles are alternately marketed as cars, as transportation aids, as status symbols, and as lifestyle enhancers, a managed care market's hot buttons will vary. Is the market looking for health care or insurance? Better service? Cost control? Better employee relations and retention? A way to meet the health needs of employees? Ease of benefits administration? And what does a particular market or prospect have in mind when it repeats that word on everyone's lips: *quality?* The answers to these questions tell you how to project your organization.

PRODUCT AND MARKETING DIVERSIFICATION

The Diversification Explosion

A decade ago, the managed care industry's membership was generally composed of PPOs, three or four models of HMOs, and indemnity plans with managed care features. They tended to specialize in the same thing: basic medical coverage.

Since then, we've seen a bewildering explosion of managed care products, services, and market diversification, including:

- point-of-service (POS) plans, which provide different coverage levels, depending on whether the participant obtains health care services from a PPO, a nonnetwork provider, or an HMO

- open-ended HMOs, which allow members to self-refer to other providers and still receive coverage, although at a reduced rate
- greater managed care organization interest in serving particular market segments, such as the Medicare (see Chapters 28 and 29), retiree (see Chapter 30), Medicaid (see Chapter 31), armed services (see Chapter 32), and workers' compensation (see Chapter 33) markets
- a growing number of optional benefits marketed as plan enhancements or as stand-alone products that can be sold separately (eg, an HMO may offer vision care either as an optional plan enhancement to health coverage or as a stand-alone benefit, where the employer contracts with another organization for basic health benefits and with the HMO only for vision coverage)
- managed care organizations providing separate services or lines of business such as utilization review services, claims administration, or workers' compensation medical services

Several related factors are driving the trend toward wider variety and specialization, including cost control concerns, the search for better ways to price and deliver care, and competitive pressures. To stay within the focus of this chapter, we will primarily restrict our attention to competitive concerns.

Diversification Advantages

The managed care organization that can offer several different financial arrangements and add-on and stand-alone products enjoys a competitive advantage because it has a better chance of being able to fulfill employers' differing needs. That versatility also enables it to promote an image of expertise and competence.

Stand-alone products may appeal to an employer that at that time only needs that one extra benefit. A stand-alone product also provides a toe-in-the-water low-risk chance to test the managed care organization. From the managed care organization's perspective, it is a foot in the door, providing an opportunity for cross-selling additional products. For example, if an employer becomes a client for an HMO's utilization review services, the HMO gains more of an opportunity to acquaint the employer with its other products and services.

Diversification Disadvantages

Diversification can be dangerous. Developing new products, financial arrangements, or the administrative and financial systems to sell existing products such as add-ons or stand-alones can be costly. New products can be difficult to price without historical data to guide underwriting. Stand-alone products are vulnerable to adverse selection. Certain market segments, particularly Medicare, entail administrative complexities and the uncertainty of changing requirements and reimbursement formulas.

New products or attempts to serve special market segments also carry the risk of taking away the managed care organization's attention and resources from what it knows best. Worse yet, they may take its attention and resources away from areas that need improvement.

Making the Choice

The decision to offer specialty products or to pursue a certain market segment should be based upon the findings of several areas in the managed care organization, including administrative, financial, and medical. The marketing area's contribution to the decision initially lies in its market research function to determine whether the market wants and will pay for the new products or marketing ventures.

But what if market research indicates considerable market demand for a product that would dangerously stretch the managed care organization's resources? Fortunately, there are ways to add new products and financial arrangements without risking large investments in time and money.

For adding stand-alone or add-on products, a private label approach may hold the solution. In this kind of arrangement, you contract with a specialty vendor to allow you to market its product under your name in such a way that the arrangement is not visible to the employer/employee. This approach holds little risk to the managed care organization, has low start-up costs, takes little time to set up, and takes advantage of the vendor's economy of scale and expertise.

Other kinds of arrangements are also possible. For example, a joint venture arrangement with an insurance company may allow a freestanding HMO to develop POS products. Reciprocating agreements with other managed care organizations outside your coverage area may allow you to expand the number of locations you offer. Joint marketing arrangements or alignments, where your organization and another help sell each other's products and services, present another possibility. This approach may be appropriate for managed care organizations and third-party administrators, who may see the same prospects for related but noncompeting reasons.

Moving Ahead

The trend of increasing specialization and variety is apt to continue in the years ahead. Several driving forces are likely to propel interest in certain areas.

Cost Drivers

Workers' compensation costs have been escalating at incredible rates in recent years. In most states, restrictive laws prevent employers from directing workers' compensation claimants only to managed care providers, where costs would be less and claimants would get back to work sooner. As cost pressures build, some states are beginning to relax restrictions on employers' abilities to direct claimants to managed care. This issue is discussed in detail in Chapter 33.

Health Drivers

The nation's interest in fitness is extending beyond the lifespan of a craze and may become a permanent lifestyle component. If so, wellness and health promotion programs could become a more frequently expected part of standard benefit packages.

Age Drivers

The cohort of aging Baby Boomers will swell the ranks of retirees in the years ahead. Employers that provide retiree benefits are already under pressure from accounting rules to reduce their current and future estimated retiree costs. These forces may drive employers to look to managed care plans to reduce those costs. Meanwhile, more managed care organizations may begin pursuing the retiree and Medicare markets to replace the retiring active employees they would otherwise lose as members. Retirees are discussed in Chapter 30, and Medicare is discussed in Chapters 28 and 29.

Reform Drivers

Public pressure to reform the health care system will continue to grow. The pressure to increase access will focus on and intensify in every area of the health care delivery system, including managed care organizations. Managed care organizations will inevitably begin serving more Medicaid recipients (see Chapter 31) and small employers, either because they see them as profitable new markets or because they are forced to serve them by legislative and regulatory directives.

PROSPECTING

Establishing Relationships

As discussed earlier, your involvement in health coalitions, business organizations, and the broker community as part of your informal market research can help you develop a network of information resources and contacts. Utilizing this network, your current customer base, and your board can help you spend more of your time in referral prospecting instead of cold calling.

Listening is crucial to establishing a relationship. Your initial objective is not to make a sale but to get a meeting with a prospect, a potential client, where you can conduct some market research and develop the opportunity to ask for another referral. Managed care marketing requires a high level of buyer trust. As a result, sales are rarely quick, and relationships play a crucial role.

Identifying Primary Prospects

Primary prospects are the people who make the initial decision about whether an employer should affiliate or contract with a managed care organization. The decision maker will vary. It could be the benefits manager, human resources director, chief executive officer, or chief financial officer.

Sometimes the initial decision maker is not even the employer. For example, your market research or conversation with an employer or broker may reveal that a case is broker controlled. Or you may find that the employer is using a consultant to evaluate managed care organizations, requiring you to direct your attention there. Perhaps the employer will not make a move until its union gives an OK.

Brokers and Consultants

In many markets, brokers and consultants play critical and somewhat overlapping roles. Both advise employers about their selection of a benefits provider, but brokers receive a commission as compensation based on a percentage of the premium as stated in the managed care organization's commission schedule. Consultants are more often employed on a project basis and are paid directly by the employer. It is possible for an employer to use a broker for most of its benefits needs and to hire a consultant for work on a specific project.

How do you find out whether an employer uses a broker? It is part of market research to determine who controls business in the community. Also, an employer will tell you whether it has a broker of record, or a broker can produce a letter from the employer stating that it is the broker of record.

A case may be broker controlled, in which case the employer essentially delegates decision making about its benefits plan to a broker. In these cases, it will be to your benefit to work with the broker. Some managed care organizations choose not to approach employers through brokers as a matter of policy, but that means they are effectively cut out from a portion of the market.

Responding to Requests for Proposal

An employer seeking a managed care provider will often issue a request for proposal (RFP) to solicit bids directly or through a consultant or broker. Although the managed care organization's response to an RFP is an essential step in the marketing process, this cannot replace the relationship-building process. An RFP is only a formal request for proposal. The informal marketing steps before and during the RFP response period can have a great bearing on the managed care organization's success in responding to the RFP.

First, consultants and employers do not simply conduct a mass mailing of RFPs to every known managed care organization. Formally or informally, they assess prospective organizations and send RFPs only to a selected list. If the RFP issuer does not consider your organization a known, active player in the community with the qualities the employer seeks, it may not even send you an RFP.

Second, consultants and employers do not develop RFPs in a vacuum. If you have a relationship with the employer and/or consultant, you may have an opportunity to influence the content of an RFP with your suggestions and comments about the capabilities it should examine before it is issued.

Third, having a relationship with the consultant and employer allows you to push for an opportunity to meet with the employer during the RFP process to identify its key buying issues. By meeting with the employer, you can determine the relative weights of importance the buyer attaches to different parts of the RFP. That meeting also provides you the opportunity to present your company in the best possible light. A good consultant will only present a factual, unbiased picture of your organization and all the others that respond. You do not want the consultant to be the only person representing your company to the employer.

The RFP will vary substantially by the size of the account and the employer's or consultant's level of experience. Smaller cases may use a less formal process than an RFP; for example, they may use a request for information (RFI) simply to request financial information, general information, and the managed care organization's schedule of benefits and prices. The RFI may be as simple as a request for the managed care organization to quote community rates for a prospective customer and to provide some demographic information about the plan's customer base such as age, sex, and ZIP codes of residences in the community rate quote.

At the other extreme, more sophisticated consultants and employers may use an RFI to gather preproposal information. The RFI may ask significant questions about your company, organizational structure, membership, profitability, how it manages care, how it manages quality, its member services, how it pays claims, where it is located, its service area, and how it interfaces with the home office.

The RFI issuer will then analyze responses to develop an RFP and also to determine the managed care organizations to which it will send the actual RFP. The RFP itself is more concerned with financial data and will ask you to give information about your claims, experience, and proposed benefits design.

Typically, the last question in an RFP will ask why your plan is best suited for the employer. This is another area where your market research investment can pay dividends. It can tell you about specific needs of the employer not addressed elsewhere in the RFP that you can emphasize here. Similarly, on the basis of your competitive intelligence research findings, you can use this question to highlight the advantages you have over other managed care organizations.

Sometimes the answer to this last question can be decisive in winning a managed care contract. Isn't it nice that you have all that solid market research to guide you?

Employee and Dependent Prospecting

Managed care marketing does not stop with the employer's agreement. The marketing process must also identify its competitors and prospective members and develop targeted messages to guarantee increased plan enrollment.

The competition will certainly include the other managed care organizations the employer offers, if any. If the employer will still provide an indemnity plan option, that too is a competitor. Finally, your competition will include the plan you replace. Even if it is gone, it will still be in the minds of employees, and they will compare it with your plan.

What does, or did, the competition offer? Your enrollment people need to understand how your program differs from its competition so that they can identify the high points of your program. There are several possible points of comparison:

- *Benefits* —When the managed care organization is competing with or replacing an indemnity plan, there are apt to be significant coverage differences. What are the points to push on your side?

- *Process*—The employee's procedure for obtaining health care from your organization will differ substantially from that for the indemnity process and possibly from that for other managed care organizations (eg, procedures may differ between PPOs and HMOs and possibly even between HMO model types, such as closed panel and open panel models).

- *Premiums*—Although your managed care organization's benefits and process may be similar to those of other organizations, the premium levels may differ.

- *Accessibility*—The locations your managed care organization offers in relation to where employees work and live may differ from those of other managed care providers.

Your analysis of the competition should go hand in hand with your analysis of the buyer's employees and dependents. Your enrollment team will need to know, for example, their average age, their education levels, whether they are blue or white collar, where they live, and their probable buying decisions.

Some rough generalizations may be helpful. Younger employee populations are likely to place more importance on well-child care, child care accessibility, and obstetric care. Cost is an issue with all groups, but it is more so with blue collar groups. Physician quality, too, is important to all groups, but higher-income groups are more likely to be interested in details about the program, provider backgrounds, and provider accessibility than in a $5 difference in premium.

Although these generalizations can be useful in a broad sense, the information you can gather through the relationships you established can be more helpful. If possible, meet with the company's human resources and benefits people to learn their perceptions of what matters to employees. Find out whether the broker or consultant on the case has any knowledge of employee interests or applicable survey information. If the plan serves union members, ask union representatives for their perceptions of employee concerns.

Your relationship with the employer can be a critical factor in the enrollment process. Ideally, the employer will:

- provide names and addresses of employees so that you can mail materials to them

- distribute your materials to employees at the workplace

- make employee attendance at enrollment meetings mandatory

- allow spouses, who may be the actual decision makers in the family when it comes to health care, to attend enrollment meetings

Managed care serves both employer and employee in different but complementary ways. That requires the preparation of different messages for each.

For example, the employer may appreciate the gatekeeper role of the primary care physician in controlling overutilization and its attendant expenses. But the gatekeeper function does not serve as a buy signal to employees and dependents. To the employee and dependent, presenting the primary care physician as their personal physician who will walk them through the system, make sure their needs are met, and serve as an advocate for their health needs speaks more to that audience's interests and still accurately portrays the primary care physician's role.

Whatever employer-oriented messages you develop for the prospecting process and whatever employee- and dependent-oriented messages you develop for the enrollment process should be consistent with the messages you present in your marketing materials. This consistency can reinforce your messages at every step of the marketing process.

MARKETING COMMUNICATIONS AND SALES PROMOTION

Advertising, public relations, and sales promotion are related but distinctly different activities that managed care organizations can use to convey positive messages about their plans to employers and employee/prospects. To capitalize on the strengths of these tools and to deploy these resources effectively, it pays to develop marketing communication strategies through an integrated approach rather than as separate promotional activities.

Start the marketing communications planning process with a review of your market research findings to identify your target business and consumer audiences. Only after you have a firm view of your intended audiences can you begin building an integrated marketing communication strategy.

Next, identify the key messages you want to deliver to your target audiences. For example, if your market research tells you consumers are most concerned about the quality of care they receive, their ability to choose where their care comes from, and cost, you will want to develop overall messages relating your plan or products to these concerns.

As you develop overall messages, develop specific, supportive statements. For example, one overall message may be that the plan provides quality care. Your supportive statements for this might inform audiences about your physician credentialing process and the primary care physician's role to ensure that care is appropriate.

Identifying overall messages and position statements allows you to develop an effective integrated marketing approach that protects you from presenting a fragmented image. Advertising, public relations, collateral materials, direct mail, and sales promotional items all have different and overlapping capabilities and limitations. But if you give your range of promotional materials a consistent message and look, you can present a capable and unified message that is stronger than the sum of its parts.

We'll look now at each of these approaches, their differences in capabilities and limitations, and how they can support each other.

Advertising

Advertising is one of the most effective means available to build name recognition and is good for communicating a broad, overall message. But at best it can only grab attention and give a few brief reasons for strengthening preference for your plan. Radio and television advertising, for example, give too little time to communicate more than a single idea. Print advertising, too, has only a few moments to capture and hold readers' attention before they turn the page. Billboards can raise name awareness, but they barely provide enough space to deliver even a brief, simple message. Advertising is also expensive.

But high costs and lack of space or time are not the only reasons why advertising is best for communicating only a broad message and establishing name recognition. Advertising tends to go to a broad audience. A large portion of any advertising message will be wasted on listeners, viewers, and readers who are not in your target audience. Also, if you offer a variety of products and present a message about a specific product, you may reach an audience whose employer offers one of your other products. Your plan could then end up competing against itself.

Public Relations

Public relations activities encompass a far greater range than the damage control role popularized in the media. They include, for example, working with the media to develop articles for trade, newspaper, and business and consumer publications. Public relations includes planning promotional events, such as organizing or participating in a health promotion worksite wellness fair. It may also include arranging local speaking opportunities for the plan's management or sponsoring a business and health meeting for an audience of employers.

With business and public interest in health care delivery at an all-time high, opportunities abound for a plan's management to speak at business and industry meetings. Seminars for employers, where the theme is clearly informational rather than marketing oriented, have great potential for establishing a plan's management as a knowledgeable, professional group. In an industry where trust and relationships are paramount, that is a goal worth pursuing.

Community events, such as road races, health screenings, and lectures on health issues open to the public, present a way to reach out to potential members. On the local level, the mere act of reminding people that you are in the community can enhance the name of your company. Community events may require large amounts of money, however. You will want to identify which events and locations best reach your target audience. Generally, schools are a good place to start.

Public relations activities, like advertising, can build name recognition and communicate single messages. They can also help establish goodwill and a sense that the plan is a member of and serves the community. But also like advertising, public relations is limited in the number of messages it can deliver.

Collateral Materials and Direct Mail

Collateral materials generally include any printed materials about the managed care organization and its products and services. Brochures, provider directories, member handbooks, newsletters, stuffers, posters, and data sheets all fall into the collateral materials category. Direct mail, however, refers to transmitting the message in a targeted fashion. For example, you can distribute collateral materials such as product brochures at an enrollment meeting, at a health fair, or as part of a direct mail promotion.

In contrast to advertising and public relations, with collateral materials and direct mail you can exercise much greater control in limiting the audience you reach. Although you can use direct mail to communicate general messages, that audience selectivity also gives you the opportunity to deliver specific information for a particular audience, in greater detail than you can with advertising. For an employee audience, however, you will want your collateral materials written simply so that everyone can understand the options you offer.

Although collateral materials and direct mail offer great flexibility, advertising and promotion are still necessary activities because they help create the conditions for direct mail and collateral materials to work. Name recognition, credibility, and a favorable impression of the plan are preconditions that must be met before recipients of direct mail and collateral materials are likely to read them.

Also, unlike the situation with advertising, the distribution channels for collaterals and direct mail are tightly controlled and are not always easily accessible. Will the employer distribute your materials? Will the employer provide employees' names and home addresses? If you do not have an employer's support, you may not be able to reach much of your intended audience.

Promotional Items and Services

Sales promotions can include both objects and services. The objects are usually giveaways, such as health education materials for members, or incentives, such as a T-shirt for achieving an exercise goal or an infant car safety seat as an incentive to enroll in a prenatal care program. Services include access to free information, free blood pressure screening, discounts on health- or sports-related purchases, free sports physicals, and discounted memberships in health clubs or day-care centers.

Sales promotional items are generally the weakest part of the promotional effort. They cannot deliver a competitive message, and they may draw more attention to themselves than the plan. They can be costly and are often given ei-

ther to people who are already in the plan or to people who have no intention of joining.

But in a market where there may be no differentiating factor between your plan and another, sales promotional items and services can make a difference. They serve as attention getters and reminders. Also, when your price is the same as or higher than that of a competitor, they communicate a value-added message: "Yes, you pay a little more here, but you get more." When they are clearly linked to your product, sales promotional items can also provide a tangible reminder of another message: "We believe in keeping you healthy."

YOUR MARKETING TEAM

Should Staff Specialize?

The larger carriers and HMOs have separate sales and marketing teams. Their marketing staffs gather research and data on what to sell and how to sell, and they play a role in product development and market research. Their sales teams sell. In other organizations, the same staff has both sales and marketing functions, which is the model we will discuss here.

Although some specialization is necessary for maximum effectiveness, there are probably as many schools of thought about marketing staff specialization as there are ways to develop that specialization.

The possibilities are many. Some managed care organizations have marketing staff dedicated to or specializing by prospect size, geography, product line, or new business versus current customers. The degree and type of specialization will depend in part on the marketing staff's size and experience and the market. The marketing director may also want to consider individual personalities and experience in assigning staff responsibilities.

The marketing staff members will have various levels of expertise. Some will be new without any established client relationships and without the expertise to establish relationships. Others may be competent at selling smaller cases but lack the expertise to establish and deal with more technically astute and experienced clients. Some may be great for selling small case HMO-only business but cannot handle the financial considerations of a larger case looking for a POS plan and experience rating.

Just as they will differ in experience, marketing staff members will have different personality traits and related skills. Some will work well as hunters, who are best at drumming up new business, and others will serve better as closers, who negotiate and finalize the sale. Still others may work well with consultants and are able to wend their way through the maze that that often entails.

Sales versus Service Representatives

Should your sales people be responsible for servicing accounts? In part, that depends on the size of the marketing organization. There is value in requiring the person who sells to be the one who services the account. After all, the individual sellers and buyers already have established relationships.

But not every seller is a good service person, and not every service person is a good seller. Also, managed care is a service-intensive business. If sales people retain responsibility for service, you take their time away from generating new business.

Some managed care organizations, especially the larger ones, balance these concerns by having an account management team to service accounts. But regardless of who has account servicing responsibilities, the marketing staff members should maintain communications and a relationship with customers. This may provide them with an early warning of client dissatisfaction and the opportunity to remedy problems. It also provides opportunities for cross-selling of additional products and for getting referrals to new prospects.

Product Specialists

Should your marketing team specialize by product? It is more realistic for smaller organizations to expect everyone to be a generalist with

an overall knowledge of all the products the organization sells. More experienced generalists can become specialists in certain products, so that anyone can go to them for assistance and advice.

Large, diverse health care organizations that market a range of HMOs, PPOs, POS plans, and other combinations are more likely to have product specialists, at least in the product development area. But the sales operation should consider the potential pitfalls of specialization carefully. Jealousy and resentment can flare if certain staff members are rewarded with exclusive privileges to sell in-demand, highly profitable products. Also, having product specialists may give the appearance of a fragmented organization and a confusing impression to the broker community.

Sales Compensation

Organizations with separate sales and marketing staffs should compensate them through different arrangements. Marketing staff who do not have a sales function can be compensated through typical salary arrangements. In addition, bonuses tied to performance and/or profitability may be appropriate.

But staff members who have a sales function should be compensated in large part through an incentive compensation (IC) program. IC uses a carefully structured set of rewards to provide selling incentives. Generally, it compensates individual sales people on the basis of a percentage of the income that their sales generate.

The managed care organization can base its specific IC structure on a number of different factors, depending upon the sales staff's responsibilities and what the organization wishes to emphasize. For example, some managed care organizations base their IC program upon a sold case's membership size.

Where sales people also service an account, some managed care organizations use a formula based on the net member gain compared to gross membership. By tying IC to net retention, the IC structure rewards the sales people for servicing the account and preventing disenrollment on the back side. For example, if a case has a membership of 500, but 400 members of the employer's group do not stay with the plan, the sales staff on the case would only get credit for 100 members.

Still other managed care organizations base IC on premium dollars and revenue brought into health plans instead of on membership numbers. This gives the sales team an incentive to sell premium increases instead of offering lower premiums to encourage a quick sale.

A common goal underlying these different arrangements is tying IC into the profitability of membership. After all, the ultimate goal of the managed care organization is not simply to sell coverage but to make money. An IC program that rewards sales people simply on the basis of case size may tempt sales people to sign up every risk they can and to withhold information from the underwriting and/or financial departments.

In addition to an IC program, managed care organizations can use a bonus program tied into business profitability, either that of the entire plan or that of the book of business that the sales representative is responsible for selling and servicing. This gives the sales staff a stronger commitment to the overall financial soundness of the organization and to helping you manage its risk.

The Health Plan Staff's Importance to the Sales Process

The sales team is only part of the managed care organization's team. The organization's medical director, provider relations staff, member services department, quality assurance staff, and providers all have marketing roles. Every encounter or interaction that a member or employer has with the plan either confirms or undermines the sale.

Business concerns about quality have moved into the health care arena. Health plan site visits are now critical to the sales process. Employers are asking managed care organizations to show them how their system works and who will handle their account. Presenting the health care delivery system and demonstrating how quality

is monitored are becoming increasingly significant in the sales process. The medical director can lend critical credibility to the plan's reputation for quality and control.

IT IS NEVER OVER

Customer Retention

Despite your best efforts, your plan is bound to lose customers and members. Some disenrollments will be involuntary. A customer's headquarters in a faraway city may consolidate the plan for all locations with another managed care organization. A member may lose eligibility because of a change in employment status or marital status.

Although there is little you can do to prevent involuntary disenrollment, you will want to try to keep voluntary disenrollment to a minimum. Even when the marketing department does not have a direct role in servicing an account, it should still keep in touch with the three primary customers of an account to determine whether their needs are being satisfied.

First, the technical person with day-to-day responsibilities, usually the benefits manager, has administrative needs. Second, the person with financial responsibilities requires financial information and cost savings data. Third, individual members need to stay satisfied.

The member services department plays a critical role in both member and customer retention. If a member has problems, often the customer's human resources person who deals with employee-raised issues will hear about it. It is important that the human resources person and the member services department people get to know each other and begin a bonding process. The account manager should maintain open communications with customers so that the organization has a chance to identify problems and work to resolve them. Member services are discussed in greater detail in Chapter 19.

Open communications with accounts also means that, when you become aware of a problem, you notify the broker, union, and/or employer immediately. You will not be able to prevent all disenrollments. Small cases especially are apt to swap providers at renewal time for penny-saving differences. But if an account does not renew, and that comes as a surprise, then shame on you. You probably were not maintaining relationships and communicating effectively with the employer.

FURTHER READING

Managed care developments are proceeding at such a pace that up-to-date information is critical for making marketing decisions. Only your market research can tell you the names of some of the most important publications you should read. These are the ones that local employers, brokers, and consultants turn to for news. The following national publications each have special strengths or values to marketing staff. Write or call for subscription rates:

- *AAPPO Journal*—The bimonthly journal of the American Association of Preferred Provider Organizations. It often serves as a forum for PPO executives to present their views on the state of the industry. It is published by Health Care Communications, Inc, One Bridge Plaza, Suite 350, Fort Lee, NJ 07024; (201) 947-5545.

- *Business Insurance*—A weekly tabloid reporting news of the insurance industry. This is a good source of news about developments in the group health industry, although some issues may provide more information about the property and casualty industry. It is published by Crain Communications, 740 North Rush Street, Chicago, IL 60611-2590; (313) 446-1611.

- *Business & Health*—A monthly employer-oriented magazine with feature articles about different aspects of employee health benefits. It is published by Medical Economics Publishing, PO Box 2082, Marion, OH 43306; (800) 526-4870.

- *Business Marketing*–A monthly magazine rarely covering health issues, but it sometimes has relevant articles about prospecting, advertising, and other marketing concerns. It is published by Crain Communications (see *Business Insurance,* above).

- *HMO Magazine*—A bimonthly magazine with feature articles about different issues relating to HMOs, often with a marketing orientation. It is published by the Group Health Association of America, 1129 20th Street NW, Suite 600, Washington, DC 20036; (202) 778-3247.

- *Managed Care Outlook*—A biweekly newsletter with rapid updates of changes or events in managed care. It is published by Capitol Publications, Inc, 1101 King Street, PO Box 1453, Alexandria, VA 22313-2053; (800) 327-7203.

- *Marion Merrell Dow Managed Care Digest*—Each year this series includes one each of an *HMO Edition*, *PPO Edition,* and *HMO-PPO Update Edition.* These provide detailed statistics on HMO/PPO trends in ownership, market penetration, enrollment, premium rates, product mix, and other vital information. It is published by Marion Merrell Dow, Managed Health Care Markets Department, 9300 Ward Parkway, Kansas City, MO 64114; (800) 362-7466.

Finance and Underwriting

If making money is a slow process, losing it is quickly done.

Ihara Saikaku
(1642–1693)

*The Japanese Family Storehouse; or,
The Millionaire's Gospel,* bk I

Chapter 25

Operational Finance and Budgeting

David L. Ward

To manage properly the ongoing operations of a managed care organization, accurate and timely financial accounting for the results of operations is crucial. Through this timely capture of revenues and expenses and proper reporting, the organization can monitor its progress against established business objectives. This chapter provides a broad overview of the mechanics of operational finance and budgeting in a managed care organization and the compilation of financial results into management tools.

BACKGROUND

Managed care organizations are typically categorized as health maintenance organizations (HMO), preferred provider organizations (PPO), or point-of-service (POS) programs. For the purposes of this discussion, the focus will be HMO financial accounting and reporting. An HMO is commonly referred to as a prepaid health plan

because it collects premium revenues in advance of the delivery of medical benefits. A fundamental difference of prepaid health plans is that the HMO provides for the delivery of health care services, either through a network of providers or through its own employees, unlike traditional indemnity insurance plans, which indemnify participants against claims incurred. Accounting and reporting for self-funded plans (ie, those health benefit plans that are provided by the HMO on an administrative services only basis) differ principally in that medical expenses (net of reinsurance) are reimbursed retrospectively whereas administrative costs remain prospective. These concepts are discussed in greater detail in the section Medical Benefits, below.

Guidance for the accounting for HMO operations may be obtained from the statement of position issued by the American Institute of Certified Public Accountants (AICPA) in 1989 entitled *Financial Accounting and Reporting by Providers of Prepaid Health Care Services*. This statement of position provides a description of the proper financial accounting and reporting of revenues, medical benefits, and administrative expenses in prepaid health plans. Additional guidance is provided on recognition of loss contingencies under short-term contracts to provide health care services. This document can be

---

David L. Ward is the President and Chief Executive Officer of CapitalCare, Inc, a health maintenance organization located in Washington, DC. Mr Ward is a Certified Public Account with broad experience in the financial management, budgeting, business planning, and operations of independent practice association model health maintenance organizations.

found in the audit guide *Audits of Providers of Health Care Services* published by the AICPA.

The financial life cycle of the HMO begins with the underwriting and rating of potential client groups, flows through the enrollment process into the billing and collection of premiums, establishes accruals for medical benefits expenses, captures administrative and other operating and nonoperating costs incurred in servicing client groups, and ends in the reporting of financial results to internal management and state and federal regulatory agencies. This monthly financial reporting is the basis for preparing and measuring performance against established budgets and business plans and for analyzing the cost effectiveness and efficiency of the delivery system. From the proper understanding and application of financial analyses, the HMO manager can forecast future operational results. Throughout the financial life cycle and the measurement, reporting, and analysis of financial results, the HMO manager should concentrate on where the dollars are spent. In its simplest form this concept means that, if 90% of expenses are associated with medical benefits, management should not spend 90% of its efforts focusing on administrative expenses. More than a few troubled HMOs have maintained tight controls over administrative expenses while letting medical benefits utilization and cost increases far outpace the rate of premium growth.

REVENUES

Premium Revenues

The largest and most significant form of revenue within the HMO is premium revenue. Premium revenue represents the amount paid by a member in exchange for the provision and administration of medical benefits. Premiums are established and paid in advance of the period for which benefits are to be provided and are due whether or not services are incurred.

As discussed in detail in Chapter 26, the premium cycle begins with the underwriting of the client, typically an employer group or individual, to evaluate the potential of providing health care coverage. During the underwriting process, the HMO reviews and evaluates information specific to the client such as demographic data (ie, the age and sex mix of employees), industry type, contribution policies of the company toward the cost of health benefits, and competition within the account. These factors are considered in accordance with established underwriting guidelines employed by the HMO's underwriters to determine whether a rate quotation should be provided to the applicant group.

Once the applicant has been determined to be eligible for coverage (ie, the group passes underwriting guidelines), a rate calculation is prepared. HMOs typically rate groups under either a community rating methodology or an experience rating methodology. A pure community rating methodology applies a standard rate to all groups within the community of risk being underwritten by the HMO. Under this rating methodology, a base revenue requirement is calculated to determine the amount needed to pay expected claims and administrative expenses and to return a profit to the HMO. This base revenue requirement is then applied to specific groups on the basis of the number of rate tiers quoted, the average family size, and the contract mix assumed for the group. A rate tier represents a classification of rates based on the number and relationship of persons covered under the employee's health care plan. Typical rating tiers include single (ie, the employee), couple, employee plus dependent, employee plus minor, and family. Rate tiers may also be developed on the basis of the age and sex of the employee.

Variations on the pure community rating methodology may be applied by using community rating by class (CRC), in which the base revenue requirement is adjusted on the basis of the specific demographics and/or industry classification of the group. An alternative community rating application is adjusted community rating (ACR), in which the community rate is adjusted for group-specific information other than demographics and industry classification.

In addition to community rating, the HMO may also employ experience rating methodologies. Under experience rating methodologies the group's rates are based on the group's actual experience with the application of a trend factor to project the increase in medical benefits cost for the contract period. Experience rating requires detailed actual claims expenses for the group being underwritten. Where rates are being quoted for new groups or groups in which the HMO has a low penetration (ie, a small percentage of employees has joined the HMO), experience rating may not provide the best results for the HMO. A much more detailed discussion of these rating methodologies is provided in Chapter 26.

As rates are developed for new and renewal accounts, the timing of rate quotations requires the ability accurately to project trend increases in medical benefits expenses. Because rates must be finalized before the enrollment of members, it is usually necessary to quote rates 3 to 4 months before the effective date for commercial groups. Rates may be quoted as far as 8 months in advance of the effective date for government agencies. When one considers that rates are typically guaranteed for one contract year, the advance quoting of rates results in instances where rates quoted in May of the current year will be in effect to cover medical benefits costs in December of the subsequent year. It is therefore critical that the underwriting function maintain a close relationship with the financial accounting and budgeting areas so as to develop accurate trend assumptions for medical benefits and administrative expenses.

Once premiums have been developed, quoted, and accepted by the group, the enrollment process begins. During the enrollment process, each employee of the group must individually enroll in the HMO. The standard HMO enrollment form requires the employee to include the name, sex, date of birth, relationship to the employee, and primary care physician (PCP) selection for each person being enrolled in the health care plan. From this detailed information the HMO billing system is able to apply the correct premium to each employee on the basis of the number and relationship of covered individuals in accordance with the rating tiers.

Because HMOs are prepaid health plans, premiums are billed in advance of the month for which benefits are being provided. These billings typically occur between the 15th and 25th

calendar day of the month before the month of coverage. The billing document usually includes a detailed listing of each employee covered under the health plan, the billing tier applicable to the coverage, and the amount due for each employee. Although the prevalent form of billing small to medium-size employer groups is through the generation of a printed invoice, a number of large groups and government entities require electronic billing via magnetic tape.

There are two methods of billing for premiums by the health plan. The first method is known as the self-billing or positive billing method. Under this method the client is responsible for adjusting the bill correctly to indicate each employee covered, the appropriate premium tier, and the premium due. Upon receipt of the premium invoice, the client group reviews the bill for accuracy and notes additions, terminations, and changes in coverage on a group transmittal form. The group transmittal form adjusts the amount due to the health plan and is the basis upon which payment is made. This form is combined with a copy of the invoice, the payment, and any applicable change or enrollment forms and is returned to the HMO.

The second billing method is referred to as a retroactive billing method. Under this method the monthly invoice prepared by the HMO reflects additions, terminations, and changes in coverage type based on information previously received by the HMO. This method is considered preferable to the self-billing method because the bill automatically adjusts for retroactive changes in the enrollment system. A key element of the retroactive billing method is that the client must pay the amount of the invoice without making adjustments to the current bill. This requires effective communication with and education of the client's accounts payable function upon implementation of the contract.

The accounts receivable function should reconcile all billings on a monthly basis to ensure that premiums have been properly paid or credited by the client in accordance with the contract and that the HMO's enrollment records are accurate. Failure to maintain enrollment records accurately and in a timely manner may result in the HMO either providing services for members who are terminated or denying benefits for members who are properly enrolled. For certain large or government clients such as the Federal Employee Health Benefits Program (FEHBP), the HMO may receive a lump sum premium payment on a regular basis without supporting detail for the amount being paid. In these situations a semiannual enrollment reconciliation should be performed with the contracting office, at a minimum, to adjust the HMO's enrollment records to those of the client. Because of the vast number of enrollment changes that may occur each month from multiple government agencies, the investment in adequate staff resources to administer the billing and collection of these accounts is a fiscally responsible decision.

Coordination of Benefits

Another source of revenue for the HMO is coordination of benefits (COB). COB represents the portion of a member's medical benefits that is the liability of another insurance carrier or managed care plan. These situations arise when a member has two health care coverages in effect for the same period. This often occurs in two–wage-earner families where both the husband, through his employer, and the wife, through her employer, maintain family coverage. In COB situations, the HMO's enrollment records should contain information about other coverages applicable to the member. By coordinating the payment of services with the other carrier, duplicate payment for medical benefits is avoided.

There are two methods of handling COB: pursue and pay, and pay and pursue. Under the pursue and pay method, the HMO investigates the availability of other coverage and determines each carrier's liability before paying the claim. In this situation, the HMO does not actually receive income but rather avoids payment of a portion of claims where it is secondary. If the HMO is the primary carrier (ie, has initial liability for the claim), there is no avoidance of claims liability. The HMO would pay the claim as if there were no alternative coverage. Because the HMO is not actually receiving a cash reimbursement under the pursue and pay method, the identifica-

tion of the amount that was avoided is captured for management reporting and as an income statement convention. If revenues are to be included in the income statement under this method of COB, medical benefits expenses should reflect the total amount of the claim, not merely the net amount paid by the HMO.

The pay and pursue method requires the HMO to pay each claim as if it were the primary carrier and then seek reimbursement from the alternative carrier. If the HMO is determined to be primary, there is no liability to the HMO by the other carrier. If the HMO is secondary, the other carrier reimburses the HMO for its primary liability. This reimbursement should be reflected in the HMO's statements as income. No adjustment is necessary to the medical benefits expenses, which are recorded at the gross amount paid. COB is discussed further in Chapter 20.

Reinsurance Recoveries

To avoid the assumption of an inordinate amount of risk for medical benefits, and usually as a condition of state licensure, the HMO must maintain reinsurance. Reinsurance is insurance coverage that is purchased by the HMO as protection against catastrophic high-cost claims. The typical reinsurance agreement includes a deductible amount expressed on a per member per year basis. This deductible, which may be $50,000, for example, is the amount of medical benefits expense that the HMO must incur for each member each year before any reinsurance for that member is applicable. Once the deductible has been met, claims above the deductible are shared on a coinsurance basis, with the HMO paying a small portion (eg, 20%) and the reinsurer being responsible for the remainder, usually up to a limit (eg, $1 million per individual member per year).

The reinsurer charges the HMO a premium for the reinsurance coverage being provided. The amount of the premium is a function of the deductible, the coinsurance level, prior reinsurance claims experience, and the number of members enrolled in the health plan. As a general rule, the lower the deductible or HMO membership level, the higher the reinsurance premium. Reinsurance premiums are appropriately accounted for as medical benefits expenses and are discussed later.

Once the deductible has been met, the HMO receives a recovery, or reimbursement, from the reinsurer. These recoveries are typically paid once the actual liability of both parties can be determined. The HMO should reflect the total cost of the claims as medical benefits expense, because the HMO actually paid the claims, and should record the recovery from the reinsurer as revenue in its statements. As a note of caution, the HMO should only record recoveries when they have been adequately determined on the basis of actual benefits provided and should avoid establishing an accrual for recoveries until such time as the reinsurer has verified the amount recoverable. This will result in the timing of recoveries occurring later in the fiscal year than the payment of reinsurance premiums because claims must accumulate to exceed the deductible.

Other Income

A source of considerable revenue is interest income from cash and investments. Assuming that the plan has adequate reserves (and profits, if applicable), there should be considerable funds on hand. Also, contracts with providers of health care services typically allow the HMO a reasonable period of time (eg, 30 days) in which to pay claims. Because premiums from clients are billed and collectible in advance of the provision of benefits, the HMO can maximize interest earnings by collecting premiums on a timely basis. These earnings from interest and investments should be reflected as revenue in the HMO's statements.

MEDICAL BENEFITS

Within the HMO, medical benefits represent the greatest area of expense and encompass all the costs of providing health care services to the HMO's enrolled membership. For financial accounting and reporting purposes, the identification and proper categorization of the costs of providing health care services are critical to the successful operation of the HMO. Medical benefits are generally accounted for in the broad categories of inpatient services, outpatient services, physician services, other medical services, ancillary services, prescription drugs, reinsurance premiums, and other medical costs. Each of these categories is discussed in more detail.

Table 25-1 indicates the typical relationship of costs associated with the various categories of medical benefits within the HMO to each dollar of premium.

Inpatient Services

Inpatient services represent the largest single component of health care costs within the HMO. For financial accounting and reporting purposes, inpatient services are defined as the cost of providing services within an inpatient facility, typically a hospital. These costs include all facility charges, such as room and board, operating room, laboratory, radiology, and pharmacy, and other ancillary charges associated with the admission and treatment of a member in the hospital. The cost of supplies and surgical implants (eg, prosthetic devices such as artificial knees, hips, cochlear ear implants, and the like) provided to the patient during surgery is also in-

Table 25-1 Typical Health Plan Medical Costs*

Category	Percentage of Expense	
Hospital		
Inpatient	28	
Outpatient	11	
Total hospital		39
Physician services		
Primary care	12	
Specialty care	20	
Total physician services		32
Other medical services		5
Ancillary services		15
Prescription drugs		9
Total medical benefits expenses		100

*Based on $5 office copay benefit plan. Excludes reinsurance premiums.

Source: Data from *Milliman & Robertson Health Cost Guidelines,* Milliman & Robertson, Inc.

cluded in this category of medical benefits expenses.

Reimbursement Models

Inpatient services may be reimbursed under a number of different methods. In developing reimbursement arrangements for hospitals, the HMO seeks to obtain reasonable discounts in exchange for increased patient volumes as a result of the hospital's participation in the network. Many factors come into consideration during the negotiation of hospital discounts. These factors may include the services provided by the hospital, local competition among hospitals, the anticipated volume of patient days from HMO patients, and the community demand for services provided by the hospital.

Reimbursement models are discussed in detail in Chapter 8, and readers are urged to familiarize themselves with the different models for reimbursement that are discussed in that chapter. Exhibit 25-1 (adapted from Exhibit 8-1 in Chapter 8) lists some varieties of hospital reimbursement models that a managed care plan may use.

The HMO must keep the claims processing system in mind when developing inpatient reimbursement arrangements. It can be frustrating and disruptive to the negotiation process to discover, after rates have been finalized, that the

---

Exhibit 25-1 Models for Reimbursing Hospitals

- Charges
- Discounts
- Per diems
- Sliding scales for discounts and per diems
- Differential by day in hospital
- Diagnosis-related groups (DRGs)
- Differential by service type
- Case rates
    Institutional only
    Bundled
- Bed leasing
- Capitation or percentage of revenue
- Ambulatory patient groups (APGs) for outpatient care
- PIP and cash advances
- Penalties and withholds

---

claims system cannot handle the terms negotiated. This results in additional administrative burdens for the claims processing staff and increases the potential for incorrect payments to the hospital.

Capture and Reporting of Data

Once the inpatient reimbursement terms have been finalized, the HMO must have a system of capturing actual admissions and length of stay data for financial accounting and reporting purposes. The capture of admission and length of stay statistics is performed within the utilization management department. From inpatient authorization information, the utilization management department should be charged with the responsibility of compiling total admissions and days incurred each month. Inpatient utilization reporting should capture sufficient detail to provide finance with the number of admissions by type (ie, medical, surgical, pediatric, or maternity), total days incurred for these admissions, and the facility in which the days were incurred. In addition to reporting current month statistics on a routine basis, utilization management should continually update prior month utilization reports for retrospective cases identified in the current month that apply to previous months. Continual updating of inpatient statistics provides the finance staff with accurate and up-to-date information upon which to base expense accruals.

In addition to monthly reporting by utilization management, the HMO's management information system (MIS) should provide regular reporting of actual claims paid statistics. The most common method of reporting claims paid statistics is through system-generated lag reports. A lag report summarizes claims paid by the month of service and the month of payment. The lag report is so named because of the lag, or lapse of time, between when services are rendered (date of service) and when the HMO actually receives the billing for such services. Lag reports may be generated on the basis of date of service versus date of receipt, date of service versus date of payment, or date of receipt versus date of payment. The preferable lag report format is date of service versus date of receipt. With this method of lagging claims, variations in the HMO's claims processing backlogs (ie, amount of claims in process of payment) do not distort the lag reports.

The lag report is updated monthly for all claims paid during the current month, regardless of the month of service. By indicating the month of service on one axis and the month of payment on the other axis, the lag report develops a lag triangle. This lag triangle is the basis for developing completion factors for each month of service on the basis of historical patterns. These completion factors are then applied to the total claims for a specific month of service, paid as of the current date, to estimate the total incurred claim liability for that month. An example of a lag report is shown in Exhibit 25-2.

Calculation of Estimated Liability

Once the finance staff has received the inpatient reporting from utilization management and the lag reports, there are two methods of estimating inpatient expense for the current month. The first method is referred to as the specific inventory method. Under this method, the number of days incurred in the current month, by type of service and facility, is input into a worksheet containing historical cost per day data for each type of service within each facility. The average cost per day for each type of service and facility is derived by dividing the total number of days paid into the total amount paid. For example, current paid claims data indicate that 100 surgical days were paid for XYZ Hospital at a total cost of $80,000. Average cost per day for surgical admissions at XYZ Hospital is therefore $800 ($80,000 divided by 100).

A note of caution in calculating average cost per day. Because paid claims data are the basis for calculating average cost per day to be used in estimating liability, the number of days paid should be adjusted downward when COB results in payment of a portion of the claim by another carrier. For example, a claim was incurred for 5 days with total allowable charges of $5,000. During the processing of the claim, it was determined that the HMO was secondary and that the primary carrier's liability was $4,200. In this ex-

ample the claim would indicate an actual payment of $800 ($5,000 – $4,200). If the number of paid days is not adjusted, the calculation would derive an average cost per day of $160 ($800 divided by 5 days). When these data are combined with other paid claims data, the total average cost per day for all admissions would be understated. It is recommended that, where COB results in a secondary payment by the HMO, the claims processing function should adjust the number of paid days accordingly to reflect the plan's overall average cost per day. In the above example, the number of paid days would be adjusted in the claims system to 1 day (on the basis of plan average cost per day of $800).

Once the average cost per day for each type of service and facility has been multiplied by the days incurred for this type of service and facility, an inpatient liability per facility is calculated. These liability amounts are then summed to arrive at an overall inpatient liability based on days reported by utilization management. After the inpatient liability by facility has been estimated, a factor must be applied for incurred but not reported (IBNR) claims. IBNR represents claims that may have occurred but have not currently been identified to the utilization management staff. These claims could result from out-of-area emergency admissions, admissions that were not precertified because of failure of network providers to follow the HMO's guidelines, or incorrect insurance carrier information being given to the hospital at the time of admission. The IBNR factor represents an additional cushion that is built into the current liability to reserve for these claims. The IBNR factor is derived through historical analysis of paid admissions versus admissions reported by utilization management. The IBNR reserve is added to the estimated liability to arrive at the total expected inpatient liability for the current month. This total amount is reflected on the income statement as inpatient expense and on the balance sheet as a liability for inpatient claims.

The second method of estimating inpatient expense is through the use of completion factors derived from lag reports. Under this method, a historical completion factor is applied to the in-

Exhibit 25-2 Example of Lag Report

XYZ Corporation
Monthly Lag Report
For the period: January 1992–December 1992
As of: January 1, 1993

Inpatient Services
Claims Paid
Month of Receipt

Service Month	Jan	Feb	Mar	Apr	May	Jun	Jul	Aug	Sep	Oct	Nov	Dec	Total
January	10	100	150	50	35	2	1		1		4	1	354
February		7	126	164	44	22	1	1		6			371
March			24	89	201	33	46	53			5	1	452
April				12	109	177	3	25	2	2	1		331
May					1	188	156	45	59	3	4	2	458
June						3	255	189	67	55	4	1	574
July							9	163	198	84	54	8	516
August								33	127	199	87	62	608
September									27	244	149	88	508
October										17	155	205	377
November											5	104	109
December												12	12
Total	10	107	300	315	390	425	471	509	481	610	468	484	4570

Inpatient Services
Completion Factors
Month of Receipt

Service Month	Cur	+1	+2	+3	+4	+5	+6	+7	+8	+9	+10	+11
January	0.03	0.31	0.73	0.88	0.97	0.98	0.98	0.98	0.99	0.99	1.00	1.00
February	0.02	0.36	0.80	0.92	0.98	0.98	0.98	0.98	1.00	1.00	1.00	
March	0.05	0.25	0.69	0.77	0.87	0.99	0.99	0.99	1.00	1.00		
April	0.04	0.37	0.90	0.91	0.98	0.99	1.00	1.00	1.00			
May	0.00	0.41	0.75	0.85	0.98	0.99	1.00	1.00				
June	0.01	0.45	0.78	0.90	0.99	1.00	1.00					
July	0.02	0.33	0.72	0.88	0.98	1.00						
August	0.06	0.31	0.71	0.88	1.00							
September	0.05	0.53	0.83	1.00								
October	0.05	0.46	1.00									
November	0.05	1.00										
December	1.00											
Jan–Jun	0.02	0.36	0.78	0.87	0.96	0.99	0.99	0.99	1.00	1.00	1.00	1.00

Note: July–December claims considered incomplete for average factor calculation.

patient claims paid for current month dates of service to estimate the current month inpatient liability. This methodology has a number of deficiencies that make it less preferable than the specific inventory method. The first deficiency of the completion factor method for estimating inpatient liability is that inpatient utilization, measured in days per thousand,* can vary widely from month to month and year to year. These variations can result from seasonality (particular times of the year when inpatient admissions are higher, such as the first quarter of the calendar year) or from changes in the severity of patient admissions.

An additional deficiency in the completion factor method is that membership in the HMO may be increasing or decreasing rapidly. When membership is growing rapidly, such as at the beginning of the year, the ability of members to schedule elective admissions as quickly as possible may be delayed as a result of membership strains on the network. As membership decreases rapidly, the potential of a high-intensity case to affect adversely overall days per thousand is increased. The completion factor method also does not consider changes in inpatient expense reimbursement arrangements that may have occurred recently. Furthermore, if the plan experiences wide variations in claims processing (ie, significant and variable backlogs in claims), the completion factor becomes severely distorted because the degree of completion is related less to utilization than to inefficiencies in the claims department.

As a result of these deficiencies, the completion factor method should be used as a back-up to the inpatient liability calculated under the specific inventory method. Where the HMO is unable to track and report admission and days incurred data on a prospective basis because of systems or staffing limitations, the completion factor method should be used to calculate inpatient liability. In these situations, the lag reports and completion factors must be continually updated to avoid material misstatement of liabilities.

---

* Days per thousand, the number of inpatient days incurred per 1,000 members covered per year, is a standard measure of utilization.

Outpatient Services

Outpatient services are generally those institutional services provided to members of the HMO in lieu of inpatient services. These services are typically provided by hospitals or free-standing ambulatory surgery centers. For financial accounting and reporting purposes, the outpatient services category may include ambulatory surgery, laboratory and radiology services provided by the outpatient division of a hospital, emergency room charges, and charges associated with transportation by ambulance.

The portion of the medical benefits expense budget associated with providing outpatient services has grown rapidly in the past few years as hospitals seek to maximize revenues and as outpatient services receive greater recognition as an alternative to costly inpatient care. In recent years, as managed care plans have sought to avoid inpatient admissions and to reduce lengths of stay for patients, hospitals have experienced decreasing occupancy levels. Together with these decreasing occupancy levels for inpatient admissions, hospitals have seen significant increases in technology and the development of additional outpatient procedures. To recapture revenues lost as a result of decreasing inpatient volumes, charges for outpatient services have escalated rapidly.

Until recently, the prevalent method of reimbursing hospitals for outpatient services was on a discount from charges basis. Under this method, the hospital provides a discount off allowable charges to the HMO. Because of the recent escalation in charges for outpatient services, HMOs are taking a more proactive approach to negotiating with hospitals for the reimbursement of these services. Current reimbursement arrangements include case rates, global rates, and discount from charges with a maximum reimbursement limitation. Outpatient reimbursement models are discussed in detail in Chapter 8, and the reader is urged to become familiar with those models.

For financial accounting and reporting purposes, the timely analysis of trends in outpatient services utilization and cost is critical to the proper estimation of liabilities. With the use of data gathered through the precertification of ambulatory surgery by utilization management, reports indicating the number, type of ambulatory surgery, and facility at which the services are provided should be generated. Reports should be prepared on a monthly basis and provided to the finance staff when inpatient reports are prepared. In addition to reports of ambulatory surgery cases prepared by utilization management, lag reports should be generated in the same format as the lag reports for inpatient services.

As with the estimation of inpatient liabilities, the preferable method of estimating outpatient liability is through the specific identification of ambulatory surgery. This method, however, typically does not capture emergency room cases or laboratory and radiology services provided on an outpatient basis. To estimate outpatient liability properly, the HMO should use the completion factor method supplemented by the specific identification of ambulatory surgery by type and facility. The completion factor method is applied by using historical per member per month (PMPM) outpatient claims expense to estimate current month liability. In times of rapidly escalating charges for outpatient services, the calculation of the outpatient liability should be performed in a conservative manner. It is better to be conservative in the preparation of the HMO's financial statements than to be underaccrued as a result of incorrect estimation of outpatient expenses.

In preparing outpatient liability calculations, the finance staff should be aware of case management activities underway within utilization management. Through the use of case management techniques, utilization management arranges for high-quality, cost-effective alternatives to inpatient care. These alternatives often involve providing additional outpatient benefits for the member (eg, home health, home intravenous antibiotics, and so forth). If the HMO's case management activities have shown significant improvement recently, historical lag analyses will not reflect the increase in outpatient activity.

Physician Services

Within the HMO, the provision of medical services occurs through a network of physicians (both PCPs and specialists), hospitals, and other ancillary providers. Through the network of PCPs, care for members is coordinated to ensure that appropriate levels of service are given to treat members' medical conditions in a cost-effective and cost-efficient manner. The PCP, also referred to as a gatekeeper, manages the patient's care through referrals to specialists and other network ancillary providers such as laboratories, pharmacies, and radiology facilities.

Primary Care Services

By the very nature of its design, the HMO provides the greatest volume of routine care services through the PCP network. These services, however, are not nearly as costly on a per episode basis as services provided in an inpatient or outpatient setting. Even at a relatively lower cost, the high volume of physician services, both PCP and specialist, represents the largest combined component of medical benefits expense. This discussion focuses on the differences between the financial accounting and reporting of PCP services and those of specialty services and the unique attributes of each.

Primary care services are the focal point of a member's health care. As a result of the control that the PCP has over the provision of health care services in a cost-effective and cost-efficient manner, most HMOs structure PCP reimbursement arrangements in a manner so as to provide financial incentives for the achievement of these objectives. These arrangements typically involve an element of risk sharing between the PCP and the HMO. Within the risk-sharing mechanisms, the PCP is rewarded for good performance and penalized for poor performance.

A standard criticism of HMOs is that physicians are encouraged to withhold services because of risk-sharing mechanisms. Although there may be isolated instances in which physicians withhold care to receive a higher financial incentive, the HMO takes great care through quality assurance and medical management initiatives to identify and eliminate practices that compromise patient care. The competent HMO manager recognizes that the lowest-cost health care is not always the highest-quality care for the patient. In this regard the determination of good performance within a risk-sharing arrangement should not be based solely on the cost of care provided but also on the quality of the care. Underutilization of health care resources when they are necessary for the treatment of a member's medical condition usually results in higher long-term medical costs and membership turnover.

The topic of primary care reimbursement is discussed in detail in Chapter 6, and the reader is urged to become familiar with that chapter. Possible models for primary care reimbursement are illustrated in Exhibit 25-3.

Once the HMO has determined the reimbursement arrangement that best meets client needs, can be administered by the claims system, and is acceptable to PCPs, the finance staff must properly account for primary care expenses. The capitation model is the easiest one under which to project costs and estimate liabilities. The automated capitation payment system calculates total PCP capitation, withhold, referral pool allocations, hospital pool allocations, and stop-loss benefits on a monthly basis. PCP capitation is recorded as primary care expense when paid. Allocations to the referral pool are recorded as specialty care expenses when funded, and hospital pool allocations are recorded as hospital expenses when funded. Conversely, accruals to withhold, referral, and hospital pools should be recorded on the balance sheet as liabilities, with reduction of the liability balances as claims are paid. During the year end settlement, pool balances are cleared except for the amount needed for IBNR.

The estimation of liability under fee-for-service and global fee reimbursement systems uses the completion factor method. By using lag analyses and historical trends for primary care expenses, the HMO can project these expenses on a PMPM basis. In applying historical PMPM expense levels to current month activity, the financial manager must be aware of trends occurring within the medical delivery system. Questions to be considered are the following: Is inpatient utilization high in the current month (eg, because there are sicker patients requiring more services)? Has the HMO increased its fee schedule or global fees? Has the HMO recently allowed PCPs to bill for additional services? There may be various answers to all these questions, and therefore the estimation of primary care expenses under these reimbursement methods requires continual analysis of current and prior month trends. When the estimated liability is developed, primary care expense is recorded on the income statement with a corresponding liability on the balance sheet. As actual claims are paid, the net amount paid is charged against the liability account.

Specialty Care Services

Specialty care services represent those services provided to members by specialists upon referral by the PCP. These services range from consultations to surgeries and all levels of service in between. HMOs typically require the PCP to document a referral to a specialist, indicating the nature and extent of services to be performed. The referral document serves as the specialist's authorization to provide services to the member.

The prevalent method of reimbursing specialists is on a fee-for-service basis against the HMO's fee schedule, although other methods may be used (see Chapter 7 for a detailed discussion). The same fee schedule that is used for reimbursing PCPs under a fee-for-service reimbursement system contains current procedural terminology (CPT) codes and fee maximums for specialty services. Although specialty services are more intensive, and therefore higher cost, than PCP services, the volume of these services

---

Exhibit 25-3 Examples of Reimbursement Models for Primary Care

- Primary care capitation
  - —Variations by age and gender
  - —Variations by other factors
  - —Carve outs
- Capitation pools for referral and institutional services
- Withholds and risk/bonus arrangements
- Reinsurance and stop-loss or threshold protection
- Fee-for-service
  - —Withholds
  - —Risk-based adjustments to fee allowances
- Budgeted fee-for-service
- Sliding-scale individual fee allowances
- Global fees

is controlled by the PCP gatekeeper through the use of referrals.

As a result of the need for a referral for a specialist to receive payment from the HMO, churning (seeing a patient more often than is medically necessary) and upcoding (using procedure codes for which reimbursement is higher than for the procedure actually performed) are not as likely to occur as in an unmanaged fee-for-service environment. The potential for unbundling or exploding (creating new billing codes where one code was used in the past) is increased, however, because of the complexity of services being provided by the specialist. To protect the HMO against unbundled claims, global fees may be developed for certain specialty procedures. A common example of the use of specialty global fees is surgery. The surgeon typically conducts a preoperative consultation, performs the actual surgery, and provides postsurgery follow-up. Because the same physician is performing all services associated with the surgery, the HMO can pay a global rate that is all inclusive.

Expense estimation for specialty services follows the lag completion methodology as discussed above for a PCP fee-for-service system. An additional step that proves useful in estimating specialty care services is an inventory of referrals from PCPs. Because a copy of the referral is necessary to pay a specialty claim, referrals are typically received and entered into the HMO's authorization system before receipt of the specialist claim. By applying a historical average cost per specialist claim to the inventory, the finance staff can project specialty care expenses on the basis of the inventory level. The lag completion method and the referral inventory projection should be used in conjunction with one another to arrive at the estimate of expense. The same questions asked in estimating PCP expenses should be asked for specialty care expenses. As with other medical expense analyses, the finance staff should routinely monitor historical expense and utilization trends when developing expense estimations.

Other Medical Services

Other medical services include those services that are of such a specialized nature that they are beyond the gatekeeper management control of the PCP. This category usually includes such services as tubal ligations, abortions, vasectomies, maternity care, chemotherapy, hemodialysis, and perhaps large case management where the HMO has assumed the role of PCP to manage catastrophic cases directly. In all these instances, the PCP cannot exercise effective control over the length of treatment (eg, for chemotherapy or hemodialysis), nor can the PCP provide alternatives to accomplish the treatment of the condition (eg, for abortions or tubal ligations). Under a PCP capitation system, the HMO often absorbs the risk for these services instead of charging the claims against the PCP's referral pool.

As with other services provided by specialists, the typical reimbursement method for other medical services is a discount fee-for-service basis, although other methods may be used, as discussed elsewhere in this book. The fee schedule is applied to the particular services provided. The HMO should not be concerned with churning or upcoding for these services because of the nature of the condition being treated. The HMO should, however, be concerned with the potential for unbundling of charges and should follow the same review concepts as developed for other fee-for-service reimbursements.

Expense estimation for other medical services is consistent with the methodology used for specialty care services and does not require further discussion here. With the exception of maternity care and large case management, the incidence of other medical services is relatively low, and therefore this category usually does not present significant financial risk to the HMO.

Ancillary Services

Within the category of ancillary services, the HMO typically classifies those services that are subcontracted to highly specialized providers. Frequent examples of these types of services are laboratory, radiology, allergy, and mental health/substance abuse management. These are usually services or subspecialties for which the HMO provides a limited network or, in many instances, an exclusive provider for the entire membership. These services are often reimbursed on a capitated basis for the HMO to control costs and to share risk with the provider of the service. The provider will usually accept capitation and share in risk in exchange for being the exclusive provider of the service to the HMO's membership.

A typical example of this approach is the provision of laboratory services. As PCPs and specialists provide care to the HMO's members, the need for laboratory analyses arises frequently. Because the HMO cannot control the frequency of referral for laboratory services, the intent is to provide these services in the least costly manner. Laboratory services typically have a high profit margin built into the amount charged for the procedure. In addition, as discussed in Chapter 12, a growing number of physicians have a financial relationship with independent laboratories or other providers of ancillary services. To control the cost of these services, the HMO contracts with a reputable clinical reference laboratory that can provide services to the entire membership. By performing laboratory analyses at a central facility, the reference laboratory can manage the per unit cost of each analysis. The reference laboratory will usually provide aggressive capitation rates to gain entrée to the physicians' offices and to capture additional laboratory business that the physician is currently sending to competitors. The HMO gains by paying a fixed PMPM cost for these services, and the laboratory gains market share in a competitive arena.

As opposed to the disadvantage of PCP capitation, which does not pass savings back to self-funded clients, ancillary capitations are such a small portion of medical care expense that the financial impact of not capturing savings is immaterial. An aggressive laboratory capitation will usually represent less than 1% of total medical benefits expense. In addition to capitating providers for these services, the HMO may also reimburse the provider under a discount fee-for-service methodology. The methodology employed for estimating expense and liability should follow the same format as previously discussed for capitation (actual expense is known at time of payment) and fee-for-service arrangements (lag completion method).

Prescription Drugs

Providing prescription drug benefits for members represents an ever increasing percentage of the HMO's total medical benefits expense. With the rapid development of new drugs and the wide variation in the cost of medications, the HMO is at the mercy of the prescribing patterns of the PCPs and specialists. Within the limitations of a managed care environment, the HMO cannot practically intervene in each network and nonnetwork physician's prescribing patterns on a prospective basis.

In an effort to control the rapid escalation in the cost of providing prescription drug benefits, many HMOs are either developing or subcontracting with pharmacy management programs. These programs control costs through the implementation of formularies (a defined listing of medications that the HMO will cover), aggressive contracting with pharmacies, and manufacturers' rebate programs. Through aggressive negotiation of pharmacy contracts, the HMO may reimburse pharmacies at a percentage discount from the average wholesale price (AWP) plus a dispensing fee for each prescription filled. Maximum allowable charge (MAC) pricing is also effective at controlling reimbursement for prescriptions. In many instances, the pharmacy management company charges a capitated fee or per claim fee for administering the processing of pharmacy claims if the HMO claims system cannot handle pharmacy benefits administration. This fee is usually charged only for the membership with pharmacy benefits. Where the pharmacy management company has negotiated manufacturers' rebates, which flow through to the HMO, the HMO should use the rebates to offset the cost of administrative fees and pharmacy benefits charged to clients. This topic is discussed in detail in Chapter 14.

In developing liability estimates for prescription drug benefits, the lag completion methodology is employed. Lags for pharmacy claims are usually completed much more quickly than those for physician claims because most pharmacies process billings on a rapid basis. Pharmacies need to receive reimbursement in a timely manner as a result of the rapid turnover of medications. Because the payment of a pharmacy claim does not usually require matching with a referral, the HMO can process these claims in a batch mode. Prescription drug utilization is directly affected by factors such as the time of year (ie, seasonality), the prevalence of flu and cold epidemics, and the termination of a member's contract period. It is not unusual to experience a dramatic rise in the number of prescriptions filled (or, more commonly, refilled) near the end of the calendar year as members prepare for changes in health care benefits. For example, if a member of the HMO can receive a prescription refill for a $5 copayment and the employer is switching coverage from the HMO to an indemnity plan with a deductible and coinsurance, it is to the member's financial benefit to have prescriptions refilled at $5 each before December 31 rather than incur the deductible and coinsurance on or after January 1 of the next year. This phenomenon is sometimes referred to in the HMO industry as the end-of-year run on the bank. Each of these factors should be considered when one is estimating liability for prescription drugs.

Reinsurance Premiums

As discussed earlier, reinsurance premiums represent the amount paid to the reinsurer in exchange for providing reinsurance against catastrophic claim costs for members. Because reinsurance recoveries are an offset to medical benefits expenses, reinsurance premiums are considered benefits expenses. Reinsurance premiums are typically paid monthly as a PMPM based on total HMO membership. Reinsurance premiums should be recorded as expenses when paid.

Calculation of Estimated Liability

As indicated in the above discussion of the financial accounting for medical benefits expenses, the monthly calculation of liabilities and expenses is a complex process. There is no exact science to the estimation of IBNR balances needed to cover outstanding claims. Therefore, the financial staff must ask a number of practical

questions as the monthly financial statements are prepared:

- Are claims backlogs being maintained at a stable rate? If not, what is the impact on lag reports and completion factors of the changes in backlog volumes?
- Do current month trends vary widely from prior months? If so, what are the underlying reasons for the variances?
- Does the finance staff have confidence in utilization reports prepared by the utilization management department and in system-generated analyses? If not, what additional analyses are needed to obtain comfort in the reported data?
- Is the HMO experiencing rapid membership growth, or has a large account recently terminated? If so, what is the impact on benefits expenses?

The most important question of all is: Does the combination of claims data, trend analyses, and the total benefits expense calculation pass the nose test? In other words, does the result smell right to an experienced manager? This is a difficult question to answer and requires that the finance staff work in concert with the medical management, claims, and management information system departments to understand and interpret the costs of providing medical benefits for the HMO's membership.

ADMINISTRATIVE EXPENSES

Administrative expenses for an HMO encompass all expenses, from lease expense for administrative offices to salaries and benefits to normal business supplies, incurred by the HMO in administering medical benefits provided to members. Within the HMO environment, accounting and reporting for administrative expenses follows standard financial accounting and reporting practices under generally accepted accounting practices (GAAP). The classification of administrative expenses for HMOs may vary depending on the model of the HMO. An independent practice association (IPA) model HMO provides for the delivery of health care services through a network of independently contracted providers. A staff model HMO employs its own primary care and specialist physicians and provides services within its own medical facilities. The differences in administrative expense classification are touched on during this general discussion.

An HMO usually groups administrative expenses into five broad categories: occupancy, administration, sales and marketing, medical management, and other expenses. The actual classification of expenses may be different for an HMO that wants to concentrate on certain administrative expense areas or has additional financial reporting needs.

Occupancy expenses typically include the cost of space occupied and equipment used for the HMO's operations. In the IPA environment, occupancy includes rent, maintenance, utilities, and depreciation expenses for furniture, fixtures, and computer equipment. Because the staff model actually provides health care services, there are also expenses associated with the depreciation of medical equipment such as X-ray machines.

Administration typically includes salaries and benefits, office supplies, travel and entertainment, and all other related expenses associated with departments that service the HMO's membership. These departments usually include executive staff, customer services, claims, human resources, finance, rating and underwriting, and management information systems.

The sales and marketing category includes all expenses associated with the selling of the HMO's products. Sales staff salaries and benefits, commissions, travel and entertainment, advertising, and public relations are usually included in this classification. Printing costs associated with open enrollment materials and marketing brochures are also included in this category.

Medical management comprises those areas that administer the provision of health care benefits. This generally includes the medical director(s) and the areas of utilization management, quality assurance, provider relations, and physician advisors.

Other expenses include items such as interest expense, intercompany allocations (if appli-

cable), and other items of expense that are not classified under one of the above categories.

In accounting and reporting for administrative expenses, the finance staff must have a thorough understanding of state and federal regulatory reporting requirements. A good source of information regarding the classification of HMO administrative expenses is included in the definitions for the annual statutory reporting form known as the orange book (so called because of the color of the report cover). In addition to regulatory requirements, certain client contracts such as the FEHBP may require detailed accounting for the cost associated with administering the group's specific benefits. Under FEHBP regulations, allocation to the contract of certain administrative expenses such as advertising, marketing, and interest expense may not be allowable for experience rated plans. These special requirements should be carefully researched and understood before the HMO's financial accounting and reporting systems are developed. The FEHBP is discussed in Chapter 27.

FINANCIAL REPORTING

A comprehensive monthly report of the HMO's operations provides management with the tools necessary to measure the achievement of business objectives. The responsibility for producing this monthly report of operations (or monthly operating report) falls within the scope of responsibility of the finance staff. HMO management relies on monthly financial reports to identify positive or negative trends in membership, revenues, medical benefits expenses, and administrative expenses. Through the early identification of trends that negatively affect the HMO's financial performance, management can undertake corrective actions to reduce financial exposures and enhance the HMO's bottom line.

The monthly report of operations should include income statements expressed in whole dollars and in PMPM. Although the whole dollar income statement is useful for showing overall financial results, the PMPM income statement is useful for analyzing the HMO's revenues and expenses in terms of the number of members enrolled. The income statements should provide line item detail for each of the medical benefits expense categories discussed above. In addition to the detail of medical benefits expenses, analyses of inpatient utilization levels (days per thousand) and cost (cost per day) trends as well as utilization and cost trends in outpatient services should be provided. The monthly balance sheet should provide detail on cash and investments, accounts receivable, restricted assets (ie, monies on deposit with regulatory agencies), medical liability balances, accounts payable, risk pool liability balances, debt, and net worth. Additional analyses of staffing levels, enrollment trending, and net worth are also recommended in a comprehensive monthly operating report prepared for management.

STATUTORY REPORTING

Because of the nature of an HMO's operations, providing health care services to enrolled members, the HMO industry is heavily regulated. Each state has a unique set of laws and regulations that govern the practices of HMOs (see Chapter 34). Through oversight functions within state regulatory agencies, the financial condition of HMOs is closely monitored. The ability of an HMO to meet its financial obligations on a timely basis protects members and providers from financial detriment. In addition to strict financial reporting requirements, states typically require that HMOs maintain deposits with the state treasurer and that insolvency protection be available to members in the event of an HMO failure. Most states require that HMO provider contracts include hold harmless language that precludes the provider of services from billing the member for claims that are the responsibility of the HMO (see Chapter 36). The absence of hold harmless language in provider contracts usually results in higher minimum net worth requirements for the HMO.

Quarterly and annual reporting to state regulatory agencies requires the use of statutory accounting practices (SAP). Under this type of reporting, emphasis is placed on the liquidity of the HMO. This reporting adjusts the HMO's net worth for nonadmitted assets such as premium receivables over 90 days old, intercompany re-

ceivables over 90 days old, and certain fixed assets such as software and computer hardware. Statutory reporting requirements may vary by state and should be researched thoroughly in the applicable HMO regulations for a particular state.

The standard form for reporting to state regulatory agencies is the orange book developed by the National Association of Insurance Commissioners (NAIC). The orange book consists of an income statement, balance sheet, statement of changes in financial position, schedule of enrollment and utilization, and various other schedules covering assets, liabilities, and net worth. In addition to financial schedules, the orange book includes a set of questions (interrogatories) about the HMO's bylaws, contracts, and operations. On a quarterly basis, most states require a portion of the orange book, usually the income statement, balance sheet, statement of changes in financial position, and enrollment and utilization schedule, to be filed within 45 days of the end of the calendar quarter. The full orange book is usually required to be filed on an annual basis by March 1. Together with the filing of this annual statement, many states require certification from an independent actuary attesting to the adequacy of the HMO's medical liabilities.

Federally qualified HMOs (see Chapter 35) and competitive medical plans (CMPs) with Medicare contracts (see Chapters 28 and 35) are also required to file quarterly and annual statutory statements with federal regulatory agencies. Federally qualified HMOs use the same orange book format for reporting to federal agencies. The financial manager of a federally qualified HMO should become familiar with federal regulatory reporting requirements.

BUDGET DEVELOPMENT

On an annual basis, the HMO should develop a comprehensive budget and business plan for the coming year. The budgeting and business planning process provides an excellent opportunity for the HMO's management to establish the company's future strategic direction. The budgeting and business planning process should include management from all operations and sales divisions within the HMO. Through a coordinated planning process, HMO management can communicate the corporate mission and objectives down to all employees within the organization.

The preferable budgeting and business planning process involves the development of a bottoms-up budget that promotes accountability among managers for the HMO's financial results and encourages active participation in the planning process. In the bottoms-up budget development process, the finance staff provides each department manager with the tools necessary to develop a comprehensive detailed administrative expense budget for his or her department. These tools may include standard expense assumptions for occupancy, supplies, insurance, utilities, and employee benefits expenses. These standard assumptions are usually developed on a full-time equivalent (FTE) basis so that the manager can calculate the total detailed administrative expenses for the department on the basis of staffing projections.

To prepare staffing projections, the sales and marketing division must have completed enrollment projections. These enrollment projections should provide detail of total enrollment by month for the budget period. As these enrollment projections are prepared, the sales and marketing division should coordinate the development of revenue budgets with the rating and underwriting staff to ensure consistency with underwriting guidelines and rate filings. The budgeting process may include the development of specific revenue and membership projections for each of the HMO's top 20 groups and aggregate projections for the HMO's remaining business.

Once enrollment and revenue projections are developed, each department manager must project the number of employees needed to service these projected enrollment volumes. In departments such as claims, customer services, and medical management, the estimation of staffing levels may be based on established ratios of service representatives to members. These ratios are usually presented as the number of FTEs per thousand members. Staffing ratios should consider changes occurring within the benefit plans marketed by the HMO. As a general rule, the more complex the benefit plan offering (eg, point of service), the more labor intensive the administration of the product.

In addition to developing detailed administrative expense budgets, each department should project its capital equipment needs for the coming year. These capital budgets help the management information system and finance departments project fixed asset and hardware requirements as membership and staffing levels increase.

Special consideration needs to be given to budgeting marketing expenses. Many marketing costs such as advertising and printing enrollment kits, special inserts, and brochures are seasonal in nature. Substantial costs are incurred in the fall and spring coincident with the heavy open enrollment seasons. The HMO needs to decide whether such expenses will be budgeted on a straight line basis (ie, spread across the entire year) or when the HMO actually expects to incur the cost. If the straight line approach is used, the HMO must consider accruing the expense as the year goes along rather than facing several months with significant expense deficits.

After each department submits its detailed staffing, administrative expense, and capital expenditures budget, the finance staff is charged with the responsibility of compiling these budgets into the HMO budget. The finance staff usually works with the medical management and management information system departments to develop medical benefits utilization and cost targets for the budget period. Where the HMO is experiencing historical seasonality trends, these factors may be applied when medical benefits budget targets are compiled. The finance staff should also prepare pro forma balance sheets, net worth projections, and cash requirements schedules as part of the budget process.

FORECASTING AND PROJECTING FINANCIAL RESULTS

The budget provides a framework for measuring the HMO's performance against established targets at regular intervals. In conjunction with the preparation of monthly reports of financial results, the HMO should prepare current year forecasts for the balance of the year. These forecasts serve as management tools for making midyear corrections in the HMO's operations. These forecasts also serve as tools to drive the decision-making process for benefit and marketing decisions. Where forecasts indicate significant negative variances in operational results, contingency planning should take place within the HMO.

In addition to current year forecasting, the HMO should prepare pro forma (ie, "what if") projections on a quarterly basis. These projections may involve any number of years into the future and should provide detailed assumptions about enrollment growth, revenue trends, medical benefits trends, administrative expense trends, and cash and net worth requirements.

CONCLUSION

As evidenced by this discussion of operational finance and budgeting for the HMO, the proper and timely accounting for revenues and expenses not only makes good management sense but is required by regulatory agencies. As the HMO manager gains experience with the development of medical expense liabilities, the ability to anticipate and adjust for adverse financial results allows the HMO to continue as a going concern and to achieve positive financial performance.

Chapter 26

Rating and Underwriting

Gregory N. Herrle

One of the more important requirements for a managed health care plan is to appropriately assess risks and establish adequate revenue to ensure the financial viability of the plan. To remain a viable entity over time, the health plan must obtain revenues that exceed expenditures by a large enough margin to support the plan's growth and risk assumption. The functions of rating and underwriting include the assessment of risk and the pricing of that risk.

These functions can be separated into three general areas:

1. establishing planwide medical cost and revenue targets or budgets
2. underwriting or selecting risk (eg, groups and/or individuals)
3. setting the premium for a specific risk

MEDICAL COST AND REVENUE TARGETS

The first step of the rating process is to establish overall medical cost and revenue targets for the managed care plan. These targets generally vary by product line (eg, large group, small group, Medicaid, Medicare, and direct pay) and by benefit plan within product line. Unique targets may be established for distinct geographic areas. Most managed care plans express their medical cost and revenue targets on a per capita or per member per month (PMPM) basis. The PMPM targets are generally established for a specific time period (eg, a calendar year or for groups effective on January 1). The overall PMPM revenue target is then converted to group-specific premiums (eg, single or family) with the use of one of the rating methodologies noted later in this chapter.

The following steps are generally used to develop a PMPM revenue target for a particular product line and effective date.

Summarize and Review Historical Plan Experience

The development of medical cost targets starts with a review of a plan's historical utilization, average charge, and average cost PMPM experience for a particular base experience period. Generally the most recent 12-month period of credible data is selected as the base experience period, although longer time periods may be used. Shorter experience periods are generally not used because of the potential for seasonal fluctuations in claims levels.

Gregory N. Herrle, FSA, is a Principal and Consulting Actuary with the Milwaukee office of Milliman & Robertson, Inc. His area of expertise is managed health care programs. He has assisted clients in the areas of product development, delivery system design and evaluation, experience analysis, health care management, and actuarial projections.

The experience data may vary depending on the structure of the managed care plan. Some plans are claims based, others use capitations, and some actually own their own facilities (eg, staff model health maintenance organizations). The process of summarizing and projecting experience data will vary depending on the plan's structure. The example provided in this discussion is representative of a claims-based delivery system.

It is useful to summarize a managed health care plan's experience data in detail by medical service category. An example of these summary data is shown in Table 26-1.

This detailed summary allows the actuary to assess the reasonableness of the experience, to review historical trends (if the information is presented for different time periods), and to verify the accuracy of the data. Utilization rates per 1,000 members per year, average charges per service, and cost PMPM should be collected. The impact of any member cost sharing should also be shown. This detail is also needed to price various benefit plans where member cost sharing varies by plan.

It is extremely important to assess the credibility of the data after the experience data are summarized. Exhibit 26-1 illustrates some of the questions that should be considered. Generally the information in Table 26-1 is summarized for a 12-month period, based on dates of service, with claims paid for some period beyond the 12 months of service (eg, January through December dates of service with claim payments through the following March). It is common for a portion of claims incurred during the 12 month experience period to be unreported and/or unpaid at the time the experience is summarized. The paid cost PMPM may be understated by claims that are incurred but not yet paid. Therefore, the utilization and cost PMPM experience data should be adjusted upward to reflect any estimated understatement.

It is also important to note the environmental characteristics of the plan during the experience period so that the claims experience can be evaluated in light of those characteristics. Some of the items to consider include membership growth, provider contracts, utilization manage-ment procedures, large claim or stop-loss experience, administrative policies (eg, coordination of benefits recoveries), and benefit levels.

Trend Historical Experience

In the claims-based example, the historical experience should be trended from the midpoint of the 12-month experience period to the midpoint of the rating period, which is also generally a 12-month period. The trending concept is shown in Figure 26-1. The selection of the trend assumption is quite critical because there is often

---

Exhibit 26-1 Experience Data Questions

- Data source?
- Reliability: Consistent with financial information?
- Date of service based?
- Claims paid through what date?
- How are the following items reflected in data?
  —Coordination of benefits (COB) recoveries
  —Stop-loss claims
  —Provider discounts (billed versus paid charges)
  —Member cost sharing
  —Provider withholds
  —Capitated services
- Definition of medical service categories
- Definition of referral and encounter services
- How are hospital and physician charges repre-sented (eg, billed charges, fee schedule, fee maxi-mum)?
- Are any services or costs excluded?
- Reasonableness of results by calendar quarter; are any data problems indicated (eg, missing data, in-correct enrollment)?
- General reasonableness of utilization rates, aver-age charge per service, and PMPM cost relative to industry experience
- Comparison of multiple group/network experi-ence within a given service area
- Comparison of enrollment data to other enroll-ment data sources within plan
- Review of historical data for underlying trends in utilization or charges; can trends be explained (eg, medical management or benefit changes, enroll-ment growth, administrative changes)? How do trends compare to competitors, industry, or expec-tations?
- Is enrollment large enough for data to be credible?
- Other reasons why historical data may not be ap-propriate predictors of future year experience

Table 26-1 Example of Experience Data

Benefit	Utilization per 1000	Allowed Average Charge ($)	Per Capita Monthly Claim Cost ($)
Hospital inpatient			
Medical	119 days	949.92	9.42
Surgical	98 days	1,146.80	9.37
Psychiatric	43 days	558.94	2.00
Alcohol and drug	23 days	410.30	0.79
Maternity	40 days	948.33	3.16
Extended care	3 days	176.42	0.04
Total	326 days		24.78
Hospital outpatient			
Emergency department	132 visits	139.38	1.53
Surgery	76 visits	1,273.03	8.06
Other outpatient services	352 services	129.43	3.81
Maternity, nondelivery	5.2 cases	390.14	0.17
Total			13.57
Physician			
Inpatient surgery	35 procedures	890.77	2.60
Outpatient surgery	343 procedures	170.93	4.89
Anesthesia	59 procedures	746.44	3.67
Inpatient visits	271 visits	34.69	0.78
Office visits	3,765 visits	27.42	8.60
Consults	98 consults	51.23	0.42
Emergency department visits	125 visits	19.57	0.20
Immunizations and injections	531 procedures	11.87	0.53
Allergy tests and injections	271 procedures	10.99	0.25
Well-baby examinations	104 examinations	24.70	0.21
Physical examinations (physician)	190 examinations	28.59	0.45
Vision, hearing, speech examinations	421 examinations	21.66	0.76
Physical therapy	308 visits	23.85	0.61
Obstetrics, deliveries	15.5 cases	1,512.34	1.95
Obstetrics, nondeliveries	9.3 cases	333.36	0.26
Radiology	800 procedures	111.58	7.44
Pathology	2,041 procedures	31.84	5.42
Outpatient mental health	358 visits	41.41	1.24
Outpatient substance abuse	37 visits	38.58	0.12
Miscellaneous medicine	238 procedures	58.99	1.17
Total			41.57
Other			
Home health care	26 visits	214.76	0.47
Ambulance	14 runs	303.41	0.35
Durable medical equipment/prosthetics	34 units	261.48	0.74
Total			1.56
Total medical costs			81.48

an 18- to 24-month difference between the midpoints of the experience period and the rating period. Exhibit 26-2 lists some of the issues to consider when one is establishing a trend assumption. Consideration should be given to both utilization and cost trends.

Adjust Projected Medical Costs

Adjust the projected medical costs for any anticipated changes in underwriting policy, utilization management, provider contracts, benefits, and administrative policies between the experi-

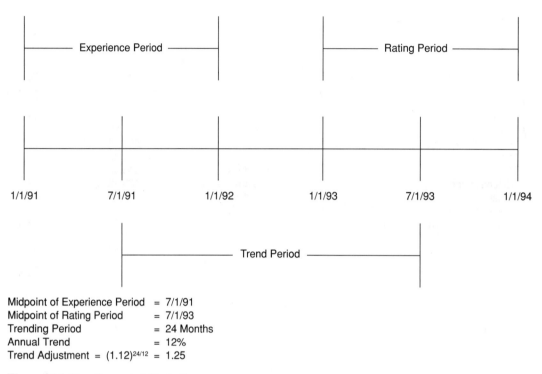

Midpoint of Experience Period = 7/1/91
Midpoint of Rating Period = 7/1/93
Trending Period = 24 Months
Annual Trend = 12%
Trend Adjustment = $(1.12)^{24/12}$ = 1.25

Figure 26-1 Trending period illustration.

ence period and the rating period. All functions of a health plan, including marketing, finance, utilization management, claims, provider contracting, and operations, should be involved in this segment of the rating process.

Develop per Member per Month Revenue Target

Develop the PMPM revenue target by adding the value of administrative expenses, risk or profit margins, state premium taxes, minimum state surplus requirements, and the net cost of reinsurance (ie, the difference between reinsurance premiums and expected recoveries) to the projected medical costs. The values of these items are generally expressed as PMPM values or as percentages of total revenue.

A simplified illustration of the trend and administrative loads is shown in Table 26-2. The trends in Table 26-2 are applied only to the medical service category subtotals in Table 26-1. In reality, trend adjustments would be applied to each of the medical service categories in Table 26-1.

Convert per Member per Month Revenue Target to Contract Premiums

Convert the PMPM revenue target to contract premiums (eg, single and family). The form of this conversion will depend on the type of group-specific rating method employed by the managed health care plan.

An example of the premium conversion process is illustrated in Exhibit 26-3 and is based on the experience period mix of contracts, average members per contract, and the targeted premium relationships (eg, the family premium is targeted at 2.7 times the single premium) shown.

UNDERWRITING

Underwriting can be defined as the process used to make judgments regarding the risk associated with enrolling a specific employer group or individual member in a managed health care program. This risk assessment leads to the establishment of a premium rate to be charged to the

Exhibit 26-2 Trend Considerations

Utilization
- Expected fee-for-service trends in the plan's service area
- The plan's historical utilization trends
- The age of the plan
- Changes in underwriting guidelines
- Changes in benefit levels or member cost sharing
- Changes in the plan's utilization management program
- Changes in the plan's delivery system or in the risk-sharing arrangements with the plan's providers

Charges
- Expected fee-for-service trends in the plan's service area
- The plan's average charge trends
- Expected changes in utilization (eg, a decrease in hospital inpatient utilization may result in higher average charges per inpatient day as a result of increasing intensity of service)
- The structure of provider contracts (eg, per diem arrangements may be expected to have different trends than discount arrangements)
- Anticipated changes in provider contracts (eg, negotiated per diems) or in the structure of the contract (eg, per diems versus discounts)

group or individual. The health care plan must ensure that a broad cross-section of risk is enrolled (ie, avoid adverse selection) to remain competitive and viable over time.

Exhibit 26-3 Community Rating Example

Medical costs PMPM	$ 90
Administrative costs PMPM	10
Revenue PMPM	$100

Contract Type	Plan Contract Mix	Plan Members per Contract	Standard Premium Loads
Single	40%	1.00	1.00
Family	60%	3.00	2.60
Total	100%	2.20	1.96

Single/per member
conversion factor $= 2.20 \div 1.96 = 1.12$
Premiums $= \$100 \times 1.12 \times 1.00 = \$112.00$
Family $= \$100 \times 1.12 \times 2.60 = \$291.20$

Traditionally, underwriting has been an integral part of insurance carrier and managed care plans. Underwriting affects the plan's:

- overall level of claims experienced
- competitive position in the marketplace
- ability to offer alternative premium rates to larger groups with better than average experience
- penetration levels in employer groups (eg, lower rates may result in lower employee

Table 26-2 Simplified Revenue Target Example

Service Category	Experience Period Paid Claims (7/1/91)	Unpaid Claims Adjustment	Adjustments*	Trends	Gross Rating Period Targets (7/1/93)	PMPM Copayment Value	Net Rating Period Targets
Hospital inpatient	$24.78	÷ 0.95	× 0.90	× (1.10)²	= $ 28.41	− $0.00	= $ 28.41
Hospital outpatient	13.57	÷ 0.95	× 1.05	× (1.15)²	= 19.84	− 0.30	= 19.54
Physician services	41.57	÷ 0.93	× 1.00	× (1.07)²	= 51.18	− 0.50	= 50.68
Other services	1.56	÷ 0.97	× 1.00	× (1.12)²	= 2.02	− 0.00	= 2.02
Total medical costs	81.48				101.45	− 0.80	= 100.65
COB recoveries							(1.50)
Net cost of reinsurance							0.40
Administration (100%)							11.71
Profit margin (3%)							3.51
Risk margin (2%)							2.34
Revenue target							$117.11

*Changes in utilization management, underwriting policy, provider contracts, and the like.

contribution rates, increased penetration, and better risk selection)

- relationship with providers, if provider satisfaction with capitation or other risk-based payments is improved
- financial performance

Some of the factors that affect a plan's risk selection include the following:

- the criteria used to select employer groups for coverage. These criteria may include definitions of eligible groups, eligible employees and dependents, minimum participation requirements, the data and information required to quote a group, coverage limitations, effective dates of coverage, and maximum rate and benefit differentials in open enrollment situations.
- benefit design. High relative benefits tend to attract higher relative risks.
- rate level and methods. High relative premiums or employee out-of-pocket contributions tend to attract higher relative risks.
- marketing and sales approach.
- the size, type, and perception of the provider network. Higher relative risks may be attracted to larger, more loosely controlled networks.
- utilization management. Aggressive utilization management programs hold costs down, which tends to lower premiums and improve selection. Strong utilization management programs may also be less attractive to high utilizers of health care services.
- an employee's out-of-pocket premium contribution. This can greatly affect a plan's risk selection, especially in an open enrollment situation.
- administration policies, to the extent that they affect a plan's costs.

Underwriting practices typically vary by type of market. Large employer groups are generally underwritten on the basis of their financial stability, history with other health plans, and certain participation requirements. Generally all employees and dependents of large groups are guaranteed coverage.

Underwriting practices in the small employer market have historically relied more on medical underwriting, the practice of basing coverage on the health history of prospective members. Traditional insurance carrier underwriting practices have caused considerable controversy among consumers, regulators, legislators, and small employers. In response to this controversy, the National Association of Insurance Commissioners adopted model small group reform legislation in 1990 and 1991 that restricts some of the underwriting and rating practices in the small group market. The ultimate fate of small group market reform on the state or federal level is unknown at the time of this writing.

Once the health plan's PMPM revenue target is established, it is generally converted to unique contract premiums on a group-by-group basis. Some of the common rating methods used by managed health care plans include community rating, community rating by class, and experience rating (adjusted community- or group-specific community rating). A specific rating method used for a group should be:

- adequate, so that total revenue covers all expenses and contributes to the health plan's profit or surplus
- competitive, to maximize penetration in an account
- predictable, to minimize year-to-year rate fluctuations
- flexible, so that the method can be adaptable to different types of groups
- simple and easy to explain and administer
- equitable, so that each group pays its fair share
- legal and in compliance with applicable state and federal regulations

The various rating methods attain these goals in different degrees. A brief description of some common group-specific rating methods follows.

Community Rating

Community rating develops group-specific rates by using the health plan's overall revenue targets and membership. The unique characteristics of a group are generally not reflected. Community rates may be expressed as a common revenue PMPM, revenue per contract, or community rate structure (eg, single and family premiums). Under pure community rating each group would receive rates designed to produce the selected plan community rating target.

Examples of these types of community rating targets are illustrated in Exhibit 26-3. Community rates can be expressed as:

- rate PMPM (eg, $100)
- rate per contract (eg, $220 = 2.20 × $100)
- rate per contract category (e.g., $112 single, $291.20 family)

Community Rating by Class

Community rating by class uses the health plan's overall revenue targets and a group's unique risk characteristics relative to the health plan's average risk characteristics to establish group-specific rates. Examples of these risk characteristics may include:

- employer industry classification
- subscriber or member age
- subscriber or member sex
- contract type (eg, single or family)
- subscriber or member health status (eg, smoker or nonsmoker)
- employees' average family size

The purpose of community rating by class is to establish a group's rates to approximate more nearly the risk associated with the group. A group's actual experience is not used, only its risk characteristics (eg, age/sex and industry). Illustrative age and sex factors are shown in Table 26-3. These factors reflect the expected revenue requirement for an employee of a particular age, sex, and contract status relative to the health plan's overall PMPM revenue target. For example, the expected revenue for a single male employee younger than 30 years is 50% (ie, 0.5) of the health plan's average PMPM revenue target.

An illustrative community rating by class calculation for a single contract is shown in Exhibit 26-4 and uses the age/sex factors given in Table

26-3. A similar calculation can be made of the family premium. Community rating by class will result in more rate variability than community rating.

Experience Rating

Experience rating develops claims costs and establishes revenue targets on the basis of a group's actual experience. Experience rating methods may rely on actual claims costs, utilization statistics (also known as group-specific community rating or adjusted community rating), loss ratios, or some combination of these approaches.

Health plans experience rate for a number of reasons: because employers want it, to compete more effectively among larger groups, as a defensive measure (because the competition is already doing it), and to reduce the variability in the health plan's profits by group. Nevertheless, there are some limitations to consider about experience rating:

- Reliable and timely information is needed by group.
- It takes more time, effort, and expertise to administer.
- Experience rating is not appropriate for all groups.
- The health plan may have to provide experience data to the group to explain the renewal rate.

A simplified example of claims-based experience rating is shown in Exhibit 26-5. The process and considerations are somewhat similar to those used in establishing the health plan's over-

Table 26-3 Illustrative Age/Sex Factors

Employee Age (years)	Single		Family	
	Male	Female	Male	Female
Younger than 30	0.5	1.2	2.9	2.8
30–39	0.7	1.3	2.8	2.6
40–49	1.0	1.4	2.7	2.5
50–59	1.4	1.5	2.9	3.1
60+	1.9	1.8	3.4	3.5

Exhibit 26-4 Community Rating by Class Example

Health plan PMPM revenue target = $100

Employee Age (years)	Single Male	Single Female	Family Male	Family Female
Under 30	5	6	7	5
30–39	4	5	6	4
40–49	3	4	5	3
50–59	2	3	4	2
60+	1	2	3	1
Total	15	20	25	15

Group's single

$$
\begin{aligned}
\text{premium} &= \$100 \times [(5 \times 0.5) + (4 \times 0.7) \\
&\quad + (3 \times 1.0) + (2 \times 1.4) + (1 \times 1.9) \\
&\quad + (6 \times 1.2) + (5 \times 1.3) + (4 \times 1.4) \\
&\quad + (3 \times 1.5) + (2 \times 1.8)] \div (15 + 20) \\
&= \$100 \times (40.4 \div 35) \\
&= \$100 \times 1.15 \\
&= \$115
\end{aligned}
$$

Exhibit 26-5 Simplified Experience Rating Example

Category	Year t	Year t−1
Paid claims PMPM	$68.00	$50.00
Incurred claims PMPM	82.00	65.00
Pooling charge PMPM	8.00	7.00
Pooled claims	(10.00)	(2.00)
Actual claims charged (2 + 3 + 4)	80.00	70.00
Plan average	$75.00	$60.00
Experience ratio (5 ÷ 6)	1.07	1.17
Credibility	60%	20%

Plan PMPM
revenue target = $100

Group's PMPM

$$
\begin{aligned}
\text{revenue target} &= \$100 \times [(1.07 \times 0.60) + (1.17 \times \\
&\quad 0.20) + (1.00 \times 0.20)] \\
&= \$100 \times 1.08 \\
&= \$108
\end{aligned}
$$

Note: t = most recent year
t–1 = one year earlier than t

all revenue target except that the approach is applied to a single group.

Exhibit 26-5 illustrates the use of multiple years of experience, credibility, and claims pooling. An important issue regarding experience rating is whether a group's historical experience is a reliable predictor of the group's future experience. The reliability of past experience will vary with the following:

- the size of the employer group. The experience of larger groups is generally more credible than that of smaller groups.
- the health plan's penetration in the employer group. The whole group's experience is relatively more credible than that of a portion of the group.
- the presence of large shock loss claims. Higher or lower than expected claims can distort a group's experience.
- the stability of the market environment. Stable enrollment and benefits make a group's historical experience more reliable.

Multiple years of experience are often used as the basis for projecting future experience to minimize the fluctuations that may occur in a group's year-to-year claims experience. Different credibility levels may be assigned to each year of experience. Generally, more credibility is given to the most recent experience.

Large claims (eg, the portion of claims in excess of $30,000 per member per year) may also be removed from the group's historical experience to minimize the impact of year-to-year fluctuations. In these situations, the group's actual large claims (ie, the portion of claims cost in excess of the pooling level) are replaced with a pooling charge, which represents the average large claims costs for the health plan. The average pooling charge must be assessed to each group if a group's large claims are removed so that the health plan charges enough revenue across all groups.

A combination of a group's historical experience and the average experience of the health plan is generally used to set the group's future rates, depending on the perceived credibility of the group's historical experience. All these experience rating concepts are illustrated in Exhibit 26-5.

A variation of experience rating known as group-specific community rating is based on utilization ratios (eg, hospital days per 1,000, prescriptions per 1,000, or office visits per 1,000) rather than claims costs. This rating method works similar to the example in Exhibit 26-5 except that the PMPM claims costs are replaced with various utilization ratios and associated weights. An example of group-specific community rating is shown in Exhibit 26-6.

Summary

As noted above, the various group-specific rating methods do not all meet the rating method objectives to the same degree. Table 26-4 shows how the rating methods meet these objectives.

CONCLUSION

Although there are a wide variety of rating methodologies, they all share a common trait: If performed properly, they can help ensure the fiscal health of the plan. The related function of underwriting is equally important. The path that each plan chooses to follow in executing these responsibilities will depend on the local competitive environment, the talents and skills of the personnel charged with carrying them out, the regulatory environment, and the marketplace demands on the plan.

Exhibit 26-6 Simplified Group-Specific Community Rating Example

	Year	
Category	t	t–1
Inpatient days per 1,000		
Group (G)	350	360
Health plan (H)	300	330
Ratio (G ÷ H)	1.17	1.09
Weight	40%	40%
Office visits per 1,000		
Group	3,300	3,200
Health plan	3,000	3,000
Ratio	1.10	1.07
Weight	50%	50%
Scripts per 1,000		
Group	5,000	4,800
Health plan	4,800	4,800
Ratio	1.04	1.00
Weight	10%	10%
Average ratio	1.12*	1.07
Credibility	60%	20%

$$*1.12 = (1.17 \times 0.40) + (1.10 \times 0.50) + (1.04 \times 0.10)$$

Plan PMPM
  revenue target = $100
Group PMPM
  revenue target = $100 × [(1.12 x 0.60) + (1.07 × 0.20) + (1.00 × 0.20)]
        = $100 × 1.09
        = $109

Note: t = most recent year
        t–1 = one year earlier than t

Table 26-4 Scorecard for Group-Specific Rating Methods

Category	Community Rating	Community Rating by Class	Experience Rating
Legal	Yes	Yes	Yes, some forms
Equitable	No	For smaller groups	Yes
Simple	Yes	Yes	In concept
Flexible	No	Somewhat	Yes
Predictable	Yes	Yes, except smaller groups	No
Competitive	Perhaps	For smaller groups	Yes
Profitable	?	?	?

Part VI

Special Market Segments

We're One
But we're not the same.

Bono (1991)

Chapter 27

The Federal Employees Health Benefit Program and Managed Care

Joel L. Michaels and Christine C. Rinn

The Federal Employees Health Benefits Program (FEHBP), with its coverage of approximately 10 million federal employees and annuitants and their dependents, represents the largest employer-sponsored health benefits program in the United States today. The FEHBP is established pursuant to the Federal Employees Health Benefits Act, 5 USC Section 8901 et seq, and is administered by the federal Office of Personnel Management (OPM). Under the FEHBP, OPM is authorized to offer certain choices of health benefits plans to federal employees. These choices include governmentwide plans and employee organization plans (which are experience rated) as well as comprehensive health plans (which are predominantly community rated). Most of the comprehensive health plans are health maintenance organizations (HMOs) and represent a significant presence by OPM as a purchaser of managed care services.

The focus of this chapter is the FEHBP's relationship to HMOs, with particular emphasis on the continuing controversy over HMO rating practices under the FEHBP. Also discussed are issues related to benefit design, federal em-

ployee–HMO relationships, federal preemption of state laws, and requirements for coverage of services rendered by non-HMO providers.

One of the key reasons why rating issues are particularly significant is that FEHBP contracting is not a competitive bidding process, and OPM does not engage in exercising its purchasing power (at least on the front end of the rate proposal process) to achieve a better rate. OPM initially relies upon the rate representations made by the contractors. At the time of this writing, OPM contracts with approximately 400 comprehensive health plans, almost all of which are community rated plans. Comprehensive plans may be either staff or group model (ie, closed panel), individual practice association, direct contract model (ie, open panel), or mixed model plans depending upon the configuration of the HMO's provider delivery system. Community rating, in its most simplistic terms, means that the costs charged to an employer group represent costs spread across the community of the HMO's enrollment and not just the experience of a particular account. HMOs that are federally qualified under the federal HMO law[1] are required to be community rated by that statute, and OPM, under the Federal Employees Health Benefits Act, has an affirmative obligation to offer to contract with federally qualified

Joel L. Michaels is a Principal, and Christine C. Rinn is an Associate, in the law firm of Michaels & Wishner, PC, in Washington, DC.

HMOs that meet the requirements of the FEHBP.[2]

The concept of what constitutes community rating has changed significantly over the years under amendments to the federal HMO law, thereby adding to the complexity of determining whether a community rate is truly being offered by the HMO to the FEHBP. In some cases, this complexity has led to abuse by certain HMO contractors who may be engaged in a pattern of selective discounting to certain nonfederal employer groups. In an effort to curb these abuses and to simplify program administration, OPM has recently moved away from community rating requirements and has focused more on how OPM rates compare with those of other HMO employer groups that are similar in size and benefits to the federal account. Because benefit design is an important element of rate development, it is necessary first to review how OPM determines its premium contribution and its approval over HMO benefit packages.

PREMIUM CONTRIBUTION AND BENEFIT DESIGN

Under 5 USC Section 8906, OPM pays a portion of the premium, and the employee or annuitant is responsible for the remainder. The government contribution has historically been set at 60% of the average premium of the Big Six (the two high-option governmentwide plans, the two largest employee organizations, and the two largest comprehensive plans). Since Aetna's withdrawal from the FEHBP as a government-wide plan in 1990, OPM has used a modified formula to develop the contribution. The government's contribution, however, is further limited by the requirement that it be no more than 75% of the plan's premium. In such a case, if OPM's contribution is more than 75% of an HMO's premium, the HMO receives a contribution from OPM equal to 75% of its premium.

As for benefit design, OPM is authorized to establish reasonable minimum standards. These minimum benefits include hospital benefits, surgical benefits, in-hospital surgical benefits, ambulatory patient benefits, supplemental benefits, and obstetric benefits.[3] Although federally quali-

fied HMOs are required to contract with OPM for the basic benefits mandated by the federal HMO law, there are typically no established minimum standards set by OPM for the benefits, deductibles, or copayments, with the exception of certain mandated coverages for mental health and substance abuse. Moreover, HMOs are usually not allowed to provide additional benefits unless the change is part of the HMO's community benefits package and is offered to all groups and not just the federal account. Of course, with the advent of the recent similarly sized subscriber group requirements discussed below, comparability of benefits with the two groups most similar in size to the federal account will be important in determining the appropriateness of the rate charged to OPM.

PREMIUM RATING UNDER THE FEDERAL EMPLOYEES HEALTH BENEFITS PROGRAM

There are two rating options under the FEHBP. One option, as discussed above, is community rating. The other option, which is not available to federally qualified HMOs (who represent the largest component of comprehensive health plans), is experience rating.[4]

Experience Rating

Under the experience rating option, carriers charge the FEHBP a rate that is based on the utilization of health care services by the federal account. This rate is retrospectively determined and should not be confused with adjusted community rating, where the experience of an account is prospectively factored into the rate charged that group. The FEHB acquisition regulations (FEHBAR),[5] which govern the FEHBP, define an experience rate as a:

> rate for a given group that is the result of that group's actual paid claims, administrative expenses, retentions, and estimated claims incurred but not reported, adjusted for benefit modification, utilization trends, and economic trends. Actual paid claims, any actual

or negotiated benefits payments made to providers of medical services for the provision of health care such as capitation not adjusted for specific groups, per diems, and Diagnostic Related Group (DRG) payments.[6]

Recent amendments to the definition of experience rate specifically recognize provider capitation payments, which represent a typical provider compensation payment arrangement utilized by HMOs, as paid claims.[7] Ironically, this amendment has particular significance for comprehensive plans even though they are predominantly community rated. As discussed later in this chapter, the expanded definition of experience rate may have removed some of the barriers faced by community rated plans in calculating a retroactive experience rate for the FEHBP as a remedy to an audit finding of defective community rating.

Community Rating

Traditional Community Rating

Before the 1991 contract year, the premium rate development of community rated carriers participating in the FEHBP was severely restricted by OPM's rating requirements. Among these requirements was the definition of a community rate as a:

> rate of payment that is equivalent to that charged on the effective date to *all subscriber groups of the carrier* for the same contract period for the same level of benefits [emphasis added].[8]

On the basis of the foregoing definition, any rating discrepancies between the rate charged to the FEHBP and that charged to any other group by the carrier that were discovered upon audit were determined to be unlawful discounts and served as the basis for findings by OPM of defective community rating. Moreover, this limitation was particularly problematic in light of the fact that HMOs were permitted to use not only traditional community rating under the federal HMO law but also community rating by class

and adjusted community rating. Community rating by class permits the introduction of classes, such as age and sex, in determining the HMO's revenue requirement for the community, and the amount charged an employer is then based upon the composition of the employer's workforce and its dependents.

Recent Changes

In light of the above, OPM has modified its rating requirements for community rating plans. The FEHBAR definition of a community rate is now a:

> rate of payment based on a per member per month capitation rate or its equivalent that applies to a combination of the subscriber groups for a comprehensive medical plan . . . .[9]

Thus, under the new regulations, OPM no longer requires that a single community rate be applicable to all a carrier's groups, including the FEHBP. The revised definition substantially relaxes the rating restrictions imposed by OPM on its community rated carriers. In fact, one of the stated purposes of the revised definition was to "recognize the increasing diversity in community rating in the insurance industry and, specifically, within the [FEHBP]."[10]

As a result, OPM began to recognize community rating by class as an acceptable rating methodology for its contractors. Until recently, the FEHBAR required the classes used by the contractors to be approved in advance by OPM, although in practice OPM did not formally approve the classes used by its contractors. OPM's failure specifically to approve the rating classes used by its contractors is coming back to haunt some of those who used industry adjustment factors as part of their community rating by class methodology. The use of industry adjustment factors is discussed in more detail later in this chapter.

OPM now recognizes adjusted community rating as an acceptable methodology for FEHBP carriers. An adjusted community rate is a:

> community rate which has been adjusted for expected use of medical re-

sources of the FEHBP group. An adjusted community rate is a prospective rate and cannot be retroactively revised to reflect actual experience, utilization, or costs of the FEHBP group.[11]

Before the adoption of the similarly sized subscriber group (SSSG) concept by OPM, which is described below, a contractor using adjusted community rating for the FEHBP was required to have the methodology as well as the criteria for deciding which groups would be rated with adjusted community rating approved by OPM in advance. The purpose of this prior approval requirement was to ensure that the FEHBP was being treated in the same manner as the carrier's commercial groups of like size.

Similarly Sized Subscriber Groups

One of the most significant changes for the FEHBP in the area of rating requirements is the concept of SSSGs. Under the FEHBAR provisions that were in effect before 1991, a contractor had to certify that the rate charged to the FEHBP was charged to all its subscriber groups that had the same contract period and benefit package as the FEHBP. Under the new provisions of the FEHBAR, contractors must certify that the rate charged to the FEHBP is "no greater than the [rate] quoted the Carrier's similarly sized subscriber groups . . . ; and that adjustments made to the [rate are] consistent with the rating methodology used to rate the carrier's similarly sized subscriber groups. . . ."[12] At the time the SSSG regulations were proposed, OPM stated that the regulations reflected OPM's new policy "to obtain the market price, including applicable discounts, accorded to the two subscriber groups arithmetically closest in size to the FEHBP group for the same basic benefit package and the same contract year."[13]

Thus, the SSSGs are the contractor's two employer groups[14] that best meet all the following conditions:

(a) Have total number of contracts at the time of the rate proposal arithmetically closest in size to the previous

September's FEHBP subscriber enrollment, as determined by OPM; (b) Purchase substantially the same basic benefit package proposed for the Federal group; and (c) Are renewed during the plan's fiscal year.[15]

Contractors were first required to certify that the FEHBP's rates were no higher than those charged to the plan's SSSGs for the 1991 contract year.

The introduction of the SSSG concept will have a significant impact on the rating practices of FEHBP contractors as well as on the outcome of audit findings of defective community rating. The SSSG regulations have been in effect for only short time, however, and it is too early to tell how they will be applied by OPM.

Industry Adjustment Factors

Some HMOs that use community rating by class used industry adjustment factors (IAFs) to adjust a group's premium rates in an effort to predict and account for that group's expected level of health care utilization. Before 1992, OPM recognized that its contractors used IAFs but prohibited their use in the premium rate development of the FEHBP. As a result, if a contractor used industry factors, OPM's rate instructions directed the contractor to use an IAF of 1 for the FEHBP, which would neither increase nor decrease the FEHBP's rates.

With the advent of the SSSG regulations discussed above, however, OPM changed its view regarding IAFs. Although the 1991 rate instructions continued to require contractors to use an IAF of 1 for the FEHBP, contractors discovered when they submitted their rate reconciliations that if either of the SSSGs received an IAF of less than 1, which would decrease that group's rates, OPM demanded the same IAF for the FEHBP. Moreover, if both SSSGs were rated with IAFs, OPM demanded the lower of the two.

OPM's decision regarding IAFs reflected the agency's position that IAFs are not legitimate predictors of health care utilization. Rather, IAFs are viewed by OPM as a means by which contractors can give discounts to their commercial accounts.

With the SSSG regulations and the relaxing of OPM's community rating requirements, OPM adopted a new policy with respect to IAFs. This new policy states that the IAF used in a contractor's proposed rate for the FEHBP may not exceed 1. OPM will examine the IAFs used to rate the SSSGs during the rate reconciliation process. Upon reconciliation, OPM will require that the IAF used for the FEHBP be no greater than 1 and no larger than the lowest IAF used in the premium rate development of an IAF.[16]

OFFICE OF PERSONNEL MANAGEMENT AUDITS AND APPEALS

As government contractors, HMOs participating in the FEHBP are subject to periodic audit by OPM. For community rated carriers, this means that OPM auditors will seek to verify that the rate charged to the FEHBP is a community rate as defined by the FEHBAR and that any benefit and other loadings to the FEHBP rate are reasonable and appropriate. To assist OPM in the conduct of audits, contractors are required to maintain their records relating to a contract year for 5 years after the expiration of that contract year.[17] The language of the record retention requirement fails to state specifically what records contractors are required to maintain. Upon audit, however, OPM will want to review state and federal rate filings, actual billings to commercial accounts, and rate worksheets used in the premium development of the audited groups.

Audits of many community rated plans typically result in findings of defective community rating and recommendations that the FEHBP is entitled to a premium adjustment as a result of the contractor's defective community rating practices. These rating practices may range from selective discounting for certain key employer groups to manipulating rates to achieve a result without a consistent rate-setting methodology. The methodology used by the OPM auditors in determining the amount of the recommended refund for the FEHBP depends on the contract year under audit. As discussed below, OPM's

remedial authority has changed over the last 6 years. With these changes, the size of the OPM claims against HMOs has increased dramatically.

In conducting an audit, it is the Office of the Inspector General that develops the audit findings and recommendations. It is the Audits Resolution Division within OPM's Office of Insurance Programs, however, that enters into the direct settlement negotiations with the contractors.

Audits of Pre-1990 Contract Years

It is not too surprising that the pre-1990 definition of a community rate, a rate charged to all the contractor's groups, led to audit findings of defective community rating. Any rating discrepancies between the FEHBP's rates and the audited groups' rates that could not be attributed to benefit differences were determined to be discounts in violation of the contractor's certificate of community rating.[18] There could be several sources of these discrepancies: using a different demographic source for the FEHBP than for commercial groups, quoting commercial groups a premium rate before state approval of the carrier's community rate, and blatant discounting. Whatever the source of the discrepancy, the result was typically the same: a finding by the OPM auditors that the contractor engaged in defective community rating and a recommendation that the contractor refund the overcharges to the FEHBP. The amount of the recommended recovery for the FEHBP depends upon the remedy used by the auditors.

Before the adoption of the FEHBAR, OPM had two options in cases of defective community rating. First, it could require the contractor to establish a true community rate. Alternatively, the contractor could experience rate the FEHBP for the contract year(s) in question. Any differences between the new rate and the rate charged were required to be returned to the FEHBP. With the promulgation of the FEHBAR in 1987, OPM's remedies were substantially strengthened with a third remedy, the so-called most favored customer remedy.[19] The most favored customer remedy, which became effective for the 1988 contract year, gives the FEHBP the benefit of the largest discount afforded another group by an audited contractor and can result in large claims against the contractor.

The most favored customer remedy became OPM's remedy of choice in initiating a claim against a contractor. Contractors who sought to employ the other two remedies, establishing a true community rate or experience rating the FEHBP, found that OPM had interpreted these remedies in such a way as to make them illusory. For example, for a contractor to establish a true community rate, OPM would require the contractor to rerate all its groups, give refunds to those groups that it overcharged, and bill those that it had undercharged. A retroactive experience rate analysis of the FEHBP was similarly impractical because OPM would not recognize provider capitation payments, which are common in the HMO industry, as claims paid for purposes of deriving the FEHBP's claims experience. Moreover, it was OPM's position that a retroactive experience rate analysis was not available to federally qualified HMOs, which are prohibited from experience rating.

Although OPM has not changed its view as to what constitutes a true community rate, a contractor's ability to perform an acceptable retroactive experience rate analysis of the FEHBP has improved. As previously mentioned, OPM has amended the definition of an experience rate specifically to recognize capitation payments as claims paid for purposes of determining the FEHBP's claims expense. In addition, OPM apparently no longer takes the position that federally qualified HMOs cannot perform a retroactive experience analysis of the FEHBP as a remedial measure. Although these changes greatly improve a contractor's chances of performing an acceptable experience rate analysis, a number of obstacles still remain. For example, for its noncapitated providers, the contractor must have claims data specific to the FEHBP. In addition, the analysis must include coordination of benefits and subrogation recoveries and must exclude marketing costs and interest expense. The HMO's administrative load cannot exceed a specific percentage of premium, which tends to range from 5% to 10%. Moreover, those administrative expenses that cannot be allocated to the FEHBP on a direct basis must be allocated on an indirect basis, typically by number of claims or member months.

Audits of Contract Year 1990 and On

The SSSG regulations replaced OPM's three remedies for defective community rating. Under the new regulations:

> If any rate established in connection with this contract was increased because (1) the Carrier furnished cost or pricing data that were not complete, accurate, or current . . . ; (2) the Carrier furnished pricing data that were not accurate . . . ; (3) the Carrier developed FEHBP rates with a rating methodology and structure inconsistent with that used to develop rates for similarly sized subscriber groups . . . ; or (4) the Carrier furnished data [or information of any description] that were not complete, accurate, and current—*then the rate shall be reduced in the amount by which the price was increased because of the defective data or information* [emphasis added].[20]

According to the *Federal Register* commentary accompanying the final regulations, the above regulation was effective January 1, 1990.[21] OPM audits of the 1990 contract year, however, continued to employ the most favored customer remedy in determining the amount of the recommended recovery for the FEHBP. Added to the apparent confusion regarding the new regulation's effective date is the confusion about how the new regulation will be implemented. The regulation states that the FEHBP's rate shall be reduced in the amount by which the price was increased because of the defective data or information. The regulation does not state "how" the rate will be reduced, however. For example, the regulation fails to address the situation where only one of the SSSGs is defectively rated. Similarly, it is not clear what adjustment the FEHBP should receive if both SSSGs receive discounts but one discount exceeds the other. It appears, however, that OPM may take the initial position that averaging of the two rates is not required, and OPM may take the largest discount afforded one of the SSSGs.

Defending and Settling Findings of Defective Community Rating

FEHBP contractors that are charged with defective community rating typically have two formal opportunities to defend themselves at the agency level. The first opportunity is in response to the findings contained in the draft audit report. The second opportunity is after receipt of the final audit report, which is issued after OPM has received the contractor's comments to the draft audit report. It is critical that both responses be comprehensive submissions that defend the contractor's rating practices, where possible, and put forth alternative analyses for the calculation of the FEHBP's damages. In this regard, there are many analyses available to a contractor. The goal, however, is to find the one that best illustrates the unreasonableness of the amount recommended by the auditors by showing that the government's actual damages as a result of the contractor's community rating practices are much lower. The contractor's analyses can have a second purpose as well: They can serve as the basis of settlement negotiations between OPM and the contractor.

If OPM and the contractor are unable to settle their dispute, the contracting officer will issue a final decision. Although settlement negotiations may continue after a final decision has been issued, once the final decision is issued the time period for appealing the government's decision starts to run. In addition, interest on the claimed amount begins to accrue 30 days after the decision is issued.

Contract appeals are subject to the Contract Disputes Act of 1978, 41 USC Section 601 et seq. In appealing the contracting officer's decision, the contractor can appeal to the Armed Services Board of Contract Appeals. Alternatively, an appeal can be made by the contractor to the US Claims Court. To date, few contractors have appealed a final decision because most OPM claims have resulted in settlement.

MISCELLANEOUS CONTRACTING ISSUES

Enrollment Reconciliations with Local Payroll Offices

A common problem faced by FEHBP contractors is the inability to obtain timely enrollment and disenrollment information from OPM and the local payroll offices. As a result, many contractors find that they are carrying FEHBP enrollees on their membership lists and paying capitation payments to providers for federal enrollees long after these individuals have been terminated from the FEHBP.

Under its contract with FEHBP carriers, OPM is obligated to maintain or cause to be maintained adequate enrollment information to allow contractors to maintain an accurate record of their FEHBP enrollees. Moreover, contractors are entitled to rely on this information. Despite these contractual obligations, however, OPM's position is that it is the responsibility of the contractors and the individual payroll offices to reconcile enrollment records to ensure that the contractor's records are accurate. Unfortunately, the majority of payroll offices are unwilling or unable to work with the contractors to reconcile their enrollment records. Thus the contractors are left without any definitive source in seeking to maintain accurate records.

At least one contractor has filed a claim with OPM seeking accurate enrollment information as well as compensation for the numerous federal enrollees who were carried on the HMO's membership lists as a result of a lack of accurate enrollment information. Although OPM and this contractor were able to settle their dispute, the situation faced by the contractor is a common one that may force other contractors to file claims against OPM.

Reimbursement for Self-Referrals to Out-of-Network Allied Health Professionals

Section 8902(k) of the Federal Employees Health Benefits Act allows federal enrollees to self-refer to various allied health professionals, contrary to the concept of a closed delivery system inherent in an HMO program. Specifically, the statute states:

> When a contract . . . requires payment or reimbursement for services which may be performed by a clinical psychologist, optometrist, nurse midwife, or nurse practitioner/clinical specialist . . . or by a qualified social worker . . . [the enrollee] shall be free to select, and shall have direct access to, such a [provider] without supervision or referral by another health practitioner and shall be entitled under the contract to have payment or reimbursement made to him or on his behalf for the services performed.[22]

Group practice HMOs are exempt from the self-referral requirement, but independent practice and mixed model HMOs are not.[23] Although the self-referral statute, in various forms, has been in existence for a number of years, OPM had not sought to enforce the law. In 1991, however, OPM notified its contractors that it would enforce the law's requirements effective with the 1992 contract year. OPM's decision was made worse for contractors by its timing. OPM announced its decision after the contractors had received OPM's acceptance of their 1992 rates. Thus the contractors could not lessen the impact of the agency's decision through appropriate rate adjustments.

In response to the harsh criticism it received and pressure from its contractors and industry trade associations, OPM announced that it would adjust contractors' rates during the 1992 rate reconciliation process to cover any additional "documented costs they may incur in providing direct access benefits."[24] OPM's decision will reduce the financial impact of the self-referral requirement on the 1992 contract year. In addition, a new law, P.L. 102-393, was recently passed to broaden the exemption from group practice plans to "comprehensive medical plans" as described in Section 8903(4). As a result, the self-referral provisions should not be an issue for HMOs for the 1993 contract year.

Federal Preemption of State Laws

FEHBP contractors can sometimes be faced with conflicting requirements as federal government contractors and as state licensed HMOs. These conflicts can relate to benefits, rates, and terms of the federal subscriber documents. In this regard, the Federal Employees Health Benefits Act contains a preemption provision that can eliminate the need for contractors to comply with some state laws that affect the contractors' FEHBP operations. The Federal Employees Health Benefits Act states:

> The provisions of any contract . . . which relate to the nature or extent of coverage or benefits (including payments with respect to benefits) shall supersede and preempt any State or local law, or any regulation issued thereunder, which relates to health insurance or plans to the extent that such law or regulation is inconsistent with such contractual provisions.[25]

Thus, Section 8902(m)(1) can preempt state-mandated benefit requirements to the extent that the state benefits are inconsistent with those offered by the contractor to the FEHBP. In addition, it is possible that the preemption clause may be used to preempt state laws that may not appear, on their face, to affect the nature of coverage or extent of benefits. For example, Section 8902(m)(1) could be used to preempt state prohibitions on such practices as subrogation, and OPM intends to publish regulations that will address this very issue. OPM also exempts itself from any state or local taxes (eg, premium taxes or local occupational taxes), so that a plan neither pays taxes nor charges OPM for such taxes as regards premium revenue from the FEHBP.

The FEHBP is also exempt from the provisions of the Employee Retirement Income Security Act (ERISA).[26] As a result, some of the protections offered by that statute to payers from state law claims by enrollees do not directly extend to FEHBP contractors.[27] The FEHBP brochure given to enrollees, however, limits recoveries to the benefits under the contract. This has been construed to limit the ability of a claimant to recover punitive damages for bad faith denials.[28] Moreover, the claims review procedures under the FEHBP are similar to those under ERISA. As a result, and similar to ERISA, it may be argued that FEHBP remedies are the sole remedies for claim denials and that state actions for claims, such as punitive damages, are preempted by Section 8902(m)(1). Although the true scope of federal preemption of state laws under Section 8902(m)(1) has not been definitively established, the case law seems to suggest that the scope of federal preemption is broad, similar to that under ERISA.

CONCLUSION

The FEHBP will continue to be the largest employer-sponsored health benefits program. OPM's ability successfully to administer this ever growing program and to retain desirable contractors will depend on its ability to demand accountability from its contractors while maintaining consistency in the application of its rules on rates and benefits. In this regard, one of the most important developments to date has been the move away from traditional community rating requirements that have limited relevance in today's market toward a focus on the FEHBP's comparability to other SSSGs. This development is viewed as favorable because the SSSG rules are more clear to HMOs and define with more precision the conduct required of them. It also prevents the application by OPM of remedies that are punitive in nature (ie, seizing the largest discount given another group regardless of comparability). Even with the SSSG rules, however, it remains to be seen how these requirements will be implemented by OPM.

Despite the adoption of the SSSG rules, pressures for overall reform of the FEHBP will probably continue. The federal enrollees themselves are often confused by the myriad benefit plan options and contractors they face every year during open season, and they may feel that they are getting fewer benefits while paying higher premiums. With the introduction of point-of-service plans in 1992, this confusion will probably increase.

Among the proposals that have been advocated by various parties in an effort to minimize confusion are those that would standardize benefit packages as well as reduce the number of FEHBP contractors. The administration's reform proposal for the FEHBP is expected by the time this book is published, and the reader is urged to research the most recent changes in FEHBP rules and regulations. Like many employers, the FEHBP may find that the benefits of competition cannot be fully realized in an environment where direct comparisons between benefits and rates among various health plan options are difficult to make.

NOTES

1. 42 USC §§ 300e et seq.
2. See 5 USC § 8902(1).
3. See 5 USC § 8904.
4. Pursuant to 42 USC § 300e-1, with limited exceptions, the premium rates charged by federally qualified HMOs must be based on a community rating system. See also 42 CFR § 417.104.
5. 48 CFR §§ 1601.101–1653.000.
6. 48 CFR § 1602.170–6 (1990).
7. See 55 Fed Reg 27406–27419 (July 2, 1990).
8. 48 CFR § 1602.170–2 (1987).
9. 48 CFR § 1602.170–2(a) (1990).
10. 54 Fed Reg 43089 (October 20, 1989).
11. 48 CFR § 1602.170–2(b) (1990).
12. 48 CFR § 1615.804–71 (1990).
13. 54 Fed Reg 43089 (October 20, 1989).
14. Under the draft version of the SSSG regulations, a government account could not be used as an SSSG. OPM reversed its position when the final regulations were published, however. Thus government accounts may be used, provided that they are community rated. OPM has indicated that proposed regulations are forthcoming that will require the inclusion of governmental accounts.
15. 48 CFR § 1602.170–11 (1990).
16. Letter from Reginald M. Jones, Jr, Assistant Director of Insurance Programs, OPM, to David O'Connor, Federal Programs Representative, Group Health Association of America, dated October 23, 1991.
17. See 48 CFR § 1652.204–70 (1990).
18. See 48 CFR § 1615.804.70 (1987).
19. 48 CFR § 1652.215–70 (1987).
20. 48 CFR § 1652.215–70 (1990).
21. 55 Fed Reg 27406 (July 2, 1990).

22. 5 USC §§ 8901 et seq.

23. See 5 USC § 8902(k)(2).

24. Letter from Constance Berry Newman, Director, OPM, to James F. Doherty, President and Chief Executive Officer, Group Health Association of America, dated October 16, 1991.

25. 5 USC § 8902(m)(1).

26. 29 USC § 1003(b).

27. See *Pilot Life Insurance Company v Dedeaux*, 481 US 41 (9187), wherein the US Supreme Court held that the civil enforcement provisions of ERISA are preemptive and provide a federal remedy for state law claims such as tortious breach of contract or bad faith conduct. Suits by enrollees challenging the denial of benefits under an employee health benefit plan may therefore be removed to federal court, where only ERISA remedies are available.

28. See *Hartenstine v Superior Court of San Bernardino County*, 196 Cal App 3d 206, (1987), cert denied, 488 US 899 (1988).

Chapter 28

Medicare and Managed Care

Carlos Zarabozo and Jean D. LeMasurier

TGIF (THE GOVERNMENT IS FRIGHTENING) UNLESS YOU KNOW YOUR ACRONYMS

Although you do not need to know too many acronyms for some dealings with the government, such as buying a postage stamp or paying

Carlos Zarabozo is Director of the Operational Analysis Staff of the Office of Prepaid Health Care Operations and Oversight (OPHCOO). He was previously Special Assistant to the Director (six directors or acting directors) of the Office of Prepaid Health Care (OPHC) or its successor organization, OPHCOO, from March 1988 through February 1992. He worked previously as a group health plan operations specialist in OPHC and in the Health Care Financing Administration's (HCFA's) San Francisco regional office.

Jean D. LeMasurier is Director of the Division of Policy and Evaluation of HCFA's Office of Coordinated Care Policy and Planning. She has developed policy, legislation, and regulations for Medicare contracts with HMOs and federally qualified HMOs and other coordinated care initiatives in HCFA's Office of Research and Demonstrations, Office of Legislation and Policy, and OPHC. In addition, she developed legislation for Medicare HMOs while serving on the US Senate Finance Committee staff.

The views expressed within the chapter are the authors' and not those of the HCFA. All addresses and telephone numbers listed were accurate at the time of publication, but such numbers and addresses occasionally change, so the authors make no warranty as to their currency.

taxes, it helps to know an acronym or two in dealing with Medicare. On the subject of health maintenance organizations (HMOs)* and Medicare, some of the acronyms that you can use at cocktail parties to sound knowledgeable (and no doubt boring) are HCFA, TEFRA, CMP, ACR, APR, COBRA, OBRA, and, especially, AAPCC. These acronyms are all addressed in this chapter.

All acronyms aside, what the government is attempting to do through emphasis on coordinated care options, one of which is HMO contracting, is bring down health care costs while improving the quality of care. Traditional Medicare was at one time a strictly fee-for-service system with reimbursement based on cost or charges. In the past few years the government has radically changed its reimbursement for Medicare services through such means as

---

*Throughout this chapter the term *HMO* is generally meant to refer to both federally qualified health maintenance organizations and organizations that are determined to be competitive medical plans (CMPs) as defined in the TEFRA legislation introducing the concept of CMPs. The initial discussion deals exclusively with risk-sharing HMOs and CMPs. It is also possible for an HMO or CMP to contract with the Health Care Financing Administration under a cost-reimbursement arrangement that limits the risk exposure of the HMO/CMP, as discussed in the latter part of the chapter.

the well-publicized prospective payment system of inpatient reimbursement based on diagnosis-related groups (DRGs) rather than reasonable cost reimbursement. In the case of HMOs, the government looked at what was happening in the private sector and found that HMOs (which in their early history had been promoted, in a sense, by the federal government) had the potential for decreasing health care costs while bringing about possible improvements in the quality of care through coordinated care.

UNDERSTANDING THE ADJUSTED AVERAGE PER CAPITA COST

If acronyms are not your favorite subject of discussion, we can get down to business and talk instead about money. As one would expect, money usually determines whether an HMO or competitive medical plan (CMP) will want to contract with the government. Under the risk payment methodology established in the law, a contract is expected to be financially advantageous to both the HMO/CMP and the government. HMOs with a Medicare risk contract are paid 95% of what the government's actuaries estimate to be the cost of medical services if the services had been obtained in traditional fee-for-service Medicare. The government should save, actuarially speaking, at least 5% compared to what would have been the fee-for-service costs for those Medicare beneficiaries who choose to enroll in an HMO, and the health plan is paid at 95% of the fee-for-service rate with the expectation that because HMOs, as organized health care delivery systems, are able to provide services more efficiently than fee-for-service their cost of providing care will be at or below the 95% level.

The government pays risk-based HMOs a prospective monthly capitation payment for each Medicare member that is akin to the premium paid to an HMO by an employer for coverage of its employees. In exchange for this capitation payment, the HMO is required to provide the full range of health care services covered under the federal Medicare program. The adjusted average per capita cost (AAPCC) is the basis of payment to HMOs and CMPs under contract to the Health Care Financing Administration (HCFA). For each county of the United States, for each Medicare member, an HMO or CMP is paid 1 of 122 possible monthly capitation amounts (which can vary significantly by county).

You can think of these 122 rate cells as 122 little amoebalike creatures floating around aimlessly in space, or you can think in the less daunting terms of the five (yes, a mere five) variables used to create 120 rate cells: age, sex, Medicaid eligibility, institutional status, and whether a person has both parts of Medicare (Part A being inpatient hospital, inpatient skilled nursing, and home health services, and Part B being all other services, such as physician services and outpatient services). This is illustrated in Exhibit 28-1.

To restate the illustration in Exhibit 28-1, once the age and sex are established, the Part A and Part B rates are different for institutionalized and noninstitutionalized individuals. The noninstitutionalized are reimbursed at different rates depending on whether they are eligible for Medicaid or not; Medicaid status does not affect the level of payment for the institutionalized. There are also two rate cells for each state for individuals with end-stage renal disease, making a total of 122 possible rate cells.

The AAPCC represents an actuarial projection of what Medicare expenses would have

---

Exhibit 28-1 The 120 "Rate Cells" That Make Up Medicare Capitation

Ages (10 age groups)

×

Part A or Part B (2)

×

Sex (2)

=

$10 \times 2 \times 2 = 40$

Institutionalized	Non-institutionalized + Medicaid	Non-institutionalized + non-Medicaid
40 cells	40 cells	40 cells

=

$40 + 40 + 40 = 120$ total cells

been for a given category of Medicare beneficiary had the person remained in traditional fee-for-service Medicare. The AAPCC rates change every calendar year.

Under the law, the HCFA's actuary is required to publish each calendar year's AAPCC rates by September 7 of the preceding year. Each July, the HCFA's Office of the Actuary is also required to publish information about the methodology and assumptions related to the AAPCC announcement for the following year. The announcement of rates is required to contain sufficient information for any HMO to reconstruct the manner in which AAPCC rates for the counties served by the HMO were derived. The HCFA's actuary also determines the actuarial equivalent of Medicare beneficiary liability amounts, expressed as a monthly average amount that Medicare beneficiaries have to pay for out-of-pocket expenses in fee-for-service Medicare (such as the coinsurance for physician services or the deductible a person pays on entering a hospital). When a Medicare beneficiary joins an HMO, the beneficiary deductible and coinsurance requirements are satisfied by having the beneficiary pay a monthly premium to the HMO and/or copayments for services. This actuarial equivalent is, in almost all cases, the maximum total of premiums and copayments an HMO may charge its Medicare members to cover Medicare beneficiary liability amounts.

The format of the published AAPCC rates consists of a listing, for all US counties, of Medicare Part A and Part B base rates for the aged and the disabled (beneficiaries younger than 65 years entitled because of their disability) together with a table of nationally used demographic factors, by which the county rates are multiplied to determine payment for a given rate cell. The published AAPCC rates are not the total projected fee-for-service rates. As published, they are 95% of the projected rates. As noted above, the upper limit of payment to a risk-based HMO/CMP contracting with the HCFA is the 95% rate.

To determine how much an HMO will be paid for its Medicare members, an HMO that is considering entering into a contract with the HCFA needs to be able to project the make-up of its Medicare population. The HMO will project how many members it will have in each rate cell of each county of its service area to determine the total payment rate and the average payment rate (APR) from the HCFA. The HCFA is able to provide a report of the demographic make-up of each US county by rate cell. The same report states how many Medicare beneficiaries are currently HMO members. This type of report can be obtained through the HCFA's Office of the Actuary.

THE ADJUSTED COMMUNITY RATE/ AVERAGE PAYMENT RATE COMPARISON

Let us assume that you are the chief financial officer of an HMO and that, having nothing better to do one morning while reading the latest *Federal Register,* you decide to figure out how much money the government will pay you under a Medicare contract. After a little bit of effort, you have figured out that the HCFA is willing to pay you an average of, let us say, $200.00 per member per month (PMPM)—more than any employer group ever considered paying you. You cannot wait to phone the HCFA and ask that a signed contract be sent to you immediately. The HCFA is more than happy to oblige, provided that you understand that you may not really be getting $200.00 PMPM. After you have determined your APR (per person) from the HCFA, the law requires that you compare this APR to your adjusted community rate (ACR) to determine whether $200.00 PMPM is an appropriate payment from the government. Your community rate is your premium for a commercial group. Your ACR computation is a statement to the HCFA's accountants of what premium you would charge for providing exactly the same Medicare-covered benefits to a community rated group account, adjusted to allow for the greater intensity and frequency of utilization by Medicare recipients (because most Medicare beneficiaries are elderly). The ACR includes the normal profit of a for-profit HMO or CMP.

If your projected premium, your ACR, equals or exceeds your projected payment, your APR—that is, if you expect your Medicare revenue to be less than or equal to your cost of providing care—then you will receive the $200.00 PMPM, or whatever the exact 95% AAPCC payment happens to be, and no more.

If, however, your ACR is lower than your projected APR—if you project, for example, that you can deliver the Medicare-covered services to the population you expect to enroll at $175.00 PMPM—then you are required to return the surplus to the government or to your Medicare beneficiaries by (1) accepting a reduced payment rate averaging $175.00 PMPM or (2) returning the difference between the ACR and APR to Medicare beneficiaries in the form of a reduced premium that would otherwise be collectible from the Medicare members, or (3) enriching the benefit package offered by the dollar equivalent of the surplus. That is, in the last case, if your ACR is $175.00 PMPM and your APR is $200.00, you would return $25.00 PMPM to the Medicare members of your HMO by providing $25.00 worth of additional benefits not covered by Medicare (such as drugs and routine eye care and glasses), reducing the premium by $25.00 per month, or offering any combination of premium reduction and benefit enrichment.

A health plan may also use what is referred to as a benefit stabilization fund, through which the government withholds a portion of the difference between the ACR and APR if the APR exceeds the ACR. The withholds can be withdrawn by the health plan in a future year so that the plan is able to offer its Medicare beneficiaries the same benefit package as in the previous year in the event that there is a reduction in the AAPCC or an increase in the ACR that would otherwise result in a reduction in the benefits available. Only a few plans have used this method of disposing of savings.

WHAT IF YOU MAKE A MISTAKE IN COMPUTING THE ADJUSTED COMMUNITY RATE/AVERAGE PAYMENT RATE?

An HMO must sign a contract lasting at least 1 year. All HMOs with Medicare contracts currently operate on a calendar year cycle to match the AAPCC cycle because the AAPCC payment rates change each year beginning on January 1.

Contracts are automatically renewable at the end of each contract period. During the contract term there can be no increase in the premium an HMO charges its Medicare members, nor can there be any reduction in the enriched benefits offered to Medicare members.

As a newly contracting HMO you can either overestimate or underestimate the ACR and APR. As noted above, the HCFA will not pay you more than the 95% AAPCC rate, but if you have overestimated an element of the ACR computation—let us say, for example, that you have overestimated the degree to which Medicare members will require more frequent visits to their primary care physicians—you pocket the difference. If you underestimate, you lose money.

Of course, the HCFA requires that you submit a new ACR computation for each year. During the first year of contracting you are permitted to use utilization data from other HMOs to come up with a Medicare ACR. After the first year you must use internal data, however, and in the case of pocketing the difference your internal data should show that the ACR of the first year had overestimated figures, leading to a windfall that will not be repeated in the coming year. If your ACR calculation had underestimated your cost, your recalculation would yield a higher ACR.

A LITTLE BIT OF HISTORY

Because you have now mastered the accounting aspects of Medicare contracting, we will take up the subject of history. The current body of law treating Medicare HMOs was passed in September 1982 as part of the Tax Equity and Fiscal Responsibility Act of 1982 (TEFRA). There were to be no TEFRA Medicare contractors until publication of final HCFA regulations on TEFRA contracting, however, which appeared in the January 10, 1985, *Federal Register*. The regulations became effective February 1, 1985.

There did exist pre-TEFRA risk contractors under rules in existence before TEFRA. The largest of these was the Group Health Cooperative of Puget Sound. There were never more than just a few health plans that chose to contract with the HCFA under the pre-TEFRA rules, although as of the beginning of 1992 there were 87 HMOs or CMPs with TEFRA risk contracts. Why the difference? TEFRA simplified the contracting requirements and brought them more in line with the way in which HMOs normally operate. Under pre-TEFRA rules, an HMO was reimbursed at 100% of the AAPCC, but it was required to file cost reports with the government to establish whether there was a loss or whether there were excess government payments at the 100% rate. If the cost of providing services was below the 100% rate, the HMO could keep only a portion of the profit or savings. If the cost of providing services (as determined through submission of a cost report by the HMO) was below the 100% level, the HMO and the government split the savings unless savings exceeded 20%. If savings exceeded 20%, the HMO retained 10% of the savings and the government kept the remainder. Losses, however, could be carried over into future years to offset the amount of savings that had to be shared with the government.

In 1982, the HCFA awarded demonstration contracts to try out the concepts of TEFRA-type risk HMOs through what were referred to as Medicare competition demonstration projects. These demonstration projects, some of which were operating under a variety of waivers of parts of section 1876 of the Social Security Act (the section entirely reworked by TEFRA), were all required to convert to TEFRA status. By the time TEFRA implementing regulations were published in January 1985, there were about 300,000 members (out of a total of about 30 million Medicare beneficiaries then) of these types of organizations. In February 1992, Medicare membership in TEFRA risk HMOs was nearly 1.4 million.

What TEFRA Did

On the payment side, TEFRA introduced the concept of sharing the wealth, to use Huey Long's phrase, whereby savings are returned to Medicare beneficiaries rather than to the government, as explained in the section above on the AAPCC. The computation of savings would be done on a prospective basis, and there would be

no retrospective adjustment and thus no cost reports filed by an HMO. As far as changes in contracting provisions, before TEFRA only plans that were federally qualified HMOs could have Medicare contracts. TEFRA modified HMO contracting rules to permit the HCFA to contract with a new type of entity, the CMP. The definition of a CMP is illustrated in Exhibit 28-2.

As of January 1992 there were 14 CMPs with Medicare contracts. As a result of the 1988 amendments to the HMO Act (the 1973 law authorizing federally qualified HMOs, Title XIII of the Public Health Service Act), the major differences that existed between federally qualified HMOs and CMPs at the time TEFRA was passed no longer exist: Federally qualified HMOs are no longer required to be separate legal entities, and they may set premium levels based on the utilization experience of groups (as opposed to the pre-1988 community rating requirement). The major remaining differences that continue to make the CMP option more feasible for certain organizations are (1) the level at which services may be provided through noncontracting providers and (2) the limitations that a CMP, but not an HMO, may impose on the scope of services. The 1988 HMO Act amendments introduced a provision allowing a feder-

---

Exhibit 28-2 Definition of a Competitive Medical Plan (CMP)

A CMP is defined as an entity that:

- is state licensed (organized under the laws of any State, to use the terminology of the regulations)
- provides health care on a prepaid, capitated basis
- provides care primarily through physicians who are employees or partners of the entity (or the services are provided through groups of physicians or individuals under contract to the CMP), *primarily* being defined under HCFA policy to be at least 51% of the services provided through the CMP (thus allowing preferred provider organizations to be CMPs)
- assumes full financial risk on a prospective basis, with provisions for stop loss, reinsurance, and risk sharing with providers
- meets the Public Health Service Act requirements of protection against insolvency

ally qualified HMO to provide up to 10% of physician services outside the HMO (ie, a self-referral option for members not wishing to use an HMO physician), whereas the requirement for the provision of medical services in a CMP is that the services be provided primarily through the CMP.

Although under a Medicare contract a CMP and an HMO would both be required to provide all Medicare-covered services, the commercial members of a CMP need not be offered certain benefits that the law requires an HMO to offer, such as home health care, mental health services, and substance abuse treatment. A CMP may also limit the scope of some of the services it is required to offer (the required services being physician services, inpatient hospital services, laboratory, radiology, emergency and preventive services, and out-of-area coverage) and is permitted to require deductibles and copayments. A federally qualified HMO may only charge nominal copayments and a deductible for the 10% of physician services the HMO is permitted to cover as out-of-plan services. A federally qualified HMO may not limit the scope of coverage except as specifically allowed in regulations (20 outpatient mental health visits per year being an example of a reduced scope of service permitted in HMO regulations).

What Congress Did after TEFRA

Only if you were out of the country during the summer of 1987 could you have escaped hearing about the government's termination of its Medicare contract with IMC, the HMO in south Florida and Tampa with 130,000 Medicare enrollees and one of the original TEFRA demonstration HMOs. Although the situation resolved itself through Humana's purchase of IMC, the contract termination and the events that led to the action generated a great deal of publicity. It is generally agreed, however, that having IMC leave the Medicare risk program was beneficial for both the HCFA and the HMO industry. The contract was terminated for IMC's failure to adhere to the 50/50 rule (although it did have a waiver of the rule, the health plan did not pursue commercial enrollments actively enough) and its failure to take corrective measures in its man-

agement and finances that had been requested by the HCFA.

Over the brief history of Medicare risk contracting, a number of new provisions of the law and regulations have been added that reflect concerns about questionable practices by, mainly, IMC. For example, the May 25, 1984, publication of the proposed TEFRA risk contracting regulations contained a provision that required all marketing material to be reviewed and approved by the HCFA before an HMO could use the material. This requirement was dropped in the January 10, 1985, publication of the final rules, only to be added later by Congress through the Consolidated Omnibus Budget Reconciliation Act of 1986 (COBRA). COBRA also required that HMOs immediately disenroll Medicare beneficiaries who requested disenrollment as of the first day of the month after the beneficiary's request; previously an HMO could retain a Medicare member for up to 60 days before disenrollment was effective.

The Omnibus Budget Reconciliation Act of 1985 (OBRA-85) introduced more requirements and restrictions on HMOs. The importance of the 50/50 requirement was re-emphasized because Congress limited the availability of waivers to government entities or to HMOs serving areas in which the Medicare/Medicaid population exceeds 50% of the total area population. Sanctions are to be imposed if an HMO fails to meet the 50/50 requirement: New enrollment can be prohibited, or the HCFA can permit new enrollment but the HMO will not be paid for the new enrollees. IMC was one of the health plans that was granted a waiver of the 50/50 rule under the prior, more liberal, criteria.

OBRA-85 requires HMOs to inform Medicare members of their rights when the beneficiaries join the HMO and annually thereafter. It was also OBRA-85 that brought about the option of disenrollment at Social Security offices for Medicare HMO members.

OBRA-85 expanded the role of peer review organizations (PROs) and a new type of entity referred to as a quality review organization (QRO) in monitoring the quality of care at HMOs by requiring PRO/QRO review of HMO inpatient care and ambulatory care. PROs and QROs are charged with the responsibility of investigating any complaint submitted to a PRO/QRO by a beneficiary regarding the quality of care rendered by an HMO. OBRA provides for fines against an HMO if it is found that the HMO substantially failed to provide adequate care.

OBRA-85 also mandates that there be a study of the physician incentive arrangements in hospitals reimbursed through the Medicare prospective payment system (DRGs) as well as incentive arrangements in HMOs with a view toward imposing restrictions on the types of incentive arrangements that have an adverse effect on patient care. After several years of pondering the issue, Congress, in OBRA-90, imposed added restrictions on Medicare-contracting HMOs that prevent them from having incentive arrangements that put physicians at substantial financial risk for services the physicians did not directly provide. If an HMO has incentive arrangements that the HCFA finds to involve such substantial financial risk, the HMO is required to have stop-loss provisions for its physicians, and the HMO must conduct beneficiary surveys to determine whether the risk arrangements affect the services members receive.

OBRA-87 required that HMOs that were terminating or not renewing a contract or were reducing their Medicare service area arrange for supplemental (Medigap) coverage to replace HMO coverage for Medicare beneficiaries affected by the HMO's decision. If an insurer imposes a waiting period for coverage of preexisting conditions, the HMO must arrange to have the waiting period waived or must otherwise provide for coverage, for up to 6 months, of services related to the preexisting condition.

OBRA-90 required Medicare-contracting HMOs to comply with Medicare requirements imposed on hospitals and other providers to make Medicare beneficiaries aware of the right to have their medical care subject to advance directives (living wills) and to have the beneficiary's instructions made part of the HMO medical record.

THE REQUIREMENTS TO OBTAIN A TEFRA CONTRACT

To obtain a TEFRA Medicare contract, a plan must be either a federally qualified HMO or des-ignated by the HCFA as a CMP. For an entity that wishes to become eligible as a CMP, the only type of application that may be submitted is a combined application to be found eligible as a CMP and to be granted a Medicare contract. An HMO or CMP must meet the following TEFRA requirements to obtain a risk contract.

Membership

A nonrural plan must have at least 5,000 (1,500 for a rural plan) prepaid capitated members for which the organization is at risk for the provision of comprehensive services (although risk may be shared by providers). The 5,000 rule may be satisfied by a parent organization that assumes responsibility for the financial risk and adequate management and supervision of health care services furnished by its subdivision or subsidiary, to cite the regulations. Even though the 5,000 rule may be met by a parent organization, however, there is a further requirement that there be a minimum membership of 1,000 at the subsidiary location before the plan may enter into a Medicare contract to establish that the subsidiary is viable and to have a valid basis for determining a Medicare ACR for the subsidiary.

An organization must have a membership that at all times during the contract does not exceed 50% combined Medicare and Medicaid enrollees. This provision (referred to as the 50/50 rule) can be waived only for government entities or if the HMO serves an area in which the population exceeds 50% Medicare/Medicaid.

Medical Services

The organization must be able to render directly or through arrangements all the Medicare services available in its service area. It must use Medicare-certified providers, that is, hospitals, skilled nursing facilities, and home health agencies. [Some skilled nursing facilities are certified only for Title XIX (Medicaid) patients, and some home health or home care agencies are not Medicare certified.] Physicians and suppliers used by the HMO may not include persons who have been barred from participation in either Medicare or Medicaid because of program abuse or fraud.

The HMO must be able to provide 24-hour emergency services and must have provisions for the payment of claims for emergency services within the service area and for out-of-area emergency or urgently needed services. All services that the HMO is required to render must be accessible with reasonable promptness, and there must be a record-keeping system that ensures continuity of care.

Open Enrollment

The law requires that a Medicare HMO have a 30-day open enrollment every year. An HMO must also have open its enrollment to Medicare enrollees disenrolled from another Medicare HMO in the area as a result of a contract non-renewal or termination. Aside from these required open enrollment periods, the HMO may have any other open enrollment period, including continuous open enrollment. During an open enrollment period the organization must enroll any Medicare beneficiary eligible to enroll who lives in the organization's service area. Medicare beneficiaries who are also Medicaid recipients may also enroll. Medicare beneficiaries who have end-stage renal disease (whether aged, disabled, or entitled to Medicare solely because of their disease), however, must be denied enrollment unless they are already an enrollee of the HMO. Medicare beneficiaries who have elected to be cared for in a Medicare-certified hospice are also prohibited from enrolling. If a person acquires end-stage renal disease after enrollment or elects hospice after enrollment, the HMO may not disenroll the individual.

The open enrollment requirement may be waived in one of three circumstances: (1) The organization will exceed 50% Medicare/Medicaid enrollment; (2) the organization will enroll a disproportionate share of enrollees in a particular AAPCC category, in which case the HCFA will permit the organization to discontinue enrollments in that AAPCC category; or (3) the organization does not have capacity to render services to any more enrollees, either commercial or Medicare. If an organization is going to limit enrollment under option (3), the HCFA must be informed 90 days before the open enrollment period so that HCFA approval can be given. In determining capacity for Medicare enrollees, the organization may set aside vacancies for expected commercial enrollees during each Medicare contract period.

Marketing Rules

An HMO must market its Medicare plan throughout the entire service area specified in the Medicare contract. All marketing material, including membership and enrollment material, must be approved by the HCFA before use. Prospective enrollees must be given descriptive material sufficient for them to make an informed choice in enrolling in an HMO. Prohibited marketing activities include door-to-door solicitation, discriminatory marketing (avoiding lower-income areas, for example), and misleading marketing or misrepresentation. These activities are subject to sanctions, including suspension of enrollment, suspension of payment for new enrollees, or civil monetary penalties (the government's euphemism for fines).

Ability To Bear Risk

An HMO or CMP must be able to bear the potential financial risk under a Medicare contract.

Administrative Ability

An organization must have sufficient administrative ability to carry out the terms of a Medicare contract. The same section of the regulations dealing with this provision mentions that an organization may not have any management, agent, or owner who has been convicted of criminal offenses involving Medicare, Medicaid, or Title XX. (The regulations are silent about what the HCFA thinks of other types of felons.)

Quality Assurance

HMOs are required under the Public Health Service Act to have quality assurance programs that are evaluated as part of the HMO qualification process. CMPs are required to have quality assurance programs to be granted a Medicare contract. The quality assurance program of a CMP must stress health outcomes to the extent consistent with the state of the art, must provide for peer review, must collect and interpret data systematically to make necessary changes in the provision of health services, and must include written procedures for remedial action to correct problems.

The Right To Inspect and Evaluate Records

The government has the right to inspect financial records as well as records pertaining to services performed under the contract and pertaining to enrollment and disenrollment of individuals. The right to inspect extends to entities related to the HMO, a right that was expanded in scope in OBRA-86.

Confidentiality of Records

The organization must adhere to relevant provisions of the Privacy Act and is required to maintain the confidentiality of the medical and nonmedical records of its Medicare members.

FLEXIBILITY IN CONTRACTING

The HCFA's view of the requirements for Medicare contracting has evolved since the early days of the risk-contracting program. Certain changes in policy have permitted expansion of Medicare risk contracting or have ensured the continuing participation of contractors. At the beginning of the TEFRA program, the HCFA maintained that there should be no difference between Medicare contracting and contracting with commercial groups with regard to the providers available to each type of member and the service area in which the HMO was being offered. In 1987, however, two changes were made that gave HMOs more flexibility in their Medicare-contracting options. One change was to allow HMOs to contract initially for less than their commercial service area as well as to drop counties from their service area at the end of any contract year. Because the HCFA's AAPCC

payment rates vary from county to county, one consequence of this change was that, in Minnesota, for example, HMOs that included rural counties in their service area were able to discontinue their Medicare contracts in the rural counties in which AAPCC payment rates were relatively low.

Another change has permitted HMOs to have differential premiums for different groups of Medicare enrollees. Under one Medicare HMO contract, premiums may vary by county, or the HMO may charge differential premiums based on the Medicare beneficiary's choice among two (or more) types of provider networks. For example, an HMO that delivers services in part through staff physicians and in part through an individual practice association (IPA) of independent physicians may charge Medicare beneficiaries less for choosing the staff option over the IPA option. In any case in which there are differential premiums among Medicare enrollees in an HMO, however, every Medicare beneficiary must receive the level of benefits and be charged no more than the maximum premium computed through the HMO-wide Medicare ACR process. That is, an HMO must treat all its Medicare members equally in computing its ACR to be submitted for HCFA approval. If the ACR requires that the HMO charge no more than $20 as a monthly Medicare premium, then all Medicare enrollees must be charged $20 or less. As long as all members are charged no more than $20, members who reside in certain counties, or members who choose a particular provider network, may be charged less than $20. The HMO would waive all or a portion of the otherwise collectible premium if the competitive situation in a particular county dictated such a practice or if the HMO wished to induce Medicare enrollees to choose one type of delivery system over another.

Employer group retirees represent a special case for which differential premiums are permitted. Often, employers or unions include, in their retiree benefit packages, additional services not covered by Medicare, and the union or employer contributes toward the individual's premium. Medicare beneficiaries who wish to enroll in a Medicare-contracting HMO offered through their employer or union may pay a higher or lower premium than individual Medicare enrollees.

WHICH OFFICE DOES WHAT, WHERE TO WRITE, AND WHOM TO CALL

We got even with H. L. Mencken for all the terrible things he said about government ("men . . . so little moved by concepts of public duty and responsibility as, say, the corps of advertising agents, or that of stockbrokers, or that of attorneys") by putting the massive headquarters of the Social Security Administration and the HCFA in the Sage of Baltimore's backyard. One of the few HCFA offices not in Baltimore is most of the Office of Prepaid Health Care Operations and Oversight (OPHCOO).

To obtain a contract, you must submit an application to the HCFA. You can obtain an application by writing to:

> HCFA Office of Prepaid Health Care
>   Operations and Oversight
> Wilbur J. Cohen Building
> 330 Independence Avenue SW
> Washington, DC 20201

Write to the same office to obtain information about and an application for federally qualified HMO status or to obtain Medicare contract eligibility as a CMP.

For information about the ACR process, you should contact:

> Division of Finance
> HCFA OPHCOO
> 1-G-2 Oak Meadows Building
> 6325 Security Boulevard
> Baltimore, MD 21207
> (410) 966-7634

The Division of Finance reviews and approves ACR submissions and is also responsible for payment activities and systems activities such as enrollment and disenrollment from HMOs.

There are 10 regional offices of the HCFA. Although an applicant would initially send an application for a Medicare contract (HMO or CMP) to the HCFA's central office, the regional offices have primary responsibility for processing Medicare contract applications and are the principal point of contact for HMOs after the HMO has a Medicare contract. The regional offices and the HCFA central office together monitor the performance of contracting HMOs through on-site visits that occur at least biannually (and more frequently if fortune shines on your HMO). Any marketing material that an HMO prepares that is not submitted with the original application submitted to the Division of Contract Administration has to be reviewed by the servicing HCFA regional office. The regional offices answer most beneficiary inquiries and investigate complaints about an HMO. They perform valuable technical assistance functions in the day-to-day Medicare operations of an HMO, including resolving problems that an HMO may be having with membership data being submitted to the HCFA, Medicare coverage issues, and liaison with Social Security offices and Medicare fiscal intermediaries. In other words, the regional office contact person is a good person to get to know, although you will also have HCFA central office contact people for systems and financial functions, and each HMO will have a central office overall plan manager.

THE STEPS OF THE CONTRACTING PROCESS

Before submitting a request for a Medicare contract as a part of a federal qualification or CMP eligibility determination, the applicant usually contacts the HCFA, if for no other reason than to obtain the most current application forms and accompanying explanatory material.

The purpose of an application for a Medicare contract is to allow the HCFA to determine whether you meet all the requirements for the granting of a contract, as listed above, and whether you have a sufficient understanding of how the requirements are to be implemented. Questions included in the application are illustrated in Exhibit 28-3.

If the organization wishes to apply as a CMP, you submit a combined application to OPHCOO. The Medicare sections of the application are reviewed by the HCFA regional office

Exhibit 28-3 Information Requested on Application for a Medicare Contract

- Types and number of providers the plan will use
- Listing of benefits
- Description of Medicare marketing strategy
- Copies of marketing material to be used
  —Evidence of coverage or subscriber agreement listing membership rules, enrollee rights, and plan benefits
  —How to use the plan to obtain services
  —Information on obtaining services after hours or in an emergency in or out of the service area
  —How to file claims from nonplan providers
  —The lock-in requirement
- Quality assurance plan
- Enrollment and disenrollment procedures, including a description of how the plan will meet the open enrollment requirement
- Plan's grievance and Medicare appeals procedures
- Other information as necessary

staff, and the financial and legal aspects (ie, the structural and contractual requirements imposed by the law) are reviewed by the OPHCOO central office staff. There will also be a site visit to decide whether you meet the criteria for designation as a CMP. If you wish to become a federally qualified HMO, you may also submit a combined application for HMO qualification and the granting of a Medicare contract; there will be a site visit to qualify you as an HMO (the qualification process is discussed in detail in Chapter 35). If you are already a federally qualified HMO, you submit a freestanding application for a Medicare contract. The evaluation of the Medicare contract application will also involve a site visit in many cases. For any of these situations, an ACR proposal must be submitted to the Division of Finance in Baltimore. Then you wait.

The Medicare application, or the Medicare portions of your combined application, is reviewed by the regional office, and comments are sent back to you. Then they wait.

You submit a reply to the comments, fix up your marketing material, promise to obey every law in the books and whatever new laws Congress passes, and so forth. Then you wait.

In the meantime, your able accountants have submitted a beautifully done ACR proposal to

Baltimore. You insisted that it be beautifully done because you know that until the ACR proposal is accepted, the HCFA will not sign a contract. Also in the meantime, you have had your management information systems staff talking with the OFM systems staff to make sure that, when you have members to accrete to your Medicare plan, your data submission will be compatible with the HCFA's requirements. Or you may choose to submit your accretions and deletions through Litton or CompuServe, each of which has a contract with the HCFA for the processing of health plan accretions and deletions. One advantage to using CompuServe or Litton is that you can have immediate verification of Medicare eligibility and identifying data, so that your submission of an accretion will be accepted by the HCFA on the first try, and you will be paid immediately for the new member. As far as how the government pays the plan, once you have a contract you will be paid through electronic funds transfer from the Treasury Department on the first day of each month.

Assuming that you have qualified your HMO or have been deemed eligible as a CMP, the HCFA finally tells you that, yes, you can have a contract. It mails you three copies of a contract to sign and return. You are done waiting. You now mobilize your Medicare marketing forces, deluge the HCFA regional office with brand new innovative marketing material on a daily basis, and (alas) wait again for the hordes of new Medicare enrollees.

WHY DO MEDICARE BENEFICIARIES JOIN A TEFRA RISK HMO?

You are now ready to market to your prospective Medicare members. There are a number of good reasons why a Medicare beneficiary would want to join your newly contracting HMO. If you know someone who is on Medicare, you know that the explanation of Medicare benefits is no fun to deal with. One advantage of HMO membership is that, for practically all services, Medicare beneficiaries do not have to be involved in any aspect of the claims payment process. Although this is a great advantage, especially to the friends and relatives of Medicare beneficiaries, the principal consideration prompting Medicare beneficiaries to join HMOs is financial. HMOs offer the full range of Medicare services at an affordable cost.

More than 70% of Medicare beneficiaries have supplemental insurance policies to cover the charges not paid by Medicare, such as the physician services coinsurance. In some areas, the cost of this type of Medigap policy exceeds the premium that a Medicare risk HMO would charge. Many physicians do not accept assignment from Medicare carriers, meaning that, in addition to the required 20% coinsurance that a beneficiary must pay and a $100 yearly deductible, the beneficiary must also pay any balance billed amount, the difference between what the physician has billed and the fee schedule payment made by the Medicare carrier, which is the upper limit of payment to that particular physician for that service. Recent changes in the law now limit the maximum liability of a Medicare recipient to balance billing by physicians who do not accept Medicare assignment. The liability maximum is determined from a formula and is a percentage above the Medicare allowed amount. Currently, Medicare covers, on the average, less than 50% of the costs of beneficiaries' medical care.

HMOs with Medicare contracts are permitted to charge Medicare members, in the form of a premium and copayments, the actuarial equivalent of the coinsurance and deductibles that is the average out-of-pocket expense for Medicare beneficiaries in fee-for-service (a figure that does not include amounts over and above what Medicare carriers pay based on the Medicare fee schedule). Thus, depending on the need for health services, an HMO enrollee could face lower out-of-pocket expenses compared to what he or she would have had to pay under fee-for-service. HMO membership also permits Medicare beneficiaries to budget specific amounts for medical expenses, even though there may be no savings in choosing the HMO option.

The extreme case, so to speak, of HMO membership being advantageous to Medicare beneficiaries exists in those competitive areas in which the marketplace has established a zero premium as the standard for TEFRA risk HMOs. These include the areas with the largest Medicare risk

HMO enrollment in the nation: south Florida and southern California. As of February 1992, about half of all Medicare risk enrollees were enrolled in health plans in these two areas. Not only do most of the beneficiaries in these areas have no premium, they also receive additional benefits not covered by Medicare, including prescription drugs and eyeglasses.

BENEFICIARY RIGHTS AND RESPONSIBILITIES

If you are a commercial member of an HMO, you know that you cannot go to any physician anywhere and expect your HMO to cover the cost of the care. If you are a Medicare beneficiary, you may not know this, even if you enrolled in a Medicare-contracting HMO. Explaining to Medicare beneficiaries how lock-in HMOs work has been a major problem. This is true partly because Medicare beneficiaries are accustomed to fee-for-service Medicare, in which a beneficiary may use almost any provider and can be assured that Medicare will pay some, if not all, of the costs of the services. It is also the case that some HMOs have enrolled Medicare beneficiaries in ways that do not adequately explain lock-in provisions (eg, such as mail-in applications). The HCFA strongly recommends that there be a face-to-face discussion of the requirements of HMO membership with prospective Medicare members. To ensure that the lock-in provision is understood, and to confirm enrollment, the HCFA sends every Medicare beneficiary a notice of HMO enrollment when the HCFA computer records are changed to annotate the individual's new HMO status.

Among the beneficiary rights is the right to remain enrolled in the health plan for the duration of the contract with the government. Involuntary disenrollment is permitted only if the person loses entitlement to Part B of Medicare, commits fraud in connection with the enrollment process or permits abuse of his or her membership card, permanently leaves the HMO's service area, fails to pay premiums or copayments, or (people who write regulations like to mention the obvious) dies. There is a provision allowing disenrollment for cause, or disruptive behavior that prevents the health plan from rendering services to the member or other members; such disenrollments have to have the prior approval of the HCFA.

Beneficiaries are guaranteed certain appeal rights for decisions made by an HMO regarding liability for Medicare services or coverage of Medicare services. The appeal rights include a provision that requires HCFA review of any decision that is adverse or partly adverse to a Medicare member. The HCFA review (which is actually done by a private entity under contract to the HCFA) can be followed by appeal to an administrative law judge (if the amount is $100 or more) and, for cases involving amounts of $1,000 or more, appeal for review at the federal court level.

Beneficiaries may voluntarily disenroll from an HMO whenever they wish. COBRA-85 requires the disenrollment to be effective the first day of the month after the month of the request. As of July 1987, beneficiaries may also disenroll from an HMO through any Social Security office.

WHAT IS DIFFERENT ABOUT HAVING A MEDICARE MEMBER?

Evaluating whether the payment an HMO will receive from the government is adequate is a necessary step in determining whether an organization will contract with the HCFA to enroll Medicare members. Another factor to be considered, which may be looked at as a cost, is that enrolling Medicare members and providing services to them is not identical to enrolling and serving a commercial population. In the commercial market, an HMO signs up a group and enrolls members through the group; in Medicare, the HMO must sign up individuals one by one (ie, retail selling). Thus the marketing strategy is different: The product is different, the means of making potential enrollees aware of the product is different, and the target of marketing is no longer a group and its representative but instead is an individual potential enrollee. These differences require an HMO to expand its marketing staff, and most HMOs with risk contracts have established a completely separate marketing department for Medicare.

There will also have to be a significant increase in the member relations staff of an HMO, again perhaps by establishing a totally separate department to deal with the Medicare membership. For a variety of reasons, Medicare beneficiaries require more hand-holding than commercial members. For example, either the member relations staff or the marketing staff will be responsible for ensuring that Medicare members understand the concept of lock-in or exclusive use of HMO providers, which is an especially difficult concept to convey to Medicare beneficiaries. The member relations staff will also be responsible for dealing with Medicare member grievances; and, along with the claims staff and medical or legal staff in the HMO, the member relations staff will probably be involved in the processing of Medicare appeals cases, which under the law must be reviewed by the HCFA when the HMO wishes to deny payment for claims or when the HMO denies a requested service.

Medicare enrollment records are not solely internal to the HMO. To be paid by the HCFA, an HMO must send its enrollment and disenrollment information to the HCFA on a monthly basis via magnetic tape or by using a commercial firm (CompuServe or Litton, currently) under contract with the HCFA to process membership data. Medicare members may disenroll at any time and may do so not only at the HMO or by writing to the HMO but also at any Social Security office. For both the enrollment and disenrollment process, there are specific regulatory requirements regarding written notice to the member and provisions regarding the timeliness of an HMO's actions.

The claims department of an HMO will be affected by a Medicare contract in that claims volume will increase for nonplan claims. For one thing, given that Medicare beneficiaries are higher utilizers of medical services, there will be a greater number of out-of-plan claims for emergency and urgently needed services. When a Medicare member uses an out-of-plan provider, a claim may be submitted to a Medicare carrier or intermediary as though the person were a fee-for-service Medicare beneficiary, but the claim will be transferred to the HMO from the Medicare carrier or intermediary (the Medicare fiscal agent for processing claims). Regulations require that an HMO process each claim received for its Medicare members and determine whether payment is appropriate. In its coordination of benefits activities, the claims department will have to become aware of Medicare coordination rules, because under a risk contract the HMO is in a sense acting as a Medicare fiscal agent in making payment decisions.

The services that are covered under the federal Medicare program are broader than services that a federally qualified HMO is required to provide to serve a commercial population. For example, durable medical equipment and skilled nursing facility services are not benefits usually available in a commercial group package. In addition to having to arrange such services, the HMO has to ensure that its utilization review staff is aware of what is and is not covered under Medicare.

All the above differences require the HMO either to expand its staff or to increase the responsibilities of its existing staff, which in either case usually means increased costs.

Another significant difference that will have to be considered when one is thinking about the consequences of obtaining a Medicare contract is the difference in the method of payment for Medicare members. The government does not pay an HMO in the same way that an employer group does, as explained above in the section on AAPCC payment. Consequently, an HMO may need to revise reimbursement arrangements with its existing providers and develop reimbursement arrangements with new providers (additional providers to expand capacity as well as new provider types, such as skilled nursing facilities and suppliers of durable medical equipment).

In establishing its guidelines for the ACR/APR computation explained above, the HCFA recognized that utilization by Medicare members is more frequent and more intensive than that of commercial enrollees. For example, if a physician is paid a capitation by the HMO to treat HMO commercial members, the same capitation would not be a reasonable payment to the physician for a Medicare member. If hospitals are paid a per diem rate for commercial HMO members, that same per diem may not be appropriate for Medicare members. The new reimbursement arrangements to take into account Medicare member utilization patterns need not result in a decrease in revenue on a per member basis, but it is important to know that there is more to Medicare contracting than just signing a contract and watching the AAPCC rates go up every year.

WHATEVER HAPPENED TO BIG BROTHER?

As of now, payments to HMOs are a minuscule part of the HCFA's budget. Of course, one person's minuscule is another person's majuscule: Payments to HMOs are minuscule in the context of a budget for Medicare health care expenditures that totals more than $110 billion. But any time an organization can receive 1 billion in payments from the government over 3 years, as is the case with the HMO that has the greatest number of Medicare enrollees, there is bound to be at least a slight amount of interest in having some government oversight.

Once any HMO, whether Medicare contracting or not, is qualified, or once a CMP is granted eligibility for a Medicare contract, the HCFA maintains ongoing monitoring of the plan. The monitoring is accomplished through self-reporting of financial and other information by the HMOs and CMPs on a quarterly basis, although if certain criteria are met, HMOs (but not CMPs) may report this information on a yearly basis. The information is reported to the OPHCOO central office on a special reporting form known as the National Data Reporting Requirements.

Specific to Medicare is a monitoring process that is performed by the OPHCOO and, principally, by the 10 regional offices of the HCFA. By the end of the first year of contracting, each plan will have a monitoring visit conducted jointly by the OPHCOO and the regional offices, during which the reviewers will determine whether the health plan is complying with regulatory requirements in such areas as insolvency arrangements, legal and financial requirements for the entity as a whole, quality of care issues, marketing practices, enrollment/disenrollment, claims payment, and grievance and appeals procedures. The reviewers follow a specific written protocol in conducting the review.

After such a monitoring visit, a report is prepared, and if necessary the HMO is required to submit a corrective action plan. Close monitoring of the plan continues until the HCFA is satisfied that the problems have been resolved. If the initial review goes well, there may not necessarily be a review of the same HMO for another 2 years.

As previously noted, Medicare risk-contracting HMOs are subject to external review of the quality of care they render. Peer review organizations, which also review the quality of care of institutional providers in fee-for-service Medicare, review an HMO's inpatient and ambulatory care. This review requirement has been the subject of a great deal of controversy among HMOs. The HMOs maintain that the review procedures are overly burdensome for the results they produce and that the methodology should be more tailored to the care rendered in a managed care system. As of the beginning of 1992, the HCFA is in the process of revising the methodology, in part on the basis of comments from the HMO industry and other outside groups such as hospital groups and the American Association of Retired Persons. To deal with another criticism of the current procedures, the new methodology will rely on random Medicare member lists as the basis for drawing review samples. Previously, no-pay bills submitted by hospitals to Medicare intermediaries (bills submitted for which the hospital did not claim any Medicare payment) were the basis of the sample. The level of submission of no-pay bills was well below the known utilization levels of members of Medicare HMOs, however, and in many cases the HCFA had to use alternative sampling methodologies.

ALTERNATIVES TO RISK CONTRACTING FOR THE RISK AVERSE

Figure 28-1 shows that cost contracting is increasing in popularity among HMOs as interest in risk contracting appears to be declining (although in the latter part of 1991 and in early 1992, business appeared to be picking up for risk, as judged from the number of applications for risk contracts that the HCFA had pending). Cost contracts are especially attractive to the faint of heart and to those burned by an unhappy experience with Medicare risk contracting: Cost contracts provide that the HMO is reimbursed by the HCFA for the reasonable cost of all services actually provided to Medicare enrollees, with the only significant cost that is not reimbursed being the profit of a for-profit contractor. Medicare enrollees of a cost-reimbursed organization are not locked into the plan. If a beneficiary chooses to use a nonplan provider, Medicare fee-for-service carriers and intermediaries will pay any claims without regard to the person's Medicare cost HMO status.

An HMO may obtain a cost contract under two different statutory provisions: the Social Security Act provision that also authorizes risk contracting (section 1876), and a provision that constitutes a fragment of a sentence in section 1833 of the Medicare law. The latter arrangement, a health care prepayment plan (HCPP) agreement, is virtually unregulated compared to the requirements of section 1876. A section 1876 contractor must be a federally qualified HMO or a CMP and must adhere to all the requirements that risk contractors follow other than PRO review of services (because there is no lock-in and no risk on the part of the cost HMO) and the requirement of holding an open enrollment to enroll beneficiaries leaving a risk HMO that is terminating its contract. An HCPP, on the other hand, may health screen, need not have an open enrollment, need not provide the full range of Medicare-covered services (only certain physician and supplier services are required), need not provide any appeal rights to members, and is not financially responsible for emergency care. Any organization that provides services to enrolled members through staff or contracted physicians may become an HCPP. Many of the HCPPs contracting with the HCFA are in fact labor or employer organizations that arrange for the provision of services exclusively to their members. As of February 1992, there were 25 HMO/CMP cost contractors, with 131,000 enrollees, and 52 HCPP contractors, with 524,000 Medicare enrollees.

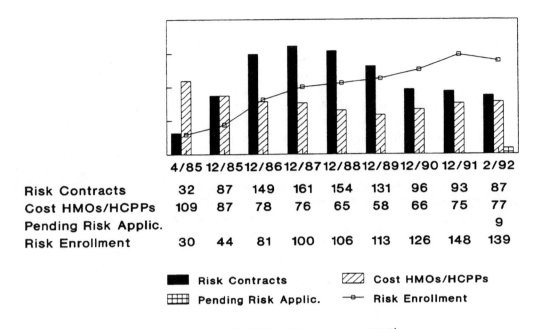

	4/85	12/85	12/86	12/87	12/88	12/89	12/90	12/91	2/92
Risk Contracts	32	87	149	161	154	131	96	93	87
Cost HMOs/HCPPs	109	87	78	76	65	58	66	75	77
Pending Risk Applic.									9
Risk Enrollment	30	44	81	100	106	113	126	148	139

■ **Risk Contracts** ▨ **Cost HMOs/HCPPs**
▦ **Pending Risk Applic.** –□– **Risk Enrollment**

Enrollment x 10,000 (i.e., 1.39 Million Enrollees in 2/92)

Figure 28-1 Medicare contracting, 1985 to 1992. *Source:* Health Care Financing Administration.

The HCFA is not enamored of cost HMOs/ CMPs because of the absence of a beneficiary lock-in, which defeats the purpose of a closed coordinated care system, and because it is uncertain whether cost HMOs/CMPs are cost effective for Medicare (in most cases HMOs/CMPs are free to pay their physicians at higher than Medicare fee-for-service payment levels). The same is true of most HCPPs, which the HCFA likes even less than cost HMOs/CMPs because of the absence of beneficiary protections. Liked or not, however, cost HMOs and HCPPs continue to be popular as a means of serving Medicare beneficiaries, including as a transition mechanism from risk when an organization decides to terminate its risk contract. It was always hoped at the HCFA that the only transition that would exist would be from cost to risk and never in the opposite direction. Reality made a reassessment necessary.

MEDICARE'S DUAL OPTION STRATEGY: A REASSESSMENT

In 1985, Medicare policy makers positioned Medicare as a dual option program: fee-for-ser-

vice and the risk HMO option. The expectation was that large numbers of Medicare beneficiaries would be enrolled in HMOs by the end of the decade. By 1991, however, only 3% of Medicare beneficiaries older than 65 years were enrolled in a risk contract HMO, and only 6% were enrolled in any type of coordinated care plan.

In contrast, by 1991, according the Health Insurance Association of America, 49% of employees younger than 65 years who received their health benefits from an employer-sponsored health plan were enrolled in a managed care plan. Managed care plans offered by employers included a broader array of options than were available to Medicare beneficiaries, such as preferred provider organizations (PPOs) and point-of-service options in addition to HMOs.

Medicare policy makers noted the divergent trends between private sector managed care enrollment and Medicare enrollment in coordinated care. Three perspectives were considered: the beneficiary, the HMO, and the Medicare program (discussed below). The result of this analysis was a revised coordinated care strategy for Medicare. The strategy incorporates four prongs, based on lessons learned from the private sector: (1) improving the Medicare risk HMO program, (2) making the choice of coordinated care more widely known to Medicare beneficiaries, (3) adopting an incremental approach to coordinated care that includes improving cost options for coordinated care (HMOs, CMPs, and HCPPs) and the addition of new coordinated care products, and (4) adding coordinated care strategies, such as case management, to Medicare fee-for-service (discussed below).

DUAL CHOICE: 1985 TO 1992

The Beneficiary Experience

By 1987, 0.9 million Medicare beneficiaries of a potential 32 million population had enrolled in a risk contract. By 1992, 1.4 million Medicare beneficiaries were enrolled. These statistics suggest that the demand from Medicare beneficiaries for enrollment in risk HMOs was low. More careful analysis, however, reveals that demand was high in some markets. For example, in Minnesota 40% of Medicare beneficiaries were enrolled in HMOs at the peak. In 1990, more than one third of Medicare beneficiaries were enrolled in HMOs in southern California and Portland, Oregon, and 27% of such beneficiaries were enrolled in south Florida. These penetration rates were similar to the rates for the nonelderly in these market areas and in some cases were higher.

Why don't more beneficiaries choose an HMO? First of all, the HMO option is not available in many areas. In addition, Medicare did not offer beneficiaries a choice when they became entitled to Medicare. Marketing was left to the HMO.

Information from focus groups suggests that beneficiaries do not necessarily understand that the HMO can be Cadillac insurance coverage. Rather, they are committed to their current physician, and unless this physician retires or they move, Medicare beneficiaries are reluctant to change their known source of health care. Additionally, many Medicare beneficiaries are not aware that expenses not covered by Medicare and supplemental policies can be covered by an HMO. The concept of coordinated care, where one is locked into a system, is not familiar to the senior population. Thus they do not seek change at a time when they may need health care coverage the most.

A recent study by the Group Health Association of America (GHAA) suggests that Medicare beneficiaries do choose HMO enrollment when the premium differential with Medigap supplemental policies is substantial. GHAA found that Medicare enrollment in the 12 highest penetrated HMO markets is similar to nonelderly enrollment when the Medicare HMO premium is low, for example, in south Florida and southern California, where the HMO Medicare premium is zero or minimal. Conversely, when HMO premiums are high relative to the cost of Medicare supplemental insurance, Medicare HMO enrollment is low. For example, when HMO premiums for Medicare enrollees were $82 per month in the Boston area, only 4% of Medicare beneficiaries chose to enroll in HMOs compared to 28% of the nonelderly population. Projections for the future show slow but steady growth in Medicare HMO risk enrollment.

The Health Maintenance Organization Experience

In 1987, 152 of more than 500 HMOs in the country had Medicare risk contracts. By 1992, the number of risk contracts had declined to 87. Four organizations had 64% of the Medicare HMO members.

HMOs are interested in Medicare contracts for several reasons. A primary reason is that HMOs sought a way to keep enrollees in the HMO after they became eligible for Medicare. Further, many HMOs felt that they could be successful in serving a broader Medicare population (eg, through an open enrollment process). For example, HMOs recognized that Medicare was paying too much for institutional care, and they determined that if their payment was based on Medicare fee-for-service they would be able to be more efficient for a population that was risky by definition.

Experience with the risk-contracting program over the last 6 years has caused HMOs to rethink their earlier enthusiasm for doing business with Medicare. First, the 5% discount from Medicare fee-for-service payment has been eroded by Medicare discounts accomplished in the 1980s (eg, DRGs for hospital care, reductions in over-priced procedures, and fee schedules for physician and supplier services). Second, marketing their product on an individual rather than a group basis, and the requirement to conduct an annual open enrollment, have been expensive. Third, the vagaries of the political process disrupted the prospective budgeting incorporated in the HMO budgets (eg, catastrophic enactment and repeal and Gramm-Rudman reductions). Finally, the Medicare method to set prospective premiums has been subject to methodological weaknesses, including adjustments for phase-in of prospective payment system (PPS) rates and working-age adjustments.

By 1991, most HMOs that remained in the Medicare risk program were concentrated in areas with high AAPCCs. Of all risk enrollees, 73% are in markets where Medicare payment is 110% of the national per capita amounts, and 58% are in areas with 132% of the national average. HMOs that were in low AAPCC areas have either dropped out of the program or shifted to cost payment arrangements.

Some organizations that had been successful in the past with risk contracts are now encountering significant projected losses. These organizations are shifting to other arrangements to serve their Medicare enrollees, such as HCPP agreements.

A number of HMOs, however, realized that the Medicare payment rate was not the only problem. Equally important was the HMO's ability to manage the care of an older and sicker population. Several companies with a corporate commitment began developing special services and programs to manage or coordinate the care of the elderly. These organizations have been successful with the Medicare population and are developing plans to expand Medicare risk contracts as a corporate goal.

Because of changing demographics, slow but steady growth in Medicare HMO contracts is projected.

Medicare's Experience

The Medicare program, like other payers, expected that the HMO enrollment would reduce program costs. The formula incorporates a 5% discount from fee-for-service expenditures. Although incentives appear to encourage efficiency, however, the evidence of savings to the Medicare program has been mixed. And some studies show net cost increases to the Medicare program.

Although Medicare administrators still believe that the HMO model offers a preferred alternative to fee-for-service with incentives for efficiency and value, there have been a number of research studies that suggest that Medicare beneficiaries who enroll in risk contracts are healthier than the average beneficiary.

On the other hand, HMOs indicate that enrollees use more services than budgeted. Many HMOs are able to offer the Medicare beneficiary additional benefits and reduced costs because Medicare payment levels are sufficiently high. Thus viewing savings from a Medicare only perspective is too narrow. One must also incorporate the impact on beneficiary costs. Additionally, HMO premium growth has been consistently below the growth in premiums for indemnity insurance (ie, Medigap).

HCFA research also suggests that large HMO penetration reduces costs in the fee-for-service sector. A 1991 study showed a direct correlation between reduced hospital costs in an area and HMO market penetration. Another study found that HMO market share decreases Medicare fee-for-service expenditures. Additional research is being conducted on how the Medicare payment method can be improved, for example, through the addition of health status adjustors.

AN INCREMENTAL STRATEGY

For coordinated care to have a significant impact, it must involve many more Medicare beneficiaries. Medicare must build on the successes of its current programs to bring the advantages of coordinated care to the 94% of Medicare beneficiaries who do not currently have a choice or, where they have a choice, choose not to enroll in a comprehensive plan.

Ultimately, Medicare would like all Medicare beneficiaries to have a choice between fee-for-service and a risk-based plan. Thus the Medicare program has adopted, and proposed, a number of changes that are intended to make the risk option more attractive for organizations to seek Medicare contracts and beneficiaries to enroll.

The realities in 1992 (when this chapter was written), however, are that many organizations are not ready to provide services on a full risk basis to Medicare beneficiaries throughout the nation. In addition, many beneficiaries are not ready to enroll with a comprehensive care organization that provides services in a single location. Thus the Medicare program has adopted an incremental coordinated care strategy that will offer a range of coordinated care products.

The Medicare program is also proposing a number of reforms to the Medicare fee-for-service program that will introduce the incentives and advantages of coordinated care systems.

Improvements to the Medicare Risk Contract Option

Medicare has worked aggressively to be a better business partner with HMOs that choose to enter risk contracts. These changes address both the supply side (ie, the number of HMOs that choose to enter risk contracts) and the demand side (ie, the number of Medicare beneficiaries who are interested in choosing a risk plan).

Recent improvements on the supply side, as noted previously, include allowing risk-contracting HMOs retroactively to enroll employer group retirees; reforming quality assurance reviews conducted by PROs to be less burdensome and more accurate (the reformed process will focus attention on problem identification and resolution instead of costly and often ineffective retrospective case review); correcting methodologic problems with the payment method, such as how PPS phase-in amounts and national coverage expansions are calculated; and decentral-

izing administration of HMO contracts to regional offices to expedite contract approval and monitoring and problem resolution.

On the demand side, Medicare is implementing a number of activities to ensure that Medicare beneficiaries understand that their choices for Medicare include not only fee-for-service but also coordinated care. For example, all Medicare publications are being revised to emphasize the theme of choice, and materials are being provided to Social Security offices to ensure that information about beneficiary options is available. Medicare is also contacting employers to ensure that they understand coordinated care options for retirees.

The HCFA has proposed a number of reforms that require legislative action. These include reforming the Medicare prospective payment method (AAPCC) to increase payment and to adjust properly for high HMO penetration levels, providing adjustments in Medicare payment for outliers (ie, those beneficiaries who consume higher than average resources), providing financial incentives for Medicare beneficiaries to join a risk plan through a refund of a portion of their Medicare Part B premium, and requiring Medicare beneficiaries to make a positive choice for fee-for-service and coordinated care at the time they become eligible for Medicare.

Alternatives to the Risk Option

Not all Medicare beneficiaries want to enroll in the full lock-in system required by the risk HMO. More flexible coordinated care arrangements should be more attractive to certain beneficiaries (eg, beneficiaries who travel or live part of the year in other locations). In addition, more flexible coordinated care options are considered a transition to the full risk HMO and an improvement over fee-for-service Medicare.

Medicare has revised its dual choice strategy to offer an incremental approach to coordinated care. Policy makers believe that a continuum of complementary coordinated care choices will allow beneficiaries to choose the arrangement that best suits them, from fee-for-service to nonenrollment models to opt-out models to risk

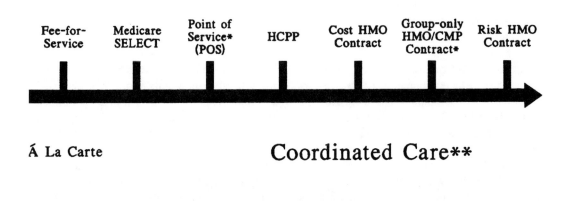

Á La Carte   **Coordinated Care****

* **Proposed Law**
** **Continuum reflects range of services included under Coordinted Care**

Figure 28-2 Range of Medicare options. *Source:* Health Care Financing Administration.

HMO models. Figure 28-2 displays the continuum currently envisioned by Medicare.

Medicare SELECT

A new coordinated care product is Medicare SELECT, recently enacted by the OBRA-90 in 15 states for a 3-year period. Medicare SELECT permits Medicare supplemental insurance companies to offer a preferred provider organization network-type product in conjunction with their Medicare supplemental insurance (Medigap). Medigap is private insurance that covers medical costs that Medicare does not pay, such as deductibles and coinsurance. In exchange for a reduced premium, Medicare SELECT policies provide a financial incentive for Medicare beneficiaries to use their network of providers. For example, if a network physician is used, the Medicare SELECT policy will pay 20% coinsurance; if a nonnetwork physician is used for nonemergency services, however, the Medicare SELECT policy may pay no coinsurance or a reduced amount.

Medicare SELECT policies are considered an incremental coordinated care product because the financial penalty to the Medicare enrollee for using out-of-network services is minimal. That is, Medicare will pay its share of the cost regardless of whether the network provider is used. In the example cited, Medicare will continue to pay 80% of the nonnetwork physician's fee.

Through Medicare SELECT, beneficiaries are provided an incentive to choose physicians and providers that authorize only medically necessary services. If beneficiaries choose a nonnetwork provider or physician, however, the cost will be limited and predictable because Medicare will continue to pay its share.

Point of Service

The next generation of coordinated care options is the point-of-service option. Ultimately, Medicare expects that this option (which requires authorizing legislation) will replace Medicare fee-for-service as we know it today. Point-of-service models are the current choice of private employers (see Chapter 23) because they provide the flexibility for employees to choose a network or nonnetwork provider on a service-by-service basis with marginal financial risk. But they also provide a financial or other incentive for employees to use a network, where care will be coordinated and unnecessary or inappropriate care minimized.

Many argue that Medicare fee-for-service is already a type of point of service because it discounts fees on the basis of volume of services. Medicare believes that this is a shortsighted analysis. Although Medicare has realized discounts from PPS and new physician and supplier fee schedules, there are few volume controls that are basic to an effective point-of-service system.

Under fee-for-service Medicare, physicians are free to order marginally necessary tests or marginally appropriate procedures and Medicare will continue to pay. Point-of-service will provide a system of health care delivery that will encourage providers to consider the episode of care and the delivery of appropriate care in the appropriate setting. It will provide enhanced value for the Medicare payment and enhanced quality for the beneficiary because the care plan will be focused on the needs of the patient rather than on the Medicare fee schedule.

Improved Cost-Contracting Models

Under the dual option strategy, Medicare deemphasized coordinated care options that are currently authorized by statute. These include cost contracts with HMOs/CMPs and agreements with HCPPs. Medicare was concerned that these cost options resulted in costs that were higher than those for fee-for-service Medicare (ie, through duplicate payment) and in the lack of incentives for cost contractors to consider total costs outside their network. In addition, HCPPs do not provide sufficient beneficiary protections. Under the incremental strategy, Medicare is proposing to redesign the current cost-contracting options through regulatory and legislative changes. Redesigned cost options permit more flexible coordinated care arrangements that allow Medicare beneficiaries to choose to go out of network for minimal penalty (ie, a modified self-referral option). They also will provide cost-contracting entities with incentives to coordinate care, to control total Medicare costs, and to ensure beneficiary protections, which are cornerstones of the risk contract model.

Modified Fee-for-Service

Medicare recognizes that even if these incremental reforms are enacted, they will take time to be implemented throughout the United States. Thus Medicare is proposing that the fee-for-service system incorporate many of the managed care features that have been successful in the private sector. One of the most promising approaches is a case management program. Under this system (which requires authorizing legislation), a potentially high-cost beneficiary is identified by a case management company and is offered a voluntary program where a case manager, together with the beneficiary's physician, will develop a plan of treatment. This treatment plan may modify Medicare-covered benefits if appropriate (eg, it will cover more home health visits). The plan must ensure cost-effective, quality care. For the Medicare beneficiary and his or her family, case management offers a more appropriate treatment plan that provides care in the most appropriate setting.

CONCLUSION

A Definite *Maybe* to Risk Contracting

If you understand how Medicare HMO payment works, and if you understand that dealing with the Medicare population is different from dealing with group accounts in more than a few minor ways, then you should have no difficulty in deciding whether it is feasible for you to enter into a Medicare risk contract with the HCFA. The key determinant of whether an HMO will want a Medicare risk contract is the payment issue. Preparation of an ACR submittal to the HCFA should not be just an exercise in accounting and statistics to satisfy a regulatory requirement. Without knowing how much the government will pay and how much it will cost to render Medicare services in a risk plan, there can be no reasoned answer to the question of whether it is a wise business decision for a particular HMO or CMP to have a risk contract. This is evident from the brief history of the TEFRA risk-contracting program, graphically represented in Figure 28-1. Even though enrollment in Medicare risk plans has grown at a steady pace, only half as many HMOs are contracting with the HCFA on a risk basis in 1992 as were contracting in 1987.

The reason given by most plans for deciding not to renew is that AAPCC rates are too low. A complete reason is probably that the AAPCC rates were too low for the costs they incurred because (choose one or more) they had adverse selection, utilization was way beyond what they expected, they projected the wrong enrollment mix, they did not get a sufficient number of enrollees to have a good risk base, and so on. The many factors that would lead an HMO not to renew a Medicare risk contract are obviously the factors that must be considered before an entity decides whether to contract with the HCFA on a risk basis. You can consult an astrologer, or you can go to the trouble of developing good data that will tell you whether your health plan should contract or not.

Other Alternatives

The incremental coordinated care strategy recognizes that not all Americans will choose risk HMOs and that not all plans are ready, willing, or able to take on a risk contract. Thus a continuum of choices is now in place, and additional options are expected to be available soon. Combined with innovations and incentives, these coordinated care options are designed to be attractive to beneficiaries and are intended to move the Medicare program away from à la carte, uncoordinated, fee-for-service.

Regardless of the approach, each plan must assess the risks and rewards of participation in the Medicare program. There are 34 million Medicare beneficiaries out there, eagerly awaiting your decision.

Additional Reading

Law and Regulations

The law governing Medicare risk and cost contracts with HMOs and CMPs is found at section 1876 of the Social Security Act or section 1395(mm) of the US Code. The fragment of a sentence that authorizes health care prepayment plans is found at section 1833(a)(1)(A) of the Social Security Act. Title XIII of the Public Health Service Act (42 USC 300e) is the law that deals with federally qualified HMOs.

Regulations for all these entities are found in Title 42 of the Code of Federal Regulations, sections 417.100 through 417.180 (federally qualified HMOs), sections 417.400 through 417.694 (cost and risk HMOs and CMPs), and sections 417.800 through 417.810 (HCPPs). (Current editions of the *Code of Federal Regulations* also

contain sections 417.200 through 417.292, which are obsolete in that they contain only pre-TEFRA contract provisions.)

For the voracious reader, the *Federal Register* of May 25, 1984, and of January 10, 1985, contain, respectively, the proposed and final versions of the TEFRA contracting regulations, which are relevant to those interested in seeing the changes between the proposed and final versions of the regulations and in knowing the types of public comments received on the regulations.

Also published in the *Federal Register* was a January 6, 1986, notice (pp 506–510) outlining the HCFA's AAPCC payment methodology. Explaining the AAPCC, and studying it, is a cottage industry of its own, as is evident from the list of additional reading materials below.

The law and regulations are available at any federal depository library, at law libraries, and through compendiums such as the *Commerce Clearing House Medicare and Medicaid Guide*. CD-ROM versions of the HCFA's regulations and manuals are also now becoming available.

Manuals

The *Medicare HMO/CMP Manual* (HCFA Publication 75) is in the process of being updated as of the beginning of 1992. The manual generally explains (in layperson's language), or expands on, the requirements contained in the law and regulations. All Medicare-contracting HMOs/CMPs/HCPPs receive the *Manual* and any updates. The *Manual* may be purchased through:

> National Technical Information
>   Service
> Department of Commerce
> 5825 Port Royal Road
> Springfield, VA 22161
> (703) 487-4630
> Publication number PB 85-953899

Reports of the General Accounting Office Related to Medicare HMOs

The first two digits indicate the year in which the report was issued.

91-03 *PRO Review Does Not Assure Quality of Care Provided by Risk HMOs*

89-46 *Medicare: Health Maintenance Organization Rate Setting Issues*

89-03 *Reasonableness of HMO Payments Not Assured*

88-12 *Physician Incentive Payments by Prepaid Health Plans Could Lower Quality of Care*

88-08 *Experience Shows Ways To Improve Oversight of HMOs*

88-07 *Issues Concerning the HealthChoice Demonstration Project*

88-05 *Improving Quality of Care Assessment and Assurance*

87-11 *Uncertainties Surround Proposal To Expand Prepaid Health Plan Contracting*

87-07 *Preliminary Strategies for Assessing Quality of Care*

General Accounting Office reports may be obtained from:

General Accounting Office
PO Box 6015
Gaithersburg, MD 20877
(202) 275-6241

Books and Journal Articles

The following monographs, all by Susan Jelley Palsbo of GHAA, are the most lucid and thorough explanation of the AAPCC:

The USPCC Explained (June 1988)
The AAPCC Explained (February 1989)
The Demographic Factors Explained (February 1990)
Medicare Capitation Explained (March 1990)

The monographs, which are all GHAA publications, are available from:

GHAA
1129 20th Street
Suite 600
Washington, DC 20036
(202) 778-3200 [Fax: (202) 331-7487]

Other pertinent materials include the following:

Adamache K, Rossiter L. The entry of HMOs into the Medicare market: implications for TEFRA's mandate. *Inquiry*. 1987;23:1314-1418.

Anderson GF, Steinberg EP, Powe NR, et al. Setting payment rates for capitated systems: a comparison of various alternatives. *Inquiry*. 1990;27:225-233.

Ash A, Ellis RP, Lezzoni L. *Clinical Refinements to the Diagnostic Cost Group Model*. Boston: Health Policy Research Consortium, Cooperative Research Center; 1990.

Ash A, Porell F, Gruenberg L, et al. Adjusting Medicare capitation payments using prior hospitalization data. *Health Care Financing Rev* 1989;10:17-29.

Barnett B. How to take the risk out of Medicare HMO management: opportunities and challenges in the 1990s. *Group Pract J*. 1989;38:29-30,32-33,36.

Brown B. The structure of quality assurance programs in risk-based HMOs/CMPs enrolling Medicare beneficiaries. *GHAA J*. 1989;10:68-82.

Dowd B, Feldman R, Wisner C. *Issues Regarding Health Plan Payments under Medicare and Recommendations for Reform*. Bloomington, MN: University of Minnesota, Division of Health Services Research and Policy; 1990.

Health Care Financing Administration (HCFA). *Expanding Medicare Coordinated Care Choices for Employer Group Retirees*. Baltimore: HCFA Office of Coordinated Care Policy and Planning; 1991.

Hill JW, Brown RS. *Biased Selection in the TEFRA HMO/CMP Program: Final Report*. Baltimore: Health Care Financing Administration; 1990.

Langwell K. Structure and performance of health maintenance organizations: a review. *Health Care Financ Rev*. 1990;12:71-79.

Langwell KM, Hadley JP. Insights from the Medicare HMO demonstrations. *Health Affairs*. 1990;9:74-89.

Langwell KP, Hadley JP. *National Evaluation of the Medicare Competition Demonstrations: Summary Report*. Baltimore: Health Care Financing Administration;1989.

Langwell K, Rossiter L, Brown R, Nelson L, Nelson S, Berman K. Early experience of health maintenance organizations under Medicare competition demonstrations. *Health Care Financ Rev.* 1987;8:37-56.

Lichtenstein R, Thomas JW, Adams-Watson J, et al. Selection bias in TEFRA at-risk HMOs. *Med Care.* 1991;29:318-331.

Lubitz J. Health status adjustments for Medicare capitation. *Inquiry.* 1987;24:362-375.

McCombs JS, Kasper MD, Riley GF. Do HMOs reduce health care costs? A multivariate analysis of two Medicare HMO demonstration projects. *Health Serv Res.* 1990;25:593-613.

McMillan A, Lubitz J. Medicare enrollment in health maintenance organizations. *Health Care Financ Rev.* 1987;8:87-94.

Morrison EM, Luft HS. Health maintenance organization environments in the 1980s and beyond. *Health Care Financ Rev.* 1990;12:81-90.

Nelson L, Brown R. *The Impact of the Medicare Competition Demonstrations on the Use and Cost of Services: Final Report.* Baltimore: Health Care Financing Administration; 1989.

Newhouse JP, Manning WG, Keeler EB, Sloss EM. Adjusting capitation rates using objective health measures and prior utilization. *Health Care Financ Rev.* 1989;10:41-54.

Pollard MR. The impact of recent legal and regulatory changes on Medicare risk contractors. *HMO/PPO Trends.* 1990;3:13-15.

Porell FW, Tompkins CP, Turner WM. Alternative geographic configurations for Medicare payments to health maintenance organizations. *Health Care Financ Rev.* 1990;11:17-30.

Porell FW, Turner WM. Biased selection under an experimental enrollment and marketing Medicare HMO broker. *Med Care.* 1990;28:604-615.

Porell FW, Wallack SS. Medicare risk contracting: determinants of market entry. *Health Care Financ Rev.* 1990;12:75-85.

Rossiter LF, Adamache KW. Payment to health maintenance organizations and the geographic factor. *Health Care Financ Rev.* 1990;12:19-30.

Scheffler RM, Rossiter LF. *Advances in Health Economics and Health Services Research.* Greenwich, CT: JAI Press. A continuing series.

Siddharthan K. HMO enrollment by Medicare beneficiaries in heterogeneous communities. *Med Care.* 1990;29:918-927.

Welch WP. Defining geographic areas to adjust payments to physicians, hospitals and HMOs. *Inquiry.* 1991;28:151-160.

Welch WP. Improving Medicare payments to HMOs: urban core versus suburban ring. *Inquiry.* 1989;26:62-71.

West J. The future of HMO Medicare risk contracts: views from the plans' perspective. *HMO/PPO Trends.* 1990;3:7-13.

Wilensky GR, Rossiter LF. Coordinated care and public programs. *Health Affairs.* 1991;10:62-77.

Chapter 29

Medicare Risk Contracting: An Industry Perspective

Jan Malcolm

As discussed fully in Chapter 28, the Tax Equity and Fiscal Responsibility Act (TEFRA) authorized the Health Care Financing Administration (HCFA) to contract with health maintenance organizations (HMOs) and competitive medical plans for the provision of services to Medicare recipients on a full risk basis; that is, the health plan, rather than the federal government, accepts risk for medical expenses. Such contracts are generally referred to as Medicare (or TEFRA) risk contracts.

Successfully holding a Medicare risk contract over time requires attention to trends, careful planning, and flexibility in managing a whole range of issues in a significantly changing environment. A risk contractor's serenity prayer might go something like this: "God (or Congress), grant me the strength to manage what variables I can control, the insight to project correctly the variables I cannot control, and the wisdom to know the difference."

If you are evaluating whether your plan should enter into a risk contract or continue a contract you already have, this chapter will pose a number of questions that may be relevant for your consideration. Although there are some similarities in strategies and capabilities among successful risk-contracting plans nationwide, there are important determinations that can only be made in the context of your own plan's situation. The questions and suggestions are organized in the following categories:

- How does your plan's mission shape your product strategies?
- What strategic decisions should you make up front?
- What marketplace opportunities and constraints will you face?
- What financial issues and trends must you understand?
- How will your plan's operations be affected?

Whatever your plan's experiences and decisions regarding Medicare risk contracting, the issues underlying the Medicare business provide a window into the future of private sector purchasing and health care reform as well.

QUESTIONS OF MISSION

How does your plan's mission shape your Medicare product strategies? Is your plan in

Jan Malcolm is Vice President for Public Policy and Programs at Group Health, Inc in Minneapolis–St. Paul, Minnesota.

business to sell insurance products or to provide medical care? Are your primary constituents your members, providers, or shareholders? These questions may seem self-evident to some and irrelevant to others. They are worth some thought, however, because the answers may have a strong bearing on whether your plan is a long-term player in risk contracting or is soon driven out by more pressing priorities.

Your plan's mission might be to offer the most competitive products possible to be the largest plan in your market. You would then evaluate risk contracting in that light. If yours is a for-profit plan, you might be inclined to contract on a risk basis for only as long as HCFA's average area per capita cost payments (AAPCCs) generate a return equal to or better than margins from your other lines of business.

Group Health, Inc (GHI), by way of illustration, is a member-governed, staff model HMO whose mission is to provide affordable high-quality care to its members. GHI considers itself a care delivery system first and an insurance entity second. As a member-governed organization GHI knows that it will always provide care to the Medicare population, particularly because the current enrollees in GHI's Medicare products are the very people who founded GHI in the 1950s. GHI's goal is to provide Medicare products of the highest value to members and under financing approaches that best fit our medical group operations. GHI has had a risk contract since the mid-1980s.

Whatever your plan's mission, your key management staff needs to have a shared understanding of how your Medicare product strategy fits that mission. Medicare products are challenging to manage, so that clear and consistent commitment and direction from the plan's leadership will be necessary.

STRATEGIC DECISIONS

Demographic reality is a pretty straightforward reason for getting into and staying in the Medicare business in some form. The population is aging, and future market share growth almost demands that you respond. A sound strategy for long-term success must address the following issues up front.

How Will Your Plan Define Success?

Will you expect your Medicare contract to produce the same financial results as commercial business, or are other results acceptable given other strategic considerations? Will you expect the same rate of growth as for other products, or are you striving for faster or more cautious growth? Is your primary market your existing enrollees as they age in to Medicare or seniors from the larger community who have not previously been your members?

Plan for a Long-Term Commitment

Plans should view Medicare risk contracting as a major commitment with long-term consequences. A risk contract is not something to be casually experimented with and easily discarded. The HCFA and many states require a plan to replace a terminating risk contract with substantially similar coverage. Any replacement product that is less favorable to seniors in terms of price or benefits will prompt negative community reaction and can cause a significant backlash from your state regulators and legislature.

Plans should understand that there is little margin for error and plan accordingly. Before entering into a risk contract, plans should try to assess its viability several years downstream, making fairly conservative assumptions. Part of having a long-term view involves knowing where you want to end up with enrollment. Some plans have enrolled so many seniors that their finances are now driven heavily by Medicare experience. They may have intended this result or just happened into it as a result of stronger than expected Medicare sales after a number of years. Either way, a heavy dependence on Medicare could be a vulnerable position for plans given the volatility of Medicare revenues and expenses.

As an example, GHI's long-term enrollment goal is to mirror our community's demographic

make-up. We do not seek to enroll a disproportionately high percentage of seniors. Several
years ago, even while our Medicare risk margins
were significantly better than our commercial
business, we slowed down the rate of enrollment
growth in our risk product. We did this to keep
our enrollment in proportion and because we
were anticipating the coming collision of increasing costs and flattening revenues.

THE MARKETPLACE

There are great rewards in bringing products
of excellent value and good care management to
the Medicare market. These products can make a
difference in peoples' lives and can demonstrate
the advantages of managed care at its best. A
risk product can provide important financial protection to seniors on fixed incomes by eliminating out-of-pocket expenses and adding needed
benefits not covered by Medicare. A risk contract with its comprehensive coverage, no paperwork, defined provider network, and care coordination systems can also greatly simplify for
seniors both insurance and care systems, which
can be bewildering.

In short, these products really meet a need,
and enrollment results can bear that out. In Minneapolis–St Paul, all the major HMOs began offering risk products in the early 1980s. Within
about 5 years, more than half the local Medicare
population had enrolled. Several of the plans
have since converted their risk contracts to
health care prepayment plans (HCPPs) or Medicare supplements, but the seniors have largely
stayed with the HMOs.

What Sells? What Can You Afford?

To some degree, marketing a risk product requires overcoming a lack of awareness among
seniors of what Medicare itself actually covers.
Collaborative community education campaigns
with local senior organizations can be effective
in this regard.

In designing your specific benefits package
and marketing strategy, you will obviously want
to know what benefits are most attractive to seniors. Do not assume that your standard commercial package is right for this population for reasons of both consumer preference and financial
risk. Do some market research, and be quite conservative in your financial projections. You may
find, for example, that access to chiropractors
and podiatrists is more important to prospective
senior members. You will certainly find that prescription drug coverage is a desirable benefit. If
your AAPCCs are high enough, and/or if your
delivery system is efficient enough, and if you
are not concerned about adverse selection, drug
coverage can be a strong marketing plus. With
high pharmacy cost trends and at the higher utilization levels of seniors, however, the financial
impact of the drug benefit in your Medicare
product will be much greater than in your commercial business.

Extended coverage of home care and
noninstitutional chronic care can also be major
selling points. For example, in addition to our
TEFRA risk contract, GHI also has one of the
four Social/HMO (S/HMO) sites in the country.
The S/HMO product is reimbursed at 100% of
the AAPCC in recognition of the fact that a less
healthy population is expected to join. Covered
benefits include the benefits of our TEFRA plan
plus prescription drugs and an annual fixed dollar benefit for long-term care services. There is
growing concern among the Medicare population and service providers with the lack of a national strategy for dealing with long-term care
coverage. Federal and state budgets probably
will not allow for the expansion of coverage that
seniors want any time soon. Given these opposing forces, we think there is an emerging private
market for long-term care coverage. Medicare
risk contractors have a major opportunity to fill
in the gap, perhaps through S/HMO contracts if
those become more widely available permanent
contracting options in the future.

What Do You Want To Be Known for?

You will need to decide what position you
want your plan to occupy in the market. Do you
want to offer the most comprehensive product?
The lowest priced? The broadest provider net-

work? The one position you probably do not want to hold is that of the most comprehensive and the highest priced plan. Traditional supplement plans may be able to pull off such a position because they can health screen applicants (except during the first 6 months after an applicant enrolls in Medicare Part B). A TEFRA risk plan, however, cannot health screen any time it is open for enrollment. It may be logical for younger seniors to purchase the cheapest product they can find and later, as their health care needs increase, move up to more comprehensive products if those are available to them.

Whatever your chosen position in the market, it is wise to do your annual pricing with an eye on long-term trends. Given the pressures of the budget deficit, it is only logical to assume that federal payments will continue to lag behind the rate of cost inflation. So, costs will continue to be shifted to the private sector to an increasing degree, or providers will deliver ever more deeply discounted services, or seniors will pay more of the total bill. It is probably a mistake intentionally to hold down your premium rates one year to gain market share and then hit the population with a large rate increase the next year. Smoothing out the predictable increases steadily is probably more palatable over the long run.

FINANCIAL TRENDS

This brings us back to the importance of understanding long-term trends in evaluating your initial decision about whether to enter into a Medicare risk contract and then in managing the product on an ongoing basis. Receiving a payment at 95% of local fee-for-service costs sounds like a good deal. Most HMOs would expect to be able to be more than 5% more efficient than the fee-for-service system. But do not forget what the payment is based on.

First, as discussed in Chapter 28, the AAPCC payment is not based on 95% of fee-for-service charges but rather on costs as experienced by the HCFA. Charges that the HCFA disallows do not count in the base. Given that Medicare pays deeply discounted prices, a risk contractor will have to be considerably more efficient than community fee-for-service utilization levels to make the finances work, unless it intends simply to pass along Medicare payment rates to its providers (and that would probably make the contracting staff's job rather difficult). Second, the HCFA's payment only covers basic Medicare services. Extra benefits that the plan wants to offer must be financed entirely out of delivery system efficiencies or by member premiums.

Think Long Term

To assess a risk contract's long-term prospects, you need to realistically project revenue and cost trends, remembering that the federal government has both the incentive (the deficit) and the ability (regulation and sheer purchasing clout) to hold its payment levels below those of the private market. In the past, the HCFA has usually attributed risk contractor terminations to plans' inexperience, inefficiency, lack of commitment or critical enrollment mass, or adverse selection. The HCFA does not usually acknowledge the impact of its deeply discounted purchasing or the resultant cost shift. The HCFA seems serious about wanting managed care and risk contracting to be at the core of its Medicare reform strategy, but as long as it can buy services for what it is now paying in the fee-for-service system, the prospects for increased capitation payments are not good.

When you are deciding to get into risk contracting, it is not enough to estimate accurately payment and cost levels for the next contract year. Look farther ahead at US per capita cost (USPCC) trends, and then look historically at how your community's AAPCC tracks with the USPCC to make your revenue forecasts.

Understand Underlying Trends

Consider whether there could be pent-up demand or existing unmet medical needs in your target population. This may be true if your market area is more rural or low income or if it has not had extensive Medicare supplement coverage previously. In the late 1980s, several Minnesota HMOs attempted to expand their Medicare risk contracts into rural communities, believing that the rural AAPCCs would be reasonably predictive of medical costs, as the urban AAPCCs had been up to that time. Utilization was much higher than expected, however, particularly for cataract surgeries, joint replacements, and other medical procedures that seniors facing large out-of-pocket expenses had considered more discretionary and thus had put off. Most of the HMOs left the rural areas, a fact for which they have not yet been forgiven by either seniors or the state legislature. Interestingly, in a few pockets where plans stayed with the risk contract, utilization returned to more normal levels within 2 or 3 years, even though the AAPCCs still understate costs as billed by the local providers.

If your local medical community has lower charge levels and more conservative practice patterns than the national average, your plan may find it hard to sustain a risk contract over time under the current AAPCC system. Efficient communities are not rewarded under today's rules. High-cost, high-utilization fee-for-service providers in an area keep the AAPCC inflating nicely, and in that ironic sense they are a risk contractor's best friends. As HMO market share in a community grows, fee-for-service costs and Medicare expenditures are moderated as a result of competitive pressures and changes in physician practice patterns.[1] It seems that the managed care/market reform strategy really does work. As measured by AAPCC trends, however, risk-contracting plans are hardly rewarded for this beneficial effect. The good news is that the HCFA seems to recognize this inequity. The President's health care reform proposals would address the problem by inflating a community with high HMO penetration at the USPCC instead of the AAPCC.

Keep an Eye on Fee-for-Service

A plan needs to factor changes in the fee-for-service environment into its forecasts. The latest round of Medicare reforms will have effects on physicians as dramatic as those caused for hospitals by diagnosis-related groups. For most high-AAPCC communities, the new resource-based relative value system (RBRVS) will have a clearly depressing effect on future increases. For

communities that already more closely approximate the HCFA's desired state in terms of primary/specialty and procedure mix, the effects will be more positive. The RBRVS system, and the tightening limits on balance billing, may increase physicians' interest in contracting with managed care plans. This could present a good opportunity for plans. Providers usually expect to be paid more through their HMO contracts than they would from Medicare on a fee-for-service basis. This may be achievable if the plan carefully selects its provider group on the basis of quality and cost effectiveness and if the benefits of efficiently managing the whole health care dollar are shared with the providers.

Analyze Trends in Your Enrolled Population

Because a plan is reimbursed at 95% of Medicare's predicted *average* costs in a community, it needs to enroll an average population to succeed. Monitoring the utilization patterns and disenrollment rates of your enrollees according to their length of enrollment can be a useful predictor of financial performance. After you have a Medicare product in place, look at what percentage of your under-65 members you successfully retain after they age in to Medicare, and look at their prior utilization patterns. Are you losing young seniors to other competitors? Do significant numbers of members disenroll within the first year? Are those disenrolling low or high utilizers? Analysis of the factors causing disenrollment can be important for quality assurance as well as product design. Measuring the average age and average length of enrollment in the plan will help you predict cost trends and can also help in targeting case management services to higher-cost individuals. Any reasonable means of assessing selection bias in your enrollment should be pursued.

The HCFA's general belief that plans benefit from favorable selection contributes to the lack of urgency that the HCFA has shown in making improvements in the accuracy of the payment system. Better data from operating plans are critical to gaining a more complete picture of selection, especially as enrollment grows over time and as populations age within the plans.

There is likely to be renewed interest in health status adjusted payments in light of the various national health care reform proposals now being debated. The HCFA is already exploring a next round of research and testing of health status adjusted payments. It may become important for plans to be able to model the effects of health status adjustments in the next few years.

How Do You Relate to Your Providers?

Returning to the original question of plan mission (What business are you really in?), how you relate to the providers in your network will heavily determine your responses to changing financial results under a risk contract. If your plan is a pure contracting entity where all the risk for medical costs is transferred to providers, your piece of the pie will be the administrative dollars, the revenue for which is significantly higher under a risk contract than that from cost contracts or supplement products. You are not likely to pull the plug on a risk contract until your providers demand it if their experience goes sour. At this point, you could relatively easily convert to another type of product and let the providers return to accepting Medicare reimbursement. If, however, your plan is provider owned or a staff model plan in which you are the provider, your analysis might lead you to a different conclusion.

An example of this analysis exists at GHI. As we evaluate our options at GHI, we have now reached the point (at the time this is written) where we are forecasting multimillion dollar losses in Medicare unless revenue trends begin to match more closely those of the commercial market. Even so, the alternative reimbursement options look even less appealing than our loss projections on our risk contract. Medicare fee-for-service reimbursement levels would cover less of our clinic cost than the risk contract. We would lose the ability to manage the entire health care dollar, to allocate resources according to member need, and to use hospital savings to help fund the shortfall in funding for primary care physician services. We would also lose the benefit and operational flexibility of a risk contract. For example, under cost-based Medicare rules, we would have to hospitalize someone for 3 days before skilled nursing facility services would qualify for reimbursement. Given that we do not see the abandonment of the Medicare market as an option for us from a mission, strategic, or regulatory point of view, the benefits flexibility and less negative financial returns still make risk contracting our preferred alternative.

OPERATIONAL REQUIREMENTS

Administrative Systems

Almost every aspect of an HMO's operations will be affected by the unique requirements of managing the Medicare business. The importance of an overall program management function to keep track of all the pieces cannot be overstated. Your plan will need to designate someone to be responsible for keeping up with ever changing regulations, policy interpretations, and operational directives from the HCFA. This function should provide a linkage among operational areas that have to implement the changes called for, and it should also be a sort of high-level auditor of the various systems and processes related to enrollment, member materials, claims and benefits administration, member services, and provider relations. The program manager will also probably be the person charged with monitoring the key performance indicators of the product, tracking the market, and planning for the future.

A key organizational decision will be whether to create a department or even a separate company that houses the full range of specialized resources needed to manage the product or whether to mainstream the operations into the various functional departments of your plan. Successful risk contractors have done it both ways. An advantage to the freestanding specialized department approach can be the degree of expertise, dedicated attention, and unified teamwork that can be developed around the product. The disadvantage is that the rest of the company outside the Medicare department may have little knowledge of or investment in the product. By contrast, in the decentralized or functional approach, ownership of the product is more broadly shared throughout the organization. The disadvantage may be that individuals working within the larger enrollment or finance departments may have other aspects to their job and may not develop either the proficiency or the investment of a dedicated staff.

Under either organizational approach, you will need to adjust staffing ratios for the Medicare population in almost all areas. Compared to those in commercial business, the Medicare enrollment and claims processes are more complex, member appeals processes are more elaborate, and individual marketing and customer service are more labor intensive. Consult with a few plans of your same model type to get some specific advice about needed staffing levels and operating requirements.

Plan for the fall to be an intensely busy time for financial analysis and product planning. At GHI, we have found it useful to have a detailed time line of when various analyses need to be completed and when decisions need to be made at various levels internally and then communicated to the HCFA, state regulators, and our members. We begin constructing scenarios and assigning committees to pursue various analyses and strategies by early summer so that, when the next year's AAPCCs come out in early September, we have a context and strategic options within which to place the revenue picture.

Medical Operations

Correctly forecasting the impact of your Medicare product(s) on clinic capacity is critical. On the basis of not only your model type (eg, staff model or independent practice association) but also your care system configuration (eg, primary care gatekeeper or open access to specialists), find out what similar plans use as ratios for frequency and intensity of clinic use by senior members. The Group Health Association of America is also a useful source of this information.[2]

The HCFA's contracting requirements have a direct impact on utilization management and quality assurance. Quality assurance processes and staffing needs must accommodate external Peer Review Organization review. These im-

pacts are also fairly model specific. Logically enough, you should staff up in concurrent review, discharge planning, and other utilization management functions to account for the expected utilization volume generated by senior members (ranging from three to five times that for commercial members).

Within the care delivery system, you should plan for the heightened importance of the triage function for ensuring timely access to needed care and to reroute care to midlevel professionals when appropriate. Systems to manage emergency out-of-plan care aggressively but appropriately will also be more important than usual, especially given the travel patterns of many seniors. Adequate and efficient physician coverage of extended care facilities will also be necessary for both quality and cost management. The need to manage the link between the acute and chronic care delivery systems may be a new challenge for your care system created by your growth in the Medicare market.

Preparing to serve growing numbers of Medicare members as the population ages requires some fundamental adjustments in the care delivery system. Like many other large plans and medical groups, GHI has established a new clinical focus on geriatric care over the last several years. The geriatric division of GHI is developing special assessment clinics, case management, and team care approaches to serve the distinct needs of the elderly in a cost-effective manner. Our history with and commitment to the Medicare population have also led us to develop our own Medicare-certified hospice program. Many of these care approaches developed for seniors now have broader application in the care of complex patients across the spectrum of age and medical conditions.

CONCLUSION

As an industry, we have now had more than a decade of experience with HMOs and other managed care plans serving all the medical needs of enrolled Medicare populations on a capitated, fully at-risk basis. We have delivered products of unprecedented value to members, saving Medicare beneficiaries many millions of dollars in out-of-pocket expenses. We have also learned to adjust our delivery systems and operations to meet better the needs of seniors. We have helped the government cap its risk and budget its expenses in our part of the Medicare program, and we believe that we have helped slow the rate of growth in total Medicare expenditures in our communities by changing practice patterns and introducing competitive market pressures.

The HCFA too has improved its systems and procedures for administering the program, and it continues to say that capitation of organized care delivery systems is the key to long-term cost and quality management.

In the process of all this learning, some plans have lost millions, others have made millions, and all of us look toward the future with similar questions. As a nation, we face even more formidable financial challenges in the future as the population ages and as medical technology increases our ability and inclination to intervene aggressively in the processes of illness, injury, and aging.

Can the HCFA and the managed care industry come up with ways of fairly reimbursing plans for long-term, sustained, desirable cost and quality management results? Can we change today's short-term incentives to game whatever payment system we are under? Can we reward rather than punish plans who insure the people who most need care? Can we restore some sense of community values and equity in health care resource deployment and consumption?

These are many of the same critical questions that managed care plans face in dealing with their commercial customers. And they are some of the fundamental questions in the health care reform debate both in the states and federally. Our maturation both as individual plans and as an industry should help us meet these challenges and apply our growing practical and policy expertise to the Medicare program. At the same time, our successes in Medicare and our ability to work in partnership with the government to solve tough problems can help ensure and strengthen our role in the health care system of the future.

REFERENCES

1. Welch WP. HMO market share and its effect on local medicare costs. *Urban Institute Working Paper;* 1991: 3840-01.

2. Group Health Association of America, 1129 20th Street NW, Suite 600, Washington, DC 20036; Telephone (202) 778-3200.

Chapter 30

Managed Care for Retirees and the Elderly

Roger S. Taylor

The US population is aging, and older people require more health care services than younger people. These two simple facts pose a major challenge to our health care system. How are we going to finance and deliver health care to retirees and the elderly in the United States? Who should be responsible for financing the health care services to this population: government,

Roger S. Taylor, MD, MPA, is the National Leader, Health Care, for The Wyatt Company, an international consulting firm specializing in human resources, financial management, and systems. He has previously served as Senior Vice President of EQUICOR, Inc, and as President of Corporate HealthCare Management, a large national utilization review company. Dr. Taylor has more than 25 years of experience in the health care field as a practicing physician, health care executive, and consultant.

Parts of this chapter were adapted with permission from "Can Managed Care Reduce Employers' Retiree Medical Liability?" by Roger S. Taylor and Bonnie Newton, from *Benefits Quarterly*, Copyright ©1991, International Society of Certified Employee Benefit Specialists.

References to individual companies' retiree health care benefit programs were taken from a combination of presentations, articles, and personal knowledge available at the time this chapter was written. The author does not represent that specific benefit provisions ascribed to an individual company in this chapter remain current at the time of this book's publication.

employers, or individuals? What is the role of managed health care in ensuring the most cost-effective delivery of these services?

This chapter summarizes changes in the demographics, financing, and delivery of health care services to the elderly in the United States. It explores how changes in employer financing of retiree health benefits could alter the way we prepare for health care costs in retirement, and it examines our early experiences with delivering health care services through employer- and government-based managed health care programs. To date, experience with managed care programs in the retiree and elderly population has been limited. From this review of financing and benefit trends and of the early successes across a range of managed care experiences, the author speculates on the direction in which managed care programs will evolve to serve the health care needs of our growing elderly population.

THE CHALLENGE OF AN AGING POPULATION

The aging of America is undeniable. Census Bureau data show that the number of people age 65 and older now exceeds 31 million and represents 12.7% of the population. In 2020, when fewer than half the Baby Boomers will be age 65 or older, the Census Bureau estimates that the number of elderly will represent almost 18% of the population. By the time the entire Baby Boom generation has reached at least age 65 in the year 2030, it is estimated that there will be 120% more elderly people than there are today, or almost 65 million. By then, people age 65 and older will represent an estimated 22% of the population.[1] Not only is the number of older Americans increasing, but older people are living longer. From 1901 to 1986 the life expectancy for a man age 65 increased by 28%, and for a woman it increased by 53%.[1] These factors combine to make individuals 85 years of age and older members of the fastest growing segment of our population.

At the same time, changing lifestyle patterns, work force reduction programs, and the mobility of our population are generally working to reduce retirement ages. Labor force participation patterns show a steady decrease in the percentage of working men age 60 and older. In 1950, 55% of men age 60 and older were in the labor force; by 1990, this had dropped to less than 21%.[2] If personal preferences hold true, the trend could continue. In an American Association of Retired Persons survey of workers ages 50 and older, 26% said they plan to retire at or before age 62, and an additional 20% said they plan to retire at ages 63 to 65.[3] Fueling this attitude is a tendency for employers to encourage older active employees to retire as part of a downsizing or restructuring effort. Because rich early retirement packages are often offered, workers who otherwise might remain in the labor force until age 65 are leaving earlier.

These demographic shifts have changed the age and productivity mix of those who receive benefits from American companies. Twenty years ago the average Fortune 500 company had 12 active employees for every retiree. Now it has 3.[4] Twenty years from now the number of retirees receiving employer-provided health benefits is projected to grow to 9 million, and the annual costs to employers will rise to $25 billion, an increase of almost 100% per employee.[5]

These trends are further complicated by the fact that older people are less healthy on average than younger people. In 1988, the elderly accounted for 33% of all health care expenses nationally, even though they accounted for only 12% of the population.[6]

Employers that provide health insurance coverage for retirees will be directly affected by these demographic trends. The older an employer's work force and the more retirees covered under the employer's health plan, the higher the employer's health insurance premiums. The aging of the work force will shorten the period in which employers can prefund benefits before retirement, and longer life expectancy will lengthen the period during which benefits will be paid. For example, it is reported that the average man retiring at age 65 in the year 2030 will require an additional 25 monthly payments of any promised benefit compared with a man age 65 retiring in 1990.[3] The average woman in the same example would require an additional 39 monthly payments. At the same time, the number of younger employees entering the work force is decreasing. Since 1972 fertility rates in the United States have been less than the replacement rate of 2.11 births per 1,000 women.

The Financial Accounting Standards (FAS) Board's release of statement 106 has added to the demographic and general health care cost pressures felt by US employers, forcing them to re-evaluate their approach to retiree health benefits for current and future retirees. This statement, known as FAS 106, requires employers to accrue liabilities for retiree health benefits during employees' active service, rather than record the cost as benefits are paid, beginning in 1993. Employers are scrambling to find ways to reduce the statement's effect on corporate balance sheets. For retirees, the net effect of FAS 106 is that they will generally have less coverage for health care costs in the future.

Federal, state, and local governments also feel the effects of changing demographics as a result of their obligation to provide for the elderly and poor. The federal government provides medical benefits for the elderly through the Medicare program under Title XVIII, Health Insurance for the Aged, of the Social Security Act. In 1973 the program was extended to entitled disabled persons and to certain individuals with end-stage renal disease. Title XVIII thus became Health Insurance for the Aged and Disabled. In 1985, Medicare was made secondary payer for all workers age 65 or older and their spouses who elected to be covered by employment-based health insurance through an employer with 20 or more employees. In 1986, Medicare was also made secondary payer for all disabled Medicare beneficiaries who continue working and are covered by larger employment-based plans (100 or more employees).

Medicare consists of two separate but coordinated programs: Part A, Hospital Insurance, and Part B, Supplementary Medical Insurance. Medicare Part A provides coverage for basic hospital inpatient services as well as limited posthospital and home health services and hospice care. Medicare Part B is optional and provides coverage for physicians' and surgeons' services, outpatient hospital, laboratory, and radiology services as well as an array of other professional services and medical supplies.[7] Both Parts A and B require the covered individual to pay deductibles and coinsurance or copayments for services rendered, and Part B is only available to those who pay the required premium.

The federal and state governments also provide additional benefits for the elderly poor who qualify for a separate program, Medicaid. The Medicaid program, established under Title XIX of the Social Security Act, provides the elderly poor with such added benefits as long-term care and some prescription drug coverage. The criteria for, and benefits from, Medicaid vary from state to state.

In some ways, the effect of demographic trends creates an even bigger challenge for government health care programs than for employment-based programs. American employers are not legally required to offer health care benefits. Yet, federal, state, and local governments have been assigned a legal obligation to care for the medical needs of the elderly and poor. Government-owned or -funded health care facilities are also viewed as having a moral obligation to be the provider of last resort for the entire population. The longer people live and the less coverage they bring with them from their employers, the more costs will be borne by government.

Furthermore, the fewer workers there are per retiree, the less employment-based tax income there will be to support these government programs. As fewer and fewer pre-65 retirees have adequate employer-based health care coverage, pressure will mount for a lowering of the eligibility age on Medicare. In 1991, legislation proposing to lower Medicare eligibility to age 60 was introduced in the Congress, and this provision is a component of several national health care reform proposals. The challenge of an aging population will have a profound effect on both government- and employer-based health care programs over the next generation.

CHANGES IN EMPLOYMENT-BASED HEALTH COVERAGE FOR RETIREES

FAS 106 has forced US employers to look squarely at the aging of their work force and their outstanding liability for retiree medical costs. For many employers, the result has been an abrupt change in their retiree medical benefit commitment to their work force. A survey by the Wyatt Company showed that more than two thirds of employers with retiree benefits had modified their plans in 1990 or 1991.[8] In the author's experience, employers have responded to FAS 106 in one or more of five principal ways. They have (1) increased cost sharing and/or capped the employer's obligation, (2) eliminated the benefit, (3) developed alternative funding mechanisms, (4) replaced the open-ended medical benefit with a defined dollar benefit or a defined contribution benefit, and/or (5) pensionized the benefit.[9]

Increased employee and/or retiree cost sharing can involve raising deductibles and/or copayments and/or decreasing the number of services covered, the levels at which services are reimbursed, or the duration of coverage. This approach also frequently involves increasing the retiree contribution and/or capping the employer contribution level to the insurance premium. For example, Bell Atlantic Corporation's 1989 collective bargaining for nonmanagement employees produced a cap on company contributions for postretirement medical coverage. Once retiree medical costs exceed that cap, employees will pay the difference. Other regional phone companies have protected their liability in some way as well.

Other companies have moved to eliminate their medical benefits for future retirees altogether. Ralston Purina, for example, continues to provide company-paid retiree health benefits to current retirees. But for future retirees, the company is phasing out its contribution to the medical plan, and eventually the retiree medical plan will be completely funded by retirees.

Employers have also pursued alternative ways to fund future health care benefits on a tax-preferred basis. Current funding vehicles that receive the most favorable tax preferences have tight limits on total annual contributions. The funding vehicles with fewer contribution restrictions generally do not qualify as FAS 106 assets and, therefore, cannot be used to reduce an employer's liability.[10] Although Congress is under considerable pressure from employers to loosen the restrictions and provide easier tax-preferred funding options, federal budget problems make such a change difficult and unlikely at this time.

In the meantime, employers are seeking innovative methods to reduce the tax obligation of these benefits. One of these shifts some of the health care cost obligation to employees, but in a tax-efficient way. Under an employee retiree medical account, employees make regular contributions from after-tax income to individual accounts. The contributions are invested in an insurance company contract that allows the account to earn interest without creating taxable income.[11]

One of the biggest problems for employers facing large future retirement populations has been the unknown nature of their financial commitment. Traditionally, health insurance has defined the benefit level to be provided. For example, a plan may pay 100% of hospitalization cost after a certain deductible has been met and 80% of physician fees up to a usual and customary level. This so-called defined service benefit approach places no intrinsic limit on employers' liability; they have little knowledge or control of the future dollar value of that benefit. A calculation of an employer's postretirement medical liability for the year 2020, for example, hinges on actuarial estimates of physician and hospital charges, utilization rates, and technology costs in that year.

To cope with this unknown and to put some logical caps on the commitment, many employers are moving to a defined dollar benefit approach, in which an employer defines a certain maximum annual dollar commitment toward the cost of retirees' annual medical coverage. The retiree has the responsibility to make up any remaining health care costs or to seek coverage elsewhere. This defined dollar benefit approach can come in a number of forms, all of which have the advantage for employers of fixing their maximum annual liability at some level that is not subject to uncontrolled increases in health care premiums. IBM, for example, has capped its retiree health liability premiums at $7,000 a year for those younger than 65 and at $3,000 for those age 65 and older. Although this contribution cap is higher than current costs, it is estimated that premiums will exceed this level by the end of the 1990s.

An alternative to the defined dollar benefit approach that also limits an employer's commitment is the defined contribution approach, in which the employer provides an annual contribution to an account set up for each active employee. The money is invested and at retirement can be drawn for the purchase of health care services or coverage. The First Bank of Boston has implemented this type of plan. Employees receive $500 in credits each year beginning at age 40. Thus an employee retiring at age 60 would receive $10,000 in credits that can be used to purchase retiree medical coverage.

Finally, some employers are moving to pensionize retiree medical benefits. Historically, full retiree health care benefits have been available to most new employees shortly after their hire date. The level of medical benefits had little to do with the employee's length of service or the contribution that the employee made to the company's success. Many employers now feel that retiree health care benefits should be earned over time, with closer tracking of the way pension benefits are accrued. This move to pensionize retiree medical benefits often combines the defined dollar benefit approach discussed earlier with service-related limitations on benefit level and eligibility.

When employers base benefits on length of service, they often incorporate three practices common in pension benefits: a minimum service requirement (in number of years); benefit or employer contribution levels based on years of service; and benefit or employer contribution levels based on retirement age.

Data General, for example, changed its retiree health plans to follow more closely a pension approach. Data General provides health coverage for retirees through a defined dollar benefit based on years of service. This approach places a variable cap on the amount that will be provided to retirees for health insurance based on length of service. The remaining cost of retiree health insurance is paid by the retiree. The cap is reviewed annually.

Traditionally, an active employee has had the option of adding his or her dependents to the plan, an option that is retained if health benefits are provided in retirement. Employers are now also considering the value of limiting dependent eligibility in some absolute way or through years of service or a defined dollar benefit formula.

And last, again borrowing from a pension approach, some employers have considered freezing the level of benefit or employer contribution for retiree health benefits at the point of retirement. A similar but more favorable approach for the retiree is to increase that benefit only gradually after retirement based on some fixed inflator such as the Consumer Price Index or the Medical Cost Index.

These early employer responses to FAS 106 increase employee responsibility for the cost of health care in retirement. They also assume that employees will stay with one company for the 20 to 35 years needed for full benefit accrual, a length of service rarely seen in today's fluid labor market. Unlike some retirement plans, however, these accrued health benefits may not be transferable upon one's leaving a job. The net effect is that these changes in employer-based health care coverage for retirees may lead to a growing population of employees who are inadequately prepared to pay for retiree medical benefits. When given an optional savings vehicle, the average younger worker may often choose to ignore this problem, preferring higher cash compensation or immediately available spending accounts. Middle-aged and older employees may be faced with difficult financial choices and limited years to fund those choices. To offset partially this effect, some employers allow older employees and current retirees to continue in the traditional health care coverage plan.

These changes in employment-based health coverage for the retirees will also have a profound impact on the development of managed health care options for the elderly. Executives of managed care organizations such as health maintenance organizations (HMOs) and preferred provider organizations (PPOs) were convinced that FAS 106 would greatly increase the demand for employer group–based managed care products aimed at retirees. That conviction was based on the assumption that employers would be scrambling for contracts that would deliver a future defined benefit for less money. What has happened to date, however, is that employers are moving away from defining the benefits due to retirees and are replacing that with a definition of the cash available for retiree health coverage. Whether that cash is available to the employees to purchase any plan of their own individual choice or whether it can only be applied to the employer's sponsored plan(s) varies by employer. It would be inconsistent with this trend for employers to create long-term commitments to a specific benefit level or even specific mechanisms (such as managed care) to deliver those benefits. This change in the direction of employer-based health coverage for retirees suggests that the traditional employer group–based managed care products created for active employees may not be appropriate for future retirees.

THE RELATIONSHIP BETWEEN EMPLOYMENT-BASED AND MEDICARE-BASED COVERAGE

The relationship between employment-based coverage for retirees and Medicare also has an effect on the development of managed care. Most employers stipulate that retirees must apply for Medicare as soon as they become eligible at age 65, and the retirees' employment-based health benefits will be reduced accordingly. The amount of reduction varies by employer. Generally there are four methods for integrating employer benefits with Medicare: coordination of benefits, maintenance of benefits, carve out, and Medigap (or supplemental plan). A coordination of benefits plan pays all unpaid covered charges up to 100% of the benefit dollars that would otherwise have been paid by the plan if Medicare were not primary. In this way, the retiree may pay nothing, because the employer's plan can be used to pay the coinsurance, deductibles, or other charges not covered by Medicare. When retirees are covered under the same plan as active employees, and when integration with Medicare is by coordination of benefits, retirees will find that their cost sharing significantly decreases when they reach age 65. A carve-out plan, on the other hand, calculates the benefit that would have been paid and reduces it by any payments from Medicare, thus preserving any cost-sharing elements present in an employer's original health plan. A maintenance of benefits approach results in coverage somewhat between the first two approaches. Employers with any of these options may or may not also reimburse retirees for their Medicare Part B premiums.

A Medigap or supplement plan uses a different approach from the approaches of the first three. Rather than integrate with Medicare coverage, the Medigap plan usually covers a limited set of specific benefits that are not currently covered by Medicare, such as reimbursement for a specified amount of Medicare's deductibles or coinsurance and coverage for specified vision and drug benefits. A Medigap policy may have its own separate set of coinsurance and deductible requirements. Some Medigap policies are available through HMOs and other managed care organizations. HCFA has also promoted the development of Medicare select programs that incorporate PPO design into this Medigap option. The majority of Medigap policies do not include managed care features.

Of the four methods discussed, a Medigap plan provides the most specific limits on employers' postretirement medical liability. The premium cost of a well-defined Medigap benefit plan is the least susceptible to changes in Medicare coverage or payment policy. A distinct disadvantage of using a Medigap policy with today's limits for future benefit needs, however,

is that those needs may be altered by changes in medical care technology, fee structures, and Medicare policy. In addition, Medigap policies have varied greatly in terms of costs, benefits, and quality, causing Congress to demand the enforcement of minimum standards in the future. Medigap policies are well suited, however, for retirees who are left to purchase their own supplemental insurance at age 65 either from their own savings funds or from an employer-supplied cash account.

None of these four ways of coordinating Medicare with employment-based coverage for retirees is particularly well suited for managed care because assigning total health care responsibility to one managed care organization requires that all funding of care be coordinated from a single source.

THE GOVERNMENT'S USE OF MANAGED CARE FOR RETIREES

The Medicare program has historically been far ahead of employers in the use of managed care with older individuals. Medicare policy changes have gradually introduced a number of techniques designed to help contain health care cost increases over the years. Inpatient services are subjected to utilization review by peer review organizations to make sure that they meet accepted criteria for admission and continued inpatient care. Hospitals are reimbursed on a prospective payment system based on each patient's diagnosis-related group. Selected surgeries require prior authorization. Physicians are paid on a discount through a federally set maximum allowable fee schedule. And, although participation in Medicare's system is voluntary, physicians are limited in how much they can charge over and above the Medicare allowed fee, whether they participate or not. Claim audits and retrospective review of services rendered are conducted on a regular basis. These audits can result in a wide range of actions, such as not paying for the specific service in question, removing a provider from the list of participating providers, and prosecuting for fraud. Each of these various techniques used by Medicare to manage costs could be considered components of a managed health care program. They do not, however, qualify as a managed health care delivery system as the term is used in this book.

Medicaid inpatient and physician payment methodologies have also been modified over the last 10 to 15 years to provide many of the same incentives for cost containment. Although no two state systems are alike, prospectively determined hospital payment systems that differentiate payment rates according to the patient's illness, rather than on the basis of cost-based reimbursement, are now the predominant method of payment used by state Medicaid programs.[12]

There is increasing interest on the part of both Medicare and Medicaid programs to increase their use of managed health care systems. The challenge of an aging population is well understood by the federal government. The Social Security Board of Trustees reported in 1991 that the Medicare Hospital Insurance Trust Fund will probably be exhausted shortly after the turn of the century and that corrective action will be needed soon to avoid the need for potentially precipitous changes later. The trustees contend that, although currently more than four covered workers support each hospital insurance enrollee, this ratio will begin to decline rapidly early in the next century. By the middle of the century, there will be only about two covered workers supporting each hospital insurance enrollee. The same board's annual report describes the Supplemental Medical Insurance Trust Fund, which is supported by general federal revenue (approximately 76%) and by premiums from beneficiaries (approximately 24%), as actuarially sound. The report expressed concerns, however, about the rapid growth in the cost of this program, which has nearly doubled in the last 5 years.[13]

Medicare, HMOs, and other governmental managed care programs are discussed later in this chapter and extensively in Chapters 28 and 29; the reader is referred to those chapters for an in-depth review of the issues.

EMPLOYER'S USE OF MANAGED CARE FOR RETIREES

Prior to the last few years, employers made little use of managed health care for their retir-

ees. This has been especially true for retirees at or beyond age 65, at which point Medicare is primarily in charge of health care coverage and delivery decisions. The current reluctance for employers to move aggressively to managed care for retirees is based on several reasons: Employers' immediate priority is to lower their FAS 106 liability (discussed above), employers are concerned that managed care may not have saved employers money on a populationwide basis, and there are some barriers to applying today's managed care products to retirees. The following is a discussion of each of these reasons and a look at why some employers are turning to managed care as a single plan solution.

Concerns about Managed Care's Savings

Managed care programs in the late 1970s and 1980s were often touted as the remedy for the soaring increases in health care costs. Today, there are four principal managed care options available to employers: HMOs, preferred provider organizations (PPOs), primary care point-of-service (POS) plans, and specialized carve-out managed care programs. Each of these approaches claims to save money in a number of ways: by controlling excessive days of hospital admissions, by controlling excessive and unnecessary procedures and services, and/or by limiting use of providers to a select group whose fees and practice patterns result in more efficient or higher-quality care.

Other chapters of this book have discussed the value of specific managed care programs in reducing costs or improving quality for the specific population served. Chapter 23 discusses employers' views on managed care. It is important here to emphasize the skepticism that exists among some employers and group benefit actuaries as to whether (or how much) these managed care programs reduce the cost of caring for an entire population. Until this concern about overall savings is resolved with hard evidence, it will limit the growth of employer-sponsored managed care in the retiree population. Because there is little experience with managed care in large groups of retiree populations, actuaries must turn to the cost experience in group employment–based populations to answer these questions.

Who Is Saving Money with Managed Care?

Many studies of the effectiveness of managed health care focus largely on the reduction in hospital utilization rates for those individuals who elected to be covered in a managed care program. Newer studies focus on outpatient utilization rates or on total employer costs for this self-selected group in managed care programs. But to reduce overall health care costs, the critical question is the impact on a total population of employees, dependents, and retirees. A few surveys have examined the differences in premium costs among types of health plans offered to employment-based groups, but the findings of these surveys are somewhat inconsistent. A survey by the Health Insurance Association of America demonstrated small differences in the average premiums of HMOs, PPOs, and traditional indemnity plans.[14] The average monthly premium for coverage under a fee-for-service plan (with preadmission certification) was within a few dollars per month of the average premium for HMOs. In a more recent survey of the four types of managed care plans (traditional indemnity, HMOs, PPOs, and POS plans), traditional insurance plans were the most expensive. The average per employee cost for indemnity plans was $3,573 in 1991; this is 6.5% higher than for PPO plans ($3,355), 8.6% higher than for POS plans ($3,291), and 17.3% higher than for HMOs ($3,046). This survey pattern varies significantly, however, in different regions of the country.[15] Results of other recent surveys generally fall between these two extremes and show a more modest difference in premiums among plan types, varying widely by employer and geographic area. It should be noted, however, that employers' costs derived from surveys are not the same as total health costs by type of managed care option. The benefit levels, employee contributions to premium, cost-sharing features, and managed care elements of these plans vary widely from employer to employer.

So where is the payoff? If HMOs and PPOs have succeeded in significantly lowering hospital utilization and discounting provider costs,

why aren't their premiums always significantly lower than those of their indemnity counterparts? One answer is that the enrollee has generally been the principal recipient of savings from managed care plans in the form of increased benefits. HMOs have historically covered a comprehensive group of benefits. They generally provide preventive care services, such as physical examinations, well baby care, and preventive diagnostic procedures, that are often not available in indemnity plans. There is generally a small or no deductible, low copayments or coinsurance levels, and limited use of lifetime benefit maximums. These extra values, in addition to no pre-existing condition exclusions or claims forms, often make the HMO an attractive benefit package. Likewise, PPOs traditionally have provided 10% to 20% higher benefit levels when services are provided in the PPO network, and many PPOs add a limited number of preventive health benefits. Furthermore, the costs associated with constructing and maintaining a provider network add significant administrative costs to both HMOs and PPOs. The net result is that to date the majority of benefits derived from any efficiencies in PPOs or HMOs have been passed on to employees as inducements to join these programs. Currently, most companies will not be willing to commit to HMOs or PPOs that might increase their benefit obligation to future retirees, especially if that conversion would not significantly reduce their FAS 106 liability.

Can Managed Care Reduce the Health Care Cost Trend Rates?

When one is analyzing the impact of managed care, it is critical to differentiate between two possible effects of cost management procedures: the effect of reducing the baseline costs, and the effect on overall trend rates. This differentiation is particularly important when one realizes that a good part of the research to date on health care cost management has focused on changes in the base costs of a health care program within a few years of implementing managed care. Examples of this might be a study of a managed mental health program that shows a decrease in cost of 40% compared with expected costs in the first year of operation. This 40% decrease could simply be a one-time reduction related to removing the heretofore undiscovered excesses in utilization. Part of the savings could also be the one-time effect of redesigning benefits or introducing provider discounts. In projecting health care costs 10 to 20 years forward to plan for future retiree medical expenses, this single reduction in claims cost is valuable, but much less so than a persistent reduction in trend rate that continues to have an effect year after year.

This point is driven home by Schwartz and Mendelson[16] in their study of the slowing of health care cost increases in the mid-1980s. They suggest that savings attributed to managed health care in the middle to late 1980s were due to decreasing excess utilization of hospital stays. But these available savings have largely been realized. Even with the significant growth in managed care operations in the late 1980s, the use of hospital bed days per 1,000 patients is no longer decreasing, and the overall rate of health care cost inflation has returned to the pre–managed care level. Schwartz and Mendelson contend that because of this one-time adjustment the basic rate of health care inflation is, in the final analysis, generally the same for HMOs and managed care as it is for indemnity health insurance.

These observations fly in the face of claims by managed care organizations over the years that they will successfully slow the spiraling increase in health care costs. Many employers, in fact, have implemented HMOs and other managed care models knowing that the increased benefits to induce employees into the network may initially cost more than the alternative indemnity plan but expecting that managed care's longer-term impact will slow the rate of health care inflation. Thus the rate of inflation is a critical variable that must be studied separately from the effects of one-time adjustments in the base due to the elimination of certain excesses in the system.

When challenged on the issue of trend rate, managed care proponents point to the rapid growth in indemnity premiums in the last few years compared with the slower growth in HMO premiums. In fact, there is evidence that they are correct. Surveys by this author's company and other consulting companies generally suggest that the growth rate in indemnity insurance premiums over the last several years has been about

21% a year but that the growth rate has been about 5% to 6% lower for HMOs. If this difference persists, it would greatly boost the claim that managed care is at least a partial solution for the problem of health care cost inflation. It will also result in a much greater difference between HMO and indemnity plan premiums than we have experienced to date.

The trend rate for PPOs has been studied less. This may be partially due to the lack of clear definitions for PPOs. The level of coverage, the value of the provider contracts, the percentage of services provided in network, and the degree of management responsibility for services provided in the network vary considerably from model to model.

Complicating any analysis of trend rates is the potential of adverse selection among health care benefit plans. For example, if an employer offers an HMO and a self-insured indemnity plan, the employer will probably pay the HMO a prepaid premium for all employees who join. The employer also pays directly for all health care claims for those staying within the indemnity plan. If the HMO selectively enrolls younger or healthier patients, then the employer is paying a higher premium than appropriate for the employees going to the HMO. That employer is also paying higher claims dollars than expected per employee for those staying in the indemnity plan. The net result is a higher net increase in costs than would otherwise be predicted for that total employee population. Some investigators studying the impact of various health care options on premiums have confirmed this trend, concluding that there is growing evidence that HMOs experience favorable selection when they are offered as an alternative to conventional coverage.[17]

As a result of adverse risk selection and cost increases, the indemnity plan in the example above must continue to increase premiums. This further drives healthier employees into HMOs, which in turn drives premiums in the indemnity plan higher. As this cycle, called the indemnity death spiral, continues, it becomes harder and harder to support separate indemnity and managed care options. Some in Congress have expressed the concern that this same adverse selection is occurring within the Medicare HMOs and have asked the Health Care Financing Adminisatration (HCFA) to implement a number of mechanisms to guard against that possibility.[18]

There are also studies suggesting the opposite: that HMOs and indemnity plans tend, on balance, to attract similar risk. A few studies even suggest that independent practice association (IPA) model HMOs attract higher-risk patients than other plans. Employers are skeptical, however. In a national survey of chief executive officers conducted by Wyatt,[19] the majority of respondents felt that HMOs have not lowered their overall health care costs, and one third said that HMOs and PPOs have actually increased their costs.

The net effect of these findings is that it is difficult to predict the overall impact of a mixture of indemnity and managed care options on the health care cost trend rate of an entire group or population. A common approach of employers' has been to assume that there is a single average trend rate for their covered population. For an employer with a large percentage of employees in an indemnity plan, the trend rate for the indemnity plan is typically assumed for the entire population. For an employer with a significant mix of managed care options, two approaches could be used: the costs and trend rate of the indemnity plan alone, or the weighted average of the employer's cost and trend rates across all plans. Both options reduce the potential positive effect that introducing managed care might have on an employer's current postretirement (FAS 106) liability. Even if most active employees choose managed care options, it's not clear what percentage will stay with managed care (and with that trend rate) through retirement. This confusion about the effectiveness of managed care to reduce overall costs and trend rates has limited the efforts by employers to apply managed care solutions to their retiree medical liability problems.

Managed Care As the Single Health Plan

One way to eliminate adverse selection among available health plan options is to offer groups a managed health plan as the sole health insurance option. Limited data are available on the success of this strategy, probably because few employers or government programs currently structure their health benefits in this way. The most common approach to a single integrated managed care plan is through the POS plan. These plans are designed to offer an HMO-like delivery system for services provided in network while retaining some of the out-of-network coverage found in PPOs. A limited number of employers have made an HMO their only choice for retiree health in those locations where an HMO is offered or made the indemnity plan's premium so high that most retirees choose the HMO. The conversion to a single POS plan is usually more acceptable to both employers and employees, however, because both cost control and choice are preserved.

Several large companies, such as Southwestern Bell and Allied-Signal, have received considerable attention for their early conversions to the POS approach. Allied-Signal claims that its network, run by CIGNA since March 1988, resulted in managed care plan costs rising 8% to 13% per year, depending on network area, compared with indemnity cost increases of 18% to 26%. Southwestern Bell Corporation's Custom Care Network, managed by the Prudential Insurance Company since April 1987, reports a similar savings experience of 7% to 12%.[20] Southwestern Bell was also a pioneer in applying this single option managed care approach to its retirees as well as to active employees. If a pre-65 retiree's ZIP code was in an area serviced by the POS network, then the POS plan was his or her only health care coverage option. Although implementation of this managed care conversion in a retiree health program required a lot of good management and communication, the results in terms of cost control and retiree acceptance have been quite positive.

POS plans studied by the Wyatt Company for the Health Insurance Association of America experienced an average reduction of 6.83% in claims costs compared with the expected claims costs before implementing the plan. The annual savings on claims costs ranged from 4.23% to 12.7% over the employers' previous mix of indemnity and HMO options. The savings for the two employers (mentioned above) that had a full 3 years' experience were above average. The plans studied represented a total of more than

500,000 covered lives.[21] It is difficult to generalize from these findings, however. POS plans have in most cases been in effect for only a short time, and substantial changes in benefits, employee contribution levels, and network channeling incentives are often made at the same time a POS plan is put in place. A portion of the reported savings is probably due to one-time events. Maintaining a single managed care plan or a limited number of plans that are highly integrated may, however, offer the greatest promise of producing the hoped for savings in overall health care costs. Not only is adverse selection eliminated, but (assuming that benefits remain stable) any savings can be directly linked to efforts of the managed care delivery system.

Barriers in the Application of Managed Care to Retirees

Managed care is spreading among the younger and employed population in the United States, with some areas of the country showing much greater penetration than others. There is much less experience, however, with managed care among retirees and the elderly. This has led to concerns that there are some barriers to applying today's managed care products to retirees.

Only a small proportion of current HMO enrollees is elderly. The Group Health Association of America (GHAA) reports that enrollees age 65 and older represented only 6% of HMO enrollment in 1988. Enrollees younger than 45 represented 77%, and 17% were between ages 45 and 65.[22] PPOs also seem to enroll fewer elderly. The average age of PPO members in a RAND Corporation study of five employers in California, Ohio, and Florida ranged from 35 to 45 years.[23]

Older Americans often are unfamiliar with or do not understand the concept of HMOs or PPOs. A Brandeis University survey of Medicare-eligible retirees showed that this group had limited interest in HMOs.[24] Only 18% said they would definitely consider an HMO, and an additional 26% said they might consider joining a prepaid health plan, such as a local HMO, where members receive all their medical services. Fewer than one quarter ruled out the possibility completely, however. A national public opinion survey by the Gallup Organization for the Employee Benefit Research Institute asked various questions about participating in HMOs and PPOs.[25] Confirming GHAA's survey, respondents age 55 and older were less likely than younger respondents to be members of HMOs or PPOs. Among those who were not members, older respondents were more likely than younger respondents to say that they were satisfied with their current provider (20% of those ages 35 to 54 and 9% of those ages 18 to 34). Older respondents were more likely than those ages 35 to 54 to say that they did not like the choice (or the lack thereof) of providers in HMOs. Younger adults (ages 18 to 34) were even more likely to say this, however. Finally, older respondents were a bit more likely to say that they were unfamiliar with HMOs and PPOs.

One company, Owens-Corning Fiberglass, conducted a survey of its retirees and found that older individuals consider individual choice of physicians critical in selecting a plan.[26] Almost half their retirees would not join a local HMO if they had to change physicians, even if the HMO charged less than their current physician. Retirees in the survey said that long family ties and trust are the most important reasons for which they select a physician. This loyalty could pose a problem to employers trying to gain retiree acceptance for HMOs and PPOs unless more retirees' physicians are in the plans.

Countering the concerns about the restrictions posed by managed care is the elderly's higher level of concern over health care costs. Elderly Americans consistently rank health care as their biggest concern. They are concerned not only about staying healthy but also about costs associated with not staying healthy. The bottom line for many older people is the challenge of balancing assets against life span. Furthermore, most retirees do not want to deal with paperwork or the dollars-and-cents issues of health care. The benefits structure of HMOs and the fact that HMOs and PPOs typically do not require any claims forms to be filed should be a major inducement for retirees to join managed care plans.

In a Louis Harris survey for Pfizer Pharmaceuticals, HMO enrollees were asked various questions about why they chose HMOs over fee-for-service plans, including which characteristics were most important in selecting their particular plan and their overall satisfaction with their health care plan. Cost issues tended to be the most important to respondents who chose HMOs over indemnity plans, with 26% citing the low per visit cost as the single most important reason for their choice, followed by 14% who cited low or no deductibles or copays as the most important reason.[27] Asked why they selected a particular HMO over others, enrollees overwhelmingly cited the ability to select their own physician (42%) as the major factor. Interestingly, the convenience of facilities (mentioned by 20% of respondents) and the absence of claims forms (mentioned by 16%) were much less important. As with most surveys of individual satisfaction, this study found that, in general, once an individual joins an HMO he or she is satisfied with the plan. In the RAND survey, PPO participants were more likely than HMO participants to be satisfied with access to care.

In conclusion, the evidence seems to suggest that older Americans lack adequate knowledge about managed health care and generally mistrust restrictions placed on their choice of providers. Nevertheless, when individuals do join and become familiar with managed health care programs and associate with a specific physician, their satisfaction level appears to be high. One would expect that an employee would be comfortable remaining with a particular managed care plan in retirement, all else being equal. Furthermore, future retirees will probably have more experience with managed care delivery mechanisms and, therefore, will be more receptive to them as retirees.

In addition to retiree preference, demographic patterns may pose some barriers to retiree participation in managed care plans. Most Americans stay in their hometown to live after they retire, but those who leave are reportedly healthier, more affluent, and less attached to family.[28] It is estimated, for example, that the state of New York lost more than 127,000 retirees to Florida between 1985 and 1990.[29] In fact, Florida attracts more retirees than any other state. Longino and Crown[29] estimate that between 1985 and 1990 the persons age 60 and older who moved to

Florida deposited an additional $6 billion into the state's economy. Arizona is the next closest, with an estimated gain of around $1 billion during the same years. Although people age 65 and older represent about 12% of the US population as a whole, they represent 19% of Florida's population and 30% of what is called the retirement belt: a seven-county region on the state's west coast.[28]

These migration patterns are expected to continue. The University of Florida's Center for Economic and Business Research predicts that by the year 2000 the retirement belt will grow by another 36%. Other states that have a higher than average proportion of the 65 and older population are Iowa, Arkansas, and Pennsylvania (with 15% of residents age 65 and older) and West Virginia, South Dakota, Missouri, Massachusetts, and Nebraska (with 14%).[6]

Rural areas also appear to be a growing retirement hot spot. Research by Glasgow[30] shows that since 1960 the net migration of adults age 60 and older has been toward rural areas. Furthermore, retired people tend to travel more. Notable among this group are the snowbirds, those from the north who spend their winters in the south. The migration of retirees to more rural areas and to sunbelt states and their propensity to travel complicate the picture for managed care, which is still predominantly delivered in more urban settings through local or regional networks of providers. An active employee who is a member of an HMO in his or her community but chooses for family reasons or personal preference to move out of the area upon retirement may not be eligible to continue HMO membership in the new location. The new location may not even have HMOs or provider networks available. Some HMOs are developing reciprocity agreements with other plans to capture migrating or traveling retirees. For example, Health Insurance Plan (HIP) of Greater New York signed a partnership agreement with Network Health Care of Florida to accommodate 50,000 HIP retirees who moved to Florida's Palm Beach, Broward, and Dade counties.[31] Other HMOs are following suit.

Further research is clearly needed on the acceptability of managed health care to retirees and on the impact of retiree migration patterns on group-based managed care products. To date, the mobility of the retiree population has limited the application of employment-based group managed care products to this population.

MANAGING PRESCRIPTION DRUG BENEFIT COSTS

Experience with managed care programs for prescription drugs is more limited than for general medical benefits in the retiree population. This may be based on the fact that Medicare, which does not cover prescription drugs, has not exercised the same leadership here that it did in other areas of cost control. This lack of managed care experience is not because drug costs have not been a problem. According to the HCFA, the average drug expenditure for elderly persons has increased by more than 250% from 1980 to 1989, partly as a result of the rise in drug utilization among the elderly. The number of annual prescriptions per elderly has increased from 12.1 in 1980 to 17.7 in 1988. And, on average, the elderly use approximately three times more prescriptions than people younger than 65.[32]

Consumers bear a disproportionate share of the cost of prescription drugs compared to other medical services, particularly the aged. Lipton[32] reports that consumers bear 9% of hospital costs, 29% of the cost of physician services, 51% of the cost of nursing home services, and 75% of the cost of drugs and medical supplies purchased through retail outlets. Furthermore, the out-of-pocket share of total prescription drug costs paid by families is higher for persons age 65 years and older than for the total population (77% and 73%, respectively). The poor elderly bear the greatest burden for drug expenses. According to a survey reported by Lipton,[32] private insurance reimbursed more than 20% of prescription drug expenses among the nonpoor elderly in 1980 but reimbursed less than 11% among the near poor elderly and less than 8% among the poor elderly. The poor were defined as those living in families whose incomes were less than or equal to the national poverty level. The near poor were those in families whose incomes were above, but less than or equal to twice, the poverty level.

A number of cost-control techniques such as cost sharing and provider discounts can save money for the insurer, employer, or government payer. There is limited information, however, about the role of comprehensive managed health care programs in controlling overall prescription drug costs. Even so, review of employer and government programs points to some useful information about what works and why. The conclusion drawn by this author is that, although cost-control techniques can save money for the sponsors of the program, their effect on total costs is less clear. Effective drug utilization review programs require a great deal of targeted one-on-one effort and/or an organized system of professional follow-up. The combination of cost-control techniques, an effective managed drug utilization review program, and a process of selecting preferred providers based in part on their cost-effective prescribing habits would have the strongest capability of controlling costs.

Pharmaceutical services and managed care are discussed extensively in Chapter 14, and the reader is referred to that chapter for an in-depth discussion of various strategies for managing this benefit cost.

MANAGING LONG-TERM CARE COSTS

Long-term care is the one major health care cost exposure for which there is little insurance available. Medicare covers short-term episodes of illnesses, not long-term care for chronic illnesses or for regular assistance in performing essential activities of daily life.[1] Medicaid provides nursing home and custodial care only for people who are poor (either poor to begin with or poor as a result of medical or other expenses). Private insurance is only a nominal source of long-term care financing, with less than 4% of the elderly and 1% of the population overall being enrolled in a long-term care program.[33] Yet long-term care insurance has grown rapidly in recent years. The number of individuals with long-term care insurance policies grew from 815,000 in 1987 to nearly 2 million in 1990. Similarly, the number of insurance companies selling long-term care insurance nearly doubled over the same period, from 75 to 143.[33] Individual policies and group association policies are the most common types of private insurance and have been available the longest. Employer-based policies are newer and less prevalent, covering 133,000 individuals, or 7% of total policy holders in 1990.

Enrollment in employers' long-term care plans is usually optional, with employees paying most or all of the premiums. Enrollees are younger on average than in other private individual plans because many participants are active workers and their spouses.

The limited coverage for long-term care and the later entry of commercial insurers in this market severely limit the amount of data available on managed long-term care programs. Much of the information known, as with other medical services, relates to the impact of cost-control techniques such as cost sharing and utilization review. But even something seemingly as basic as utilization review has proven difficult in this new product area. The need for long-term care services cannot be as objectively defined in review criteria as the need for other medical services. There is no inherent limit to the amount of custodial or support services a person can consume. And the degree of help available from family and friends strongly influences the need for outside assistance, although this variable is hard to control through utilization review.

The most extensive experience to date with techniques designed to manage long-term care cost and utilization resides in state Medicaid preadmission screening (PAS) programs for nursing homes. A large study of 31 state-administered nursing home PAS programs in 1986 was designed to go beyond the question of whether PAS could control the utilization and cost of nursing homes (which it had been shown to do) and to study its ability to control all long-term care services.[34] These services were defined broadly to include health, social, housing, and income services provided to chronically ill and physically disabled older people over an extended period of time. Although the PAS programs in 29 states and the District of Columbia varied greatly, they generally included a comprehensive on-site assessment of the client's needs and a recommendation concerning what

long-term care services were needed and where they should have been provided. The assessment generally included an evaluation of the client's physical and mental health, functional status, and formal and informal social supports. In some cases, home care services were then provided to those at risk for nursing home placement to prevent institutionalization.

The results of the study's written survey and phone interview, with 81% of the state PAS programs participating, was disappointing. The study concluded that PAS was not an effective utilization control measure for long-term care, noting that, although PAS in some states may divert nursing home candidates to home care, the increased utilization of home care may offset any potential cost savings. The study went on to suggest some possible reasons for this failure and some changes that could improve future results. The investigators also reminded readers that PAS still serves a number of other valuable functions beyond any role in cost containment, such as helping individuals make difficult decisions about how and where they should receive long-term care services.

One concern that developed in the study was the question of when people are at risk for nursing home placement. For example, if one applies the PAS program only to those who apply for nursing home admission, it may be too late to consider other alternatives. If the program provides its special treatment to a broader group of so-called at-risk individuals, it may actually be spending considerable resources educating and referring people to community services who are not truly at risk for institutionalization. These concerns suggest that PAS for long-term care might be more effective in the context of a broader continuum of managed care, where the individual is known over a longer period of time and an approach to all health and social needs can be better integrated.

Two attempts better to integrate long-term care coverage with other aspects of an elderly person's life are continuing care retirement communities (CCRCs) and life care at home (LCAH) programs. CCRCs combine the financing and delivery of long-term care within a single organizational context and insure residents against the catastrophic costs of long-term care. CCRCs offer housing and related services that often include medical, preventive health, and nursing home care. Two thirds of CCRCs provide their contracting members with some level of nursing home insurance, and the other third provides nursing care on a purely fee-for-service basis. Experience with CCRCs suggests that lifetime utilization of nursing home beds under a fully insured access-guaranteed system such as CCRC is comparable to lifetime use in the general population, at least through 85 years of age. The pattern of use of nursing homes appears to be different, however, in that the chance of admission is 50% greater and the length of stay is shorter for CCRC residents.[35] This pattern probably represents a more dynamic use of nursing beds for short recovery stays and may well be associated with decreased use of acute hospital beds (although this correlation was not studied).

LCAH programs offer a variation of CCRC at lower cost by providing most of the same benefits to elderly who prefer to remain in their own homes instead of moving to a central campus. LCAH programs generally provide comprehensive protection for both nursing home and home- and community-based care by using a number of managed care and risk management techniques to control costs. A strong case management system is a common feature.[35] LCAH programs are new and still face numerous challenges before their cost and service impact is fully known.

INTEGRATING ALL HEALTH SERVICE NEEDS THROUGH MANAGED CARE

Many of the programs discussed in this chapter that are designed to provide health care coverage for the elderly fail to provide the broad coverage needed and/or fail to manage the total cost and quality of the care delivered. Medicare has significant cost-sharing features but fails to cover prescription drugs or long-term care. Employment-based retiree programs are often limited, rarely cover long-term care, and are not generally subject to coordinated management with Medicare. In addition, the large number of claims administrators, the geographic disper-

sion, and the variations in coverage and administrative policies make it difficult to develop managed care programs for the elderly through employment-based financing. State programs are generally limited to the poor and do not usually integrate well with Medicare from a management perspective, although some managed care Medicaid programs are experimenting with ways to improve such integration. And finally, the cost pressures in all these systems make it difficult for them to focus on issues of managed care integration as opposed to opportunities to cost shift to others.

A number of important attempts, however, have been made to integrate the funding and management of all health care services for the elderly. One such attempt that is discussed in greater detail in Chapters 28 and 29 is the Medicare HMO risk contract. In this program, funding from Medicare is paid to the HMO for each Medicare-eligible enrollee. That amount, calculated at 95% of the HCFA's projected cost in the fee-for-service environment, is combined with any premium charged by the HMO and is used to pay for all covered services. Although few Medicare HMOs provide extensive long-term care benefits, prescription drug benefits are not uncommon. This integrated approach is strongly supported by the Department of Health and Human Services (DHHS). Despite the early problems and instability of this program, the number of participating HMOs and enrollees is growing. Medicare HMOs may in fact be the vehicle to provide cost-effective, high-quality acute care to older persons.[34]

There are at least three new variables that must be considered by an otherwise successful HMO when entering the Medicare HMO market: the payment rate by the HCFA for that area, the level of supplemental benefits to be offered, and the capacity of the administrative and provider structure to manage the Medicare-eligible population. Of these three variables the most common concern is the HCFA's payment rate and the anticipated change in that rate over time. Regardless of the payment source, estimating the future medical cost of an older group of people is more difficult than for an actively employed group. The cost curve is more skewed, and prior year costs are not as good a predictor of future costs. But for reasons still being debated, the calculated HCFA payment rates for some areas of the country seem just too low to support the delivery of Medicare benefits through a private prepaid product such as an HMO. The more successful Medicare HMO contractors have avoided areas where rates appear inadequate. The combination of disagreements about rate adequacy and the administrative hassles associated with government contracting led to many of the early HMO defections from this program.

Early Medicare HMOs were also overly optimistic about their ability to control costs more effectively than the HCFA. This optimism led them to add rich supplemental benefits for small additional premiums. Most successful Medicare HMOs have avoided rich prescription drug benefits or other such supplemental offerings that may drive up premiums and/or attract a less healthy mix of Medicare-eligible individuals to their plan. And finally, many of the early Medicare HMO failures resulted from inadequate preparation for the differences in working with this population. The administrative and staff time involved in individual sales and enrollment for Medicare HMOs is always much greater than for group marketing and enrollment. The elderly also take much more coaching to understand fully the nature of the HMO product and the limitations on physician and hospital access. In addition, depending on the HMO's structure, primary care physician gatekeepers may have a larger role in managing retiree medical services than for otherwise comparable employed HMO members. And most important, if there is any weakness in an HMO's management, provider contracts, or incentives, the Medicare population will expose that weakness quickly and at a significant cost.

These three variables and the many other barriers to success that arise in any HMO, however, should not dissuade potential Medicare contractors. The growth of Medicare HMOs and many federal reviews of these programs suggest that Medicare HMOs can successfully deliver cost-effective quality medical care at a profit.

The federal government has looked for ways to expand beyond individually marketed Medicare HMOs. Specific interest has developed in ways to integrate Medicare with employment-based group plans. In 1987 Congress authorized DHHS to make agreements with a maximum of three employment-related groups, such as employers or unions, to pay a fixed per capita amount from Medicare in exchange for the groups' taking responsibility for paying Medicare-covered health care services for their retirees and employees along with the supplemental benefits usually provided by the group. These plans are called Medicare-insured groups (MIGs).

Employers' initial reception of MIGs has been cool. Early interest in the program was expressed by a number of older manufacturing or mining industries with large retiree populations and high health costs. The HCFA payment rate for MIGs had problems similar to those of Medicare HMOs. In addition, the HCFA's payment formula did not take into account the higher historical costs of these specific groups. The cash flow and savings value of these MIGs were also limited by the fact that they would only apply to retirees who lived in an area in which the MIG operated a managed health care program. These and other contractual issues have slowed the progress of what otherwise could be a good idea.

At the time of this writing, there are no results on how well MIGs can control costs. One potential MIG sponsor, Amalgamated Life Insurance Company, has proposed Philadelphia as the initial site for its MIG. Two other potential MIG sponsors decided not to proceed with the final development phase. Another potential sponsor, Deere and Company, may proceed to development.[36] One would expect that a MIG may look similar to a Medicare HMO. The added advantage to both the HCFA and future analysts studying managed care in the elderly is that MIGs will operate on a group basis and will not be as subject to the individual enrollment selection biases of Medicare HMOs.

The longest experience with integrating the financing and management of all health care services for the elderly is through social HMOs (S/HMOs). This approach was designed to control costs while expanding long-term care services. The demonstration model, designed by Brandeis University in 1980, was sponsored by the HCFA with waivers from Medicare and Medicaid. The

S/HMO model includes the following basic organizational and financing features: (1) A single structure provides a full range of acute and chronic care services to Medicare beneficiaries who enroll on a voluntary basis and pay a monthly premium; (2) a coordinated case management system is established to authorize long-term care to those who meet certain disability and financial criteria; (3) S/HMOs serve a cross-section of the elderly population, including both functionally impaired and unimpaired; and (4) financing is accomplished through prepaid capitations by pooled funds from Medicare, Medicaid, and member premiums.[37]

In a 5-year review of the results of the four S/HMO demonstration projects by Harrington and Newcomer,[37] the importance of a managed care orientation is clear. Two S/HMO sponsors included HMOs: Medicare Plus II by Kaiser Permanente Northwest in Portland, Oregon, and Seniors Plus by Group Health, Inc in Minneapolis–St Paul, Minnesota. The other two, Elderplan (based in Brooklyn, New York) and Senior Care Action Network Health Plan (based in Long Beach, California), were established by non-HMO entities. The two S/HMOs sponsored by HMOs that added these projects as new products to their existing service plans appeared to be better able to control utilization of acute and ambulatory care. In part, this was because the established HMOs were able to economize by using their existing service delivery networks and physician experience in controlling utilization. All four organizations experienced financial problems associated with starting up and running S/HMOs. Although the initial problems were partially overcome, it remains to be determined whether S/HMOs can become viable financial organizations or product lines after their demonstration periods are over. Harrington and Newcomer[37] suggested a number of options designed to make S/HMOs more financially viable.

There are also some individual employer efforts to integrate better the employment-based health care coverage for their retirees with the coverage and services provided by government programs and the community. A number of companies have expanded their employee assistance programs to include elder care assistance. These expanded programs can help active employees better understand how to get needed care for their aging family members and can also provide valuable assistance to retirees. Some elder care assistance programs even serve as ombudsmen on behalf of retirees to make sure they get the most service from the social programs to which they are entitled. This kind of one-on-one effort can also be used to help retirees better understand and utilize managed care programs.

Some employers have gone beyond providing assistance and advice and more actively coordinate the care provided to their retirees. For example, they may expand their case management services used with active employees to assist in the coordination of care and financing issues with retirees. At the cutting edge of this approach is the geriatric assessment program known as Generation sponsored by Southern California Edison. This pilot program, now in its third year, aims to help retirees better manage their health care while trying to reduce retiree health care costs through coordinated care. The program, initially based in a single company-sponsored clinic, is designed for retirees and their spouses age 55 years and older. It provides a complete health assessment screening, including a questionnaire, a personal interview by the health care team, a review of all medications taken, and an evaluation of the individual's support system. The health care team features a physician, pharmacist, geriatric social worker, and other health professionals as needed. The result of all this is a care plan that includes short-term and long-term goals for any problem picked up in the process. Six-month follow-ups are scheduled to ensure that the care plan remains current and that the team remains available to provide advice and encouragement. The program provides strong empiric evidence that the quality of care has improved in specific cases as well as anecdotal evidence that it is saving costs. The program has also received a lot of favorable attention, capturing the Aging Leadership Award from the Washington Business Group on Health.[38]

One might hope that these various experiments in integrating health care management and funding would provide us with a clear picture of the one best way to do it right. Unfortunately, few successful programs have been around long enough to provide all the needed answers. There is still disagreement about issues as fundamental as the criteria for defining needed care. For example, case management is a common feature of all the S/HMOs as they attempt to manage the utilization and cost of long-term care services. Yet when a study analyzed care plan decisions at each of the four S/HMO sites for the same seven patients, significant differences were found in eligibility determination and allocation of care plans as well as in the types and mix of services prescribed. The range of approaches underscored the difficulties in managing long-term care, even in more integrated programs such as S/HMOs, and the lack of accepted standards for care planning and long-term care resource allocation. Abrahams et al, in a 1989 study, concluded, "we need new avenues of research, as well as thinking, about clinical practice that will now focus on how long-term care resource allocation decisions are made, what influences those decisions, and how such influences affect both cost and quality outcomes."[39(p736)]

CONCLUSION

The aging of the US population and the yet uncontrolled annual increases in health care costs present a formidable challenge to all of us. American public policy, as well as future purchasers, providers, and consumers of health care, will be greatly affected by these trends. Demographic projections suggest not only that we will have more older people but that we will have fewer working-age people to support future employer- or government-sponsored health care programs. These trends underscore the urgent need for the development and promotion of managed health care programs specifically aimed at retirees and the elderly. Currently, we have a good deal of experience in the use of specific techniques to control health care plan sponsors' costs in programs for retirees and the elderly. Many of those techniques, however, result in cost shifting or fragmentation of the financing and delivery of health services. We have only limited experience with applying full managed health care systems to this population.

The funding and promotion of managed health care for retirees through employment-based insurance programs has been restricted by a number of factors. Currently the most important of these factors is FAS 106, which requires employers to accrue liabilities for retiree health benefits during employees' active service rather than record the cost as benefits are paid. This FAS 106 requirement, which goes into effect for larger employers in 1993, has caused a major shift in the way employers view their obligation to guarantee retiree medical benefits. The resulting move by many employers away from a defined benefit approach to retiree health coverage also has had the effect of moving employers' attention away from the development of managed health care programs for future retirees.

Another factor restricting the development of employment-based funding of managed health care programs for retirees is the skepticism among many employers as to whether managed care saves them money in the long run. Much of the early savings were thought to be lost to employers through extra benefits provided to induce employees to join managed care. Some employers are also concerned that managed care savings may be a one-time event, with future health care trend rates being essentially unaffected. Others acknowledge that HMO and PPO premiums and/or trend rates may be lower than those in nonmanaged care, but they are concerned that these are false savings based on a maldistribution of health risks among benefit plan options. The result of all these concerns is at least a mild general skepticism among employers regarding the ability really to manage future overall costs with currently available managed care products.

There are, however, some strong and compelling success stories with managed health care in both the active and the retiree populations. HMOs and other managed health care systems have effectively controlled the cost and quality of care delivered to their membership. POS plans, especially when offered as a single health plan option (or in a coordinated way with HMO options), have also shown great promise. Medicare HMOs and isolated examples of managed health programs in the pre-65 retiree population have proven that these programs can deliver quality health care services in a cost-effective way to retirees and the elderly. Results from S/HMOs, CCRCs, and early LCAH programs suggest that we can expand the scope of managed care coverage to include a much broader range of elder care needs.

Nonetheless, there are a number of barriers to the use of managed health care in the retiree population. Many retirees are unfamiliar with managed care options and are concerned about any limitations on their choice of providers, especially if their physician is not in the plan under consideration. The mobility of retirees also has limited the ability of an employer-based group contract to provide managed care to the many locations where retirees may move or vacation. This may be part of the reason that most managed care programs for older people have not been group products but individual enrollment products sold locally. Given that health care costs and the hassle of submitting claims forms are major concerns of the elderly, however, it is logical to assume that managed health care will become an increasingly attractive option to this group over time.

Few of the currently available managed health care products address the full range of coverage needed by our aging population. Prescription drug and long-term care benefits particularly are lacking. Although there is limited information about the use of managed care systems for the elderly in these two areas, it appears that properly structured managed care programs can be effective in controlling drug and long-term care costs and quality. Further research is needed in this area, and a great deal of product development and integration is needed as well.

As employers complete the redesign of their retiree medical benefits in response to FAS 106, emphasis will eventually move away from liability and funding issues and will again be on benefits. It is then that managed health care options for retirees could begin playing a more significant role in the group benefit market. Further research and product development could greatly increase the speed at which this evolution occurs. The HMO community must be responsive

to the concerns of adverse selection and the perverse effect the HMOs could be having on indemnity rates. Employers and managed health care executives should explore lower benefit plan options, experience rating, and integrated premium strategies to ensure that managed care offerings have the desired effect on overall average group health premiums. Likewise, employers will need to limit strictly the number of health plan choices and/or integrate those choices to manage overall costs better.

Further research is needed in both employment-based and government-sponsored programs to define the effects of the various managed care delivery structures and interventions, including whether these effects have a one-time or long-term impact on health cost trends. Special carve-out medical management products such as managed prescription drug programs will need to address the same issues. Those managed health care plans that apply to an entire employer group (such as all pre-65 retirees) or to an entire community's population (such as all Medicare-eligible individuals) will produce more useful data and more clear-cut results.

All retirees and elderly need health care coverage for a reasonably comprehensive baseline of benefits, regardless of whether it is purchased by employers, individuals, or the government. Managed health care programs undoubtedly will play a significant role in providing that coverage because they can deliver more benefits to enrollees for less money than nonmanaged care plans. And, as the buying elderly public becomes more sophisticated about managed care options, the elderly will increasingly demand accessibility to reasonable coverage for prescription drugs and protection against the catastrophic costs of long-term care. The elderly population is currently an open market for properly designed and delivered managed care products. The most successful products will be those that do the best job of limiting the overall growth in both enrollee and sponsor costs while retaining as much flexibility and portability as possible. These products will be judged by their ability to make quality care accessible in a cost-effective way to the entire population they serve.

REFERENCES

1. Friedland RB. *Facing the Costs of Long Term Care*. Washington, DC: Employee Benefit Research Institute; 1990.

2. Schieber SJ. Can our social insurance system survive the demographic shifts of the 21st century? Paper presented at the Spring 1991 Pension Research Council Symposium; May 9–10, 1991; Philadelphia, PA.

3. Finkel ML. Cost of retiree health benefits. In: *Health Care Cost Management—A Basic Guide*. Brookfield, WI: International Foundation of Employee Benefit Plans; 1991.

4. Logan GC. What to do about retiree medical funding after FAS 106. *Benefits Law J*. 1991;4:5–17.

5. Cole GE Jr. How will companies cope with the skyrocketing costs of retiree health benefits? *Employee Benefits J*. 1989;14.

6. Bureau of the Census. *Current Population Reports* (series P-25, no 1044). Washington, DC: Government Printing Office; 1989.

7. Social Security Administration. Health care. *Soc Secur Bull*. (Ann Statistical suppl). 1991;50–61.

8. The Wyatt Company. Tidal wave of retiree medical redesign. *Wyatt Comparison*. 1992;1:3–8.

9. Taylor RS, Newton B. Can managed care reduce employers' retiree medical liability? *Benefits Q*. 1991;7:58–72.

10. Davis J. Retiree health benefits: issues of structure, financing and coverage. *Employee Benefit Research Institute Issue Brief*. 1991;112:1–25.

11. Miner W. Innovative funding program debuts at Ball Corporation. *Wyatt Commun*. 1991;9(2):36.

12. Commerce Clearinghouse. ProPAC publishes reports on PPS methods and results. *Medicare Medicaid Guide*. 1991;679:17.

13. Commerce Clearinghouse. Social Security trustees report on status of Medicare trust funds. *Medicard Medicaid Guide*. 1991;655:5.

14. Gabel J, DiCarlo S, Sullivan C, Rice T. Employer-sponsored health insurance, 1989. *Health Aff*. 1990;9(3):161–175.

15. A. Foster Higgins. *Health Care Benefit Survey, 1991*. Princeton: A. Foster Higgins; 1992.

16. Schwartz WB, Mendelson DN. Hospital cost containment in the 1990s: hard lessons learned and prospects for the 1990s. *N Engl J Med*. 1991;324(15):1037–1042.

17. Jensen GA, Morrissey MA. The premium consequences of group health insurance provisions. Paper presented at the American Public Health Association Meeting; November 14, 1988; Boston, MA.

18. Taylor RS. Filling the gaps in HMOs and PPOs. *J Health Care Benefits*. 1991;19:27.

19. The Wyatt Company. *Management USA: Leading a Changing Workforce*. Washington, DC: Wyatt; 1990.

20. Atlantic Information Services. Point-of-service plans holding down employer costs. *Inside Health Care Financing*; suppl to *Management Care Week*. June 24, 1991:1–2.

21. The Wyatt Company. *Cost Analysis of State Legislative Mandates on Six Managed Health Care Practices*. Washington, DC: Wyatt; 1991.

22. Group Health Association of America (GHAA). *HMO Industry Profile*. Washington, DC: GHAA; 1991;2.

23. Hosek SD, Marquis MS, Wells KB. *Health Care Utilization in Employer Plans with Preferred Provider Organization Options*. Santa Monica: RAND Corp; 1990.

24. Leavitt TD. Post retirement benefits: what do retirees want? *Compens Benefits Manag*. 1989;5(3):215–225.

25. The Gallup Organization. *Public Attitudes on HMOs and PPOs*. Washington, DC: Employee Benefit Research Institute; 1990.

26. Geisel J. Doctor loyalty deters retiree use of HMOs. *Bus Insur*. 1987 (December):1,70.

27. Pfizer, Inc, Louis Harris and Associates, Inc. *National Survey of HMO Enrollees*. New York: Louis Harris and Associates; 1988.

28. Edmondson B. Is Florida our future? *Am Demogr*. 1987 (June):38–43, 68–69.

29. Longino CF Jr, Crown WH. The migration of old money. *Am Demogr*. 1989 (October):28–31.

30. Glasgow N. A place in the country. *Am Demogr*. 1991 (March):24–30.

31. Grobman M. Wrestling with the retiree market. *HMO Mag*. 1991(July-August):17–20.

32. Lipton HL. Drug economics and the elderly: prescriptions for change. *Bus Health*. 1988;5:8–11.

33. Horkitz K. Long-term care financing and the private insurance market. *Employee Benefit Research Institute Issue Brief*. 1991;117:1–24.

34. Polich CL, Iversen LH. State preadmission screening programs for controlling utilization of long-term care. *Health Care Financ Rev*. 1987;9:43–49.

35. Cohen M. Life care: new options for financing and delivering long-term care. *Health Care Financ Rev*. 1988 (ann suppl):139–143.

36. Commerce Clearinghouse. Managed care. *Medicaid Medicare Guide*. 1992;687;15.

37. Harrington C, Newcomer R. Social health maintenance organizations' service use and costs, 1985–89. *Health Care Financ Rev*. 1991;12:37–52.

38. Bureau of National Affairs. SCE experiments with managed care in pilot geriatric assessment program. *Benefits Today*. March 6, 1992;9:73.

39. Abrahams R, Capitman R, Levtz W, Macko P. Variations in care planning practice in the social/HMO: an exploratory study. *Gerontologist*. 1989;29:725–736.

Chapter 31

Medicaid and Managed Care

R. Robert Herrick

Medicaid is a program operated by the states that uses both federal and state funding to provide health services for poor persons. Medicaid began as a fee-for-service program in 1966. It has incurred significant cost inflation over the past 25 years that has paralleled that of the private sector. During this period, Medicaid expenditures were often the fastest growing segment of state budgets and the second largest state spending category in fiscal year 1990.[1] Medicaid payment systems, however, have been much slower to adapt to recent health cost-containment methods whose effectiveness has been demonstrated by private sector initiatives.[2,3]

Managed care approaches for Medicaid recipients have been generally encouraged by some state Medicaid agencies and by the Health Care Financing Administration (HCFA) over the past decade. A few state efforts to enroll Medicaid recipients in systems of managed care were even begun in the early 1970s, with mixed results.[4,5]

Until the mid-1980s, though, managed care had little impact on the number of Medicaid recipients enrolled and therefore little overall im-

R. Robert Herrick is President of Robert Herrick Associates, Inc., a managed care consulting and management firm. He was formerly Vice President of Public Programs for HealthAmerica Corporation and has 20 years of experience in managed care.

pact on Medicaid costs. By mid 1990, HCFA reports[6] showed 3,009,246 Medicaid enrollees in managed care systems, which is about 14% of all Medicaid recipients. Enrollment nationwide rose by 19% from June 1989 to June 1990. About half these Medicaid recipient enrollees (1,592,810) are in seven health insuring organizations (HIOs), which act primarily as capitation-reimbursed fiscal agents rather than as managers of care. This managed care enrollment was in only 28 states and the District of Columbia, but it did include those states with the largest Medicaid populations.

Although the number of federally and state-qualified health maintenance organizations (HMOs) was more than 600, only 127 federally and state-qualified HMOs and 66 prepaid health plans (PHPs) that manage care had contracts in 1990 with state Medicaid agencies to enroll recipients.[6]

The total number of managed care entities serving Medicaid is now 200 nationwide, but there has been no increase in the number of states with Medicaid managed care programs since 1986. Twenty-two states have no Medicaid managed care program. There is continued policy pressure at both state and federal levels to reduce Medicaid program costs by enrolling more eligibles in managed care systems. Medicaid contracting, however, has proven to be more difficult for HMOs and other managed care programs than for the private sector or commercial market.[7]

MEDICAID MARKET

The current national Medicaid market consists of approximately 24 million eligibles in the 50 states and the District of Columbia and is continually growing as the federal government expands eligibility. In 1989 Medicaid benefit payments were more than $58 billion, with the federal government paying 55% of the total.[1] Managed care programs generally have access to serve only those eligible persons covered by Aid to Families with Dependent Children (AFDC), and the Aged, the Blind, and Disabled, excluding long-term care.

The Medicaid market has widely varying characteristics by state. Understanding four of these characteristics is crucial to understanding this market:

1. *Regulations*—Medicaid programs have certain basic regulations required by the HCFA that are nationally consistent; each state program has its own unique regulatory requirements, however.
2. *Eligible categories*—Different categories of eligible persons have different health and sociologic concerns and may require small to large amounts of health services resources.
3. *Benefits*—Medicaid benefits and limitations on copayments and services are different from commercial managed care benefits.
4. *Access*—Geographic access to services by eligible persons is a greater problem than for commercial enrollees in most communities.

The effect of each of these characteristics on enrollment and service of Medicaid eligibles in managed care systems is discussed below.

Regulations

Managed care organizations that have operated in multiple states and seek to serve Medicaid eligibles in more than one state find little consistency beyond the basic HCFA requirements for all programs. Eligibility rules vary, categories of eligibility vary, enrollment and marketing rules vary, benefits vary, provider subcontract requirements vary, reimbursement methods and limitations vary, and even state reporting requirements designed to meet the same HCFA reporting requirements vary. Therefore, each state Medicaid program must be approached with a customized plan to serve its eligibles.

Eligible Categories

Although percentages may vary among states and will vary more dramatically within regions of states, overall statewide typical percentages of eligible Medicaid beneficiaries are as follows:

- 70% are beneficiaries of AFDC and related programs. These beneficiaries typically include 65% persons from birth through 17 years, 30% women of childbearing ages who are heads of families, and 5% other heads of families. Most health services for this category are related to birthing.

- 15% are aged, blind, and disabled persons covered by supplemental security income benefits, including some who are also covered by Medicare. Most health problems are related to aging or disability.

- 10% are general relief or general assistance persons who are mostly ages 20 through 50. The most frequent health problem is substance abuse. (The HCFA reports usually exclude general relief because it is not a federally funded category.)

- 5% are other categories, including refugees. Major health concerns of these categories of beneficiaries vary widely among categories.

Therefore, both the managed care service delivery systems and the costs of health care will vary by category. Serving the overall Medicaid population requires systems that focus on health problems ranging from birthing to aging to substance abuse.

Some states contract with managed care systems to serve only AFDC eligibles. Other states require a managed care contractor to enroll and serve all categories. In still other states, general relief or general assistance is a locally (county or city) contracted category not included in the statewide program.

Benefits

Medicaid-eligible persons always have limited income and usually receive most of their income from state or federal programs. Medicaid benefits are therefore usually more comprehensive than those of commercial health insurance programs. Also, Medicaid programs usually prohibit significant copayments or deductibles because they form a barrier to access to needed care for persons of limited income. Some states do allow small copayments (eg, $1 or less), but these are too small to restrain unnecessary utilization in the manner that high copayments and deductibles are believed to function for commercial enrollees. Most states will also require the managed care contractor to provide all mandated Medicaid benefits and services other than long-term care. Long-term care patients are usually disenrolled from the managed care system and revert to the Medicaid fee-for-service system. Although Medicaid benefits vary by state, a typical list of benefits from the Ohio Medicaid program AFDC is shown in Exhibit 31-1.

Some states have restricted payment for inpatient services under fee-for-service Medicaid by using either diagnosis-related group (DRG) or per diem payments as a way to limit the state's cost liability. The managed care contractor, however, may be expected to provide the unlimited inpatient days benefit consistent with federal or state HMO qualification requirements. Because benefits for Medicaid eligibles include some that are not typically included in most commercial HMO programs (eg, dental services, chiropractic services, or eyeglasses), the contractor is required to arrange for these services for Medicaid recipient enrollees only, even if Medicaid constitutes only a small portion of the HMO's total enrollees. States are usually unwilling to contract for only those benefits provided by the HMO to its commercial enrollees, with remaining benefits being paid by state fee-for-service Medicaid. Whenever benefits for

Exhibit 31-1 Medicaid Typical Benefits: Capitation Contract, Ohio, Scope of Services by Service Type

---

The following types of services will be provided to covered persons by HMO at least to the extent such services are covered by Ohio Medicaid:

1. Inpatient hospital services
2. Outpatient hospital services
3. Laboratory and X-ray services
4. Early and periodic screen diagnosis and treatment of covered persons under 21 years of age (EPSDT)
5. At-risk pregnancy services
6. Family planning services and supplies for covered persons of childbearing age
7. Physician services, whether furnished in the office, the covered person's home, a hospital, or elsewhere
8. Medical care and any other type of remedial care recognized under state law furnished by licensed practitioners within the scope of their practice as defined by state law
9. Home health care services
10. Private duty nursing services
11. Clinic services
12. Physical therapy, occupational therapy, and services for covered persons with speech, hearing, and language disorders
13. Prescribed drugs
14. Ambulance and ambulette transportation
15. Emergency services
16. Dental services
17. Mental health services, except community mental health clinic services and inpatient care in state-operated psychiatric facilities
18. Podiatric services
19. Chiropractic services
20. Physical medicine services
21. Durable medical supplies and equipment
22. Vision care services
23. Nurse midwife services
24. Nursing facility services for rehabilitation of injury or illness
25. Other limited practitioner services
26. Hospice care services

Source: Ohio Department of Human Services, HMO Provider Agreement, 1992.

Medicaid eligibles exceed those of commercial enrollees, the identity of Medicaid recipients enrolled in managed care systems must be clearly known to providers, just like under fee-for-service Medicaid reimbursement systems. In some Medicaid managed care programs, it was a program objective to make the provider network blind to the source of reimbursement, but that is usually no longer possible.

Access

Most managed care systems initially grew by providing services to employees and their dependents and by being geographically accessible to these persons. Although some Medicaid enrollees in the various categories may live in all neighborhoods in a community, the residences of most Medicaid eligibles are usually concentrated in the low-income neighborhoods. Many Medicaid enrollees may therefore have difficulty obtaining transportation to the provider sites that were developed to serve commercial enrollees. The managed care system needs to concern itself with accessibility to improve the appropriate use of services.

In addition to geographic access, many Medicaid eligibles have not had access to private physicians in the past and have resorted to inappropriate use of emergency departments for all their care.[8] Enrollees new to managed care therefore may have both unmet health needs and utilization habits that initially raise their cost of care. New Medicaid enrollees may also have difficulty learning to access services in a managed care system.[9] An outreach program by the managed care system is a cost-effective way to teach new Medicaid eligibles how to use the system appropriately.[10]

MEDICAID MANAGED CARE CONTRACTS

State Medicaid agencies have sought to contract with various managed health care systems on a capitation payment basis for about two decades. Because Medicaid was enacted by Congress as a fee-for-service program under Title XIX of the Social Security Act, state agencies face two types of restrictions.

First, state requirements vary from state to state and may allow contracting only with HMOs, or they may allow contracts with other entities such as community health centers. Some states still do not allow any Medicaid capitation contracting.

Second, federal requirements periodically have been changed by Congress to limit the contracting latitude of state agencies. Such requirements limit the authority of the Secretary of the Department of Health and Human Services to waive various fee-for-service requirements that are the basis for the original Medicaid program.

States have been encouraged by the HCFA to develop demonstration managed care programs that are intended to control Medicaid costs. Some have succeeded, others have not.[5,11]

Managed care contracts with state Medicaid agencies that reimburse on the basis of a fixed capitation payment per enrollee now seem to be limited to:

- federally qualified HMOs
- state-qualified HMOs
- prepaid health plans (PHPs), including community health centers
- health insuring organizations (HIOs) acting only as fiscal agents

States also have the option of acting as their own HMO and contracting directly on a capitation basis with providers. Some state Medicaid agencies have assumed this role as manager of health care, as contrasted with their traditional role of claims reimburser.

In one state, it became a requirement of HMO licensure that each HMO must be willing to provide Medicaid services. In other states, access to state employees for HMO enrollment has been granted only if the HMO contracts with the Medicaid agency also. These requirements forcing HMOs to participate in Medicaid have produced little increase in Medicaid enrollment.

Most capitation contracts for Medicaid services are for voluntary enrollment of Medicaid eligibles. Even so, 1.6 million individuals in the 1990 Medicaid managed care systems enrollment are in universal enrollment programs in a few states. This represents about half of all Medicaid managed care enrollees. The form of these programs is the HIO.

HIOs have long been allowed by federal regulations, but few states have contracted in this manner. HIOs initially were statewide or regional fiscal agents contracting with the state Medicaid agency to receive a capitation payment, then paying providers on a fee-for-service basis. These HIOs enrolled all eligible persons residing within the contract region on a universal or mandatory basis. In 1983, the HIO concept was applied to managed care systems for a primary care network in Louisville, Kentucky, and subsequently for other programs.[12] Congress effectively restricted further development of universal Medicaid enrollment managed care systems in 1985, however, by requiring that they meet the same rules as HMOs for mix of commercial and Medicaid enrollment. HMOs are required by federal law to have no more than 75% Medicaid and/or Medicare enrollment. Because an HIO is a contract program with the state Medicaid agency only and not a commercial HMO, it cannot meet this requirement.

The only state that started its Medicaid program as a managed care system was Arizona in 1982. Arizona, under HCFA demonstration waivers, has subsequently contracted only with PHPs for providing service to Medicaid recipients.

Contracts with state Medicaid agencies vary from state to state in their complexity and their rigidity. In some states, all Medicaid managed care contracts within the state must be identical in service scope, marketing requirements, and rate structure. These states do not allow for differences in the delivery system among HMOs. They also require special services for Medicaid enrollees that are not included in typical HMO commercial contracts. They furthermore may require modification of the entire provider subcontract structure to serve Medicaid enrollees. Other states are less rigid and are more willing to customize the Medicaid managed care contract to the specific organizational entity providing the services, thus allowing for regional delivery systems differences and for the managed care entity to serve Medicaid recipients in the same manner in which it serves its commercial enrollees. In these cases, the HMO or other managed care system can use its customary provider subcontracts to provide Medicaid services.

ENROLLMENT AND MARKETING

Enrollment of Medicaid recipients is significantly more difficult than commercial enroll-

ment for several reasons. Managed care systems with Medicaid contracts do not have access to names or addresses of potential enrollees because federal and state regulations treat this as confidential information. Also, Medicaid recipients do not pay for their own coverage and can have no significant copayments or deductibles. Therefore, there is never a financial incentive for the Medicaid eligible to enroll in the HMO, as often occurs with commercial enrollees.

Medicaid eligibles are usually not required to make a positive selection between managed care and fee-for-service care; they are automatically enrolled in the fee-for-service system and must take action on their own to seek a managed care system for their health care.

Enrollment is continuous throughout the year and is not concentrated in discrete time periods that would allow for focused informational efforts. Use of print and electronic media therefore is generally ineffective for enrolling Medicaid eligibles.

Marketing and enrollment of Medicaid have been most successful if one of the two following methods was used:

1. positive choice, with the use of managed care enrollment representatives, not neutral state workers, to explain the managed care system
2. door-to-door marketing in high-density Medicaid-eligible neighborhoods, encouraging word-of-mouth referrals

Both of these methods have in the past led to abuses in some regions, but methods to avoid the abuses are available without eliminating the enrollment method.

In most regions, the only positive incentives for a Medicaid-eligible person to enroll in a managed care program are access to physicians and good service. Quality of care may also be an incentive but is not quantifiable by enrollees. There are no out-of-pocket savings incentives. Benefits are usually so comprehensive that benefit additions are not available to serve as an incentive to enroll. Various states have also placed restrictions on marketing, such as not allowing representatives to enroll inside the state or county eligibility offices or not allowing representatives to approach a recipient unless the Medicaid recipient requests information first.

Retention of Medicaid enrollees is also more difficult. Most states allow disenrollment after 30 days for any reason, and enrollees lose their Medicaid eligibility at a much higher rate than the rate at which employees change employers. Therefore, the turnover rate in Medicaid managed care is higher than that in commercial care, with an accompanying effect on use of services.[10] Some states are now offering a 6-month guarantee of eligibility to new Medicaid enrollees, but enrollees are not locked in and are still free to disenroll monthly.

Because of initial enrollment and retention problems, the cost of Medicaid marketing and enrollment is higher than that of typical commercial marketing. The goals of managed care marketing should be to inform adequately the Medicaid beneficiaries of their health care choices and to assist them in choosing the best program to meet their needs. Ideally, the state Medicaid agency should require positive choice and provider information adequate for eligibles to select the best health care program. Few do, in spite of the clear cost incentive of 5% to 10% savings to the state and federal government for persons who enroll in capitated managed care systems.

MEDICAL MANAGEMENT: QUALITY ASSURANCE AND UTILIZATION REVIEW

Medicaid contract requirements for quality assurance and utilization review vary among states. Some states simply require that the managed care system abide by the requirements of its federal or state qualification, thus treating Medicaid enrollees the same as commercial enrollees. In other states, a separate review system is required for Medicaid managed care contracts. In some states, the Medicaid contract also requires that the quality audit of Medicaid service records also be extended to include non-Medicaid service records in the same HMO, with the entire audit being made part of the public record. Because fee-for-service Medicaid is not audited for outpatient quality, no comparisons can be

made. All managed care contracts contain a requirement that an independent audit of both inpatient and outpatient services provided to Medicaid eligibles be performed, although fee-for-service Medicaid programs usually audit only inpatient care.

The states also vary in their requirements for subcontracting with providers. Some states accept the physician, hospital, and other provider subcontracts approved by the state licensing and federal or state qualification requirements for managed care systems. Other states require provider subcontracts to be rewritten to include Medicaid-specific language and terms. Some states require all managed care system providers also to be fee-for-service Medicaid contractors. No states allow a provider dropped from fee-for-service Medicaid for fraud or abuse to become a subcontractor for a managed care Medicaid contractor.

Effective utilization review and quality assurance programs not only are required for Medicaid contracts but are essential to the cost-effective management of Medicaid services. For example, there is a high incidence of costly, high-risk births in the fee-for-service Medicaid AFDC population. Both to achieve healthy outcomes and to control costs, early prenatal care, continuity of care, and effective birthing care are needed. Effective medical management of high-risk births is a dramatic example of the outcome and cost-control advantages achievable by managed care systems.

Utilization of fee-for-service Medicaid by beneficiaries is generally high. Managed care systems have shown the ability to achieve a more than 50% reduction of hospital days, a 70% reduction of emergency department visits, and a slight increase in physician visits compared to fee-for-service Medicaid. Exhibit 31-2 indicates the control and savings achievable by managed care programs for AFDC Medicaid eligibles in selected urban areas.

FISCAL MANAGEMENT AND CAPITATION RATES

In the early years of Medicaid managed care contracting, some states required Medicaid capi-

Exhibit 31-2 Ranges of AFDC Medicaid Utilization—US Urban Areas

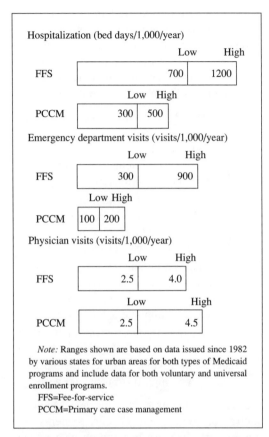

Hospitalization (bed days/1,000/year)

	Low	High
FFS	700	1200

	Low	High
PCCM	300	500

Emergency department visits (visits/1,000/year)

	Low	High
FFS	300	900

	Low	High
PCCM	100	200

Physician visits (visits/1,000/year)

	Low	High
FFS	2.5	4.0

	Low	High
PCCM	2.5	4.5

Note: Ranges shown are based on data issued since 1982 by various states for urban areas for both types of Medicaid programs and include data for both voluntary and universal enrollment programs.
FFS=Fee-for-service
PCCM=Primary care case management

tation rates to be based on commercial rates. Resulting rates were generally too low to pay for even the reduced inpatient utilization achievable by the managed care systems. The Medicaid population is actually sicker than the private sector commercial population; that is, a higher proportion of eligibles have health problems. States now pay higher rates for Medicaid in proportion to the higher service requirements, however. Currently all states that contract Medicaid services to managed care systems will pay for managed care at either (1) 90% to 95% of the regional fee-for-service Medicaid claims cost for a comparable population adjusted to a per eligible per month capitation rate, or (2) a bid rate, submitted by the managed care system, that may not exceed 95% of fee-for-service claims costs or claims plus state administrative costs.

Rates are usually regionalized by county within the state, thus recognizing the actual medical cost differences between urban and rural areas. Data for capitated rates by service or benefit by region, however, have been developed only recently in most states and may not accurately portray the actual cost of services.

Managed care systems should not assume that they can routinely provide effective care at 95% of fee-for-service Medicaid rates. The major reason is that most states have artificially suppressed provider reimbursements, especially for physicians, over the past few years. Medicaid payment schedules for physician services in most states are at 50% to 70% of commercially prevailing fees. Other Medicaid providers may receive a higher proportion of commercial reimbursement, but still not 100%. The states have therefore shifted some of the cost of Medicaid to the providers. Thus the managed care system probably cannot reimburse its providers for Medicaid services at its commercial rates either. Although some studies have shown that Medicaid fee-for-service utilization rates have increased when unit cost reimbursement was reduced, the effective management of care may not be able to show enough reduction of utilization to allow payment of its providers at prevailing rates equivalent to commercial capitation.

Thus, although Exhibit 31-2 shows that Medicaid hospitalization can be more than halved in a managed care system, overall financial management is still difficult because the fee-for-service payment rates, on which 95% capitation is based, are so low.

Capitation rates are also sensitive to the mix of categories of eligibles. The typical capitation cost of the AFDC population is about half the cost of the aged/blind/disabled population and two thirds the cost of general assistance. Enrollment mix is therefore important unless the state reimburses the managed care system with a different capitation rate for each category of eligible persons.

In a few states or regions within states, where Medicaid enrollment in managed care represents more than 50% of the eligible beneficiaries, the fee-for-service claims costs database is no longer valid as a base for capitation rating. In these areas, states must resort to other methods of rate development, usually by projecting Medicaid managed care experience for inflation or by using fee-for-service data on a comparable population in another community.

Many HMOs experienced severe payment problems over retroactive eligibility for coverage in early Medicaid contracts with states both for adding new enrollees and for late terminations due to loss of Medicaid eligibility. In most contracts now, states will provide a monthly list of enrolled eligibles and will pay the HMO on the basis of that list at the beginning of each month. Therefore retroactive additions and terminations should no longer be a major problem.

In the future, states can be expected to squeeze the managed care capitation rates from 95% of fee-for-service claims to 90% or less. One state already requires HMOs serving Medicaid to take an automatic rate reduction in the second year of the Medicaid contract. Some states also make an age/sex adjustment to the capitation rate in the second year and beyond based on the actual enrollment in the HMO. These reductions will occur because states are always under severe budget pressures for tax-generated revenue. As this trend continues, some HMOs in some states may find that they can no longer reduce utilization further, relative to the fee-for-service claims level, and will be forced to drop their Medicaid contract or shift costs to their other lines of business.

CONCLUSION

Medicaid managed care contracting continues to become more complex each year with increasing governmental limitations on enrollment, increasing service requirements, and increasing reporting and audit requirements, all of which raise administrative service costs. Even in 1980, Vignola and Strumf stated, "The administrative complexities alone would appear to be enough to dissuade may HMOs from seeking Medicaid contracts."[4]

Yet despite the complexities and higher administrative costs, HMOs and other managed care systems find that they can provide well-managed health services to Medicaid beneficiaries for 95% of the fee-for-service Medicaid costs in most communities. HMOs also find that Medicaid beneficiaries have predictable health

needs and can learn to use managed care systems effectively. Hence, if marketed and managed properly, a managed care system can serve Medicaid enrollees well at reasonable profit.

Key elements that require more administrative attention to achieve cost-effective management for Medicaid enrollment compared to private sector enrollment are as follows:

- The Medicaid contract capitation rate should be no less than 95% of actual fee-for-service Medicaid costs until the managed care system achieves its own track record of services utilization.

- Active and continuous marketing to Medicaid eligibles needs to be conducted to achieve and maintain a reasonable balance of high- and low-risk enrollees.

- An outreach program to teach Medicaid enrollees how to access and use managed care services effectively is needed to help control costs and improve outcomes.

- Effective monitoring and control of utilization of high-cost services (eg, effective prenatal care for AFDC enrollees to reduce the frequency of high-risk births) are needed.

Several elements could improve Medicaid contracting with managed care systems and subsequently increase penetration of capitated systems in the Medicaid market:

- contract flexibility by state and federal agencies to allow managed care systems to enroll and serve Medicaid enrollees in the same manner in which they serve commercial enrollees

- guaranteed eligibility for more than 30 days, including eligibility for a period of time that extends beyond the loss of welfare payments

- contracting assurance for more than a 1-year term, for fixed rates or ensured rate inflation, and for stop-loss provided by the state for unpredictable high-cost services (eg, organ transplantation or acquired immunodeficiency syndrome)

- universal enrollment in regions where sufficient choice of competing HMOs or capitation contracting providers is available to enrollees to ensure adequate access and choice of providers

Both the HCFA and the states are expected to continue to encourage contracting for Medicaid services with managed care systems as data continue to show overall quality care being provided at cost savings to the state and federal governments.

REFERENCES

1. Wilensky GR. From the Health Care Financing Administration: Recent Medicaid expansions. *JAMA.* 1991;265(19):2461.

2. Freund DA, Hurley RE. Managed care in Medicaid: selected issues in program origins, design and research. *Annu Rev Public Health.* 1987;8:137–163.

3. Freund DA, et al. Evaluation of the Medicaid competition demonstrations. *Health Care Financ Rev.* 1989;11:2.

4. Vignola ML, Strumf GB. *Medicaid Beneficiaries in Health Maintenance Organizations: Utilization Cost, Quality, Legal Requirements; An Annotated Bibliography.* Washington, DC: American Public Welfare Association and Department of Health and Human Services; 1980.

5. Anderson MD, Fox PD. Lessons learned from Medicaid managed care approaches. *Health Aff.* 1987 (Spring);6(1):71–86.

6. Thompson D. *Report on Medicaid Capitation Enrollment in Capitated Plans as of June 30, 1990.* Washington, DC: Department of Health and Human Services; 1990.

7. Gaul GM. HMOs and the poor. *Phila Inq.* November 2, 1986.

8. Hurley RE, Freund DA, Taylor DE. Emergency room use and primary care case management: evidence from four Medicaid demonstration programs. *Am J Public Health.* 1989;79:7.

9. Ware JE, et al. Comparison of health outcomes at a health maintenance organization with those of fee-for-service care. *Lancet.* 1986(May 3):1017–1022.

10. Wintringham K, Bice TW. Effect of turnover on use of services by Medicaid beneficiaries in a health maintenance organization. *Group Health J.* 1985;1:12–18.

11. Freund DA. *Medicaid Reform: Four Studies in Case Management.* Washington, DC: American Enterprise Institute; 1984.

12. Herrick RR. *Medicaid Health Insuring Organizations.* Washington, DC: GHAA Group Health Institute; 1985.

Chapter 32

CHAMPUS and the
Department of Defense Managed Care Programs

John F. Boyer and Larry Sobel

The Military Health Services System (MHSS) is a large and complex health care system designed to provide, and to maintain readiness to provide, medical services and support to the armed forces during military operations and to provide medical services and support to mem-

John F. Boyer is a Navy Nurse Corps officer on active duty currently assigned as Director, Coordinated Care Policy, in the Office of the Assistant Secretary of Defense (Health Affairs). In this capacity, he serves as the principal policy adviser to the Deputy Assistant Secretary of Defense for Health Services Financing in matters related to the delivery and financing of health care. He holds master's degrees in both nursing and management as well as a PhD in public administration and policy analysis.

Larry Sobel is currently the Deputy Director, Coordinated Care Operations and a senior health care program analyst for the Deputy Assistant Secretary of Defense for Health Services Financing in matters related to managed care operations. He has more than 15 years of experience in managed health care. He holds an AB from Harvard College and a JD from Harvard Law School.

The views expressed within the chapter are those of the authors and not necessarily those of the Department of Defense.

A portion of the chapter was adapted from J. Boyer, D. Fant, S. Lillie, and C. Pool, "An Overview of Managed Health Care in the Department of Defense," *Medical Interface*, vol 4, no 11, November 1991, pp. 15–22, copyright © 1991, Medicom International, Inc.

bers of the armed forces, their dependents, and others entitled to Department of Defense (DOD) medical care. To accomplish these missions, the Army, Navy, and Air Force operate more than 1,000 medical and dental treatment facilities, including 148 hospitals, located throughout the world. To augment this direct health care system, the DOD also offers care indirectly to certain beneficiaries via the Civilian Health and Medical Program of the Uniformed Services (CHAMPUS). This chapter will focus on a discussion of CHAMPUS, both the traditional medical benefits program and its managed care demonstration programs, and on DOD's recently developed coordinated care program (CCP).

CHAMPUS is a program of medical benefits provided by the US government under public law.[1] Specified categories of individuals qualify for these benefits by virtue of their relationship to one of the seven uniformed services (US uniformed services include the Army, Navy, Air Force, Marine Corps, Coast Guard, the Commissioned Corps of the Public Health Service, and the Commissioned Corps of the National Oceanic and Atmospheric Administration). In general, persons eligible for CHAMPUS benefits include families of active duty service members; retired service members, their spouses, and their unmarried children; survivors of active duty or retired service members; and certain former spouses of members of the military. Active duty members of the services are not covered by CHAMPUS, nor, in general, are retirees, survivors, or family members of a retiree if they are eligible for Medicare. Today, there are approximately 6 million CHAMPUS-eligible beneficiaries,[2] and the annual program budget has grown to approximately $3.9 billion.[3]

LEGAL AUTHORITY AND RESPONSIBILITIES

Title X, Chapter 55, of the US Code authorizes the Secretary of Defense, the Secretary of Health and Human Services, and the Secretary of Transportation jointly to prescribe regulations for the administration of CHAMPUS. Title X, Chapter 55, also authorizes the Secretary of Defense to administer CHAMPUS for the Army, Navy, Air Force, and Marine Corps under DOD jurisdiction, the Secretary of Transportation to administer CHAMPUS for the Coast Guard (when the Coast Guard is not operating as a service in the Navy), and the Secretary of Health and Human Services to administer CHAMPUS for the Commissioned Corps of the US Public Health Service and the National Oceanic and Atmospheric Administration.

The Secretary of Defense has delegated authority to the Assistant Secretary of Defense for Health Affairs [ASD(HA)] to provide policy guidance, management control, and coordination for CHAMPUS.[4] The Secretary of Health and Human Services has delegated authority to the Assistant Secretary for Health, Department of Health and Human Services (DHHS), to consult with the Secretary of Defense or a designee and to approve and issue joint regulations implementing Title X, Chapter 55.[5] The Secretary of Transportation has delegated authority to the Commandant, US Coast Guard, to consult with the Secretary of Defense or a designee and to approve and issue joint regulations implementing 10 USC, Chapter 55.[5]

In 1974, the Office of CHAMPUS (O-CHAMPUS) was established as a field activity under the policy guidance and direction of the ASD(HA) to supervise and administer the program.[6] Today, within the Office of the ASD(HA), OCHAMPUS falls under the purview of the Deputy Assistant Secretary of Defense (Health Services Financing). In carrying out one of the most important responsibilities of the agency, the Director, OCHAMPUS develops for issuance (subject to approval by the administering secretaries) such policies or regulations as required to administer and manage CHAMPUS effectively.

MEDICAL BENEFITS PROGRAM

Although similar in structure to an insurance program in many respects, CHAMPUS is not an insurance program. That is, CHAMPUS does not involve a contract guaranteeing the indemnification of an insured party against a specified loss in return for a paid premium. Further, CHAMPUS is not subject to state regulatory bodies or agencies that control the insurance industry generally. Instead, CHAMPUS is a program whereby the federal government pays for certain medically or psychologically necessary services provided by an authorized health care professional to eligible beneficiaries. Specifics about program eligibility, basic program benefits, provider authorization, claims processing, and other program features are detailed in a DOD regulation.[7]

PROGRAM FUNDS

The funds used by CHAMPUS are furnished by the Congress through the annual Appropriations Acts to the DOD and the DHHS. These funds are further disbursed by agents of the government under contracts negotiated in accordance with provisions of the Federal Acquisition Regulation by the Director, OCHAMPUS.[8] These agents, commonly referred to as fiscal intermediaries (FIs), receive claims against CHAMPUS and adjudicate the claims in accordance with administrative procedures and instructions prescribed in their contracts. The funds expended for CHAMPUS benefits are federal funds provided to CHAMPUS FIs solely to pay CHAMPUS claims and are not a part of, or obtained from, the CHAMPUS FI's funds related to other programs or insurance coverage. CHAMPUS FIs are reimbursed for the adjudication and payment of CHAMPUS claims at a rate (generally fixed price) prescribed in their contracts.

RECENT CHAMPUS EXPERIENCE

Benefits covered under CHAMPUS roughly parallel those of high-option programs available under other public and major private health care plans. CHAMPUS coverage includes most inpatient and outpatient health services, a substantial portion of physician and hospital charges, medical supplies and equipment, and mental health services. Because CHAMPUS beneficiaries pay no premiums, and because in recent years other health benefit programs have instituted increasingly greater limits on benefits, CHAMPUS has become one of the most generous health benefit plans available in the United States today. Not surprisingly, then, in the last several years CHAMPUS has experienced substantial growth in program costs and utilization. Indeed, since 1985 both CHAMPUS expenditures and CHAMPUS claims have more than doubled.[9]

CHAMPUS MANAGED CARE DEMONSTRATIONS

Faced with such statistics, the DOD has implemented a number of demonstration programs in recent years to test the feasibility of employing certain managed care mechanisms and to explore their impact on the delivery of health care services under CHAMPUS. The demonstrations, which vary in design and scope, test cost and utilization management controls in a variety of health care settings. The projects range in size from small-scale demonstrations at a single site for a given population to system-wide implementation of managed care mechanisms. Among the principal demonstration programs at this time are the following:

- the CHAMPUS reform initiative (CRI)
- the New Orleans managed care demonstration

- several catchment area management (CAM) projects
- the southeast region/preferred provider organization (SER/PPO) demonstration
- The contracted provider arrangement (CPA)–Norfolk.

The CHAMPUS Reform Initiative

CRI is a demonstration program designed to improve CHAMPUS through competitive selection of a financially at-risk contractor to underwrite delivery of CHAMPUS health care services. The primary goal of CRI is to improve the program's quality and cost effectiveness through the application of proven managed health care techniques. In February 1988, in accordance with requirements of the Federal Acquisition Regulation, the DOD awarded a contract to Foundation Health Corporation to conduct the demonstration in California and Hawaii. Approximately 800,000 CHAMPUS-eligible beneficiaries reside within the demonstration area, or about 14% of the total number of program eligibles. Foundation Health began delivery of health care services in August 1988, subcontracting with three health plans and offering two alternatives to the standard CHAMPUS program: CHAMPUS Prime and CHAMPUS Extra.

In CHAMPUS Prime, which is similar to a health maintenance organization (HMO), beneficiaries enroll, select a primary care provider, and are required to obtain all their care through that provider. The designated provider can be on staff in one of the military treatment facilities (MTFs) located in the demonstration area or a participating civilian provider. Enrollees also may be referred to participating specialists as needed. Beneficiaries pay only a small cost for each office visit or hospital day, and little paperwork is involved.

CHAMPUS Extra is essentially a preferred provider organization (PPO) plan. Beneficiaries may seek care from either a network provider or a nonnetwork provider; if they use the former, however, their portion of the allowable fee for the service is reduced by 5% on an already discounted provider fee. The beneficiaries' out-of-pocket costs are, therefore, reduced, although they pay somewhat more than CHAMPUS Prime enrollees.

From numerous surveys conducted by independent, objective investigators, satisfaction with CRI in general, as well as with the medical care received therein, appears to be high among all beneficiary categories. The most popular features of CHAMPUS Prime among beneficiaries include the smaller copayments, reduced paperwork, and reasonable visit fees. From the provider's perspective, the patient referral system and the professionalism shown in the program's utilization and quality management functions are most commonly cited.

One of the key principles governing CRI is that the program will be continued only if the actual cost is likely to remain below what CHAMPUS would have paid without CRI. The RAND Corporation has issued two interim reports that describe early periods in the demonstration, and final, comprehensive RAND evaluation of CRI is expected in 1993.

In addition to features common to many managed care plans, the CRI also includes several innovative features that contribute to its apparent successes. CHAMPUS service centers, established in all military hospitals and clinics in the demonstration area, employ 100 health care finders, currently all registered nurses, who coordinate all patient referrals. These personnel now are managing more than 10,000 referrals per month.

Another feature of CRI is an effort called resource sharing, wherein agreements between the CRI contractor and MTFs are established. Under these agreements, the contractor provides personnel, supplies, or equipment to an MTF to enhance patient care capability. By 1992, more than 200 resource-sharing agreements had been executed. Enhancing the capacity of MTFs by selectively increasing staff and materiel resources, resource sharing has enabled the facilities to operate more productively and therefore has proved to be a valuable component of the CRI demonstration.

The current CRI demonstration is scheduled to continue until August 1993, and a competitive procurement is currently underway to award a follow-on managed care contract for California and Hawaii.

New Orleans Managed Care Demonstration

Congressionally directed, the New Orleans demonstration project was designed to test the application of managed care techniques in an area without an inpatient MTF. After a competitive procurement, a contract was awarded in June 1991 to Foundation Health Federal Services, a wholly owned subsidiary of Foundation Health Corporation. Health services delivery under the demonstration began on December 1, 1991, and will continue until February 28, 1996. The design features of the project are similar to those of the CRI: a risk-based contract with a triple option (ie, HMO, PPO, and standard CHAMPUS), provider networks, and comprehensive utilization management and quality assurance programs. Of the eligible population of approximately 24,000 CHAMPUS beneficiaries residing in the greater New Orleans area, more than 4,000 enrolled in the HMO option during the first 4 months of operation, far exceeding expectations.

Catchment Area Management Demonstration Projects

CAM projects were initiated to pursue alternative management techniques within CHAMPUS in an effort to contain costs at the local level. Under CAM, a military hospital commander has responsibility for managing the delivery and financing of health care services for the entire beneficiary population residing in the hospital's catchment area (an area surrounding the facility, specified by ZIP codes, with a radius of roughly 40 miles).

In these projects, CHAMPUS funds are allocated to the hospital commander, who is then responsible for distributing the combined CHAMPUS and direct care system funds appropriately for all services within the catchment area. Although funding is limited to that which would have been spent in the absence of a demonstration, commanders are given authority to pursue alternative health care delivery methods that are not generally possible outside the demonstration area.

Within the guidelines of demonstration authority and the overall design approach established by the DOD, the Army, Navy, and Air Force have implemented separate demonstration projects. The first CAM site became operational in June 1989, and currently the program is operational at five demonstration sites. Each has attempted to maximize the opportunities for innovation available through CAM to take advantage of local geographic and health care environments. Therefore, although there is a central CAM design, significant operational differences, both interservice and intraservice, exist among CAM sites.

Among the design features common to all CAM sites are a health care finder service, enhanced claims management, enrollment, and modifications to the standard CHAMPUS benefit package. The health care finder service coordinates outpatient and inpatient care with providers and facilities under agreement with the hospital. The majority of the demonstration sites are operating under a family practice/designated provider health care model; one site has maintained a traditional practice model.

All service demonstrations require voluntary enrollment as a condition of CAM participation. Enrollees are expected to use participating providers as directed by health care finders. Eligibility is limited to CHAMPUS-eligible beneficiaries within the catchment area, with the family being the unit of enrollment. The minimum enrollment period is 1 year. In addition, all service CAM demonstrations include a variety of benefit modifications that have been designed to make CAM more appealing to beneficiaries and to maximize voluntary enrollment. All the service benefit plans contain reduced or eliminated deductibles and/or copayments. Rates are discounted for some inpatient and outpatient services.

All the CAM designs also include both utilization management and quality assurance features. Preadmission review of inpatient care and retrospective case review are the common mechanisms applied. Some sites also conduct case management of either all patients or those with selected high-cost diagnoses. All contract civilian providers are subject to the same utilization and quality management procedures as military providers.

Claims processing functions under CAM have been simplified to relieve beneficiaries of the paperwork of claims preparation and submission. Although all the claims processing functions are similar in concept, implementation of the simplified claims processing functions is site specific, depending upon demonstration design and FI requirements and capabilities.

The Southeast Region Preferred Provider Organization

The SER/PPO demonstration was undertaken as a response to congressional direction to modify a regional CHAMPUS FI contract to implement managed care techniques. The primary goals were to reduce CHAMPUS cost growth and to improve beneficiary satisfaction by organizing an accessible, cost-efficient network of health care providers.

In July 1990, an FI contract was awarded to Wisconsin Physicians Service. Under the contract, a PPO has been established in a five-state southeast region of the United States to offer beneficiaries a low-cost alternative to standard CHAMPUS. To develop PPO networks and to perform utilization management, Wisconsin Physicians Service subcontracted with a national firm having expertise in those areas. In the design of the demonstration, participants retain freedom of choice and do not enroll, but they have several incentives to use preferred providers. In particular, there are fee discounts, a 5% reduction in coinsurance rates, and direct claims filing by providers. The program, which now covers nearly 900,000 beneficiaries in 20 military hospital catchment areas, is viewed as a support contract for individual hospital commanders in establishing relationships with civilian providers.

Additional features of the demonstration include a quality assessment program and contractor personnel on site in the military hospitals. A key component, as in CRI and the CAM demonstration projects, is that the military hospital is considered the most preferred provider. Further, civilian networks are seen as complementing, rather than competing with, the MTFs.

Today, where PPOs are operational, management reports are provided to military hospital commanders on all aspects of the networks, including percentage of network use by beneficiaries, type and cost of services delivered, utilization review activity, savings from provider discounts, and estimates of savings from utilization review.

Contracted Provider Arrangement–Norfolk

For some time, CHAMPUS costs for mental health care have represented an increasing portion of the CHAMPUS budget. Before 1986, the Tidewater area of Virginia presented a particular concern because per capita costs for mental health care were found to be twice the national average. As a result of this finding, the CPA-Norfolk demonstration project was initiated to test the effects of cost and utilization controls on the delivery of mental health services in this area. The design of this demonstration included an at-risk, fixed-price contract for all necessary mental health services; case management as a prerequisite for payment; a contracted provider network with negotiated rates; claims processing and administrative functions performed by the contractor; a partial hospitalization benefit; and independent quality monitoring.

After a competitive procurement process, the DOD contracted with Sentara First Step for delivery of services, and operations commenced on October 1, 1986. Sentara First Step implemented all features of the design, including intake and case management processes, a network of preferred providers with significantly reduced rates, and an internal quality assurance program. For government monitoring purposes, an external quality monitoring effort was undertaken through a separate contract with SysteMetrics/McGraw Hill. Delivery of services by Sentara First Step under the demonstration ceased on March 31, 1989, and after another procurement effort a follow-on contract was awarded to First Hospital Corporation–Options (FHC-Options).

Under the current contract, FHC–Options is responsible for all mental health care provided to CHAMPUS beneficiaries in the geographic region of the demonstration. Utilization management of all inpatient care as well as of all outpatient care beyond the 23rd visit is required. The present contractor has been allowed to reduce or eliminate cost-sharing requirements as an inducement for beneficiaries to use those providers who joined the preferred provider network. All contracted providers are required to accept assignment on all claims and may not bill CHAMPUS beneficiaries for charges above the allowable amount. Additionally, all non-contracted providers are required to comply with utilization management activities at least 95% of the time or risk losing certification as CHAMPUS-authorized providers for a period of 1 year.

At this point in the demonstration, the DOD believes that the CPA-Norfolk model is generally practical and effective. Additionally, available data show that access to care in the CPA area is at least as good as, and perhaps better than, access for beneficiaries in the rest of the country. Dialog currently continues between the DOD and the contractor, however, to refine the criteria used under this contract to assess the appropriateness in level and intensity of care.

THE MILITARY HEALTH SERVICES SYSTEM COORDINATED CARE PROGRAM

In general, the demonstrations discussed above have been successful in providing evidence that innovations in the delivery and financing of health care services can help in containing the rising costs of health care, at least in the short term. They also have shown that such approaches can have a positive effect on provider and beneficiary behavior. Therefore, many features of the DOD demonstration projects are being incorporated into the recently introduced MHSS CCP.

The MHSS CCP is a DOD initiative designed to provide MTF commanders with the tools, authority, and flexibility needed to perform the health care/medical mission more effectively. The CCP will enable the DOD to accomplish better the medical mission by improving beneficiary access to health care services, controlling health care costs, and ensuring quality care to all MHSS beneficiaries.

Systemwide improvements being implemented to support and complement local health care delivery networks include reforms of CHAMPUS provider payment methods, establishment of specialized treatment facilities (STFs) to provide high-technology/high-cost health care services in the most cost-effective manner, new approaches to contracting for health care services, establishment of participation agreements with civilian providers to accept CHAMPUS assignment, and improvements in the efficiency and accuracy of claims processing. Because of the scope, magnitude, and complexity of the MHSS, and the extensive nature of the CCP reforms, the program will be phased in over a 3-year period beginning in fiscal year 1992.

The features of the CCP can be divided into four major areas: the delivery of care, the organization of health care delivery, accountability, and controlling/measuring costs.

The Delivery of Care

The linchpin of the delivery system will be a primary care provider: a specific primary care clinic, site, provider, or group of providers with which each enrolled beneficiary will establish and maintain a medical affiliation.

Some differences in the delivery of care will occur geographically because of differences in the relative capacity of MTFs. In some areas, MTFs have the ability to deliver extensive primary and specialty care. In other areas, MTF commanders must rely upon civilian providers to deliver care not available within the facility. In still other areas, beneficiaries rely completely on civilian providers.

Because the CCP is based largely on decentralized execution, certain features of the program vary among locations. Many program features, however, will be uniform. When the CCP is fully operational, some of the features that will be the same or similar across all regions of the country include the following:

- *an enrollment system*—The enrollment process will be designed to allow each

MTF commander to know the beneficiaries for whom he or she will be responsible and therefore to plan and budget better for the population served.

- *incentives based upon enrollment status and network provider use*—Beneficiaries will have financial incentives to enroll in managed care plans and to use network providers. Such differentials are designed as incentives to use the system that better ensures high-quality care and lower costs.

- *primary care managers*—MTF commanders will have the flexibility to assign each enrolled beneficiary, or to allow each beneficiary to choose, a primary care manager who will have overall responsibility for managing the care provided to a beneficiary or family. The primary care manager may be either a practice site or a single primary care provider.

- *greater uniformity in scope of covered services*—To minimize beneficiary confusion, the services covered throughout the CCP will be as uniform as possible so that all enrolled beneficiaries are treated equitably. This is a particular concern at the local level, where it is important that an enrollee with a civilian primary care manager not have different benefits from those of an enrollee with an MTF primary care manager.

- *utilization management and quality assurance programs*—Refinement and expansion of existing utilization management and quality assurance policies throughout the MHSS will permit the DOD and the service medical departments to ensure quality improvement and cost effectiveness of coordinated care programs within and among geographic regions.

- *claims processing*—A national, uniform claims processing system for CHAMPUS is currently under development and will include centralized files containing deductible, catastrophic cap, and other health insurance information. Such improvements are being designed to provide more accurate payment of claims, to reduce delays in claims processing, and to reduce regional variation in claims payments.

- *communications strategies*—A critical responsibility of managers at all levels is to communicate all changes in the way health care is delivered and received in the CCP to all those affected. An extensive education program for both beneficiaries and health care providers is being developed to inform participants of the phased transition from the traditional framework for health care delivery to the CCP. Education will focus on informing beneficiaries of the options available in seeking health care and ensuring that beneficiaries understand how they can maintain and improve their own health status through family risk management, diet, exercise, and appropriate use of health services.

The Organization of Health Care Delivery

In the CCP, local MTF commanders will be responsible for health care costs, quality, and access in their service areas. They will be required to ensure that CCP health care networks are sufficient to provide enrolled beneficiaries access to care. Commanders may approach the procurement of civilian providers' services in one or more of the following ways. They may set up their own local networks by contracting through competitive procurements or provider agreements; they may elect technical assistance from a consultant on issues of network contracting, the quality of networks, network development, and so forth; or they may contract with provider networks already in existence.

In those locations where there are overlapping catchment areas, network decisions may be more complex. Thus the ASD(HA) will designate a lead agent (ie, one of the uniformed services) to coordinate health care delivery. The lead agent will work collaboratively with the other services in the area so that each will have a participatory role. Such coordination will increase cost efficiency and decrease beneficiary confusion.

For certain high-technology/high-cost procedures, STFs will be established on a regional or national level. The designation, which will be made by the ASD(HA), will be based on readiness, cost, and quality of care considerations. If a beneficiary does not use an STF when one is designated and available, he or she will be responsible for paying the full cost of the care.

Accountability

A goal of the CCP is to combine centralized direction and monitoring with decentralized (ie, local) accountability and execution. Local execution will enable MTF commanders to better serve the needs of beneficiaries. Centralized monitoring means that the performance of the delivery system must be measurable, which requires the development of new performance and outcome measures and a timely information flow.

The CCP outcome measures will assist MHSS managers in making better decisions about quality, utilization, and costs in delivering care to both enrolled and nonenrolled beneficiaries. To increase accountability, comparative performance data with respect to quality, cost, and access will be provided by the services to the ASD(HA), and vice versa.

Controlling/Measuring Costs

A guiding principle of the CCP is to optimize MHSS resources. Resource allocation and financing mechanisms will be designed to encourage improved efficiency and effectiveness. Congress has mandated that the DOD use diagnosis-related groups (DRGs) and a similar disease-based measure for ambulatory care [ambulatory visit groups (AVGs) or ambulatory patient groups (APGs)] for resource allocation. Using DRG/AVG-APG data will allow service managers to have better information about the output of MTFs and will permit service managers to monitor the relative performance of MTFs. When linked with data on MTF budgets for supplies, labor, facility maintenance, and CHAMPUS costs, MHSS managers will be able not only to analyze the relationships between resource inputs and outputs in their service areas but also to analyze better the relative cost of care provided in all components of the CCP.

Although traditionally MTF commanders have managed only the service operation and maintenance funds for MTFs, under the CCP commanders also will be responsible for managing the funds that pay CHAMPUS claims. Controlling both CHAMPUS and MTF operation and management funds will provide commanders the financial flexibility and authority to ensure that beneficiaries in their service areas receive the care they need.

Summary of the Coordinated Care Program

In sum, the CCP represents a major overhaul in the way health care is managed in the MHSS. Major CCP components include an enrollment system, cost-sharing incentives, a system of primary care managers and health care networks, and improved utilization management and quality assurance programs. MTF commanders will be aided by changes in how the delivery of care is organized and financed and by incentives that optimize MTF utilization.

COMPARISON WITH MEDICARE

Finally, it may be useful to compare the development of managed care under the Medicare and CHAMPUS programs. A significant difference in this development is that, after a brief demonstration period, the Medicare HMO risk program was implemented through permanent statutory and regulatory authorities. In contrast, all the major CHAMPUS managed care programs have been implemented under demonstration authority[10] and, usually, through competitive procurements. More specifically, only recently has the Health Care Financing Administration begun to test a Medicare PPO product. On the other hand, the CHAMPUS managed care demonstrations currently operating are extremely varied, including a multibillion dollar, triple-option, risk-based program; a much smaller triple-option, risk-based program in an area without a military hospital; a five-state, dual-option, cost plus incentives reimbursement project; and five similar service-designed managed care projects that are managed by MTF commanders at the local level.

Although the long-range goal of the DOD is a uniform, nationwide CCP for all MHSS beneficiaries, significant differences among DOD managed care programs will continue to exist in the near term. Many of these differences will disappear as current demonstrations end and new projects begin, but some differences in management mechanisms may be necessary to accommodate differences in population concentrations ranging from regional, risk-based, contractor-supported programs to strictly local MTF commander initiatives.

A second significant difference between the Medicare HMO risk program and CRI, the major CHAMPUS risk-based contract, is in the reimbursement mechanism. Whereas Medicare HMOs are totally at risk for cost overruns in the enrolled program, there are adjustments in CRI in the fixed price paid to the contractor for circumstances outside contractor control (eg, the work load in the MTF). Also, there is risk sharing (and sharing in savings) between the contractor and the DOD for cost overruns (and underruns) in the contract price. Additionally, the CRI contractor is at risk for the entire CHAMPUS population residing in California and Hawaii, not just those beneficiaries in the enrolled option. As a result, there are no issues of adverse selection or skimming with which to contend. In fact, it is in the contractor's best financial interest to have the individuals with the more severe health problems enroll in the more closely managed HMO option.

CONCLUSION

Although the term *coordinated care* is coming into more general use as an alternative to the term *managed care*, coordinated care in the DOD has another level of meaning beyond that in Medicare and commercial programs. In addition to the usual and important functions of a primary care manager coordinating different types and levels of care, coordinated care in the MHSS includes the essential function of coordination between the military direct care system and the civilian health care system. Along with quality, cost, and access, integrating the CHAMPUS and direct care systems has been a focal point of the managed care demonstrations and will continue to be a major challenge as the DOD's CCP is implemented nationwide.

REFERENCES

1. The Dependents Medical Care Act of 1956, Pub L No 84-569, 70 Stat 250, as amended by the Military Medical Benefits Amendments of 1966, Pub L No 89-614, 80 Stat 862, Pub L 98-94, 97 Stat 614, codified as amended in 10 USC, Sections 1071-1106.

2. *DEERS Enrollment Statistics (Stat 2) Report, as of March 4, 1992.* Monterey, CA: Defense Manpower Data Center; March 5, 1992 (run date).

3. US DOD FY 1993 Defense Health Program, amended President's budget, January 1992, page 6.

4. DOD Directive 5136.1, "Assistant Secretary of Defense (Health Affairs)," April 15, 1991.

5. The Dependents Medical Care Act of 1956, op. cit.

6. DOD Directive 5105.46, "Civilian Health and Medical Program of the Uniformed Services," December 4, 1976.

7. Department of Defense Regulation, DOD 6010.8-R, "Civilian Health and Medical Program of the Uniformed Services (CHAMPUS)," July 1991. DOD components and other uniformed services may obtain copies of this regulation through their own publication channels. Other federal agencies and the general public may obtain copies from the US Department of Commerce, National Technical Information Service, 5285 Port Royal Road, Springfield, VA 22161.

8. Federal Acquisition Regulation, April 1, 1984.

9. US Department of Defense. Office of the Civilian Health and Medical Program of the Uniformed Services (OCHAMPUS). *CHAMPUS Chartbook of Statistics.* Aurora, CO: Department of Defense; December 1985 and August 1990.

10. See, in general, 10 USC, Chapter 55, Section 1092.

Chapter 33

Workers' Compensation Medical Benefits: A Practical Framework for Implementing New Cost Containment Strategies

David S. Iskowe

There are few concepts today that are more broadly defined than, or subject to as much interpretation as, medical cost containment. To some, cost containment represents services such as medical fee schedule audits, independent medical examinations, or rehabilitation services. Others, when asked to define the term, will quickly note preferred provider organizations (PPOs), health maintenance organizations (HMOs), or hospital precertification programs. The reason for such broad interpretation becomes understandable when one considers that two separate and distinct medical insurance systems, operating under vastly different rules, dominate the funding of employee medical benefits: group health insurance and workers' compensation insurance.

The rules and basis for payment of medical benefits vary greatly between these two systems,

David S. Iskowe, a certified public accountant, is President and Chief Operating Officer of FOCUS Healthcare Management, Inc. He has extensive operational experience in the development and ongoing management of medical cost-containment programs in both group health and casualty areas.

and for a variety of reasons the workers' compensation system has traditionally been viewed as separate from and unaffected by changes in the much larger group health system. The behavior of employees and medical providers in both systems, however, is inextricably linked. For example, in the face of dramatic increases in medical expenses, a growing number of employers have significantly reduced the level of group health benefits provided to employees. Through no coincidence, an October 1987 *Business Week* feature noted that savvy employees and medical providers are using the workers' compensation system to pay medical expenses that are no longer covered by group health plans.

To best understand and effectively apply new medical cost containment strategies within the workers' compensation system, group health and workers' compensation should be viewed as two highly interactive systems that share a strikingly similar set of problems. Therefore, much of the following discussion will involve an explanation and comparison of the two systems along with sharing of those unique issues to consider when one is adapting medical cost containment initiatives now common in the group health setting within the framework of the workers' compensation system.

GROUP HEALTH AND WORKERS' COMPENSATION INSURANCE: A CONTRAST IN PURPOSE

The majority of today's employers have established a group health insurance plan for the benefit of full-time employees and their eligible dependents. In contrast to the workers' compensation system, employers generally have significant control and discretion over the level and extent of medical benefits available to employees under the plan. Such control is usually exercised through various cost-sharing requirements (eg, the meeting of deductible amounts before the insurance program begins). Cost sharing, or benefit levels, may vary significantly from one company to the next, depending on the company's individual philosophy or competitive considerations. More often than not, an employee will also make some monthly contribution to the overall cost of the insurance program.

Workers' compensation laws, first introduced in 1911, essentially create a *no fault system* designed to protect the interests of both workers and employers. In exchange for guaranteed compensation for a work-related injury, an employee relinquishes his or her right to file a damage suit against the employer. With workers' compensation benefits as the sole remedy for disabilities resulting from a workplace injury, employers are protected against unpredictable and unreasonable damage awards. Far different from group health, benefits payable to an injured employee are generally dictated to an employer on the basis of applicable state law. Such benefits are intended to cover most of the worker's economic loss associated with treatment of the injury. Such payments may include cash benefits for both physical impairment and disability; medical benefits, usually without dollar limits; and rehabilitation benefits for both medical and vocational rehabilitation. There are no deductibles to be met by an injured employee because the employer is generally required to assume full and unlimited responsibility for medical and rehabilitative care resulting from the work-related injury.

THE MEDICAL COST DILEMMA: DIFFERENT SYSTEMS SHARING THE SAME PROBLEMS

Over the past decade, escalation in group health medical benefits has been relentless, nearly doubling every 5 years. In August 1985, a *Harvard Business Review* article noted that expenses for health care costs are rising at such a fast rate that, if they went unchecked, in 8 years they might eliminate all profits for the average Fortune 500 company and the largest 250 nonindustrials. By 1986, the medical cost component of the Consumer Price Index (CPI) surpassed the overall CPI by a margin of 7 to 1, the largest gap between the two indexes ever recorded. In response, group health insurers rapidly introduced, throughout the 1980s, new concepts in medical cost containment. Having both the control and the discretion to dictate changes quickly in medical benefit levels, programs such as precertification of hospital admissions as a prerequisite for receiving full benefits became quite common. Further, PPOs were introduced and rapidly incorporated within group health plans, with employers offering increased benefits to employees if they sought care from discounted preferred providers. By 1987, approximately 60% of all group health insurers had incorporated hospital utilization review or PPO programs as basic elements of their health insurance plans. As we enter the 1990s, virtually all federal and private insurers now have in place some form of PPO, HMO, or managed indemnity plan option as the foundation for group health coverage.

In a pattern strikingly similar to that of group health, the workers' compensation system has experienced an extraordinary spiral of increases in the cost of medical benefits over the past decade. As previously noted, in 1986 the medical cost component surpassed the overall CPI by a margin of 7 to 1. In numerous states during 1986, workers' compensation payments increased by twice the medical component of the CPI. Such factors have caused most workers' compensation insurers dramatic increases in loss ratios (the ratio of claims incurred to premium revenues), which have averaged between 110% and 120% over the past few years. The problem has reached such proportions that some carriers now require premium increases as high as 300% to fund underwriting risks. Further, as a result of regulatory limits on the amount of rate increases, a number of carriers have withdrawn from and ceased writing policies in certain markets entirely. In an April 1988 feature in *Business Insurance*, Kevin M. Ryan, President of the National Council of Compensation Insurers, remarked that the medical care system had spun out of control and that workers' compensation insurers were among the principal victims of that chaos. Mr. Ryan further noted that medical costs then represented 40% of all workers' compensation payments and were expected to rise to 50% by the year 2000. An October 1991 industry analysis by Edmund Kroll of Needham & Company noted that 1990 workers' compensation medical costs had increased 50% *faster* (approximately 17%) than the already hyperinflationary 11% rise in overall medical costs. Finally, in a May 1992 feature in *Business Insurance*, William Hager, the current President of the National Council of Compensation Insurers, stated, "The workers' compensation crisis is exacerbated by unbridled health care costs, which may be the ultimate doom of the compensation system, unless drastic and immediate cost containment and reform measures are adopted."

Despite the positive impact of new medical cost containment programs now common in the group health setting, most workers' compensation payers have only recently introduced techniques such as hospital utilization review or PPOs and are still in the midst of adapting these tools to the unique culture of the workers' compensation system. Further complicating implementation of these programs is growing evidence that the success of recent cost containment initiatives in group health may be spurring cost shifting by medical providers to the workers' compensation system. A recent Workers' Compensation Research Institute (WCRI) brief un-

derscored this trend and further raised the specter that provider behavior may differ when reimbursed under workers' compensation. In this study, for a demographically similar patient population, Liberty Mutual paid 225% more for treatment of back disorders than did Blue Cross and Blue Shield of Minnesota. The only unadjusted variable in the equation was the coverage type under which the provider would be reimbursed—workers' compensation or group health system.

WORKERS' COMPENSATION: ADAPTING TOOLS FROM THE GROUP HEALTH SYSTEM

No legislation precludes workers' compensation insurers from implementing medical cost containment programs that prospectively and concurrently monitor providers to ensure that injured employees are receiving reasonable, appropriate, and necessary medical care. As testimony, John C. Morrison, outgoing Board Chairman of the National Council of Compensation Insurers, sounded a call to arms for insurers to confront the escalating medical benefits crisis. According to Morrison, the workers' compensation system is one of the last remaining public or private insurance schemes with few or no cost containment provisions. Further confirming this stance, the International Association of Industrial Accident Boards and Commissions (IAIABC), at its September 1988 annual convention, formally endorsed medical cost containment measures as a key way of managing workers' compensation medical benefits. As a first step toward this goal, the IAIABC revised existing standards to include reference to reasonable and necessary medical care to encourage introduction of relevant medical cost containment strategies similar to those now commonplace in the group health setting, within the context of workers' compensation medical benefits.

As we enter the new decade, a 1990 survey by the Insurance Research Council indicates that workers' compensation carriers have, in fact, made significant progress over the past few years to introduce new managed care programs.

Of the survey respondents, 44% had contracted with PPOs, and 64% were reviewing proposed hospitalizations to determine whether a hospital stay was necessary. Spurred by continuing loss ratios of over 120%, the level of participation by workers' compensation carriers in managed care programs will no doubt continue to grow rapidly, as will the scope of available managed care services, particularly in the area of outpatient care.

The balance of this chapter concentrates on exploring the two most prominent new medical cost containment programs being introduced to the workers' compensation system: PPOs and hospital utilization review (HUR) programs. Particular emphasis will be placed upon those distinctions to consider when one is adapting such programs from the group health setting into the workers' compensation system.

HOSPITAL UTILIZATION REVIEW PROGRAMS

The goal of an effective hospital utilization program is to limit hospital admissions to only those cases that are medically appropriate. This is accomplished through preventing hospitalizations when care can be provided safely in an outpatient setting and avoiding unnecessary preoperative days or admissions on days (such as holidays and weekends) when few hospital-level services will be provided. Depending on the approach of a given utilization review vendor, concurrent review may or may not be incorporated within the core precertification program. The concurrent review element monitors, through dialog with the hospital and/or admitting physician, the appropriate length of stay throughout a patient's confinement period.

Although data are limited as a result of the relative newness of hospital utilization programs within the workers' compensation system, early results are rapidly confirming savings opportunities comparable with those enjoyed by group health insurers. In a recent *Business Insurance* article entitled "Cost Containment Strategies Also Effective for Work Comp," a panel of experts concluded that mechanisms such as PPOs and utilization review programs, for years in use to control employer health care benefit costs,

can be applied to workers' compensation cases with surprisingly successful results. This conclusion is more significant than it may appear at face in that the workers' compensation system lacks the leverage of benefit differentials (or penalties) that are used in group health to maximize employee and provider compliance with HUR programs. Further supporting such conclusions are the actual findings by FOCUS Healthcare Management, a medical risk management company serving the workers' compensation industry. FOCUS systematically sampled 100 workers' compensation cases for which, at the request of the workers' compensation insurer, hospital precertification and concurrent review services were performed. When notified in advance of an injured employee's hospital admission, FOCUS was able either to reduce the length of stay or to avoid a medically unnecessary admission entirely in approximately 25% of the cases. In recognition of such findings, in late 1991 a number of state workers' compensation commissions enacted legislation either requiring providers to request preauthorization of all proposed nonemergency hospital admissions or requiring workers' compensation carriers formally to establish and submit for state approval their medical utilization review programs. No doubt, the emergence of legislation of this nature will increasingly provide workers' compensation payers the leverage to introduce more assertively HUR programs for work-related claims.

There are some fundamental distinctions to consider when one is adapting an HUR program within the workers' compensation environment.

The Role of the Claims Adjustor

When a work-related injury is reported to the insurance carrier, a claims adjustor will be assigned to the case to manage and settle the financial exposure arising from the claim. The claims adjustor focuses foremost on those cases where the injury has caused lost time from work because alleged permanent physical or vocational disability benefits arising from such lost-time claims now represent approximately 55% (medical being 45%) of total workers' compensation benefit costs.

Acknowledging that the level and duration of medical care will probably drive the amount of disability benefits, independent HUR programs have slowly gained acceptance by claims adjustors as a tool to lend objectivity to what often becomes an adversarial relationship among the claimant (as the patient is commonly called), the insurance carrier, and the attending provider. The claims adjustor will typically initiate first contact with the HUR vendor and will inform the review nurse of any special factors to consider when reviewing the case. For example, because of the high percentage of claims that are represented by an attorney, the claims adjustor will typically expect to be notified by the review nurse before giving formal notice to a provider of denial of certification.

In addition to obtaining regular telephone updates throughout the hospital stay, and in stark contrast to the situation with a group health review, the claims adjustor will expect to receive a final clinical report for each individual claim file where HUR has been performed. When the adjuster is reporting on the medical event, the clinical report will be expected to include considerations relative to pre-existing conditions; whether any treatment during the hospital confinement may have been unrelated to the workplace injury; whether the injury, on its own merits, appears to have a causal relationship with the workplace; observations on progress relative to maximum medical improvement; and physical restrictions and light duty alternatives that in turn can translate into opportunities to expedite return to work and to contain disability costs.

Medical Criteria and Clinical Documentation

The vast majority of work-related injuries involve some form of trauma, repetitive motion, or other orthopedic/neurologic impairment. In performing adequate utilization review of medical care provided to injured employees, a far more narrowly defined but comprehensive approach to medical criteria development is necessary than is typical of most medical review organizations, which orient programs to the much more broad range of care applicable to group health

benefits recipients. Further, with growing frequency, attorneys for both claimants and certain provider groups with practices highly dependent on workers' compensation volume are requesting to review those explicit guidelines or criteria used to deny certification of a stay. The points to be made here are:

1. Criteria for evaluating diagnoses and proposed procedures common to musculoskeletal injuries must be both comprehensive and worthy of consensus approval by practicing specialists, particularly in orthopedics and neurosurgery. This becomes quite challenging with a growing trend toward alleged soft tissue claims, mostly in the back or neck areas, that are of nonspecific diagnosis (ie, without objective physical findings) but are accompanied by chronic pain complaints that, with surprising frequency, result in a recommended surgical procedure.

2. The high level of attorney involvement and potential bad faith complaints in workers' compensation cases makes standardization of nurse review notes essential, including the rationale behind any conclusions reached by a physician advisor participating in the case. When performing internal quality checks on file documentation, remember that appeals within the workers' compensation system seldom start with the HUR vendor's medical director but rather with notification from an attorney or a state commission.

Establishment of Causality

In appreciation of benefit coverage issues unique to workers' compensation, the HUR vendor must provide specific training and guidelines that will assist a review nurse to recognize disparities between the reported mechanism of injury and the proposed medical treatment plan. Such disparities can trigger a recommendation to a claims adjustor to consider whether the proposed medical treatment, although medically appropriate, may not be causally related to the workplace injury and, therefore, not compensable under the workers' compensation statute. Emphasis should also be placed on recruiting physician advisors and review nurses with occupational medicine or orthopedic expertise who are capable of determining whether the effect of workplace trauma or a minor movement probably resulted in an alleged workplace injury (eg, a disc herniation) or whether the ailment probably arose as a result of a chronic degenerative condition that should be covered under group health rather than workers' compensation.

Quality Assurance

Any reputable utilization review company should obviously have formally documented quality assurance programs to ensure that proper clinical judgments are being made by both review nurses and physician advisors. Claimants injured in the workplace deserve quality care, and the presence of a thorough quality assurance program may ultimately become the most important consideration to a workers' compensation carrier when selecting an HUR organization. Confidence in being able to demonstrate that the HUR vendor is not defense oriented but rather managed on the basis of objective and well-documented quality assurance standards will be key in situations where an attorney may challenge the consistency and quality of your medical review recommendations.

Recognition of the Issues Unique to Workers' Compensation

A utilization review organization's ability to perform effectively in the workers' compensation systems will be measured by its sincere appreciation and respect for the cultural differences between the group health and workers' compensation systems. As mentioned previously, the workers' compensation system does not have the absolute financial leverage of group health, whereby penalties can be assessed for lack of compliance with a utilization program. Claimants tend to view workers' compensation benefits as an entitlement and can easily be in-

fluenced to seek legal involvement. On the basis of the above factors, a well-structured HUR program must be designed, to the extent possible, as largely transparent to the claimant. Accordingly, the leverage in a successful workers' compensation program will largely result from the review organization's ability to maximize the information exchange among the claims adjustor, the claimant's provider, and itself. Hospital admissions departments and physicians, as a result of the predominance of existing group health precertification programs, often now automatically call the insurer in advance of elective admissions. A thoughtful plan for communication with frequently used providers, distributed by the workers' compensation insurer, can successfully ride the coattails of familiar notification requirements already in place throughout the group health insurance system. Finally, a well-coordinated effort between the claims adjustor and the HUR organization should minimize unnecessary care, optimize quality of care, and ensure that the workers' compensation carrier only assumes responsibility for medical care related to the workplace injury.

PREFERRED PROVIDER ORGANIZATIONS

The major growth of PPOs in the group health system first began to take hold in 1983. There currently are well over 500 PPOs serving the group health system. Some of these PPOs are hospital only, but the majority also include an extensive network of primary and specialty care physicians. The basic economics behind PPOs is that, in return for the promise of new patient volume, medical providers will offer significant discounts from their usual and customary fees. As a result of the combination of a developing oversupply of physicians, reduced admissions at hospitals because of utilization review programs, and the overall competitiveness that has emerged in the health care market, many providers are now willing to discount their fees to insurers so that, at a minimum, they do not lose any of their existing market share.

No legislation precludes workers' compensation insurers from implementing preferred arrangements, now commonplace in the group health setting, for the delivery of medical benefits to injured employees. In fact, 24 states presently have workers' compensation statutes that generally allow an employer to designate those providers from whom an employee must receive initial care for a work-related injury. In those states, this obviously provides an opportunity to direct employees to selected or preferred providers. A March 1987 article in *Business and Health* noted that, even in a state where after 30 days an employee could demand a change to a provider of his or her choice, in practice such requests were found to occur in less than 5% of the cases.

In the adaptation of the PPO concept to the workers' compensation system, of some debate is whether the PPO should attempt to secure significant discounts from both hospital and physician providers. Virtually all group health PPOs require both hospitals and physicians to provide discounts. However, a PPO for workers' compensation payors may be better served by "hospital only" discount arrangements and enlist physicians, whether or not they accept discounts, based on their willingness to cooperate with the claims adjuster, be considerate of return to work issues, and practice quality medical care. The major drawback to discounted physician PPOs has been a concern that churning—or the practice of increasing the volume of services to recapture reduced fees due to discounts—will occur. Second, in fee schedule states (of which there are presently 30), allowable fees may already be quite low, and many question whether or not quality physicians would be willing to participate in a program requiring discounts below an already reduced mandatory schedule.

The proper response to these questions requires evaluation on a state-by-state basis. First, to attract the attention of quality providers, you must be able to demonstrate some ability to channel injured employees and, in turn, favorably affect a provider's income. In a state such as Georgia, where employers and insurers can make efforts to direct patients to preferred providers through assertive worksite posting and supervisor training programs, the likelihood of recruiting and maintaining a network of high-

quality physicians while receiving significant discounts from the state fee schedule is extremely high. The fact that Georgia's state fee schedule is considered reasonable by the provider community also improves the likelihood of substantial discounts. As to the issue of churning, group health PPO experience has confirmed that consistent application of two techniques can effectively minimize the potential for such problems: careful credentialing, or meaningful acceptance criteria, of PPO providers, and an active and formal physician quality assurance and utilization review program.

In states where the regulatory climate is favorable to employers, a workers' compensation PPO configured to include both hospitals and physicians can be successful. A useful set of guidelines for evaluating the overall quality of any given hospital only or physician and hospital PPO are the following:

- *availability*—Do the hospitals and physicians within the PPO network provide ready access, in terms of both hours and location, to major employers in a given service area? Unlike a typical group health PPO, where the distribution of providers is usually based on residential considerations, an effective workers' compensation PPO must key on industrial concentrations throughout the community.

- *accessibility*—Can an injured employee expect immediate walk-in access to timely care as well as access to a provider who is skilled and equipped to treat minor trauma commonly arising from workplace injuries? Further, do PPO provider locations allow for timely scheduling of follow-up appointments, because such visits often strongly influence the date of return to work? Most group health PPOs, where a high percentage of primary care physicians are specialists in internal medicine or pediatrics, have difficulty meeting the unique accessibility requirements of the workers' compensation system.

- *accountability*—Does the administrator of the PPO display adequate supervisory oversight of the network, and are there vehicles to provide information about, and to obtain input from, patients, carriers, and adjustors? The ideal mechanism for a feedback loop is for representatives of the PPO to make regular visits to field offices of carriers to make sure that quality and/or service issues are identified promptly and resolved. Also to be considered is whether providers included in the PPO are known to be cooperative and accountable for reasonable requests made by workers' compensation insurers.

- *acceptability*—In the design and ongoing refinement of the PPO network, does the administrator solicit input from its carriers and adjustors on physicians and hospitals that are best suited to the profile required in the workers' compensation system? If care is not acceptable or of perceived quality and cooperation, one can be assured that a claimant's attorney will let the insurer know.

- *appropriateness*—Because *appropriate* refers to the actual content of clinical care, it is best assessed and ensured by medical professionals engaged in peer review. Probably the best that a carrier can do in this regard is to ask for documented evidence of the PPO's in-house quality assurance program and how physicians and hospitals are credentialed and regularly monitored to ensure that the initial selection of them as preferred was the right one and, foremost, that high-quality care is being delivered to injured employees. Quality management is discussed in Chapter 15.

The ability to develop effective mechanisms to direct or channel patients, regardless of whether the PPO includes physicians or is hospital only, will be key to the long-term survival of quality preferred networks within the workers' compensation system. Many of the current workers' compensation PPO arrangements, predominantly on the west coast, principally take advantage of discounts on existing traffic patterns of injured workers rather than actively trying to increase the market share, and in turn revenues, of participating providers. Experiences in group health have confirmed that a cost-effective program, with minimal churning, is short lived under such an arrangement.

Workers' compensation insurers and PPO organizations need to be prepared to correspond with policy holders, whether through the posting process or through other forms of direct contact, to initiate a channeling effort. Utilization review companies, by instruction from the workers' compensation insurer whom they serve, should consistently ask about dual privileges at preferred hospitals in an effort to redirect admissions at the time of precertification. Clearly, through thoughtful PPO management, there is little doubt that PPO arrangements can be an enduring and successful cost containment alternative within the workers' compensation system.

CONCLUSION

The arena of worker's compensation has significant differences from the group health market, but there are many similarities to effective medical management programs. The differences are related to benefit coverage, the individual state laws concerning worker's compensation benefits, and the nature of the injuries. Nevertheless, the worker's compensation market is subject to significant improvements by application of managed care techniques to reduce inappropriate utilization and enhance quality of care.

Part VII

Relationships with Government Regulatory Agencies

A wise government knows how to enforce with temper or to conciliate with dignity.

George Grenville
(1769)

Chapter 34

State Regulation

Erling Hansen and Garry Carneal

The organizational structure of managed health care plans is usually the determining factor of how they are regulated by the states. Many different forms of managed care now exist.

Forty-seven states have enacted enabling legislation and regulations that govern the organization and operation of health maintenance organizations (HMOs). About half of all states formally regulate preferred provider organizations (PPOs), 24 have enacted standards and licensing requirements for utilization review activities, and a few directly oversee exclusive provider organizations (EPOs). In instances where managed care arrangements are not formally regulated by the state, laws governing health insurance companies may be used. For example, in the District of Columbia, Hawaii, Oregon, and Wisconsin, where enabling legislation has not been enacted, HMOs are regulated through other insurance provisions applicable to

---

Erling Hansen is General Counsel, and Garry Carneal is Associate General Counsel, of Group Health Association of America (GHAA), the national trade group of HMOs and similar managed care companies. Among other duties, they are responsible for GHAA's state government relations activities, including liaison with the National Association of Insurance Commissioners and the National Association of HMO Regulators.

prepayment plans or, when applicable, by the federal HMO Act.

This chapter will focus on the state regulation of HMOs. HMOs serve as the best case study because they have been regulated for the longest period of time and by the most states. An attempt is made in this chapter to identify basic HMO state regulatory requirements, but specific regulatory criteria will vary from state to state. Many of the regulatory concerns detailed below are based on the *HMO Examination Handbook*, which was adopted by the National Association of Insurance Commissioners (NAIC) in December 1988.

THE REGULATORY PROCESS

HMOs are regulated on the state level usually by more than one state agency. Typically, regulatory supervision is shared by the departments of insurance and health. Insurance regulators assume principal responsibility for the financial and consumer aspects of HMO operations. Health regulators focus on quality of care issues, utilization patterns, and the ability of participating providers to provide adequate care. In a few instances, other state subdivisions may be charged with some supervisory duties. By way of example, whereas insurance-based managed care typically falls under the jurisdiction of California's Department of Insurance, the Department of Corporations regulates HMOs organized under the California Knox Keene Act.

In addition to enabling statutes and regulations, other sources of authority are used to govern HMO operations. From time to time, regulators will supplement their regulations with written policy statements, usually as the direct result of an inquiry from an HMO or other interested party. Internal office policies are also developed as HMO regulators deal with specific issues.

Several organizations play an important role in the development of HMO guidelines. In 1972, the NAIC adopted the Model HMO Act. The NAIC wanted to create a model bill that clearly authorizes the establishment of HMOs and provides for an ongoing regulatory monitoring system. The Model Act, or substantial portions thereof, has now been enacted by 27 states. The NAIC, along with the National Association of HMO Regulators, continues to develop new regulatory guidelines for the HMO industry.

HMO LICENSURE

Licensure is obtained by applying for a certificate of authority. An organization may be incorporated for the sole purpose of becoming licensed as an HMO, or an existing company may sponsor an HMO product line through a subsidiary or affiliated organization. Applications are usually processed by the insurance department and, among other items, include the following documents: corporate bylaws, sample provider and group contract forms, evidence of coverage form, financial statements, financial feasibility plan, description of service area, internal grievance procedures, and the proposed quality assurance program. Payment of licensing fees is usually required, and about one third of states assess premium taxes against HMOs.

The licensure and recertification process provides state officials with a mechanism to make sure that the HMO is operating properly and is in compliance with all the applicable laws and regulations. If an HMO fails to submit to this oversight, it will probably be considered engaging in the unauthorized practice of insurance and may be subject to criminal and civil penalties.

Certificate of Need

In addition to obtaining a certificate of authority, HMOs may be subject to a state's certificate of need law. Thirty-four states and the District of Columbia have certificate of need statutory provisions that regulate the construction, alteration, or licensing of a health care facility. Certificate of need approval may also be required for the acquisition of equipment and changes in the level of services or beds. Insofar as HMOs operate and run health care facilities, regulatory permission may be required to carry out these types of activities.

Enrollee Information

The Model Act has set forth certain requirements for communicating information about the plan to HMO enrollees. Enrollees are entitled to receive a copy of the individual and group contracts. Misleading, confusing, and unjust provisions are prohibited. Each contract must contain basic information describing eligibility requirements, covered benefits, out-of-pocket expenses, limitations and exclusions, termination or cancellation of policies, claims processing, grievance procedures, continuation of benefits, conversion rights, subrogation rights, term of coverage, and grace period after nonpayment of premiums. Regulators require that these plan documents be filed with and approved by the regulatory body in charge of reviewing contracts.

In addition to individual and group contacts, the Model Act requires HMOs to make other disclosures. Every enrollee is entitled to receive a document referred to as the evidence of coverage, which describes the essential features and services of the HMO. Plans must also provide details on how services can be obtained through the HMO network and a telephone number at the plan to answer additional questions. Upon member enrollment or re-enrollment, HMOs must provide a list of their providers to members. Within 30 days after a material change in the plan, HMOs must notify enrollees of any such change if it has a direct impact upon enrollees.

Provider Issues

HMOs are required to execute written contracts with their participating providers. Upon an initial application for a certificate of authority, and periodically thereafter, regulators will review sample contracts for primary care, specialty care, and other ancillary services. Contracts must contain a number of provisions, including a list of covered services, how physicians will be paid, hold-harmless language, the contract term, termination procedures, and obligation to adhere to HMO quality assurance and utilization management programs. Examples of such contracts are given in Chapter 36.

Regulators are also concerned about provider risk-sharing arrangements. Most HMOs share the risk for the cost of health care with their providers (principally primary care physicians) through performance-based reimbursement, including capitated payment mechanisms, and periodically through withholds and pooling arrangements. Under capitation, a provider is usually compensated on a fixed, prepaid basis (eg, per member per month). In addition, providers may participate in a withhold arrangement where the HMO withholds a portion of the provider's payment (eg, 20%) during a 12-month period to cover excess medical expenses; if money is still left at the end, the provider will receive it. See Chapter 6 for a full discussion of compensation models. Regulators carefully scrutinize these types of reimbursement formulas to make sure that the quality of care is not compromised. There is growing concern among regulators about the amount of risk assumed by providers, particularly whether the solvency of the provider is unreasonably jeopardized.

Filing Requirements

State regulators employ a number of methods to make sure that the HMO stays in compliance with the law after it is licensed. Typically, an annual report must be filed with the insurance department. The content of the report can include audited financial statements, a list of participating providers, an update and summary concerning enrollee grievances handled during the year, and any additional information that regulators deem necessary and appropriate to make a proper review of the organization.

The Model Act also requires the filing of a schedule of premium rates or a methodology for determining premium rates with the insurance department. Regulators will normally approve of the schedule or methodology if the premiums are not excessive, inadequate, or unfairly discriminatory.

In addition, states impose a duty on HMOs to update regulators automatically if there are changes in the documents that were part of the initial filing to obtain a certificate of authority (or part of the annual filings). Permanent records are kept by regulators, including primary care physician agreements, specialist provider contracts, group and individual contracts, certificate of coverage, and other pertinent information.

Quality Assurance Program

Examination of an HMO's quality assurance program (see Chapter 15) begins with a review of relevant documents, including a comprehensive description of the program. Regulators will then make an assessment as to how well the HMO is carrying out its responsibilities. Preventive care activities, program administration, provider credentialing, utilization review procedures, risk management, provider payment mechanisms, accessibility of HMO services, medical records, claims payment procedures, and management information services will be carefully reviewed in the quality assurance evaluation. Some states, notably Kansas and Pennsylvania, require an HMO to obtain an independent external review of its quality assurance program from approved review agencies, such as the National Committee for Quality Assurance (see Chapter 21).

Grievance Procedures

The Model Act requires the establishment of a grievance procedure to assist in the resolution of enrollee complaints. States often specify how these grievances should be handled. Typically, regulators require that each HMO form a grievance committee that hears the complaints. Enrollees must be informed of their right to a hearing when they join the HMO. Decisions by the committee may be appealed within the HMO, and if necessary the state may step in to hear the complaint. The number of grievances filed and processed by an HMO must also be reported on a regular basis to the appropriate regulatory body. See Chapter 19 for further discussion of this issue.

Insolvency Protection

The Model Act establishes specific capital, reserve, and deposit requirements for HMOs to protect consumers and other interested parties against insolvency. Before a certificate of authority will be issued, an initial net worth requirement of $1.5 million is called for. After issuance, a minimum net worth must be maintained by the HMO equal to the greater of $1 million, 2% of annual premiums on the first $150 million of premiums and 1% on the excess, the sum of 3 months' uncovered health care costs, or the sum of 8% of annual health expenditures (except those paid on a capitated basis or a managed hospital payment basis) and 4% of annual hospital expenses paid on a managed payment basis.

The Model Act also requires a deposit of $300,000 with the insurance department. The deposit is considered an admitted asset of the HMO in the determination of its net worth, but it is used to protect the interests of HMO enrollees or to cover the administrative costs if the HMO goes into receivership or liquidation.

In most states, HMOs are required also to include hold-harmless clauses in their provider contracts (see Chapter 36). In situations where the HMO fails to pay for covered medical care, such clauses prohibit providers from seeking collection from the enrollees. California and New York have statutory hold-harmless requirements protecting enrollees even in the absence of a contractual provision.

A few states also require that HMOs participate in guaranty fund programs. These programs are established by a state to provide funding to cover an HMO's potential liabilities for health care services if the HMO becomes insolvent. Regulators may use this money to reimburse nonparticipating providers, to pay for the continuation of benefits, and to cover conversion costs. Guaranty funds have been almost universally implemented in states for life, health, and accident insurance policies. Only a few states, however, require HMO participation in their life and health guaranty associations. In four states, HMOs reinsure each other through a stand-alone HMO guaranty association or insolvency assessment fund. The NAIC Model Act includes a provision to establish an insolvency assessment fund based on a law in the Commonwealth of Virginia. The NAIC drafting notes accompanying this section, however, specifically state that this mechanism is not recommended for all states because there may be inadequate premium volume or too few HMOs to make an assessment feasible.

States often require HMOs to establish contingency plans for insolvency that allow for the continuation of benefits to the enrollees during the contract period for which premiums have been paid. If necessary, insurance departments will call for HMOs to take further precautions to safeguard enrollee benefits. These additional measures might include the purchasing of additional insurance, entering into contracts where providers promise to continue to provide services in the event that the HMO ceases operation, setting aside additional insolvency reserves, or securing letters of credit.

If a regulator determines that the financial condition of the HMO threatens its enrollees, creditors, or the general public, the regulator is usually given broad discretion to order the HMO to take specific actions as necessary to rectify the situation. Such action plans may include reducing potential liabilities through reinsurance, suspending the volume of new business for a period of time, or increasing the HMO's capital and surplus contributions.

Financial Examinations and On-Site Visits

Regulators can also conduct specialized inquiries, which often examine HMO finances, marketing activities, and quality assurance programs. The objective in these regulatory reviews is to determine the HMO's financial solvency and statutory compliance and whether any trends can be identified that may cause problems down the road.

For example, the Model Act requires that the insurance department complete a detailed examination of the HMO's financial affairs at least once every 3 years. The NAIC *HMO Examination Handbook* sets forth specific procedures for examining HMO balance sheet assets and liabilities. The goals are to verify ownership and stated amounts of the assets and to ensure the adequacy of the HMO's net worth to meet existing and future liabilities. Examiners may look at an HMO's existing cash resources; investments; premium receivables; interest receivables; prepaid expenses; restricted assets; leasehold arrangements; accounts payable; unpaid claims; unearned premiums; outstanding loans; statutory liability; building, land, equipment, and inventory lists; as well as other company assets and costs.

If the HMO is undercapitalized or otherwise short of funding, regulators will usually provide an opportunity for the HMO to straighten out its affairs. Regulators take financial shortfalls seriously, however, and will suspend or revoke an HMO's license if necessary, in order to protect consumer interests.

As part of the examination process, regulators may drop by for an on-site visit to see the HMO's operations first hand, to complete a review of plan documents, and to assess the efficiency and soundness of plan operations. The on-site visit may be relatively brief or can take place over a period of days. Occasionally, regulators will contact participating providers and enrollees directly to verify how the HMO is operating.

MULTISTATE OPERATIONS

With many HMOs now operating in more than one state, HMOs must comply with the regulations of each jurisdiction. Most states mandate that foreign HMOs meet the same requirements applicable to domestic HMOs. States may also require that out-of-state HMOs register to do business under the appropriate foreign corporation law and appoint an agent for service of process.

Multistate operations can become expensive if plans are subject to a multitude of financial examinations and other regulatory requirements. To alleviate this concern, some states permit regulators who are considering the application of a foreign HMO to accept financial reports and other information from the HMO's state of origin. The NAIC has also established guidelines for coordinating examinations of HMOs licensed in more than one state. The coordinated examination is called for by the lead state, where the HMO is domiciled, and other interested states are encouraged to participate.

Occasionally, regulations in one state may adversely affect or hinder the operations of an HMO licensed in another state. For example, an out-of-state HMO cannot review the medical necessity or appropriateness of care delivered to its enrollees on an emergency basis in Nevada unless the HMO is licensed as a utilization review agent in that state.

Historically, the general rule in group insurance has been that the policy is subject to the law of the state in which it is issued. A policy issued in state A would be subject to filing and approval in state A and would also be subject to the other insurance laws of that state, including mandated benefits. Unfortunately, this general rule has been eroded by extraterritorial application of state insurance law. The laws of state B may require that any resident of state B covered under a group health policy receive the same coverage that would be required had the group policy been issued in state B.

The benefits arena has been further clouded by states adopting legislation and regulation, both formal and informal, that permit various types of managed care arrangements. State A may allow PPOs but not EPOs; State B may allow both forms. It may therefore be impermissible for the insurance policy filed in state A to provide for an EPO, although state B has approved policy language for that arrangement. In some cases state A may consent to the group policy containing different provisions for state B if these are in accordance with the laws of state B.

SELF-INSURED ARRANGEMENTS

Under self-insured arrangements where the employer assumes the financial risk of its employees' health care costs, regulators can do little to supervise the attempts of employers to manage the health plan. Self-insured arrangements are usually employee benefit plans under the Employee Retirement Income Security Act (ERISA) of 1974 and are exempted from state regulation. In essence, these plans are not considered insurance companies for the purpose of any state law governing insurance activities. With the growing trend by employers to become self-insured, state regulators have expressed concern over the lack of authority to protect consumers under these arrangements. It is now common for large employers to use managed care in a self-insured arrangement, thereby avoiding most state regulation, mandated benefits, premium taxes, and so forth.

OTHER REGULATED MANAGED CARE PRODUCTS

Some states do supervise other managed care product lines such as PPOs [also referred to as preferred provider arrangements (PPAs)] and specific managed care activities such as utilization review. Generally speaking, however, fewer states have enacted legislation covering non-HMO products.

Preferred Provider Organizations

PPO/PPA regulatory supervision is not as intense as HMO oversight. For example, the NAIC's HMO Model Act has 34 sections, whereas the PPA Model Act has 9 sections and provides only a few guidelines. This stems in part from the anticipation that participants in PPAs will already be regulated under other laws and that no new corporate entity will necessarily be created.

Administrative Services Only

Regulated entities such as insurance companies and HMOs can effectively offer a non-regulated managed care product under an administrative services only arrangement with an employer that assumes the financial risk of the benefits plan.

Exclusive Provider Organizations

EPOs by definition are not regulated because they coordinate health services in self-insured plans and administrative services only arrangements.

Hybrids

In addition to the ERISA exemption, regulatory oversight is diminished by the fact that many managed care products are hybrids and are not easily categorized. For example, an HMO that offers a point of service (POS) product is similar to a PPA that utilizes a gatekeeper. An HMO or PPA that offers a network of providers under a self-insured plan is similar to an EPO. Conversely, a POS plan that utilizes both a licensed HMO and a licensed indemnity carrier to provide in-network and out-of-network benefits, respectively, may be subject to double the regulation because there are two entities, each with different requirements.

HOW MUCH REGULATION?

Ironically, a number of managed care experts are expressing concern that state HMO regulation is becoming too burdensome. A prime example is the proliferation of state legislation mandating one benefit after another. Because mandated benefits usually cover specialty services, these provisions reduce the ability of HMOs to cover basic health care services, as funds must be rerouted to provide the new specialty service. States have also begun enacting "any willing provider" legislation, which requires HMOs to accept nonparticipating providers into their network. This takes away the ability of HMOs to manage care through their closed provider network of credentialed physicians and often dictates that HMOs accept new provider classes into the network, such as chiropractors, podiatrists, acupuncturists, osteopaths, and family therapists. Mandated benefits, any willing provider provisions, and similar types of initiatives are commonly referred to as anti–managed care laws and are symptomatic of too much regulation.

HMO enabling laws may also be too restrictive if they do not authorize product innovation. For example, only a handful of states have enacted legislation that allows HMOs to offer POS products under the HMO license. Under these arrangements, enrollees are able to self-refer, on a limited basis, outside the HMO provider network. Employers increasingly ask HMOs to offer POS products as a health benefits option that encourages individuals to become familiar with managed care while retaining some freedom to choose providers. Regulators typically view the out-of-network option as an insurance product that should only be offered under an insurance license.

In addition to the pure quantity of regulations, the quality or method of regulating is important. For example, when is an HMO financially sound? Unfortunately, regulators do not have crystal balls to assist them in setting the proper capital, deposit, and reserve requirements. Even the procedures used in accounting to determine the HMO's net worth and liabilities can make a big difference in calculating available funds for insolvency protection. Whereas the HMO industry prefers using the generally accepted accounting principles, which require accrual accounting, regulators prefer statutory accounting principles, which use a cash basis and set aside certain assets that would not be of value if the HMO became insolvent.

CONCLUSION

Although there are certain levels of uniformity in regulation from state to state, wide variability also exists. In all events, however, the state regulatory process is designed to ensure that the consumer is treated fairly and consistently, including protection from plan failure.

Chapter 35

The Hows and Whys of Federal Qualification and Eligibility

Elisabeth A. Handley

IN THE BEGINNING

In its infancy, the health maintenance organization (HMO) industry faced considerable opposition from organized medicine, restrictive state laws, and difficulty in finding start-up funding. Recognizing these problems and the possibilities that HMOs offered in health care delivery, Congress passed Title XIII of the Public Health Service Act in 1973. This legislation was significant to the then struggling HMO industry because it signaled a national policy of support and recognition.

The HMO Act, as it is known, gave HMOs a big boost by authorizing funding for grants, loans, and loan guarantees for their development and support. Importantly, this law also established organizational and operating requirements for HMOs that were to be federally qualified and provided for their continued regulation.

Elisabeth A. Handley is the Deputy Director of the Office of Prepaid Health Care Operations and Oversight in the Health Care Financing Administration.

The author wishes to thank Steve Balcerzak, Sylvia Hendel, Sid Lindenberg, Dick Malsbary, and Marjorie Swiecicki for their help with this chapter.

The views expressed within the chapter are the author's and not those of the Health Care Financing Administration. Addresses and telephone numbers were current at the time of publication, but the author cannot verify their accuracy over time.

Over the years, congressional interest in managed care has evolved. In the 1970s Congress provided money and credibility for this fledgling industry. It provided greater flexibility and introduced a new population to managed care when, in 1982, it enacted legislation creating competitive medical plans (CMPs) to serve Medicare beneficiaries.

Congress envisioned CMPs as the new breed of managed care entities that would go beyond serving the people who already had access to managed care: the working population. It envisioned CMPs enrolling a brand new population previously neglected by managed care organizations: Medicare beneficiaries (who are elderly or disabled).

The shift to serving a different population (one that is by definition sicker), Congress recognized, necessitated providing CMPs with more flexibility than federally qualified HMOs. Building on the successes of the federal qualification process, however, Congress declared that CMPs must meet certain organizational and operating requirements to be found as eligible organizations. Many of these eligibility standards are identical to those applied to federally qualified HMOs.

Congressional interest in managed care has continued beyond the creation of CMPs. With the passage of the HMO Act amendments of

1988, Congress allowed federally qualified HMOs to adopt some of the innovations that preferred provider organizations and insurance companies had devised. During the presidential race of 1992, President Bush and Bill Clinton made managed care an important part of their health reform proposals.

This chapter focuses on the federal qualification and eligibility processes for HMOs and CMPs. It explains what federal qualification and eligibility are, the differences between HMOs and CMPs, the different kinds of applications for qualification and eligibility, qualification and eligibility review procedures, what to expect after qualification or eligibility, the advantages and disadvantages of qualification and eligibility, and tips on succeeding at obtaining qualification and eligibility. The reader is referred to Chapter 28 for an in-depth discussion of Medicare risk contracting.

WHAT ARE QUALIFICATION AND ELIGIBILITY?

Federal qualification and eligibility are terms that describe the federal government's certification process for managed care organizations. In the broadest terms, this process may be equated to seeking and receiving the federal government's Good Housekeeping Seal of Approval. This process may also be likened to taking a snapshot of an organization at a given point in time and ensuring that specific items are both present and present in a certain configuration.

Organizations interested in federal qualification as an HMO or eligibility as a CMP submit an application to the US Department of Health and Human Services (DHHS). HMOs that are preoperational, transitional, or operational may apply for federal qualification. Through these applications and the reviews that accompany them, the HMO or CMP demonstrates that it meets federal standards for its health service delivery system, financial viability, marketing activities, and legal and organizational status.

It is important to note that federal qualification and eligibility are entirely voluntary. HMOs and CMPs apply for them only if they so desire. As of April 1, 1992, 434 HMOs and 17 CMPs have voluntarily applied and been found either qualified or eligible.

For HMOs, the federal law that describes the qualification process is contained in Title XIII of the Public Health Service Act. The federal regulations that implement Title XIII and contain specific requirements that HMOs must meet may be found at section 42 of the Code of the Federal Regulations Part 417 (42 CFR 417.100 through 417.180).

For CMPs, eligibility standards are mandated in section 1876 of the Tax Equity and Fiscal Responsibility Act (TEFRA). The implementing federal regulations for CMPs may be found at section 42 of the Code of Federal Regulations Part 417 (42 CFR 417.400 through 417.810). HMOs and CMPs interested in applying for qualification or eligibility receive these regulations when they request an application kit.

Both sets of regulations specify HMO and CMP requirements and the issue areas to be reviewed. Generally, these include the HMO's or CMP's health service delivery system, its financial picture (eg, CMPs and HMOs must be fiscally sound), its marketing activities, and its legal and organizational status. The review confirms that the provisions are met. Exhibit 35-1 details the key review areas for CMP and HMO eligibility and qualification. Specific review areas for both HMOs and CMPs may be found in the regulations cited above.

DIFFERENCES BETWEEN HEALTH MAINTENANCE ORGANIZATIONS AND COMPETITIVE MEDICAL PLANS

Table 35-1 lists some of the differences between HMOs and CMPs.

QUALIFICATION OR ELIGIBILITY APPLICATIONS: WHICH TO USE WHEN

The Office of Prepaid Health Care Operations and Oversight (OPHCOO) is a part of the Health Care Financing Administration (HCFA) within the larger DHHS. OPHCOO is the federal government entity responsible for qualification and

Exhibit 35-1 CMP and HMO Eligibility and Qualification Review Areas

Legal
- Organized under state law
- Insolvency arrangements
- Provider agreements
- Subscriber agreements
- Board oversight (HMOs only)
- Management ability to control HMO/CMP operations
- Staff capability

Financial Viability
- Performance
- Budget assumptions
- Cost and revenue projections
- Capitalization

Health Services Delivery
- Availability, accessibility, and continuity of health services
- Quality assurance
- Utilization controls
- Physician risk arrangements
- Management information systems
- Feedback to physicians
- Evidence of physician willingness to serve Medicare population

Marketing
- Enrollment projections and assumptions
- Strategy
- Marketing materials
- 5,000 minimum commercial members (1,500 rural)
- 50% Medicare or Medicaid membership/50% commercial membership rule (all CMPs and HMOs that plan to contract with Medicare)

Source: US Department of Health and Human Services, Office of Prepaid Health Care Operations and Oversight.

Table 35-1 Key Differences between HMOs and CMPs

HMO	CMP
Must be community rated, with some flexibility	May be community or experience rated
Comprehensive benefits requirements	More flexibility in benefits design
Few limitations as to time or cost of benefits	May limit benefits as to time and cost
Services provided almost solely by HMO health professionals; up to 10% of basic health services may be provided by out-of-plan providers	Services provided primarily through CMP health professionals; 49% may be provided by out-of-plan providers
Dual choice mandate by employer applies	No dual choice mandate

Source: US Department of Health and Human Services, Office of Prepaid Health Care.

330 Independence Avenue SW
Washington, DC 20201
(202) 619-0840

There are four different applications that an HMO or CMP may complete and submit to the OPHCOO:

1. Qualification application (Title XIII), with option of Medicare contract (Title XVIII), HCFA-901-2/91
2. CMP Medicare contract application (Title XVIII), HCFA-901-2, 2/91
3. Qualified HMO Medicare contract application (Title XVIII), HCFA-901-1, 2/91
4. Application for Medicare Health Care Prepayment Plan (HCPP) agreement (Title XVIII), HCFA-6/90.1

Qualification Application

The federal qualification application may be used to apply for federal qualification only or for both federal qualification and a Medicare contract simultaneously. That is, because federal qualification (or eligibility) is a prerequisite for a Medicare contract, HMOs (and CMPs) can do one-stop shopping through the OPHCOO by applying for both qualification and a Medicare

eligibility review. It has staff located in both Washington, DC, and Baltimore, Maryland. In addition, federal government employees in DHHS's 10 regional offices also participate in qualification and eligibility reviews.

To obtain HMO qualification or CMP eligibility, a prepaid plan must complete an application form provided by the HCFA. These applications forms may be obtained from:

Office of Prepaid Health Care Operations and Oversight
Office of Operations, Health Care Financing Administration
Room 4360 HHS Cohen Building

contract at the same time.

This multipurpose application is also used for federal qualification of a regional component of an HMO. Federal regulations [Part 42 CFR 417.104(b)(4)] define a regional component as ". . . geographically distinct and separate from any other regional component . . . [that] provides substantially the full range of basic health services to its members, without extensive referral between components of the organization for these services." HMOs sometimes establish regional components so that they may establish a separate community rate for each separate component.

Competitive Medical Plan Medicare Contract Application

Entities that apply for CMP eligibility also benefit from the one-stop shopping concept noted above: The two applications for eligibility and a Medicare risk or cost contract are combined. Thus an organization that wishes to become eligible and to have a Medicare risk or cost contract would complete only the CMP eligibility application. CMPs that later end their Medicare contracts must relinquish their CMP status because it is only associated with having a Medicare risk or cost contract.

Qualified HMO Medicare Contract Application

Already qualified HMOs that are interested in a risk or cost contract with the federal government to provide health care to Medicare beneficiaries must complete the qualified HMO Medicare contract application. This application may also be completed if the HMO wants to expand its Medicare contract service area within the currently federally qualified service area or if it is requesting a separate Medicare contract for an already federally qualified regional component.

Application for Medicare Health Care Prepayment Plan Agreement

The remaining type of application, application for Medicare HCPP, is used by CMPs or entities not needing to be federally qualified that

wish to serve Medicare beneficiaries and to be reimbursed on a cost basis. HCPPs furnish non-institutional Medicare benefits to a defined population on a prepaid basis. See Chapter 28 and the federal regulations (42 CFR 417.800 ff) for further details.

Service Area Expansions

If an HMO or CMP wants to expand the service area that has already been federally qualified or found eligible, it should complete the qualification application or the CMP Medicare contract application. Both applications indicate that only asterisked items need to be filled in for an expansion. For example, if an HMO had been federally qualified in the Maryland counties of Montgomery and Prince Georges and it wanted to serve people in Howard County as well, it would submit a service area expansion for that county by using the qualification application.

QUALIFICATION AND ELIGIBILITY REVIEW PROCEDURES

When a qualification or eligibility application is received, it is assigned to a plan manager within the Office of Operations. The Office of Operations is a subunit of OPHCOO that is responsible for qualification and eligibility determinations, Medicare contracting with HMOs and CMPs, and oversight of regional offices' monitoring of Medicare contracting HMOs and CMPs.

The plan manager serves as the legal reviewer in most instances and manages and coordinates the review of the application by other specialists in the finance, health services delivery, and Medicare (if applicable) areas. Specialists who review the health services delivery and Medicare portions of an application are located in the 10 regional offices. As of September 1, 1992, all 10 regional offices began handling the health services delivery and Medicare portions of applications. Together, the plan manager and the specialists form a team that reviews the application.

The OPHCOO sometimes uses outside consultants from the health care industry as specialists. These consultants may include HMO/CMP chief executive officers, medical directors, and others. Their addition brings a valuable operational perspective to the review process.

The qualification and eligibility review processes are generally completed within 5 months of the receipt of an application, provided that the applicant organization furnishes all required information and that user fees are submitted (see below for details about user fees). To ensure timely determinations, the OPHCOO has established an application review process, which consists of the following steps:

1. Initial review
2. Intensive review
3. Site visit
4. Post-site visit and determination of qualification and eligibility

The discussion of the application process relies heavily on internal working papers used by staff in the OPHCOO. It comes from the standard operating procedures application process used by plan managers and regional office staff in reviewing applications. This document is not distributed to the public because it is used solely by staff members in performing their jobs. Questions about applications may be directed to the address or phone number listed above.

Initial Review

Before the intensive review begins, the plan manager acknowledges receipt of the application and, along with the regional office, performs the initial review of the application. During the initial review, the plan manager evaluates whether the information is sufficient for him or her to be able to go to the next step, the intensive review. On the basis of this review, the plan manager sends one of two letters to the applicant. The first is a completeness letter, which states whether a site visit will be conducted and gives a general time frame for the visit.

The second possibility is an incompleteness letter, which ". . . inform[s] the applicant of the inadequacy of information and gives instructions in the preparation of an appropriate

response."[1(p8)] Information must be returned by the HMO or CMP within 60 days to complete the application. Once the additional information is returned, the plan manager (along with the regional office) determines that the application is ready for the intensive review and informs the HMO of this fact in writing.[1]

Intensive Review

After the completeness check is finished, the Plan Manager and specialists begin the intensive review of the application. As noted in the OPHCOO's standard operating procedures, the purpose of the in-depth review is[1(p12)]:

> . . . to evaluate a) consistency and adequacy of submitted information; b) operational and policy conformance with the Public Health Service and Social Security Acts, regulations, OPHCOO policies; and c) identification of policy issues requiring decisions.

Each individual prepares a written report of his or her findings called a desk report. According to the OPHCOO, the purpose of the desk report is to[1(p12)]:

> (1) identify documentation required as additional justification and substantiation of data in the application, (2) communicate specific areas the plan needs to prepare to address during the site visit, and (3) identify individuals the specialty reviewers will need to interview during the visit. Basically, any information that is not clearly/fully presented in the application can be requested in the desk report. The desk report will be enclosed in the site visit (or off-site) letter which will be mailed to the applicant.

Site Visit

The next step in the review process is the site visit. During this step, the qualification or eligibility team visits the HMO or CMP to verify information provided in the application and to explore important issues in depth.

Site visits last 1.5 to 2.5 days. While on site, the team conducts a series of group and individual interviews and reviews plan documentation. There are three distinct activities that occur during the site visit: the opening session, specialist reviews, and the closing session.

When the site visit team members arrive on the first day, they hold an orientation meeting during which they introduce themselves and receive an overview of the plan (from the plan), including a brief review of the plan's history. For the next hour, the site visit team then discusses the HMO's or CMP's organization and operation, concentrating on the relationship among the financial, health services, Medicare (if applicable), and legal aspects of the entity.

Midmorning, the site visit team divides up to review the financial, Medicare (if applicable), health services delivery, and legal systems. The organization generally prepares a written schedule for each of the reviewers to use in meeting with key staff. These meetings continue into the second day of the site visit.

On the second day, the plan manager holds a closing session. At this time, the team identifies any additional information that may be required to finalize the review. The applicant then has 14 days to submit the additional material.

Post–Site Visit Analysis and Determination of Qualification or Eligibility

After the site visit is completed and the HMO or CMP has submitted the requested materials, each reviewer analyzes the additional material (as well as information gathered from the application and on site). As a final step, each reviewer prepares and submits a report to the plan manager recommending approval or disapproval for his or her specialty area.

The plan manager then prepares a comprehensive report (called a program advisory committee report) that contains a recommendation for qualification or eligibility (and a Medicare contract, if applicable). This recommendation is reviewed and approved by the program advisory committee. The committee comprises the

OPHCOO director and deputy, OPHCOO senior staff members, the plan manager, and specialty reviewers.

The OPHCOO may render the following determinations[1(pp20–21)]:

> (1) Approval, if the applicant meets all requirements; (2) Intent to Deny, if the applicant can correct its deficiencies within 60 days; or (3) Disapproval, if the issues are determined unresolvable within the next 60 days. A denial notification may be sent without an intent to deny, if it is evident that the applicant will be unable to resolve outstanding issues within 60 days. A denial notification may also be sent if the applicant does not satisfactorily resolve all issues addressed in the intent to deny letter within 60 days.

Applicants who have received an intent to deny or a denial may request a conference with the plan manager and specialty reviewers, and, according to OPHCOO procedures, "At that time, the HMO's proposed response to the issues or other matters is reviewed."[1(p23)]

After a qualification determination, HMO qualification applicants (but not CMP eligibility applicants) must sign assurances that they meet and will continue to meet the applicable requirements of the regulations. HMOs have 30 days from the date of the determination of qualification to return their assurances. It is only when these assurances are signed and notarized that the applicant becomes qualified.

Designation of Federal Qualification

The OPHCOO describes three designations of federal qualification for which an HMO may qualify upon signing and returning the assurances.

Operational

An operational qualified HMO is a plan that provides basic and supplemental health services to all its members and is organized and operates in accordance with regulatory requirements. The plan must sign written assurances within 30 days of the OPHCOO determination that it will continue to provide health services as specified in the regulatory requirements for qualification. It is eligible for a Medicare contract when the signed assurances are returned to the OPHCOO.

Preoperational

A preoperational qualified HMO is an entity that the HCFA has determined will, when it becomes operational, be a qualified HMO. The assurances include specific requirements that must be met by the HMO before it becomes operational. The plan must sign the documented assurances within 30 days of the date of the OPHCOO determination notification stating that it qualifies as a preoperational HMO. It must become operational within 60 days after signing the assurances, and the Secretary of Health and Human Services must be informed in writing. The OPHCOO must determine that the plan is an operational qualified HMO within 30 days of the plan's notification to the OPHCOO of its operational status.

A preoperational HMO has no enrollees and is not eligible for a Medicare contract at the time of preoperational qualification because of Medicare contract enrollment requirements. The HMO is eligible for a Medicare contract when it becomes operational and meets the Medicare enrollment requirements.

Transitional

A transitional qualified HMO already operates a prepaid health care delivery system that the HCFA has determined meets the requirements for qualification. It is considered a qualified HMO for the purpose of compliance by an employer in accordance with regulatory requirements. The employer must include the HMO in its health benefits plan as long as the HMO's qualification has not been revoked.

A transitional qualified HMO has enrollees, is operational, and meets all Title XIII requirements except those concerning the qualified commercial benefits package. The transitional qualified HMO may continue its prequalification contracts with employers until renewal of the annual employer contract, at which time the qualifiable benefits must be provided.[1]

AFTER QUALIFICATION

Monitoring

Once an HMO or CMP has been qualified or found eligible, it must continue to comply with applicable federal laws and regulations. Coordinated care specialists in each of the HCFA's 10 regional offices monitor the HMO or CMP to ensure compliance with Medicare requirements. Additionally, the plan manager in Washington, DC, communicates with the regional office staff person if problems arise with the HMO's or CMP's compliance.

Federally qualified HMOs without Medicare contracts are monitored differently. They are supervised by central office staff. Monitoring visits occur only if a complaint is made against the HMO or if staff determine that sufficient cause exists to perform an on-site review.

Regional office staff do site visits of HMOs and CMPs with Medicare contracts. Post–contract award visits are conducted for each entity with a Medicare contract between the 6th and 12th month after the effective date of the contract, depending upon the size of the Medicare membership. Comprehensive visits occur every 2 years. For example, on site, regional office staff will verify that health care services are still available and accessible to members, that the organization remains fiscally viable, and that the plan's Medicare appeals process is functioning smoothly. Interim visits may also take place on an as needed basis. They might be done, for example, for the regional office to investigate an allegation of a problem or to assess whether a corrective action plan has been instituted and has been successful.

Financial Reporting Requirements

Federally qualified HMOs and eligible CMPs are also required to prepare and submit financial reports to the OPHCOO on a periodic basis. This filing is part of the HMO national data reporting requirements and includes three basic financial statements: a balance sheet, an income statement, and a statement of change in financial position. The report is accompanied by several supporting schedules and utilization reports.

Central office staff regularly review these reports to ensure the continued fiscal soundness of the organization.

ADVANTAGES OF QUALIFICATION AND ELIGIBILITY

HMOs and CMPs that obtain federal qualification and eligibility have several distinct advantages over those that do not. These advantages include increased credibility with employers, greater potential market share through the dual choice mandate, a shortened Medicare risk-contracting process, and the identification of strengths and weaknesses by the review team.

Credibility with Employers

Perhaps the most important advantage of qualification and eligibility is how these distinguish HMOs and CMPs from their competitors. By obtaining qualification or eligibility, the HMO or CMP has demonstrated that it meets stringent standards, something that its competitors may not be able to do. Not only can the HMO or CMP sell the employer on the fact that it has already met these standards, it can also note its continued compliance with these standards over time to retain its federal qualification or eligibility.

Through the qualification or eligibility reviews, the employer may be assured that the HMO or CMP will be offering its employees health care that is more closely regulated and scrutinized than that of an HMO or CMP without federal qualification or eligibility. Employers may perceive that their employees will receive better health care from these organizations, which in effect have a federal seal of approval. Many large employers will only offer HMOs that are federally qualified.

Dual Choice

Another important advantage of qualification relates to potential market share. Because of the substantial opposition HMOs were experiencing in marketing their products in the early 1970s,

Congress enacted a dual choice mandate within Title XIII of the Public Health Service Act.

Dual choice means that employers of 25 or more persons with employees residing in an HMO's service area, employers who are required to pay minimum wage, and employers who offer their employees health benefits to which they contribute must give employees the option of joining an HMO. The HMO must, in accordance with federal procedures, ask to be included in a health benefits program; the employer must then give the HMO marketing opportunities at least equal to those given the current indemnity carrier.[2]

Thus federally qualified HMOs are practically guaranteed access to the employer marketplace (the dual choice mandate applies only to HMOs, not to CMPs). Of note, however, is the fact that federal regulations require only the offering of two HMOs: a group or staff model (closed panel) and an individual practice association model (open panel). An employer is not required to offer multiple HMOs of the same type unless the second HMO can prove that it has a unique service area. Moreover, in 1988 Congress put a sunset on the dual choice provision: It will end in 1995.

Shortened Medicare Contracting Process

HMOs that wish to contract with the federal government to serve Medicare beneficiaries under a risk arrangement must be qualified before they can contract. Thus those who have already been qualified have shortened the amount of time it will take them to obtain a Medicare contract because they have already completed one critical step and are ready to begin the Medicare contract application process itself.

Identification of Strengths and Weaknesses

HMOs and CMPs that apply for qualification and eligibility undergo a rigorous review process. Although the federal government charges HMOs (but not CMPs) for the cost of this review (see below), the review may provide the organization with important information about its strengths and weaknesses in critical operational areas such as health service delivery, fiscal soundness, and legal issues. Because the review is performed by outsiders who have no stake in the operation of the HMO or CMP, management may gain a valuable perspective to which it might not otherwise have been exposed. Plans often use this information to make improvements and changes.

DISADVANTAGES OF QUALIFICATION AND ELIGIBILITY

User Fees

Congress, through the user fee statute, encourages federal agencies to charge for services in certain circumstances so that the provision of the service is self-sustaining. Effective July 13, 1987, the federal government published a final regulation that requires prepaid plans seeking qualification or an expansion of their service area, or a CMP seeking qualification as an HMO, to pay the federal government specific user fees. There is no cost for CMP eligibility reviews.

For an entity seeking qualification as an HMO or an HMO seeking qualification of a regional component as an HMO in itself, the user fee is $18,400. If the OPHCOO determines that no site visit is needed for an HMO seeking qualification of a regional component, $8,000 will be returned to the applicant. An HMO seeking expansion of its service area is required to pay $6,900 in user fees. A CMP seeking HMO qualification must pay $3,100.

Less Flexibility in Offerings

HMOs that are federally qualified must offer certain benefits to meet qualification standards. In some instances, this may mean that the organization is offering a richer benefit package than other non–federally approved HMOs or than it would have wanted to offer on its own. A richer benefit package may make it harder for the HMO to compete in its community, at least with indemnity products. It should be noted, however, that vis-à-vis other HMOs it is likely that competitors are qualified and thus offer at least

the same minimum package. Furthermore, many states have enacted laws that require the offering of minimum benefits that may duplicate federal benefit requirements.

In addition to benefit requirements, federally qualified HMOs (but not CMPs) have somewhat less flexibility in premium rate development than non–federally qualified plans (ie, plans that are regulated only by the state). In some instances, a non–federally qualified HMO may be allowed to use premium rate methodologies (eg, retrospective experience rating) that are not allowed under federal qualification, although it should be noted that current federal regulations regarding rating are considerably more flexible than they were in the past.

TIPS ON SUCCEEDING

HMOs and CMPs that have decided that they want to obtain federal qualification or eligibility may want to follow some of the tips described below. These tips are both procedural and substantive.

Procedural Issues

Accurately Represent the Local Situation

Sometimes the application that is submitted does not match what the review team finds when it goes on site. This is especially true when the HMO or CMP uses consultants to prepare the application or when corporate offices frame the information for a local office. It is important that the staff the review team interviews be familiar with the operations and systems represented in the application. In one recent incident, the local office had not even had access to the application prepared by its corporate headquarters and was surprised (and embarrassed) to learn about what it was supposedly doing at the local site when interviewed by OPHCOO staff.

Occasionally HMOs or CMPs submit an application right before a major change in the health care delivery system or in top management. If these are not the systems that are currently in use or are brand new systems that were instituted just as the application was being prepared, then the HMO or CMP must educate itself about the systems to be able to respond to questions effectively. Otherwise, depending upon the severity of the problem, the HMO or CMP may appear disorganized and lacking in sufficient administrative capability to manage the plan.

For example, an HMO may have lost a major contract with an individual practice association that it was counting on to provide the majority of health services to enrollees. Without the agreement or a replacement for it, the HMO does not have an adequate number of providers, and the reality that was reflected in the application no longer exists. The processing of the application will be delayed because the organization will have to get new providers or demonstrate that it has signed contracts with them.

Applicants have sometimes submitted less than up-to-date information. Most commonly the material that is out of date is the subscriber agreement, either for commercial enrollees or for the Medicare population.

In many cases a legal reviewer will have spent many hours reviewing the benefits described in the agreement. When the reviewer calls the HMO or CMP to discuss the plan's shortcomings, the HMO or CMP then discovers to everyone's dismay that the subscriber agreement that was a part of the application was outdated. This not only leads to a waste of time but delays the processing of the application because an extra step must be added to the process: The reviewer will have to compare the old to the new to see which comments are still valid.

Build Up Expertise

Corporations (regional or national) that seek federal qualification or eligibility in many different places should consider having one person put together all the applications. This would build expertise and allow for quality control because this individual will have learned the OPHCOO's procedures and policies by submitting multiple applications. Additionally, it would mean that all local offices would not need to go through the learning curve and that one person could build a relationship with federal government staff. Critical to the success of this strategy, however, is ensuring that the individual

and the local staff work together.

Allow Sufficient Time

HMOs and CMPs should consider their reasons for applying and their own time table before submitting an application and plan accordingly. If, for example, an HMO wanted to become federally qualified to be offered to a specific employer, it should back up the date of the application submittal from the date of the employer's open enrollment (allowing time for marketing materials printing too). It is also good to let the OPHCOO know what that date is at the outset. Keeping in mind that it generally takes around 5 months to get an application reviewed and allowing extra time for unanticipated situations will help ensure that the review is accomplished in time for the open enrollment.

The timeliness of OPHCOO processing of an application will be affected by the HMO's or CMP's ability to respond to requests for information from reviewers. In planning for the future as suggested above, HMOs and CMPs would be well advised to keep in mind that the information flow needs to work both ways. For the reviewers to do their job, they must have certain information. The amount of time that it takes to produce that information may impinge upon their ability to provide an evaluation of whether the entity meets federal requirements.

Brand new entities that are completing an application and having it reviewed should considering allotting 1 year. This will allow them sufficient time to think through various aspects of the application and to guarantee that all systems are in place and that all information is complete before submission of the application. During this time, for example, an HMO or CMP could acquire insolvency coverage that meets federal requirements.

Work done on the front end will save time on the back end. To illustrate, in the past year more than one HMO prepared an application that did not really contain a network of physicians to serve enrollees (because they had not yet signed contracts with physicians). In the end, these HMOs withdrew their applications and later resubmitted them. Because they were applying for federal qualification, they had paid the user fee of $18,400. When they reapplied later, they had to pay $18,400 more. This example also exemplifies why it is vital to ensure that the application is complete before it is submitted.

Work with the State Early and Often

One of the requirements for both federal qualification and CMP eligibility is that the organization be state licensed. Although the OPHCOO does not mandate that the license has been acquired when it receives an application, it does require that the state license be applied for before it will begin processing the application. In several recent instances, HMOs and CMPs have underestimated how much time it would take to receive state approval. Consequently, the federal reviewers completed their reviews but could not go any further until the state licensure was obtained. If that takes a while, the information in the application may become too old and in need of updating, which will add to the delay in processing. Developing a good working relationship with the state reviewers early on and being familiar with their requirements will eliminate delays.

Provide Documentation

In the application and the regulations that accompany the application package sent to applicants, federal requirements are delineated. Through the application process, the federal government is evaluating whether the applicant meets the requirements. This is done by verifying the information contained in the application, obtaining additional information as needed, and interviewing selected personnel.

Some HMOs or CMPs, however, want OPHCOO reviewers to accept their word that they either meet requirements now or will take a specific action in the future to do so. This is not acceptable: Documentation must demonstrate that requirements are or will be met. To illustrate, copies of a sample of signed provider agreements demonstrate that an HMO or CMP has been successful in establishing a network of physicians. This depicts the ability to sign up physicians rather than just the ability to prepare a provider contract. Providing documentation on the front end will speed up the review process

and help the organization achieve qualification or eligibility more quickly.

Be Flexible

HMOs and CMPs should be flexible during the review process. The managed care industry is evolving and the organizations submitting applications illustrate this evolution. Their applications contain systems and structures that are new. Although OPHCOO and regional office staff have a lot of experience in reviewing HMOs and CMPs, it takes time to evaluate innovative, new structures and systems. To facilitate the review and to speed it up, plans should identify what is unique about their system and how it fits federal requirements.

Substantive Issues

The Health Service Delivery System Is Critical

Many HMOs and CMPs have problems when they submit an application in meeting the health service delivery system requirements. Most of these problems can be overcome with time and effort, but the application process will be much smoother and quicker if health service delivery requirements are in order at the outset. Frequently, they are not.

Applicants should consider the health service delivery system from the perspective of the enrollee when building a network and when submitting the application that details how the network looks. Health services must be available and accessible to the enrollee. Physicians should be near the people whom they will be seeing, there should be contracting hospitals throughout the service area, and all specialties should be represented on the HMO's or CMP's roster.

For example, one HMO proposed to expand its area into a new county and said that it would have certain physicians as a part of its network. Upon investigation, it became clear that a number of the physicians had not specifically agreed to contract with the HMO (one even lived out of state), there were too few physicians to serve the projected enrollment, some physicians were very geographically distant from where the enrollees lived, a number of the physicians listed as being available were indeed not accepting new patients, and there was no agreement with a hospital to serve enrollees in a heavily populated county.

The application requires that maps be provided by the organization depicting what the service area is and where the providers are. Providing a clear map with easily identifiable providers spread throughout the service area will help the reviewer determine that services are indeed available and accessible to enrollees and may serve as a way of ensuring that requirements are met by the people who prepare the application. For example, a map noting one primary care physician, three specialists, and no hospitals in a large metropolitan county would portray graphically the inadequacy of the HMO's proposed network.

Some of the other key health service delivery deficiencies detected in applications include weak quality assurance and utilization control programs. Specifically, quality assurance programs were not fully developed or operational, they were not in place for all parts of the delivery system, they focused on inpatient services only, and there were no links between member services departments and the quality assurance staff. Thus complaints were not tracked so that problems could be rectified.

Poor utilization controls discovered have included weak medical management (with little feedback provided by the HMO or CMP to the physicians about their performance), provider risk arrangements that were either unclear or inadequate, and a lack of hospital and ambulatory controls in place.

When constructing the health service delivery system and preparing applications, organizations should keep in mind that whatever is prepared for the application may end up being used by multiple parties. Nowadays, many employers are interested in HMOs' and CMPs' quality assurance programs. Hence the quality assurance program may be viewed by employers and others and may be important for marketing (to employers) purposes. Concomitantly, devoting a lot of time and effort to this area on the front end may serve the organization well.

The Full Financial Picture Is Essential

Another area in which HMOs and CMPs have experienced problems is financial. Financial deficiencies that reviewers have encountered include declining net income, unsubstantiated financial projections, and inadequate insolvency protection. All these must be overcome for federal qualification or CMP eligibility to be awarded. If, for example, an HMO plans to use the resources of its parent company to meet the HCFA's financial requirements, it must demonstrate that the money is available and set aside for no other purpose and cannot be touched by the parent company.

Benefits Must Be Comprehensive

HMOs that are federally qualified must provide basic health services without limits on time or cost. In some instances, HMOs are the only insurers in an area that have such a generous benefit package because indemnity insurers have reduced benefits. HMOs may perceive that it is difficult for them to compete in a marketplace with indemnity insurers or non–federally qualified HMOs that offer reduced benefits. Thus, in their applications, these HMOs may propose a reduced benefit package for federal qualification.

To be federally qualified, however, the benefit package must be comprehensive and unlimited as to time and cost. The HMO Act leaves little flexibility on what the benefits may consist of. HMOs that wish to provide a less comprehensive benefit package might consider CMP eligibility as an alternative to federal qualification if this is an issue for them and if they are also applying for a Medicare risk or cost contract.

CONCLUSION

Federal qualification and eligibility are voluntary seals of approval that HMOs and CMPs may wish to pursue. Federal approval brings with it both advantages and disadvantages. Chief among these are increased credibility with employers and ease in Medicare contracting at the cost of user fees and continued federal oversight. Obtaining qualification or eligibility is a systematic process that may take up to 1 year from when the decision is made to seek it. That time requirement can be shortened considerably if a plan is properly prepared.

REFERENCES

1. Department of Health and Human Services (DHHS). *Standard Operating Procedures Application Process.* Washington, DC: DHHS; February 1992.

2. Department of Health and Human Services (DHHS). *Employers, HMOs and Dual Choice.* Washington, DC: DHHS; 1978.

Part VIII

Legal Issues

Deceive not thy physician, confessor, nor lawyer.

George Herbert
(1593–1633)
Jacula Prudentum (1651), 105

Chapter 36

Legal Issues in Provider Contracting

Mark S. Joffe

The business of a managed health care plan is to provide or arrange for the provision of health care services. Most managed health care plans such as health maintenance organizations (HMOs) or preferred provider organizations provide their services through arrangements with individual physicians, individual practice associations (IPAs), medical groups, hospitals, and other types of health care professionals and facilities. The provider contract formalizes the managed health care plan–provider relationship. A carefully drafted contract accomplishes more than mere memorializing of the arrangement between the parties. A well-written contract can foster a positive relationship between the provider and the managed health care plan. Moreover, a good contract can provide important and needed protections to both parties if the relationship sours.

This chapter is intended to offer to the managed health care plan and the provider a practical guide to reviewing and drafting a provider contract. In the appendices that follow the chapter are an HMO–primary care physician agreement and an HMO–hospital agreement. These con-

tracts, which have been provided solely for illustrative purposes, have been annotated by the author. Although these agreements are used by an HMO, most provisions have equal applicability to other managed care plans.

Contracts need not be complex or lengthy to be legally binding and enforceable. A single-sentence letter agreement between a hospital and a managed health care plan that says that the hospital agrees to provide access to its facility to enrollees of the managed health care plan in exchange for payment of billed charges is a valid and binding contract. The only additional language that may need to be part of a contract is a provision required under the managed health care plan's license (such as an HMO license) for inclusion in the contract (eg, a hold-harmless clause). If a single-paragraph agreement is legally binding, why is it necessary for managed health care plan–provider contracts to be so lengthy? The answer is that many terms of the contract, although not required, perform useful functions by articulating the rights and responsibilities of the parties.

An ideal contract or contract form does not exist. Appropriate contract terms vary depending on the issues of concern and objectives of the parties, each party's relative negotiating strength, and the desired degree of formality.

Mark S. Joffe is an attorney in private practice in Washington, DC, and specializes in legal and business issues affecting managed health care organizations.

Although the focus of this chapter is explaining key substantive provisions in a contract, the importance of clarity cannot be overstated. A poorly written contract confuses and misleads the parties. Lack of clarity increases substantially the likelihood of disagreements over the meaning of contract language. A contract should not only be written in simple, commonly understood language but should be well organized so that either party is able to find and review provisions as quickly and easily as possible.

The following discussion is designed to provide a workable guide for managed health care plans and providers to draft, amend, or review contracts. Much of the discussion is cast from the perspective of the managed health care plan, but the points are equally valid from the provider's perspective. Most of the discussion relates to contracts directly between the managed health care plan and the provider of services. When the contract is between the managed health care plan and an IPA or medical group, the managed health care plan needs to ensure that the areas discussed below are appropriately addressed in both the managed health care plan's contract and the contract between the IPA or medical group and the provider.

GENERAL ISSUES IN CONTRACTING

Key Objectives

The managed health care plan should divide key objectives into two categories: those that are essential and those that, although not essential, are highly desirable. Throughout the negotiations process a managed health care plan needs to keep in mind both the musts and the highly desirable objectives. Not infrequently, a managed health care plan or a provider will suddenly realize at the end of the negotiation process that it has not achieved all its basic goals. The managed health care plan's key objectives will vary. If the managed health care plan is in a community with a single provider of a particular specialty service, merely entering into a contract on any terms with the provider may be its objective. On the other hand, the managed health care plan's objectives might be quite complex, and it

may demand carefully planned negotiations to achieve them.

"Must" objectives may derive from state and federal regulations, which may require or prohibit particular clauses in contracts. Managed health care plans need to be aware of these requirements and make sure that their contracting providers understand that these provisions are required by law.

Beyond the essential objectives are the highly desirable ones. Before commencing the drafting or the negotiation of the contract, the managed health care plan should list these objectives and have a good understanding of their relative importance. This preliminary thought process assists the managed health care plan in developing its negotiating strategy.

Annual Calendar

Key provider contracts may take months to negotiate. If the contemplated arrangement with the provider is important to the managed health care plan's delivery system, the managed health care plan will want to avoid the diminution of its bargaining strength as the desired effective date approaches.

The managed health care plan should have a master schedule identifying the contracts that need to be entered into and renewed. This schedule should include time lines that identify dates by which progress on key contract negotiations should take place. Although such an orderly system may be difficult to maintain, it may protect the managed health care plan from potential problems that may arise if it is forced to operate without a contract or to negotiate from a weakened position.

Letter of Intent Compared to Contract

The purpose of a letter of intent is to define the basic elements of a contemplated arrangement or transaction between two parties. A letter of intent is used most often when the negotiation process between two parties is expected to be lengthy and expensive (eg, a major acquisition). A letter of intent is a preliminary, nonbinding agreement that allows the parties to ascertain whether they are able to agree on key terms. If the parties agree on a letter of intent, the terms of that letter serve as the blueprint for the contract. For the most part, managed health care plans do not use letters of intent for provider contracts; a letter of intent should be considered an option, however, when the contemplated arrangement is complex.

Negotiating Strategy

Negotiating strategy is determined by objectives and relative negotiating strength. Except in circumstances in which the relative negotiating strength is so one-sided that one party can dictate the terms to the other party, each party should identify for itself before beginning negotiations the negotiable issues, the party's initial position on each issue, and the extent to which it will compromise. Because a managed health care plan may use the same contract form as the contract for many providers, the managed health care plan needs to keep in mind the implications of amending one contract for the other contracts that use the same form.

A recurring theme presented at conference sessions discussing provider contracting and provider relations is the need to foster a win-win relationship, where both parties perceive that they gain from the relationship. The managed health care plan's objective should be fostering long-term, mutually satisfactory relationships with providers. When managed health care plans have enough negotiating strength to dictate the contract terms, they should exercise that strength cautiously to ensure that their short-term actions do not jeopardize their long-term goals.

CONTRACT STRUCTURE

As mentioned above, clarity is an important objective in drafting a provider contract. A key factor affecting the degree of clarity of a contract is the manner in which the agreement is organized. In fact, many managed health care plan contracts follow fairly similar formats. The contract begins with a title describing the instrument (eg, "Primary Care Physician Agreement"). After this is the caption, which identifies the names of the parties and the legal action taken, along with the transition, which contains words signifying that the parties have entered into an agreement. Then, the contract includes the recitals, which are best explained as the *whereas* clauses. These clauses are not intended to have legal significance but may become relevant to resolve inconsistencies in the body of the contract or if the drafter inappropriately includes substantive provisions in them. The use of the word *whereas* is merely tradition and has no legal significance.

The next section of the contract is the definitions section, which includes definitions of all key contract terms. The definitions section precedes the operative language, including the substantive health-related provisions that define the responsibilities and obligations of each of the parties, representations and warranties, and declarations. The last section of the contract, the closing or testimonium, reflects the assent of the parties through their signatures. Sometimes, the drafters of a provider contract decide to have the signature page on the first page for administrative simplicity.

Contracts frequently incorporate by reference other documents, some of which will be appended to the agreement as attachments or exhibits. As discussed further below, managed health care plans frequently reserve the right to amend some of these referenced documents unilaterally.

The contract's form or structure is intended to accomplish three purposes: to simplify a reader's use and understanding of the agreement, to facilitate amendment or revision of the contract where the contract form has been used for many providers, and to streamline the administrative process necessary to submit and obtain regulatory approvals.

Clarity and efficiency can be attained by using commonly understood terms, avoiding legal or technical jargon, using definitions to explain key and frequently used terms, and using well-organized headings and a numbering system. The ultimate objective is that any representative of the managed health care plan or the provider who has an interest in an issue be able to find easily the pertinent contract provision and understand its meaning.

Exhibits and appendixes are frequently used by managed health care plans to promote efficiency in administering many provider contracts. The managed health care plan, to the extent possible, could design many of its provider contracts or groups of provider contracts around a core set of common requirements. Exhibits may be used to identify the terms that may vary, such as payment rates and provider responsibilities. This approach has several advantages. First, it eases the administrative burden in drafting and revising contracts. Second, if an appendix or exhibit is the only part of the contract that is being amended and it has a separate state insurance department provider number, the managed health care plan need only submit the amendment for state review. Third, when a contract is under consideration for renewal and the key issue is the payment rate, having the payment rate listed separately in the appendix lessens the likelihood that the provider will review and suggest amending other provisions of the contract.

COMMON CLAUSES, PROVISIONS, AND KEY FACTORS

Table of Contents

Although a table of contents has no legal significance, the reader will be greatly assisted in finding pertinent sections in a long contract. One common failing in contract renegotiations is neglecting to update the table of contents after the contract has been amended.

Definitions

The definitions section of a contract plays an essential role in simplifying the structure and the reader's understanding of a contract. The body of the contract often contains complicated terms that merit amplification and explanation. The use of a definition, although requiring the reader to refer back to an earlier section for a meaning, simplifies greatly the discussion in the body of the agreement. A poorly drafted contract will define unnecessary terms or define terms in a manner that is inconsistent with their use in the body of the agreement.

Defined terms are frequently capitalized in a contract to alert the reader that the word is defined. Definitions are almost essential in many contracts, but their use may complicate the understanding of the agreement. Someone who reads a contract will first read a definition without knowing its significance. Later, when he or she reads the body of the contract, he or she may no longer recall a term's meaning. For this reason, someone reviewing a contract for the first time should read the definitions twice: initially and then in the context of each term's use. Definitions sections tend to err on the side of containing too many definitions. A term that is used only once in a contract need not be defined. On the other hand, a critical reader of a contract will identify instances in which the contract could be improved by the use of additional definitions.

An occasional defect in some contracts is that the drafter includes substantive contract provisions in definitions. A definition is merely an explanation of a meaning of a term and should not contain substantive provisions.

Terms that are commonly defined in a managed care context are *member, subscriber, medical director, provider, physician, primary care physician, emergency, medically necessary, and utilization review program*. Some of these terms, such as *medically necessary*, are crucial to readers' understanding of the parties' responsibilities and should be considered carefully in the review of a contract. The managed health care plan should ensure that these terms are consistent, if appropriate, with those in other contracts (eg, the group enrollment agreement).

Provider Obligations

Provider Services

Because the purpose of the agreement is to contract for the provision of health services, the description of those services in the contract is important. As mentioned above, the recitation of services to be furnished by the provider could be either set out in the contract or set out in an exhibit or attachment. An exhibit format frequently allows the party more flexibility and administrative simplicity when it amends the exhibited portion of the agreement, particularly when the change requires regulatory approval.

The contract needs to specify to whom the provider is obligated to furnish services. Although the answer is that the provider furnishes services to covered enrollees, the contract needs to define what is meant by a covered enrollee, explain how the provider will learn who is covered, and assign the responsibility for payment if services are furnished to a noncovered person.

Provider contracts should also cover adequately a number of other provider responsibilities, including their responsibilities to refer or to accept referrals of enrollees, the days and times of days the provider agrees to be available to provide services, and substitute on-call arrangements, if appropriate.

If the provider is a hospital, the contract will include language identifying the circumstances in which the managed health care plan agrees to be responsible or not responsible for services provided to nonemergency patients. A fairly common provision in hospital contracts states that the hospital, except in emergencies, must as a prerequisite to admit have the order of the participating physician or other preadmission authorization. The hospital contract also should have an explicit provision requiring that the managed health care plan be notified within a specified period after an emergency admission.

A good provider contract must be supplemented by a competent provider relations program to ensure that problems that arise are resolved and that the providers have a means to answer questions about their contract responsibilities.

Nondiscriminatory Requirements

Provider agreements frequently contain clauses obligating the provider to furnish services in the same manner as the provider furnishes services to nonmanaged health care patients (ie, not to discriminate on the basis of payment source). In addition, a clause is used to prohibit other types of discrimination on the basis of race, color, sex, age, religion, and national origin. A related clause that is often omitted in contracts is a provision that requires compliance with all nondiscrimination requirements under federal, state, and local law. A managed health care plan with a federal contract will violate federal law if its subcontractors violate the nondiscrimination requirements. The contract should address this potentiality. Finally, with the Americans with Disabilities Act effective, contracts should also contain provisions prohibiting discrimination on the basis of disability in accordance with the requirements of the Act.

Compliance with Utilization Review Standards and Protocols and the Quality Assurance Program

The success of the managed care organization is dependent on its providers being able and willing to control unnecessary utilization. To do so, the providers need to follow the utilization review guidelines of the managed health care plan. The contract needs to set out the provider's responsibilities in carrying out the managed health care plan's utilization review program. The managed health care plan's dilemma is how to articulate this obligation in the contract when the utilization review program may be quite detailed and frequently is updated over time. One option used by some managed care organizations is to append the utilization review program to the contract as an exhibit. A second option is merely to incorporate the program by reference. In either case, it is important for the managed health care plan to ensure that the contract allows it to amend the utilization review standards in the future without the consent of the provider. If the managed health care plan does not append a cross-referenced standard, the managed health care plan should give each provider a copy of the guidelines and any amendments. Without this documentation, the provider might argue that he or she did not agree to the guidelines or subsequent amendments.

The contract needs to inform providers of their responsibilities to cooperate in efforts by the managed health care plan to ensure compliance and the implications of the provider not meeting the guidelines.

The same basic concepts and principles apply to the provider's acceptance of the managed health care plan's quality assurance program. Some managed health care plans tend to equate their utilization review and their quality assurance programs. This attitude not only reflects a misunderstanding of the objectives of the two programs but is likely to engender the concern or criticism of government regulators who view the two programs as being separate.

The contract should include a provision requiring the provider to cooperate both in furnishing information to the managed health care plan and in taking corrective actions, if appropriate.

Acceptance of Enrollee Patients

A provider contract, particularly with a physician or physician group, will need a clause to ensure that the provider will accept enrollees regardless of health status. This provision is more important when the risk-sharing responsibilities with the providers are such that the physician has an incentive to dissuade high utilizers from becoming part of his or her panel. Most provider contracts with primary care physicians also include a minimum number of members that the physician will accept into his or her panel (eg, 250 members). The contract should also include fair and reasonable procedures for allowing the provider to limit or stop new members added to his or her panel (at a point after the provider has accepted at least the minimum number of members) and a mechanism to notify the managed health care plan when these changes take place.

Enrollee Complaints

The contract should require the provider to cooperate in resolving enrollee complaints and to notify the managed health care plan within a specified period of time when any complaints are conveyed to the provider. The provider should also be obligated to advise the managed health care plan of any coverage denials so that the managed health care plan might anticipate future enrollee complaints.

Maintenance and Retention of Records and Confidentiality

Provider contracts should require the provider to maintain both medical and business records for specified periods of time. For example, these agreements could provide that the records must

be maintained in accordance with federal and state laws and consistent with generally accepted business and professional standards as well as whatever other standards are established by the managed health care plan. If the managed health care plan participates in any public or private payer program that establishes certain specific records retention requirements, those requirements should be conveyed to the providers. The contract should state that these obligations survive the termination of the contract.

The managed health care plan also needs a legal right to have access to books and records. The contract will want to state that the managed health care plan, its representatives, and government agencies have the right to inspect, review, and make or obtain copies of medical, financial, and administrative records. The provider would want the availability of this information to be limited to services rendered to enrollees, after reasonable notice, and during normal business hours. The cost of performing these services is often an issue of controversy. If there are no fees for copying these records, the contract should so state.

In addition to the availability of books or records, the managed health care plan might also want the right to require the provider to prepare reports identifying statistical and descriptive medical and patient data and other identifying information as specified by the managed health care plan. If such a provision is included in the contract, the managed health care plan should inform the provider of the types of reports it might request to minimize any future problems. Finally, the provider should be obligated to provide information that is necessary for compliance with state or federal law.

An often neglected legal issue is how the managed health care plan obtains the authority to have access to medical records. Provider agreements periodically contain an acknowledgment by the provider that the managed health care plan is authorized to receive medical records. The problem with this approach is that the managed health care plan might not have the right to have access to this information, and, if it does not, an acknowledgment of that right in the contract has no legal effect. Some state laws give insurers and HMOs, as payers, a limited right of access to medical records. Managed health care plans should review their state law provisions on this issue and their plan's procedures for obtaining the appropriate consents of their members to have access to this information. Many managed health care plans obtain this information through signatures that are part of the initial enrollment materials. These consents could also be obtained at the time health services are rendered. Although the clause acknowledging the right of access may make it easier to persuade a reluctant provider to release an enrollee's medical records, the managed health care plan needs to remember that that statement, or for that matter similar statements in the group enrollment agreement, do not confer that right. Finally, the contract should explicitly state that the provisions concerning access to records should survive the termination of the agreement.

A related provision almost always included in provider contracts is a requirement that the provider maintain the confidentiality of medical records. A common clause is a provision that will only release the records in accordance with the terms of the contract, in accordance with applicable law, or upon appropriate consent. State law will frequently allow disclosure of information without patient identifiers for purposes of research or education. Managed health care plans and providers need to be sensitive to confidentiality concerns with regard to minors, incompetents, and persons with communicable diseases for which there are specific state confidentiality statutes governing disclosure of information.

A medical records issue may arise when a managed health care plan wants the right to perform certain medical tests outside the hospital before an enrollee's admission. The contract between the managed health care plan and the hospital may allow for such tests and the inclusion of the test results into the hospital's medical records. The hospital may insist that the results of the tests be in a format acceptable to the hospital's medical records committee, that the laboratory results be properly certified, and that the duties performed shall be consistent with the proper practice of medicine.

Payment

The payment terms of the agreement often represent the most important provision for both the provider and the managed health care plan. As mentioned earlier, the payment terms are frequently set forth in an exhibit appended to the contract and are cross-referenced in the body of the agreement. A number of payment issues should be covered in the contract. For example, who will collect the copayments? If the managed health care plan pays the provider on a fee-for-service basis, a provision needs to state that unauthorized or uncovered services are not the responsibility of the managed health care plan. From the provider's perspective, he or she needs a clear understanding of what is necessary for a service to be authorized. If the provider submits claims to the managed health care plan, the contract should set out the manner in which the claim is to be made and either identify the information to be provided in the claim or give the managed health care plan the right to designate or revise that information in the future. If the contract specifies the information to be included in a claim, the managed health care plan should also have the unilateral right to make changes in the future.

The agreement should also obligate the provider to submit claims within a specified period and the managed health care plan to pay claims within a certain number of days. The latter requirement should not apply to contested claims. Also, special provisions will apply to claims for which another carrier may be the primary payer. A common way to address this issue in a balanced manner is to allow a 2-month period for collection from the purported primary carrier. If unsuccessful, the managed health care plan would pay while awaiting resolution of the dispute.

The contract needs also to address reconciliations to account for overpayments or underpayments. To avoid these issues from lingering an inordinately long period of time, some managed health care plans limit the adjustment period to a specified time period (eg, 6 months). Also, some managed health care plans use contract provisions that do not allow for a reconciliation if the amount in controversy falls below a specified amount.

The most complex aspects of provider contracts are often the risk-sharing arrangements (see Chapter 6), particularly where several risk pools are established and distributions are determined through complicated formulas. Although the primary objective of these arrangements is to create incentives to discourage unnecessary utilization, the complexity of many of these arrangements has confused providers and engendered their distrust when their distribution falls below expectations. Some managed health care plans that had complex risk-sharing arrangements are now realizing that simpler, more understandable arrangements are preferable. If the arrangement designed by the managed health care plan is somewhat complex, the provider's understanding will be greatly enhanced by the use of examples that illustrate for providers the total payments they will receive in different factual scenarios.

In recent years, as providers gain more experience with managed health care plans, they are becoming more sophisticated in analyzing and evaluating payment arrangements and are more aware of the ability or inability of managed health care plans to produce the volume promised. A growing number of contracts are being renegotiated in light of the actual volume of patients a managed health care plan is able to deliver to the provider. Contracts are also now beginning to allow volume as a factor affecting payment amount.

Some of the payment-related issues that should be addressed in a contract are as follows: What if services are provided to a person who is no longer eligible for enrollment? What if services are provided to a nonenrollee who obtained services by using an enrollee's membership card? Who has the responsibility to pursue third-party recoveries? What are the notice requirements when the nonresponsible party finds out about a potential third-party recovery? Some managed health care plans allow their providers to collect and keep third-party recoveries, whereas others will require that the information be reported and deducted. One sensitive issue is the potential liability of a managed health care

plan if a provider collects from Medicare inappropriately when another carrier under the Medicare secondary payer rules had primary responsibility. Under the regulations of the Health Care Financing Administration (HCFA), the managed health care plan is legally responsible and may be forced to pay back the HCFA even if the payment was received by the provider without the knowledge of the managed health care plan. Managed health care plans should include a contract provision transferring the liability to the provider in this circumstance.

Another issue that should be addressed in the contract is the responsibility of the managed health care plan as a secondary carrier if the provider bills the primary carrier an amount greater than the amount the provider would have received from the managed health care plan. From the managed health care plan's perspective, it will want a contract provision relieving the managed health care plan of any payment responsibility if the provider has received at least the amount he or she would have been entitled to under the managed health care plan–provider contract.

Hold-Harmless and No Balance Billing Clauses

Virtually all provider contracts contain a hold-harmless clause under which the provider agrees not to sue or assert any claims against the enrollee for services covered under the contract, even if the managed health care plan becomes insolvent or fails to meet its obligations. A no balance billing clause is similar (and may be used synonymously) and states that a provider may not balance bill a member for any payment owed by the plan, regardless of the reason for nonpayment; the provider may bill the member for any amount that the member is required to pay, such as copayment or coinsurance, or for services not covered under the schedule of benefits (eg, cosmetic surgery). Many state insurance departments (or other agencies having regulatory oversight in this area) will not approve the provider forms without inclusion of a hold-harmless clause with specific language. The HCFA also has adopted recommended model hold-harmless language applicable to federally qualified HMOs that was approved by the National Association of Insurance Commissioners.

Relationship of the Parties

Provider contracts usually contain a provision stating that the managed health care plan and the provider have an independent contractual arrangement. The purpose for this provision is to refute an assertion that the provider serves as an employee of the managed health care plan. The reason is that under the legal theory of respondeat superior the managed health care plan would automatically be liable for the negligent acts of its employees. Although managed health care plans frequently include a provision such as this in their provider contracts, it has limited value. In a lawsuit against the managed health care plan by an enrollee alleging malpractice, the court is likely to disregard such language and to focus on the relationship between the managed health care plan and the provider and the manner in which the managed health care plan represented the provider in evaluating whether the managed health care plan should be vicariously liable.

A related clause frequently used in provider contracts states that nothing contained in the agreement shall be construed to require physicians to recommend any procedure or course of treatment that physicians deem professionally inappropriate. This clause is intended, in part, to affirm that the managed health care plan is not engaged in the practice of medicine, an activity that the managed health care plan may not be permitted to perform. Another reason for this clause is to protect the managed health care plan from liability arising from a provider's negligence.

Use of Name

Many provider contracts limit the ability of either party to use the name of the other. This is done by identifying the circumstances in which the party's name may or may not be used. Contract clauses may allow the managed health care plan the right to use the name of the provider for the health benefits accounts, the enrollees, and the patients of the participating providers. Otherwise the party needs the written approval of the other party. The use applies not only to the name but to any symbol, trademark, and service mark of the entity. The managed health care plan and the provider will want to ensure that proprietary information is protected. The contract should require that the provider keep all information about the managed health care plan confidential and prohibit the use of the information for any competitive purpose after the contract is terminated. With medical groups frequently switching managed care affiliations, this protection is important to the managed health care plan.

Notification

The managed health care plan needs to ensure that it is advised of a number of important changes that affect the ability of the provider to meet his or her contractual obligations. The contract should identify the information that needs to be conveyed to the managed health care plan and the time frames for providing that information. For example, a physician might be required to notify a managed health care plan within 5 days upon loss or suspension of his or her license or certification, loss or restriction of full active admitting privileges at any hospital, or issuance of any formal charges brought by a government agency. Although specific events should be identified in the contract, a broad catch-all category should also be included, such as an event that if sustained would materially impair the provider's ability to perform the duties under the contract.

In a hospital contract, the corresponding provisions would be when the hospital suffers from a change that materially impairs its ability to provide services or if action is taken against it regarding certifications, licenses, or federal agencies or private accrediting bodies.

Insurance and Indemnification

Insurance provisions in contracts are fairly straightforward. The managed health care plan wants to ensure that the provider has resources to pay for any eventuality. The contract will state particular insurance limits, provide that the limits will be set forth in a separate attachment, or leave it up to the managed health care plan to specify. A hospital agreement may require only that the limits be commensurate with limits contained in polices of similar hospitals in the state. There also should be a provision requiring the provider to notify the managed health care plan of any notification of cancelations of the policy. Another needed notification in a physician context is notification of any malpractice claims.

Cross-indemnification provisions in which each party indemnifies the other for damages caused by the other party are common in contracts. One weakness of the clause is that some professional liability carriers will not pay for claims arising from these clauses because of general exclusions in their policies for contractual claims. Although these clauses are frequently used, this limitation and the fact that a provider should still be liable for his or her negligent acts suggest that these indemnification clauses are not essential.

Term, Suspension, and Termination

One section of most contracts identifies the term of the contract and the term of any subsequent contract renewals. Many contracts have automatic renewal provisions if no party exercises its right to terminate. Both managed health care plans and providers should give careful thought to these issues: the length of the contract and the renewal periods.

Some contracts give a right of suspension to the managed health care plan. In suspension, the contract continues, but the provider loses specific rights. For example, if a provider fails to follow utilization review protocols a specified number of times, the provider will not be assigned new HMO members or perhaps will receive a reduction in the amount of payment. The advantage of a suspension provision is that total termination of a contract might be counterproductive for the managed health care plan, but a suspension might be sufficiently punitive to persuade the provider to improve.

Termination provisions fall into two categories: termination without cause, and termination with cause. The value of having a provision that allows the managed health care plan to terminate without cause is that the managed health care plan need not defend a challenge by the provider on the substantive issue of whether the grounds were met. A 90-day period is fairly common. If the managed health care plan has the right to terminate without cause, frequently the provider will also be given that right. A regulatory issue to be aware of is that some state laws require providers to continue to provide services for a specified period of time after their contract has terminated. These requirements relate to the state's requirements for the managed health care plan to have protections against insolvency and have to be reflected in the contract.

Terminations with cause allow the health plan to terminate faster and should be used in situations where the managed health care plan needs to act quickly. The contract might establish two different categories: one for immediate termination and another for termination within a 30-day period. Many contracts give either party a period of time to cure any contract violations. This time period, although useful to the managed health care plan if it has allegedly violated the agreement, extends the period of time in which it can terminate the contract. Grounds for termination for cause may be suspension or revocation of license, loss of hospital privileges, failure to meet accreditation and credentialing requirements, failure to provide services to enrollees in a professionally acceptable manner, and refusal to accept an amendment to the contract agreement. A general clause also allows for termination if the provider takes any actions or makes any communications that undermine or could undermine the confidence of enrollees in the quality of care provided by the managed health care plan.

The contract should be clear that a provider, upon termination, is required to cooperate in the orderly transfer of enrollee care, including records, to other providers. The provider also should cooperate in resolving any disputes. Finally, the provider should continue to furnish services until the services being rendered to enrollees are complete or the managed health care plan has made appropriate provisions for another provider to assume the responsibility. The contract should also be clear that the provider is entitled to compensation for performing these services. In general, too little consideration has been given to preparing for contract terminations. When the provider and the managed health care plan enter into a contract, little thought is given to what will occur when the contract ends. Often, relationships end acrimoniously, and it is in both parties' best interest to consider how their interests will be protected in the event the contract is terminated.

Declarations

In declarations, the parties provide answers to a number of "what if" questions. These clauses are common to all contracts.

A force majeure clause relieves a party of responsibility if an event occurs beyond its control. In a provider contract this instance is more likely to arise if the provider is no longer able to provide services. In considering force majeure clauses, the parties need to distinguish between events that are beyond a party's control and those that disadvantage a party but for which the party should still be obligated to perform the contract's responsibilities.

A choice of law provision identifies the law that will apply in the event of a dispute. Absent a violation of public policy in the state in question, a court will apply the agreed-upon law. Frequently, lawyers draft contracts using the state in which their client is located without consideration of the advantages and disadvantages of the underlying law. In provider contracts where the managed health care plan and the provider are located in the same state, this clause has little relevance.

A merger clause specifies that only the language in the agreement shall constitute the contract. Such a clause prevents a party from arguing that oral conversations or other documents not included in the contract modify the contract's terms.

A provision allowing or not allowing parties to assign their rights is frequently included in contracts. Provider contracts usually prohibit a provider from assigning its rights under a contract. Some contracts are silent on the right of the managed health care plan to assign the contract. Silence would allow the managed health care plan to assign the contract. An option is to allow the managed health care plan to assign the contract only to an affiliate or a successor without the written consent of the provider.

A clause identifying how the contract will be amended is almost always included in a provider contract. A contract will frequently give the managed health care plan the unilateral right to amend the contract absent an objection by the provider. This procedure is necessary when the managed health care plan has a large provider panel and it is administratively difficult to obtain the signatures of all the providers.

A severability clause allows the contract to continue if a court invalidates a portion of the contract. This is a common provision in a contract, but it is unlikely that the problem will arise.

Contracts also set forth a notice requirement identifying how notices are provided to parties and to whom. The manner in which notice is provided is important. If a notice requires that the communication be conveyed by certified mail with return receipt requested, an alternative form of delivery is not valid. Parties should consider what is administratively feasible before agreeing on how notice will be given.

Closing

Both parties need to confirm that the parties identified at the beginning of the contract are the parties that sign the contract. Also, if a corporation is one of the parties, the signatory needs to be authorized on behalf of the corporation to sign the agreement.

CONCLUSION

The provider contract establishes the foundation for the working relationship between the managed health care plan and the provider. A good contract is well organized and clearly written and accurately reflects the full intentions of the parties. In drafting and reviewing provider contracts, the managed health care plan and the provider need to keep in mind their objectives in entering the relationship, the relationship of this contract to other provider contracts and agreements, and applicable regulatory requirements.

The appendixes to this chapter contain two sample provider contracts. The author has annotated each contract to point out strengths and weaknesses of the provisions. These two contracts are provided for illustrative purposes and are not represented as ideal agreements.

AGREEMENT BETWEEN

_____

AND
PRIMARY CARE PHYSICIAN

THIS AGREEMENT, made and entered into the date set forth on the signature page hereto, by and between _____, Inc, a _____ corporation (hereinafter referred to as "HMO"), which is organized and operated as a health maintenance organization under the laws of the State of _____ and the individual physician or group practice identified on the signature page hereto (hereinafter referred to as "Primary Care Physician").

WHEREAS, HMO desires to operate a health maintenance organization pursuant to the laws of the State of _____;

WHEREAS, Primary Care Physician is a duly licensed physician (or if Primary Care Physician is a legal entity, the members of such entity are duly licensed physicians) in the State of _____, whose license(s) is (are) without limitation or restriction;[1] and

WHEREAS, HMO has as an objective the development and expansion of cost-effective means of delivering quality health services to Members, as defined herein, particularly through prepaid health care plans, and Primary Care Physician concurs in, actively supports, and will contribute to the achievement of this objective; and

WHEREAS, HMO and Primary Care Physician mutually desire to enter into an Agreement whereby the Primary Care Physician shall provide and coordinate the health care services to Members of HMO.

---

[1]Although there is nothing wrong with having a statement here that the primary care physician's license is not restricted, the body of the contract, as is the case in this contract in Section IV.H, needs to contain this requirement and provide that the failure to maintain the license is grounds for termination.

NOW, THEREFORE, in consideration of the premises and mutual covenants herein contained and other good and valuable consideration, it is mutually covenanted and agreed by and between the parties hereto as follows:

PART I.   DEFINITIONS

A. *Covered Services* means those health services and benefits to which Members are entitled under the terms of an applicable Health Maintenance Certificate which may be amended by HMO from time to time.[2]

B. *Emergency Services* means those Medically Necessary services provided in connection with an "Emergency," defined as a sudden or unexpected onset of a condition requiring medical or surgical care which the Member secures after the onset of such condition (or as soon thereafter as care can be made available but which in any case not later than twenty-four (24) hours after onset) and in the absence of such care the Member could reasonably be expected to suffer serious physical impairment or death. Heart attacks, severe chest pain, cardiovascular accidents, hemorrhaging, poisonings, major burns, loss of consciousness, serious breathing difficulties, spinal injuries, shock, and other acute conditions as HMO shall determine are Emergencies.[3]

C. *Encounter Form* means a record of services provided by Physician to Members in a format acceptable to the HMO.[4]

D. *Health Maintenance Certificate* means a contract issued by HMO to a Member or an employer of Members specifying the services and benefits available under the HMO's prepaid health benefits program.

E. *Health Professionals* means doctors of medicine, doctors of osteopathy, dentists, nurses, chiropractors, podiatrists, optometrists, physician assistants, clinical psychologists, social workers, pharmacists, occupational therapists, physical therapists, and other professionals engaged in the delivery of health services who are licensed, practice under an institutional license, and are certified or practice under other authority consistent with the laws of the State of _____.

F. *Medical Director* means a Physician designated by HMO to monitor and review the provision of Covered Services to Members.

G. *Medically Necessary* services and/or supplies means the use of services or supplies as provided by a hospital, skilled nursing facility, Physician or other provider required to identify or treat a Member's illness or injury and which, as determined by HMO's Medical Director or its utilization review committee, are: (1) consistent with the symptoms or diagnosis and treatment of the Member's condition, disease, ailment or injury; (2) appropriate with regard to standards of good medical practice; (3) not solely for the convenience of the Member, his or her physician, hospital, or other health care provider; and (4) the most appropriate supply or level of service which

---

[2]This definition notes the HMO's right to revise the covered services that the primary care physician is required to provide. If the physicians were capitated for those services, a mechanism would need to be available to revise the capitation rate accordingly. If the services were not limited to HMO enrollees [eg, covered persons under an administrative services only (ASO) arrangement with a self-insured employer], this definition would have to be written more broadly.

[3]The definition for emergency services would be coordinated with the definition used in the HMO's group enrollment agreement. The examples are a useful method of illustrating the types of conditions that are considered emergencies. Some contracts will exclude deliveries during the last month of pregnancy while the mother is traveling outside the service area.

[4]By stating that the encounter form must be acceptable to the HMO, the contract allows the HMO to change its requirements in the future.

can be safely provided to the Member.[5] When specifically applied to an inpatient Member, it further means that the Member's medical symptoms or condition requires that the diagnosis or treatment cannot be safely provided to the Member as an outpatient.[6]

H. *Member* means both a Subscriber and his or her eligible family members for whom premium payment has been made.[7]

I. *Participating Physician* means a Physician who, at the time of providing or authorizing services to a Member, has contracted with or on whose behalf a contract has been entered into with HMO to provide professional services to Members.

J. *Participating Provider* means a Physician, hospital, skilled nursing facility, home health agency or any other duly licensed institution or Health Professional under contract with HMO to provide professional and hospital services to Members.

K. *Physician* means a duly licensed doctor of medicine or osteopathy.

L. *Primary Care Physician* means a Participating Physician who provides primary care services to Members (eg, general or family practitioner, internist, pediatrician or such other physician specialty as may be designated by HMO) and is responsible for referrals of Members to Referral Physicians, other Participating Providers and if necessary non-Participating Providers. Each Member shall select or have selected on his or her behalf a Primary Care Physician.

M. *Referral Physician* means a Participating Physician who is responsible for providing certain medical referral physician services upon referral by a Primary Care Physician.

N. *Service Area* means those counties in _____ set forth in Attachment A and such other areas as may be designated by HMO from time to time.

O. *Subscriber* means an individual who has contracted, or on whose behalf a contract has been entered into, with HMO for health care services.

PART II.   OBLIGATIONS OF HMO

A. *Administrative Procedures.* HMO shall make available to Primary Care Physician a manual of administrative procedures (including any changes thereto) in the areas of recordkeeping, reporting, and other administrative duties of the Primary Care Physician under this Agreement. Primary Care Physician agrees to abide by such administrative procedures including, but not limited to, the submission of HMO Encounter Forms documenting all Covered Services provided to Members by Primary Care Physician.[8]

B. *Compensation.* For all Medically Necessary Covered Services provided to Members by Primary Care Physician, HMO shall pay to Primary Care Physician the compensation set forth in Attachment B.[9] Itemized statements on HMO Encounter Forms, or approved equivalent, for all Cov-

---

[5]This clause gives the HMO the authority to deny coverage for a medically appropriate procedure where another procedure is also appropriate. Although this clause does not explicitly address the subject, it is intended to give the HMO the right to cover the most cost-effective, medically appropriate procedure. An alternative way of addressing the issue is to state explicitly as one of the criteria that the procedure performed is the least costly setting or manner appropriate to treat the enrollee's medical condition.

[6]This last sentence is a good addition to the definition. It makes clear the preference of outpatient care over inpatient care.

[7]*Member* is usually regarded as synonymous with *enrollee*. The definition of *member* should be consistent with the definition used in the group enrollment agreement.

[8]This paragraph allows the HMO to designate and amend the information, including the claims form, that the primary care physician provides the HMO without obtaining the prior approval of the primary care physician.

[9]This contract reimburses primary care physicians on a fee-for-service basis. Attachment B also sets forth alternative language if an HMO pays its primary care physicians on a capitated basis.

ered Services rendered by Primary Care Physician must be submitted to HMO within ninety (90) days of the date the service was rendered in order to be compensated by HMO. The purpose of the risk sharing/incentive compensation arrangement set forth in Attachment B is to monitor utilization, control costs of health services, including hospitalization, and to achieve utilization goals while maintaining quality of care.

C. *Processing of Claims.* HMO agrees to process Primary Care Physician claims for Covered Services rendered to Members. HMO will make payment within thirty (30) days from the date the claim is received with sufficient documentation. Where a claim requires additional documentation, HMO will make payment within thirty (30) days from date of receipt of sufficient documentation to approve the claim.[10]

D. *Eligibility Report.* HMO shall provide Primary Care Physician with a monthly listing of eligible Members who have selected or have been assigned to Primary Care Physician.

E. *Reports.* HMO will provide Primary Care Physician with periodic statements with respect to the compensation set forth in Attachment B and with utilization reports in accordance with HMO's administrative procedures. Primary Care Physician agrees to maintain the confidentiality of the information presented in such reports.

PART III.   OBLIGATIONS OF PRIMARY CARE PHYSICIAN

A. *Health Services.* Primary Care Physician shall have the primary responsibility for arranging and coordinating the overall health care of Members, including appropriate referral to Participating Physicians and Participating Providers, and for managing and coordinating the performance of administrative functions relating to the delivery of health services to Members in accordance with this Agreement. In the event that Primary Care Physician shall provide Member non-Covered Services, Primary Care Physician shall, prior to the provision of such non-Covered Services, inform the Member:

1. of the service(s) to be provided,
2. that HMO will not pay for or be liable for said services, and
3. that Member will be financially liable for such services.[11]

For any health care services rendered to or authorized for Members by Primary Care Physician for which HMO's prior approval is required and such prior approval was not obtained, Primary Care Physician agrees that in no event will HMO assume financial responsibility for charges arising from such services, and payments made by HMO for such services may be deducted by HMO from payments otherwise due Primary Care Physician.[12]

B. *Referrals.* Except in Emergencies or when authorized by HMO, Primary Care Physician agrees to make referrals of Members only to Participating Providers, and only in accordance with HMO policies. Primary Care Physician will furnish such Physicians and providers complete information on treatment procedures and diagnostic tests performed prior to such referral. Upon referral, Primary Care Physician agrees to notify HMO of referral. In the event that services required by a Member are not available from Participating Providers, non-Participating Physi-

---

[10]This paragraph allows the HMO to delay payment to the physician while waiting for sufficient documentation.

[11]This prior notification requirement is an important requirement and often required by state law.

[12]It is important for the HMO to make sure that the physicians know the circumstances or conditions for which prior HMO approval is required.

cians or Providers may be utilized with the prior approval of HMO. HMO will periodically furnish Primary Care Physician with a current listing of HMO's Participating Referral Physicians and Participating Providers.

C. *Hospital Admissions.* In cases where a Member requires a non-Emergency hospital admission, Primary Care Physician agrees to secure authorization for such admission in accordance with HMO's procedures prior to the admission. In addition, the Primary Care Physician agrees to abide by HMO hospital discharge policies and procedures for Members.[13]

D. *Primary Care Physician's Members.* The Primary Care Physician shall not refuse to accept a Member as a patient on the basis of health status or medical condition of such Member, except with the approval of the Medical Director. Primary Care Physician may request that he/she does not wish to accept additional Members (excluding persons already in Primary Care Physician's practice that enroll in HMO as Members) by giving HMO written notice of such intent thirty (30) days in advance of the effective date of such closure. Primary Care Physician agrees to accept any HMO Members seeking his/her services during the thirty (30) day notice period. Primary Care Physician agrees to initiate closure of his/her practice to additional Members only if his/her practice, as a whole, is to be closed to additional patients or if authorized by HMO. A request for such authorization shall not be unreasonably denied. HMO may suspend, upon thirty (30) days prior written notice to Primary Care Physician, any further selection of Primary Care Physician by Members who have not already sought Primary Care Physician's services at the time of such suspension.

In addition, a physician who is a Participating Provider may request, in writing to HMO, that coverage for a Member be transferred to another Participating Physician. Participating Physician shall not seek without authorization by HMO to have a Member transferred because of the amount of services required by the Member or because of the health status of the Member.

E. *Charges to Members.* Primary Care Physician shall accept as payment in full, for services which he/she provides, the compensation specified in Attachment B. Primary Care Physician agrees that in no event, including, but not limited to, non-payment, HMO insolvency or breach of this Agreement, shall Physician bill, charge, collect a deposit from, seek compensation, remuneration or reimbursement from, or have any recourse against Subscriber, Member, or persons other than the HMO acting on a Member's behalf for services provided pursuant to this Agreement. This provision shall not prohibit collection of copayments on HMO's behalf made in accordance with the terms of the Health Maintenance Certificate between HMO and Subscriber/Member. Primary Care Physician further agrees that:

1. this provision shall survive the termination of this Agreement regardless of the cause giving rise to termination and shall be construed to be for the benefit of the HMO Member, and that

2. this provision supersedes any oral or written contrary agreement now existing or hereafter entered into between Primary Care Physician and Member, or persons acting on their behalf.[14]

F. *Records and Reports.*

1. Primary Care Physician shall submit to HMO for each Member encounter an HMO Encounter Form which shall contain such statistical and descriptive medical and patient data as

---

[13]Here, again, it is important for the HMO to ensure that the primary care physicians have full notice of all the requirements for prior authorization and discharges.

[14]State regulatory agencies often dictate the precise language of this clause.

specified by HMO. Primary Care Physician shall maintain such records and provide such medical, financial and administrative information to HMO as the HMO determines may be necessary for compliance by HMO with state and federal law, as well as for program management purposes. Primary Care Physician will further provide to HMO and, if required, to authorized state and federal agencies, such access to medical records of HMO Members as is needed to assure the quality of care rendered to such Members. HMO shall have access at reasonable times, upon request, to the billing and medical records of the Primary Care Physician relating to the health care services provided Members, and to information on the cost of such services, and on copayments received by the Primary Care Physician from Members for Covered Services. Utilization and cost data relating to a Participating Physician may be distributed by HMO to other Participating Physicians for HMO program management purposes.

2. HMO shall also have the right to inspect, at reasonable times, Primary Care Physician's facilities pursuant to HMO's credentialing, peer review and quality assurance program.

3. Primary Care Physician shall maintain a complete medical record for each Member in accordance with the requirements established by HMO. Medical records of Members will include the recording of services provided by the Primary Care Physician, specialists, hospitals, and other reports from referral providers, discharge summaries, records of Emergency care received by the Member, and such other information as HMO requires.[15] Medical records of Members shall be treated as confidential so as to comply with all federal and state laws and regulations regarding the confidentiality of patient records.[16]

G. *Provision of Services and Professional Requirements.*

1. Primary Care Physician shall make necessary and appropriate arrangements to assure the availability of physician services to his/her Member patients on a twenty-four (24) hours per day, seven (7) days per week basis, including arrangements to assure coverage of his/her Member patients after-hours or when Primary Care Physician is otherwise absent, consistent with HMO's administrative requirements. Primary Care Physician agrees that scheduling of appointments for Members shall be done in a timely manner. The Primary Care Physician will maintain weekly appointment hours which are sufficient and convenient to serve Members and will maintain at all times Emergency and on-call services. Covering arrangements shall be with another Physician who is also a Participating Provider or who has otherwise been approved in advance by HMO. For services rendered by any covering Physician on behalf of Primary Care Physician, including Emergency Services, it shall be Primary Care Physician's sole responsibility to make suitable arrangements with the covering Physician regarding the manner in which said Physician will be reimbursed or otherwise compensated, provided, however, that Primary Care Physician shall assure that the covering Physician will not, under any circumstances, bill HMO or bill Member for Covered Services (except copayments), and Primary Care Physician hereby agrees to indemnify and hold harmless Members and HMO against charges for Covered Services rendered by physicians who are covering on behalf of Primary Care Physician.

---

[15]This paragraph contains an important requirement. The primary care physician serves as a gatekeeper and the coordinator of care for this HMO. To serve this function, the primary care physician needs information from referral providers. There, of course, needs to be a requirement in the contracts with referral physicians that this information be provided to the applicable primary care physician.

[16]For this sentence to be effective, the HMO needs to ensure that its staff and the primary care physician understand state and federal confidentiality laws. Special requirements often arise in some areas, such as for acquired immunodeficiency syndrome and mental health and substance abuse services.

2. Primary Care Physician agrees:

    (a) not to discriminate in the treatment of his/her patients or in the quality of services delivered to HMO's Members on the basis of race, sex, age, religion, place of residence, health status, disability, or source of payment, and

    (b) to observe, protect and promote the rights of Members as patients. Primary Care Physician shall not seek to transfer a Member from his/her practice based on the Member's health status, without authorization by HMO.

3. Primary Care Physician agrees that all duties performed hereunder shall be consistent with the proper practice of medicine, and that such duties shall be performed in accordance with the customary rules of ethics and conduct of the applicable state and professional licensure boards and agencies.

4. Primary Care Physician agrees that to the extent he/she utilizes allied Health Professionals and other personnel for delivery of health care, he/she will inform HMO of the functions performed by such personnel.

5. Primary Care Physician shall be duly licensed to practice medicine in _____ and shall maintain good professional standing at all times. Evidence of such licensing shall be submitted to HMO upon request. In addition, Primary Care Physician must meet all qualifications and standards for membership on the medical staff of at least one of the hospitals, if any, which have contracted with HMO and shall be required to maintain staff membership and full admission privileges in accordance with the rules and regulations of such hospital and be otherwise acceptable to such hospital. Finally, Primary Care Physician shall be a duly qualified provider under the Medicare program. Physician agrees to give immediate notice to HMO in the case of suspension or revocation, or initiation of any proceeding that could result in suspension or revocation, of his/her licensure, hospital privileges, or Medicare qualification status or the filing of a malpractice action against the Primary Care Physician.

H. *Insurance.* Primary Care Physician, including individual Physicians providing services to Members under this Agreement if Primary Care Physician is a legal entity, shall provide and maintain such policies of general and professional liability (malpractice) insurance as shall be necessary to insure the Primary Care Physician and his/her employees against any claim or claims for damages arising by reason of personal injuries or death occasioned, directly or indirectly, in connection with the performance of any service by Primary Care Physician. The amounts and extent of such insurance coverage shall be subject to the approval of HMO. Primary Care Physician shall provide memorandum copies of such insurance coverage to HMO upon request.[17]

I. *Administration.*

1. Primary Care Physician agrees to cooperate and participate in such review and service programs as may be established by HMO, including utilization and quality assurance programs, credentialing, sanctioning, external audit systems, administrative procedures, and Member and Physician grievance procedures. Primary Care Physician shall comply with all determinations rendered through the above programs.

2. Primary Care Physician agrees that HMO may use his/her name, address, phone number, picture, type of practice, applicable practice restrictions, and an indication of Primary Care Physician's willingness to accept additional Members, in HMO's roster of physician participants and other HMO materials. Primary Care Physician shall not reference HMO in any

---

[17]The HMO should have this insurance information on file. Thus the HMO, as a matter of course, should request this information and require notification of changes in the insurance coverage.

publicity, advertisements, notices, or promotional material or in any announcement to the Members without prior review and written approval of HMO.

3. Primary Care Physician agrees to provide to HMO information for the collection and coordination of benefits when a Member holds other coverage that is deemed primary for the provision of services to said Member and to abide by HMO coordination of benefits and duplicate coverage policies. This shall include, but not be limited to, permitting HMO to bill and process forms for any third party payor on the Primary Care Physician's behalf for Covered Services and to retain any sums received. In addition, Primary Care Physician shall cooperate in and abide by HMO subrogation policies and procedures.

4. Primary Care Physician agrees to maintain the confidentiality of all information related to fees, charges, expenses, and utilization derived from, through, or provided by HMO.

5. In the event of:

   (a) termination of this Agreement,

   (b) the selection by a Member of another Primary Care Physician in accordance with HMO procedures, or

   (c) the approval by HMO of Primary Care Physician's request to transfer a Member from his/her practice,

   Primary Care Physician agrees to transfer copies of the Member's medical records, X-rays, or other data to HMO when requested to do so in writing by HMO, at the reasonable, customary and usual fee for such copies.

6. In the event that this Agreement is terminated by either HMO or Primary Care Physician, Primary Care Physician shall return to HMO any and all materials used by Primary Care Physician in the provision of services to HMO Members. Upon termination of the Agreement, the Primary Care Physician shall not use any information obtained during the course of the Agreement in furtherance of any competitors of the HMO.

7. Primary Care Physician warrants and represents that all information and statements given to HMO in applying for or maintaining his/her HMO Primary Care Physician Agreement are true, accurate and complete. The HMO Physician application shall be incorporated by reference into this Agreement. Any inaccurate or incomplete information or misrepresentation of information provided by Primary Care Physician may result in the immediate termination of the Agreement by HMO.

8. Primary Care Physician shall cooperate with HMO in complying with applicable laws relating to HMO.

PART IV. MISCELLANEOUS

A. *Modification of This Agreement.* This Agreement may be amended or modified in writing as mutually agreed upon by the parties. In addition, HMO may modify any provision of this Agreement upon thirty (30) days prior written notice to Primary Care Physician. Primary Care Physician shall be deemed to have accepted HMO's modification if Primary Care Physician fails to object to such modification, in writing, within the thirty (30) day notice period.[18]

B. *Interpretation.* This Agreement shall be governed in all respects by the laws of the State of _____. The invalidity or unenforceability of any terms or conditions hereof shall in no way

---

[18]This is a common provision and useful in simplifying the administrative work associated with amending the agreement. Needless to say, it is important for the HMO to explain clearly the nature of the amendment to the primary care physician.

affect the validity or enforceability of any other terms or provisions. The waiver by either party of a breach or violation of any provision of this Agreement shall not operate as or be construed to be a waiver of any subsequent breach thereof.

C. *Assignment.* This Agreement, being intended to secure the services of and be personal to the Primary Care Physician, shall not be assigned, sublet, delegated or transferred by Primary Care Physician without the prior written consent of HMO.

D. *Notice.* Any notice required to be given pursuant to the terms and provisions hereof shall be sent by certified mail, return receipt requested, postage prepaid, to HMO or to the Primary Care Physician at the respective addresses indicated herein. Notice shall be deemed to be effective when mailed, but notice of change of address shall be effective upon receipt.[19]

E. *Relationship of Parties.* None of the provisions of this Agreement is intended to create nor shall be deemed or construed to create any relationship between the parties hereto other than that of independent entities contracting with each other hereunder solely for the purpose of effecting the provisions of this Agreement. Neither of the parties hereto, nor any of their respective employees, shall be construed to be the agent, employer, employee or representative of the other, nor will either party have an express or implied right of authority to assume or create any obligation or responsibility on behalf of or in the name of the other party. Neither Primary Care Physician nor HMO shall be liable to any other party for any act, or any failure to act, of the other party to this Agreement.

F. *Gender.* The use of any gender herein shall be deemed to include the other gender where applicable.

G. *Legal Entity.* If Primary Care Physician is a legal entity, an application for each Physician who is a member of such entity must be submitted to and accepted by HMO before such Physician may serve as a Primary Care Physician under this Agreement.

H. *Term and Termination.* The term of this Agreement shall be for three (3) years from the "effective date" set forth on the signature page. This Agreement may be terminated by either party at any time without cause by prior written notice given at least sixty (60) days in advance of the effective date of such termination. This Agreement may also be terminated by HMO effective immediately upon written notice if Primary Care Physician's (or if a legal entity, any of the entity's physicians') medical license, Medicare qualification or hospital privileges are suspended, limited, restricted or revoked, or if Primary Care Physician violates Part III(E), (G)(3), (G)(5), (H), (I)(1) or (I)(4) herein. Upon termination, the rights of each party hereunder shall terminate, provided, however, that such action shall not release the Primary Care Physician or HMO from their obligations with respect to:

1. payments accrued to the Primary Care Physician prior to termination;

2. the Primary Care Physician's agreement not to seek compensation from Members for Covered Services provided prior to termination; and

3. completion of treatment of Members then receiving care until continuation of the Member's care can be arranged by HMO.

In the event of termination, no distribution of any money accruing to Primary Care Physician under the provisions of Attachment B shall be made until the regularly scheduled date for such

---

[19]Before adopting this paragraph, an HMO should consider whether it is necessary to require that all notifications be sent by certified mail, return receipt requested. If the HMO has a large provider panel, it might prefer the right to send information by regular mail.

distributions. Upon termination, HMO is empowered and authorized to notify Members and prospective Members, other Primary Care Physicians, and other persons or entities whom it deems to have an interest herein of such termination, through such means as it may choose.

In the event of notice of termination, HMO may notify Members of such fact and assign Members or require Members to select another Primary Care Physician prior to the effective date of termination. In any event, HMO shall continue to compensate Primary Care Physician until the effective date of termination as provided herein for those Members who, because of health reasons, cannot be assigned or make such selection during the notice of termination period and as provided by HMO's Medical Director.

IN WITNESS WHEREOF, the foregoing Agreement between _____ and **Primary Care Physician**, is entered into by and between the undersigned parties, to be effective this ____ day of _____, 19___.

PRIMARY CARE PHYSICIAN

_____

_____

By: _____

(Name of Individual Physician
or of Group Practice—Please
Print)

_____

(Mailing Address)

_____

(Date)

_____

(City, State, ZIP)

_____

(Telephone Number)

_____

(Taxpayor Identification Number)

_____

(DEA#)

_____

(Signature)

_____

(Name and Title if signing as authorized
representative of Group Practice)

_____

(Date)

ATTACHMENT B
COMPENSATION SCHEDULE
PRIMARY CARE PHYSICIAN AGREEMENT

I. Services Rendered by Physicians

For Covered Services provided by Primary Care Physician in accordance with the terms of this Agreement, HMO shall pay Primary Care Physician his/her Reimbursement Allowance, less any applicable copayment for which the Member is responsible under the applicable Health Maintenance Certificate, and less the Withhold Amount, as described below. "Reimbursement Allowance" shall mean the lower of (i) the usual and customary fee charged by Primary Care Physician for the Covered Service, or (ii) the maximum amount allowed under the fee limits established by HMO.

II. Withholds from Reimbursement Allowance

HMO shall withhold from each payment to Primary Care Physician a percentage of the Reimbursement Allowance ("Withhold Amount") and shall allocate an amount equal to such withhold to an HMO Risk Fund. HMO shall have the right, at its sole discretion, to modify the percentage withheld from Primary Care Physician if, in its judgment, the financial condition, operations or commitments of the HMO or its expenses for particular health services or for services by any particular Participating Providers warrant such modification.

III. Withhold Amount Distributions

HMO may, at its sole discretion, from time to time distribute to Primary Care Physician Withhold Amounts retained by HMO from payments to Primary Care Physician, plus such additional amounts, if any, that HMO may deem appropriate as a financial incentive to the provision of cost-effective health care services. HMO may, from time to time, commit or expend Withhold Amounts, in whole or in part, to assure the financial stability of or commitments of the HMO or health care plans or payors with or for which the HMO has an agreement to arrange for the provision of health care services, or to satisfy budgetary or financial objectives established by HMO.

Subject to HMO's peer review procedures and policies, a Primary Care Physician may be excluded from any distribution if he/she does not qualify for such distribution, for example, if he/she has exceeded HMO utilization standards or criteria. No Primary Care Physician shall have any entitlement to any funds in the HMO Risk Fund.

IV. Accounting

Primary Care Physician shall be entitled to an accounting of Withhold Amounts from payments to him/her upon written request to HMO.

ATTACHMENT B (ALTERNATE)
CAPITATION PAYMENT
PRIMARY CARE PHYSICIAN AGREEMENT

Compensation

I. Capitation Allocation

The total monthly amounts paid to Primary Care Physician will be determined as follows:

For each Member selecting Primary Care Physician ("selecting" also includes Members assigned to a Primary Care Physician), 90 percent of the monthly Primary Care Service capitation set forth below for Primary Care Services shall be paid by HMO to Primary Care Physician by the 5th day of the following month. The capitation shall be set according to the particular benefit plan in which each Member is enrolled. Where the capitation is not currently adjusted for age and/or sex, HMO reserves the right to make such age and/or sex adjustment to the capitation rates upon thirty (30) days notice. In consideration of such payments, Primary Care Physician agrees to provide to Members the Primary Care Services set forth in Attachment C hereto.

Health Plan shall allocate the remaining 10 percent of the monthly capitation payments to a Risk Reserve Fund which fund is subject to the further provisions of this Attachment. The capitation payments to Primary Care Physician for Primary Care Services, subject to the above withhold, are as follows:

Coverage Plans

Age/Sex	*Commercial Plan__* *Capitation Payment*	*Commercial Plan__* *Capitation Payment*	*Commercial Plan__* *Capitation Payment*
0–24 Months/M/F	$ _____	$ _____	$ _____
2–4 Years/M/F	$ _____	$ _____	$ _____
5–19 Years/M/F	$ _____	$ _____	$ _____
20–39 Years/F	$ _____	$ _____	$ _____
20–39 Years/M	$ _____	$ _____	$ _____
40–49 Years/F	$ _____	$ _____	$ _____
40–49 Years/M	$ _____	$ _____	$ _____
50–59 Years/F	$ _____	$ _____	$ _____
50–59 Years/M	$ _____	$ _____	$ _____
>60 Years/F	$ _____	$ _____	$ _____
>60 Years/M	$ _____	$ _____	$ _____

Primary Care Physician is financially liable for all Primary Care Services rendered to Members under the above capitation. If Primary Care Physician fails to do so, HMO may pay for such services on behalf of Primary Care Physician and deduct such payments from any sums otherwise due Primary Care Physician by HMO.

Appendix 36-B

Sample Hospital Agreement

_____.

HEALTH MAINTENANCE ORGANIZATION
PARTICIPATING HOSPITAL AGREEMENT[20]

THIS AGREEMENT, made and entered into the date set forth on the signature page hereto, by and between _____ (the "Hospital"), a facility duly licensed under the laws of the State of _____ and located at _____, and _____ ("HMO"), a corporation organized under the _____ law, and located at

_____.

WHEREAS, HMO provides a plan of health care benefits (the "Plan") to individuals and their eligible family members and dependents who contract with HMO or who are the beneficiaries of a contract with HMO for such benefits ("Members"), and in connection with such Plan, arranges for the provision of health care services, including Hospital Services, to such Members; and

WHEREAS, the Hospital desires to provide Hospital Services to Members in accordance with the terms and conditions of this Agreement as hereinafter set forth; and

WHEREAS, HMO desires to arrange for the services of the Hospital for the benefit of the Members of the Plan.

NOW, THEREFORE, in consideration of the foregoing recitals and the mutual covenants and promises herein contained and other good and valuable consideration, receipt and sufficiency of which are hereby acknowledged, the parties hereto agree and covenant as follows:

---

[20]For consistency, the HMO has used the same definitions for this agreement and the preceding primary care physician agreement. This agreement also uses some of the same provisions as in the primary care physician agreement. Comments made to those provisions in the primary care physician agreement will not be repeated here.

PART I. DEFINITIONS

A. *Covered Services* means those health services and benefits to which Members are entitled under the terms of the applicable Health Maintenance Certificate, which may be amended by HMO from time to time.

B. *Emergency Services* means those Medically Necessary services provided in connection with an "Emergency," defined as a sudden or unexpected onset of a condition requiring medical or surgical care which the Member receives after the onset of such condition (or as soon thereafter as care can be made available but not more than twenty-four (24) hours after onset) and in the absence of such care the Member could reasonably be expected to suffer serious physical impairment or death. Heart attacks, severe chest pain, cardiovascular accidents, hemorrhaging, poisonings, major burns, loss of consciousness, serious breathing difficulties, spinal injuries, shock, and other acute conditions as HMO shall determine are Emergencies.

C. *Health Maintenance Certificate* means a contract issued by HMO to a Member or an employer of Members specifying the services and benefits available under the HMO's prepaid health benefits program.

D. *Hospital Services* means all inpatient services, emergency room, and outpatient hospital services that are Covered Services.

E. *Medical Director* means a Physician designated by HMO to monitor and review the provision of Covered Services to Members.

F. *Medically Necessary* services and/or supplies means the use of services or supplies as provided by a hospital, skilled nursing facility, Physician or other provider required to identify or treat a Member's illness or injury and which, as determined by HMO's Medical Director or its utilization management committee, are: (1) consistent with the symptoms or diagnosis and treatment of the Member's condition, disease, ailment or injury; (2) appropriate with regard to standards of good medical practice; (3) not solely for the convenience of the Member, his/her Physician, hospital, or other health care provider; and (4) the most appropriate supply or level of service which can be safely provided to the Member. When specifically applied to an inpatient Member, it further means that the Member's medical symptoms or condition requires that the diagnosis or treatment cannot be safely provided to the Member as an outpatient.

G *Member* means both an HMO subscriber and his/her enrolled family members for whom premium payment has been made.

H. *Participating Physician* means a Physician who, at the time of providing or authorizing services to a Member, has contracted with or on whose behalf a contract has been entered into with HMO to provide professional services to Members.

I. *Participating Provider* means a Physician, hospital, skilled nursing facility, home health agency or any other duly licensed institution or health professional under contract with HMO to provide health care services to Members. A list of Participating Providers and their locations is available to each Member upon enrollment. Such list shall be revised from time to time as HMO deems necessary.

J. *Physician* means a duly licensed doctor of medicine or osteopathy.

K. *Primary Care Physician* means a Participating Physician who provides primary care services to Members (eg, general or family practitioner, internist, pediatrician, or such other physician specialty as may be designated by HMO) and is responsible for referrals of Members to referral Physicians, other Participating Providers, and if necessary, non-Participating Providers.

PART II. HOSPITAL OBLIGATIONS

A. Hospital shall provide to Members those Hospital Services which Hospital has the capacity to provide. Such services shall be provided by Hospital in accordance with the provisions of its Articles of Incorporation and bylaws and medical staff bylaws and the appropriate terms of this Agreement.

B. Hospital shall render Hospital Services to Members in an economical and efficient manner consistent with professional standards of medical care generally accepted in the medical community. Hospital shall not discriminate in the treatment of members and, except as otherwise required by this Agreement, shall make its services available to Members in the same manner as to its other patients.[21] In the event that an admission of a Member cannot be accommodated by Hospital, Hospital shall make the same efforts to arrange for the provision of services at another facility approved by HMO that it would make for other patients in similar circumstances. In the event that Hospital shall provide Member non-Covered Services, Hospital shall, prior to the provision of such non-Covered Services, inform the Member:

1. of the service(s) to be provided,

2. that HMO will not pay for or be liable for said services, and

3. that Member will be financially liable for such services.

C. Except in an Emergency, Hospital shall provide Hospital Inpatient Services to a Member only when Hospital has received certification from HMO in advance of admission of such Member. Services which have not been so approved or authorized shall be the sole financial responsibility of Hospital.[22]

D. If, and to the extent that, the Hospital is not authorized to perform preadmission testing, the Hospital agrees to accept the results of qualified and timely laboratory, radiological and other tests and procedures which may be performed on a Member prior to admission. The Hospital will not require that duplicate tests or procedures be performed after the Enrollee is admitted, unless such tests and procedures are Medically Necessary.

E. In an Emergency, Hospital shall immediately proceed to render Medically Necessary services to the Member. Hospital shall also contact HMO within twenty-four (24) hours of the treatment of the emergency treatment visit or emergency admission. HMO has twenty-four (24) hour on-call nurse coverage for notification of Emergency Services or admits.

If Hospital fails to notify HMO within the required time period, neither HMO nor the Member shall be liable for charges for Hospital Services rendered subsequent to the required notification period that are deemed by HMO not to be Medically Necessary.[23]

F. Hospital shall cooperate with and abide by HMO's programs that monitor and evaluate whether Hospital Services provided to Members in accordance with this Agreement are Medically Necessary and consistent with professional standards of medical care generally accepted in the

---

[21]This requirement serves the same purpose as its counterpart in the primary care physician agreement of requiring the hospital to treat HMO members in the same manner as fee-for-service patients.

[22]A growing issue, not addressed in this provision, is the HMO's responsibility for hospital charges incurred to provide a medical screening examination, as required by Section 1867 of the Social Security Act, to enrollees seeking care from the hospital's emergency department. The hospital may want to seek an explicit statement requiring the HMO to cover the cost of that examination.

[23]To avoid disputes, the hospital and HMO need a common understanding of the meaning of the term *Medically Necessary*. The definition of that term used in this contract favors the HMO by allowing for its interpretation.

medical community. Such programs include, but are not limited to, utilization management, quality assurance review, and grievance procedures. In connection with HMO's programs, Hospital shall permit HMO's utilization management personnel to visit Members in the Hospital and, to the extent permitted by applicable laws, to inspect and copy health records (including medical records) of Members maintained by Hospital for the purposes of concurrent and retrospective utilization management, discharge planning, and other program management purposes.

G. Hospital shall cooperate with HMO in complying with applicable laws relating to HMO.

PART III.   LICENSURE AND ACCREDITATION

Hospital represents that it is duly licensed by the Department of Health of the State of _____ to operate a hospital, is a qualified provider under the Medicare program, and is accredited by the Joint Commission on the Accreditation of Healthcare Organizations ("Joint Commission"). Hospital shall maintain in good standing such license and accreditation and shall notify HMO immediately should any action of any kind be initiated against Hospital which could result in:

1. the suspension or loss of such license;
2. the suspension or loss of such accreditation; or
3. the imposition of any sanctions against Hospital under the Medicare or Medicaid programs.

Hospital shall furnish to HMO such evidence of licensure, Medicare qualification and accreditation as HMO may request.

PART IV.   RECORDS

A. Hospital shall maintain with respect to each Member receiving Hospital Services pursuant to this Agreement a standard hospital medical record in such form, containing such information, and preserved for such time period(s) as are required by the rules and regulations of the _____ Department of Health, the Medicare program, and the Joint Commission. The original hospital medical records shall be and remain the property of Hospital and shall not be removed or transferred from Hospital except in accordance with applicable laws and general Hospital policies, rules, and regulations relating thereto; provided, however, that HMO shall have the right, in accordance with paragraph (B) below, to inspect, review, and make copies of such records upon request.

B. Upon consent of the Member and a request for such records or information, Hospital shall provide copies of information contained in the medical records of Members to other authorized providers of health care services and to HMO for the purpose of facilitating the delivery of appropriate health care services to Members and carrying out the purposes and provisions of this Agreement, and shall facilitate the sharing of such records among health care providers involved in a Member's care. HMO, and if required, authorized state and federal agencies, shall have the right upon request to inspect at reasonable times and to obtain copies of all records that are maintained by Hospital relating to the care of Members pursuant to this Agreement.

PART V.   INSURANCE AND INDEMNIFICATION

A. Hospital shall secure and maintain at its expense throughout the term of this Agreement such policy or policies of general liability and professional liability insurance as shall be necessary to insure Hospital, its agents and employees against any claim or claims for damages arising by reason of injury or death, occasioned directly or indirectly by the performance or nonperformance of any service by Hospital, its agents or employees. Upon request, Hospital shall provide HMO with a copy of the policy (or policies) or certificate(s) of insurance which evidence compliance with the foregoing insurance requirements. It is specifically agreed that coverage amounts in general conformity with other similar type and size hospitals within the State of _____ shall be acceptable to HMO and be considered satisfactory and in compliance with this requirement.[24]

B. Hospital and HMO each shall indemnify and hold the other harmless from any and all liability, loss, damage, claim or expense of any kind, including costs and attorney's fees, arising out of the performance of this Agreement and for which the other is solely responsible.

PART VI.   MEDICAL STAFF MEMBERSHIP

Notwithstanding any other provision of this Agreement, a Participating Physician may not admit or treat a Member in the Hospital unless he/she is a member in good standing of Hospital's organized medical staff with appropriate clinical privileges to admit and treat such Member.[25]

PART VII.   HMO OBLIGATIONS

A. HMO shall provide to or for the benefit of each Member an identification card which shall be presented for purposes of assisting Hospital in verifying Member eligibility. In addition, HMO shall maintain other verification procedures by which Hospital may confirm the eligibility of any Member.

B. HMO shall provide thirty (30) days advance notice to Hospital of any changes in Covered Services or in the copayments or conditions of coverage applicable thereto.

C. HMO will, whenever an individual, admitted or referred, is not a Member, advise Hospital within thirty (30) days from the date of receipt of an invoice from Hospital for services to such an individual. In such cases, Hospital shall directly bill the individual or another third party payor for services rendered to such individual.

D. In the event continued stay or services are denied after a patient has been admitted, HMO or its representative shall inform the patient that services have been denied.

PART VIII.   USE OF NAME

Except as provided in this paragraph, neither HMO nor Hospital shall use the other's name, symbols, trademarks or service marks in advertising or promotional material or otherwise. HMO shall have the right to use the name of Hospital for purposes of marketing, informing Members of the identity of Hospital and otherwise to carry out the terms of this Agreement. Hospital shall have the right to use HMO's name in its informational or promotional materials with HMO's prior approval, which approval shall not be unreasonably withheld.

PART IX.   COMPENSATION

Hospital will be compensated by HMO for all Medically Necessary Covered Services provided to Members in accordance with the provisions of Attachment A annexed hereto and incorporated herein.[26]

---

[24]This paragraph reflects the difference in relative bargaining strength that the HMO has with hospitals and physicians. Although the HMO–primary care physician agreement gives the HMO the right to approve malpractice coverage, no such right is contained in the HMO–participating hospital agreement. Another factor may be that the concern of inadequate coverage may be greater for a physician than a hospital.

[25]Requiring the HMO's physicians to comply with the hospital's medical staff requirements is important and reasonable.

[26]Attachment A provides for payment as a percentage of charges. By structuring the agreement in this manner, the HMO is able to negotiate different payment arrangements with hospitals without revising the body of the agreement.

PART X.   PAYMENT TO HOSPITAL BY HMO

For Hospital Services rendered to Members, Hospital shall invoice HMO at Hospital's current charges. [**Alternative**: For Hospital Services rendered to Members, Hospital shall invoice HMO.[27]] Except for Hospital Services which HMO determines require further review under HMO's utilization management procedures, or when there are circumstances which are beyond the control of HMO, including submission of incomplete claims, HMO shall make payment of invoices for Hospital Services within thirty (30) calendar days after the HMO's receipt thereof. HMO authorized copayments shall be collected by the Hospital from the Member and the Member shall be solely responsible for the payment of such copayments. All billings by Hospital shall be considered final unless adjustments are requested in writing by Hospital within sixty (60) days after receipt of original billing by HMO, except for circumstances which are beyond the control of Hospital.[28] No payment shall be made unless the invoice for services is received within sixty (60) days after the date of discharge of the Member or date of service, whichever occurs later. Hospital shall interim bill HMO every thirty (30) days for patients whose length of stay is greater than thirty (30) days.

PART XI.   PROHIBITIONS ON MEMBER BILLING

Hospital hereby agrees that in no event, including, but not limited to, nonpayment by HMO, HMO's insolvency or breach of this Agreement, shall Hospital bill, charge, collect a deposit from, seek compensation, remuneration or reimbursement from, or have any recourse against a Member or persons other than HMO acting on a Member's behalf for services provided pursuant to this Agreement. This provision shall not prohibit collection of copayment on HMO's behalf in accordance with the terms of the Health Maintenance Certificate between HMO and Member. Hospital further agrees that:

1. this provision shall survive the termination of this Agreement regardless of the cause giving rise to termination and shall be construed to be for the benefit of the Member; and
2. this provision supersedes any oral or written contrary agreement now existing or hereafter entered into between Hospital and Member, or persons acting on their behalf.

PART XII.   INSPECTION OF RECORDS

Upon request, and at reasonable times, HMO and Hospital shall make available to the other for review such books, records, utilization information and other documents or information relating directly to any determination required by this Agreement. All such information shall be held by the receiving party in confidence and shall only be used in connection with the administration of this Agreement.

PART XIII.   COORDINATION OF BENEFITS

Hospital agrees to cooperate with HMO toward effective implementation of any provisions of HMO's Health Maintenance Certificates relating to coordination of benefits and claims by third parties. Hospital shall forward to HMO any payments received from a third party payor for authorized Hospital Services where HMO has made payment to Hospital covering such Hospital Services and such third party payor is determined to be primarily obligated for such Hospital Services under applicable Coordination of Benefits rules. Such payment shall not exceed the amount paid to Hospital by HMO. Except as otherwise required by law, Hospital agrees to permit HMO to bill and process forms

---

[27]This broader alternative language along with the cross-reference to Attachment A in the preceding paragraph allows the body of the contract to be used for any type of payment arrangement. An alternative Attachment A is offered that establishes per diem rates for inpatient stays and a percentage of charges for outpatient services.

[28]To avoid potential disputes, the hospital and the HMO should have some general understanding of the meaning of the term *beyond the control of Hospital.*

for any third party payor on Hospital's behalf, or to bill such third party directly, as determined by HMO. Hospital further agrees to waive, when requested, any claims against third party payors for its provision of Hospital Services to Members and to execute any further documents that reasonably may be required or appropriate for this purpose. Any such waiver shall be contingent upon HMO's payment to Hospital of its (HMO's) obligations for charges incurred by Member.

PART XIV.   TERM AND TERMINATION

A. This Agreement shall take effect on the "effective date" set forth on the signature page and shall continue for a period of one year or until terminated as provided herein.

   1. Either party may terminate this Agreement without cause upon at least ninety (90) days written notice prior to the term of this Agreement.

   2. Either party may terminate this Agreement with cause upon at least thirty (30) days prior written notice.

B. HMO shall have the right to terminate this Agreement immediately by notice to Hospital upon the occurrence of any of the following events:

   1. the suspension or revocation of Hospital's license;

   2. the suspension, revocation or loss of the Hospital's Joint Commission accreditation or Medicare qualification; or

   3. breach of Part II(E) or Part XI of this Agreement.

C. HMO shall continue to pay Hospital in accordance with the provisions of Attachment A for Hospital Services provided by Hospital to Members hospitalized at the time of termination of this Agreement, pending clinically appropriate discharge or transfer to an HMO designated hospital when medically appropriate as determined by HMO. In continuing to provide such Hospital Services, Hospital shall abide by the applicable terms and conditions of this Agreement.

PART XV.   ADMINISTRATION

Hospital agrees to abide by and cooperate with HMO administrative policies including, but not limited to, claims procedures, copayment collections, and duplicate coverage/subrogation recoveries. Nothing in this Agreement shall be construed to require Hospital to violate, breach, or modify its written policies and procedures unless specifically agreed to herein.

PART XVI.   MEMBER GRIEVANCES

Hospital agrees to cooperate in and abide by HMO grievance procedures in resolving Member's grievances related to the provision of Hospital Services. In this regard, HMO shall bring to the attention of appropriate Hospital officials all Member complaints involving Hospital, and Hospital shall, in accordance with its regular procedure, investigate such complaints and use its best efforts to resolve them in a fair and equitable manner. Hospital agrees to notify HMO promptly of any action taken or proposed with respect to the resolution of such complaints and the avoidance of similar complaints in the future. The Hospital shall notify the HMO after it has received a complaint from an HMO Member.

PART XVII.   MISCELLANEOUS

A. If any term, provision, covenant or condition of this Agreement is invalid, void or unenforceable, the rest of the Agreement shall remain in full force and effect. The invalidity or unenforceability of any term or provision hereof shall in no way affect the validity or enforceability of any other term or provision.

B. This Agreement contains the complete understanding and agreement between Hospital and HMO and supersedes all representations, understandings or agreements prior to the execution hereof.

C. HMO and Hospital agree that, to the extent compatible with the separate and independent management of each, they shall at all times maintain an effective liaison and close cooperation with each other to provide maximum benefits to Members at the most reasonable cost consistent with quality standards of hospital care.

D. No waiver, alteration, amendment or modification of this Agreement shall be valid unless in each instance a written memorandum specifically expressing such waiver, alteration, amendment, or modification is made and subscribed by a duly authorized officer of Hospital and a duly authorized officer of HMO.

E. Hospital shall not assign its rights, duties, or obligations under this Agreement without the express, written permission of HMO.

F. None of the provisions of this Agreement are intended to create nor shall be deemed to create any relationship between HMO and Hospital other than that of independent entities contracting with each other hereunder solely for the purpose of effecting the provisions of this Agreement. Neither of the parties hereto, nor any of their respective employees shall be construed to be the agent, employer, employee or representative of the other.

G. This Agreement shall be construed in accordance with the laws of the State of _____.

H. The headings and numbers of sections and paragraphs contained in this Agreement are for reference purposes only and shall not affect in any way the meaning or interpretation of this Agreement.

I. Any notice required or permitted to be given pursuant to the terms and provisions of this Agreement shall be sent by registered mail or certified mail, return receipt requested, postage prepaid, to:

_____

_____

_____

_____

_____

_____

and to Hospital at:

_____

_____

_____

_____

_____

IN WITNESS WHEREOF, the foregoing Agreement between _____

and Hospital is entered into by and between the undersigned parties, to be effective the _____ day of

_____,1992.

By: _____

Title: _____

Date: _____

HOSPITAL

By: _____

Title: _____

Date: _____

ATTACHMENT A

PARTICIPATING HOSPITAL COMPENSATION

Subject to the terms and conditions set forth in this Agreement, HMO shall pay Hospital
_____ (_____%) of Hospital's schedule of charges effective _____
as submitted and approved by HMO, for Medically Necessary Covered Services provided to Members.

ATTACHMENT A (ALTERNATE)

PARTICIPATING HOSPITAL COMPENSATION

Subject to the terms and conditions set forth in this Agreement, HMO shall pay Hospital, as follows:

Service	Type of Reimbursement	Total Reimbursement
Inpatient care		
Nonmaternity- secondary	Per Diem	$_____
Nonmaternity- tertiary	Per Diem	$_____
Maternity	Per Diem	$_____
Psychiatric	Per Diem	$_____
Well newborn children	Per Diem	$_____
Outpatient care		
Other than outpatient surgery	Percentage Discount	___%
Outpatient surgery		Hospital will be reimbursed (1) the percentage discount stated above, (2) any guaranteed maximum "global" rate program adopted by the Hospital for ambulatory surgical procedures,[29] or (3) 125 percent[30] of the per diem payment amount had the Enrollee been admitted to the Hospital, whichever is least.

---

[29]If Medicare adopts a global fee for reimbursement of outpatient hospital costs, an increasing number of HMO-hospital contracts are likely to adopt a similar approach.

[30]This percentage commonly varies from 100% to 125%.

Chapter 37

Legal Issues and Antitrust Considerations in the Establishment of Credentialing and Other Selection Criteria

William G. Kopit and Mark E. Lutes

Traditional indemnity insurance had little or nothing to say about who provided care. Managed care, on the other hand, is predicated on the notion that covered persons may be channeled to efficient and/or low-cost providers. It is becoming increasingly clear that courts will determine that, at some level, channeling of covered persons to designated providers gives rise to a duty of care with respect to the selection and retention of the providers. Moreover, the federal and state antitrust laws, and an increasing number of other state statutes, impose parameters on the criteria employed in selection and retention decisions. Likewise, the procedures employed to make such decisions are, in some cases, influenced by state common law or the desire to take advantage of statutory immunities. This chapter is therefore designed to outline the considerations relevant to managed care credentialing and selection decisions and to offer some practical suggestions for the development of selection criteria in various potential environments.

The authors are partners with the Washington, DC, office of Epstein, Becker & Green, PC, where they represent a variety of managed care payers and health care providers. Epstein Becker has, since 1974, counseled hundreds of HMOs, PPOs, and insurers. The firm has also been involved in several landmark health care antitrust cases.

THE WELLSPRINGS OF CREDENTIALING

The selection and credentialing of providers by managed care entities is being driven by a variety of factors. First, there is generally a desire on the part of the managed care entities to provide, or to arrange for the provision of, high-quality health care services to their members. Second, there are requirements that providers be credentialed in some regulatory schemes, most frequently those licensing health maintenance organizations (HMOs) and occasionally those authorizing insurers and other payers to incorporate preferred provider organizations (PPOs) into their coverages.

A third cause is the increasing demand from payers for cost-effective provider networks. Those managed care entities that bear insurance type risk have an obvious interest in safeguarding their bottom lines by contracting, where marketing demands permit, only with the most efficient providers of care. Risk-bearing managed care organizations (MCOs) find their impulse to contract with the most efficient providers constrained by the demands of employers and beneficiaries for access to providers perceived to be the premier institutions or specialists and for geographic ease of access.

Those managed care entities that do not bear traditional insurance type risk are not, however, immune from comparable pressure carefully to select participating providers. Self-funded plans and their agents (third-party administrators and insurers operating on an administrative services only basis) that contract with these entities may base selection and renewal decisions on their perception of the network's contribution or potential contribution toward the goal of controlling costs. Moreover, poor provider selection and retention decisions can cost the network money where it receives a performance-based service fee.

THE TORT LIABILITY IMPERATIVE

From a legal, and arguably a financial, perspective the strongest impetus behind appropriate provider selection criteria is a concern for the tort liability that might arise should beneficiaries be injured by contracting providers where adequate criteria might have prevented the injury from occurring.

Managed Care Arrangements in Which a Duty Might Arise

Courts in a number of jurisdictions have found that hospitals have a duty to their patients properly to credential and supervise their medical staff, including independent contractors. For example, in *Johnson v. Misericordia Community Hospital,*[1] the court held that the failure by a hospital to investigate a medical staff applicant's qualifications gives rise to a foreseeable risk of harm and therefore that a duty to exercise care in the selection of the staff exists. It is not difficult to foresee the extension of an equivalent duty to HMOs that directly employ their physicians or employ them through one or more medical groups.[2]

The widespread imposition of such a duty on individual practice association (IPA) or open panel model HMOs may be the next evolutionary step.* For instance, in *Harrell v Total Health Care, Inc,*[3] an IPA model HMO was explicitly held to have a duty to reasonably investigate the reputation of its participating physicians.[4] The

court's rationale was that, where an HMO lists physicians and requires patients to utilize only those physicians to obtain all but emergency coverage, "there is an unreasonable risk of harm to subscribers if the physicians listed . . . are unqualified or incompetent."[5] In another instance where an appeals court allowed the case to go forward against an IPA model HMO on an imputed liability theory, the complaint alleged that the HMO was negligent in failing to qualify or oversee its physicians and hospitals and in not requiring its physicians and hospitals "to provide adequate evidence of skill, training and competence. . . ."[6]

There is a substantial question as to whether a comparable duty will or should be imposed in the context of other types of managed care arrangements. One might speculate that the lynchpin with respect to a court's imposition of such a duty will be the degree to which the managed care arrangement restricts the covered person's choice of health care provider. Thus it is most likely that managed care that uses effective channeling arrangements, such as self-funded plans that limit covered persons' provider choices to a designated network, will have exposure under this theory. On the other hand, a benefits plan that incorporated a pure point-of-service (POS) election of in-network or out-of-network care, with no more than a modest financial incentive to choose an in-network provider, arguably should have little exposure.

The more interesting question concerns that vast middle ground of PPOs or POS plans with significant channeling. A duty to credential and otherwise establish appropriate selection criteria may arise in this context if a court determines that, on the basis of all the facts and circumstances (including the message conveyed by subscriber materials, the operation of the utilization management program, other communications by the plan, and the strength of the finan-

---

*In this section the term *IPA model HMO* is used to describe all HMOs with physicians practicing in private offices and generally not in a multi-specialty group setting. Thus, the term includes HMOs that contract directly with physicians in private practice and those that contract with private practice physicians through IPAs.

cial incentives), the covered person could reasonably expect some effort on the part of the MCO to assess provider competency. Of course, the mere fact that a duty to apply appropriate selection criteria may exist does not mean that an MCO should be responsible for a particular harm to a covered person resulting from the actions of one of its participating providers. The imposition of liability should also require proof that proper selection criteria or other monitoring would have disclosed information indicating that the provider was likely to engage in the tortious conduct, that a reasonable MCO would have been convinced to exclude the provider from its panel, and that the MCO, had it acted on such information, might have prevented the injury to the covered person.

The Scope of a Managed Care Organization's Duty To Credential

Liability for a negligent tort is based on a breach of a duty of care. The inquiry is into whether a reasonable person of ordinary prudence would have acted under the circumstances as the defendant did. To date, there is not a large body of case law suggesting what the scope of credentialing and recredentialing by an MCO found to have duties in these areas should be. MCOs can look for clues to the *Harrell* decision, however, and to several outside accreditation or regulatory compilations.

In *Harrell,* the court did enumerate the components of a reasonable credentialing or recredentialing investigation. It did, however, criticize the fact that defendant Total Health Care's credentialing program consisted merely of a review to determine whether the applicant was licensed, had admitting privileges at a hospital, and could dispense narcotics. The court noted that the HMO conducted no personal interviews and did not check references or otherwise verify the information contained in the provider's application.

A second source of guidance for MCOs comes from the standards set by the National Committee for Quality Assurance (NCQA). Other sources include the standards of the American Association of Preferred Provider Or-

ganizations, the Health Care Quality Improvements Act (HCQIA), the now defunct MCO standards of the Joint Commission on Accreditation of Healthcare Organizations, and, to some extent, state law.* By tracking the elements of the NCQA standards and distilling the wisdom of these other sources, an MCO might come up with a strong set of criteria.

The NCQA standards urge MCOs, inter alia, to conduct credentialing by:

- maintaining written policies and procedures for the credentialing and re-credentialing of physicians and dentists every 2 years according to the policies and procedures adopted by the MCO's governing body and implemented through a designated credentialing committee

- conducting credentialing of, at a minimum, all physicians and other licensed independent practitioners listed in the MCO's member literature

- obtaining, at a minimum, the applicant's license, DEA/CDS certificate where applicable, a training assessment, work history, professional liability history, evidence of good standing at a hospital, and evidence of adequate medical malpractice insurance coverage

- obtaining a statement by the applicant as to disciplinary activity, physical and mental status, license history, criminal record, lack of impairment, and the correctness and completeness of the application

- making inquiries to the National Practitioner Data Bank and the applicable state licensing board and as to Medicare and Medicaid sanction activity

- using an integrated appraisal process including member complaints, quality review results, utilization management records, and member satisfaction surveys

---

*Typically, state laws governing preferred provider arrangements do not establish credentialing requirements. Although HMO statutes and regulations may require the HMO to maintain such a system, they are typically not prescriptive as to its contents.[7]

- visiting each primary care physician's office to review the site and the physician's record keeping
- maintaining a written description of delegated activities and the delegate's accountability
- maintaining a mechanism for suspension, reduction, or termination of participation of providers

The standards with respect to formal delegation, to verification of experience, training, and claims history, to primary care office site visits, to the delegation system, and to policies and procedures for discipline do not currently prevent accreditation but are, in effect, targets for MCOs. This is an apparent acknowledgment by NCQA that, for example, primary care office site visits are probably not the norm among MCOs in most places in the country.

The standard as to the integration of the MCO's member complaint, utilization management, and quality review programs with the credentialing program is currently applied by the NCQA in accreditation reviews. For most MCOs, however, such integration is informal if it takes place at all. Likewise, the credentialing of independently practicing practitioners other than physicians is currently not widespread, although MCO liability for the torts of these providers is equally plausible.

The NCQA standards do not require that the applicant be interviewed, although the dicta in *Harrell* suggested that interviews would be a reasonable precaution. Maryland's proposed HMO credentialing standards would go beyond the NCQA model and require credentialing programs to delineate the services to be provided by the applicant to the HMO's members. Privilege delineation obviously has a hospital analog. In *Privilege Delineation: Legal Implications of Adopting Clinical Competence Guidelines*, Nancy E. Ator has outlined the issues for hospitals to consider in adopting the American College of Physicians' guidelines for the assessment of the cognitive and technical skills or knowledge to be possessed by applicants for privileges in approximately 100 procedures. Implementation issues equivalent to those discussed in

Ator's document would arise where MCOs attempt to specify the types of services and procedures to be performed by contracting providers (Ator's document is available through the National Health Lawyers Association). In the future, privilege delineation might become customary for certain MCOs, particularly those that provide rather than merely arrange for services.

The Delegation of Credentialing Responsibilities

The NCQA target standard with respect to the delegation of credentialing functions points to an area of risk that many MCOs have, to date, ignored. Actually, the problem is pervasive in managed care. Self-funded employers delegate the credentialing of the preferred provider networks with which they contract to PPOs. Insured employers delegate the credentialing function to their insurers, which may credential directly contracted providers but frequently delegate credentialing to PPOs outside their corporate family. Likewise, insured employers offering HMO products in effect delegate the credentialing of HMO providers to the HMO. The HMO in turn may delegate the decisions to an IPA or a medical group. The IPA or medical group (or the HMO itself, where it uses a direct contract format) may in turn rely upon the credentialing done by a county medical society or hospital. PPOs have also been known to rely on the credentialing performed by a hospital and to use county medical society credentialing services.

Tort law does not prevent delegation, but a party with a duty to use reasonable care in provider selection cannot escape that duty through delegation absent a release from the persons owed the duty.* Thus an MCO with exposure in

---

*This is not to suggest that each of the delegating entities in any of the delegation scenarios in the previous paragraph has an established duty to credential. As discussed above, that duty is likely to be a function of the degree of channeling that the managed care arrangement involves and of the reasonable expectations of covered persons as to the delegating entity's role.

this area would want, at a minimum, to conduct a due diligence type review of the proposed contractor's standards and procedures before making the delegation. Ideally, such a review would not be confined to a review of the contractor's statement of standards and procedure manual but would also include an inspection of some randomly selected provider files to determine whether the documentation alleged to be maintained is complete and up to date. Moreover, such a due diligence inspection might take place at regular intervals. The NCQA target standard requires that the contractor's effectiveness be monitored.

The risks involved in delegation of credentialing might be managed in several other ways as well. For instance, the service agreement between the parties should specify what standards will apply in network recruitment and maintenance. The HMO, insurer, or self-funded payer may also want to retain the right to approve new providers and sites and to terminate or suspend individual providers. This sort of reservation of powers is in fact mandated by the NCQA target standard. Additionally, the MCO might seek indemnification from the contractor for losses related to the contractor's negligence in performing these functions. Alternatively, the MCO may require the contractor to name it as an insured party in its professional liability coverage. Of course, part of the due diligence review would involve an inquiry into whether the contractor maintained such coverage, the acts or omissions encompassed by the coverage, and the coverage's limits.

Practical Tort Liability Risk Management

Formal credentialing systems and an adequate record as to the credentialing that has taken place may prove to be an effective defense for employers and MCOs against allegations of corporate negligence. Medical groups will, however, have more direct liability for the torts of their employees. They may not significantly reduce this risk by maintaining fancy credentialing records. Thus medical groups probably lack incentives to cooperate with employers and MCOs in this area. (For a thoughtful discussion of these problems, see *The Credentialing Process and Its Implications: A Medical Group Perspective*, by Stephen T. Newman and available through the National Health Lawyers Association.) These groups will therefore have to be made aware that credentialing is a significant issue for the MCOs with which they contract. The MCOs in turn will have to be cognizant of the paperwork demands they are placing on the groups, particularly where the group services the covered persons of a large number of MCOs. Ideally, the MCOs in an area, with regulatory assistance or otherwise, would standardize their credentialing information requirements to ease the burden on these groups. Additionally, they would avoid midstream changes to such requirements even if one or more potential new accounts desired different information than that which the MCO previously gathered from the group.

There are also those who believe that MCOs best manage their risk in this area not by maintaining extensive files on the background of all providers but by focusing their efforts on identifying and excluding those most likely to be bad apples. For instance, Alan Bloom, long-time legal counsel to Maxicare, advocates that HMOs concentrate their credentialing efforts on first-time applicants and unknown providers. He also believes that provider office visits are more important than all the paperwork verification in the world.

This school of thought has a number of other important aspects to it. For instance, the school of practical risk management emphasizes verification of insurance coverage on the theory that, where the allegedly negligent provider's insurance is adequate, plaintiff's counsel will be less likely to name the MCO as a codefendant. Likewise, this school emphasizes that MCOs should avoid creating malpractice defense problems by scrupulously adhering to stated policies and by thorough investigation of enrollee complaints. Bloom, in fact, believes that NCQA type credentialing has the wrong emphasis. He believes that enrollees are better served if MCOs spend their time verifying the availability and accessibility of services (eg, through office visits and appointment audits) rather than creating a paper trail as to providers' qualifications.

STRUCTURING THE CREDENTIALING PROCESS

A provider has far fewer rights in the context of managed care network selection than in the context of hospital staff privileges and membership. Nevertheless, insofar as physicians are accustomed to the procedural formality associated with hospital medical staff determinations, and because, given the paucity of case law on provider exclusions in the managed care context, courts may seek guidance from hospital case law, it is useful to compare and contrast MCO provider credentialing to hospital privilege law.

Procedural Protections Might Emanate from Hospital Law

The Fifth and Fourteenth Amendments to the US Constitution prohibit the federal and state governments from depriving any person of life, liberty, or property without substantive and procedural due process. A liberty interest has sometimes been found to be involved in hospital staff privilege cases where the physician claims damage to his or her professional standing. A property interest has sometimes been found to exist with respect to the continuation of previously granted hospital staff privileges.

Public hospitals are government entities, and therefore physician exclusions will fall within the ambit of due process protections. The courts in a majority of jurisdictions have, however, been reluctant to extend constitutional due process protections in the context of private hospital credentialing decisions.[8] Thus, for private hospitals, judicial review of credentialing decisions is generally confined to an inquiry as to whether the hospital followed its own bylaws.[9] Some courts go so far as to deem the medical staff bylaws to be a contract between the hospital and the medical staff's members.[10]

In most states, where no specific statutory breach is alleged, a court's review of an MCO's credentialing decision should be similarly confined. First, the court will determine whether any contractual grievance procedure existed, and, if so, whether it was observed. Second, the court is likely to consider whether all internal proce-

dures were observed (eg, whether the stated credentialing process was complied with).

In a few jurisdictions, the courts have looked beyond the procedure applied by a private hospital and have reviewed the substance of the hospital's decision.[11] New Jersey courts, for instance, have reasoned that the public interest in quality care permits courts to determine whether medical staff selections are not arbitrary, capricious, or unreasonable. This approach was first enunciated in *Greisman v Necomb Hospital*[12] and was based on findings that even private hospitals receive a substantial portion of their revenues from public funds, receive tax benefits, and often constitute virtual monopolies in their areas. California courts have applied common law fair process theory out of a concern that denial of medical staff membership would effectively impair the applicant's right to fully practice his or her other profession.[13]

Arguably, neither theory supports the application of judicial review to the substance of MCO credentialing decisions. The *Greisman* rationale should not apply because MCOs are, more often than not, taxable entities, and only rarely will the credentialing decision of a single MCO have the market impact of a hospital's credentialing decision. Likewise, the California fair process rules should not apply because the applicant for participation in an MCO's network will generally not have his or her practice impaired by the MCO's decision to the same degree that, in some locales, it could be impaired by an adverse hospital credentialing decision. Of course, the California courts should probably distinguish between the impact of credentialing decisions made by the sole facility in a community and those made by facilities in markets with several hospital options. The fair process rationale also assumes that the provider should not be expected to move to relieve the economic pain of the exclusion. In any case, in the MCO situation other comparable sources of revenue are likely to be available to the excluded provider, so that movement is unlikely to be necessary.

Particularly in fair process jurisdictions, MCOs may elect to extend limited procedural rights to excluded providers despite the absence of direction in the case law to do so. Such extensions can serve several purposes. First, the fair process procedures would satisfy any rights imported by a court from hospital law to the MCO context. Second, the procedures can create an appearance of fairness that meets provider expectations derived from the hospital setting and mollifies potential litigants.

Moreover, the record created by such procedures may provide the reviewing court with the basis to resolve the case upon defendant's motion to dismiss or for summary judgment. Absent special circumstances, the MCO's risk of liability should be relatively low in provider exclusion cases. The defendant's goal, however, is to resolve the case in a manner that minimizes time and legal fee expenditures. Fair process procedures can be helpful in reaching that goal.

In some cases MCOs will borrow from hospital case law the notion that greater procedural rights should apply in considering the revocation of privileges or a decision not to renew existing credentials than in the context of an initial application for privileges.[14] These entities may, for example, choose not to afford providers appeal type rights where an initial application for privileges is denied. On the other hand they would extend fair process type rights in recredentialing or in for cause termination situations.

What Are the Components of Fair Process?

Again, an MCO may elect to extend modest procedural rights to providers either out of concern that, if the action is challenged, the court will apply fair process type standards or because it believes that the resultant internal records will be the evidence a court will require to resolve the case upon a preliminary motion. Importantly, the MCO need not accord the provider full-blown constitutional type due process. Procedural safeguards that should satisfy common law fair process requirements will generally revolve around notice and an opportunity to address the issues and correct any errors in the record.

More specifically, the procedure might call for notice citing the applicable standards and a statement as to the basis for the denial.[15] The MCO may also want to incorporate an opportunity for the provider to be heard. That opportunity could simply be an opportunity to respond in writing, or it could take the form of a hearing, although not necessarily a hearing with the panoply of constitutional safeguards such as the rights to counsel and cross-examination of witnesses.[16] Finally, fair process may provide for an unbiased decision-making body (eg, one that is not controlled by direct economic competitors of the applicant).[17]

State Law Constraints

Although there are relatively few common law constraints on MCO credentialing, some jurisdictions place explicit statutory requirements on provider selection by MCOs. The impact of these requirements is largely a function of the specific language of the applicable state statute. Therefore, generalizations are difficult. Thus this section will only identify the types of state statutory constraints and the classes of MCOs that each affects. With these categories in mind, an MCO must assess the regulatory environment in the states in which it operates.

Provider selection by HMOs is sometimes constrained by a requirement that the plan make members of certain classes of providers a part of its panel. The classes that may be mandated include psychologists; optometrists; licensed clinical social workers; licensed registered nurses with counseling experience; licensed marriage, family, and child counselors; podiatrists; chiropractors; and nurse midwives. For example, California has a statute that can be interpreted to require a plan to give reasonable consideration to providers in a number of categories, although the plan may consider such factors as professional qualification, accessibility, and utilization experience.[18]

Because managed care accounts for an increasing share of health care financing, MCOs can expect that political pressure will grow to require them to contract with all providers or members of particular classes of providers. Thus provider selection by insurers offering preferred provider arrangements is sometimes affected by any willing provider requirements.

The any willing provider statute in Virginia has, to date, received the most judicial attention.[19] Two separate cases have been brought. In both cases the health care bar believes that the court gave the insurer considerable discretion to set participation criteria, which took into consideration such factors as geographic location, relative cost of the applicants, and the insured's previous utilization of the facilities.[20] Although several federal health financing proposals would preempt such state statutes,[21] until such time as a federal preemption law is passed MCOs will have to monitor carefully state legislative developments in this area.

In contrast, the provider selections of self-funded employers utilizing preferred panel arrangements are probably beyond the reach of these statutes because of the preemption of state laws relating to self-funded employee welfare benefit plans by Section 514(a) of the Employee Retirement Income Security Act (ERISA) of 1974.[22] These plans, however, may be indirectly affected when they contract with freestanding networks brokered by insurers unless the insurer differentiates its recruitment of providers for its insured product from its recruitment of providers for its noninsured product. The two cases noted below that construe Virginia's any willing provider statute in an insured context did not reach the issue of whether ERISA might preempt the statute's application.

IMPACT OF THE HEALTH CARE QUALITY IMPROVEMENT ACT

The HCQIA of 1986[23] has become a significant influence on credentialing in the sector of the managed care industry subject to it. Its impact falls in three related categories. First, it is having its intended effect where HMOs are querying the National Practitioner Data Bank created by the HCQIA to improve the credentialing of health care entities and to reduce their tort liability exposure. Second, the HCQIA is visible in efforts to make quality-related credentialing decisions in a manner that preserves eligibility for the HCQIA's immunity from damages and liability. Finally, and perhaps unexpectedly, the HCQIA is visible in efforts by HMOs to structure their credentialing so as to minimize the occasions in which reporting to the Data Bank must occur.

Affected Managed Care Organizations

Among MCOs, the impact of the HCQIA has been felt predominantly by HMOs. HMOs are clearly eligible for the HCQIA damages immunity and have an obligation to report certain adverse actions against the clinical privileges of physicians and dentists as described below.

HMOs acquired this burden and blessing by virtue of being deemed a health care entity in the statute.[24] It might be argued that all HMOs do not equally meet the definitional subcategory to which HMOs are assigned: that of an entity that "provides health care services and that follows a formal peer review process for the purpose of furthering quality health care."[25] For example, IPA or open panel model HMOs have long argued that they do not provide care but rather arrange for that care with licensed providers or groups of providers. The HCQIA, however, does not differentiate among model types in its treatment of HMOs.

Arguably, many insurers and other payers that incorporate preferred provider arrangements into their coverage directly or indirectly include peer review processes and provide health care services, at least with respect to their preferred level of benefits, to the same degree as an IPA model HMO. PPOs are not expressly deemed to be health care entities by the HCQIA or regulations, however. There is also no case law on point (eg, instances where a PPO has claimed the immunity as a defense in litigation). The official position of the Department of Health and Human Services (DHHS) is that Data Bank access is granted to all applicants that, in good faith, certify that they meet the care provision and utilization review prerequisites. Nonetheless, PPOs, unlike HMOs, were not issued Data Bank reporting numbers when the Data Bank became operational and thus must affirmatively seek to participate. It should be noted, however, that it may be possible for a PPO to raise an HCQIA defense to an antitrust or other suit without having reported to the Data Bank previously because the statute does not link a failure to report to a revocation of health care entity status except where an administrative procedure revoking such status has taken place.

Health Care Quality Improvement Act Immunity

Immunity Continued to Professional Review Actions

Significantly, the immunity available to a health care entity is only available with respect to professional review actions or recommendations taken in the course of professional review activity. Professional review activities are any that relate to the determination of privileges or membership or a change or modification of such privileges or membership.[26] To qualify for immunity, however, a professional review action must be based on the "competence or professional conduct of an individual physician (which conduct affects or could affect adversely the health or welfare of patients). . . ."[27] Thus health care entities can only find damages liability shelter under the HCQIA where the health care entity's decision is based on the competence or conduct of the physician or dentist. As described below, certain of the reporting requirements establishing the HCQIA's and a hospital's obligation to request information from the Data Bank also apply to health care practitioners other than physicians and dentists. Actions with respect to nonphysicians, however, do not qualify for Section 11111 immunity. Section 11137, however, which immunizes the act of reporting, also covers nonphysician practitioners.

The statute and the regulations make clear that actions based on certain factors (eg, lack of membership in a professional association or a physician's advertising practices) are not deemed to be based on competence or conduct adversely affecting the health and welfare of patients.[28] *The National Practitioner Data Bank Users Guidebook* also expands the reach of this exception, in the reporting context,* to exclude

such items as an adverse action based on failure to complete a chart even though such a failure arguably has quality implications.[29] Nonetheless, there remains substantial room for judicial clarification as to what health care entity actions will be protected.

Although the presence of such ambiguity is not likely to prevent a health care entity from asserting the defense, it can significantly hamper its development of credentialing and recredentialing procedures. As discussed below, a professional review action only qualifies for immunity if, inter alia, it is taken after certain procedural safeguards are observed. Therefore, health care entities such as HMOs are encouraged to maximize the opportunities for immunity by incorporating HCQIA type procedures into their credentialing programs. Given the cumbersome nature of the procedures, however, an HMO will only want to apply the procedures where the potential for immunity is clear. There is ambiguity as to what types of professional review actions will be reportable because they are deemed to be based on competence or conduct that adversely affects, or could adversely affect, a patient's health or welfare, so that the development of appropriate procedures is made difficult.

Designing Credentialing To Comply with HCQIA Procedural Requirements

Assuming that the HMO or other health care entity's credentialing decision is sufficiently related to competence or conduct to be deemed a professional review action, it must still satisfy several procedural standards to qualify for immunity. First, there must be a "reasonable effort to obtain the facts of the matter."[30] Second, the action must be preceded by "adequate notice and hearing procedures."[31]

The HCQIA sets out relatively elaborate procedures that, if followed, are statutorily deemed to be adequate. At the notice stage, the physician is given a written statement of the proposed action and the reasons underlying it, at least 30 days to request a hearing, and a summary of his or her hearing rights.[32] If a hearing is requested, it must be held within 30 days.[33] The HCQIA also dictates the composition of the tribunal and the rights of the physician (eg, to be represented

---

*The HCQIA's requirement that certain adverse professional review actions against clinical privileges be reported to the Data Bank partially overlaps the immunity provision. Where the *Guidebook* or DHHS policy deem a matter not to be a reportable professional review action, arguably the immunity would not extend to the action either. On the other hand, it may be argued that there is a broader number of professional review actions eligible for the damages immunity than those that are reportable.

by an attorney, to call and examine witnesses, to present evidence, and to submit a written statement).[34] This section of the HCQIA is quoted in Chapter 9 of this book.

The procedures need not be followed before an action where the delay of the action could result in "imminent danger to the health" of the HMO's enrollees.[35] Likewise, it does not preclude summary suspension of privileges, membership, or participation while an investigation is being conducted.[36] Most important, immunity may be granted if the health care entity applies procedures other than those prescribed in the statute if they are "fair to the physician under the circumstances."[37]

In sum, the HCQIA calls for more extensive, hospital medical staff type, procedural guarantees than those to which many MCOs are accustomed. Therefore, MCOs frequently have to modify their credentialing and recredentialing practices to strengthen their claim to immunity. Because of the burden that HCQIA type procedures impose and the limited scope of the preemption, however, MCOs may wish to design two-track procedures that apply full-blown HCQIA protections only where there is a reasonable likelihood that the MCO's efforts will entitle it to HCQIA immunity.

Other Conditions to Immunity

Even if the HMO or other health care entity's professional review action is based on concerns as to professional competence or conduct, it will be denied the benefits of the immunity if the court finds that the action was not taken in the reasonable belief that it would further quality health care or was not "warranted by the facts known."[38] These requirements, it may be argued, authorize a court to conduct a fishing expedition into the defendant's intent and do not further the congressional goal of reducing the deterrent effect of litigation on peer review. If so, these conditions to the immunity vitiate the HCQIA's effectiveness in promoting peer review by making it relatively rare for a court to dispose of an excluded physician's or dentist's damages claims on preliminary motion.[39] For example, in *Manion v Evans*, the defendants' motion to dismiss on HCQIA grounds (that motion was converted into a motion for summary judgment) was

denied in part because the plaintiff raised an issue as to the true motivations of the defendants' peer review actions.[40]

Data Bank's Impact

The HCQIA also created the Data Bank. The Data Bank was intended to facilitate the identification and discipline of health care professionals who engage in unprofessional behavior. The Health Resources and Services Administration (HRSA) within the DHHS has contracted with the UNISYS corporation to administer the Data Bank for a 5-year period.

The Data Bank collects three types of reports: reports as to malpractice payments, reports as to certain adverse actions against licenses, and reports as to adverse actions against clinical privileges. The HCQIA obligates hospitals to query the Data Bank with respect to applicants during initial credentialing and subsequently at 2-year intervals. The impact of the Data Bank on MCO credentialing is discussed below.

Designing Credentialing To Comply with Data Bank Reporting Requirements

MCOs that are health care entities within the meaning of the HCQIA have an obligation to report adverse actions against the clinical privileges of physicians and dentists on Data Bank forms to the relevant licensure board. The boards are then obligated to inform the Data Bank. An adverse action against clinical privileges is deemed to have occurred in two cases, each of which is discussed below.

Actions in excess of 30 days. The first case is where a professional review action adversely affects clinical privileges for more than 30 days.[41] Professional review actions, however, are confined to those based on a physician's or dentist's competence or conduct that "could affect adversely the health or welfare of a patient or patients."[42] Significantly, at Data Bank briefing conferences, HRSA took the position that a denial of privileges based on threshold eligibility requirements is not reportable because it is not based on the individual's competence or conduct but rather on the health care entity's surrogate measures of the likelihood of such competence or conduct occurring.[43] The Data Bank Help

Line personnel advise that health care entities be granted reasonable discretion in this regard but recommend that the entity conduct its reporting according to internally adopted written guidelines.

Consequently, an MCO concerned with provider community sentiment and seeking not to discourage applications may have the option of using the exception to structure its process to minimize its reporting obligations. It could apparently adopt a policy classifying a number of key criteria (eg, board eligibility or certification) as administrative or threshold. Its policy would logically not call for the reporting of exclusions based on these criteria on the grounds that a true (individualized) professional review action had not taken place.

Application withdrawals. The second case in which the regulations deem a reportable professional review action to have occurred involves the surrender of privileges. A surrender is reportable either when the physician or dentist is under investigation related to possible incompetence or improper professional conduct or when it occurs in return for not conducting an investigation.[44] Also relevant is the statement in the *National Practitioner Data Bank Users Guidebook* published by HRSA that actions are not reportable until final.[45]

Thus an MCO desiring to minimize its reporting obligations arguably might craft a credentialing or recredentialing procedure that does not involve an investigation until its later stages. A provider who has not met threshold criteria could be advised of such a failure and asked whether he or she wished his or her application to be reviewed by the committee with investigative authority. Upon being advised of the committee's obligations to report any adverse determinations it reaches, he or she might choose to withdraw the application before that review began. In doing so, the MCO may have partially reconciled its need to avoid negative surprises (eg, Data Bank reports) for its applicants with its Data Bank reporting obligations.

Penalties for Failure To Report

A health care entity that substantially fails to report could lose its immunity for 3 years.[46] Sig-

nificantly, immunity is not lost until after an DHHS investigation, an opportunity for correction, and publication of the entity's name in the federal register. If DHHS judges material facts to be in dispute, a request for a hearing might be granted. The loss of immunity is not retroactive, but a failure to comply makes arguments claiming the immunity more difficult.

Querying the Data Bank

Again, hospitals are required by the HCQIA to obtain Data Bank information at the time they consider physicians, dentists, and other health care practitioners for clinical privileges or medical staff membership. They are then required to query the Data Bank again at 2-year intervals.

Under the statute, other health care entities that have entered into, or may be entering into, employment or affiliation relationships with a physician, dentist, or practitioner voluntarily can also request information from the Data Bank.[47] Nevertheless, as a practical matter, MCOs may be required to query the Data Bank. Although there are, to date, no cases establishing such a duty, MCOs that qualify as health care entities within the meaning of the HCQIA may, in the future, face allegations that they have been negligent in their credentialing and recredentialing where they have failed to take advantage of the availability of the Data Bank. It is also conceivable that the 2-year recredentialing interval imposed on hospitals by the HCQIA may be alleged to be the standard of care for other health care entities as well.

Where MCOs choose to access the Data Bank, they will currently find that doing so can build delay into their credentialing or recredentialing procedures. In late 1991, HRSA reported that more than 1 million queries had been logged. Although HRSA claims that a response to a single query takes an average of only 5 working days, it admits that a response to a request for data on multiple names takes an average of 20 working days. Single name requests are given priority because HRSA presumes that these are usually first-time requests for privileges or affiliation.

One approach in managing this delay is to proceed with the credentialing decision but to be prepared to terminate the provider if unanticipated adverse information is reported by the Data Bank. The groundwork for such a strategy involves requiring the applicant for new or renewed credentials to warrant that he or she has disclosed everything that the Data Bank will report and, in the provider's contract, to make a breach of such a warranty grounds for immediate termination. Providers named in any type of report received by the Data Bank are furnished a copy of the report by the Data Bank so they are aware of all information in the Data Bank.

Also of interest is the amount and types of information that MCOs that choose to query the Data Bank will receive (clearly, obtaining information from the Data Bank should be only a part of a broader check or verification of education, licensure, training, disciplinary history, and professional record). The information available is currently relatively limited because it only pertains to reportable events that occurred after the Data Bank opened for business on September 1, 1990. Second, the type of information currently in the Data Bank varies depending upon the type of provider. The Data Bank contains reports as to malpractice payments made on behalf of physicians, dentists, and other licensed or certified practitioners. The Data Bank can only be relied upon for information as to adverse actions against clinical privileges with respect to physicians and dentists, however, because the reporting of such actions with respect to other practitioners is voluntary. Last, the Data Bank has, since its inception, been accumulating reports as to adverse licensure actions against physicians and dentists. The Data Bank has not been accepting reports as to adverse licensure actions against other health care practitioners, however, because HRSA has not promulgated the regulations necessary to effectuate reporting by the relevant licensure boards.

Where reporting as to a particular type of action or payment is required, the information received from the Data Bank will not be up to the minute. The Data Bank report verification procedures impose a 30-day stay on the release of information. Moreover, insurers and others who make malpractice payments have 30 days from the date of payment to make their reports, and state licensing boards need not report an action against a physician's or dentist's license for 30 days. Adverse actions against clinical privileges are to be reported within 15 days of the action, but because the reports are made to the licensure boards it may be another 15 days before they are transmitted by the board to the Data Bank. Thus there may be as much as a 60-day lag time between an event and the release of a report by the Data Bank.

ANTITRUST CONSTRAINTS ON PROVIDER EXCLUSIONS

It is important to recognize that the focus of antitrust law is the welfare of the consumer, not the welfare of individual competitors. Consumer welfare is promoted by preventing conduct by individual firms or by groups of firms acting together to prevent markets from functioning competitively.[48] As discussed below, when given full play in managed care, the consumer focus of antitrust reduces MCOs' exposure in the provider selection/contracting areas. Although the purposes of antitrust law are simple, analysis by courts is more complex and requires defining competition and measuring both procompetitive and anticompetitive effects. This is particularly true in the managed care field, where an action may benefit one group of consumers but cause harm to another group.

Although there are only a few statutes to consider, the language in these statutes is broad and ambiguous. Thus antitrust law, to a large extent, is common law in the sense that individual cases must be analyzed to ascertain what types of conduct are illegal and how the court determined its conclusion.[49] The Sherman Act and the Clayton Act are the major statutes to consider, although in the provider exclusion context the cases are predominantly Sherman Act cases. Most states also have antitrust statutes. They vary widely in scope and penalties. More often than not, however, courts construing state antitrust statutes look for guidance to Sherman Act cases. Thus this section discusses the antitrust implications of MCO credentialing in the context of Sherman Act precedent.

Statutory Basis

Sherman Act Section 1 Cases

Section 1 of the Sherman Act, 15 USC § 1, provides in relevant part that:

> Every contract, combination in the form of trust or otherwise, or conspiracy, in restraint of trade or commerce among the several states, or with foreign nations, is hereby declared to be illegal.

Thus a major issue in Section 1 cases is whether, as a factual matter, the conduct in question was the result of an agreement or the result of unilateral conduct. Regardless of purpose or effect, unilateral conduct cannot violate Section 1. An agreement may be formal or informal, however. What is required is only that some understanding or meeting of the minds is present. Nevertheless, if the challenged conduct is as consistent with individual as with joint conduct, a conspiracy may not be inferred.[50]

The parties accused of making an agreement must be capable as a matter of law of making such an agreement. Thus questions have arisen as to whether a company and a subsidiary are capable of forming an agreement for purposes of Section 1 analysis. A key question that arises is whether one entity controls the other or whether the entities are under common ownership.[51] If so, then the concerted action requirement of Section 1 is probably not met.[52] Thus Section 1 conspiracies will not be present between managed care payers and their corporate parents or their controlled subsidiaries.

For the same reason, a corporation generally cannot be found to conspire with its officers, directors, or employees. If a corporate official or director has an independent economic interest in a particular transaction, however, he or she may be viewed as a separate actor capable of entering into a conspiracy with the corporation.[53] This independent stake exception has been the source of considerable anxiety in the application of antitrust law to managed care.

Sherman Act Section 2 Cases

Section 2 of the Sherman Act, 15 USC § 2, provides in relevant part that:

> Every person who shall monopolize, or attempt to monopolize, or combine or conspire with any other person or persons, to monopolize any part of the trade or commerce among the several states, . . . shall be deemed guilty of a felony . . .

The elements of the offense of monopolization are "the possession of monopoly power" and "the willful acquisition, maintenance, or use of that power by anticompetitive or exclusionary means or for anticompetitive or exclusionary purposes."[54] Monopoly power is the power to control price or to exclude competition in some relevant market. Exclusionary or predatory conduct, consciously designed to injure a smaller competitor, by a firm with market power will generally support a claim of monopolization. This conduct must be distinguished from growth or development as a consequence of a superior product, business acumen, or historic accident.[55]

Attempted monopolization involves a specific intent to monopolize the relevant market, some overt act in furtherance of that intent, and a dangerous probability of successful monopolization.

Market Power Focus

In most cases, the assessment of the competitive consequences of conduct involves a determination of the existence, or nonexistence, of market power within a properly defined market.

> Liability in antitrust law almost always requires proof of market power. This is because market power is an essential ingredient of injury to consumers. Market power means the ability to injure consumers by curtailing output and raising price; no possible injury, no market power; no market power, no violation; injury to consumers is, therefore, an essential ingredient of liability.[56]

To determine an MCO's market power it is first necessary to define a relevant market comprising both a product market and a geographic market. Where MCOs do not have the ability to curtail output or raise price, they will not be determined to have market power. Therefore, except where the offense is per se illegal, the MCO's exposure to antitrust liability should be limited to situations where it has market power.

Another factor that will be examined by the courts is the extent, if any, of anticompetitive effect. Again, in a limited number of cases, the so-called per se cases, the effect can be presumed from the nature of the conduct. In most cases, however, the effect must be demonstrated, or at least inferred, from the increase in market power.[57] Courts will place more emphasis on the actual or likely competitive effect of conduct rather than on the reason why the conduct was undertaken.[58] Defining what types of conduct constitute an unreasonable effect on competition is difficult, but MCOs must question conduct that fixes or stabilizes any competitive variable, such as price, quality, or services offered, or significantly increases the market power of those participating in the agreement.[59]

Application to Provider Contracting

Provider Contracting by Nonprovider Controlled MCOs

As indicated above, recent court decisions have granted nonprovider controlled MCOs significant latitude to engage in hard bargaining with providers.* Indeed, the antitrust laws expect that competitors will conduct their business aggressively, even heavy-handedly. The focus of the antitrust laws is the consumer welfare fostered by competition, not the welfare of individual competitors.[61]

Thus an MCO can lawfully drive a hard bargain with providers because (in the usual case) consumers will benefit (ie, through lower premiums). Only conduct that exceeds the bounds of mere hard bargaining (ie, conduct that is predatory or exclusionary) will violate the Sherman

Act.* Unfortunately, the demarcation is not always crystal clear.

An MCO's unilateral decision not to deal with a particular provider generally does not run afoul of the antitrust laws, even if the MCO has a dominant market position.[63] If the decision results from an agreement between the MCO and the provider's competitors, however, an unlawful boycott may be found to exist. The Supreme Court, in *Northwest Wholesale Stationers, Inc v Pacific Stationery & Printing Co,* 472 US 284 (1985), indicated that boycotts will be viewed as per se unlawful (ie, unlawful regardless of purpose or intent) if they involve joint efforts to disadvantage competitors by directly denying them relationships that they need to compete. Thus the boycotting firm(s) generally must possess a dominant market position and thus be an essential facility, and the conduct must fall outside plausible notions of enhancing efficiency. In *Reazin v Blue Cross & Blue Shield,*[64] Blue Cross terminated its contract with a hospital that was under common ownership with a competing HMO. A jury awarded the competing hospital and HMO $7.8 million under the Sherman Act based in part on its finding that Blue Cross' actions were undertaken in concert with the terminated hospital's competitors. Based on evidence of Blue Cross' dominant market share and in light of its unreasonable conduct, Blue Cross also was found to have engaged in monopolizing conduct in violation of Section 2 of the Sherman Act. Unlike the court in *Ball Memorial,* the *Reazin* court (on essentially similar facts) found that Blue Cross did not face meaningful potential competition from other indemnity insurers.

---

*Providers have been notoriously unsuccessful in challenging the contracting policies of nonprovider controlled MCOs. The courts have upheld a variety of contracting practices by plans, even those with alleged market power, on the grounds that the plans, fundamentally, are purchasers of services.[60]

*As previously noted, Section 1 of the Sherman Act prohibits concerted action in restraint of trade, which encompasses both per se violations (price fixing, division of markets, and some forms of boycotts and tying arrangements, all of which are condemned without regard to their purpose or actual effect) and other unreasonable restraints competition (which are judged on the basis of their actual effect on consumers). Section 2 of the Sherman Act condemns unilateral conduct that creates or perpetuates a monopoly through predatory or exclusionary acts as well as conspiracies to achieve those ends. In general, a unilateral actor has greater freedom under the Sherman Act than persons acting in concert.[62]

The court accepted evidence that Blue Cross' market position was so entrenched by its leverage over hospitals that its only meaningful competition would come from HMOs and PPOs, such as the plaintiff.

Evidence at the Reazin trial showed that at least 27 meetings had taken place between Blue Cross and the competitor hospitals, mostly in the context of discussing the development of a new HMO/PPO with the hospitals, and that the termination of the plaintiff hospital had been discussed at some of those meetings. Evidence also showed that the competitor hospitals agreed to give Blue Cross a better discount, and the jury inferred a conspiracy to reduce competition from those facts. The weakness in the *Reazin* court's holding is that it is not at all clear that Blue Cross actually extracted a promise of discounts from the competitor hospitals in exchange for its termination of the plaintiff. The Sherman Act does not impose liability unless the weight of the evidence excludes the possibility of unilateral decision making by the alleged conspirators.[65]

Reazin stands as a prime example of the boycott liability risk that will persist for MCOs even where they are not themselves provider controlled. Whereas there would be no liability if the nonprovider controlled MCO was not an essential facility and acted unilaterally, liability can be present where a horizontal conspiracy can be alleged between the MCO and other interested providers.

Similar legal questions may arise if an MCO's provider negotiations are used to control the providers' relationships with third parties. Illustrative is *Westchester Radiological Associates v Empire Blue Cross & Blue Shield,*[66] a case involving facts potentially applicable to any MCO with a large market share. Empire Blue Cross and Blue Shield required its Blue Cross contracting hospitals to bundle radiologist services as part of the hospital package. That is, Empire bought radiologist services for hospital patients exclusively from its contracting hospitals and not from the radiologists directly. As a consequence, Empire prohibited radiologists from billing directly for their services under Blue Shield and effectively required them to have

hospital contracts. The price terms of those hospital contracts were constrained, in turn, by Empire's hospital payment negotiations. Empire's restrictions also effectively prohibited radiologists from balance billing Blue Cross/Blue Shield subscribers. An association of radiologists challenged those policies, claiming that Empire employed them to fix prices for radiology services and to monopolize the health insurance market.

The district court initially denied a motion to dismiss by Blue Cross, citing language in the *Kartell* case[67] suggesting that it is unlawful for a third force to come between willing buyers (patients) and sellers (radiologists). Ruling on a subsequent motion for summary judgment, however, a different judge of the same court rejected that theory, both generally and as it applied to Empire. The court viewed Empire as the patient's intermediary for the purchase of radiologist services. Accordingly, the court found that Empire had not violated the Sherman Act but merely had acted as a rational buyer of medical and hospital services. The court noted that even a buyer with market power (which it assumed Blue Cross possessed) is not prohibited from negotiating a good price or specifying what it will buy.

Provider Contracting by Provider Controlled MCOs

Decisions made by a provider controlled MCO with respect to the membership of the controlling providers' competitors can lead to claims of concerted action in restraint of trade in violation of Section 1 of the Sherman Act.[68] The membership decisions of a financially integrated provider controlled MCO organization, however, should be regarded as a unilateral refusal to deal and are treated as the membership decisions of nonprovider controlled MCOs.

Even if the adoption of a particular selection standard or a resultant provider exclusion was viewed as the product of concerted action, such conduct would not violate the antitrust laws unless it unreasonably restrained trade. Agreements among providers regarding the operation of an MCO, including the implementation of selective criteria, should not be presumed unlawful but should be analyzed under the "rule of reason."[69] Under the rule of reason the plaintiff must first establish the existence of market power. In many cases a formal market definition will be a prerequisite to this analysis. In certain cases where market power appears obvious, however, direct evidence of effect may be sufficient.[70] Assuming that market power is established, the court will then determine whether there has been an anticompetitive effect on consumers. This can be established by direct proof of the effect, or by proof of an anticompetitive purpose that permits an inference of anticompetitive effect.[71] Thus, rule of reason analysis involves an assessment of a credentialing decision's purpose and effect. Hospital staff privileges decisions are typically analyzed in this manner. The application of the rule of reason to alleged boycotts in the MCO context is equally appropriate.

An MCO's decision, for instance, to limit provider participation would not be viewed as anticompetitive in purpose if it can be demonstrated that the organization had no need for additional providers in one or more specialties or geographic areas. Likewise, a reasonable purpose might be intended if the organization did not posses the administrative capacity to accept new providers. MCOs also have a legitimate interest in controlling costs. Utilization records might therefore form a legitimate basis for exclusions.

In addition to arguments relating to the legitimate purpose of an exclusion, an MCO can defend such a decision on the ground that it has no anticompetitive effect. Because the antitrust laws are concerned with competition and not individual competitors, a court should measure effect from the consumer's point of view. In the context of a limitation on provider participation in an MCO, the antitrust analysis of effect properly should focus on the competitive alternatives for members/consumers—whether there have been any changes in quality, price, or output—to determine whether competition has decreased. Under this construction an individual physician would have difficulty demonstrating a Section 1 violation because his or her exclusion would have little effect on consumers' options. Clearly,

a physician or group is not entitled to relief under the antitrust laws merely because it loses out to another competitor in providing services to an HMO.[72]

It should be noted that an excluded provider may also challenge a provider controlled MCO's credentialing or sanctioning decisions under Section 2 of the Sherman Act. It is unlikely, however, that the exclusion of a provider would be considered an unlawful exercise of, or an attempt to gain, monopoly power. In many cases, the MCO will not have the requisite market power to support such claims. Proof of market power aside, it is unlikely that an excluded physician could demonstrate that the exclusion amounted to monopolizing conduct or that he or she could demonstrate, as is required for the attempt offense, a specific intent to destroy competition or to build a monopoly. Because the excluded provider would compete in a different market than the MCO, it is unlikely that the provider could demonstrate a dangerous probability of success of the MCO to monopolize the market relevant to the provider's injuries.[73]

Recent Significant Provider Contracting Cases Compared

The complexity of Sherman Act analysis in the provider contracting context is evident in the contrasting decisions of *Hahn* and *Hassan*. These decisions graphically point out the possibilities for disparate judicial treatment depending upon whether a provider controlled MCO is treated as a financially integrated single entity or as a vehicle for a provider boycott.

In *Hassan v Independent Practice Associates*,[74] two physicians who had been terminated from participation in an HMO health plan brought a Sherman Act suit against the plan's IPA, alleging price fixing and a group boycott. The plan paid the defendant IPA a capitation amount and retained 12% of the capitation as a risk withhold. The withhold was to be paid to the IPA when sufficient surplus was available to the HMO. The IPA paid its members on a fee-for-service basis according to a maximum fee schedule, which it established. The plaintiffs charged that they were the subject of a boycott.

The court rejected the group boycott claims, finding first that the IPA's 20% market share did not give it sufficient market power to harm competition even if the IPA were engaged in a boycott. There was apparently little evidence in the case as to whether the IPA actually controlled the plan. Evidence showed that the plan and the IPA had the same executive, the same office, and the same staff (who were detailed to the IPA by the plan), which the court apparently interpreted to indicate a lack of control by the IPA. Subscribers, the public, and the IPA (which owned the plan) were represented on the board, although the court's opinion does not indicate the proportion of seats held by the physicians or any evidence of control in fact (of which the plaintiffs apparently offered none). Moreover, the court found that the exclusion of the plaintiff physicians, in any event, was for legitimate business reasons, having been in reaction to the plaintiffs' objections to the IPA's cost containment policies. Thus, the court concluded that the exclusion was justified as enhancing the efficiency of the plan.

The *Hassan* decision stands somewhat in contrast to *Hahn v Oregon Physicians' Service*.[75] In that case, the Ninth Circuit Court of Appeals reversed a summary judgment in favor of a physician controlled Blue Shield plan. The plan had been sued by podiatrists who claimed that their categorical exclusion from Blue Shield participation constituted an unlawful boycott. The podiatrists also alleged that the plan had engaged in price fixing by virtue of the fact that the claims of participating physicians were paid at a higher rate than the claims of nonparticipating podiatrists.

In the court's opinion, evidence that the physicians represented a majority of the plan's board raised at least an inference that the plan was a conspiracy among the physicians and not an independent provider of health care. The court concluded that the board members, even if not themselves competitors of the plaintiffs, conceivably could have acted out of joint and reciprocal self-interest with those Blue Shield physicians who did compete with the plaintiffs. In addition, the court noted an absence of evidence that the plaintiffs' categorical exclusion

was motivated by cost or other legitimate business considerations, whereas other evidence tended to show that physicians who practice in any of 20 specialties may provide foot care in competition with plaintiffs. Thus the court sent the case back for trial.

Significantly, after considering (and denying) a motion for rehearing, the court issued a new opinion[76] that contained two important revisions. First, the court backed off from its joint and reciprocal conduct standard in favor of a slightly relaxed test for inferring that the Blue Shield board was the instrument of a conspiracy. The court stated that there was evidence that:

> the physician board members, even if not themselves competing directly with podiatrists, shared similar economic interests with those board members and [plan] physicians who did compete directly, and that therefore the [Blue Shield] board as a whole may have acted in the anticompetitive interests of those member physicians who compete with podiatrists for the provision of foot care.[77]

The court also added a footnote indicating that control of a health plan by providers may be less probative of an unlawful conspiracy in the HMO context:

> We recognize, however, that this rule [ie, that a plan may reimburse member and nonmember providers differently only if not controlled by providers] may not be applicable to some health plans, such as health maintenance organizations, in which "persons who would otherwise be competitors pool their capital and the risks of loss as well as the opportunities for profit. . . " In such an arrangement, involving a "functionally integrated group of doctors," it is the doctors, rather than the patient or insurer, who bear the economic risk.[78]

There are clear factual distinctions between *Hahn* and *Hassan*. First, as the court's added footnote points out, evidence of economic integration was lacking in *Hahn*. Thus provider control of the plan might be suspected.[79] The *Hahn* case also raises the issue of physician exclusion of nonphysician competition, which has always engendered close scrutiny in the antitrust context.[80]

CONCLUSION

Managed care, when successful, is generally built upon the channeling of covered persons to cost-effective providers. With that direction may come allegations of MCO liability for the torts of the contracted providers. One of the risk management tools that can be applied is the credentialing and recredentialing of providers.

An MCO credentialing program in a few instances will be dictated by state regulation. More commonly it will be devised to comply with NCQA or equivalent standards and to minimize unnecessary reporting to the National Practitioner Data Bank. At the same time, the program should account for antitrust concerns in structuring a selection process that is not conducive to anticompetitive conspiracies.

REFERENCES

1. 301 NW 2d 156 (1981).

2. See *Stelmach v Physicians Multi-Specialty Group, Inc*, No 53906 (Mo Ct App, June 13, 1989) (medical group contracting with HMO has responsibility to verify the credentials of its physicians).

3. 1989 WL 153066 (Mo App), transferred to 781 SW2d 58 (Mo Ct App 1989).

4. For a discussion of a variety of tort liability theories affecting HMOs see Tiano, *The Legal Implications of HMO Cost Containment Measures*, 14 Seton Hall Legislative J 1, 79 (1990).

5. *Harrell v Total Health Care*, 1989 WL 153066 at *13.

6. *Boyd v Albert Einstein Medical Ctr*, 547 A2d 1229 (Pa Super Ct 1988).

7. But see 19 Md Reg Issue No 5, at 587 (to be codified at Md Regs Code tit 10, § 10.07.11) (proposed rule establishing minimum standards for HMO credentialing and recredentialing).

8. See, eg, *Mahmoodian v United Hosp Ctr, Inc*, 404 SE 2d 750 (W Va), *cert denied*, 112 S Ct 185 (1991); *Stiller v La Porte Hosp, Inc*, 570 NE2d 99 (Ind Ct App 1991); *Barrows v Northwestern Memorial Hosp*, 525 NE2d 50 (Ill 1988); *Lakeside Community Hosp, Inc v Levenson*, 710 P2d 727 (Nev 1985).

9. See, eg, *Gianetti v Norwalk Hosp*, 557 A2d 1249 (Conn 1991); *Gates v Holy Cross Hosp*, 529 NE2d 1014 (Ill App Ct 1988); *Jain v Northwest Community Hosp*, 385 NE2d 108 (Ill App Ct 1978).

10. See, eg, *Anne Arundel General Hosp v O'Brien*, 432 A2d 483 (Md Ct Spec App 1981); *Contra Weary v Baylor Univ Hosp*, 360 SW2d 895 (Tex 1962).

11. Jurisdictions with recent case law prescribing so-called common law fair process include West Virginia and Wisconsin. See *Mahmoodian v United Hosp Ctr, Inc*, 404 SE2d 750 (W Va), *cert denied*, 112 S Ct 185 (1991); *Boden Steiner v St Michael's Hosp*, 451 NW 2d 804 (Wis Ct App 1989).

12. 192 A2d 817 (NJ 1963).

13. See, eg, *Rosenblit v Superior Court*, 282 Cal Rptr 819 (Ct App 1991); *Ascherman v Saint Francis Memorial Hosp*, 119 Cal Rptr 507 (Ct App 1975).

14. See, eg, *Anton v San Antonio Community Hosp*, 567 P2d 1162 (Cal 1977).

15. See generally *Ezekial v Winkley*, 572 P2d 32 (Cal 1977); *Silver v Castle Memorial Hosp*, 497 P2d 564, *cert denied*, 409 US 1048 (Haw 1972).

16. See *Anton v San Antonio Community Hosp*, 567 P2d 1162, 1176–77 (Cal 1977).

17. See *Appelbaum v Board of Directors*, 163 Cal Rptr 831 (Ct App 1980).

18. Cal Health & Safety Code §§ 1373(h)(2) and 1373.11.

19. See *HCA Health Servs v Metropolitan Life Ins Co*, 752 F Supp 202 (ED Va 1990), *appeal withdrawn*, 1992 WL 31159 (4th Cir Va); *St Mary's Hosp v Blue Cross & Blue Shield*, No CH-91-588 (Henrico County Cir Ct, Oct 4, 1991) (filed under seal). Both of these cases reviewed an insurer's recruitment of its hospital network, not a physician panel.

20. Touse, "Insurers Potential Liability Exposure," National Health Lawyers Association Conference, "The Law of Utilization Management and Quality Assurance" (1992).

21. See, eg, S1812 (Bentsen); S1227 (Kennedy "Health America"); and HR1565 (Johnson) in the 102nd Congress.

22. See *Mullenix v Aetna Life & Casualty Ins Co*, 912 F2d 1406 (11th Cir 1990).

23. The HCQIA is codified at 42 USC §§ 1101–11152.

24. 42 USC § 11151(4)(A)(ii).

25. Id.

26. 42 USC § 11151(10).

27. 42 USC § 11151(9).

28. 42 USC § 11151(9); 45 CFR § 60.3.

29. *National Practitioner Data Bank Users Guidebook,* Health Resources Administration, Department of Health and Human Services, at 27.

30. 42 USC § 11112(a)(2).

31. Id.

32. 42 USC § 11112(b)(1).

33. 42 USC § 11112(b)(2).

34. 42 USC § 11112(b)(3).

35. 42 USC § 11112(c)(1).

36. 42 USC § 11112(c)(1).

37. 42 USC § 11112(a)(3).

38. 42 USC § 11112(a).

39. These concerns have also been expressed by medical groups. See, eg, *Second Opinion—National Practitioner Data Bank's Impact on Medical Groups,* 5 The Medical Staff Counselor No 2, at 65 (Spring 1991).

40. Memorandum and Order, No 3:89CV7436 (ND Ohio, July 8, 1991).

41. 45 CFR § 60.9(a)(1)(i).

42. 45 CFR § 60.3.

43. Hackney, *The National Practitioner Data Bank: A Step Toward More Effective Peer Review,* 24, J Health & Hosp L 201, 204 (July 1991).

44. 45 CFR § 60.9(a)(1)(ii).

45. *Guidebook* at 43.

46. 42 USC § 1133(c)(1).

47. 45 CFR § 60.11(a).

48. *Reiter v Sonotone Corp,* 442 US 330 (1979).

49. See Miles, *Health Care Antitrust Issues,* in Gosfield Ed *Health Law Handbook,* 549 (1989).

50. *Todarov v DCH Healthcare Auth,* 921 F2d 1438 (11th Cir 1991); *Market Force, Inc v Wauwatosa Realty Co,* 906 F2d 1167 (7th Cir 1990).

51. *Century Oil Tool, Inc v Prod Specialties, Inc,* 734 F2d 1316 (5th Cir 1984).

52. *Copperweld Corp v Independence Tube Corp,* 467 US 752 (1984).

53. *Johnston v Baker,* 445 F2d 424 (3d Cir 1971).

54. *Aspen Skiing Co v Aspen Highlands Skiing Corp,* 472 US 585, 610 (1985).

55. *Berkey Photo, Inc v Eastman Kodak Co,* 603 F2d 263 (2d Cir 1979), *cert denied,* 444 US 1093 (1980).

56. *Drs Steuer & Latham PA v National Medical Enters,* 672 F Supp 1489, 1504 (DSC 1987), *aff d,* 846 F2d 70 (4th Cir 1988) (quoting *Fishman v Estate of Wirtz,* 807 F2d 520, 586 (7th Cir 1986) (Easterbrook, J, dissenting in part)).

57. The effects of the challenged conduct must be on competition, not on merely a competitor. *Capital Imaging Assocs v Mohawk Valley Medical Assocs,* 725 F Supp 669, 677 (NDNY 1989).

58. *Ball Memorial Hosp, Inc v Mutual Hosp, Inc,* 784 F2d 1325, 1334–37 (7th Cir 1986).

59. Miles, supra note 69, at 550.

60. See *Ball Memorial,* supra note 80 (selective contracting for hospital services); *Barry v Blue Cross,* 805 F2d 866 (9th Cir 1986) (selective contracting for physician services); *Kartell v Blue Shield,* 749 F2d 922 (1st Cir 1984), *cert denied,* 471 US 1029 (1985) (ban on balance billing by physicians); *Pennsylvania Dental Ass'n v Medical Serv Ass'n,* 815 F2d 270 (3d Cir), *cert denied,* 484 US 851 (1987) (UCR schedule); *Royal Drug Co v Group Life & Health Ins,* 737 F2d 1433 (5th Cir 1984), *cert denied,* 469 US 1160 (1985) (pharmacy agreements).

61. *Reiter v Sonotone Corp,* 442 US 330 (1979); *Brunswick Corp v Pueblo Bowl-O-Mat, Inc,* 429 US 477 (1977).

62. See *Copperweld Corp v Independence Tube Corp,* 467 US 752, 767, 775 (1984).

63. See *Ball Memorial,* supra note 82.

64. 663 F Supp 1360 (D Kan 1987), *aff d in part,* 899 F2d 951 (10th Cir), *cert denied,* 110 S Ct 3241 (1990).

65. *Matsushita Elec Indus Co v Zenith Radio Corp,* 475 US 574 (1986); *Monsanto Co v Spray-Rite Serv Corp,* 465 US 752 (1984).

66. 707 F Supp 708 (SDNY 1989).

67. *Westchester Radiological Assocs,* 707 F Supp at 712 (citing *Kartell,* 749 F2d at 924).

68. Arrangements with providers are not protected under the McCarran-Ferguson exclusion from federal antitrust law. Thus the Supreme Court indicated in *Royal Drug* that the relationship between an insurer and its suppliers was not the business of insurance. 440 US at 230 n37. Similarly, the Supreme Court had held that contracts between an insured and a utilization/peer review organization are not the business of insurance. *Union Labor Life Ins Co v Pireno,* 458 US 119 (1982). Nevertheless, where the relationship between the insurer and its subscribers is central to the relationship, the spreading of risk is involved, and the business of insurance is therefore implicated.

69. The agreement between an HMO and IPA that excludes some providers is a vertical nonprice restraint that is analyzed under the rule of reason. *Capital Imaging Assocs v Mohawk Valley Medical Assocs,* 725 F Supp at 677.

70. See *FTC v Indiana Federation of Dentists, 476 US 447 (1986).*

71. See *Chicago Board of Trade v United States,* 246 US 231 (1918).

72. *Capital Imaging Assocs v Mohawk Valley Medical Assocs,* 725 F Supp at 677.

73. *Capital Imaging Assocs v Mohawk Valley Medical Assocs,* 725 F Supp at 678.

74. 698 F Supp 679 (ED Mich 1988).

75. 860 F2d 1501 (9th Cir), *superseded by,* 868 F2d 1022 (9th Cir 1988), *cert denied,* 493 US 486 (1989).

76. *Hahn v Oregon Physicians' Serv,* 868 F2d 1022 (9th Cir 1988).

77. *Hahn v Oregon Physicians' Serv,* 868 F2d at 1030.

78. *Hahn v Oregon Physicians' Serv,* 868 F2d at 1029 n5 (citations omitted).

79. In contrast to most HMOs, the limited integration present in most provider sponsored PPO arrangements increases the antitrust risks of such arrangements. See *Preferred Physicians, Inc,* 52 Fed Reg 45970 (1987) final consent order issued, 53 Fed Reg 10367 (1988) (barring a physician controlled PPO from dealing with any third party on collective terms, where the PPO was composed of a majority of a leading hospital's medical staff). As *Preferred Physicians* suggests, antitrust risk for PPOs is greater where membership is "overinclusive" and potential market power accordingly is greater. See also FTC Enforcement Policy with Respect to Physician Agreements to Control Medical Prepayment Plans, 46 Fed Reg 48982 (1981); *Blue Cross v Kitsap Physicians Serv,* 1982-1 Trade Cas (CCH) ¶ 64,588 (WD Wash 1981).

80. See, eg, *Wilk v American Medical Ass'n,* 719 F2d 207 (7th Cir 1983), *cert denied,* 467 US 1210 (1984), *on remand,* 671 F Supp 1465 (ND Ill 1987).

Chapter 38

Medical Management and Legal Obligations to Members

James L. Touse

Managed care organizations (MCOs) are subject to a variety of legal and regulatory obligations related to development and operation of their medical management programs. This chapter will briefly discuss those obligations and MCOs' potential legal liability to members if they fail to satisfy those obligations and will suggest what can be done to minimize that liability exposure while still accomplishing such organizations' medical management objectives.

The terms *medical management program* or *medical management activities* are used to refer to the types of activities that MCOs utilize to control the cost and to assess the quality of

James L. Touse is the Western Regional Counsel of the AEtna Life Insurance Company. He is responsible for providing legal counsel to AEtna Health Plans managed care organizations and employee benefits operations located throughout the western United States. Mr Touse has previously served as legal counsel to other insurance companies, health maintenance organizations, and the Ohio Department of Insurance.

The views presented in this chapter are solely those of the author and do not necessarily reflect the position of the AEtna Life and Casualty Company. Those views are intended to stimulate consideration and discussion concerning an evolving area of the law and should not be interpreted to describe procedural standards applicable to AEtna or any other managed care organizations in conducting medical management activities.

health care services provided to their members. Those activities can be broadly categorized as utilization management, quality assurance, and dispute resolution programs. Utilization management activities may include referral management programs; preadmission, concurrent, and retrospective review programs; utilization reporting and evaluation programs; case management programs; and provider incentive arrangements. MCOs' quality assurance activities may include provider selection, credentialing, or privileging programs; quality assessment studies; total quality management programs; peer review activities; and medical policy or protocol development programs. Although MCOs' member and provider grievance programs may not traditionally be considered medical management activities, they are included in the definition because such programs may permit MCOs to identify and resolve disputes related to their other medical management programs.

There has been a continuing evolution in MCOs' structure, membership, and medical management activities during the past decade. In 1981, 95% of covered Americans younger than 65 were covered by indemnity health insurance plans. In 1990 only 24% of the population had such coverage; 22% were covered by health maintenance organizations (HMOs), 37% by preferred provider organizations (PPOs), and 17% by managed indemnity plans (MIPs).[1] The trend toward ever more tightly managed health benefit programs, including exclusive provider organizations (EPOs) and point of service (POS) programs underwritten or administered by large national insurers or regional HMOs, is likely to continue. There has also been a significant consolidation of the entities offering group health benefits during the past decade.

The statutory and common (ie, case) law related to MCOs' medical management obligations and liability exposure is also in a state of rapid evolution. There has also been a great deal of confusion and speculation concerning the implications of the relatively few cases that have addressed MCOs' medical management obligations. As an example, *Wickline v State of California*[2] (*Wickline*) has been widely interpreted as holding that the failure to offer physicians a right to appeal a nonauthorization decision constitutes a defect in the design of the organization's medical management program. Although the *Wickline* opinion stated that the failure to provide an appeal mechanism might be negligent, that theory was discussed in dicta, or a statement of opinion, that did not support the ultimate decision in that case. In *Wickline,* the court actually decided that Medi-Cal, the California Medicaid agency, was not negligent, despite its failure to provide an appeal procedure, because the attending physician was ultimately responsible for making treatment decisions concerning the care of his patient. Other reported cases have also contributed to the confusion because they have suggested potential theories of liability that have not been widely accepted by other courts. Those cases should not be dismissed because they illustrate the types of issues that should be considered when one is developing or operating a medical management program, but it is important to emphasize that there are currently few settled legal rules related to MCOs' medical management obligations.

If there is any generally accepted rule, it is that MCOs must act in a reasonable manner and in accordance with their legal obligations when making medical management determinations. If an organization acts reasonably, it should be able to avoid any catastrophic legal liability exposure while still conducting effective medical management activities.

An MCO's medical management obligations to members are fundamentally based upon its organizational structure and relationships with employers, regulators, providers, and members. The following sections of this chapter will briefly summarize MCOs' most significant medical management obligations to its members.

REGULATORY OBLIGATIONS

It is clearly beyond the scope of this chapter to evaluate the multitude of state and federal statutes, rules, and regulations (laws) applicable to MCOs' medical management activities. An MCO must comply with all applicable laws, however, because the failure to do so may result in disciplinary action being taken against that organization.

The term *MCO* is used throughout this chapter, but it might be equally appropriate to refer to managed care programs, products, or arrangements. Those distinctions are most relevant when one is determining which laws are applicable to an MCO's medical management activities. Many regulations are only applicable to a specific type of MCO structure. Types of MCOs are described in Chapter 2.

HMOs are generally required to establish medical management programs pursuant to state HMO laws. As an example, the National Association of Insurance Commissioners (NAIC) Model HMO Act (see Chapter 34), which has served as a model for a majority of the states' HMO statutes, requires HMOs to "effectively provide or arrange for the provision of basic health care services on a prepaid basis"[3] and to "assure that the health care services provided to enrollees shall be rendered under reasonable standards of quality of care consistent with prevailing professionally recognized standards of medical practice."[4] HMOs are generally required to incorporate a hold-harmless provision in all agreements with participating providers, which prohibits providers from holding members financially responsible for the cost of covered services even if the HMO fails to pay the provider for those services.[5] See Chapter 36 for an example of this provision. HMOs are also required to establish a grievance procedure to address and attempt to resolve member grievances, including grievances related to such organizations' medical management activities.[6] This topic is addressed in Chapter 19.

If the HMO is federally qualified (see Chapter 35), it will also have to comply with the requirements of the federal HMO statute. That statute requires federally qualified HMOs to have an ongoing quality assurance program that stresses health outcomes and provides peer review of the process followed in providing services to members. It also requires qualified HMOs to have an effective procedure for collecting, evaluating, and reporting information concerning the utilization of services to the Secretary of the Department of Health and Human Services (DHHS).[7]

Regulatory oversight of an HMO's medical management activities varies, depending on the jurisdiction where the HMO is licensed and whether it is federally qualified. HMOs are generally required to describe their proposed medical management programs in their license applications and periodically to report information concerning their medical management activities to regulators after they are licensed. The licensing agency may also periodically audit licensed HMOs' medical management records and activities to ensure that such organizations are conducting medical management activities in accordance with applicable laws. The Model HMO Act empowers the state regulatory agency to fine and suspend or revoke the licenses of HMOs that fail to comply with those obligations.[8] The Secretary of DHHS may also revoke the qualification of any HMO that fails to comply with the assurances made in its qualification application concerning its medical management activities.[9]

There are fewer regulatory requirements applicable to PPO, POS, EPO, or MIP products underwritten or administered by insurers; Blue Cross and Blue Shield organizations; or other third-party benefit administrators. A number of states have enacted "any willing provider" or "limited practitioner" statutes that limit an MCO's discretion to refuse to accept an appli-

cant as a participating provider (see Chapter 37). As an example, Section 6 of the NAIC Preferred Provider Arrangements Model Act states:

> Health care insurers may place reasonable limits on the number or classes of preferred providers which satisfy the standards set forth by the health care insurer, provided that there (shall) be no discrimination against providers on the basis of religion, race, color, national origin, age, sex or marital status, and further provided that selection of preferred providers is primarily based on, but not limited to, cost and availability of covered services and the quality of services performed by the providers.

Most states also have adopted some version of the NAIC Unfair Claims Settlement Practices Model Regulation, which establishes minimum standards governing how an insurer processes and notifies claimants of its claim determinations. In general, such statutes require insurers to act fairly and expeditiously when evaluating claims and, if they deny a claim, to send written notice to a member that specifies the contract provision upon which that denial is based.

Eighteen states have enacted utilization review statutes and/or regulations that may affect MCOs' medical management activities.[10] There is little uniformity among those statutes, but they frequently regulate such matters as the hours of operation, staffing, review criteria, and reconsideration procedures of utilization management organizations operating in that state. The failure to comply with those obligations may limit an organization's ability to conduct utilization management activities in that state.

There is a question concerning whether those statutes or other state laws regulating MCOs' medical management activities are preempted by the Employee Retirement Income Security Act (ERISA) of 1974.[11] ERISA provides that, if a benefit plan is governed by ERISA, it preempts "any and all State laws insofar as they now or hereafter relate to any employee benefit plan."[12] The Supreme Court has stated that the preemption provision should be liberally construed as:

"a law 'relates to' an employee benefit plan, in the normal sense of the phrase, if it has a connection with or reference to such a plan."[13] The ERISA preemption provision is subject to the savings clause, however, which states, "nothing in this subchapter shall be construed to exempt or relieve any person from any law of any State which regulates insurance banking, or securities."[14]

The apparent conflict between the broad preemption of any law related to an ERISA benefit plan and the savings clause was addressed in *Pilot Life Insurance Co v Dedeaux*[15](*Pilot Life*). In that case, the Supreme Court decided that ERISA preempted a bad faith judgment against an insurance company because Mississippi's bad faith law was not specifically directed at regulating an insurer's activities and was not, therefore, saved from preemption by the savings clause.

As will be noted throughout this chapter, issues related to the scope of ERISA's preemption of state laws have and will continue to significantly affect MCOs' medical management obligations to members. Courts have been wrestling with the question of when a state law that affects MCOs' medical management activities relates to a ERISA benefit plan since the *Pilot Life* decision was issued in 1987. It certainly can be argued MCOs' medical management activities relate to the administration of an employer's benefit plan. As an example, in *Varol v Blue Cross and Blue Shield of Michigan* (*Varol*), the Court decided that ERISA preempted an action claiming that Blue Cross' medical management activities conflicted with a Michigan statute that prohibited nonproviders from interfering with a provider's diagnosis or treatment of patients. The court stated, "these state law claims do not have a 'remote and tenuous' connection with the benefit plan, but go directly to the essence of the plan—the preauthorization and managed care requirements."[16]

If ERISA is applicable, MCOs acting as administrators of benefit plans must comply with specified claims procedures whenever the organization denies a claim for benefits, which presumably includes a denial of authorization to render services. Those regulations require the plan administrator to notify members of the denial of a claim and to establish a procedure by which a member may request reconsideration of that denial within a reasonable time period, which may not be less than 60 days after the date that the member receives that claim denial notice. That notice must give, in a manner calculated to be understood by the claimant, the reasons for the denial, the contractual provisions upon which the denial is based, a description of any additional information needed to complete or perfect a claim, and a description of what the claimant should do to request reconsideration of the claim denial decision.[17] HMO grievance procedures that comply with the federal HMO Act are deemed to satisfy ERISA's claims procedures pursuant to subsection j of that regulation. The Secretary of the Department of Labor may fine an administrator, and either the Secretary or a plan participant or beneficiary may initiate a civil action to compel an administrator to comply with those regulatory obligations in addition to other enforcement provisions that will be described in greater detail later in this chapter.[18]

MCOs must review and understand all applicable laws affecting the structure and operation of their medical management activities. It is, therefore, advisable to implement a regulatory compliance program to ensure that the MCO is aware of and complies with those laws. Information concerning existing or proposed laws may be available from state or national trade associations, legal publications, or the organization's legal counsel.

MCOs' descriptions of their medical management programs or activities in license applications or other regulatory filings should be objective, accurate, and achievable. The failure to achieve promised objectives may provide a basis for a regulatory action against the organization. It may also provide a basis for actions by members who allege that the MCO is not complying with its regulatory obligations.

MCOs should relate their medical management activities to the terms of their benefit agreements, whenever possible, to preserve the right to assert that state laws that adversely affect those activities are preempted by ERISA. The advantages and suggested methods of complying with applicable ERISA rules and regulations will be discussed in greater detail elsewhere in this chapter.

CONTRACTUAL OBLIGATIONS TO MEMBERS

Obligations Based on Group Agreements

Employers, government entities, unions, associations, and other groups contract with MCOs to provide or administer health care benefits to eligible employees, dependents, or members. Those groups are increasingly requiring MCOs to contractually describe their medical management programs in detail. They are also evaluating and overseeing contracting MCOs' medical management activities because of their concern that the group might be held liable for negligence or for breaching its fiduciary duties pursuant to ERISA if it fails to exercise reasonable care when selecting and supervising the activities of its contracting MCOs.[19]

Certain groups may also request that contracting MCOs agree to indemnify or hold the group harmless against any liability related to the contracting MCOs' medical management activities. If a member sues the group on the basis of an MCO's activities, that indemnification obligation may require the MCO to assume responsibility for all legal expenses and damages arising from that lawsuit.

Government benefit programs, such as the Federal Employees Health Benefit and Medicare programs, require participating MCOs to comply with specified medical management requirements as a condition of participating in those programs. As an example, the standard contract for federal employee health benefits obligates contracting entities to develop and implement a quality assurance program that includes specific procedures for addressing the utilization of services, credentialing of providers, risk arrangements with providers, and member satisfaction with the contracting organization's benefit program.

Failure to comply with commitments made in the MCO's agreements with groups may result in the termination of the organization's contract to provide services to individuals covered by that group. More important, for purposes of this discussion, those agreements and the evidence or certificate of coverage distributed to members (collectively referred to as benefit agreements) describe the organization's contractual obligations to members related to their medical management activities.

Obligations Based on Members' Benefit Agreements

Most medical management issues have, to date, related to the denial of benefits or authorization to provide services to members when such services allegedly should have been covered pursuant to an MCO's benefit agreement. Those cases have generally considered whether the denial of coverage was reasonable based upon the terms of that benefit agreement.

There have been dramatic developments related to MCOs' contractual obligations to their members during the past decade. During that period, the bad faith theory of liability has been accepted by certain state courts, most notably California.[20] That theory of liability has, in turn, been preempted in many cases by the *Pilot Life* decision.

The basis for a bad faith action is an allegation that an MCO breached its implied duty of good faith and fair dealing when it denied benefits or authorization to provide covered services to its members. The law implies, "Every contract imposes upon each party a duty of good faith and fair dealings in its performance and enforcement."[21] While *Pilot Life* held that ERISA preempts bad faith actions if a benefit plan is governed by ERISA, MCOs cannot ignore their potential bad faith liability exposure because ERISA is not applicable to government, church, or nongroup benefit plans.[22]

A recent Texas case, *Hedrick v Sanus Texas Health Plan, Inc*[23] (*Hedrick*), dramatically demonstrates why an organization cannot ignore its potential bad faith liability exposure when making medical management determinations. It has been reported that the health plan agreed to pay approximately $14 million to a Dallas city employee to settle that case after a jury award of $13.75 million because of the probability that the jury award would have been trebled in accordance with the Texas unfair trade practices statute. The jury concluded that the HMO had acted in bad faith when denying coverage for a bone marrow transplant because the bone marrow transplant was not excluded from coverage by the organ transplant exclusion of the member's benefit agreement. More important, from a bad faith perspective, the HMO reportedly made that determination without clarifying the status of bone marrow transplants, despite its assurances that it had requested such clarification from Sanus' national headquarters. The denial of coverage also permitted the HMO to earn a small profit for the year and triggered an employee profit-sharing program, which apparently helped convince the jury that the HMO had acted in bad faith in denying coverage for that transplant.

Other bad faith cases have held insurers liable for failing to act reasonably when making medical management determinations that have resulted in the denial of benefits to a member. Examples of such bad faith conduct include failing to contact the member's attending physician concerning the member's condition before denying coverage on the basis of a pre-existing condition,[24] failing to obtain pertinent sections of a patient's medical records and not requiring medical review of a claim before determining that services were not medically necessary,[25] or failing to inform a member of his or her right to appeal an adverse determination.[26]

In *Hughes v Blue Cross of Northern California*[27] (*Hughes*), the California Court of Appeals upheld an award of $150,000 in compensatory damages and $700,000 in punitive damages against Blue Cross on the basis of Blue Cross' denial of claims totalling $17,000 for psychiatric inpatient services that its medical director deemed to be not medically necessary. The court upheld that jury verdict, noting:

> there was evidence that the denial of respondent's claim was not simply the unfortunate result of poor judgment

but the product of the fragmentary medical records, a cursory review of the records, the consultant's disclaimer of any obligation to investigate, the use of a standard of medical necessity at variance with community standards, and the uninformative follow-up letters sent to the treating physician. The jury could reasonably infer that these practices, particularly the reliance on a restrictive standard of medical necessity and the unhelpful letter to the treating physician, were all rooted in established company practice. The evidence hence was sufficient to support a finding that the review process operated in conscious disregard of the insured's rights.[28]

That is one of the best statements of an organization's obligations pursuant to the implied covenant of good faith and fair dealing: It must not disregard the insured's rights when making medical management determinations.

The *Hughes* case also illustrates the scope of the ERISA preemption of state law because it was subsequently overturned by the Supreme Court of California.[29] The court concluded that California's bad faith common law was preempted by ERISA based on the *Pilot Life* decision because Ms. Hughes' benefit plan was governed by ERISA.

Pilot Life held that any actions by a ERISA plan participant or beneficiary are subject to the enforcement provisions of ERISA. Those enforcement provisions permit participants or beneficiaries to initiate civil actions: "to recover benefits due to him under the terms of his plan, to enforce his rights under the terms of the plan, or to clarify his rights to future benefits under the terms of the plan."[30] That statute also permits courts, at their discretion, to award reasonable attorney fees and costs to either party in such an enforcement action.[31] ERISA has, therefore, significantly lowered the stakes in contract actions governed by ERISA because those enforcement provisions do not permit a court to award the type of compensatory or punitive damages that might be awarded in a bad faith action.

ERISA may limit the damages that may be awarded against an administrator, but it does not relieve an MCO of its responsibility to act in a reasonable manner when making medical management determinations. Plan administrators are required to act as fiduciaries when making benefit determinations, pursuant to Section 1104 of ERISA.

That fiduciary duty prohibits an administrator from acting in an arbitrary and capricious manner when making benefit determinations. Although that general fiduciary duty is well established, a number of recent cases have addressed the question of what constitutes arbitrary and capricious behavior and whether the courts should make an independent evaluation (referred to as a de novo review) of the basis of the administrator's determination. In *Brunch v Firestone Tire and Rubber Company*,[32] the Supreme Court stated that a court may conduct a de novo evaluation of an administrator's determination unless the administrator has been specifically granted the authority to make discretionary benefit and eligibility determinations in its group agreement with the sponsor of an ERISA benefit plan.

If the administrator has been granted such discretionary authority, the courts generally defer to the administrator's benefit determination unless that determination is clearly unreasonable. In *Jett v Blue Cross and Blue Shield of Alabama*, the Court stated, "the function of the court is to determine whether there was a reasonable basis for the decision based on the facts known to the administrator at the time that the decision was made."[33] A subsequent decision by the 11th Circuit Court, in *Brown v Blue Cross and Blue Shield of Alabama*,[34] indicated, however, that an administrator does not have unlimited discretion when making such determinations, particularly if it is administering an insured benefit plan. The court stated:

> When a plan beneficiary demonstrates a substantial conflict of interest . . . the burden shifts to the fiduciary to prove that its interpretation of plan provisions committed to its discretion was not tainted by self-interest. That is, a wrong but apparently reasonable interpretation is arbitrary and capricious if it advances the conflicting interest of the fiduciary at the expenses of the affected beneficiary[35]

The court remanded (ie, returned) the case to the lower court to determine whether Blue Cross' failure to review hospital records before denying coverage based upon its determination that hospital emergency services were not medically necessary was arbitrary and capricious.

Those cases demonstrate that the arbitrary and capricious standard is not a fixed standard of conduct. Rather, it is a variable standard that is used to evaluate whether an administrator acted in a reasonable manner when making a medical management determination based upon the circumstances of the case being reviewed. The following conduct has been determined to be arbitrary and capricious: relying on undisclosed medical criteria that are more restrictive than the policies utilized by other insurers,[36] basing an adverse determination on an ambiguous provision of the member's benefit agreement,[37] or failing to comply with the notification and reconsideration procedures mandated by ERISA if that failure precluded the member from requesting reconsideration of an adverse benefit determination.[38]

As was noted above, ERISA permits courts to award attorney fees and legal costs to a member if an administrator acts in an arbitrary and capricious manner. In *Egert v Connecticut General Life Insurance Co*,[39] the insurer utilized inconsistent and undisclosed medical coverage policies to deny coverage for Ms. Egert's infertility treatments. The court ordered the insurer to pay for treatments that had been rendered, ordered it to cover future infertility treatments, and awarded Ms. Egert $160,000 in legal fees and costs to "deter plan administrators from developing unreasonable interpretations of ERISA plans as a means of wrongly denying coverage to plan participants."[40] Clearly, the possibility that an administrator will be required to pay a member's legal expenses should encourage administrators to adopt reasonable medical management policies and procedures, even if ERISA preempts a bad faith action based upon the administrator's medical management determinations.

Certain federal courts and legislators have also expressed concern that the limitations imposed by the ERISA enforcement provisions do not permit the courts to adequately compensate members for the damages caused by an arbitrary and capricious determination. In *Blue Cross and Blue Shield of Alabama v Lewis*,[41] the District Court stated that the U.S. Supreme Court's decision in *Ingersoll–Rand v McClendon*[42] could be interpreted to permit courts to award extra-contractual or even punitive damages if an administrator makes an arbitrary and capricious determination, even though the member's benefit plan is governed by ERISA. The court relied on that interpretation to order the lower court to conduct a jury trial to determine whether Blue Cross could enforce the subrogation provision of its benefit agreement, despite the fact that ERISA does not provide for a jury trial in an ERISA enforcement action. Although that decision appears to be in direct conflict with *Pilot Life* and has not been followed by other courts, it illustrates that ERISA is subject to a variety of interpretations. It is possible that future court decisions may expand the scope of the damages that may be awarded against an ERISA plan administrator, particularly if the court is convinced that an arbitrary and capricious decision has caused damages that cannot be remedied by the mere payment of benefits and legal fees to the member.

Several bills also introduced during the 1991 session of Congress would have restricted or eliminated the preemption of state laws in actions against insurers when acting as ERISA plan administrators. Those bills were not enacted, but they illustrate that Congress might amend ERISA so that future determinations are subject to different review standards or enforcement provisions than those currently applicable in ERISA actions.

Contractual Obligations to Providers Based on Members' Benefit Agreements

There have been relatively few reported breach of contract cases between MCOs and their participating providers. That probably reflects the fact that, until recently, most members were covered by some type of indemnity benefit program. If an indemnity insurer denied coverage for unnecessary or unauthorized services, the provider simply billed the member, and the member sued the insurer on the basis of its claimed breach of the insurer's contractual obligations to that member.

If MCOs require participating providers to hold members harmless against the cost of such services, there will probably be a significant increase in the number of breach of contract actions between providers and MCOs. In such actions, there will probably be a question concerning whether the action is based on a breach of the provider's participation agreement or the member's benefit agreement.

That issue is an important one. If the action is based on the benefit agreement, the provider's action against the MCO may be subject to ERISA. If ERISA is not applicable, the action against the MCO will be based on the state's breach of contract laws.

Even if state common law is not preempted by ERISA, however, an MCO should not be liable for bad faith it if breaches a provider's contract, even in those states that permit members to bring bad faith actions against insurers. In *Foley v Interactive Data Corporation*,[43] the California Supreme Court emphasized that the special relationship between an insurer and its insured, which provides the basis for a bad faith action against an insurer, does not exist in most other circumstances. The court distinguished between an insurance contract, which is generally not subject to negotiation and is intended to protect the insured against a risk of loss, from most other contractual relationships, where the contract is subject to negotiation and provides adequate legal remedies if the other party breaches that contract, to justify its decision that the bad faith theory of liability is only applicable to actions against insurers.

Although an MCO may not be liable for bad faith, it will still be liable for all contractual damages permitted by state law if its refusal to pay a provider breaches the terms of its participation agreement with that provider. The same type of conduct that has been found to breach a member's benefit agreement, such as the failure to thoroughly investigate medical management issues or reasonably interpret applicable contractual provisions or medical policies before denying benefits, would presumably also provide a basis for a provider's breach of contract action against an MCO.

If a member's benefit plan is subject to ERISA, there have been conflicting court decisions concerning the question of whether a provider's action against an MCO is subject to ERISA. In *Lifetime Medical Nursing Services, Inc. v New England Health Care Employees Welfare Fund,*[44] the District Court decided that ERISA was not applicable because providers are not included in the definition of beneficiaries who are entitled to bring ERISA enforcement actions. The court recognized, however, that ERISA might be applicable if the member had assigned his right to receive benefits to the home health care agency in that case. In another case, *Kennedy v Connecticut General Life Insurance Company,*[45] CIGNA refused to pay a chiropractor's claim because he had agreed to waive the copayment required by his patient's benefit plan. The court concluded that the provider had accepted an assignment of benefits, so his action was subject to ERISA. Further, because the provider had agreed to hold the member harmless pursuant to his agreement to waive applicable copayments, the court held that the member had no claim to assign to the provider, so the provider had no claim against the insurer pursuant to the member's benefit agreement. If that reasoning is accepted by other courts, it might prevent participating providers from bringing actions against MCOs administering ERISA benefit plans for their denial of payment for medical management reasons, if providers are required to hold members harmless for the cost of such services pursuant to the terms of their participation agreements.

Recommendations

MCOs have a contractual obligation to make reasonable benefit determinations whether or not a member's benefit plan is governed by ERISA. The failure to satisfy those obligations may create a liability exposure for the MCO, although the organization's exposure may be significantly reduced if the member's benefit plan is governed by ERISA.

The ability to make benefit determinations to control the cost of providing covered services to members is one of the fundamental purposes of a medical management program. An MCO will not be competitive if it is unable to deny claims for services that are specifically excluded or limited by the benefit agreement or for services that are not medically necessary or appropriately authorized as required by members' benefit or providers' participation agreements. MCOs should not permit their potential liability exposure to deter them from making appropriate benefit determinations, provided that they can prove that those determinations are reasonable. The inability to prove that the organization acted reasonably, and in good faith, may have truly catastrophic consequences, as demonstrated by the *Hedrick* decision. Therefore, it is recommended that MCOs should:

- periodically update their benefit agreements to ensure that they clearly express and appropriately limit such organizations' contractual obligations to members. As examples, MCOs should incorporate specific definitions (eg, of medical necessity, emergency services, experimental or investigational procedures, and custodial care) and specifically explain any exclusions or limitations (eg, of dental, cosmetic, rehabilitation, mental health, and other services) to avoid any ambiguity concerning what services are covered by those benefit agreements.

- monitor significant court decisions or proposed legislation affecting their contractual obligations to members through trade publications or seminars and discussions with their legal counsel to ensure that their benefit agreements do not contain ambiguous provisions. As an example, the *Hedrick* decision demonstrates the risk of not including bone marrow or tissue transplants as a specific exclusion if the organization in-

tends to exclude coverage for those transplants.

- make a reasonable effort to ensure that any
medical management issues are thoroughly
investigated before the organization makes
an adverse benefit determination. As an example, it may be advisable to develop a
general checklist of the type of information
that should be obtained before an adverse
determination is made and to document that
an organization has fully and fairly evaluated the circumstances of each case. That
checklist might ask reviewers to indicate
whether they reviewed applicable provisions of a member's benefit agreement,
reviewed relevant medical policies, contacted the member's attending physi-
cian(s), obtained pertinent medical information, referred any medical policy issues
to a qualified medical professional for
evaluation, and generally followed established policies or procedures before making an adverse determination.

- ensure that medical reviewers are appropriately qualified to make benefit determinations pursuant to an organization's review
procedures, industry standards, and any applicable utilization review statutes. As an
example, it may be appropriate to require
medical management nurses to refer disputes concerning benefit determinations to
the organization's medical director or a
consulting review physician if nurses are
not qualified to independently resolve such
disputes pursuant to applicable regulations
or general industry practices.

- make a good faith effort to ensure that
medical policies are consistent with the
organization's other internal policies, generally accepted standards of medical practice, and the terms of its benefit agreements. As an example, it may be advisable
to submit proposed medical policies and review criteria to a panel of physicians for approval to ensure that such policies are not
overly restrictive or at variance with community standards. After those policies have
been approved, it may be advisable to distribute them to participating providers to

demonstrate that the organization is not
basing determinations on undisclosed policies and to minimize potential disputes
with those providers. The organization is
unlikely to be held liable for breaching its
contractual obligations to members if the
attending physician either does not render
services or is able to request an exception to
a known policy limiting the coverage of
those services. The advantages of being
able to resolve disputes cooperatively to
avoid litigation concerning such disputes
should outweigh the added expense if certain providers use those policies to game
the MCO's medical management requirements.

- refer cases involving unique medical issues
to a peer review committee or an external
review body to provide an independent
evaluation of those issues. Providing such
independent review, particularly in cases
where the attending physician requests
such review, should help demonstrate that
the organization has exercised reasonable
care to ensure that its determinations are
consistent with accepted standards of medical practice and were not influenced by a
claimed conflict of interest.

- grant the organization discretionary authority to make eligibility and coverage determinations in group agreements if groups
agree to delegate such authority to the
MCO. Reserving such discretionary authority should limit the de novo review of
an organization's benefit determinations if
the group's benefit plan is governed by
ERISA.

- comply with ERISA's notice and reconsideration requirements. Although HMOs
generally are required by statute to implement more extensive grievance procedures
than those required by ERISA, many
HMOs' claim denial notices do not contain
the specific information required by
ERISA. The failure to provide adequate notices to members might be deemed to be arbitrary and capricious pursuant to ERISA,
or bad faith conduct pursuant to state law, if
the failure to provide such notice deprives

members of their right to request reconsideration of erroneous benefit determinations. Even though non-HMO MCOs are not generally required to adopt HMO-like grievance procedures, pursuant to state laws or ERISA, it may be advisable for such organizations to do so, if feasible, to ensure that members and providers are able to submit any relevant information before the organization makes its final benefit determination. Establishing such procedures may also help avoid costly and time-consuming litigation because many benefit disputes can be settled during the grievance process.

- ensure that their participation agreements specifically state that providers are assignees of members' rights to benefits to emphasize that any disputes between the parties should be resolved in accordance with ERISA. Notices denying payment to providers should comply with ERISA's notice and reconsideration requirements to ensure that such benefit determinations are not deemed to be arbitrary and capricious if the provider initiates a breach of contract action against the MCO pursuant to ERISA.

- contractually require providers to resolve any disputes concerning the organization's medical management determinations in accordance with a specified dispute resolution procedure (though MCOs are not required to maintain provider dispute resolution procedures). That requirement may prevent providers from putting members in the middle of disputes concerning medical issues because the members do not possess the medical expertise necessary to effectively request reconsideration of an adverse determination. It may also help avoid litigation by permitting providers to dispute cases in which the organization has denied payment because of the provider's failure to comply with applicable medical management requirements.

- refer questions concerning the interpretation of members' benefit agreements to their legal counsel. Acting upon the advice of counsel may establish that the determination was reasonable and made in good faith. Referring such cases to counsel may also provide protection against the disclosure of sensitive information because an organization may be able to claim the privilege against the disclosure of attorney-client communications if information is submitted to counsel in anticipation of litigation concerning a medical management determination.

NONCONTRACTUAL OBLIGATIONS TO MEMBERS

The legal actions discussed in the preceding subsection were based on allegations that MCOs or other payors breached their contractual obligations to members. The growth of MCOs during the past decade has resulted in an increase in the number of cases alleging that such organizations also have noncontractual obligations to members as a result of their relationships with participating providers.

Such actions differ from contract actions because they allege that an organization acted in a negligent manner or should be held liable for the negligence of its participating providers, even though it has fully performed its contractual duties to members. Those lawsuits also seek to recover damages for a member's physical injuries instead of damages caused by the denial of contractual benefits. Such noncontractual actions have generally alleged that an organization should be held liable because it was negligent in designing or operating its medical management program, negligent in selecting or supervising its participating providers, or responsible for the negligence of a participating provider because of its relationship with that provider.

Negligent conduct is defined as "conduct which falls below the standard established by law for the protection of others against unreasonable risk of harm."[46] In other words, MCOs are required to exercise the level of care that would be exercised by a reasonably prudent organization in similar circumstances to avoid causing foreseeable injuries to their members.

Like so many other medical management issues, there have been few cases specifically addressing MCOs' noncontractual medical management obligations. One of the most significant unresolved issues is whether such negligence actions are preempted by ERISA. It clearly can be argued that an MCO's medical management activities relate to the administration of a ERISA benefit plan if the organization's claimed negligence results in an inappropriate denial of benefits to a member. There is a greater question concerning whether ERISA should be applicable if a member alleges that the organization's medical management activities caused or contributed to injuries suffered by that member because requiring the payment of contractual benefits would arguably not compensate the member for those injuries.

The answer to the question of whether ERISA preempts noncontractual actions against an administrator is critically important. If such claims are preempted, MCOs should not be held liable for negligence because ERISA's enforcement provisions only require the payment of contractual benefits and do not provide for payment of damages for a member's injuries. If ERISA is not applicable, members will be able to circumvent the damage limitations imposed by ERISA if they can establish that the organization was negligent or should be held liable for its participating providers' negligence.

Several recent cases illustrate the current uncertainty concerning the scope of ERISA's preemption of such negligence actions. In *Altieri v Agna Dental Health, Inc,* the court dismissed a member's negligence action on the basis of CIGNA's alleged negligence in investigating a participating dentist's competence during its credentialing process. The court concluded that such claims have a substantial enough effect on a benefit plan to trigger preemption because "plaintiff's negligence, misrepresentation . . . and breach of contract claims have one central feature: the circumstances of [the plaintiff's] medical treatment under his employer's [dental] services plan."[47]

That broad interpretation of ERISA's preemption provision is in conflict with the narrower interpretation adopted in *Independence HMO, Inc. v Smith.*[48] In that case, the court decided that ERISA did not preempt an ostensible agency action against the HMO or require Ms.

Smith to comply with the HMO's grievance procedure because her negligence claim for injuries caused by a participating provider was not based on her entitlement to contractual benefits pursuant to ERISA. That action was characterized as a run-of-the-mill negligence action that did not have a substantial impact on Ms. Smith's ERISA benefit plan and was, therefore, held not to be preempted by ERISA.

The conflict among the federal district courts concerning whether ERISA preempts negligence actions against a plan administrator will presumably ultimately be resolved by the federal appeals courts or the Supreme Court. That decision will certainly have a significant impact on MCOs' liability exposure related to their medical management activities. If the courts ultimately decide that MCOs may be held liable for negligence, it will dramatically increase such organizations' liability exposure because ERISA's procedural and enforcement provisions will not be applicable in such actions. Even if the courts ultimately decide that ERISA preempts such actions, however, MCOs must still be aware of their potential noncontractual liability exposure for negligence because certain members will not be covered by ERISA benefit plans.

Negligent Design of Medical Management Procedures

Wickline was the first widely reported case that suggested that MCOs might be held liable for the negligent design of their medical management programs. As was noted in the introductory section of this chapter, the court ultimately decided that Medi-Cal was not liable for its failure to authorize Ms. Wickline's continued hospitalization because her attending physician had discharged her without any effort to appeal that nonauthorization determination. The court concluded that the attending physician was solely responsible for the consequences of his decision to discharge Ms. Wickline, which is consistent with the generally accepted principle that an attending physician has the ultimate responsibility for making treatment decisions concerning the care of his or her patients.[49]

In another negligent design case, *Bush v Dake*[50] (*Bush*), the court indicated that an MCO might be liable for negligence if it implements an incentive compensation arrangement that encourages participating providers to withhold necessary treatment from members to maximize their reimbursement from the organization. That case conflicts with the decision in *Pulvers v Kaiser Foundation Health Plan,* however, which held that "the use of such incentive plans is not only recommended by professional organizations . . . but that they are specifically required by Section 1301 of the Health Maintenance Act."[51]

MCOs clearly must be concerned about their potential liability if a latent defect in the design of their medical management programs contributes to a reasonably foreseeable injury to a member. In my opinion, however, most MCOs should have a fairly limited liability exposure from the design of their programs because their programs should be comparable to those of other MCOs. Their program designs should, therefore, satisfy the standard of care of the managed care industry, particularly in light of the statutory requirements of state and federal law. The decision in *Wickline* also indicates that the courts will continue to hold physicians primarily responsible for their treatment decisions despite an MCO's benefit determinations, especially if the physician does not appeal those determinations.

Although MCOs are unlikely to be held liable on the basis of the design of their programs, the recent *Wilson v Blue Cross of Southern California52* (*Wilson*) decision may signal a trend toward holding MCOs liable if they are negligent in the administration of their medical management programs. In that case, the court stated that Blue Cross might be held liable for negligence, even though the attending physician failed to request reconsideration of its denial of authorization to continue Mr. Wilson's hospitalization, notwithstanding its decision in *Wickline*. The court reversed a lower court's judgment in favor of Blue Cross and remanded the case for trial on the basis of its determination that Blue Cross would not have authorized continued hospitalization even if Mr. Wilson's attending physician had appealed the denial of authorization in accordance with Blue Cross' informal reconsideration policy.

The *Wilson* decision has been interpreted to erode the traditional distinction between a physician's obligation to make treatment decisions and a payor's obligation to make benefit determinations. It is important to emphasize that the decision in that case simply reversed a summary judgment in favor of Blue Cross, and the trial court subsequently decided that Blue Cross should not be held liable for negligence because its failure to authorize continued hospitalization did not directly contribute to Mr. Wilson's death.

Despite the trial court's decision, the *Wilson* opinion indicates that MCOs may have a duty to exercise reasonable care when making medical management determinations, even if the attending physician does not challenge those determinations. The basis of that duty is the argument that MCOs should be held jointly liable with the attending physician for the consequences of their medical management decisions because, as in *Wilson,* it is reasonably foreseeable that a denial of authorization will effectively preclude an attending physician from providing necessary covered services if the patient cannot afford to pay for those services.

If that theory becomes widely accepted and is not preempted by ERISA, it could become one of the most significant expansions of MCOs' medical management obligations to their members. Virtually any medical management determination might be deemed to be negligent, even if neither the attending physician nor the member disputes that determination, if a jury concludes that an MCO did not exercise reasonable care in investigating or evaluating the circumstances of a case before making an adverse benefit determination. The best defense against being held liable for such administrative negligence, however, is to be able to demonstrate that the organization exercised reasonable care when making such medical management determinations in accordance with its internal policies or procedures, generally accepted medical management practices, and its contractual obligations to members and providers.

Corporate Negligence Related to the Selection and Supervision of Participating Providers

There are a number of cases in which hospitals have been held to be independently liable for negligence (referred to as corporate negligence) on the basis of their failure to exercise reasonable care when selecting or supervising their staff physicians. The landmark case holding hospitals liable for such corporate negligence is *Darling v Charleston Community Memorial Hospital.*[53] In that case, the court concluded that the hospital had an independent duty to oversee the care provided to patients in accordance with applicable licensing regulations, accreditation standards, and the hospital's own bylaws. The court rejected the hospital's argument that it should not be held liable for the physician's negligence, noting, "the state licensing regulations and the defendant's bylaws demonstrate the medical profession and other responsible authorities regard it as both desirable and feasible that a hospital assume certain responsibilities for the care of the patient."[54]

Similar issues can be raised concerning an MCO's obligation to exercise reasonable care in selecting and supervising its participating providers, particularly because MCOs, like hospitals, are subject to licensing regulations and may participate in national accreditation programs. The most widely reported case addressing an MCO's potential liability for such corporate negligence is *Harrell v Total Health Care*[55] (*Harrell*). In that case, a member's negligence action against the HMO was dismissed on the basis of a unique provision of the Missouri Health Services Law that immunizes nonprofit HMOs against liability in such circumstances. The Missouri Court of Appeals stated, however, that the HMO might have been held liable absent such immunity because it failed to exercise reasonable care when credentialing the participating specialist who negligently caused Ms. Harrell's injuries. The court noted that the HMO had solicited applications from specialists by mail and had limited its evaluation of such applications to determining whether the applicant was licensed, could dispense narcotics, and had hospital admitting privileges but had not conducted personal interviews, checked references, or otherwise investigated the applicant's credentials before accepting him or her as a participant. The court concluded that the HMO had failed to conduct a reasonable investigation and had,

therefore, created a foreseeable risk of harm to members who were required to utilize that specialist. Because most other state statutes do not provide the same type of immunity provided by the Missouri statute, the failure to appropriately credential and supervise participating providers may create a significant liability exposure for MCOs on the basis of the rationale of the *Harrell* case and analogous cases in which hospitals have been held liable for their negligent selection or supervision of staff physicians.

Secondary Liability for Participating Providers' Negligence

An employer is generally liable for the conduct of its employees because of a legal theory called respondeat superior. The basis of that theory is that the employer is able to control its employees' conduct and should, therefore, be responsible if an employee injures another while acting within the scope of his or her duties. A staff model MCO might be held liable for the conduct of its employees on the basis of that theory because it is able to direct and control how employees perform their duties.

Several recent cases have raised the question of whether MCOs that contract with participating providers should also be held liable for the negligence of such providers if the MCO has some right to control a provider's conduct or if the member reasonably believes that the provider is acting as an agent of the organization when treating that member. In such cases, courts have usually followed the generally accepted rule that a contracting party should not be held liable for the negligence of an independent contractor.[56] In *Williams v Good Health Plus, Inc.,*[57] the court not only refused to hold the plan liable for the actions of its contracting provider but emphasized that an HMO could not practice medicine pursuant to the Texas Medical Practice Act and could not, therefore, be held liable for negligence related to the provision of medical services to members.

In *Schleier v Kaiser Foundation Health Plan,*[58] however, the court held Kaiser liable for the malpractice of a contracting cardiologist. It based that decision on the fact that the HMO restricted members' access to a limited number of physicians, paid those physicians to provide services that the HMO was obligated to provide pursuant to its benefit agreement, and had some right to control the physicians' behavior. The court concluded that those were all attributes of an employer-employee relationship and therefore held the HMO to be vicariously liable for the contracting specialist's negligence.

Even if an MCO does not control the conduct of participating providers, several cases have raised the question of whether an MCO can be held liable if it creates the appearance that a provider is acting as its employee or agent. The most widely reported case discussing an MCO's potential liability for the negligence of such an ostensible or apparent agent is *Boyd v Albert Einstein Medical Center*.[59] In that case, the court reversed a summary judgment granted to the HMO because it concluded that there was a question of fact concerning whether the contracting provider was acting as the HMO's ostensible agent when he negligently treated Ms. Boyd. The court noted that the HMO advertised that its participating providers were competent, required members to utilize network physicians, required primary care physicians to refer members to participating specialists, made capitation payments to primary care physicians to treat members, and exercised some control over the physicians' conduct pursuant to the terms of its participation agreement. On that basis, the court concluded that it might have been reasonable for Ms. Boyd to believe that her primary care physician was acting as an agent of the HMO when he instructed her to have diagnostic tests performed at his office instead of at the hospital emergency department. Because Ms. Boyd died of a heart attack after leaving the emergency department, the court remanded the case to the trial court to determine whether the HMO should be held liable for its participating physician's negligence in failing to authorize the hospital to perform the diagnostic tests that would have disclosed the condition that caused Ms. Boyd's death.

In *DeGenova v Ansel*,[60] which follows the *Boyd* decision, the court stated that a tort claim for personal injuries caused by an ostensible agent was only remotely related to a claim for

ERISA benefits, so that action was not preempted by ERISA. That case, together with the *Schleier* and *Boyd* decisions, represents another potentially significant expansion of MCOs' noncontractual obligations to their members. These decisions indicate that, if an organization restricts a member's choice of physicians and either controls or is reasonably believed to control how a participating provider renders services, the MCO may be held vicariously liable for the provider's malpractice and that such actions may not be preempted by ERISA.

Recommendations

It appears likely that MCOs' efforts to refer members to cost-effective providers and to require those providers to comply with the organizations' medical management requirements will increasingly expose MCOs to actions claiming that such organizations have not satisfied their noncontractual obligations to those members. Although the scope and even the existence of such noncontractual obligations are far from settled, it is appropriate to implement preventive measures to minimize an MCO's noncontractual liability exposure related to its medical management activities as follows:

- Clearly explain the independent contractor relationship between the organization and its participating providers in certificates, brochures, and other documents distributed to members and in providers' participation agreements. Such provisions should also emphasize that providers are solely responsible for all treatment decisions and explain that providers or members may appeal adverse benefit determinations.

- If feasible, establish a dispute procedure permitting providers to request reconsideration of an MCO's medical management determinations. That procedure should provide for an expedited appeal procedure to review any nonauthorization of services that the attending physician believes are urgently needed. Establishing such formal appeal procedures should help avoid claims, such as those made in *Wickline* and *Wilson*, that the provider's inability to appeal a nonauthorization determination effectively precluded a member from receiving necessary covered services.

- An organization's quality assurance programs should evaluate access, apparent underutilization, and patient complaints to ensure that its utilization management procedures and financial incentives do not encourage providers to undertreat their patients.

- The organization's credentialing and network adequacy criteria or procedures should be set forth in writing and approved by the governing body. That credentialing program should establish specific and objective participation criteria to assess applicants' professional competence and qualifications. Incomplete applications or applications indicating that a provider does not meet the MCO's participation requirements (eg, no staff privileges at a participating hospital) should not be accepted for further review.

- Applicants who satisfy the MCO's objective screening criteria should be subject to peer review evaluation of their professional reputation, qualifications, and experience. The organization's medical management staff should attempt to verify an applicant's professional references, malpractice history, insurance coverages, hospital privileges, and licensure before referring an applicant for such peer review evaluation.

- MCOs should conduct their medical management activities in accordance with any applicable regulatory requirements, their own policies and procedures, and any generally accepted industry standards to demonstrate that they are exercising reasonable care when making medical management determinations.

- Any questions concerning a participating provider's conduct or competence should be thoroughly investigated, and appropriate action should be taken to address any deficiencies to demonstrate that the MCO is appropriately supervising its participating providers. The organization should adopt a sanction procedure that permits it to terminate the participation of those providers who are unable or unwilling to comply with the organization's medical management requirements. That procedure should permit the organization to immediately terminate a provider's participation if that provider's incompetence, misconduct, or general reputation creates a risk of harm to the organization or its members (see Chapter 9).

- An MCO should not delegate medical management responsibilities to another entity (eg, an IPA) unless that entity's medical management programs are comparable to the organization's own programs. If it delegates such duties to another entity, the MCO should retain the right to audit the other entity's activities to ensure that entity is exercising reasonable care when performing those delegated medical management activities.

- Medical policies should be structured as guidelines, and providers should be encouraged to request exceptions to those guidelines if they believe that an exception is warranted on the basis of the factual circumstances of a case or changes in medical practices or technology to minimize the risk that the organization might be alleged to exert control over the providers' treatment decisions. Medical policy statements should also emphasize that the MCO has the authority to make benefit determinations but that providers are responsible for making treatment decisions in consultation with their patients.

- MCOs should require providers to purchase adequate malpractice insurance coverage. An organization should also consider purchasing professional liability coverage, if it is available at reasonable cost, because it may be added as a deep pocket if a member initiates a malpractice action against a participating provider. Even if the MCO is not held liable, such coverage should reimburse the organization for attorney fees and expenses incurred in defending against such lawsuits.

CONCLUSION

In conclusion, MCOs have a variety of regulatory, contractual, and noncontractual obligations related to the organization and operation of their medical management programs. Although the laws concerning MCOs' liability, if they fail to satisfy those obligations, are rapidly changing and evolving, the fundamental issue in all the cases discussed in this chapter has been whether an organization acted reasonably when conducting its medical management activities.

An MCO's medical management activities are likely to be found to be reasonable if the organization clearly explains and appropriately limits its obligations in contracts, solicitation materials, and other documents; complies with its contractual and regulatory obligations; acts in accordance with its own policies and procedures and generally accepted industry practices; makes a good faith and well-documented investigation of the circumstances of each case; attempts to ensure that members receive high-quality care in an appropriate and cost-effective manner; offers reasonable appeal procedures to members and providers; and balances its cost containment objectives against its members' and providers' interests in receiving payment for necessary medical services. If an MCO conducts medical management activities in such a fair, reasonable, and well-documented manner, that organization, and the managed care industry as a whole, will be able to achieve essential medical management objectives without having to be overly concerned about the regulatory or legal liability consequences of those activities.

REFERENCES

1. Faltermayer, "Let's Really Cure the Health System," *Fortune*, March 23, 1992, p. 54.
2. 183 Cal App 3d 1064, 228 Cal Rptr 661 (1986).
3. Section 4(B)(3) of the Model HMO Act.
4. Section 7 of the Model HMO Act.
5. Section 13(d) of the Model HMO Act.
6. Section 11 of the Model HMO Act.
7. 42 USC 300e(c)(6) and (8).
8. Section 25 of the Model HMO Act.
9. 42 USC 300e-11.
10. "GHAA Survey: Utilization Review Laws and Proposals," October, 1991.
11. 29 USC 1001 et seq.
12. 29 USC 1144(a).
13. *Shaw v Delta Air Lines, Inc*, 463 US 95, 96–97, 103 S Ct 2890 (1983).
14. 29 USC 1144(b)(2)(A).
15. 481 US 41, 107 S Ct 1549 (1987).
16. 708 F Supp 826, 832 (ED Mich) (1989).
17. 29 CFR 2560.503–1.
18. 29 USC 1131 and 1132.
19. Scogland, "Fiduciary Duty: What Does It Mean?" 24 *Tort & Ins L J* 803 (1989).
20. See Kornblum, "Bad Faith and Punitive Damages Litigation in the US," 23 *Tort & Ins L J* 812 (1989).
21. *Restatement of the Law of Contracts* 2d, Section 205 (1986).
22. 29 USC 1003(b).
23. No 2864 Somervell Cty, 18 Jud Dist Ct (May 1991).
24. *Linthiacum v Nationwide Life Insurance Company*, 723 P2d 675 (Az) (1986).
25. *AEtna Life Insurance Company v Lavioe*, 505 So 2d 1050 (AI) (1986).
26. *Sarchett v Blue Cross of California*, 43 Cal 3d 1 (1987).
27. 245 Cal Rptr 273 (1988).
28. *Hughes* at 858–59.
29. *Hughes v Blue Cross of California*, 255 Cal Rptr 813 (1989).
30. 29 USC 1132(a)(1)(b).
31. 29 USC 1132(g).
32. 828 F2d 134 (3rd Cir 1987), aff'd in part 489 US 101 (1989).
33. 890 F2d 1137, 1139 (11th Cir) (1989).
34. 898 F2d 1556 (11th Cir) (1990).
35. *Brown* at pp 1566–67.
36. *Bucci v Blue Cross and Blue Shield of Connecticut, Inc*, 764 F Supp 728 (D Ct) (1991).
37. *Kunin v Benefit Trust Life Insurance Company*, 910 F2d 534 (9th Cir), *cert denied* 111 S Ct 581 (1991).
38. *DePina v General Dynamics Corp*, 674 F Supp 46 (ED Mass) (1987).
39. 768 F Supp 216 (ND 111) (1991).
40. *Egert* at p 218.
41. 753 F Supp 345, 374 (ND AI) (1990).
42. 111 St Ct 478 (1990).
43. 47 Cal 3d 654 (1988).
44. 730 F Supp 1192 (DRI) (1990).
45. 924 F2d 698 (7th Cir) (1991).

46. *Restatement (Second) of Torts*, Section 282.

47. 753 F Supp 61, 64 (D Comm 1990), citing *Rollo v Maxicare of Louisiana, Inc*, 695 F Supp 245, 248 (ED La) (1988).

48. 733 F Supp 983 (ED Pa 1990).

49. See Boyd, "Cost Containment and the Physician's Fiduciary Duty to the Patient," 39 *DePaul L Rev* 131 (1989).

50. No 86-25767-NM (Mich Cir Ct, Saginaw Cty, April 27, 1989).

51. 99 Cal App 3d 560, 565 (1980).

52. 271 Cal Rptr 876, 222 Cal App 3d 660 (1990).

53. 33 ILL 2d 326, 211 NE 2d 253 (1965), *cert denied*, 383 US 946 (1966).

54. *Darling* at p 257.

55. 1989 WL 153066 (Mo Ct App) (1989), aff'd on other grounds 781 SW2d 58 (Mo 1989).

56. See *Mitts v HIP of Greater New York*, 478 NYS 2d 911 (App Div 1984).

57. 743 SW 2d 373 (Tx App 1987).

58. 876 F2d 174 (1989).

59. 547 A2d 1229 (Pa Super 1988).

60. 382 Pa Super 213, 555 A2d 147 (1988).

Glossary of Terms, Jargon, and Common Acronyms

Answer me in one word.

William Shakespeare
(1564–1616)
As You Like It, III, ii, 238

Editor's note: The definitions given here are not necessarily the last word. In fact, it is entirely possible that some managers in the industry will have differing opinions regarding some of these definitions. In those cases, the author wishes to state, "These definitions work for me." It is also possible that health reform legislation could change the definitions of some of these terms after the publication of this book.

AAPCC—Adjusted average per capita cost. The HCFA's best estimate of the amount of money it costs to care for Medicare recipients under fee-for-service Medicare in a given area. The AAPCC is made up of 122 different rate cells; 120 of them are factored for age, sex, Medicaid eligibility, institutional status, and whether a person has both Part A and Part B of Medicare. The 2 remaining cells are for individuals with end stage renal disease.

AAPPO—American Association of Preferred Provider Organizations. A trade organization for PPOs.

Accrual—The amount of money that is set aside to cover expenses. The accrual is the plan's best estimate of what those expenses are and (for medical expenses) is based on a combination of data from the authorization system, the claims system, the lag studies, and the plan's prior history.

ACR—Adjusted community rate. Used by HMOs and CMPs with Medicare risk contracts. A calculation of what premium the plan would charge for providing exactly the Medicare-covered benefits to a group account adjusted to allow for the greater intensity and frequency of utilization by Medicare recipients. The ACR includes the normal profit of a for-profit HMO or CMP. The ACR may be equal to or lower than the APR (see below) but can never exceed it.

ACS contract—See ASO.

Actuarial assumptions—The assumptions that an actuary uses in calculating the expected costs and revenues of the plan. Examples include utilization rates, age and sex mix of enrollees, and cost for medical services.

Adverse selection—The problem of attracting members who are sicker than the general population (specifically, members who are sicker than was anticipated when the budget for medical costs was developed).

AMCRA—American Managed Care and Review Association. A trade association representing managed indemnity plans, PPOs, MCOs, and HMOs. Tends to focus on issues important to open panel types of plans. Also see GHAA.

APG—Ambulatory patient group. A reimbursement methodology developed by 3M Health Information Systems for the HCFA.

APGs are to outpatient procedures what DRGs are to inpatient days. APGs provide for a fixed reimbursement to an institution for outpatient procedures or visits and incorporate data regarding the reason for the visit and patient data. APGs prevent unbundling of ancillary services.

APR—Average payment rate. The amount of money that the HCFA could conceivably pay an HMO or CMP for services to Medicare recipients under a risk contract. The figure is derived from the AAPCC for the service area adjusted for the enrollment characteristics that the plan would expect to have. The payment to the plan, the ACR, can never be higher than the APR, but it may be less.

ASO—Administrative services only. A contract between an insurance company and a self-funded plan where the insurance company performs administrative services only and does not assume any risk. Services usually include claims processing but may include other services such as actuarial analysis, utilization review, and so forth. Also see ERISA.

Assignment of Benefits—The payment of medical benefits directly to a provider of care rather than to a member. Generally requires either a contract between the health plan and the provider, or a written release from the subscriber to the provider allowing the provider to bill the health plan.

AWP—Average wholesale price. Commonly used in pharmacy contracting, the AWP is generally determined through reference to a common source of information.

Balance billing—The practice of a provider billing a patient for all charges not paid for by the insurance plan, even if those charges are above the plan's UCR or are considered medically unnecessary. Managed care plans and service plans generally prohibit providers from balance billing except for allowed copays, coinsurance, and deductibles. Such prohibition against balance billing may even extend to the plan's failure to pay at all (eg, because of bankruptcy).

Capitation—A set amount of money received or paid out; it is based on membership rather than on services delivered and usually is expressed in units of PMPM. May be varied by such factors as age and sex of the enrolled member.

Case Management—Also referred to as Large Case Management. A method of managing the provision of health care to members with catastrophic or high cost medical conditions. The goal is to coordinate the care so as to both improve continuity and quality of care as well as lower costs. This generally is a dedicated function in the utilization management department.

CHAMPUS—Civilian Health and Medical Program of the Uniformed Services. The federal program providing health care coverage to families of military personnel, military retirees, certain spouses and dependents of such personnel, and certain others.

Churning—The practice of a provider seeing a patient more often than is medically necessary, primarily to increase revenue through an increased number of services. Churning may also apply to any performance-based reimbursement system where there is a heavy emphasis on productivity (in other words, rewarding a provider for seeing a high volume of patients whether through fee-for-service or through an appraisal system that pays a bonus for productivity).

CLM—Career limiting move. A boneheaded mistake by a manager. What this book is designed to try to prevent.

Closed panel—A managed care plan that contracts with physicians on an exclusive basis for services and does not allow those physicians to see patients for another managed care organization. Examples include staff and group model HMOs. Could apply to a large private medical group that contracts with an HMO.

CMP—Competitive medical plan. A federal designation that allows a health plan to obtain eligibility to receive a Medicare risk contract without having to obtain qualification as an HMO. Requirements for eligibility are somewhat less restrictive than for an HMO.

COA—Certificate of authority. The state-issued operating license for an HMO.

COB—Coordination of benefits. An agreement that uses language developed by the National Association of Insurance Commissioners and prevents double payment for services when a subscriber has coverage from two or more sources. For example, a husband may have Blue Cross and Blue Shield through work, and the wife may have elected an HMO through her place of employment. The agreement gives the order for what organization has primary responsibility for payment and what organization has secondary responsibility for payment.

COBRA—Consolidated Omnibus Reconciliation Act. A portion of this Act requires employers to offer the opportunity for terminated employees to purchase continuation of health care coverage under the group's medical plan (also see Conversion). Another portion eases a Medicare recipient's ability to disenroll from an HMO or CMP with a Medicare risk contract.

Coinsurance—A provision in a member's coverage that limits the amount of coverage by the plan to a certain percentage, commonly 80%. Any additional costs are paid by the member out of pocket.

Community rating—The rating methodology required of federally qualified HMOs and of HMOs under the laws of many states, and occasionally indemnity plans under certain circumstances. The HMO must obtain the same amount of money per member for all members in the plan. Community rating does allow for variability by allowing the HMO to factor in differences for age, sex, mix (average contract size), and industry factors; not all factors are necessarily allowed under state laws, however (also see Experience rating).

CON—Certificate of need. The requirement that a health care organization obtain permission from an oversight agency before making changes. Generally applies only to facilities or facility-based services.

Conversion—The conversion of a member covered under a group master contract to coverage under an individual contract. This is offered to subscribers who lose their group coverage (eg, through job loss, death of a working spouse, and so forth) and who are ineligible for coverage under another group contract (also see COBRA).

Coordinated care—The federal government's term for managed care. Presumably a "kinder and gentler" way of saying it.

Copayment—That portion of a claim or medical expense that a member must pay out of pocket. Usually a fixed amount, such as $5 in many HMOs.

CPT-4—*Current Procedural Terminology,* 4th edition. A set of five-digit codes that apply to medical services delivered. Frequently used for billing by professionals (also see HCPCS).

Credentialing—The most common use of the term refers to obtaining and reviewing the documentation of professional providers. Such documentation includes licensure, certifications, insurance, evidence of malpractice insurance, malpractice history, and so forth. Generally includes both reviewing information provided by the provider as well as verification that the information is correct and complete. A much less frequent use of the term applies to closed panels and medical groups and refers to obtaining hospital privileges and other privileges to practice medicine.

DAW—Dispense as written. The instruction from a physician to a pharmacist to dispense a brand-name pharmaceutical rather than a generic substitution.

Days per Thousand—A standard unit of measurement of utilization. Refers to an annualized use of the hospital or other institutional care. It is the number of hospital days that are used in a year for each thousand covered lives.

Death spiral—An insurance term that refers to a vicious spiral of high premium rates and adverse selection, generally in a free-choice environment (typically, an insurance company or health plan in an account with multiple other plans, or a plan offering coverage to potential members who have alternative choices, such as through an association). One plan, often the indemnity plan competing with managed care plans, ends up having continually higher premium rates such that the only members who stay with the plan are those whose medical costs are so high (and who cannot change because of provider loyalty or benefits restrictions such as pre-existing conditions) that they far exceed any possible premium revenue. Called the death spiral because the losses from underwriting mount faster than the premiums can ever recover, and the account eventually terminates coverage, leaving the carrier in a permanent loss position.

Deductible—That portion of a subscriber's (or member's) health care expenses that must be paid out of pocket before any insurance coverage applies, commonly $100 to $300. Common in insurance plans and PPOs, uncommon in HMOs. May apply only to the out-of-network portion of a point-of-service plan.

Direct Contract Model—A health plan that contracts directly with private practice physicians in the community, rather than through an intermediary such as an IPA or a medical group. A common type of model in open panel HMOs.

Disenrollment—The process of termination of coverage. Voluntary termination would include a member quitting because he or she simply wants out. Involuntary termination would include leaving the plan because of changing jobs. A rare and serious form of involuntary disenrollment is when the plan terminates a member's coverage against the member's will. This is usually only allowed (under state and federal laws) for gross offenses such as fraud, abuse, nonpayment of premium or copayments, or a demonstrated inability to comply with recommended treatment plans.

DME—Durable medical equipment. Medical equipment which is not disposable (ie, is used repeatedly) and is only related to care for a medical condition. Examples would include wheelchairs, home hospital beds, and so forth. An area of increasing expense, particularly in conjunction with case management.

DSM III-R—*Diagnostic and Statistical Manual of Mental Disorders,* 3rd edition, revised. The manual used to provide a diagnostic coding system for mental and substance abuse disorders. Far different from ICD-9-CM (see below).

DRG—Diagnosis-related groups. A statistical system of classifying any inpatient stay into groups for purposes of payment. DRGs may be primary or secondary, and an outlier classification also exists. This is the form of reimbursement that the HCFA uses to pay hospitals for Medicare recipients. Also used by a few states for all payers and by some private health plans for contracting purposes.

Dual choice—Sometimes referred to as Section 1310 or mandating. That portion of the federal HMO regulations that requires any employer with 25 or more employees that reside in an HMO's service area, pays minimum wage, and offers health coverage to offer a federally qualified HMO as well. The HMO must request it. This provision sunsets in 1995. Another definition, unrelated to the previous one, pertains to point of service; see POS.

Dual option—The offering of both an HMO and a traditional insurance plan by one carrier.

DUR—Drug utilization review.

EOB—Explanation of benefits (statement). A statement mailed to a member or covered insured explaining how and why a claim was or was not paid; the Medicare version is called an EOMB (also see ERISA).

EPO—Exclusive provider organization. An EPO is similar to an HMO in that it often uses primary physicians as gatekeepers, often capitates providers, has a limited provider panel, and uses an authorization system, etc. It is referred to as exclusive because the member must remain within the network to receive benefits. The main difference is that EPOs are generally regulated under insurance statutes rather than HMO regulations. Not allowed in many states that maintain that EPOs are really HMOs.

ERISA—Employee Retirement Income Security Act. One provision of this Act allows self-funded plans to avoid paying premium taxes, complying with state-mandated benefits, or otherwise complying with state laws and regulations regarding insurance, even when insurance companies and managed care plans that stand risk for medical costs must do so. Another provision requires that plans and insurance companies provide an explanation of benefits (EOB) statement to a member or covered insured in the event of a denial of a claim, explaining why the claim was denied and informing the individual of his or her rights of appeal.

Experience rating—The method of setting premium rates based on the actual health care costs of a group or groups.

FAR—Federal Acquisition regulations. The regulations applied to the federal government's acquisition of services, including health care services (also see FEHBARS).

Favored nations discount—A contractual agreement between a provider and a payer stating that the provider will automatically provide the payer the best discount it provides anyone else.

Fee schedule—May also be referred to as Fee Maximums or as a Fee Allowance Schedule. A listing of the maximum fee that a health plan will pay for a certain service, based on CPT billing codes.

FEHBARS—Federal Employee Health Benefit Acquisition Regulations. The regulations applied to OPM's purchase of health care benefits programs for federal employees.

FEHBP—Federal Employee Health Benefits Program. The program that provides health benefits to federal employees. See OPM.

Formulary—A listing of drugs that a physician may prescribe. The physician is requested or required to use only formulary drugs unless there is a valid medical reason to use a nonformulary drug.

FPP—Faculty practice plan. A form of group practice organized around a teaching program. It may be a single group encompassing all the physicians providing services to patients at the teaching hospital and clinics, or it may be multiple groups drawn along specialty lines (eg, psychiatry, cardiology, or surgery).

FTE—Full-time equivalent. The equivalent of one full-time employee. For example, two part-time employees are 0.5 FTE each, for a total of 1 FTE.

Gatekeeper—An informal, though widely used term that refers to a primary care case management model health plan. In this model, all care from providers other than the primary care physician, except for true emergencies, must be authorized by the primary care physician before care is rendered. This is a predominant feature of almost all HMOs.

GHAA—Group Health Association of America. A trade association representing managed care with a focus on HMOs, both open and closed panel plans. Considered the premier trade organization for the managed care industry. Also see AMCRA.

Group model—An HMO that contracts with a medical group for the provision of health care services. The relationship between the HMO and the medical group is generally very close, although there are wide variations in the relative independence of the group from the HMO. A form of closed panel health plan.

Group practice—The American Medical Association defines group practice as three or more physicians who deliver patient care, make joint use of equipment and personnel, and divide income by a prearranged formula.

HCFA—Health Care Financing Administration. The federal agency that oversees all aspects of health financing for Medicare and also oversees the Office of Prepaid Health Care Operations and Oversight (OPHCOO).

HCFA-1500—A claims form used by professionals to bill for services. Required by Medicare and generally used by private insurance companies and managed care plans.

HCPCS—HCFA Common Procedural Coding System. A set of codes used by Medicare that describes services and procedures. HCPCS includes CPT codes, but also has codes for services not included in CPT such as DME and ambulance. While HCPCS is nationally defined, there is provision for local use of certain codes.

HMO—Health maintenance organization. The definition of an HMO has changed substantially. Originally, an HMO was defined as a prepaid organization that provided health care to voluntarily enrolled members in return for a preset amount of money on a PMPM basis. With the increase in self-insured business, or with financial arrangements that do not rely on prepayment, that definition is no longer accurate. Now the definition needs to encompass two possibilities: a health plan that places at least some of the providers at risk for medical expenses, and a health plan that utilizes primary care physicians as gatekeepers (although there are some HMOs that do not).

IBNR—Incurred but not reported. The amount of money that the plan had better accrue for medical expenses that it knows nothing about yet. These are medical expenses that the authorization system has not captured and for which claims have not yet hit the door. Unexpected IBNRs have torpedoed more managed care plans than any other cause.

ICD-9-CM—*International Classification of Diseases,* 9th revision, clinical modification. The classification of disease by diagnosis codified into 6-digit numbers. The ICD-10 will use alphanumeric codes and is scheduled for publication in late 1992 or 1993.

IPA—Independent practice association. An organization that has a contract with a managed care plan to deliver services in return for a single capitation rate. The IPA in turn contracts with individual providers to provide the services either on a capitation basis or on a fee-for-service basis.

JCAHO (Joint Commission)—Joint Commission for the Accreditation of Healthcare Organizations. A not-for-profit organization that performs accreditation reviews primarily on hospitals, other institutional facilities, and outpatient facilities. Most managed care plans require any hospital under contract to be accredited by the Joint Commission.

Lag study—A report that tells managers how old the claims are that are being processed and how much is paid out each month (both for that month and for any earlier months, by month) and compares these to the amount of money that was accrued for expenses each month. A powerful tool used to determine whether the plan's reserves are adequate to meet all expenses. Plans that fail to perform lag studies properly may find themselves staring into the abyss.

Line of business—A health plan (eg, an HMO, EPO, or PPO) that is set up as a line of business within another, larger organization, usually an insurance company. This legally differentiates it from a freestanding company or a company set up as a subsidiary. It may also refer to a unique product type (eg, Medicaid) within a health plan.

LOS/ELOS/ALOS—Length of stay/estimated length of stay/average length of stay.

Loss ratio—See medical loss ratio.

MAC—Maximum allowable charge (or cost). The maximum, although not the minimum, that a vendor may charge for something. This term is often used in pharmacy contracting; a related term, used in conjunction with professional fees, is *fee maximum.*

Managed health care—A regrettably nebulous term. At the very least, is a system of health care delivery that tries to manage the cost of health care, the quality of that health care, and access to that care. Common denominators include a panel of contracted providers that is less than the entire universe of available providers, some type of limitations on benefits to subscribers who use non-contracted providers (unless authorized to do so), and some type of authorization system. Managed health care is actually a spectrum of systems, ranging from so-called managed indemnity, through PPOs, POS, open panel HMOs, and closed panel HMOs. For a better definition, the reader is urged to read this book and formulate his or her own.

Mandated benefits—Benefits that a health plan are required to provide by law. This is generally used to refer to benefits above and beyond routine insurance-type benefits, and it generally applies at the state level (where there is high variability from state to state). Common examples include in-vitro fertilization, defined days of inpatient mental health or substance abuse treatment, and other special-condition treatments. Self-funded plans are exempt from mandated benefits under ERISA.

MCE—Medical care evaluation. A component of a quality assurance program that looks at the process of medical care.

MCO—Managed care organization. A generic term applied to a managed care plan. Some people prefer it to the term *HMO* because it encompasses plans that do not conform exactly to the strict definition of an HMO (although that definition has itself loosened considerably). May also apply to a PPO, EPO, or OWA.

Medical loss ratio—The ratio between the cost to deliver medical care and the amount of money that was taken in by a plan. Insurance companies often have a medical loss ratio of 92% or more; tightly managed HMOs may have medical loss ratios of 75% to 85%, although the overhead (or administrative cost ratio) is concomitantly higher. The medical loss ratio is dependent on the amount of money brought in as well as the cost of delivering care; thus, if the rates are too low, the ratio may be high, even

though the actual cost of delivering care is not really out of line.

Member months—The total of all months that each member was covered. For example, if a plan had 10,000 members in January and 12,000 members in February, the total member months for the year to date as of March 1 would be 22,000.

MeSH—Medical staff–hospital organization. See PHO.

MET—Multiple employer trust. See MEWA.

MEWA—Multiple employer welfare association. A group of employers who band together for purposes of purchasing group health insurance, often through a self-funded approach to avoid state mandates and insurance regulation. By virtue of ERISA, such entities are regulated little, if at all. Many MEWAs have enabled small employers to obtain cost-effective health coverage, but some MEWAs have not had the financial resources to withstand the risk of medical costs and have failed, leaving the members without insurance or recourse.

MIS—Management information system. The common term for the computer hardware and software that provides the support for managing the plan.

Mixed model—A managed care plan that mixes two or more types of delivery systems. This has traditionally been used to describe an HMO that has both closed panel and open panel delivery systems.

MLP—Midlevel practitioner. Physician's assistants, clinical nurse practitioners, nurse midwives, and the like. Nonphysicians who deliver medical care, generally under the supervision of a physician but for less cost.

NAHMOR—National Association of HMO Regulators.

NAIC—National Association of Insurance Commissioners.

NCQA—National Committee on Quality Assurance. A not-for-profit organization that performs quality-oriented accreditation reviews on HMOs and similar types of managed care plans.

Network model—A health plan that contracts with multiple physician groups to deliver health care to members. Generally limited to large single or multi-specialty groups. Distinguished from group model plans that contract with a single medical group, IPAs that contract through an intermediary, and direct contract model plans that contract with individual physicians in the community.

OBRA—Omnibus Reconciliation Act. What Congress calls the many annual tax and budget reconciliation acts. Most of these acts contain language important to managed care, generally in the Medicare market segment.

Open enrollment period—The period when an employee may change health plans; usually occurs once per year. A general rule is that most managed care plans will have around half their membership up for open enrollment in the fall for an effective date of January 1. A special form of open enrollment is still law in some states. This yearly open enrollment requires an HMO to accept any individual applicant (ie, one not coming in through an employer group) for coverage, regardless of health status. Such special open enrollments usually occur for 1 month each year. Many Blue Cross and Blue Shield plans have similar open enrollments for indemnity products.

Open panel—A managed care plan that contracts (either directly or indirectly) with private physicians to deliver care in their own offices. Examples would include a direct contract HMO and an IPA.

OPHCOO—Office of Prepaid Health Care Operations and Oversight. The latest name for the federal agency that oversees federal qualification and compliance for HMOs and eligibility for CMPs. Old names were HMOS (Health Maintenance Organization Service), OHMO (Office of Health Maintenance Organizations), and OPHC (Office of Prepaid Health Care). Once part of the Public Health Service, now part of the HCFA.

OPL—Other party liability. See COB.

OPM—Office of Personnel Management. The federal agency that administers the FEHBP. This is the agency with which a managed care plan contracts to provide coverage for federal employees.

OWA—Other weird arrangement. A general acronym that applies to any new and bizarre

managed care plan that has thought up a new twist.

Par provider—Shorthand term for participating provider (ie, one who has signed an agreement with a plan to provide services). May apply to professional or institutional providers.

PAS norms—The common term for Professional Activity Study results of the Commission on Professional and Hospital Activities. Broken out by region; the Western region has the lowest average LOS, so it tends to be used most often to set an estimated *LOS*. Available as *LOS: Length of Stay by Diagnosis,* published by CPHA publications, Ann Arbor, MI.

PCP—Primary care physician. Generally applies to internists, pediatricians, family physicians, and general practitioners and occasionally to obstetrician/gynecologists.

Per diem reimbursement—Reimbursement of an institution, usually a hospital, based on a set rate per day rather than on charges. Per diem reimbursement can be varied by service (eg, medical/surgical, obstetrics, mental health, and intensive care) or can be uniform regardless of intensity of services.

PHO—Physician-hospital organization. These are legal (or perhaps informal) organizations that bond hospitals and the attending medical staff. Frequently developed for the purpose of contracting with managed care plans. Sometimes called a MeSH.

PMPM—Per member per month. Specifically applies to a revenue or cost for each enrolled member each month.

PMPY— Per member per year. The same as PMPM, but based on a year.

POS—Point of service. A plan where members do not have to choose how to receive services until they need them. The most common use of the term applies to a plan that enrolls each member in both an HMO (or HMO-like) system and an indemnity plan. Occasionally referred to as an HMO swing-out plan, an out-of-plan benefits rider to an HMO, or a primary care PPO. These plans provide a difference in benefits (eg, 100% coverage rather than 70%) depending on whether the member chooses to use the plan (including its providers and in compliance with the authorization system) or go outside the plan for services. Dual choice refers to an HMO-like plan with an indemnity plan, and triple choice refers to the addition of a PPO to the dual choice. An archaic but still valid definition applies to a simple PPO, where members receive coverage at a greater level if they use preferred providers (albeit without a gatekeeper system) than if they choose not to do so.

PPA—Preferred provider arrangement. Same as a PPO but sometimes used to refer to a somewhat looser type of plan in which the payer (ie, the employer) makes the arrangement rather than the providers.

PPO—Preferred provider organization. A plan that contracts with independent providers at a discount for services. The panel is limited in size and usually has some type of utilization review system associated with it. A PPO may be risk bearing, like an insurance company, or may be non–risk bearing, like a physician sponsored PPO that markets itself to insurance companies or self-insured companies via an access fee.

PPS—Prospective payment system. A generic term applied to a reimbursement system that pays prospectively rather than on the basis of charges. Generally it is used only to refer to hospital reimbursement and applied only to DRGs, but it may encompass other methodologies as well.

Precertification—Also known as preadmission certification, preadmission review, and precert. The process of obtaining certification or authorization from the health plan for routine hospital admissions (inpatient or outpatient). Often involves appropriateness review against criteria and assignment of length of stay. Failure to obtain precertification often results in a financial penalty to either the provider or the subscriber.

PRO—Peer Review Organization. An organization charged with reviewing quality and cost for Medicare. Established under TEFRA. Generally operates at the state level.

PTMPY—Per thousand members per year. A common way of reporting utilization. The most common example is hospital utilization, expressed as days per thousand members per year.

QA or QM—Quality assurance (older term) or quality management (newer term).

RBRVS—Resource-based relative value scale. This is a relative value scale developed for the HCFA for use by Medicare. The RBRVS assigns relative values to each CPT code for services on the basis of the resources related to the procedure rather than simply on the basis of historical trends. The practical effect has been to lower reimbursement for procedural services (eg, cardiac surgery) and to raise reimbursement for cognitive services (eg, office visits).

Reinsurance—Insurance purchased by a health plan to protect it against extremely high cost cases (also see Stop loss).

Risk contract—Also known as a Medicare Risk Contract. A contract between an HMO or CMP and the HCFA to provide services to Medicare beneficiaries under which the health plan receives a fixed monthly payment for enrolled Medicare members, and then must provide all services on an at-risk basis.

Self-insured or self-funded plan—A health plan where the risk for medical cost is assumed by the company rather than an insurance company or managed care plan. Under ERISA, self-funded plans are exempt from state laws and regulations such as premium taxes and mandatory benefits. Self-funded plans often contract with insurance companies or third-party administrators to administer the benefits (also see ASO).

Service plan—A health insurance plan that has direct contracts with providers but is not necessarily a managed care plan. The archetypal (and virtually only) service plans are Blue Cross and Blue Shield plans. The contract applies to direct billing of the plan by providers (rather than billing of the member), a provision for direct payment of the provider (rather than reimbursement of the member), a requirement that the provider accept the plan's determination of UCR and not balance bill the member in excess of that amount, and a range of other terms. May or may not address issues of utilization and quality.

Shadow pricing—The practice of setting premium rates at a level just below the competition's rates whether or not those rates can be justified. In other words, the premium rates could actually be lower, but to maximize profit the rates are raised to a level that will remain attractive but result in greater revenue. This practice is generally considered unethical and, in the case of community rating, possibly illegal.

Shoe box effect—When an indemnity-type benefits plan has a deductible, there may be beneficiaries who save up their receipts to file for reimbursement at a later time (ie, save them in a shoe box). Those receipts then get lost, or the beneficiary never sends them in, so the insurance company never has to pay.

Staff model—An HMO that employs providers directly, and those providers see members in the HMO's own facilities. A form of closed panel HMO.

Stop loss—A form of reinsurance that provides protection for medical expenses above a certain limit, generally on a year-by-year basis. This may apply to an entire health plan or to any single component. For example, the health plan may have stop-loss reinsurance for cases that exceed $100,000. After a case hits $100,000, the plan receives 80% of expenses in excess of $100,000 back from the reinsurance company for the rest of the year. Another example would be the plan providing a stop loss to participating physicians for referral expenses over $2,500. When a case exceeds that amount in a single year, the plan no longer deducts those costs from the physician's referral pool for the remainder of the year.

Subrogation—The contractual right of a health plan to recover payments made to a member for health care costs after that member has received such payment for damages in a legal action.

Sutton's law—"Go where the money is!" Attributed to the Depression-era bank robber Willy Sutton, who, when asked why he robbed banks, replied "That's where the money is." Sutton apparently denies ever having made that statement. In any event, it is a good law to use when determining what needs attention in a managed care plan.

TEFRA—Tax Equity and Fiscal Responsibility Act. One key provision of this Act prohibits employers and health plans from requiring full-time employees between the ages of 65 and 69 to use Medicare rather than the group health plan. Another key provision codified Medicare risk contracts for HMOs and CMPs.

TPA—Third-party administrator. A firm that performs administrative functions (eg, claims processing, membership, and the like) for a self-funded plan or a start-up managed care plan (also see ASO).

Triple option—The offering of an HMO, a PPO, and a traditional insurance plan by one carrier.

UB-82—The common claim form used by hospitals to bill for services. Some managed care plans demand greater detail than is available on the UB-82, requiring the hospitals to send additional itemized bills. The UB-92 will replace the UB-82 in 1993.

UCR—Usual, customary, or reasonable. A method of profiling prevailing fees in an area and reimbursing providers on the basis of that profile. One common technology is to average all fees and choose the 80th or 90th percentile, although a plan may use other technologies to determine what is reasonable. Sometimes this term is used synonymously with a fee allowance schedule when that schedule is set relatively high.

Unbundling—The practice of a provider billing for multiple components of service that were previously included in a single fee. For example, if dressings and instruments were included in a fee for a minor procedure, the fee for the procedure remains the same, but there are now additional charges for the dressings and instruments.

Underwriting—In one definition, this refers to bearing the risk for something (ie, a policy is underwritten by an insurance company). In another definition, this refers to the analysis of a group that is done to determine rates or to determine whether the group should be offered coverage at all. A related definition refers to health screening of each individual applicant for insurance and refusing to provide coverage for pre-existing conditions.

Upcoding—The practice of a provider billing for a procedure that pays better than the service actually performed. For example, an office visit that would normally be reimbursed at $45 is coded as one that is reimbursed at $53.

URAC—Utilization Review Accreditation Commission. A not-for-profit organization that performs reviews on external utilization review agencies (freestanding companies, utilization management departments of insurance companies, or utilization management departments of managed care plans). Its sole focus is managed indemnity and PPOs, not HMOs or similar types of plans. States often require certification by URAC for a utilization management organization to operate.

Wraparound plan—Commonly used to refer to insurance or health plan coverage for copays and deductibles that are not covered under a member's base plan. This is often used for Medicare.

Index

as percentage of gross national product, 257
consumer portion, 365
long–term care, 365–367
managed care in reducing, 360–362
outpatient, increases in, 289
rate of increase in medical benefits, 393
Coverage
broadening, for elderly, 367–370
CHAMPUS, 384
describing, state HMO regulation on, 404–405
legal liability to members, 485–491
Medicaid, 375–376
mental health treatment, 131–132
pharmacy benefits, 144–145, 149
physician understanding of, 96
policy manual, 225–226
substance abuse treatment, 131–132
workers' compensation, 393
Credentialing. *See also* Accreditation
accreditation review of, 242
checking, in hiring process, 35
closed panel HMOs, 39–40
committee, 26
defining, 502
delegation of, legal issues in, 464–465
Health Care Quality Improvement Act, 463,
468–472
impetus for, 461–462
independent practice association, 234
legal issues
corporate negligence, 493–494
delegating responsibility, 464–465
duty to care, 462–464
hospital case law, 466–468, 494
limiting liability exposure, 495–496
mental health care providers, 139–140, 141
National Committee for Quality Assurance
guidelines, 463–464, 465, 478
open panel HMOs, 49–50
pharmaceutical services, 157
preferred provider organizations, 234
provider selection, state regulated, 467–468
quality assurance system, 234–235
substance abuse care providers, 139–140, 141
visits vs. reports, 465
Crisis care
emergency care contracts, 127
mental health treatment, 131
substance abuse, 131
Current procedural terminology, 64, 72, 226, 291,
502
Customer service. <u>See</u> Consumer affairs department

D

Death spiral, 502
Debt, 246
Deductible, 256
defined, 502

in Medicaid, 375
partial payment pharmacy programs, 145–146
reinsurance, 284–285
Demographics/statistics
adjustments in capitation payments per, 56
age, and geography, 364
age, in managed care enrollment, 363
age of labor force, 354
benefits design and, 269
employee, market assessment of, 271–272
enrollment trends, 481–482
in calculating adjusted average per capita cost,
322
in considering Medicare contract, 346–347, 348–
349
in enrollment process, 282
Medicaid, managed care enrollment and, 373
Medicaid beneficiaries, 374
Medicaid market, 374
Department of Commerce, 266
Department of Labor, 266
Dependent coverage, 256
Detoxification, 132
Diagnosis–related groups, 75
defining, 502
in hospital reimbursement, 83
in Medicaid benefits, 375
in military health care, 389
Diagnostic and Statistical Manual (DSM), 132
Diagnostic services
physician–owned, 123
utilization management, 122–126
Direct contracting, 21, 263–264, 502
Direct mail, 273–274
Directory of services, 249
Disabled persons, 374, 429
Discharge planning, 108–109
in utilization review accreditation, 238–239
Disciplinary procedures, for provider, 98–100,
253–254
Drucker, Peter, 3
Drug Enforcement Agency, 39, 234
Drugs. <u>See</u> Pharmacy services; Substance abuse
Due process, in sanctioning physician, 98–100
Dunn & Bradstreet, 266

E

Elderly. *See* Age issues
Emergency care
alternatives to hospital admission, 127
contracting for, 127
utilization management, 126–128
Employee assistance programs, mental health care
in, 135–136
Employee Retirement Income Security Act (ERISA),
318–319, 468, 483–485, 486–489, 490–493, 503

I

Q

Quality assurance. *See also* Quality management
  accreditation, 242–244
  accrediting, 241–244
  administrative burden, 236–237
  adverse event monitoring, 235
  as a condition of licensure, 232
  case audits in, 162–163
  follow–up care, 236
  in accrediting preferred provider organizations, 240
  in HMOs, 233
  in Medicare risk contracts, 351
  in preferred provider organizations, 233, 234
  in provider contract, 429–430
  in state regulation of HMOs, 405
  in utilization review firms, 233–234
  in workers' compensation system, 397
  Medicaid requirements, 378
  Medicare requirements, 328–329, 339
  mental health care provider network, 138–141
  peer review in, 162–163
  procedural standards, 164
  process analysis, 162–163
  risk management, 166
  role of credentialing in, 234–235
  role of outcome studies, 164
  role of practice guidelines, 235
  sentinel event monitoring, 235
  structural issues, 162
  surveying member satisfaction, 164–166, 236

Quality management. *See also* Quality assurance
  claims department standards, 213–214
  committee, 26, 163
  consumer affairs performance standards, 202
  evaluating physician compliance, 194–195, 196
  issues in managed care, 161, 169–170
  National Committee for Quality Assurance, 232
  of pharmaceutical services, 155–158
  organizational goals, 167
  outcome measurement in, 168–169
  physician participation, 95
  protocols in, 167–168
  trends in, 166–169

Quality of care
  drug formularies and, 152, 155–156
  in HMOs, 233
  issues in managed care, 161
  Medicare requirements, 326–327
  member complaints, 205
  monitoring mental health treatment, 135, 141
  physician perception of, in managed care, 95
  risk–bonus arrangements, 76–77, 290–291
  sanctioning physician for inadequate, 98–100

Quality screens, mental health, 135

R

Rate quotations, 283
Rating methodologies
  calculating Medicare reimbursement, 323–324
  community, 16, 174, 282, 304–305, 311–314, 500, 501
  establishing medical costs, 299–302
  establishing revenue targets, 299–302
  experience, 16, 174, 282–283, 305–307, 312–313, 503
  Federal Employee Health Benefits Program audits, 315–317
  in Office of Personnel Management contracts, 311, 312–314
  role of, 282–283, 304, 307
  self–insured benefit options, 16
  similarly sized subscriber groups, 314–315, 316–317, 319
Recertification, role in quality assurance, 234–235
Recruiting medical staff
  advertising, 34
  checking credentials, 35
  closed panel HMO primary care physicians, 33–37
  in direct contract model HMOs, 21
  in individual practice associations, 20
  interview process, 37
  maintaining provider network, 53–54
  management role in, 10
  mental health care provider network, 137–138
  National Practitioner Data Bank, 36–37
  open panel HMO primary care physicians, 43–47
  qualifying candidates, 35–36
  role of medical director, 46–47
  role of recruiter, in open panel HMO, 46
  through agencies, 34–35
  timing, 33–34, 45–46
Referrals
  capitation pools in open panel HMOs, 57–58
  data management, 116–117, 252–253
  managing consultant authorizations, 77, 117–119
  patient self–referrals, 120, 127, 136
  reimbursement methods, 291–292
  reviewing, 119–120, 194
  selecting, 117
  to contracted, capitated consultants, 73–74
  to physician–owned services, 123
  utilization management, 117–121, 252–253
Refunds, 230
Regulation. *See* Government legislation/regulation
Rehabilitation facilities, 112–113
Reimbursement/payment systems. *See also* Capitation
  abuses in, 65, 67–68, 153–154, 228–229, 229–230, 432
  accreditation and, 240

Peter Reid Kongstvedt, MD, FACP, is a Partner in the Washington, D.C. office of Ernst & Young. He is responsible for both leading and assisting consulting projects for clients in the Eastern U.S., as well as numerous other responsibilities in the firm. Ernst & Young is one of the largest health care consulting firms in the country.

Dr. Kongstvedt has extensive experience in managed care. He has served primarily in operational and leadership roles in a Blue Cross Blue Shield plan, in numerous HMOs, and in the insurance industry. In addition, Dr. Kongstvedt has served on a number of state and national level health care policy and strategy committees. Prior appointments include serving on the Governor's Pennsylvania Health Care Cost Containment Council, serving as a Medical Services Reviewer for the Department of Health and Human Services, and serving on the Nebraska State Board of Health.

Dr. Kongstvedt is a board-certified internist. He received his undergraduate and medical degrees from the University of Wisconsin. He is a Fellow in the American College of Physicians and a member of a number of professional societies.